Red Dot Design Yearbook 2017/2018

Edited by Peter Zec

reddot award
product design

About this book

"Working" presents the current best products relating to the workplace. All of the products in this book are of outstanding design quality and have been successful in one of the world's largest and most renowned design competitions, the Red Dot Design Award. This book documents the results of the current competition in the field of "Working", also presenting its most important players – the design team of the year, the designers of the best products and the jury members.

Über dieses Buch

„Working" stellt die aktuell besten Produkte rund um das Themengebiet „Arbeitsplatz" vor. Alle Produkte in diesem Buch sind von herausragender gestalterischer Qualität, ausgezeichnet in einem der größten und renommiertesten Designwettbewerbe der Welt, dem Red Dot Design Award. Dieses Buch dokumentiert die Ergebnisse des aktuellen Wettbewerbs im Bereich „Working" und stellt zudem seine wichtigsten Akteure vor – das Designteam des Jahres, die Designer der besten Produkte und die Jurymitglieder.

Contents
Inhalt

Professor Dr Peter Zec
Preface of the editor
Vorwort des Herausgebers

Dear Readers,

The Red Dot Award has been recognising outstanding product design for more than 60 years. The challenge of filtering out the best designs of the year from the large mass of entries is the responsibility of design experts from all over the globe who we appoint to the Red Dot jury. It is a task that requires a great deal of specialist knowledge and a keen instinct. All of the products and innovations have to be scrutinised, held and tested as well as viewed and evaluated within the overall context of global developments in the respective field. In view of these facts, one thing is certain: Even in the future, it will not be possible to replace the work of the jurors by means of algorithms or robots.

By contrast, artificial intelligence is on the rise in many other areas covered by the "Working" volume of the Red Dot Design Yearbook 2017/2018. From industrial and service robots to information technology, the Internet of Things or sensor-based assistance systems, never before has the Red Dot Award: Product Design seen so many intelligent products that will forever change the world of work. In the case of products from the work and technology-based environment, there is also always a special focus on user-centred design, where the person is at the core of the development and design process. This process gives rise to products that are easy and safe to use, virtually foolproof from the outset. Minimising risk in this way is especially important in industry, but also in the medical field.

On the following pages, we will introduce you to "Working" products that won over our expert jury this year with their design quality. They are all of excellent design quality and have won an award in one of the world's largest and most renowned design competitions. You will find winning products from other aspects of life in the remaining three yearbook volumes, "Living", "Doing" and "Enjoying".

I wish you an inspiring read.

Sincerely, Peter Zec

Liebe Leserin, lieber Leser,

seit mehr als 60 Jahren zeichnet der Red Dot Award herausragendes Produktdesign aus. Die Herausforderung, die jeweils besten Entwürfe eines Jahrgangs aus der großen Masse an Einreichungen herauszufiltern, obliegt Designexperten aus aller Welt, die wir in die Red Dot-Jury berufen. Es ist eine Aufgabe, die viel Fachwissen und Fingerspitzengefühl erfordert. Sämtliche Produkte und Innovationen müssen genau betrachtet, angefasst und getestet sowie im Gesamtkontext der globalen Entwicklungen im jeweiligen Bereich gesehen und evaluiert werden. Vor diesem Hintergrund ist eines sicher: Die Arbeit der Juroren wird auch künftig nicht durch Algorithmen oder Roboter ersetzt werden können.

In vielen anderen Bereichen, die wir mit dem Band „Working" des Red Dot Design Yearbooks 2017/2018 abdecken, ist hingegen die künstliche Intelligenz auf dem Vormarsch. Ob Industrie- oder Serviceroboter, Informationstechnik, Internet der Dinge oder sensorgestützte Assistenzsysteme – noch nie zuvor wurden so viele intelligente Produkte zum Red Dot Award: Product Design eingereicht, die die Arbeitswelt dauerhaft verändern werden, wie in diesem Jahr. Bei Produkten aus dem arbeits- und technologieorientierten Umfeld liegt dabei immer auch ein besonderer Fokus auf einer nutzerorientierten Gestaltung, bei der der Mensch im Zentrum des Entwicklungs- und Gestaltungsprozesses steht. Am Ende dieses Prozesses stehen Produkte, die einfach und sicher zu handhaben sind, sodass eine Fehlbedienung von Anfang an weitestgehend ausgeschlossen wird. Eine solche Risikominimierung ist sowohl in der Industrie als auch im medizinischen Bereich besonders wichtig.

Auf den folgenden Seiten zeigen wir Ihnen Produkte aus dem Bereich „Working", die unsere Expertenjury in diesem Jahr mit ihrer Designqualität überzeugen konnten. Sie alle sind von herausragender gestalterischer Güte, ausgezeichnet in einem der größten und renommiertesten Designwettbewerbe der Welt. Siegerprodukte aus anderen Lebensbereichen finden Sie in den drei weiteren Jahrbuchbänden „Living", „Doing" und „Enjoying".

Ich wünsche Ihnen eine inspirierende Lektüre.

Ihr Peter Zec

The title "Red Dot: Design Team of the Year"
is bestowed on a design team that has
garnered attention through its outstanding
overall design achievements. This year,
the title goes to the Canyon Design Team
led by Lars Wagner and Peter Kettenring.
This award is the only one of its kind in the
world and is extremely highly regarded
even outside of the design scene.

Mit der Auszeichnung „Red Dot: Design Team
of the Year" wird ein Designteam geehrt,
das durch seine herausragende gestalterische
Gesamtleistung auf sich aufmerksam ge-
macht hat. In diesem Jahr geht sie an das
Canyon Design Team unter der Leitung von
Lars Wagner und Peter Kettenring. Diese
Würdigung ist einzigartig auf der Welt und
genießt über die Designszene hinaus höchstes
Ansehen.

In recognition of its feat, the Red Dot:
Design Team of the Year receives the "Radius"
trophy. This sculpture was designed and
crafted by Weinstadt-Schnaidt based
designer Simon Peter Eiber.

Als Anerkennung erhält das Red Dot: Design
Team of the Year den Wanderpokal „Radius".
Die Skulptur wurde entworfen und angefertigt
von dem Designer Simon Peter Eiber aus
Weinstadt-Schnaidt.

2017	Canyon Design Team
2016	Blackmagic Industrial Design Team led by Simon Kidd
2015	Robert Sachon & Bosch Home Appliances Design Team
2014	Veryday
2013	Lenovo Design & User Experience Team
2012	Michael Mauer & Style Porsche
2011	The Grohe Design Team led by Paul Flowers
2010	Stephan Niehaus & Hilti Design Team
2009	Susan Perkins & Tupperware World Wide Design Team
2008	Michael Laude & Bose Design Team
2007	Chris Bangle & Design Team BMW Group
2006	LG Corporate Design Center
2005	Adidas Design Team
2004	Pininfarina Design Team
2003	Nokia Design Team
2002	Apple Industrial Design Team
2001	Festo Design Team
2000	Sony Design Team
1999	Audi Design Team
1998	Philips Design Team
1997	Michele De Lucchi Design Team
1996	Bill Moggridge & Ideo Design Team
1995	Herbert Schultes & Siemens Design Team
1994	Bruno Sacco & Mercedes-Benz Design Team
1993	Hartmut Esslinger & Frogdesign
1992	Alexander Neumeister & Neumeister Design
1991	Reiner Moll & Partner & Moll Design
1990	Slany Design Team
1989	Braun Design Team
1988	Leybold AG Design Team

Red Dot: Design Team of the Year 2017
Canyon Design Team

For the first time in the history of the competition, the "Red Dot: Design Team of the Year" honorary award and the "Radius" challenge trophy are being bestowed on a design team in the bicycle industry. Led by Lars Wagner and Peter Kettenring, the Canyon Design Team is being honoured for its consistently high design achievements which are pioneering for the cycling sector and bicycle design. Honoured with numerous prizes within the Red Dot Design Award, Canyon Bicycles, like no other company in the bicycle industry, stands for the combination of technology, design and quality.

Erstmals in der Geschichte des Wettbewerbs gehen die Ehrenauszeichnung „Red Dot: Design Team of the Year" und der Wanderpokal „Radius" an ein Designteam aus der Fahrradindustrie. Unter der Leitung von Lars Wagner und Peter Kettenring wird das Canyon Design Team für seine kontinuierlich hohe Gestaltungsleistung ausgezeichnet, die wegweisend ist für die Radsportbranche und das Fahrraddesign. Mit zahlreichen Auszeichnungen im Red Dot Design Award steht Canyon Bicycles wie kein anderes Unternehmen in der Fahrradindustrie für die Verbindung von Technologie, Design und Qualität.

Building the best bike
Das beste Fahrrad bauen

"To me, influencing the design of a product means the realisation of a dream: to be able to express myself through my own products."

„Die Einflussnahme auf die Gestaltung eines Produkts bedeutet für mich die Verwirklichung eines Traumes: mich über die eigenen Produkte ausdrücken zu können."

Roman Arnold, Founder and Managing Director Canyon Bicycles

When Roman Arnold founds Canyon Bicycles GmbH in 2002, his claim is no less than to build the best bicycles in the world. With Canyon, he realises his dream to be able to express himself through his own products. In doing so, the technical and creative quality of the bicycles presents itself as calm and unobtrusive as Roman Arnold himself. Each Canyon bike appears simple and clear. At the same time, form and visual design of the bicycles convey a high degree of precision and dynamics, also reflected in Roman Arnold's uncompromising will to succeed.

Born at the racetrack, grew up in the garage

Canyon is a prime example of how the success of companies and brands can be inseparably linked to the life story of their founder. Roman Arnold, born in 1963, learns to ride a bicycle at the age of three. Still today, he clearly recalls the feeling of riding a used "Puky" bicycle all by himself and without support for the first time. It was a feeling of great freedom. For his 15th birthday, however, he indicates his wish for a moped. Two years of anticipation and looking forward to this birthday gift pass by. Then, in the summer vacation, shortly before his birthday and on the way to Italy, he observes a group of cyclists on their way through the Alps with sporty bicycles. From now on, his interest is awakened. Back in Germany, his father buys him a racing bike: a Peugeot PY10.

From now on, interest turns into passion. Roman Arnold trains on his racing bike and participates in cycle races. His father as well as his two brothers, Franc and Lothar, accompany him. The more passionate and successful Roman Arnold goes racing, the more difficult it becomes to obtain better accessories and fitting spare parts for his racing bike. And as Roman's father doesn't want to just stand around by the roadside during his son's cycle races, he decides to buy accessories and spare parts in Italy. Back home in the family garage, the bicycles are "made fit" for the races. And while Roman Arnold takes part in contests, his father starts a business of selling spare parts and accessories from a small trailer. The result is a small family business as a sideline enterprise.

Als Roman Arnold im Jahr 2002 die Canyon Bicycles GmbH gründet, hat er keinen geringeren Anspruch, als die besten Fahrräder der Welt zu bauen. Mit Canyon verwirklicht er seinen Traum, sich über die eigenen Produkte ausdrücken zu können. Die technische und gestalterische Qualität der Fahrräder präsentiert sich dabei so unaufgeregt und unaufdringlich wie Roman Arnold selbst. Jedes Canyon-Bike wirkt einfach und klar. Zugleich vermitteln die Form und die visuelle Gestaltung der Fahrräder eine hohe Präzision und Dynamik, die sich auch im unbedingten Erfolgs- und Siegeswillen von Firmengründer Roman Arnold widerspiegeln.

An der Rennstrecke geboren, in der Garage aufgewachsen

Canyon ist ein Musterbeispiel dafür, wie der Erfolg von Unternehmen und Marken untrennbar mit der Lebensgeschichte ihres Gründers verbunden sein kann. Roman Arnold, geboren 1963, lernt mit drei Jahren, Fahrrad zu fahren. An das Gefühl, als er zum ersten Mal ganz allein und ohne Halt auf einem gebrauchten Puky-Rad fährt, erinnert er sich bis heute. Es ist ein Gefühl großer Freiheit. Zu seinem fünfzehnten Geburtstag wünscht er sich zunächst ein Mofa. Zwei Jahre lang fiebert er darauf hin. Im Sommerurlaub, kurz vor seinem Geburtstag, sieht er dann auf dem Weg nach Italien eine Gruppe von Radfahrern, die in den Alpen mit sportlichen Zweirädern unterwegs sind. Von nun an ist sein Interesse geweckt. Zurück in Deutschland, kauft sein Vater ihm ein Rennrad: ein Peugeot PY10.

Aus Interesse wird Leidenschaft. Roman Arnold trainiert auf seinem Rennrad und nimmt an Radrennen teil. Sein Vater und seine beiden Brüder Franc und Lothar begleiten ihn. Je leidenschaftlicher und erfolgreicher Roman Arnold Rennen fährt, desto schwieriger wird es, besseres Zubehör und passende Ersatzteile für sein Rennrad zu bekommen. Und weil Romans Vater bei den Radrennen seines Sohnes nicht nur am Straßenrand stehen will, entschließt er sich, in Italien Zubehör und Fahrradteile einzukaufen. In der Garage der Familie werden die Fahrräder für die Rennen fit gemacht. Und während Roman Arnold Wettkämpfe bestreitet, startet sein Vater mit dem Verkauf von Ersatzteilen und Zubehör aus einem kleinen Anhänger. Es entwickelt sich ein kleiner Familienbetrieb im Nebenerwerb.

The design of the simplest things is often most complicated. The trend is towards system integration.
Die Gestaltung der einfachsten Dinge ist oft am kompliziertesten. Der Trend geht in Richtung Systemintegration.

Growing and growing up

With good quality and a service specifically oriented to the needs of customers, the Arnold family is soon making a name for itself in the scene. But shortly after Roman Arnold's high school graduation, the family is hit by a stroke of fate: the father dies. At this point, Roman Arnold has just turned 18 years old. Together with his brother Franc, he decides to continue the garage business. For this objective, Roman Arnold completes an apprenticeship as a wholesales and export/import merchant, immediately followed by an apprenticeship as a bicycle mechanic. In 1985, after the completion of the apprenticeship, Roman and Franc Arnold open up a shop with the name "Rad Sport Arnold" in Koblenz, Germany. Behind the shop counter and in the workshop, they directly experience the hour of birth and growth phase of the mountain bikes. With their sale of exclusive branded bicycles, spare parts and accessories as well as their bicycle repair service, the small business becomes known not only to amateur cyclists. The Koblenz-based company becomes an insider's tip among pros and top athletes as well. In 1990, the brothers decide to pursue different career paths. Franc Arnold founds the company RTI Sports. By the end of the 1990s, RTI Sports focuses exclusively on high-quality bicycle accessories for the specialist retail trade.

Roman Arnold takes a step-by-step approach to the manufacture of in-house bicycles. The first mountain bikes are produced in Asia according to Roman Arnold's ideas and concepts. They enter the market in 1996. Based on his experiences in cycling and in the immediate contact with customers, he develops a special sense for new models. Without any detour via the commercial trade channels, the bicycles are coming directly

Wachsen und erwachsen werden

Mit guter Qualität und einem Service, der unmittelbar auf die Bedürfnisse der Kunden abgestimmt ist, macht sich die Familie Arnold in der Szene bald einen Namen. Doch kurz nach dem Abitur von Roman Arnold trifft die Familie ein Schicksalsschlag. Der Vater stirbt. Roman Arnold ist gerade einmal 18 Jahre alt. Er entscheidet gemeinsam mit seinem Bruder Franc, den Garagenbetrieb weiterzuführen. Für dieses Ziel absolviert Roman Arnold zunächst eine Ausbildung zum Groß- und Außenhandelskaufmann und unmittelbar darauf zum Zweiradmechaniker. Nach Abschluss der Ausbildung eröffnen Roman und Franc Arnold im Jahr 1985 ein Ladenlokal mit dem Namen „Rad Sport Arnold" in Koblenz. Hinter der Ladentheke und in der Werkstatt erleben die beiden die Geburtsstunde und Wachstumsphase der Mountainbikes hautnah mit. Der Verkauf exklusiver Markenfahrräder, von Ersatz- und Zubehörteilen sowie die Reparatur von Fahrrädern macht das kleine Unternehmen nicht nur bei Hobbyradfahrern bekannt. Auch unter Profis und Spitzensportlern avanciert das Koblenzer Unternehmen zu einem Geheimtipp. 1990 trennen sich die beruflichen Wege der Brüder. Franc Arnold gründet die Firma RTI Sports, die sich Ende der 1990er Jahre ausschließlich auf hochwertige Fahrrad-Zubehörteile für den Fachhandel konzentriert.

Roman Arnold tastet sich Schritt für Schritt an die Herstellung eigener Fahrräder heran. Die ersten Mountainbikes werden nach Roman Arnolds Vorstellung in Asien produziert. Sie kommen 1996 auf den Markt. Aufbauend auf seinen Erfahrungen im Radsport und im unmittelbaren Kontakt mit den Kunden entwickelt er ein Gespür für neue Modelle. Ohne Umweg über den Handel kommen die Fahrräder direkt vom Hersteller zum Kunden.

Engineering and design in perfection: Ultimate CF Evo LTD. Precision and simplicity at the highest level.
Ingenieurskunst und Design in Perfektion: Ultimate CF Evo LTD. Präzision und Einfachheit auf höchstem Niveau.

from the manufacturer to the customer. Roman Arnold's breakthrough to success is paved with his move to the Internet. In 1998, he manages to secure the international domain name canyon.com for his company, thereby being well ahead of his time. In 2002, Radsport Arnold is renamed to Canyon Bicycles GmbH based in Koblenz. To improve the characteristics and quality of his bicycles, Roman Arnold is looking for a new material. He follows a recommendation to try it at the Institute for Composite Materials in Kaiserslautern, Germany. The young doctoral candidate Michael Kaiser is working at the Institute when, in 2003, Roman Arnold stands in front of the door of the research institute. He needs a racing bike made of carbon – namely and if possible, the world's best racing bike. Michael Kaiser works for weeks and months, even late nights and weekends. The final result is the Canyon F10 racing bike which obtains score values that have never been achieved before.

At the international bicycle trade fair Eurobike 2004, the bike is presented for the first time. It weighs merely 3.7 kg – unimaginable at that time. The carbon frame weighs merely 818 grams. The new development is a technical crossing of borders with which Canyon underlines its aspiration as a technology leader in the industry. In an interview, former Canyon design engineer Hans-Christian Smolik explains: "The bike is a carrier of technology. We want to show how light and stable a racing bike can be." In 2005, the "Canyon F10 Carbon Ultimate" serial product, derived from this pioneer product, is honoured in the Red Dot Design Award. In retrospect, Michael Kaiser explains the influence of the material on bicycle design: "In the final analysis, carbon is carbon fibre reinforced plastic. It is a composite material because two materials are combined with each other: carbon fibres, on the one hand, which are embedded into a matrix, on the

Der Durchbruch gelingt Roman Arnold mit dem Schritt ins Internet. 1998 sichert er sich die internationale Domain canyon.com und ist seiner Zeit damit weit voraus. 2002 wird aus Radsport Arnold die Canyon Bicycles GmbH mit Sitz in Koblenz. Um die Eigenschaften und die Qualität seiner Fahrräder zu verbessern, ist Roman Arnold auf der Suche nach einem neuen Werkstoff. Er folgt einer Empfehlung, es am Institut für Verbundwerkstoffe in Kaiserslautern zu versuchen. Dort arbeitet der junge Doktorand Michael Kaiser, als im Jahr 2003 Roman Arnold vor der Tür des Forschungsinstituts steht und ein Rennrad aus Carbon braucht – und zwar das beste Rennrad der Welt, wenn möglich. Michael Kaiser arbeitet über Wochen und Monate, bis im Jahr 2004 mit dem Canyon F10 ein Rennrad entsteht, das nie erreichte Werte erzielt.

Erstmals vorgestellt wird das Rad auf der Eurobike 2004. Es bringt gerade einmal 3,7 kg auf die Waage. Unvorstellbar für die damalige Zeit. Der Carbonrahmen wiegt lediglich 818 g. Die Neuentwicklung ist ein technischer Grenzgang, mit dem Canyon seinen Anspruch auf Technologieführerschaft in der Branche unterstreicht. In einem Interview erläutert der damalige Canyon-Konstrukteur Hans-Christian Smolik: „Das Rad ist ein Technologieträger, mit dem wir zeigen wollen, wie leicht und stabil ein Rennrad sein kann." 2005 wird das aus diesem Pionierprodukt abgeleitete Serienprodukt „Canyon F10 Carbon Ultimate" im Red Dot Design Award ausgezeichnet. Michael Kaiser erläutert rückwirkend den Einfluss des Materials auf das Fahrraddesign: „Letztlich ist Carbon ein kohlenstofffaserverstärkter Kunststoff. Es ist ein Verbundwerkstoff, weil man zwei Materialien miteinander kombiniert: Das sind Kohlenstofffasern, die man in eine Matrix einbettet", so Michael Kaiser. „Das Schöne an diesem Werkstoff ist, dass man eine unendliche Anzahl an Gestaltungsmöglichkeiten hat.

other," Michael Kaiser explains. "The beauty of this material is that it gives you a sheer unlimited number of design options. I can combine thousands of different fibres with thousands of different plastics systems. One can render the material either very stiff or very soft, one can make it flexible, elastic or plastic, even thermally or electrically conductive. Actually one can do anything with it." After the success of the Canyon F10, Michael Kaiser considers a job switch from the Institute for Composite Materials to Canyon. By now, he feels a close bond between himself and the company, as he has long since been inspired by the passion expressed by staff and company. In 2007, the moment has arrived. Michael Kaiser becomes the first permanent employee to work in the development department of Canyon Bicycles. What follows is the successive build-up of the development department, the testing laboratory and the quality assurance management. Today, there are nearly 100 staff employed in these areas.

Staying in motion to keep the balance

The Canyon F10 does not yet wear the striking logo of the Canyon bikes, yet it marks a milestone in the bicycle industry and company history of Canyon with regard to technology and design. The teamwork performed by Michael Kaiser as engineer, Hans-Christian Smolik as constructor and Lutz Scheffer as designer clearly states the working principle pursued by Canyon: engineers and designers engage in mutual collaboration to arrive at the best solution. Lutz Scheffer at that time takes care of the development of the product portfolio und the bicycle design. After researching and applying the composite material carbon, Roman Arnold adds more designers to the team. Starting in 2005, the Munich-based KMS Team oversees the complete Canyon brand development which also includes a new corporate design with a new logo and new corporate typeface. In 2007, the corporate design is honoured in the Red Dot Award: Communication Design. In 2009, the award for the new Canyon Home follows. The new building not only reflects the dynamic growth of the company; in the "showroom", the customer learns to understand the areas of technology, design and quality and can directly experience the products and the brand. And the customers' interest in high-quality bicycles with regard to technology and design is growing unstoppably.

In retrospect, Michael Kaiser recalls: "To us, the subject of design in product development has always been an important factor. In 2009, we decided to redefine industrial design as a strategic subject with the objective to play a leading role in the entire industry. Subsequently, we have expanded our product and graphic design team successively, celebrating many successes since then." The design results are impressive. In the last six years, Canyon has won the Red Dot: Best of the Best award six times for, among others, the Speedmax CF SLX triathlon bike and the Aeroad CF SLX racing bike whose design was masterminded by Darmstadt-based Artefakt design studio. The team around Tomas Fiegl and Achim Pohl develops a reduced design language for the racing bikes and time trial machines made of carbon, underlying the attributes of the brand.

Ich kann Tausende von verschiedenen Fasern mit Tausenden von verschiedenen Kunststoffsystemen zusammenbringen. Man kann das Material sehr steif oder sehr weich machen, man kann es flexibel, elastisch oder plastisch, ja sogar wärme- oder elektrisch leitfähig machen. Man kann eigentlich alles machen." Nach dem Erfolg der Canyon F10 denkt Michael Kaiser lange über den Wechsel vom Institut für Verbundwerkstoffe in Kaiserslautern zu Canyon nach. Er fühlt sich inzwischen eng mit dem Unternehmen verbunden, weil ihn die Leidenschaft der Mitarbeiter und die des Unternehmens schon längst angesteckt haben. Im Jahr 2007 ist es so weit. Michael Kaiser wird der erste fest angestellte Mitarbeiter in der Entwicklung von Canyon Bicycles. Was folgt, ist der sukzessive Aufbau der Entwicklungsabteilung, des Prüflabors und des Qualitätswesens. Heute sind knapp 100 Mitarbeiter in diesen Bereichen beschäftigt.

In Bewegung bleiben, um die Balance zu halten

Das Canyon F10 trägt noch nicht den markanten Schriftzug der Canyon-Bikes, markiert aus technologischer und gestalterischer Sicht aber einen wichtigen Meilenstein in der Fahrradbranche und in der Unternehmensgeschichte von Canyon. Die Teamarbeit von Michael Kaiser als Ingenieur, Hans-Christian Smolik als Konstrukteur und Lutz Scheffer als Designer macht das Arbeitsprinzip von Canyon deutlich: Ingenieure und Designer arbeiten gemeinsam an der besten Lösung. Lutz Scheffer kümmert sich damals um die Entwicklung des Produktportfolios und des Fahrraddesigns. Nach der Erforschung und Anwendung des Verbundwerkstoffs Carbon zieht Roman Arnold weitere Designer hinzu. Ab 2005 gestaltet KMS Team aus München die komplette Markenentwicklung von Canyon, die auch ein neues Corporate Design mit neuem Logo und eigener Hausschrift beinhaltet. Das Corporate Design wird 2007 im Red Dot Award: Communication Design ausgezeichnet. 2009 folgt die Auszeichnung für das neue „Canyon Home". Der Neubau spiegelt nicht nur das dynamische Wachstum des Unternehmens wider, im Showroom lernt der Kunde auch die Bereiche Technologie, Design und Qualität verstehen. Hier kann er die Produkte und die Marke hautnah erleben. Und das Interesse der Kunden an technologisch wie gestalterisch hochwertigen Fahrrädern wächst unaufhaltsam.

Rückblickend erinnert sich Michael Kaiser: „Uns war das Thema ‚Design' in der Produktentwicklung schon immer sehr wichtig. Im Jahre 2009 haben wir uns entschlossen, Industriedesign als strategisches Thema neu zu definieren, mit dem Ziel, hier führend in der gesamten Branche werden zu wollen. Wir haben danach sukzessive unser Produkt- und Grafikdesignteam ausgebaut und seitdem viele Erfolge feiern dürfen." Die Designbilanz ist beeindruckend. In den letzten sechs Jahren wird Canyon sechs Mal mit dem Red Dot: Best of the Best ausgezeichnet, unter anderem für das Triathlonrad „Speedmax CF SLX" und das Rennrad „Aeroad CF SLX", die aus der Feder des Darmstädter Designbüros Artefakt stammen. Das Team um Tomas Fiegl und Achim Pohl entwickelt eine reduzierte Formensprache für die Rennräder und Zeitfahrmaschinen aus Carbon, die die Attribute der Marke unterstreichen.

Design captures the city. With integrated LED lighting as well as theft-proof wheels and saddle, the Commuter is ideal for the urban space.
Design erobert die Stadt. Mit integrierter LED-Beleuchtung sowie diebstahlsicheren Laufrädern und Sattel ist der Commuter ideal für den urbanen Raum.

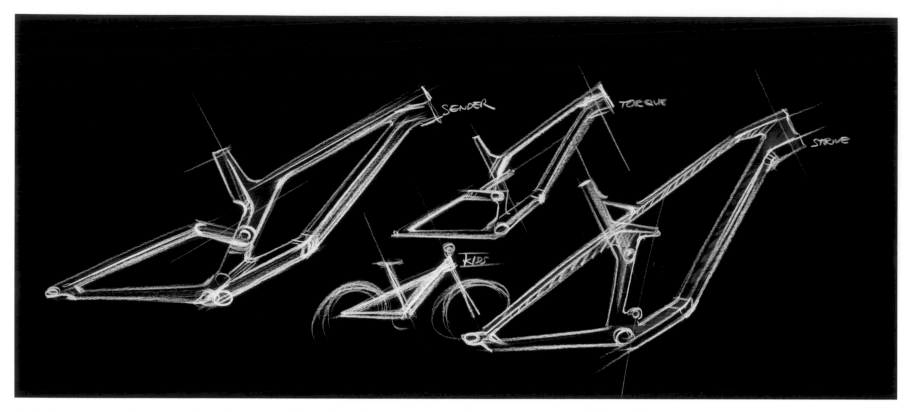

The first step involves a freehand sketch. Later the draft follows. Then, line management and frame aesthetics play a highly crucial role.
Im ersten Schritt wird frei von Hand entworfen. Später folgt der Entwurf. Die Linienführung und Ästhetik des Rahmens spielen dann eine entscheidende Rolle.

In 2017, the Canyon in-house design team receives not one but two "Red Dot: Best of the Best" awards: for the Roadlite CF fitness bike by Fedja Delic and for the Inflite CF SLX, designed by Alexander Forst and Lars Wagner. Numerous awards for the mountain bikes Strive CF, Sender CF and Nerve AL by Canyon designer Peter Kettenring and constructor Vincenz Thoma, as well as for the Commuter urban bike, round off the picture and demonstrate that Canyon, like hardly any other manufacturer in the industry, is outstandingly successful in combining the different bicycle types under a singular design and brand language. The form of each bicycle, whether for the road or for off-road, conveys simplicity, precision and dynamics. As Senior Industrial Designer, Lars Wagner is in charge of the Road Bikes section. He has been active for Canyon since 2010. Senior Industrial Designer Peter Kettenring is responsible for the Mountain Bikes section; he joined Canyon in 2012. Both Lars Wagner and Peter Kettenring studied industrial design in Darmstadt and speak the same language with regard to the design of Canyon bikes. Bringing the bicycles into an aesthetic form that renders the brand attractive yet making the design unobtrusive is the exciting task of the Canyon Design Team. The self-image and aspiration to always develop, design and build the best bicycle is a challenge and motivation, as the single models always have to combine a mixture of different development objectives. Racing cyclists, for instance, always strive for a bike as lightweight as possible which is supposed to be stiff and thus efficient in propulsion at the same time, yet it must not be uncomfortable. Triathletes want the aerodynamically optimised model, while mountain bikers want perfect kinematics.

Im Jahr 2017 wird das Canyon In-house Design Team dann gleich zweimal mit dem Red Dot: Best of the Best ausgezeichnet: für das Fitness-Bike „Roadlite CF" von Fedja Delic und für das „Inflite CF SLX" aus der Feder von Alexander Forst und Lars Wagner. Zahlreiche Auszeichnungen für die Mountainbikes „Strive CF", „Sender CF" und „Nerve AL" von Canyon-Designer Peter Kettenring und Konstrukteur Vincenz Thoma sowie für das Urban Bike „Commuter" runden das Bild ab und veranschaulichen, dass es Canyon wie kaum einem anderen Hersteller der Branche gelingt, die unterschiedlichen Fahrradtypen unter einer Design- und Markensprache zu verbinden. Die Form jedes Fahrrads, ob für die Straße oder für das Gelände, vermittelt Einfachheit, Präzision und Dynamik. Als Senior Industrial Designer verantwortet Lars Wagner den Bereich „Roadbikes". Er ist seit 2010 für Canyon tätig. Verantwortlich für den Bereich „Mountainbikes" ist Senior Industrial Designer Peter Kettenring, der 2012 zu Canyon kommt. Lars Wagner und Peter Kettenring haben beide Industriedesign in Darmstadt studiert und sprechen dieselbe Sprache, wenn es um die Gestaltung der Canyon-Bikes geht. Die Fahrräder in eine ästhetische Form zu bringen, die die Marke attraktiv, das Design aber unaufdringlich macht, ist die spannende Aufgabe des Canyon Design Teams. Das Selbstverständnis und der Anspruch, immer das beste Fahrrad entwickeln, gestalten und bauen zu wollen, ist Herausforderung und Motivation, müssen die einzelnen Modelle doch immer einen Mix aus verschiedenen Entwicklungszielen in sich vereinen. Rennradfahrer etwa streben stets nach einem möglichst leichten Bike, das zugleich steif und somit vortriebseffizient sein soll, andererseits aber nicht unkomfortabel sein darf. Triathleten suchen das aerodynamisch optimierte Modell, Mountainbiker die perfekte Kinematik.

3D rendering and result. By means of computer modelling, a virtual model results that constitutes the materiality and functionality.
The result is a high-quality carbon frame which captivates through aesthetic form and innovative features.
3D-Darstellung und Ergebnis. Mittels der Modellierung am Computer entsteht ein virtuelles Modell, das die Materialität und Funktionalität
darstellt. Das Resultat ist ein hochwertiger Carbonrahmen, der durch ästhetische Form und innovative Funktionen besticht.

All these parameters are gauged by Canyon in static and dynamic quality controls; moreover, the designers are in the wind tunnel for regular testing. With the endoscope and the first computer tomography images in the bicycle industry, all safety-relevant components are literally x-rayed. This applies to the development of new component parts, but the serially produced carbon forks and cockpits are also tested to 100 per cent. Canyon mounts its own bikes in a state-of-the-art facility in Koblenz and sells them via the Internet. The customers are able to experience the wide range of products online or in the Canyon Home, and eventually, for instance, to ride the same bicycle as the numerous professionals under contract with Canyon. The Canyon websites are available in 16 different languages. The bikes are shipped worldwide.

Something that, in retrospect, reads like a self-evident and natural course of things is by no means a straightforward path. Any cyclist knows that, in the face of obstacles and uncertainties, technical defects or material weaknesses, the shortest route from start to finish is not a straight line. This is in no way different for Roman Arnold and Canyon. And this is precisely what makes the success for Canyon so remarkable, because in the areas of technology, quality and design, the company repeatedly arrives at solutions no one had foreseen – not even industry insiders.

All diese Parameter werden von Canyon in statischen und dynamischen Qualitätsprüfungen gemessen, zudem sind die Entwickler regelmäßig für Tests im Windkanal. Mit einem Endoskop und dem ersten Computertomographen in der Fahrradbranche werden alle sicherheitsrelevanten Bauteile zudem buchstäblich durchleuchtet. Das trifft auf die Entwicklung neuer Teile zu, aber auch die in Serie gefertigten Carbongabeln und Cockpits werden zu 100 Prozent geprüft. Canyon montiert seine Bikes in einer hochmodernen Fabrik in Koblenz und vertreibt sie über das Internet. Die Kunden können online oder im Canyon Home die verschiedenen Produktwelten erleben und am Ende zum Beispiel sogar das gleiche Fahrrad wie die zahlreichen Profis fahren, die bei Canyon unter Vertrag stehen. Die Internetseiten von Canyon sind heute in 16 verschiedenen Sprachen verfügbar. Die Fahrräder werden weltweit verschickt.

Was sich rückwirkend wie selbstverständlich liest, ist kein geradliniger Weg. Jeder Radsportler weiß, dass angesichts von Hindernissen und Unwägbarkeiten, technischen Defekten oder Materialschwächen die kürzeste Verbindung zwischen Start und Ziel keine gerade Linie ist. Das ist für Roman Arnold und Canyon nicht anders. Gerade das macht den Erfolg für Canyon so bemerkenswert, weil das Unternehmen im Bereich Technologie, Qualität und Design immer wieder auf Lösungen kommt, mit denen keiner gerechnet hat, nicht einmal Brancheninsider.

Vincenz Thoma, Sandro Groll, Christian Hellmann, Wanjo Koch, Michael Kaiser, Lars Wagner, Peter Kettenring, Roman Arnold,
Fedja Delic, Sebastian Hahn, Dennis Fiedler, Christopher Herd

Red Dot: Design Team of the Year 2017
Interview
Peter Kettenring, Senior Industrial Designer Mountain Bikes
Lars Wagner, Senior Industrial Designer Road Bikes

Mr Kettenring, Mr Wagner, what does cycling actually mean?

P. Kettenring: Roman Arnold, the founder and CEO of Canyon once said: "When I learned to cycle, I felt great freedom for the first time." Basically, cycling is about moving oneself forward independently.

That sounds like a philosophy for life. Cycling to find out something about oneself!

L. Wagner: Absolutely. Almost everyone remembers the first time they rode a bike on their own. It's an emotional moment: the first time cycling alone, without your parents, just on your own steam. Bicycles are an important part of our life experience.

This year was the first time that a children's bike, the Offspring by Canyon, won in the Red Dot Design Award, and two years ago an urban bike called the Commuter won the award. How do these types of bikes fit with the Canyon brand with its origins in race bikes?

L. Wagner: Of course we did consider whether a kid's bike or a lifestyle product like the Commuter fits with our history and our brand. But this step can make absolute sense and be successful if we pay very close attention to transferring the design and quality features that characterise our brand and identity to new areas.

How can you know what kind of bicycle might be in demand in the future?

L. Wagner: That's mainly the job of the product manager, who forms a team together with the designer and the engineer and continuously looks at new types of bikes. The development may well start from scratch, or new trends emerge on the market. Customers are also a source of ideas for entirely new types of bikes. We then use these ideas to create a new overall concept.

Herr Kettenring, Herr Wagner: Fahrrad fahren – was bedeutet das eigentlich?

P. Kettenring: Roman Arnold, der Gründer und CEO von Canyon, hat einmal gesagt: „Als ich Rad fahren lernte, hatte ich erstmals das Gefühl großer Freiheit." Im Prinzip dreht es sich darum, sich selbst zu bewegen, selbst voranzukommen.

Das klingt nach Lebensphilosophie. Rad fahren, um etwas über sich selbst zu erfahren!

L. Wagner: Durchaus. Fast jeder weiß noch, wann er das erste Mal alleine mit dem Fahrrad gefahren ist. Das ist ein emotionaler Moment: das erste Mal allein unterwegs sein, ohne die Eltern, ganz einfach aus eigener Kraft. Das Fahrrad ist ein wichtiger Teil unserer Lebenserfahrung.

In diesem Jahr wurde mit dem Offspring erstmals ein Kinderfahrrad von Canyon im Red Dot Design Award ausgezeichnet, vor zwei Jahren ein Urban Bike, das Commuter. Wie passen diese Fahrradtypen zur Marke Canyon, die aus dem Radsport kommt?

L. Wagner: Natürlich haben wir überlegt, ob ein Kinderrad oder ein Lifestyle-Produkt wie das Commuter zu unserer Geschichte und Marke passen. Wenn man aber sehr genau darauf achtet, die Design- und Qualitätsmerkmale, die unsere Marke und Identität prägen, auf neue Bereiche zu übertragen, dann kann dieser Schritt durchaus sinnvoll und erfolgreich sein.

Woher weiß man, welches Fahrrad in der Zukunft gefragt sein könnte?

L. Wagner: Das ist im Wesentlichen die Arbeit des Produktmanagers, der zusammen mit dem Designer und dem Ingenieur ein Team bildet und sich immer wieder mit neuen Fahrradtypen auseinandersetzt. Die Entwicklung kann durchaus bei null beginnen, oder es entwickeln sich neue Trends im Markt. Auch die Kunden kommen mit Ideen für ganz neue Fahrradtypen. Und wir entwickeln aus diesen Ideen dann ein neues Gesamtkonzept.

So it is possible to reinvent the wheel?

P. Kettenring: Maybe not the wheel, but certainly the bicycle. Bike design has undergone a lot of change, and this will continue to be the case.

L. Wagner: Interestingly, the bicycle is much older than the car, but the classic ideas of industrial design came comparatively late to the bicycle industry. Bicycle design is still a relatively new discipline. This means that we have not yet reached a stage where no more innovation is possible. Development is a continuous process.

P. Kettenring: For example, we developed a Shapeshifter function for the Strive mountain bike. The bike looks like a traditional mountain bike but allows the rider to choose between two different geometries at the touch of a button and to tune the bike to different trail conditions on the fly: uphill and downhill. It's like having two bikes in one.

How would you describe the difference between the past and the present?

P. Kettenring: In the past, when bike frames were still welded together using individual tubes, the work of the designer was limited to the artwork. Nowadays we receive a geometric sketch made up of lines. The geometric sketch provides a framework for us to move within, but as designers we can also make our own suggestions for turning points, kinematics or tube cross-sections. We have become very confident about what we do.

Das Rad lässt sich also doch neu erfinden?

P. Kettenring: Das Rad vielleicht nicht, das Fahrrad schon. Im Fahrraddesign hat sich viel geändert, und es wird sich noch vieles ändern.

L. Wagner: Interessanterweise ist das Fahrrad viel älter als das Automobil. Der klassische Gedanke des Industriedesigns ist aber relativ spät in der Fahrradindustrie angekommen. Das Fahrraddesign ist eine noch relativ junge Disziplin. Wir sind also noch nicht an einem Punkt angekommen, der keine Innovationen mehr zulässt. Die Entwicklung geht immer weiter.

P. Kettenring: Für das Mountainbike „Strive" haben wir beispielsweise eine Shapeshifter-Funktion entwickelt. Das Rad sieht aus wie ein traditionelles Mountainbike, erlaubt dem Fahrer aber, ganz einfach per Knopfdruck zwischen zwei unterschiedlichen Geometrien zu wählen und das Rad während der Fahrt auf unterschiedliche Geländesituationen abzustimmen: bergauf und bergab. Man hat im Prinzip zwei Räder in einem.

Wie lässt sich der Unterschied zwischen gestern und heute beschreiben?

P. Kettenring: Früher, als die Fahrradrahmen noch aus einzelnen Rohren zusammengeschweißt wurden, reduzierte sich die Arbeit des Designers auf das Artwork. Heute erhalten wir eine Geometrieskizze, die aus Linien besteht. Die Geometrieskizze ist einerseits ein Rahmen, in dem wir uns bewegen, andererseits können wir als Designer eigene Vorschläge machen für Drehpunkte, Kinematik oder Rohrquerschnitte. Inzwischen wissen wir sehr gut, was wir tun.

"Simplicity, precision and dynamics are basic elements of our design language."

„Einfachheit, Präzision und Dynamik sind elementare Bestandteile unserer Designsprache."

Lars Wagner, Senior Industrial Designer Road Bikes

L. Wagner: If you look at frame development alone, you will understand that technology also creates whole new design possibilities for the designer and whole new shapes for the bike.

What is the role of the bicycle frame? It combines aesthetics with function.

L. Wagner: Yes, exactly. The bicycle frame is form and structure, volume and sculpture. If you imagine that everything we design always also affects the function, then there is a lot hanging on the frame, quite literally. Basically we draw the frame and structure it with areas of differing brightness so that the light edges and surfaces become visible. In general we try to use edges sparingly but very consciously, as the edges always also symbolise technical precision. The freeform surfaces stand for the distribution of power and the rigidity as well as for bionic shapes.

P. Kettenring: On the one hand we want to reduce the frame to the essentials, but that doesn't mean we simply weld round tubes together. If we apply the ideas of simplicity, precision and dynamics to the frame in a formal aesthetic way, then we emphasise a light edge that connects the rear end of the frame with the main frame. This is an essential point. We can reduce other downstream or subordinate edges a little using lower contrast. Basically, contrast is created where light and shade converge.

L. Wagner: Wenn man sich allein die Rahmenentwicklung anschaut, dann versteht man, dass sich durch die Technologie auch ganz neue Gestaltungsmöglichkeiten für den Designer und ganz neue Formen für das Fahrrad ergeben.

Welche Rolle spielt der Fahrradrahmen? Er vereint ja Ästhetik und Funktion.

L. Wagner: Ja, genau. Der Fahrradrahmen ist Form und Struktur, Volumen und Skulptur. Wenn man sich vorstellt, dass alles, was wir gestalten, immer auch Auswirkungen auf die Funktion hat, dann hängt buchstäblich sehr viel am Rahmen. Im Prinzip ist es so, dass wir den Rahmen zeichnen und mit unterschiedlich hellen Flächen strukturieren, sodass die Lichtkanten und Flächen sichtbar werden. Wir versuchen grundsätzlich, mit den Kanten sparsam, aber sehr deutlich umzugehen, da die Kanten immer auch die technische Präzision symbolisieren. Die Freiformflächen stehen für die Kraftverteilung und die Steifigkeit sowie für bionische Formen.

P. Kettenring: Einerseits wollen wir den Rahmen auf das Wesentliche reduzieren, andererseits bedeutet das nicht, dass wir einfach Rundrohre miteinander verschmelzen. Wenn wir die Gedanken der Einfachheit, Präzision und Dynamik formalästhetisch auf den Rahmen übertragen, dann betonen wir eine Lichtkante, die den Hinterbau und den Hauptrahmen verbindet. Das ist etwas Wesentliches. Andere Kanten, die nach- oder untergeordnet sind, können wir durch einen geringeren Kontrast etwas zurücknehmen. Der Kontrast bildet sich im Prinzip dort, wo sich Licht und Schatten treffen.

"Canyon succeeds better than almost any other manufacturer in combining the different bikes under one design and brand language."

„Canyon gelingt es wie kaum einem anderen Hersteller, die unterschiedlichen Fahrräder unter einer Design- und Markensprache zu verbinden."

Peter Kettenring, Senior Industrial Designer Mountain Bikes

How would you describe the design process at Canyon?

P. Kettenring: We start with a rough 3D sketch. Then we make a 3D print. Next we can use picture editing to change gradients. After that, the draft design goes back into the CAD system.

L. Wagner: The 3D print allows us to check the design. We don't use traditional modelling. Instead we print smaller true-to-scale models and components in house. The parts are then assembled in the technical workshop. After all, we work with very different components, and each one has to fit. As designers we also create the final shapes, and the engineer is responsible for the interfaces to the other mounting parts. As a result, we know exactly what the bike ultimately has to look like and will look like.

P. Kettenring: Artwork is still a very important topic, because the lettering, logos and colours are linked very closely to the design. The lines and the edges of the frame are reflected in and enhanced through the artwork, preventing them from disappearing during the painting stage. But we never create effects that do not exist in the form. By the time the finished bike is wheeled into our office, it's already like an old friend.

L. Wagner: Yes, it's already familiar, we have seen each other before.

Wie lässt sich der Designprozess bei Canyon beschreiben?

P. Kettenring: Wir beginnen mit einer groben Skizze. Dann wird ein 3D aufgebaut. Anschließend besteht die Möglichkeit, im Bildbearbeitungsprogramm Verläufe zu ändern. Von da aus geht der Entwurf dann wieder ins CAD-System.

L. Wagner: Der 3D-Druck dient uns dann zur Überprüfung des Designs. Wir haben keinen klassischen Modellbau, sondern drucken kleinere Maßstabsmodelle und Bauteile bei uns im Haus. In der Technikwerkstatt werden dann die Teile zu einem Ganzen zusammengefügt. Wir arbeiten ja mit ganz unterschiedlichen Komponenten. Und die müssen alle passen. Da wir als Designer auch die finalen Formen gestalten und der Ingenieur die Schnittstellen zu den anderen Anbauteilen übernimmt, wissen wir sehr genau, wie das Fahrrad am Ende aussehen muss und wird.

P. Kettenring: Auch das Thema „Artwork" ist nach wie vor sehr wichtig, da Schrift, Grafik und Farbgebung sehr eng mit der Formgebung verbunden sind. Die Linienführung und die Kanten der Rahmen werden aufgegriffen und durch das Artwork verstärkt, sodass sie nicht durch den Lackiervorgang verschwinden. Es werden aber niemals Effekte erzeugt, die formal nicht da sind. Wenn dann irgendwann das fertige Fahrrad in unser Büro rollt, ist es schon ein alter Bekannter.

L. Wagner: Ja, man kennt sich. Man hat sich schon mal gesehen.

The corporate design stems from the brand agency KMS Team in Munich. The Canyon lettering emphasises the simplicity, precision and dynamics of the bikes.

L. Wagner: The lettering is a real stroke of luck. It doesn't wear over time and never gets boring.

But Canyon design involves even more than that.

L. Wagner: Depending on the type of bike, there are different requirements in terms of aerodynamics, weight, rigidity and comfort. Bringing these opposing factors into harmony with each other is what we do, and that's what makes it exciting.

P. Kettenring: At the same time, Canyon succeeds better than almost any other manufacturer in combining the different bikes under one design and brand language. Every line, every detail and every shape should convey simplicity and precision.

Yet designing simplicity can be very complex.

L. Wagner: Of course we do always try to simplify the bikes. The frame is the structure that keeps the different elements and parts in place. That automatically leads to a certain complexity, because certain connections have to be made. We try to reduce this complexity.

P. Kettenring: The best simplification is one that not only reduces the design but also improves the function. That is a challenge and a difficulty at the same time. Not only do you take something away, you also create an improvement.

How does the idea for a functional yet aesthetic solution come about?

P. Kettenring: At Canyon, there is a very close working relationship between designers and engineers. This team work is hugely instructive. Designers learn from engineers, and engineers learn from designers. And we also always explain why we want to find different solutions for certain details from a design perspective.

L. Wagner: We generally create a team of three persons who are responsible for a project: the product manager, the engineer and the designer. The product manager has the last word if the engineer and the designer can't agree on something.

Is this team structure specific to Canyon?

P. Kettenring: Other companies are generally organised into departments. But often the project teams organised in departments don't sit together at one table from the beginning. So that is a very specific way of working at Canyon.

Das Corporate Design stammt von der Markenagentur KMS Team aus München. Der Schriftzug „Canyon" unterstreicht die Einfachheit, die Präzision und die Dynamik der Fahrräder.

L. Wagner: Der Schriftzug ist ein absoluter Glücksfall. Er verschleißt sich nicht und wird nie langweilig.

Das Canyon-Design umfasst aber noch mehr.

L. Wagner: Je nach Fahrradtyp geht es um unterschiedliche Anforderungen mit Blick auf Aerodynamik, Gewicht, Steifigkeit und Komfort. Diese Gegensätze zu einem harmonischen Ganzen zu verbinden, macht unsere Arbeit aus und bringt die Spannung.

P. Kettenring: Gleichzeitig gelingt es Canyon wie kaum einem anderen Hersteller, die unterschiedlichen Fahrräder unter einer Design- und Markensprache zu verbinden. Jede Linie, jedes Detail, jede Form soll Einfachheit und Präzision vermitteln.

Die Gestaltung der Einfachheit kann aber durchaus komplex sein.

L. Wagner: Natürlich versuchen wir auch immer, die Fahrräder zu vereinfachen. Der Rahmen ist die Struktur, die verschiedene Elemente und Teile an Ort und Stelle hält. Das führt automatisch zu einer gewissen Komplexität, weil bestimmte Verbindungen hergestellt werden müssen. Wir versuchen, diese Komplexität zu reduzieren.

P. Kettenring: Die beste Vereinfachung ist die, die nicht nur eine gestalterische Reduktion, sondern auch eine verbesserte Funktion erzielt. Das ist Herausforderung und Schwierigkeit zugleich. Man nimmt nicht nur etwas weg, sondern schafft auch noch eine Verbesserung.

Wie entsteht die Idee zu einer ebenso funktionalen wie ästhetischen Lösung?

P. Kettenring: Bei Canyon gibt es eine sehr enge Zusammenarbeit zwischen Designern und Ingenieuren. Diese Teamarbeit schult ungemein. Designer lernen von Ingenieuren, und Ingenieure lernen von Designern. Und wir erklären auch immer, warum wir bestimmte Details aus gestalterischer Sicht gerne anders gelöst hätten.

L. Wagner: Wir bilden in der Regel ein Team aus drei Personen, die für ein Projekt verantwortlich sind: Produktmanager, Ingenieur und Designer, wobei der Produktmanager das letzte Wort hat, wenn sich Ingenieur und Designer einmal nicht einigen sollten.

Ist diese Teamstruktur eine Besonderheit bei Canyon?

P. Kettenring: Aus anderen Unternehmen kennt man vorrangig die Organisation in Form von Abteilungen. Die in Abteilungen organisierten Projektteams sitzen aber häufig nicht von Anfang an an einem Tisch. Das ist schon sehr spezifisch für die Arbeit bei Canyon.

So the common understanding of the project team shortens communication channels?

L. Wagner: I think so. We know immediately what the other person is talking about. There are lots of things we don't even need to talk about, because they are obvious for us, particularly amongst designers.

P. Kettenring: I agree. Of course there are always situations where we need to discuss details and have different opinions, but the basic understanding of the brand and the design is a given.

To what extent does the management influence design?

L. Wagner: We are lucky in that our CEO Roman Arnold has a strong affinity for design. His overarching motto of "Building the best bike" emphasises how he sees himself and what he expects. He is the one who motivates all of us over and over again to develop the best bike.

P. Kettenring: Roman Arnold also expressly requested that the bikes should be of high quality and consistent in their appearance. In the same way that the frame should not only be the aesthetic form but also the functional structure, we aim to design even the smallest of details in a functional and aesthetic way. As an owner-managed business, we have the advantage that Roman Arnold truly embraces the overarching motto of "Building the best bike" in practise. This claim is not based simply on economic considerations alone. Instead, it stems from his passion for cycling.

So what role does the design play for customers?

L. Wagner: To help our customers better understand how a bike is created, we have presented examples on the topics of technology, design and quality in our showroom. For us, there is also a moment of acknowledgement when we see the joy and satisfaction on the faces of our customers as they leave the showroom with their new Canyon bike. Cycling simply has an emotional dimension.

P. Kettenring: Our customers are delighted with their new bikes. And happy customers are always also a confirmation of the work we do. Of course we also design bikes that we would like to ride ourselves. And when a new bike comes on the market, it's nice to observe the intense discussions in social media and Internet forums about the design, and not just about the test reports of trade journals. Canyon has recognised this, and maybe even contributed to this perception. It simply demonstrates the general importance of design today.

Is customers' interest in design also reflected in the specialist magazines? Is the topic of design also a topic discussed in the specialist media?

P. Kettenring: Unfortunately, design is not one of the assessment criteria used in the tests by the trade journals. It is a topic that has not yet made it to the print media, but it is very present in social media.

Das gemeinsame Verständnis des Projektteams verkürzt die Kommunikation?

L. Wagner: Ich habe schon das Gefühl. Wir wissen ja sofort, worüber der andere spricht. Über viele Dinge müssen wir gar nicht reden, weil sie für uns selbstverständlich sind, insbesondere zwischen uns Designern.

P. Kettenring: Das sehe ich auch so. Natürlich gibt es immer auch Situationen, in denen es um Details geht und man anderer Meinung ist, aber das grundsätzliche Verständnis für die Marke und das Design ist einfach gegeben.

Inwieweit nimmt die Geschäftsführung auf die Gestaltung Einfluss?

L. Wagner: Wir haben das Glück, dass unser Geschäftsführer Roman Arnold sehr designaffin ist. Sein Leitgedanke „Building the best bike" unterstreicht sein Selbstverständnis und seinen Anspruch. Er ist es, der uns alle immer wieder motiviert, das beste Fahrrad zu entwickeln.

P. Kettenring: Roman Arnold hat auch den konkreten Wunsch geäußert, dass die Fahrräder hochwertig und wie aus einem Guss aussehen. So, wie der Rahmen nicht nur ästhetische Form, sondern auch funktionale Struktur sein soll, haben wir auch den Anspruch, die kleinsten Details funktional und ästhetisch zu gestalten. Als inhabergeführtes Unternehmen haben wir den Vorteil, dass Roman Arnold den Leitgedanken „Building the best bike" lebt. Dieser Anspruch geht nicht einfach nur auf wirtschaftliche Überlegungen zurück, sondern resultiert aus seiner Leidenschaft für das Radfahren.

Welche Rolle spielt denn das Design für die Kunden?

L. Wagner: Damit auch unsere Kunden die Entwicklung eines Fahrrads besser verstehen, haben wir die Themen „Technologie", „Design" und „Qualität" beispielhaft in unserem Showroom dargestellt. Für uns ist es zudem ein Moment der Bestätigung, wenn man die Freude und Zufriedenheit in den Gesichtern der Kunden sehen kann, die mit ihrem neuen Canyon-Fahrrad den Showroom verlassen. Rad fahren ist einfach etwas Emotionales.

P. Kettenring: Unsere Kunden freuen sich riesig über ihr neues Fahrrad. Und die Freude der Kunden ist immer auch eine Wertschätzung unserer Arbeit. Natürlich gestalten wir auch Fahrräder, die wir selbst gerne fahren möchten. Wenn dann aber ein neues Fahrrad auf den Markt kommt, lässt sich sehr schön beobachten, wie in den Sozialen Medien und in den Internetforen intensiv über das Design diskutiert wird und nicht nur über die Testberichte der Fachzeitschriften. Canyon hat das erkannt. Vielleicht hat Canyon diese Wahrnehmung auch gefördert. Es zeigt einfach, welche generelle Bedeutung das Thema „Design" heute hat.

Spiegelt sich das Designinteresse der Kunden auch in den Fachmagazinen wieder? Ist Design auch ein Thema in den Fachmedien?

P. Kettenring: In den Tests der Fachmagazine ist Design leider kein Bewertungskriterium. Das Thema ist in den Printmedien noch nicht angekommen, in den Sozialen Medien dagegen schon.

Dr Michael Kaiser, Technical Managing Director Canyon Bicycles GmbH

Roman Arnold, Founder and Managing Director Canyon Bicycles GmbH

L. Wagner: The traditional media are of course important for Canyon's success. For race bikes, Tour magazine publishes a well-known Tour Test. And when we start a new project, everyone knows that we want to win that test. But we don't design new bikes just to have a new sales argument. The technical or design changes we make are based on the desire to build the best bike.

What role does the material play in bicycle design?

L. Wagner: The low-end models include bikes with an aluminium frame, while the higher-end models have carbon frames.

P. Kettenring: Normally we design the carbon model first, and apply the carbon model to the different segments. The impetus comes from the high-end models.

Traditionally it has been relatively easy to tell a bike with an aluminium frame from one with a carbon frame on account of the welded seams, isn't that so?

P. Kettenring: But the new models are making this optical distinction increasingly difficult, because the aluminium frames now also look like they are made from a single cast part.

L. Wagner: It goes without saying that we design new models without transitions and welded seams, using technology to try to get aluminium frames closer to the ideal, which is a carbon frame.

L. Wagner: Natürlich sind auch die klassischen Medien für den Erfolg von Canyon wichtig. Im Rennradbereich veröffentlicht das Tour-Magazin einen bekannten Tour-Test. Und wenn wir ein neues Projekt beginnen, ist jedem klar, dass wir diesen Test gewinnen wollen. Wir gestalten aber keine neuen Fahrräder, nur um ein neues Verkaufsargument zu haben. Die technischen oder gestalterischen Veränderungen, die wir vornehmen, basieren auf dem Anspruch, das beste Fahrrad zu bauen.

Welche Rolle spielt das Material für das Fahrraddesign?

L. Wagner: Bei den Einsteigermodellen findet man Fahrräder mit Aluminiumrahmen. Im gehobenen Segment kommen Carbonrahmen zum Einsatz.

P. Kettenring: Im Normalfall gestalten wir zuerst das Carbonmodell und übertragen das dann auf die unterschiedlichen Segmente. Der Impuls geht vom High-End-Bereich aus.

Traditionell lassen sich die Fahrräder mit Aluminiumrahmen aufgrund der Schweißnähte relativ leicht von den Fahrrädern mit Carbonrahmen unterscheiden, oder?

P. Kettenring: Die neuen Modelle machen diese optische Unterscheidung aber zusehends schwieriger, da die Aluminiumrahmen auch schon wie aus einem Guss aussehen.

L. Wagner: Wir gestalten neue Modelle natürlich übergangslos und ohne Schweißnähte und versuchen mithilfe der Technologie auch im Aluminiumbereich, uns dem Idealzustand der Carbonrahmen anzunähern.

What conditions does Canyon use to test its own bikes? The question of material quality is always also relevant for safety.

L. Wagner: Generally there are between 10 and 20 bikes assembled that are ridden and tested on road or off road by professionals, but also of course by the development team.

P. Kettenring: In addition, the quality of the pre-series production models is tested on static and dynamic test stations in the lab in order to meet norms and standards and to have similar testing stands to the bike magazines that test our bikes.

L. Wagner: What we want to achieve is a frame that is flexible vertically and rigid horizontally. The direction of the fibre in the carbon is designed accordingly. In the tests on the test station, we can see very clearly how the individual components work under pressure or tensile forces.

P. Kettenring: For example, there is a dedicated test station for the Strive with its Shapeshifter function. This station tests the durability of the bearings and seals in continuous rain and in off-road conditions with mud running down the tubes.

L. Wagner: We literally look right through the frames, and we were the first company in the bike industry to use computer tomography for quality testing.

What trends are you currently watching in bicycle design?

P. Kettenring: One trend is definitely system integration. Nowadays the customer gets a bike specially tailored to his or her needs, and no longer has to replace the components.

L. Wagner: E-bikes will also have a role to play in the future of Canyon. But of course that does mean abandoning the fundamental idea of cycling, which is to move oneself forward on one's own steam. It is almost a philosophical question.

All the more astounding how strongly Canyon has grown so far without e-bikes.

L. Wagner: If your motivation is to build the better product, you don't necessarily have to be the first on the market with a whole new type of bike.

P. Kettenring: The key moment is when you ride an e-bike for the first time. It is a completely new and different feeling. And that requires a new solution.

Mr Wagner, Mr Kettenring, thank you for speaking with us and congratulations on the title of honour, "Red Dot: Design Team of the Year".

Unter welchen Bedingungen testet Canyon die eigenen Fahrräder? Die Frage der Materialqualität ist ja immer auch sicherheitsrelevant.

L. Wagner: In der Regel sind 10 bis 20 Fahrräder aufgebaut, die von Profis, aber natürlich auch von der Entwicklungsabteilung auf der Straße oder im Gelände gefahren und getestet werden.

P. Kettenring: Zudem werden im Prüflabor die Modelle der Vorserienproduktion auf statischen und dynamischen Prüfständen mit Blick auf ihre Qualität überprüft, um Normen und Standards zu erfüllen und um ähnliche Prüfbedingungen zu haben wie die Fahrradmagazine, die unsere Fahrräder testen.

L. Wagner: Wir wollen ja erreichen, dass der Rahmen vertikal flexibel und horizontal steif ist. Entsprechend wird die Faserrichtung des Carbons darauf ausgelegt. Und in den Tests auf dem Prüfstand sieht man sehr genau, wie die einzelnen Bauteile unter Druck oder Zug arbeiten.

P. Kettenring: Für das Strive mit Shapeshifter-Funktion gibt es beispielsweise einen eigenen Prüfstand. Hier geht es um die Haltbarkeit der Lager und Dichtungen, wenn es dauerhaft regnet und im Gelände der Schlamm an den Rohren herunterläuft.

L. Wagner: Wir durchleuchten die Rahmen regelrecht und waren das erste Unternehmen in der Fahrradindustrie, das einen Computertomographen zur Qualitätsprüfung eingesetzt hat.

Welche Trends verfolgen Sie aktuell im Fahrraddesign?

P. Kettenring: Ein Trend ist sicherlich in der Systemintegration zu sehen. Heute erhält der Kunde ein speziell auf ihn abgestimmtes Fahrrad und muss gar nicht mehr die Komponenten austauschen.

L. Wagner: E-Bikes werden auch bei Canyon in Zukunft eine Rolle spielen. Allerdings verabschiedet man sich dann natürlich von dem grundsätzlichen Gedanken des Fahrrads, sich selbst aus eigener Kraft fortzubewegen. Das ist schon fast eine philosophische Frage.

Umso erstaunlicher ist, wie stark Canyon bisher ohne das Thema „E-Bike" gewachsen ist.

L. Wagner: Wenn man den Anspruch hat, das bessere Produkt zu bauen, muss man nicht unbedingt als erster mit einem ganz neuen Fahrradtyp auf dem Markt vertreten sein.

P. Kettenring: Der Schlüsselmoment ist halt der, wenn man das erste Mal E-Bike fährt. Es ist ein ganz anderes, neues Gefühl. Und das verlangt nach einer neuen Lösung.

Herr Wagner, Herr Kettenring, vielen Dank für das Gespräch und herzlichen Glückwunsch zur Ehrenauszeichnung „Red Dot: Design Team of the Year".

"The cyclist must be convinced by the product.
Only when the cyclist is convinced that it is a
fast bike will he really go fast."
„Der Fahrer muss vom Produkt überzeugt sein.
Nur wenn der Fahrer überzeugt ist, dass es ein
schnelles Rad ist, wird er auch schnell fahren."

Dr Michael Kaiser, Technical Managing Director Canyon Bicycles GmbH

Canyon Speedmax CF SLX
Design: Artefakt industriekultur, Darmstadt & Canyon Bicycles GmbH, Koblenz

Red Dot: Best of the Best
The best designers of their category
Die besten Designer ihrer Kategorie

The designers of the Red Dot: Best of the Best
Only a few products in the Red Dot Design Award receive the "Red Dot: Best of the Best" accolade. In each category, the jury can assign this award to products of outstanding design quality and innovative achievement. Exploring new paths, these products are all exemplary in their design and oriented towards the future.

The following chapter introduces the people who have received one of these prestigious awards. It features the best designers and design teams of the year 2017 together with their products, revealing in interviews and statements what drives these designers and what design means to them.

Die Designer der Red Dot: Best of the Best
Nur sehr wenige Produkte im Red Dot Design Award erhalten die Auszeichnung „Red Dot: Best of the Best". Die Jury kann mit dieser Auszeichnung in jeder Kategorie Design von außerordentlicher Qualität und Innovationsleistung besonders hervorheben. In jeder Hinsicht vorbildlich gestaltet, beschreiten diese Produkte neue Wege und sind zukunftsweisend.

Das folgende Kapitel stellt die Menschen vor, die diese besondere Auszeichnung erhalten haben. Es zeigt die besten Designer und Designteams des Jahres 2017 zusammen mit ihren Produkten. In Interviews und Statements wird deutlich, was diese Designer bewegt und was ihnen Design bedeutet.

Aruliden

"We always strive to simplify the complex."
„Wir sind stets bemüht, das Komplexe zu vereinfachen."

Was your award-winning product based on a particular design approach?
We needed to make sure that we created a hardware product that worked hand in hand with the software, ensuring that the hardware is a real extension of the technology within it. We created a very simple and intuitive experience. The intuitive gesture commands mean you can interact with content naturally and comfortably. The tools require no batteries – pens write like pens and erasers remove content like erasers should.

How do you define design quality?
There needs to be a strong basis for the existence of a product. If there is not a good reason for this product being made, then it doesn't matter.

Liegt Ihrem ausgezeichneten Produkt ein bestimmter Gestaltungsansatz zugrunde?
Wir mussten sicherstellen, dass wir eine Hardware hervorbringen, die zur Software passt, damit die Hardware eine wirkliche Fortführung der enthaltenen Technologie ist. Wir haben eine ganz einfache und intuitive Nutzererfahrung geschaffen. Intuitive Gestensteuerung bedeutet, dass man mit dem Inhalt natürlich und bequem umgehen kann. Die Geräte brauchen keine Batterien – ein Stift schreibt wie ein Stift und ein Radierer entfernt Inhalte, genau wie es ein Radierer tun sollte.

Wie definieren Sie Designqualität?
Es muss für die Existenz eines Produktes einen triftigen Anlass geben. Wenn es keinen guten Grund gibt, ein Produkt zu machen, ist es unbedeutend.

reddot award 2017
best of the best

Manufacturer
Google, New York, USA

Jamboard
Digital Collaborative Whiteboard

See page 78
Siehe Seite 78

Tomasz Augustyniak

"It's important to ask appropriate questions to get the best answers."

„Es ist wichtig, geeignete Fragen zu stellen, um die besten Antworten zu erhalten."

What was your goal when you designed your award-winning product?
My goal was to design a functional work-station which would perfectly complement different interiors, both modern and classic.

Was your award-winning product based on a particular design approach?
The main idea was to put height-adjustable work surfaces literally "in the frame" – to create both independent workplaces and linear groups of benches.

What do you see as being the biggest challenges in your industry at present?
I believe that, in this age of fast technological development, the challenge is the appropriate use of technology in all areas of life so that it serves people and is used to meet real human needs.

Welches Ziel verfolgten Sie bei der Gestaltung Ihres ausgezeichneten Produktes?
Mein Ziel war es, einen funktionalen Arbeitsplatz zu gestalten, der unterschiedliche Interieurs perfekt ergänzen würde – ob modern oder klassisch.

Liegt Ihrem ausgezeichneten Produkt ein bestimmter Gestaltungsansatz zugrunde?
Die Kernidee war, aus höhenverstellbaren Arbeitsflächen sowohl individuelle Arbeitsplätze als auch lineare Gruppen von Schreibtischen erschaffen zu können.

Worin sehen Sie aktuell die größten Herausforderungen in Ihrer Branche?
Ich glaube, dass die Herausforderung in diesem Zeitalter der schnellen technologischen Entwicklungen darin liegt, Technologie in allen Lebensbereichen angemessen anzuwenden, damit sie den Menschen dient und eingesetzt wird, um echte menschliche Bedürfnisse zu erfüllen.

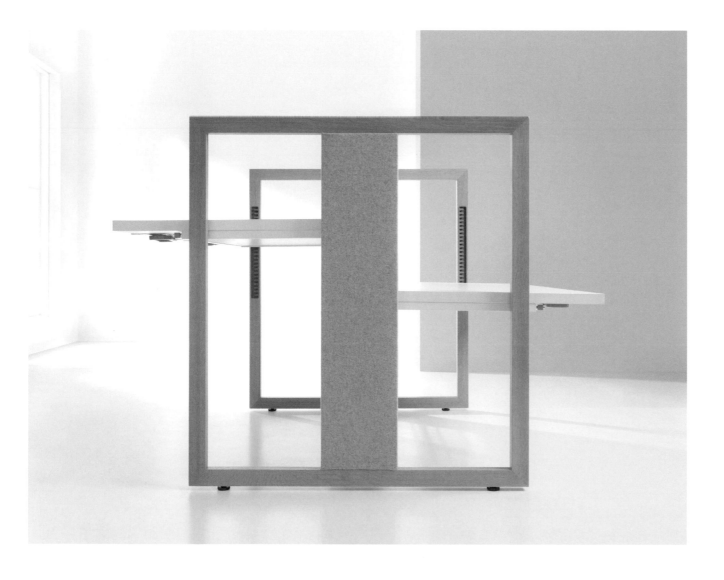

reddot award 2017
best of the best

Manufacturer
Mikomax Smart Office, Lodz, Poland

Stand Up
Office Desk
Büroschreibtisch

See page 82
Siehe Seite 82

David Bonneywell
Boss Design

"Dieter Rams: 10 Principles of Good Design."

„Dieter Rams: 10 Thesen für gutes Design."

What was your goal when you designed your award-winning product?
To create the most beautiful, functional chair, requiring minimal adjustment by the user. A new approach to how we use furniture in an office environment was needed.

What do you see as being the biggest challenges in your industry at present?
Global trade has made it easy for us all to buy cheap furniture, so a lot of the middle market has been drawn into buying inferior-quality products against short-term replacement cycles – a practice that is causing our industry to have a greater impact on the environment than it should.

Welches Ziel verfolgten Sie bei der Gestaltung Ihres ausgezeichneten Produktes?
Den schönsten funktionalen Stuhl zu gestalten, der vom Benutzer nur minimale Anpassungen erfordert. Ein neuer Ansatz, wie wir Möbel im Büroumfeld einsetzen, war nötig.

Worin sehen Sie aktuell die größten Herausforderungen in Ihrer Branche?
Der globale Handel hat es uns leicht gemacht, billige Möbel zu kaufen. Ein Großteil des mittleren Marktsegments ist dazu verleitet worden, Produkte minderwertiger Qualität zu kaufen, die innerhalb kurzer Zeit ersetzt werden müssen – eine Praxis, die dazu führt, dass unsere Branche eine größere Auswirkung auf die Umwelt hat, als sie haben sollte.

reddot award 2017
best of the best

Manufacturer
Boss Design, Dudley,
West Midlands, Great Britain

Trinetic
Office Chair
Bürostuhl

See page 86
Siehe Seite 86

Waku Tsuchiyama, Alexander Hurford
Okamura Corporation

"Keep it simple. So the design concept can speak for itself."

„Mach es einfach. Damit das Designkonzept für sich selbst spricht."

Was your award-winning product based on a particular design approach?
The design ethos was basically a simplistic systematic style that enables our customers to easily customise the product to suit their needs.

Do you have a role model?
Alberto Meda. He has a pure engineering approach to solving complex problems but at the same time he creates truly simple beautiful products.

How do you define design quality?
As a delicate balance between functionality, beauty and originality.

What do you see as being the biggest challenges in your industry at present?
As we are a big manufacturer of office furniture it will always be the ecology. Finding ways to use less material is paramount.

Liegt Ihrem ausgezeichneten Produkt ein bestimmter Gestaltungsansatz zugrunde?
Das Designethos beruhte im Kern auf einem stark vereinfachten, systematischen Stil, der es unseren Kunden ermöglicht, das Produkt leicht an ihre Bedürfnisse anzupassen.

Haben Sie ein Vorbild?
Alberto Meda. Er verfolgt zur Lösung komplexer Probleme einen reinen Engineering-Ansatz. Dabei kreiert er gleichzeitig wirklich schlichte, schöne Produkte.

Wie definieren Sie Designqualität?
Als ein empfindliches Gleichgewicht zwischen Funktionalität, Schönheit und Originalität.

Worin sehen Sie aktuell die größten Herausforderungen in Ihrer Branche?
Da wir ein großer Hersteller von Büromöbeln sind, wird es immer die Ökologie sein. Weniger Material zu verwenden, ist von größter Bedeutung.

reddot award 2017
best of the best

Manufacturer
Okamura Corporation, Yokohama, Japan

PRECEDE
Office System
Bürosystem

See page 96
Siehe Seite 96

Adrià Guiu, Iñaki Remiro
GR Industrial Design

"Function, Form and Emotion."

„Funktion, Form und Emotion."

What was your goal when you designed your award-winning product?
Observation enabled us to achieve a powerful solution that balanced user needs with the requirements of Lamy's brand heritage. The digital world is changing permanently, but when it comes to design it is still possible to produce something enduring. That belief was at the heart of this project from the start.

Was your award-winning product based on a particular design approach?
Observe, empathise and devise. Simply by paying close attention to the world around us – both the cultural and natural world – a designer can come up with products that will improve the environment we live in.

Welches Ziel verfolgten Sie bei der Gestaltung Ihres ausgezeichneten Produktes?
Beobachtungen erlaubten es uns, eine leistungsstarke Lösung zu finden, die die Bedürfnisse der Nutzer mit den Anforderungen von Lamys Markenerbe in Einklang brachte. Die digitale Welt verändert sich permanent, doch wenn es um Design geht, ist es immer noch möglich, etwas Dauerhaftes zu schaffen. Dieser Glaube stand von Anfang an im Mittelpunkt dieses Projektes.

Liegt Ihrem ausgezeichneten Produkt ein bestimmter Gestaltungsansatz zugrunde?
Beobachten, sich in andere hineinversetzen und Ideen entwickeln. Allein dadurch, dass man genau auf seine Umgebung achtet – damit meine ich sowohl das kulturelle Umfeld als auch die Natur –, kann man als Designer Produkte gestalten, die die Welt, in der wir leben, verbessern.

reddot award 2017
best of the best

Manufacturer
C. Josef Lamy GmbH, Heidelberg, Germany

LAMY screen
Stylus

See page 122
Siehe Seite 122

Adam Sjöberg, Christian Högstedt, Mikael Erlandsson, Anton Hoffman
FLIR Systems

"Why, why, why and what it is good for?
Question everything to find the essence."

„Warum, warum, warum und wozu ist es gut?
Alles hinterfragen, um den Kern zu erfassen."

What was your goal when you designed your award-winning product?
To create an advanced product that was suitable for industrial environments, as well as bringing the user experience to completely new levels.

What inspires you?
Snow falling on cars – creating awesome shapes.

How do you maintain a work-life balance?
The passion for design makes the difference between work and the rest of life blurry and greyed out. You're a designer even when you're not designing.

What do you see as being the biggest challenges in your industry at present?
To communicate the possibilities with infrared technology and design experiences.

Welches Ziel verfolgten Sie bei der Gestaltung Ihres ausgezeichneten Produktes?
Ein fortgeschrittenes Produkt zu schaffen, das für industrielle Umgebungen geeignet ist. Gleichzeitig wollten wir die Nutzererfahrung auf völlig neue Ebenen bringen.

Was inspiriert Sie?
Schnee, der auf Autos fällt und so großartige Formen bildet.

Wie erhalten Sie sich Ihre Work-Life-Balance?
Aufgrund unserer Leidenschaft für Design verwischt die Grenze zwischen Arbeit und dem Rest des Lebens und ist undeutlich. Man ist Designer, selbst wenn man gerade nicht am Gestalten ist.

Worin sehen Sie aktuell die größten Herausforderungen in Ihrer Branche?
In der Kommunikation der Möglichkeiten, die die Infrarot-Technologie und Designerfahrungen bieten können.

reddot award 2017
best of the best

Manufacturer
FLIR Systems, Täby, Sweden

FLIR Exx-Series
Thermal Imaging Camera
Wärmebildkamera

See page 128
Siehe Seite 128

Jürgen R. Schmid
Design Tech

"Simple is the opposite of undemanding."
„Einfach ist das Gegenteil von anspruchslos."

reddot award 2017
best of the best

Manufacturer
ELGAN-Diamantwerkzeuge GmbH & Co. KG,
Nürtingen, Germany

Contour Honing Tool
Konturhonwerkzeug

See page 132
Siehe Seite 132

Erik Veurman
Nedap N.V.

"Design for human beings."
„Design für Menschen."

Was your award-winning product based on a particular design approach?
With "design for human beings" I mean that product design often revolves around a product's end-users, but there are so many more human beings involved in the life cycle of a product. Our award-winning MidRanger is designed also for the people that produce it, that market and sell it.

Is there a product that you have always dreamed about realising someday?
Playing a key role in the design of a new car has always been a dream. To me, the automotive industry is the absolute pinnacle of industrial design. Car manufacturers are in such a competitive market that they don't have room to slack off any part of the life cycle design.

Liegt Ihrem ausgezeichneten Produkt ein bestimmter Gestaltungsansatz zugrunde?
Mit „Design für Menschen" meine ich, dass sich Produktdesign oft um die Endnutzer eines Produktes dreht, aber es so viel mehr Menschen gibt, die an seinem Lebenszyklus beteiligt sind. Unser ausgezeichneter MidRanger wurde auch für die Menschen konzipiert, die ihn produzieren, vermarkten und verkaufen.

Welches Produkt würden Sie gerne einmal realisieren?
Eine Schlüsselrolle im Design eines neuen Autos zu spielen, war schon immer mein Traum. Für mich ist die Automobilindustrie der absolute Gipfel des Industriedesigns. Die Automobilhersteller befinden sich in einem so umkämpften Markt, dass sie es sich nicht leisten können, irgendein Detail im Gestaltungszyklus zu vernachlässigen.

reddot award 2017
best of the best

Manufacturer
Nedap N.V., Groenlo, Netherlands

MidRanger
RFID Reader for Libraries
RFID-Lesegerät für Bibliotheken

See page 156
Siehe Seite 156

Scope Design & Strategy bv

"Understanding clients and exceeding expectations
in challenging design projects."

„In anspruchsvollen Designprojekten muss man die Kunden verstehen
und ihre Erwartungen übertreffen."

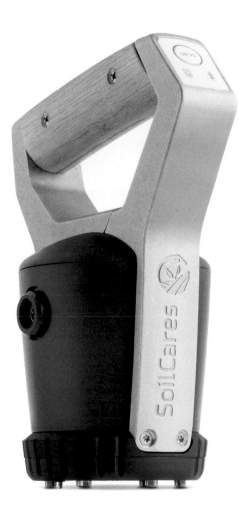

What was your goal when you designed your award-winning product?
Create a clever and attractive tool that enables small-acre farmers all over the world to increase their yield.

Was your award-winning product based on a particular design approach?
Charged with enthusiasm and curiosity we create, evaluate and revise our creations until they fit.

What inspires you?
The idea that our results can make a difference. When all aspects of our creation are aligned, the overall result has the maximum impact.

What does winning the Red Dot: Best of the Best mean to you?
It is a recognition and sincere compliment and for our clients it is a confirmation of the level of our innovation.

Welches Ziel verfolgten Sie bei der Gestaltung Ihres ausgezeichneten Produktes?
Ein raffiniertes und ansprechendes Werkzeug zu gestalten, das Kleinbauern weltweit verwenden können, um ihren Ernteertrag zu steigern.

Liegt Ihrem ausgezeichneten Produkt ein bestimmter Gestaltungsansatz zugrunde?
Wir gestalten, beurteilen und verbessern unsere Entwürfe mit Enthusiasmus und Neugier, bis sie passen.

Was inspiriert Sie?
Der Gedanke, dass unsere Lösungen einen Unterschied machen können. Wenn alle Aspekte unseres Entwurfs aufeinander abgestimmt sind, hat das Endergebnis die größtmögliche Wirkung.

Was bedeutet die Auszeichnung mit dem Red Dot: Best of the Best für Sie?
Es ist eine Anerkennung und ein ehrliches Kompliment, und für unsere Kunden eine Bestätigung unseres Innovationsniveaus.

reddot award 2017
best of the best

Manufacturer
SoilCares, Wageningen, Netherlands

Soil Scanner
Bodenscanner

See page 184
Siehe Seite 184

Jürgen R. Schmid
Design Tech

"Simple is the opposite of undemanding."
„Einfach ist das Gegenteil von anspruchslos."

What was your goal when you designed your award-winning product?
We knew that this product would only be a success if we could radically simplify the complex operating sequence – the loading and unloading of vehicles with heavy materials or components – without requiring additional equipment such as forklifts and pallet trucks. xetto can move loads vertically and horizontally and, in addition, independently loads itself onto the transporter together with the general cargo.

Do you have a role model?
I am fascinated by personalities who are brave enough not to be put off from driving their visions forward despite opposition.

How do you maintain a work-life balance?
I only take on projects that are challenging and seemingly unsolvable. That drives me and gets me going.

Welches Ziel verfolgten Sie bei der Gestaltung Ihres ausgezeichneten Produktes?
Uns war klar, dass dieses Produkt nur dann erfolgreich sein wird, wenn wir den komplizierten Bedienablauf – das Be- und Entladen von Fahrzeugen mit schweren Materialien oder Bauteilen – radikal vereinfachen, ohne dafür mehrere Geräte wie Stapler und Hubwagen einzusetzen. xetto kann Lasten vertikal und horizontal bewegen und verlädt sich zudem selbständig mit dem Stückgut in den Transporter.

Haben Sie ein Vorbild?
Ich bin fasziniert von Persönlichkeiten, die mutig sind, sich nicht beirren lassen und ihre Visionen auch gegen Widerstände vorantreiben.

Wie erhalten Sie sich Ihre Work-Life-Balance?
Ich übernehme nur Projekte, die mich herausfordern und scheinbar unlösbar sind. Das treibt mich an und bringt mich in „Flow".

reddot award 2017
best of the best

Manufacturer
HOERBIGER Automotive Komfortsysteme GmbH, Schongau, Germany

xetto®
Innovative Transport and Loading System
Innovatives Komfort-Beladesystem

See page 190
Siehe Seite 190

Peng Chen
Shenzhen Pudu Technology Co., Ltd.

"A design is called 'design', because it has solved problems."

„Ein Design heißt ‚Design', weil es Probleme gelöst hat."

What was your goal when you designed your award-winning product?
I wanted to design a cool and practical robot to help many people.

Do you have a role model?
Dieter Rams is my idol. I adore him. In particular, he put forward ten theses on good design. That is my source of enlightenment and guidance.

How do you maintain a work-life balance?
Do what you like, like what you do.

What do you see as being the biggest challenges in your industry at present?
Products need to be more and more diversified and must even be able to cross industries. That requires us to learn more about technology and information.

Welches Ziel verfolgten Sie bei der Gestaltung Ihres ausgezeichneten Produktes?
Ich wollte einen coolen und praktischen Roboter gestalten, um vielen Menschen zu helfen.

Haben Sie ein Vorbild?
Dieter Rams ist mein Idol. Ich bewundere ihn. Vor allem weil er zehn Thesen über gutes Design aufgestellt hat. Sie sind meine Orientierungshilfe und Quelle der Erleuchtung.

Wie erhalten Sie sich Ihre Work-Life-Balance?
Tu das, was du liebst, liebe das, was du tust.

Worin sehen Sie aktuell die größten Herausforderungen in Ihrer Branche?
Produkte müssen immer verschiedenartiger werden und sie müssen auch für den branchenübergreifenden Einsatz geeignet sein. Das erfordert, dass wir mehr über die Technologien lernen und uns besser informieren.

reddot award 2017
best of the best

Manufacturer
Shenzhen Pudu Technology Co., Ltd.,
Shenzhen, China

PuduBOT
Service Robot
Serviceroboter

See page 226
Siehe Seite 226

Yi Chen, Feizi Ye, Tingting Xue, Bin Zheng, Haichen Zheng, Yong Zheng, Jian Sun, Ye Tian, Xue Mei, Fan Li

Intelligent Steward Co., Ltd.

"No boasts, no repeat mistakes."

„Man darf nicht prahlen oder wiederholt Fehler machen."

What was your goal when you designed your award-winning product?
Our goal is finding a way to make users feel the product's vitality through our design. In contrast to general tooling products, we think robots should be proactive. This lively performance comes from the designer's recognition and comprehension of 'initiative thinking' and 'vivid expression'.

Was your award-winning product based on a particular design approach?
Actually, we hope BeanQ can be understandable and fun even in a non-working status. That's why we used an unconventional design approach. We referred to animation design at the beginning and devoted a lot of attention to developing BeanQ's character, form, habits, background story and even world view.

Welches Ziel verfolgten Sie bei der Gestaltung Ihres ausgezeichneten Produktes?
Unser Ziel war es, dem Nutzer die Vitalität des Produktes mithilfe unseres Designs zu vermitteln. Anders als übliche Werkzeugprodukte sollten Roboter, so glauben wir, proaktiv sein. Die lebendige Funktionsweise rührt daher, dass der Designer erkannt und verstanden hat, dass ‚eigeninitiatives Denken' und ein ‚lebhafter Ausdruck' wichtig sind.

Liegt Ihrem ausgezeichneten Produkt ein bestimmter Gestaltungsansatz zugrunde?
Wir hoffen, dass BeanQ, selbst wenn er nicht im Funktionsmodus ist, verständlich ist und Spaß macht. Deshalb haben wir einen unkonventionellen Gestaltungsansatz gewählt. Wir haben uns anfangs auf Animationsdesign gestützt und viel Zeit in die Entwicklung eines Charakters, einer Form, der Gewohnheiten, des Hintergrunds und sogar der Weltanschauung von BeanQ investiert.

reddot award 2017
best of the best

Manufacturer
Intelligent Steward Co., Ltd., Beijing, China

Pudding BeanQ
Robot for Early Childhood Education
Roboter für die frühkindliche Erziehung

See page 228
Siehe Seite 228

Zhou Shu, Feng Zhiqun, Dai Nanhai, Fei Zhaojun, Zhao Tianyu, Yi Zuowei
Haier Innovation Design Center

"Not all efforts will result in success, but giving up must result in failure."

„Nicht alle Bemühungen führen zum Erfolg, aber wenn man aufgibt, scheitert man unweigerlich."

Was your award-winning product based on a particular design approach?
Our core design approach focused on user benefit. Due to serious air pollution in China, all of us focus on air safety. So users want to buy an air purifier which is a form of home furnishing.

What do you see as being the biggest challenges in your industry at present?
After years of development, the current phenomenon of product homogenisation is quite serious because of the increasing focus on innovating details. But we believe that as time goes by, users' needs will change. So we can't give up our desire to keep innovating.

Liegt Ihrem ausgezeichneten Produkt ein bestimmter Gestaltungsansatz zugrunde?
Unser Hauptaugenmerk lag auf dem Anwendernutzen. Aufgrund der gravierenden Luftverschmutzung in China sind wir alle auf die Qualität der Luft fokussiert. Nutzer wollen daher einen Luftreiniger kaufen, der zu einem Teil der Inneneinrichtung wird.

Worin sehen Sie aktuell die größten Herausforderungen in Ihrer Branche?
Nach Jahren der Weiterentwicklung besteht durch den zunehmenden Fokus auf Detailinnovationen aktuell die Gefahr der Vereinheitlichung von Produkten. Allerdings glauben wir, dass die Anforderungen der Nutzer sich im Laufe der Zeit verändern. Daher dürfen wir unser Bestreben, weiterhin Neuerungen einzuführen, nicht aufgeben.

reddot award 2017
best of the best

Manufacturer
Haier Group, Qingdao, China

S-BOX
Air Purifier
Luftreiniger

See page 242
Siehe Seite 242

Fabian Kollmann – Bosch Thermotechnik GmbH
Markus Mottscheller – designaffairs GmbH

"Create substance with added value."

„Substanz mit Mehrwert schaffen."

What was your goal when you designed your award-winning product?
The features of the successfully launched Buderus "Titanium Design" collection clearly showcase this. In the strategic development of the generic design platform, our primary aim was to bring the Buderus brand values to the fore by means of the design. The high-quality glass front with integrated interfaces provides a design that will stand the test of time and that addresses the topic of connectivity, thereby fully meeting the requirements of end customers.

What do you see as being the biggest challenges in your industry at present?
The buzzwords of the heating technology sector are digitalisation, networking and decarbonisation. In addition, we as designers are required to bring a high level of systemic thinking to the table.

Welches Ziel verfolgten Sie bei der Gestaltung Ihres ausgezeichneten Produktes?
Die Merkmale der erfolgreich in den Markt eingeführten Buderus „Titanium Design"-Linie manifestieren sich darin deutlich. Bei der strategischen Entwicklung der generischen Designplattform ging es vor allem darum, die Buderus-Markenwerte gestalterisch herauszuarbeiten. Mittels der hochwertigen Glasfront mit integrierten Interfaces wird das Thema Konnektivität zukunftsgerecht gestaltet und kann die Erwartungen der Endkunden so bestens erfüllen.

Worin sehen Sie aktuell die größten Herausforderungen in Ihrer Branche?
Die Schlagworte der Heiztechnikbranche sind Digitalisierung, Vernetzung und Dekarbonisierung. Von uns Designern wird zudem ein hohes Maß an systemischem Denken gefordert.

reddot award 2017
best of the best

Manufacturer
Bosch Thermotechnik GmbH, Buderus
Deutschland, Wetzlar, Germany

Buderus Logatherm WLW196i AR T
Air-to-Water Heat Pump
Luft-Wasser-Wärmepumpe

See page 252
Siehe Seite 252

Classico Design Team
Hiroki Yoshitomi – Yoshio Goodrich Design

"If you are inexperienced, it means you have room to grow."

„Wenn man unerfahren ist, bedeutet dies, dass man Raum zum Wachsen hat."

What was your goal when you designed your award-winning product?
To create a stethoscope which ten per cent of doctors all over the world feel enjoy using with a sense of excitement. Our goal was to motivate them and improve the quality of medical care.

What do you see as being the biggest challenges in your industry at present?
Our industry is supposed to be one step ahead of the world, but going too far ahead makes our work unrealistic. Balance is important.

Where will your industry be in ten years?
Software programs and hardware will develop further in the future. How we deal with that determines the path our industry will take.

Welches Ziel verfolgten Sie bei der Gestaltung Ihres ausgezeichneten Produktes?
Ein Stethoskop zu entwickeln, das zehn Prozent der Ärzte weltweit mit Freude und Begeisterung verwenden. Unser Ziel war, sie zu motivieren und die Qualität der medizinischen Betreuung zu verbessern.

Worin sehen Sie aktuell die größten Herausforderungen in Ihrer Branche?
Unsere Branche soll der restlichen Welt einen Schritt voraus sein, aber wenn man sich zu weit nach vorne bewegt, wird die Arbeit unrealistisch. Das Gleichgewicht ist wichtig.

Wo wird Ihre Branche in zehn Jahren stehen?
Softwareprogramme und Hardware werden sich auch in Zukunft weiterentwickeln. Wie wir damit umgehen, wird für den Weg, den unsere Branche einschlägt, entscheidend sein.

reddot award 2017
best of the best

Manufacturer
Classico, Inc., Tokyo, Japan

U scope
Stethoscope
Stethoskop

See page 274
Siehe Seite 274

Design Team MMID/Dräger

"A good product has excellent functionality, is user focused
and exceeds users' needs."

„Ein gutes Produkt bietet eine hervorragende Funktionalität,
ist auf den Nutzer ausgerichtet und übertrifft dessen Erwartungen."

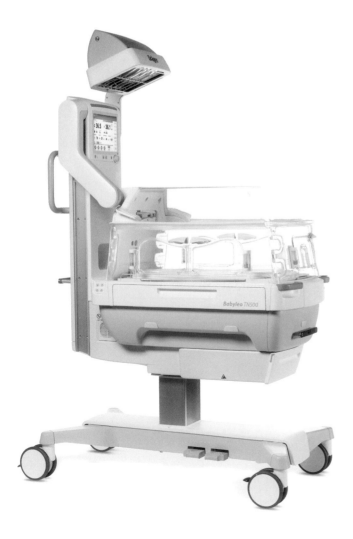

Was your award-winning product based on a particular design approach?
With our integrated product development approach, we help our clients to realise excellent products. Integrated product development is about combining different disciplines in a coherent, efficient and effective development process and knowledge environment. By combining this expertise with the experience of the Dräger design team, we lift product development to a higher level. We strongly believe that collaboration is the key to innovation.

What inspires you?
We are open to letting new ideas, different visions, cultures and lifestyles inspire us to surprising insights.

Liegt Ihrem ausgezeichneten Produkt ein bestimmter Gestaltungsansatz zugrunde?
Mit unserem integrierten Produktentwicklungsansatz helfen wir unseren Kunden, hervorragende Produkte zu verwirklichen. Dabei geht es darum, verschiedene Disziplinen in einem einheitlichen, effizienten und wirksamen Entwicklungsprozess und Wissensumfeld zusammenzuführen. Durch die Kombination dieses Know-hows mit der Erfahrung des Dräger-Designteams heben wir die Produktentwicklung auf ein höheres Niveau. Wir sind der festen Überzeugung, dass Zusammenarbeit der Schlüssel zur Innovation ist.

Was inspiriert Sie?
Wir sind offen dafür, uns von neuen Ideen, verschiedenen Visionen, Kulturen und Lebensweisen inspirieren zu lassen und so zu überraschenden Erkenntnissen zu gelangen.

reddot award 2017
best of the best

Manufacturer
Drägerwerk AG & Co. KGaA,
Lübeck, Germany

Dräger Babyleo® TN500 IncuWarmer

See page 276
Siehe Seite 276

Patrick Mainville, Richard Paré, François Gaucher
ALTO Design Inc.

"Vision to inspire. Design to believe in."

„Eine Vision, die inspiriert. Ein Design, an das man glauben kann."

What was your goal when you designed your award-winning product?
Because point-of-care testing devices like the revogene system are meant to simplify and streamline the clinician's workflow, ease of use, intuitiveness and optimal ergonomics were top-of-mind goals during all stages of the design process.

What inspires you?
Simplicity and relevance; however, these considerations alone are not enough to make a product rise above the melee. A product also needs to have a distinctive personality in order to carry the brand, especially when it comes to a new company.

Welches Ziel verfolgten Sie bei der Gestaltung Ihres ausgezeichneten Produktes?
Da Point-of-Care-Testgeräte wie revogene dazu gedacht sind, die Arbeitsabläufe von Klinikern zu vereinfachen und zu optimieren, waren eine einfache Handhabung, eine intuitive Benutzung und optimale Ergonomie in allen Phasen des Designprozesses vorrangig.

Was inspiriert Sie?
Schlichtheit und Relevanz. Allerdings reichen diese Gesichtspunkte alleine nicht aus, um ein Produkt von der Masse abzuheben. Ein Produkt muss auch eine eigenständige Persönlichkeit haben, um die Marke zu transportieren, besonders wenn es sich um ein neues Unternehmen handelt.

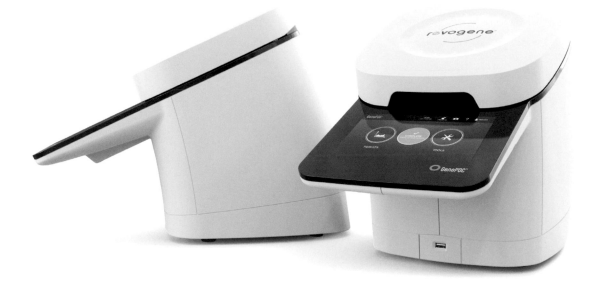

reddot award 2017
best of the best

Manufacturer
GenePOC, Quebec, Canada

revogene™
System for Microbial Testing
System für mikrobielle Untersuchungen

See page 294
Siehe Seite 294

Daniel Goodland, Edison Lee, Corey Banham, Seokbong Yang, Andrei Burean
Unitron Product & Design Team

"Putting patients at the centre of design innovation."

„Die Patienten müssen im Mittelpunkt der Designinnovation stehen."

What was your goal when you designed your award-winning product?
When a person makes the important step to try hearing aids for the first time, discretion is always a very important consideration. With that mind, our goal was to design the smallest, most discrete wireless hearing aid in the world, without compromising on technology or performance.

What do you see as being the biggest challenges in your industry at present?
Our industry is working towards creating more seamless and well-designed experiences that allow for hearing aid wearers to benefit from the sound amplification they need through technology that is both seamless and transparent.

Welches Ziel verfolgten Sie bei der Gestaltung Ihres ausgezeichneten Produktes?
Wenn jemand das erste Mal den wichtigen Schritt macht, ein Hörgerät auszuprobieren, ist Diskretion immer ein sehr wichtiger Gesichtspunkt. In Anbetracht dessen war unser Ziel, das kleinste, diskreteste drahtlose Hörgerät der Welt zu gestalten, ohne in Hinblick auf Technologie oder Leistung Kompromisse einzugehen.

Worin sehen Sie aktuell die größten Herausforderungen in Ihrer Branche?
Unsere Branche arbeitet darauf hin, ein nahtloseres und gut gestaltetes Erlebnis zu schaffen, das es den Trägern von Hörgeräten ermöglicht, von der Tonverstärkung, die sie brauchen, zu profitieren dank einer Technologie, die sowohl nahtlos als auch transparent ist.

reddot award 2017
best of the best

Manufacturer
Unitron, Kitchener, Ontario, Canada

Moxi Now
Hearing Aid
Hörgerät

See page 308
Siehe Seite 308

Philipp Kampas, Ashana Hohgräve
Ottobock HealthCare

"People are at the heart of our design which is clean and minimalist."

„Unser Design stellt den Menschen in den Mittelpunkt. Es ist klar und minimalistisch."

Is there a product that you have always dreamed about realising someday?
A prosthesis whose external shape provides the weight-bearing structure. It would be designed through an additive process with the user in mind and would be shaped in accordance with his or her individual wishes. The mechatronic that makes it work would be integrated into the design process in the form of modules.

Where will your industry be in ten years?
The increasing availability of digital manufacturing technology will transform our industry. We will need to develop business models that combine the possibilities of customisation with our knowledge of high-quality, functional products.

Welches Produkt würden Sie gerne einmal realisieren?
Eine Prothese, deren äußere Form zugleich die tragende Struktur ist. Sie wird durch additive Verfahren direkt nach dem Vorbild des Anwenders und dessen individuellen Wünschen geformt. Die funktionsgebende Mechatronik wird in Form von Modulen in den Designprozess integriert.

Wo wird Ihre Branche in zehn Jahren stehen?
Die zunehmende Verfügbarkeit digitaler Fertigungstechnologien wird unsere Industrie verändern. Es gilt Geschäftsmodelle zu entwickeln, die die Möglichkeit zur Individualisierung mit unserem Know-how für hochqualitative und funktionelle Produkte vereinen.

reddot award 2017
best of the best

Manufacturer
Ottobock Health Care Products GmbH, Vienna, Austria

System Electric Greifer DMC VariPlus
System-Elektrogreifer DMC VariPlus
Hand Prosthesis
Handprothese

See page 316
Siehe Seite 316

Mauricio Noronha, Rodrigo Brenner
Furf Design Studio

"The world does not need another product. However, it cries out for more poetry, romance and love and through design we can bring this to life."

„Die Welt braucht kein weiteres Produkt. Sie schreit allerdings förmlich nach mehr Poesie, Romantik und Liebe. Design kann das lebendig werden lassen."

What was your goal when you designed your award-winning product?
The democratisation of self-esteem.

Was your award-winning product based on a particular design approach?
The light and romantic Brazilian essence. Each element of design is synthesised as a poet carefully selects every written word. With no excess or scarcity. Bossa Nova. We mass-produce emotions.

What inspires you?
Poetry. Meaning. Eternity.

What does winning the Red Dot: Best of the Best mean to you?
The honour to be granted this award at 26 years old is an unforgettable achievement, a dream that has come true.

Welches Ziel verfolgten Sie bei der Gestaltung Ihres ausgezeichneten Produktes?
Die Demokratisierung des Selbstwertgefühls.

Liegt Ihrem ausgezeichneten Produkt ein bestimmter Gestaltungsansatz zugrunde?
Das leichte und romantische brasilianische Wesen. Jedes Element eines Designs wird synthetisiert, genau wie ein Dichter sorgfältig jedes geschriebene Wort auswählt. Ohne Exzess oder Mangel. Bossa Nova. Wir sind Serienhersteller von Emotionen.

Was inspiriert Sie?
Poesie. Bedeutung. Ewigkeit.

Was bedeutet die Auszeichnung mit dem Red Dot: Best of the Best für Sie?
Es ist ein unvergessliches Erlebnis, diese Auszeichnung im Alter von 26 Jahren zu erhalten. Es ist ein Traum, der wahr geworden ist.

reddot award 2017
best of the best

Manufacturer
ETHNOS Produtos Ortopédicos,
Rio de Janeiro, Brazil

Confetti
Prosthetic Leg Cover
Prothetische Beinverkleidung

See page 318
Siehe Seite 318

Michiel Knoppert, James Hallar
Dell Experience Design Group

"Simplify the complexities of technology, for more
 natural human interactions."
„Vereinfache die technologische Komplexität für eine
 natürlichere menschliche Interaktion."

What was your goal when you designed your award-winning product?
The goal was to close the gap between paper and digital as well as to close the gap between the advanced personal tech you have at home and the workstation that you have at work. We want people to be able to work as naturally on Canvas as on paper, to be able to organise thoughts, leave notes and create reminders that can easily reside in the digital workspace.

Where will your industry be in ten years?
We are moving into a new era of computing. The ability for computers to interpret our intent will change everything.

Welches Ziel verfolgten Sie bei der Gestaltung Ihres ausgezeichneten Produktes?
Das Ziel war, die Lücke zwischen Papier und der digitalen Welt zu schließen wie auch die Lücke zwischen der fortschrittlichen Technologie, die man zu Hause hat, und der am Arbeitsplatz. Wir möchten, dass Menschen genauso natürlich mit Canvas arbeiten, wie sie es mit Papier tun. Sie sollen ihre Gedanken ordnen können, sich Notizen machen und Erinnerungsstützen schaffen, die am digitalen Arbeitsplatz aufbewahrt werden können.

Wo wird Ihre Branche in zehn Jahren stehen?
Wir bewegen uns auf ein neues Zeitalter der Informatik zu. Die Fähigkeit von Computern, unsere Intention zu interpretieren, wird alles verändern.

reddot award 2017
best of the best

Manufacturer
Dell Inc., Round Rock, Texas, USA

Dell Canvas 27
Interactive Computer Work Surface
Interaktive Computer-Arbeitsfläche

See page 328
Siehe Seite 328

Logitech Design Team and Feiz Design

"We strive to design experiences that transcend their functional value
and are loved by people."

„Wir sind bestrebt, Erfahrungen zu gestalten, die über ihren funktionalen Wert
hinausgehen und von Menschen geliebt werden."

What was your goal when you designed your award-winning product?
To reimagine and create a beautiful keyboard based on the key consumer insight that people are using multiple devices (phone, tablet, computer) interchangeably.

Where will your industry be in ten years?
The change we are going to experience in the next ten years is going to be one of the most transformational periods in our lifetime: augmented and virtual reality, artificial intelligence, voice control, self-driving cars to name but a few, all provide Logitech with the opportunity to transform its brands, categories and experiences.

Welches Ziel verfolgten Sie bei der Gestaltung Ihres ausgezeichneten Produktes?
Eine schöne Tastatur neu zu konzipieren und zu gestalten, aufbauend auf der wichtigen Erkenntnis zum Nutzerverhalten, dass die Menschen viele Endgeräte (Mobiltelefon, Tablet, Computer) nebeneinander verwenden.

Wo wird Ihre Branche in zehn Jahren stehen?
Die Veränderung, die wir in den nächsten zehn Jahren erleben werden, wird noch in unserem Leben eine Zeit größten Wandels herbeiführen: Augmented und Virtual Reality, künstliche Intelligenz, Sprachsteuerung, autonom fahrende Autos, um nur ein paar Dinge aufzuzählen, werden Logitech die Möglichkeit geben, seine Marken, Kategorien und Erfahrungen neu zu gestalten.

reddot award 2017
best of the best

Manufacturer
Logitech, Newark, California, USA

Logitech K780
Multi-Device Wireless Keyboard
Kabellose Multi-Device-Tastatur

See page 348
Siehe Seite 348

Blackmagic Industrial Design Team

"Fostering true creativity by making the highest quality video
affordable to everyone."

„Wir fördern wahre Kreativität, indem wir höchste Videoqualität
für jedermann bezahlbar machen."

How do you define design quality?
Design quality is the unseen attention
to detail that makes a product feel intuitive. It is the thinking that the designer
does, so that the user doesn't have to.

**What do you see as being the biggest
challenges in your industry at present?**
The design industry has witnessed a
paradigm shift; the designer's role is no
longer quarantined to aesthetics around
predetermined packages of technology;
we are now empowered to inject our
thinking from the very early stages of the
development process. This has resulted
in better designed, more purposeful
products and has translated into financial
rewards for businesses willing to adopt
this strategy. The real challenge for the
design industry now, is to ensure we are
equipping the next generation of designers with the skills to operate in this
broader landscape

Wie definieren Sie Designqualität?
Designqualität ist die unsichtbare Detail-
genauigkeit, die ein Produkt intuitiv
erscheinen lässt. Sie ist zudem Ergebnis
der Gedanken, die sich der Designer macht,
damit es der Nutzer nicht tun muss.

**Worin sehen Sie aktuell die größten
Herausforderungen in Ihrer Branche?**
Die Designbranche hat einen Paradigmen-
wandel erlebt. Die Rolle des Designers
beschränkt sich nicht mehr nur auf ästhetische Aspekte im Rahmen vorgegebener
Technologieprodukte. Uns wird heute ermöglicht, unsere Ideen bereits in frühen
Stadien des Entwicklungsprozesses einzu-
bringen. Das hat zu besser gestalteten,
zweckmäßigeren Produkten geführt und
macht sich allgemein als finanzieller Vorteil für Unternehmen bemerkbar, die bereit
sind, diese Strategie zu übernehmen. Die
wirkliche Herausforderung wird nun sein,
sicherzustellen, dass wir die Nachwuchs-
generation von Designern mit den notwen-
digen Fertigkeiten wappnen, damit sie
in diesem erweiterten Umfeld arbeiten
können.

reddot award 2017
best of the best

Manufacturer
Blackmagic Design Pty Ltd,
Melbourne, Australia

Blackmagic Broadcast Suite
Broadcast Equipment

See page 386
Siehe Seite 386

Offices
Büro

Jamboard
Digital Collaborative Whiteboard

Manufacturer
Google, New York, USA

Design
Aruliden, New York, USA

Web
www.google.com/jamboard
www.aruliden.com

reddot award 2017
best of the best

Easily connected
In our globalised world, it is not too uncommon a sight anymore that people are working together despite being at very different locations, constantly exchanging information and developing ideas. Against this backdrop, Jamboard opens up new ways toward interaction across distance. Its design merges the advantages of time-proven whiteboards as used in offices with the possibilities offered by the latest technology. The aim of the design was to use the analogue familiarity of the whiteboard for a comfortable interface by combining it with digital convenience. Thus, as natural to use as a traditional whiteboard, Jamboard connects directly with another Jamboard via the Internet. This allows teams to jot down notes, sketch out plans or frame up ideas collaboratively. All Jamboard actions are rendered interactively and delivered in real time, independent of where team members are located. Jamboard thus delivers the ability to collaborate as if all co-workers were in the same room. The form and materials have been chosen to suit both the environment it is used in and the functionality it offers. Showcasing a modern, furniture-inspired aesthetic, the board fits easily in almost any workspace. With its integrated HD camera and built-in Wi-Fi, this innovative solution thus facilitates uncomplicated collaboration and interaction across distances – it exudes a lightness that is fun to use and inspiring.

Einfach verbunden
In einer globalisierten Welt ist es an der Tagesordnung, dass sich an unterschiedlichen Orten befindende Menschen zusammenarbeiten und sich dabei stetig über Ergebnisse und Vorschläge miteinander austauschen. Das Jamboard eröffnet vor diesem Hintergrund neue Wege für eine umfassende Interaktion. Seine Gestaltung vereint die Vorteile des im Büroalltag bewährten Whiteboards mit den Möglichkeiten aktueller Technologien. Zielsetzung der Gestaltung war es, die analoge Vertrautheit des Whiteboards für ein komfortables Interface zu nutzen und mit der digitalen Welt zu kombinieren. Das Jamboard lässt sich auf ähnlich natürliche Art und Weise verwenden wie ein klassisches Whiteboard und ist direkt mit einem anderen Jamboard über das Internet verbunden. Teams können Notizen machen, Pläne skizzieren oder gemeinsam eine Idee entwickeln. All diese Aktionen erfolgen interaktiv und in Echtzeit, ganz gleich, wo sich die Teammitglieder befinden. Das Jamboard erlaubt eine Kommunikation, als befänden sich alle in einem Raum. In Form und Material ist es der Umgebung, in der es eingesetzt wird, und seiner Funktionalität entsprechend gestaltet. Mit einer an Möbeln orientierten, modernen Ästhetik fügt es sich leicht in jedes Arbeitsumfeld ein. Über eine eingebaute HD-Kamera und integriertes Wi-Fi ermöglicht diese innovative Lösung eine unkomplizierte Art der Kommunikation und Interaktion – es entsteht eine Leichtigkeit, die Spaß macht und die Arbeit beflügelt.

Statement by the jury
The Jamboard allows teams to easily collaborate independently of the location of the team members. Sophisticated in technology and form, it establishes a novel, self-reliant visual appearance. The intuitively approachable and via stylus easy-to-operate interface is just as fascinating as the clear and fresh look of the device. The overall design of the Jamboard is of high quality and aesthetically pleasing. This is a pathbreaking product that opens up undreamt of possibilities.

Begründung der Jury
Mit dem Jamboard können sich Teams unabhängig vom Standort der Mitarbeiter leicht untereinander austauschen. Formal wie technologisch ausgereift, definiert es eine neue, eigenständige Formensprache. Dabei begeistert das mittels Stylus einfach bedienbare, intuitiv zugängliche Interface ebenso wie die klare, frische Formgebung. Die gesamte Gestaltung des Jamboard ist ästhetisch ansprechend und hochwertig. Es ist ein wegweisendes Produkt, das ungeahnte Möglichkeiten eröffnet.

Designer portrait
See page 30
Siehe Seite 30

Evo®
Schwenkbarer Monitor Arm
Monitorarm

Manufacturer
Innovative, Easton, USA
In-house design
Web
www.innovativeworkspace.com/evo

The newly redesigned Evo monitor arm combines ergonomic function and intuitive ease of use with a slim design and special space-savings. Quick and easy to install, Evo's modern look and clean lines make it the ideal complement for any workspace. The arm floats the monitor weightlessly above the work surface where it can be effortlessly repositioned with one-touch monitor adjustment. It is available in flat white, silver or vista black finish and comes in single or dual versions.

Statement by the jury
The Evo monitor arm convinces with the clarity of its design. Its conclusive construction allows easy and convenient handling.

Der neuerlich umgestaltete Monitorarm Evo vereint ergonomische Funktion und intuitive Bedienfreundlichkeit mit einem schlanken Erscheinungsbild und spart in verschiedener Hinsicht Platz. Er ist schnell und einfach zu montieren, und seine moderne Anmutung und seine klaren Linien machen ihn zur idealen Ergänzung jedes Arbeitsplatzes. Der Monitorarm, der den Bildschirm gleichsam über der Arbeitsfläche schweben lässt, kann mit nur einer Berührung mühelos neu positioniert werden. Er ist in Mattweiß, Silber und Vistaschwarz sowie in einer Einfach- und in einer Doppelversion erhältlich.

Begründung der Jury
Der Monitorarm Evo besticht durch seine gestalterische Klarheit. Seine schlüssige Konstruktion ermöglicht eine einfache und praktische Handhabung.

mangroovv
Desk for Tablets
Schreibtisch für Tablets

Manufacturer
blue object oHG, Hamburg, Germany
In-house design
Armin Müller, Kai Trebesius
Web
www.blueobject.de

The mangroovv is an application-oriented solution for work routines in the mobile world. At a weight of only 950 grams and featuring an automatic folding mechanism, the unconventional desk is easy to transport and set up. The frame is adjustable in height, allowing different working positions both sitting and standing. A tablet can be used easily with only one hand. In addition, the magnetic ball-joint allows continuous adjustments of the operation angle. The table is available in three versions, while head and foot elements come in a stained or black lacquered finish.

Statement by the jury
The mobile mangroovv desk fascinates with its user-oriented construction and easy handling, which allow an optimal adaptation to modern work environments and conditions.

Bei mangroovv handelt es sich um eine anwendungsorientierte Lösung für den Arbeitsalltag in einer mobilen Welt. Mit dem Gewicht von 950 Gramm und der Klappautomatik lässt sich der unkonventionelle Schreibtisch problemlos transportieren und aufstellen. Das Gestell ist in der Höhe variabel, sodass Arbeiten im Sitzen ebenso möglich sind wie eine Nutzung als Stehpult. Ein Tablet lässt sich leicht mit nur einer Hand anbringen. Das magnetische Kugelgelenk ermöglicht zudem die stufenlose Einstellung des passenden Arbeitswinkels. Der Tisch ist in drei Ausführungen erhältlich, Kopf- und Fußteil können auch gebeizt oder schwarz lackiert gewählt werden.

Begründung der Jury
Der mobile Schreibtisch mangroovv besticht durch seine nutzerorientierte Konstruktion und leichte Handhabung, die eine optimale Anpassung an moderne Arbeitsumgebungen und -bedingungen ermöglicht.

Ollin
Dynamic Monitor Arm
Dynamischer Monitorarm

Manufacturer
Colebrook Bosson Saunders,
London, Great Britain
In-house design
Web
www.colebrookbossonsaunders.com

With its innovative technical cord, the Ollin monitor arm supports tablets, monitors and laptops from 0 kg up to 9 kg in weight, making it suited for the technology of today and the screen technology of the future as it becomes lighter and more mobile. Ollin's adjustability and responsive movements mean the screen can be ideally positioned to meet a wide range of requirements, ensuring a relaxed interaction between users and their technology, which in turn improves their well-being.

Mit seiner innovativen technischen Seil-konstruktion trägt der Monitorarm Ollin Tablets, Monitore und Laptops bis 9 kg, was ihn für die Technologie von heute ebenso geeignet macht wie für die immer leichtere und mobilere Bildschirmtech-nologie von morgen. Durch seine Einstell-barkeit und Bewegungsempfänglichkeit lassen sich Bildschirme einer großen Band-breite von Anforderungen entsprechend bestmöglich positionieren, was ein ent-spanntes Verhältnis zwischen dem Nutzer und seiner Technologie verspricht. Dies erhöht wiederum das Wohlbefinden des am Schirm Arbeitenden.

Statement by the jury
The Ollin monitor arm convinces with an impressive interplay of technology and functionality. The unobtrusive de-sign submits itself to user benefits.

Begründung der Jury
Der Monitorarm Ollin überzeugt mit einem eindrucksvollen Zusammenspiel aus Tech-nologie und Funktionalität. Die zurück-genommene Gestaltung ordnet sich dem Anwendernutzen unter.

Stand Up
Office Desk
Büroschreibtisch

Manufacturer
Mikomax Smart Office,
Lodz, Poland

In-house design
Mikomax Smart Office

Design
Tomasz Augustyniak,
Poznan, Poland

Web
www.mikomaxsmartoffice.pl

reddot award 2017
best of the best

Active balance

The constant development of modern work environments often entails rapid changes in requirements with regard to workplace concepts. Stand Up is marked by a perfectly thought-out functionality that allows it to easily adjust to changes in workplace scenarios. It centres on the idea of creating an office desk for daily use that facilitates a healthy balance between sitting and standing. Thanks to its sophisticated design, this office desk with height-adjustable worktop guarantees quick and easy switching between different work positions. Featuring an innovative, patented mechanism, it makes the raising of the work surface an easy operation with no need for an electrical supply. Thus users can intuitively adjust and switch between different worktop heights in a matter of seconds. In an uncomplicated manner, the office desk thus adds flexibility to daily work processes and supports a healthy work posture. In addition, it also promotes lively interaction with colleagues as well as work and communication in project teams. Furthermore, the design with upholstered panels improves workplace acoustics and offers the ability to personalise settings. The office desk showcases clear and timeless aesthetics with worktop edges that do away with joints thanks to the use of laser technology. Boasting a dynamic and elegant look, the design positively facilitates everyday work processes – promoting an active and healthy work climate.

Aktive Balance

In einer sich stetig wandelnden Arbeitswelt ändern sich oft rasch die Anforderungen, was die Konzeption des Arbeitsplatzes betrifft. Stand Up zeichnet sich durch eine perfekt durchdachte Funktionalität aus und lässt sich leicht an wechselnde Arbeitssituationen anpassen. Im Mittelpunkt stand die Zielsetzung, einen Schreibtisch zu gestalten, der in der täglichen Arbeit eine gesunde Balance zwischen Sitzen und Stehen ermöglicht. Dieser Tisch mit höhenverstellbarer Arbeitsplatte gewährleistet durch seine ausgereifte Gestaltung einen problemlosen Wechsel zwischen verschiedenen Arbeitspositionen. Ein innovativer patentierter Mechanismus erlaubt dabei eine einfache Bedienung, welche rein mechanisch, ohne elektrische Unterstützung erfolgt. Intuitiv können die Nutzer mittels dieses Mechanismus innerhalb von Sekunden unterschiedliche Höhen der Arbeitsplatte einstellen. Auf unkomplizierte Art und Weise lässt sich so im Arbeitsprozess eine Flexibilität erreichen, die eine gesunde Körperhaltung unterstützt. Darüber hinaus wird dadurch die lebendige Interaktion mit Kollegen sowie die Arbeit und Kommunikation in Projektteams begünstigt. Die Gestaltung mit gepolsterten Paneelen verbessert die Akustik am Arbeitsplatz und bietet Möglichkeiten der Personalisierung. Dank des Einsatzes von Lasertechnologie sind die Übergänge nahtlos, was diesem Schreibtisch eine zeitlose, klare Ästhetik verleiht. Er wirkt ebenso elegant wie dynamisch. Durch Design wird hier der alltägliche Arbeitsprozess erleichtert – und für ein aktives und lebendiges Arbeitsklima gesorgt.

Statement by the jury

Based on an innovative design idea, this office desk is perfectly suited to contemporary workplaces. Its work surface can be raised or lowered intuitively via a simple and self-explanatory mechanism for easy adjustment to the requirements of different work scenarios. The reduced design language and carefully crafted, high-quality finishes lend Stand Up an appearance that is both modern and elegant.

Begründung der Jury

Auf der Basis einer innovativen Gestaltungsidee ist dieser Schreibtisch perfekt geeignet für das heutige Arbeitsleben. Seine Arbeitsplatte lässt sich mittels eines einfachen, selbsterklärenden Mechanismus intuitiv auf und ab bewegen und so leicht den verschiedenen Arbeitsszenarien anpassen. Die reduzierte Formgebung und die sorgfältig bearbeiteten, hochwertigen Oberflächen verleihen Stand Up zudem eine moderne und elegante Anmutung.

Designer portrait
See page 32
Siehe Seite 32

Masterlift 4
Sit Stand Desk
Steh-Sitz-Tisch

Manufacturer
Inwerk GmbH, Meerbusch, Germany
In-house design
Karl Bell
Web
www.inwerk.de
www.inwerk-bueromoebel.de

The Masterlift 4 sit stand desk presents itself in a consciously reduced design. The frame, as a circulating loop, lends the desk stability. Two solid steel plates support the table top, showing only a filigree line at the sides. The electrically height-adjustable desk allows frequent changes of posture, while the Masterguide monitor analysis system encourages users to actively interrupt usual seating habits in customisable intervals. The electric linear drive is integrated in the columns, while the continuously adjustable cross-beam also functions as a cable channel.

Bewusst reduziert präsentiert sich der Steh-Sitz-Tisch Masterlift 4. Der umlaufende Rahmen verleiht dem Tisch seine Standfestigkeit. Zwei massive Stahlplatten tragen die Tischplatte und erscheinen seitlich nur als filigrane Linie. Der elektrisch höhenverstellbare Schreibtisch ermöglicht regelmäßige Haltungswechsel am Arbeitsplatz, wobei das Monitor-Analysis-System Masterguide den Anwender dazu animiert, das gewohnte Sitzen im selbst wählbaren Rhythmus aktiv zu unterbrechen. Der elektrische Linearantrieb ist in die Säulen integriert, die stufenlos verstellbare Traverse fungiert zugleich als Kabelkanal.

Statement by the jury
The Masterlift 4 appeals with its sophisticated construction that skilfully combines handling, stability and contemporary design.

Begründung der Jury
Der Masterlift 4 gefällt seiner durchdachten Konstruktion wegen, die Handhabung, Stabilität und zeitgemäße Formgebung gekonnt miteinander verbindet.

startUP
Desk
Schreibtisch

Manufacturer
L&C stendal,
Stendal, Germany
Design
studio contempus,
Büro für Innenarchitektur (Oliver Ringel),
Beesenstedt, Germany
Web
www.lc-stendal.de
www.bdia.org/ringel
www.studio-contempus.de

With clear lines, the design of the startUP desk reflects subtle details of Modernism and implements them in a contemporary form. The eye-catching chrome-plated sled-base frame lends the desk stability and its characteristic appearance. The work surface is a blockboard with real oak veneer and a polished hard wax finish. Two recessed, stainless steel cable ducts in the desktop allow well-organised cable management for lighting and communication technology.

Statement by the jury
The startUP desk appeals with a clear and lightweight look as well as a sophisticated construction that places a special emphasis on practical handling.

Der Schreibtisch startUP greift mit seiner klaren Linienführung Akzente der Klassischen Moderne auf und setzt diese zeitgemäß um. Blickfang ist das glanzverchromte Kufengestell, das ihm seinen stabilen Stand und charakteristischen Ausdruck verleiht. Die Arbeitsfläche bildet eine echtholzfurnierte Tischlerplatte mit hartwachspolierter Oberfläche. Zwei in die Schreibtischplatte eingelassene Kabeldurchgänge aus Edelstahl ermöglichen eine geordnete Kabelführung für Beleuchtung und Kommunikationstechnik.

Begründung der Jury
Klar und leicht in der Anmutung gefällt der Schreibtisch startUP zugleich aufgrund seiner ausgereiften Konstruktion, die besonderen Wert auf eine praktische Handhabung legt.

TRIMAT DESK
Desk
Schreibtisch

Manufacturer
Ora Office s.c.p.a.,
Pomezia (Rome), Italy
Design
Danesi Design,
Possagno (Treviso), Italy
Web
www.oraoffice.it
www.danesidesign.it

The dynamic appeal of this desk is based on its technical appearance with an asymmetrical shape. The choice of materials lends it a modern look: its elegant harmony is the result of an innovative balance of essential yet functional forms. The elaborate, desk-carrying wooden leg is elegantly clad in ceramic slabs and mounted on an L-shaped chrome-plated steel profile that houses the electrical wiring and intersects the top.

Statement by the jury
The Trimat desk skilfully combines different materials. The distinctive design turns it into the dominating centre of the office.

Die Dynamik dieses technisch anmutenden Schreibtischs basiert auf seiner asymmetrischen Gestaltung, und die Wahl der Materialien lässt ihn modern wirken. Die elegante Harmonie ist das Ergebnis eines innovativen Gleichgewichts wesentlicher und zugleich funktionaler Formen. Das durchdachte, den Schreibtisch tragende Bein aus Holz ist stilvoll mit keramischen Platten verkleidet und auf einem L-förmigen Profil aus verchromtem Stahl montiert, das die elektrische Verkabelung birgt und durch einen Teil der Tischplatte läuft.

Begründung der Jury
Der Schreibtisch Trimat verbindet gekonnt unterschiedliche Materialien miteinander. Das markante Design lässt ihn zum dominierenden Mittelpunkt im Büro werden.

Trinetic
Office Chair
Bürostuhl

Manufacturer
Boss Design, Dudley,
West Midlands, Great Britain

In-house design
Boss Design

Web
www.bossdesign.com

reddot award 2017
best of the best

The magic of adaptability
With their Aluminium Chair, designers Charles and Ray Eames lent the office chair a timeless design appearance back in the 1950s. Since then, office chairs have undergone many changes, especially since the technology to enhance sitting comfort has constantly evolved to achieve ever better seat ergonomics. Against this backdrop, the design of Trinetic has emerged as an impressive advancement providing perfect, dynamic support without the need for manual user adjustments. At first glance, this chair adopts a classic appearance reduced to the essential, showcasing a well-balanced and timeless design. Its flowing aluminium structure houses an innovative mechanism that implies a high degree of individual adjustability: with this chair, the seated person only varies the sitting height, whereas all other settings follow almost imperceptibly by themselves, providing users with a unique experience of sitting comfort. Embodying a sophisticated system, three independent pivot points combine and interact to achieve the best possible kinetic sitting position. This kind of automatic self-adjustment also offers the advantage that several different people can sit on the same chair throughout the course of a work project or when working in teams. The timeless elegance of this office chair fascinates as much as its special, highly dynamic adaptability.

Die Magie der Anpassung
Mit dem Aluminium Chair verliehen die Designer Charles und Ray Eames in den 1950er Jahren auch dem Bürostuhl eine zeitlose Formensprache. Der Bürostuhl hat seither viele Veränderungen erfahren, vor allem die Technologie für den Sitzkomfort wurde stetig überarbeitet, um auf diese Weise eine noch bessere Sitzergonomie zu erreichen. Der Gestaltung von Trinetic gelingt hier eine beeindruckende Neuentwicklung, die eine perfekte, dynamische Anpassung an den jeweiligen Sitzenden ermöglicht. Dieser Stuhl wirkt auf den ersten Blick klassisch und auf das Wesentliche reduziert. Seine Formensprache ist ausgewogen und zeitlos. Seine fließende Aluminiumstruktur verbirgt einen innovativen Mechanismus, der ein hohes Maß an individueller Anpassung impliziert: Der Sitzende variiert bei diesem Stuhl nur die Höhe der Sitzfläche, kaum wahrnehmbar geschehen alle weiteren Einstellungen von selbst, was zu einem einzigartigen Komforterlebnis führt. Auf raffinierte Weise werden drei unabhängige Drehpunkte miteinander kombiniert, die kinetisch perfekt zusammenarbeiten für den bestmöglichen Sitzkomfort. Diese Art der selbständigen Anpassung hat außerdem den Vorteil, dass in Arbeitsgruppen und bei Teamarbeit verschiedene Menschen denselben Stuhl benutzen können. Die zeitlose Eleganz dieses Bürostuhls begeistert ebenso wie seine besondere, überaus dynamische Adaptionsfähigkeit.

Statement by the jury
Thanks to sophisticated technology, the Trinetic office chair can adapt perfectly to its user. Its innovative design merges ergonomics and functionality with a high degree of aesthetic appeal. This office chair fascinates particularly with its reduction to the essential and its highly advanced ergonomics. It is both clear and light in appearance, emotionalising users. The technology used is cleverly hidden inside, so that the material and form can fully reveal their appeal.

Begründung der Jury
Dank einer ausgeklügelten Technologie kann sich der Bürostuhl Trinetic perfekt dem Sitzenden anpassen. Seine innovative Gestaltung vereint Ergonomie und Funktionalität mit einem hohen Maß an Ästhetik. Dieser Bürostuhl fasziniert mit einer Reduktion auf das Wesentliche und seiner hochentwickelten Ergonomie. Er erscheint ebenso klar wie leicht und emotionalisiert den Betrachter. Da seine Technologie auf sehr smarte Weise verborgen ist, können zudem Form und Materialität ihre ganze Wirkung entfalten.

Designer portrait
See page 34
Siehe Seite 34

TEA 1322
Conference Swivel Chair
Konferenzdrehstuhl

Manufacturer
RIM CZ s.r.o.,
Otrokovice, Czech Republic
Design
Massimo Costaglia Design,
Santa Giustina in Colle, Italy
Web
www.rim.cz
www.massimocostaglia.com

The TEA 1322 conference swivel chair shows a well-balanced design and the combination of modern technology with high utility. Its characteristic design feature are the distinctive aluminium armrests that connect the backrest and seat. The conference swivel chair is optionally available with a rocking mechanism as well as an auto-return function. A four-star aluminium base lends the chair stability. The armrests are also available in a standard anthracite PUR version.

Statement by the jury
The TEA 1322 conference swivel chair convinces with a design that expressively integrates into conference halls and meeting rooms while also fulfilling ergonomic requirements.

Eine ausgewogene Gestaltung und die Verbindung von moderner Technik und hohem Nutzwert zeichnen den Konferenzdrehstuhl TEA 1322 aus. Charakteristisches Gestaltungsmerkmal sind die markanten Armlehnen aus Aluminium, die Rückenlehne und Sitzfläche miteinander verbinden. Der Konferenzdrehstuhl kann optional mit einer Wippmechanik sowie einer Auto-Return-Funktion ausgestattet werden. Stabilen Halt gibt ein Vierfußgestell aus Aluminium. Die Armlehnen sind wahlweise auch in der Standardvariante aus PUR in Anthrazit erhältlich.

Begründung der Jury
Der Konferenzdrehstuhl TEA 1322 überzeugt mit einem Design, das sich ausdrucksstark in Konferenzräume und Sitzungssäle integriert und gleichzeitig ergonomischen Ansprüchen genügt.

TEA 1301
Swivel Chair
Bürodrehstuhl

Manufacturer
RIM CZ s.r.o.,
Otrokovice, Czech Republic
Design
Massimo Costaglia Design,
Santa Giustina in Colle, Italy
Web
www.rim.cz
www.massimocostaglia.com

With luxurious materials such as leather and polished aluminium, the TEA 1301 swivel chair is well suited for use in representative offices. The characteristic element of the chair are its armrests, connecting the seat in an extravagant line with the backrest, which is available in different heights. Increasing ergonomic needs are met by the integrated counter pressure adjustment of the backrest as well as an ergorelax mechanism that allows four lock-in positions.

Statement by the jury
Timeless aesthetics in combination with high functionality make this office swivel chair practical and elegant.

Mit seinen luxuriösen Materialien wie Leder und poliertem Aluminium eignet sich der Drehstuhl TEA 1301 für die Ausstattung repräsentativer Büros. Markenzeichen des Stuhls sind seine Armlehnen, die den Sitz in einer ausgefallenen Linienführung mit der Rückenlehne verbinden. Diese ist in verschiedenen Höhen verfügbar. Steigenden ergonomischen Anforderungen tragen außerdem eine integrierte Gegendruckeinstellung der Lehne sowie eine Ergorelax-Mechanik Rechnung. Sie ermöglicht die Arretierung des Stuhls in vier Positionen.

Begründung der Jury
Zeitlose Ästhetik in Kombination mit hoher Funktionalität macht den Bürodrehstuhl praktikabel und elegant.

Collection S – MartinStoll
Office Chair Series
Bürostuhl-Serie

Manufacturer
Kinnarps AB, Worms, Germany
Design
NOA Intelligent Design (Michael Lammel, Markus Heller),
Aachen, Germany
Web
www.kinnarps.com
www.noa.de

The office chair series Collection S is inspired by the iconic aesthetics of the Kollektion/S from the year 1986. The segmented upholstery, the designed seaming and the distinctive armrests are reminiscent of their predecessor and translate into a contemporary design language. With different materials for shells and cushions, the series allows for a wide variety of configurations. The production of the series focuses on a holistic ecological solution: the leathers are chrome-free tanned; the wood is obtained from sustainable sources, while all parts are glue-free and can be dismounted for recycling.

Die Bürostuhl-Serie Collection S ist inspiriert von der ikonischen Ästhetik der Kollektion/S aus dem Jahr 1986. Die segmentierte Polsterung, die gestalteten Nähte und die prägnanten Armlehnen sind dem Vorläufer nachempfunden und in eine aktuelle Formensprache übersetzt worden. Mit unterschiedlichen Materialien für Sitzschalen und Füllungen lässt sich der Stuhl vielseitig konfigurieren. Bei der Produktion der Serie steht ein ganzheitlicher Herstellungsprozess im Mittelpunkt: Das Leder wird chromfrei gegerbt, alle Hölzer stammen aus nachhaltig bewirtschafteten Quellen und der Verzicht auf Kleber ermöglicht eine werkstoffspezifische Demontage.

Statement by the jury
Featuring a sophisticated and creative combination of classical and modern forms, the Collection S office chair series impresses with sustainable production.

Begründung der Jury
Anspruchsvoll in der gestalterischen Verbindung klassischer und moderner Formen beeindruckt die Bürostuhl-Serie Collection S mit einer nachhaltigen Herstellung.

FLIP FLAP
Office Chair
Bürostuhl

Manufacturer
ITOKI Corporation, Tokyo, Japan
Design
ITO Design, Cham, Switzerland
Web
www.itoki-global.com
www.ito-design.com

The design of the Flip Flap office chair was inspired by the Japanese art of paper folding, Origami. A form language with a traditional yet also futuristic appeal combines with sophisticated ergonomics in the backrest. The upholstery is designed to continuously respond to the user, providing comfort and support with every movement. Height, depth and position of the armrests can be adjusted individually. The frame of the chair is available in black or white plastic.

Die Gestaltung des Bürostuhls Flip Flap ist von der japanischen Papierfaltkunst Origami inspiriert. Die traditionelle und zugleich futuristisch anmutende Formensprache der Rückenlehne verbindet sich mit einer anspruchsvollen Ergonomie. Die Polster sind so geformt, dass sie sich dem Nutzer durchgehend anpassen und bei jeder Bewegung unterstützenden Komfort bieten. Höhe, Tiefe und Position der Armlehnen können individuell variiert werden. Das Stuhlgestell ist in schwarzem oder weißem Plastik erhältlich.

Statement by the jury
The Flip Flap office chair shows a self-reliant design that at the same time integrates high ergonomic functionality.

Begründung der Jury
Den Bürostuhl Flip Flap zeichnet eine eigenständige Gestaltung aus, die zugleich hohe ergonomische Funktionalität integriert.

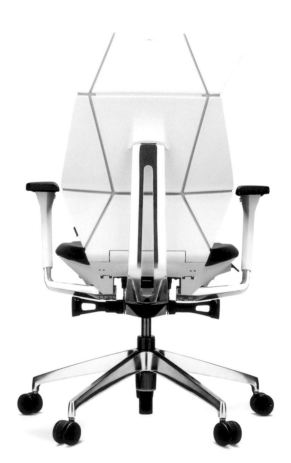

Contessa II
Office Chair
Bürodrehstuhl

Manufacturer
Okamura Corporation,
Yokohama, Japan
Design
Italdesign Giugiaro (Massimo Borrelli),
Turin, Italy
Web
www.okamura.jp
www.italdesign.it

High seating comfort and intuitive handling go hand in hand in the Contessa II office chair. The backrest with its breathable mesh fabric gently conforms to the user's movements, while the ring-shaped construction of the seat provides stability. Levers for height and reclining adjustments are conveniently located in the armrests. Available in a wide variety of colours and three different chair variations, the Contessa II blends into various office interiors.

Hoher Sitzkomfort und intuitive Bedienbarkeit gehen bei dem Bürodrehstuhl Contessa II Hand in Hand. Die Rückenlehne passt sich mit ihrem luftdurchlässigen Mesh-Textilgewebe sanft den Bewegungen des Nutzers an, während der ringförmige Aufbau der Sitzfläche Stabilität verleiht. Sitzhöhe und Neigung der Rückenlehne des Stuhls können bequem über in den Armlehnen integrierte Hebel verstellt werden. Mit einer großen Farbvielfalt und drei wählbaren Stuhlmodellen fügt sich Contessa II in unterschiedliche Büroeinrichtungen ein.

Statement by the jury
Available in a variety of configurations, the Contessa II office chair skilfully combines ease of use, flexibility and ergonomics with an elegant appearance.

Begründung der Jury
Es gelingt dem in verschiedenen Ausführungen erhältlichen Bürodrehstuhl Contessa II, Handhabbarkeit, Flexibilität und Ergonomie gekonnt mit einem eleganten Erscheinungsbild zu verbinden.

rollingframe 52
Office Chair
Bürostuhl

Manufacturer
Alias SpA, Grumello del Monte (Bergamo),
Italy
Design
Alberto Meda, Milan, Italy
Web
www.alias.design
www.albertomeda.com

The backrest and seat of the rollingframe 52 are made of extruded aluminium and give the office chair its harmonious structure. The armrests are also delicately curved, underlining the lightness of the construction. The seat width of the height-adjustable chair was increased by 10 per cent in the course of the development and offers an optimised seating comfort. The five-star base with castors provides stability. The covers are made of polyester mesh and are optionally available in fabric or leather.

Statement by the jury
The rollingframe 52 office chair catches the eye with its dynamic, flowing design, which lends it a clean appearance with high recognition value.

Rückenlehne und Sitzfläche des Bürostuhls rollingframe 52 bestehen aus fließgepresstem Aluminium und formen seine harmonische Struktur. Auch die Armlehnen sind fein geschwungen und unterstreichen die Leichtigkeit der Konstruktion. Die Sitzfläche des höhenverstellbaren Stuhls wurde im Rahmen der Entwicklung um zehn Prozent vergrößert und bietet so einen optimierten Sitzkomfort. Stabilität verleiht der Fünfsternfuß mit Rollen. Die Bezüge sind aus Polyesternetzgewebe und wahlweise in Stoff oder Leder erhältlich.

Begründung der Jury
Der Bürostuhl rollingframe 52 fällt durch seine dynamische, fließende Linienführung auf. Diese verleiht ihm ein klares Erscheinungsbild mit hohem Wiedererkennungswert.

ELODIE
Office Chair
Bürostuhl

Manufacturer
Gaber S.r.l., Caselle di Altivole, Italy
Design
Marc Sadler, Milan, Italy
Web
www.gaber.it
www.marcsadler.it

Straightforward, versatile and functional, the Elodie office chair blends into any work environment. The adjustable backrest with three different heights is intuitive in use and adapts automatically to the user's weight. In addition, the sophisticated double-shell structure of the backrest enables sound absorption, significantly contributing to an optimised work environment through the reduction of background noise. A powerful colour accent is set by the seat of the chair. The backrest comes in a choice of seven different colour tones.

Statement by the jury
The Elodie office chair sets powerful and eye-catching accents in colour and design. The innovative construction of the backrest skilfully combines function and design.

Geradlinig, vielseitig und funktional fügt sich der Bürostuhl Elodie in jede Arbeitsumgebung ein. Intuitiv zu bedienen ist die dreifache Höhenverstellung der Rückenlehne, die sich automatisch dem Gewicht des Nutzers anpasst. Die ausgefeilte Doppelschalenkonstruktion der Lehne unterstützt außerdem die Geräuschabsorption und trägt durch die Reduktion von Schallwellen wesentlich zu einer optimierten Arbeitsumgebung bei. Einen kräftigen Farbakzent setzt die Sitzfläche des Stuhls, die Lehne kann aus sieben verschiedenen Farbtönen gewählt werden.

Begründung der Jury
Der Bürostuhl Elodie setzt farblich und gestalterisch aufmerksamkeitsstarke Akzente. Die innovative Konstruktion der Rückenlehne verbindet gekonnt Funktion und Design.

Fern
Task chair
Bürostuhl

Manufacturer
Haworth GmbH,
Bad Münder am Deister, Germany
In-house design
Design
ITO Design, Nuremberg, Germany
Web
www.haworth-europe.com
www.ito-design.com

The source of inspiration for the design and function of the Fern desk chair was nature: the design language and construction of the backrest are reminiscent of a fern leaf. Its core element is the wave-like Wave Suspension. The innovative technology is integrated into the slim, clearly structured backrest and provides central back support and great freedom of movement. The edge-free design and the flexible materials of the backrest furthermore ensure a high sitting comfort. Intuitive in use, Fern adjusts quickly and easily to the individual requirements of users.

Statement by the jury
The Fern task chair fascinates with the rigorous realisation of the design approach. Its ergonomics are well thought-through to the last detail and meet the demands of modern workplace design.

Inspirationsquelle für Gestaltung und Funktion des Schreibtischstuhls Fern war die Natur: Formensprache und Aufbau der Rückenlehne nehmen Bezug auf ein Farnblatt. Sein Herzstück ist die wellenartige Wave Suspension. Die innovative Technik ist in die schlanke, strukturierte Lehne integriert und sorgt für eine zentrale Rückenunterstützung und große Bewegungsfreiheit. Das kantenfreie Design und das flexible Material des Rückenteils fördern zusätzlich einen hohen Sitzkomfort. Intuitiv in der Bedienung, lässt sich Fern schnell und einfach an die individuellen Bedürfnisse des Nutzers anpassen.

Begründung der Jury
Der Schreibtischstuhl Fern begeistert mit der konsequenten Umsetzung des Gestaltungsansatzes. Die Ergonomie ist bis ins Detail durchdacht und entspricht den Anforderungen an moderne Arbeitsplatzgestaltung.

Novo
Office Chair
Bürostuhl

Manufacturer
Exemplis LLC, Cypress, USA
In-house design
Web
www.sitonit.net

The characteristic element of the Novo office chair is its arch-shaped lines. The interplay with the stacked rectangular forms of the backrest lends the chair an expressive appearance. With frame and backrest, different structures and materials meet in a clearly defined way. The filigree mesh fabric of the backrest is breathable, while the seat with its high-quality padding adapts to the posture of the user. The seat height and depth are adjustable to individual ergonomic needs. The chair allows versatile configurations and thus blends customisably into different office environments.

Kennzeichnend für den Bürostuhl Novo ist seine bogenförmige Linienführung. Im Zusammenspiel mit den aufeinander aufbauenden rechteckigen Formen der Lehne entsteht seine ausdrucksstarke Anmutung. Mit Rahmen und Sitzfläche treffen auch verschiedene Strukturen und Materialien klar definiert aufeinander. Das filigrane Textilnetzgewebe der Rückenlehne ist atmungsaktiv, während sich die Sitzfläche mit einer hochwertigen Polsterung der Haltung des Nutzers anpasst. Auch lassen sich Sitzhöhe und -tiefe den ergonomischen Bedürfnissen entsprechend individuell einstellen. Der Stuhl ist vielseitig konfigurierbar und fügt sich so passgenau in die jeweilige Büroumgebung ein.

Statement by the jury
In its grey version and with stylishly rounded armrests, the Novo office chair obtains a clear and elegant aesthetic, which additionally receives a modern appeal thanks to its distinctive form.

Begründung der Jury
In seiner grauen Ausführung und mit den stilvoll gerundeten Armlehnen gewinnt der Bürostuhl Novo eine klare und elegante Ästhetik, die durch die prägnante Formgebung zusätzlich eine zeitgemäße Note erhält.

PRECEDE
Office System
Bürosystem

Manufacturer
Okamura Corporation,
Yokohama, Japan

In-house design
Alexander Hurford,
Waku Tsuchiyama

Web
www.okamura.jp

reddot **award 2017**
best of the best

Systematic understatement
Equipping workplaces with office systems is a highly contemporary trend as it allows the furniture to easily adapt to changes within the company. Against this backdrop, the design of Precede offers flexibility in a creative way, as the system comprises work desks and meeting tables as well as partitions and executive desks. The individual components share a common design language that lends the overall office space a subtle tone with an elegant appearance. Glass panel partitions incorporate an essential element of the series. They structure any given space, exude an impression of transparency and showcase flowing, homogeneous transitions. Furthermore, the work desks integrate structural features of bench tables and single desks, allowing multiple, diverse layouts in a single system. These desks have been fabricated to render an impression of sophisticated material comfort, which is underlined by the natural texture of the finishes. Both the doors and drawers are equipped with a quiet and soft-closing mechanism aimed at a high-quality and pleasant operating feel. The Precede office system thus creates spaces where staff can work in a shared spirit of comfort and cooperation and, in so doing, turns into a visual expression embodying a company's individual corporate culture.

Understatement mit System
Die Ausstattung mit Bürosystemen ist sehr zeitgemäß, da so das Mobiliar leicht Veränderungen in Unternehmen und Büros mitvollziehen kann. Die Gestaltung von Precede schafft auf kreative Art und Weise Flexibilität, das System umfasst dabei Arbeits- und Besprechungstische sowie Trennwände und Chefschreibtische. Die einzelnen Komponenten vereint eine ähnliche Formensprache, mit der sie dem gesamten Büro eine dezent wirkende Eleganz verleihen. Die Trennwände aus Glas sind ein wesentliches Element der Serie. Sie strukturieren den Raum, vermitteln einen Eindruck von Transparenz und ermöglichen fließende, homogene Übergänge. Da die Arbeitstische auch Schreibtische für Einzelarbeitsplätze einschließen, werden viele verschiedene Anordnungen innerhalb eines Systems möglich. In Form und Farbgebung sind die Tische auf einen gehobenen Komfort ausgerichtet, was von der natürlich anmutenden Textur ihrer Oberflächen unterstrichen wird. Die Türen wie auch die Schubladen sind mit einem gedämpft und leise arbeitenden Schließmechanismus ausgestattet, weshalb ihre Handhabung sehr angenehm ist. Das Bürosystem Precede kreiert so Räume, in denen die Menschen im Sinne einer gemeinsamen Idee von Komfort und Kooperation arbeiten können, und wird damit zum sichtbaren Ausdruck von Unternehmenskultur.

Statement by the jury
The Precede office system fascinates with elegant table leg covers and beautiful finishes. The design yields a minimalism that convinces particularly with a streamlined appearance of clarity and precision. The series impresses with its high-quality implementation and a sophisticated system character that makes it suitable for a variety of different layouts. In addition, its well-thought-out modularity facilitates spaces to be partitioned into both single workspaces and complex group arrangements.

Begründung der Jury
Das Bürosystem Precede begeistert mit seinen schönen Oberflächen und eleganten Tischbeinen. Seiner Gestaltung gelingt ein Minimalismus, dessen durchgehend klare und präzise Formensprache besonders überzeugt. Die Serie beeindruckt mit ihrer hochwertigen Ausführung sowie dem ausgefeilten Systemcharakter, der sie für ganz unterschiedliche Szenarien geeignet macht. Die durchdachte Modularität ermöglicht dabei ebenso eine räumliche Aufteilung in Einzelarbeitsplätzen wie auch komplexe Gruppenanordnungen.

Designer portrait
See page 36
Siehe Seite 36

yuno
Stacking Table
Stapeltisch

Manufacturer
Wiesner-Hager Möbel GmbH, Altheim, Austria
Design
B4K (Andreas Krob), Wolfhalden, Switzerland
Web
www.wiesner-hager.com
www.b4k.ch

The sophisticated design of the yuno stacking table enables compact and space-saving storage without the need to fold the frame. Featuring a special interconnecting frame, the tables can be interlocked longitudinally without extra linking devices when set up in rows or for banquets. Small castors integrated into the glides further facilitate the handling of the minimalist-functional table and complement its modern design concept.

Die durchdachte Gestaltung des Stapeltisches yuno erlaubt eine dichte und platzsparende Lagerung, ohne dass das Gestell eingeklappt werden muss. Versehen mit einer speziellen Gestellverschränkung lassen sich mehrere Exemplare zudem ohne Zusatzelement längsseitig bei Bankett- und Reihenaufstellungen miteinander verbinden. Kleine Rollen in den Gestellgleitern erleichtern die Handhabung des minimalistisch-funktionalen Tisches zusätzlich und runden das moderne Gestaltungskonzept ab.

Statement by the jury
The yuno stacking table scores with an innovative and clear design concept that focuses on efficient and practical handling.

Begründung der Jury
Der Stapeltisch yuno punktet mit einem innovativen, klaren Gestaltungskonzept, das den Fokus auf eine effiziente und praktische Handhabung legt.

Note
Meeting Table
Konferenztisch

Manufacturer
bürotime, Istanbul, Turkey
In-house design
Arif Akıllılar, Utkan Kızıltuğ
Web
www.burotime.com

The Note meeting table displays an expressive yet timeless appearance. Its core feature is the Y-shaped legs, lending the table its characteristic silhouette. In combination with its slim and elegant desktop, the meeting table turns into a work place with high recognition value. Harmonious lines convey consistency in a fast-paced, dynamic work world.

Statement by the jury
The Note meeting table convinces with its distinctive yet unobtrusive design, which turns it into a representative eye-catcher in meeting and conference rooms.

Der Konferenztisch Note wird geprägt durch sein ausdrucksvolles und zugleich zeitloses Erscheinungsbild. Sein Herzstück sind die Y-förmigen Tischbeine. Sie machen die charakteristische Silhouette des Tisches aus. In Kombination mit seiner schlanken und eleganten Arbeitsfläche wird der Konferenztisch zu einem Arbeitsplatz mit hohem Wiedererkennungswert. Seine ausgewogene Linienführung vermittelt Beständigkeit in einer schnelllebigen, dynamischen Arbeitswelt.

Begründung der Jury
Der Konferenztisch Note überzeugt durch sein markantes und dennoch zurückhaltendes Design, das ihn zum repräsentativen Blickfang in Besprechungs- und Konferenzräumen macht.

kinema active conference chair
Swivel Chair
Drehstuhl

Manufacturer
Kinema GmbH, Olpe, Germany
In-house design
Stefan Zoell
Web
www.mykinema.com
Honourable Mention

Featuring a compact design, the kinema active conference chair ensures an active sitting position at the workplace. The sophisticated design and ergonomic concept with its newly developed mechanics allow vertical movements as well as adjustments to desk heights from 65 to 130 cm. Thanks to the simple change from regular sitting to elevated sitting and stand-up sitting, daily work situations are provided with new agility and quality. The well-balanced Stand-Sit-Support-Dynamics improve physical well-being and support concentration and receptivity in daily work routines.

Statement by the jury
The kinema active conference chair fascinates with its dynamic, well thought-through design, which meets the high ergonomic demands on modern office furniture.

Der kompakt gestaltete kinema active conference chair sorgt für eine aktive Sitzhaltung am Arbeitsplatz. Das raffinierte Design- und Ergonomiekonzept ermöglicht mit einer neu entwickelten Mechanik vertikale Bewegungen und eine Anpassung an Tischhöhen im Nutzungsbereich von 65 bis 130 cm. Durch den leichten Wechsel vom regulären zum erhöhten Sitzen und Stehsitzen erfahren alltägliche Arbeitssituationen eine neue Agilität und Qualität. Die ausgewogene Steh-Sitz-Stützdynamik verbessert das körperliche Wohlbefinden und fördert die Konzentrations- und Aufnahmefähigkeit im Arbeitsalltag.

Begründung der Jury
Der kinema active conference chair begeistert mit seiner dynamischen, durchdachten Gestaltung, die den hohen ergonomischen Anforderungen an moderne Büromöbel gerecht wird.

se:line
Conference Swivel Chair
Konferenzdrehstuhl

Manufacturer
Sedus Stoll AG,
Waldshut-Tiengen, Germany
In-house design
Judith Daur
Web
www.sedus.com

The se:line conference and management chair combines a reduced and ergonomic design language with innovative functionality. Its armrests function as spring-tension storage, creating a clean and lightweight look even below the seat, since the design does without the usual mechanisms. Thanks to the chair's synchronous motion sequence, all users experience the same amount of backrest pressure regardless of their body weight. This automatic weight adjustment reduces the handling to height adjustments and the locking of the backrest.

Statement by the jury
The clean aesthetics of the se:line conference and management chair ties in with the sophisticated and innovative functionality of the armrests.

Der Konferenz- und Managementstuhl se:line verbindet eine reduzierte und zugleich ergonomische Formensprache mit innovativer Funktionalität. Die Armlehnen übernehmen die Funktion des Federkraftspeichers. So wird eine leichte und aufgeräumte Anmutung auch unterhalb des Sitzes ermöglicht, da die gewohnte Mechanik nicht benötigt wird. Der synchrone Bewegungsablauf ist dabei so austariert, dass der Anlehndruck unabhängig vom Nutzergewicht annähernd gleich empfunden wird. Diese automatische Gewichtsanpassung reduziert die Bedienung auf eine Höhenverstellung und eine Lehnenarretierung.

Begründung der Jury
Die aufgeräumte Ästhetik des Konferenz- und Managementstuhls se:line geht einher mit einer durchdachten und innovativen Funktion der Armlehnen.

DIADEM
Conference Chair
Konferenzstuhl

Manufacturer
Nurus A. Ş., Istanbul, Turkey
Design
Design Ballendat, Simbach am Inn, Germany
Web
www.nurus.com
www.ballendat.com

With its minimalist design and slim construction, the Diadem conference chair blends very well into different environments and is particularly well suited for highly frequented work places such as conference halls, meeting rooms or waiting lounges. The distinctive geometric form of the legs together with the steel armrests lend it elasticity and support a dynamic, flexible sitting experience. The curved backrest very naturally adapts to the user's posture, ensuring high seating comfort.

Mit seinem minimalistischen Design und seiner schlanken Bauweise fügt sich der Konferenzstuhl Diadem sehr gut in sein Nutzungsumfeld ein und eignet sich besonders für hoch frequentierte Arbeitsorte wie Konferenzsäle, Besprechungsräume und Wartelounges. Die markante geometrische Form des Fußgestells und die Armlehnen aus Stahl verleihen ihm Elastizität und unterstützen ein dynamisches, flexibles Sitzen. Die gebogene Rückenlehne passt sich ganz natürlich der Haltung des Nutzers an und sorgt so für hohen Sitzkomfort.

Statement by the jury
Distinctive and at the same time light in its design, the fully recyclable Diadem conference chair also fascinates in terms of its ecological aspects.

Begründung der Jury
Prägnant und zugleich leicht in der Formgebung, begeistert der ausnahmslos recycelbare Konferenzstuhl Diadem auch unter ökologischen Aspekten.

Penne
Chair
Stuhl

Manufacturer
Lammhults Möbel AB, Lammhult, Sweden
Design
Läufer & Keichel (Julia Läufer, Marcus Keichel),
Berlin, Germany
Web
www.lammhults.se
www.laeuferkeichel.de

The Penne chair unites simple design in Scandinavian tradition with novel materials. Its legs, made of lightweight laminated wood tubes, reduce the weight while also providing the same high degree of stability as conventional wooden chairs. Penne is certified for use in commercial properties, and its unobtrusive yet expressive aesthetics qualify it for a wide variety of events. Legs and seat are connected by screws and not glued, so that the chair is easy to disassemble and recycle.

Der Stuhl Penne vereint schlichtes Design in skandinavischer Tradition mit neuartigen Materialien. Seine Beine aus Leichtbau-Schichtholzrahmen reduzieren das Gewicht, bieten aber gleichzeitig eine ebenso hohe Stabilität wie konventionelle Holzstühle. Penne ist für den Objekteinsatz zertifiziert und seine zurückhaltende und doch ausdrucksstarke Ästhetik qualifiziert ihn für vielfältige Anlässe. Beine und Sitzfläche sind über Schrauben miteinander verbunden und nicht verklebt. So lässt sich der Stuhl leicht auseinandernehmen und einfach recyceln.

Statement by the jury
The Penne chair finds a harmonious balance between innovative technology, craftsmanship and an unmistakable design language.

Begründung der Jury
Der Stuhl Penne findet eine ausgewogene Balance zwischen innovativer Technik, handwerklichem Können und unverwechselbarer Formensprache.

LessThanFive
Chair
Stuhl

Manufacturer
Coalesse, USA
In-house design
Coalesse Design Group (John Hamilton)
Design
Michael Young Ltd. (Michael Young), Hong Kong
Web
www.coalesse.de
www.michael-young.com

The distinctive feature of this chair is the material. Made of carbon fibre, the LessThanFive stands out through a sophisticated design and high resilience. Its visual impact is based on its simple yet equally expressive lines. At a weight of less than 2.3 kg and available in six colours, the chair opens up a wide creative freedom and blends flexibly into various room and office environments. High demands on functionality are furthermore fulfilled through its stackability.

Die Besonderheit dieses Stuhls ist das Material. Aus Carbonfaser handgefertigt, besticht LessThanFive durch eine raffinierte Formgebung und hohe Belastbarkeit. Seine visuelle Wirkung beruht auf einer schlichten und gleichermaßen ausdrucksstarken Linienführung. Mit einem Eigengewicht von weniger als 2,3 kg und sechs Farbausführungen eröffnet der Stuhl einen großen Gestaltungsspielraum und lässt sich flexibel in verschiedene Raum- und Büroumgebungen einfügen. Der hohe Anspruch an die Funktionalität wird darüber hinaus durch seine Stapelbarkeit erfüllt.

Statement by the jury
The chair combines ambitious design with an innovative choice of material and high-quality craftsmanship. Being truly lightweight, it is characterised by high resilience and flexible applications.

Begründung der Jury
Der Stuhl vereint anspruchsvolles Design mit innovativer Materialauswahl und handwerklicher Qualität. Selbst ein Leichtgewicht, zeichnet er sich durch hohe Belastbarkeit und flexible Einsatzmöglichkeiten aus.

Metrik
Cantilever Chair
Freischwinger

Manufacturer
Wilkhahn, Wilkening+Hahne GmbH + Co.KG,
Bad Münder, Germany
Design
whiteID GmbH & Co. KG,
Schorndorf, Germany
Web
www.wilkhahn.de
www.white-id.com

Metrik is a chair that appears to be cast in one piece. Backrest, seat and armrests of the cantilever chair create a monolithic body whose form-fit connection with the tubular steel frame is only revealed by a narrow gap. The anatomically designed cushioning of the backrest and seat provides highly comfortable seating. Six colours for body and frame as well as a wide variety of cover options allow versatile combinations with different desk concepts and office chairs. In this way, Metrik blends into the overall design concept in accordance with user preference.

Statement by the jury
The Metrik cantilever chair is characterised by its dynamic appearance. It is flexible in use and adapts to different interior styles.

Metrik ist ein Stuhl, der wie aus einem Guss wirkt. Rückenlehne, Sitzfläche und Armlehnen des Freischwingers bilden einen monolithisch erscheinenden Körper, dessen formschlüssige Verbindung mit dem Stahlrohrgestell nur an einer schmalen Fuge ablesbar ist. Die körpergerechte Polsterung von Lehne und Sitzfläche schafft einen hohen Sitzkomfort. Sechs Korpus- und Gestellfarben sowie zahlreiche Bezugsvarianten lassen vielseitige Kombinationen mit verschiedenen Tischkonzepten und Bürostühlen zu. So fügt sich Metrik nach den Wünschen des Nutzers in die Gesamtgestaltung ein.

Begründung der Jury
Der Freischwinger Metrik zeichnet sich durch seine dynamische Anmutung aus. Er lässt sich flexibel einsetzen und passt sich unterschiedlichen Einrichtungsstilen an.

Pi A.1
Chair
Stuhl

Manufacturer
Arvo Piiroinen Oy, Salo, Finland
Design
Fokkema & Partners Architecten, FOKlab
research department, Delft, Netherlands
Web
www.piiroinen.com
www.fokkema-partners.nl

Special features of the Pi A.1 chair are the quality and processing of the used material: a deformable veneer that is flexed three-dimensionally in the production process lends the chair its lightweight appeal and reliable rigidity. The design provides effective protection against back strain and supports a healthy sitting posture. Chair legs and seat are connected by a seamless metal frame. This combination of materials contributes to the stability of the construction and defines its appealing and self-reliant appearance.

Statement by the jury
The Pi A.1 chair pleases with its well thought-through and committed construction. Sophisticated in production and materials, it catches the eye in particular with its flowing-filigree design.

Eine Besonderheit des Stuhls Pi A.1 ist die Beschaffenheit und Verarbeitung des verwendeten Materials: Verformbares Furnierholz, das im Herstellungsprozess dreidimensional gebogen wird, verleiht dem Stuhl seine leichte Anmutung und eine zuverlässige Festigkeit. Gleichzeitig trägt die Formgebung zur Entlastung des Rückens bei und unterstützt eine gesunde Sitzhaltung. Stuhlbeine und Sitz sind über einen nahtlosen Metallrahmen miteinander verbunden. Diese Materialkombination trägt zur Stabilität der Konstruktion bei und prägt ihr ansprechendes und eigenständiges Erscheinungsbild.

Begründung der Jury
Der Stuhl Pi A.1 gefällt aufgrund seiner durchdachten und engagierten Konstruktion. Anspruchsvoll in Produktion und Material, fällt er vor allem mit seiner fließend-filigranen Gestaltung ins Auge.

Fiore
Shell Chair
Schalenstuhl

Manufacturer
Bürositzmöbelfabrik Friedrich-W. Dauphin
GmbH & Co. KG, Offenhausen, Germany
Design
Dauphin Entwicklungs- und
Beteiligungs GmbH, Dauphin Design-Team
(Jessica Engelhardt), Hersbruck, Germany
Web
www.dauphin.de

With its clear forms and versatile design, the Fiore shell chair is especially suited for modern, multi-functional office rooms. Its great variability leaves room for individual design solutions. The seat shell is available in many versions, as a moulded-wood shell, in flexible plastic and with a diverse range of upholstery styles. Armrests can be added, and users can choose between different frame designs, colours and surfaces. This lends each chair a unique character.

Statement by the jury
The Fiore shell chair convinces with modern aesthetics. The combination of wooden seat shell, elegant armrests and filigree coaster is optimally coordinated.

Mit seinen klaren Formen und einem vielseitigen Design eignet sich der Schalenstuhl Fiore besonders für moderne, multifunktional genutzte Büroräume. Seine große Variabilität lässt Raum für individuelle Gestaltungslösungen. Die Sitzschale ist in verschiedenen Ausführungen erhältlich und steht als Formholzschale, aus flexiblem Kunststoff und mit verschiedenen Polstern zur Wahl. Armlehnen können ergänzt und unterschiedliche Gestellformen, Farben und Oberflächen gewählt werden. So erhält jeder Stuhl seinen ganz eigenen Charakter.

Begründung der Jury
Der Schalenstuhl Fiore besticht mit einer modernen Ästhetik. Die Kombination aus hölzerner Sitzschale, eleganten Armlehnen und filigranem Rollengestell ist optimal abgestimmt.

Bonito
Wooden-Shell Chair
Holzschalenstuhl

Manufacturer
ZÜCO Bürositzmöbel AG,
Rebstein, Switzerland
Design
Design Ballendat (Martin Ballendat),
Simbach am Inn, Germany
Web
www.zueco.com
www.ballendat.com

An accentuated light and airy appearance characterises the Bonito chair. The lively design of the slim wooden-shell, available in light oak or fine walnut, lends the chair its unique form. The high quality of the materials and their precise manufacturing round off the design concept. Fabrics and leathers as cover materials and the choice between four-legged or rotating chair models allow versatile variations.

Statement by the jury
High-quality standards in regard to materials and manufacturing characterise the wooden shell chair Bonito. The lively, open design of the backrest catches the eye.

Seine betont leichte und luftige Erscheinung kennzeichnet den Stuhl Bonito. Das schwungvolle Design der schlanken Holzschale, wahlweise aus heller Eiche oder feinem Nussbaum, verleiht dem Stuhl seine unverkennbare Form. Die Hochwertigkeit der Materialien und deren edle Verarbeitung runden das Gestaltungskonzept ab. Stoffe und Leder als Bezugsmaterialien und die Auswahl zwischen einem Vierfuß- und Drehstuhlmodell ermöglichen vielseitige Variationen.

Begründung der Jury
Ein hoher Qualitätsanspruch an Materialien und Verarbeitung zeichnet den Holzschalenstuhl Bonito aus. Die schwungvolle, offene Gestaltung der Rückenlehne zieht die Blicke auf sich.

Occo
Multi Purposal Chair
Multifunktionsstuhl

Manufacturer
Wilkhahn, Wilkening+Hahne GmbH+Co.KG,
Bad Münder, Germany
Design
jehs + laub gbr, Stuttgart, Germany
Web
www.wilkhahn.de
www.jehs-laub.com

The Occo chair is marked by a specially shaped recess in the seat shell. Moreover, the shape and different thicknesses of the material render the seat area stable yet the back extremely flexible. These features also define the iconographic name of this range: the chair's front and back is dominated by an O-shaped appearance, whereas it resembles a double C when viewed from the side. Available in four frame types with three types of cushioning and six shell colours, Occo is highly versatile, offers a vast variety of design options, and easily integrates into many different work and home environments.

Statement by the jury
The Occo chair stands out with a distinctive seat shell that lends it both a characteristically expressive structure and stability.

Charakteristisch für den Stuhl Occo ist die speziell geformte Aussparung der Sitzschale. Formverlauf und Materialstärken machen die Sitzfläche stabil und die Rückenpartie zudem sehr flexibel. Gleichzeitig entsteht so die Zeichenhaftigkeit des Programmnamens: In der Frontal- und Rückansicht dominiert die O-förmige Anmutung, im Profil das doppelte C. In vier Gestell-, drei Polstervarianten und sechs Schalenfarben erhältlich, bietet Occo eine große Gestaltungsvielfalt und lässt sich problemlos in unterschiedliche Wohn- und Arbeitsräume integrieren.

Begründung der Jury
Der Stuhl Occo punktet mit einer markanten Sitzschale, die ihm seine charakteristische expressive Struktur und darüber hinaus auch Stabilität verleiht.

ARTISO®
Conference Chair
Konferenzsessel

Manufacturer
KÖHL GmbH Sitzmöbel, Rödermark, Germany
Design
Volker Reichert, Gelnhausen, Germany
Web
www.koehl.com
www.volkerreichert.com

The Artiso conference chair fulfils high standards in ergonomics and comfort. Fitted with high-quality pocket springs, the seat encourages active sitting and ensures a pleasant sitting experience. For enhanced ergonomic functionality, a 360-degree Ergo-Disc hinge allows a flexible and dynamic positioning of the seat shell. With its distinctive design, four different frame types and exclusive upholstery materials such as leather, felt and wool fabric, the conference chair offers a wide range of individual design options.

Der Konferenzsessel Artiso erfüllt hohe Ansprüche an Ergonomie und Komfort. Die mit hochwertigen Taschenfederkernen versehene Sitzfläche ermöglicht aktives und klimatisiertes Sitzen. Um die ergonomische Funktionalität zu erweitern, erlaubt ein flexibles Ergo-Disc-Gelenk die bewegliche 360-Grad-Lagerung der Sitzschale. Markant in der Formgebung, bietet der Konferenzsessel mit vier verschiedenen Gestellvarianten und ausgesuchten Bezugsmaterialien wie Leder, Filz und Wollstoffen eine Vielzahl individueller Gestaltungsmöglichkeiten.

Statement by the jury
The conference chair combines conclusive design and functionality at a high level. With an expressive appearance, it also meets ergonomic requirements.

Begründung der Jury
Auf hohem Niveau verbindet der Konferenzsessel schlüssige Formgebung und Funktionalität. Ausdrucksstark in der Gestaltung, genügt er gleichzeitig ergonomischen Ansprüchen.

Myra
Armchair
Armsessel

Manufacturer
Metalmobil, Tavullia, Italy
Design
Emilio Nanni, Bazzano, Italy
Web
www.metalmobil.com
www.emilionanni.it

The Myra armchair embodies lightness, comfort and elegance. The curve as the defining element of the upholstered surfaces in combination with the curved shape of the seat and its straight-lined, filigree base frame lend the upholstered chair its unique appearance. Myra combines a contemporary design with high-grade and diligent manufacturing. Eye-catching are the seams in contrasting colours. A wide selection of materials and colours allows versatile combinations. The frame is available in beech wood or steel.

Statement by the jury
A markedly lightweight, delicate form characterises the Myra armchair. With its modern yet at the same time unobtrusive appearance, it is very well suited to different interiors.

Der Armsessel Myra verkörpert Leichtigkeit, Komfort und Eleganz. Die Kurve als prägendes Element der Polsterflächen in Verbindung mit der kurvig geformten Sitzfläche mit einem geradlinigen, filigranen Untergestell verleiht dem Polsterstuhl ein unverwechselbares Aussehen. Myra kombiniert zeitgemäße Formgebung mit hochwertiger und sorgfältiger Herstellung. Origineller Blickfang sind die Nähte in Kontrastfarben. Eine große Auswahl an Materialien und Farben erlaubt vielseitige Kombinationen. Das Gestell ist in den Varianten Buchenholz und Stahl erhältlich.

Begründung der Jury
Die betont leichte, feine Form kennzeichnet den Armsessel Myra. Mit seinem modernen und zugleich zurückhaltenden Aussehen eignet er sich sehr gut für unterschiedliche Interieurs.

Chic Air
Seating Furniture
Sitzmöbel

Manufacturer
Profim sp. z o.o., Turek, Poland
Design
Agence Christophe Pillet (Christophe Pillet),
Paris, France
Web
www.profim.eu
www.christophepillet.com

The Chic Air line merges the aesthetics of classic seating furniture with a sophisticated design approach. Angular geometric forms meet with delicate sections to create a contemporary appearance. Unconventional yet subtle, the chairs and benches integrate very well into conference and meeting spaces. Following the same design idiom, the slightly lowered armchair turns into an elegant eye-catcher. The furniture is available with an option of leather and high-quality textiles for the finish, which can also be combined individually.

Die Serie Chic Air vereint die Ästhetik klassischer Sitzmöbel mit einem raffinierten Gestaltungsansatz. Kantige, geometrische Formen verbinden sich mit filigranen Linien und schaffen eine zeitgemäße Anmutung. Unkonventionell und doch dezent, lassen sich Sitzbank und Stuhl sehr gut in Besprechungs- und Konferenzräume einfügen. In derselben Formensprache gehalten, wird der etwas abgesenkte Sessel zu einem eleganten Eyecatcher. Als Bezugsmaterialien stehen Leder und hochwertige Stoffe zur Auswahl. Diese können zudem individuell kombiniert werden.

Statement by the jury
The seating furniture of the Chic Air line is marked by an elegant combination of classic and modern design idioms that makes it blend with style into many interiors.

Begründung der Jury
Die Sitzmöbel der Serie Chic Air prägt die gelungene Verbindung klassischer und moderner Formgebung, die sich stilvoll in unterschiedliche Interieurs einfügt.

LIPS
Pouf
Hocker

Manufacturer
Nurus A. Ş., Istanbul, Turkey
In-house design
Web
www.nurus.com

The name "Lips" already emphasises the underlying idea of the design: the dynamic form of the upholstered pouf is reminiscent of a mouth. Its rounded base allows gentle rocking movements that activate the muscles of the user and support active sitting. When not in motion, Lips provides high comfort by supporting a relaxed sitting position. Complementing accessories comprise a holder that provides space for tablets and other technical devices.

Der Name „Lips" verweist bereits auf die dem Design zugrundeliegende Idee: Die schwungvolle Form des gepolsterten Hockers ist einem Mund nachempfunden. Mit seiner abgerundeten Standfläche ermöglicht er leichte schaukelnde Bewegungen, die die Muskeln des Nutzers anregen und aktives Sitzen fördern. Auch in ruhiger Position bietet Lips hohen Komfort, indem er eine entspannte Sitzposition unterstützt. Ergänzendes Accessoire ist eine Halterung, die Platz für Tablets und andere technische Geräte schafft.

Statement by the jury
With its unusual shape, the upholstered Lips pouf sets a creative highlight in offices and is an appealing alternative to common seating furniture.

Begründung der Jury
Mit seiner ausgefallenen Formgebung setzt der gepolsterte Hocker Lips kreative Akzente im Büro und stellt eine ansprechende Alternative zu gängigen Sitzmöbeln dar.

se:works
Modular Sofa Programme
Modulares Sofaprogramm

Manufacturer
Sedus Stoll AG,
Waldshut-Tiengen, Germany
In-house design
Falk Blümler
Web
www.sedus.com

With versatile combinations and multi-functional use, the se:works modular sofa programme complies with the different requirements of modern work environments. The parametric basic structure facilitates centimetre-precise adaptations, allowing the creation of comfortable work and meeting areas even in small rooms. Besides standard formations such as U-shapes, banks and circles, it allows for numerous individual designs. Practical tables and trays are very easily integrated.

Statement by the jury
The se:works modular sofa programme fascinates with its application-oriented, ergonomic design and high variability.

Vielseitig kombinierbar und multifunktional einsetzbar, entspricht das modulare Sofaprogramm se:works den unterschiedlichen Anforderungen an moderne Arbeitsumgebungen. Die parametrische Grundstruktur lässt zentimetergenaue Anpassungen zu. Selbst in kleinen Räumen entstehen so komfortable Arbeits- und Gesprächsinseln. Neben Standardformationen wie U-Form, Bank und Kreis sind zahlreiche individuelle Gestaltungsvarianten möglich. Praktische Tische und Ablagen können sehr einfach integriert werden.

Begründung der Jury
Das modulare Sofaprogramm se:works fasziniert durch seine anwendungsorientierte, ergonomische Gestaltung und hohe Variabilität.

Harbor Work Lounge
Loungechair
Loungestuhl

Manufacturer
Haworth GmbH,
Bad Münder am Deister, Germany
In-house design
Nicolai Czumaj-Bront
Web
www.haworth-europe.com

The Harbor Work Lounge is an ergonomic workplace and comfortable lounge chair all in one. Elegant in design, it meets the demands of various work situations thanks to its sophisticated functionality. The comfortable swivel chair features work surfaces that are equally suitable for right- or left-handed persons. An integrated sliding table provides users with space for a notebook and documents. A mobile phone, personal objects or drinks find a place on the compact suede side wing. An aluminium cast foot lends the chair stability while the seat is available partly or fully upholstered.

Statement by the jury
Highly expressive and comfortable in its appearance, the Harbor Work Lounge scores with its carefully thought-out functionality.

Die Harbor Work Lounge ist ergonomischer Arbeitsplatz und bequemer Loungesessel in einem. Stilvoll in seiner Formgebung, wird er aufgrund seiner ausgefeilten Funktionen verschiedenen Arbeitssituationen und -ansprüchen gerecht. Der komfortable Drehstuhl verfügt über Arbeitsflächen, die sich für Rechts- und Linkshänder gleichermaßen eignen. Eine integrierte Gleitplatte fungiert als Ablage für Laptop und Schreibunterlagen. Mobiltelefon, persönliche Gegenstände oder auch Getränke finden auf einem kompakten Seitenflügel aus Veloursleder Platz. Ein Aluminiumguss-Fuß gibt der Sitzschale Halt, die nach Wunsch voll oder teilweise gepolstert geliefert wird.

Begründung der Jury
Gleichermaßen ausdrucksstark und komfortabel im Erscheinungsbild, besticht die Harbor Work Lounge durch wohlüberlegte Flexibilität.

enAble
Office Furniture System
Büromöbelsystem

Manufacturer
Fursys Inc., Seoul, South Korea
In-house design
Fursys R&D Center
Web
www.globalfursys.com

The development of the enAble office furniture system placed particular emphasis on being well balanced in relation to cost, practicability and efficiency. The result is a solution that is minimal with a timeless appearance and high functionality. Thanks to numerous configuration options, the office furniture is quickly and effortlessly combined and adjusted to different spatial conditions and work habits. The table height is mechanically adjustable between 65 and 117 cm, while small cabinet and drawer units can be added individually.

Bei der Entwicklung des Büromöbelsystems enAble lag das Hauptaugenmerk auf einem ausgewogenen Verhältnis von Kosten, Praktikabilität und Effizienz. Das Ergebnis verbindet ein reduziertes, zeitloses Erscheinungsbild mit hoher Funktionalität. Dank zahlreicher Konfigurationsoptionen lassen sich die Büromöbel schnell und mühelos kombinieren und an verschiedene Räumlichkeiten sowie Arbeitsgewohnheiten anpassen. Die Tischhöhe ist mechanisch zwischen 65 und 117 cm einzustellen, kleine Schrank- und Schubladenelemente können individuell ergänzt werden.

Statement by the jury
A sophisticated concept, great variability and the consideration of individual work environments characterise the enAble office furniture system.

Begründung der Jury
Eine durchdachte Konzeption, große Variabilität und die Berücksichtigung individueller Arbeitsumgebungen zeichnen das Büromöbelsystem enAble aus.

Gispen HUBB
Modular Furniture System
Modulares Möbelsystem

Manufacturer
Gispen, Culemborg, Netherlands
Design
Mecanoo architecten, Delft, Netherlands
Web
www.gispen.com
www.mecanoo.nl

Hubb is a modular furniture system designed to create dynamic work and study environments in which a wide range of activities can take place simultaneously. Only a few elements with a seemingly straightforward basic shape are needed to form endless combinations. Made from steel, beechwood and PET-felt, Hubb offers a highly sustainable future-proof interior solution that can easily be reconfigured to meet new requirements.

Statement by the jury
The Hubb furniture system is convincingly and skilfully designed. While offering versatile combinations, it always keeps its own, distinctive character.

Das modulare Möbelsystem Hubb ermöglicht die Gestaltung dynamischer Arbeits- und Studienumgebungen, in denen eine Vielzahl an Aktivitäten gleichzeitig stattfinden kann. Nur wenige der geradlinig geformten Elemente reichen aus, um eine Vielzahl an Kombinationen umzusetzen. Aus Stahl, Buchenholz und PET-Filz gefertigt, bietet Hubb eine nachhaltige, zukunftsorientierte Einrichtungslösung, die immer wieder flexibel angepasst werden kann, um neuen Anforderungen gerecht zu werden.

Begründung der Jury
Das Möbelsystem Hubb ist schlüssig und gekonnt konzipiert. Vielseitig kombinierbar, behält es dabei stets seinen eigenen, prägnanten Charakter.

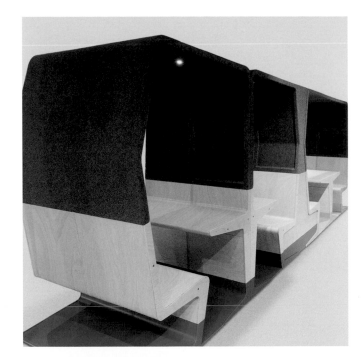

Divisio Frameless Screen
Screen
Seitenblende

Manufacturer
Steelcase Werndl AG,
Rosenheim, Germany
In-house design
Web
www.steelcase.com

The discreetly designed Divisio Frameless Screen gives desks structure and creates a space for concentrated working. With an easy to use clamping bracket, the screen element is effortlessly installed on work surfaces with a thickness of 19 to 38 mm, and is also easily removed again. Thanks to its rounded corners and its fabric covers that are available in various colours, Divisio Frameless Screen lends office interiors a warm, natural atmosphere. Furthermore, the surface is magnetic and allows a flexible and personal design of the workplace.

Statement by the jury
The appearance of the Divisio Frameless Screen is functional and reduced to the essential. It thus harmoniously blends into any environment.

Die schlicht gestaltete Seitenblende Divisio Frameless Screen gibt Schreibtischen Struktur und schafft Raum für konzentriertes Arbeiten. Mithilfe des einfach zu bedienenden Klemmbügels ist das Trennelement mühelos an Arbeitsflächen mit einer Dicke von 19 bis 38 mm anzubringen und auch wieder leicht zu entfernen. Aufgrund seiner abgerundeten Kanten und seines farblich variablen Stoffbezugs verleiht Divisio Frameless Screen Büroeinrichtungen eine warme, natürliche Atmosphäre. Die Oberfläche ist zudem magnetisch und macht eine flexible und persönliche Gestaltung des Arbeitsplatzes möglich.

Begründung der Jury
Das Erscheinungsbild der Seitenblende Divisio Frameless Screen ist funktional und auf das Wesentliche reduziert. So fügt sie sich harmonisch in jedes Umfeld ein.

Acoustic Element Wave
Akustikelement Welle
Suspended, Table and Wall Module
Hänge-, Tisch- und Wandmodul

Manufacturer
HEY-SIGN GmbH, Meerbusch, Germany
In-house design
Bernadette Ehmanns, Sonja Zilz, Reimund Braun
Web
www.hey-sign.de

The characteristic form of the Wave acoustic range merges a wave-like design with high-quality natural materials and high utility. All hanging, table and wall modules are completely covered with felt made of 100 per cent pure new wool. The materiality is the key element of the design, visually separating open office and living environments, while at the same time absorbing noise and improving acoustics. The sound-absorbing quality of the wool felt is further enhanced by the dense manufacturing of the material. The modules are available in 50 different colours.

Statement by the jury
User-friendly and consistent in form and design, the Wave acoustic range embraces the advantages of the natural felt material.

Die charakteristische Form der Akustikserie Welle vereint fließende Formgebung mit hochwertigen Naturmaterialien und einem hohen Nutzwert. Dabei sind die Hänge-, Tisch- und Wandmodule komplett mit Filz aus reiner Schurwolle ummantelt. Die Materialität steht im Vordergrund, trennt offene Büro- und Wohnwelten optisch und schirmt diese zugleich auch akustisch ab. Die schalldämmende Wirkung des Wollfilzes wird durch die dichte Verarbeitung des Materials noch verstärkt. Die Module sind in 50 verschiedenen Farben erhältlich.

Begründung der Jury
Formschlüssig und nutzerfreundlich macht sich die Akustikserie Welle die Vorzüge des natürlichen Materials Filz zu eigen.

se:wall
Wall and Partition System
Stellwandsystem

Manufacturer
Sedus Stoll AG, Waldshut-Tiengen, Germany
In-house design
Falk Blümler
Web
www.sedus.com

The se:wall wall and partition system allows flexible organisation of the workplace. Its slim and lightweight appearance elegantly blends into office environments while functional rails clearly define the contours of each individual element. Their technical appearance and precision purposefully contrast with the soft shapes of the seamlessly fabric-covered areas, which feature a sound-absorbing core made of polyester fleece. A wide range of connecting and functional elements offer a variety of possibilities for individual configurations.

Statement by the jury
The se:wall wall and partition system scores with a convincing concept, comfortable handling and emotionally appealing, harmonious aesthetics.

Das Stellwandsystem se:wall ermöglicht eine flexible Arbeitsplatzorganisation. Sein schlank und leicht gehaltenes Erscheinungsbild fügt sich elegant in die Bürolandschaft ein. Funktionsschienen geben jedem einzelnen Element eine klar definierte Kontur. Mit ihrer technischen Anmutung und Präzision bilden sie einen bewussten Kontrast zu den weichen Formen der fugenlos bespannten Stoffflächen, die über einen schallabsorbierenden Kern aus Polyestervlies verfügen. Verschiedene Verbindungs- und Funktionselemente bieten individuelle Konfigurationsmöglichkeiten.

Begründung der Jury
Das Stellwandsystem se:wall besticht mit einem schlüssigen Konzept, komfortabler Handhabung und emotional ansprechender, harmonischer Ästhetik.

PAIS
Adaptable Privacy Screen
Blendensystem

Manufacturer
Franz Blaha
Sitz- und Büromöbel Industrie GmbH, Korneuburg, Austria
Design
Brigitta Nemeth, Vienna, Austria
Web
www.blaha.co.at
www.brigittanemeth.com
Honourable Mention

The Pais privacy screen system combines flexibility and design. The elements partition workplaces in a convenient and visually appealing way. Easy to use, they are quickly set up and positioned. If required, the mobile privacy screens are quickly rolled up and ready for transport. In this way, they help to define and add a personal touch to individual workplaces in open-plan or co-working offices. Acting as a privacy screen and magnetic pinboard at the same time, the partitions also have sound-absorbent qualities. Produced from environmentally-friendly materials, the system is available in three different sizes.

Statement by the jury
Lightness in design and handling characterises the Pais adaptable privacy screens. Highly flexible in use, they fulfil the requirements of work environments, which are becoming increasingly mobile.

Das Blendensystem Pais vereint Flexibilität und Design. Die Elemente trennen Arbeitsbereiche praktisch und optisch ansprechend voneinander ab. Leicht in der Handhabung, lassen sie sich einfach justieren und positionieren. Bei Bedarf sind die mobilen Trennblenden schnell zusammengerollt und transportbereit. So helfen sie dabei, den eigenen Raum in Großraum- oder Co-working-Büros zu definieren und ihm eine persönliche Note zu geben. Sichtschutz und magnetische Pinnwand zugleich, sind die Trennblenden darüber hinaus auch akustisch wirksam. Das aus umweltfreundlichen Materialien gefertigte System ist in drei verschiedenen Formaten erhältlich.

Begründung der Jury
Leichtigkeit in Design und Handhabung zeichnet das Blendensystem Pais aus. Äußerst flexibel einsetzbar, entspricht es den Anforderungen einer mobiler werdenden Arbeitswelt.

SoundLeaves
Acoustic Panel Range
Akustikpaneel-Serie

Manufacturer
Incatro Room Acoustics,
Roermond, Netherlands
In-house design
Web
www.incatro.com

The SoundLeaves acoustic panels ensure a calm environment at the workplace and are particularly suited to open-plan offices. Users can easily place one or more panels on their desks. On the one hand, the panel absorbs sound and creates privacy at the same time, for meetings for example. On the other, colleagues can still be seen. The organically shaped elements come in a number of versions for use either on the desk or for fixing on a wall and in a range of colours.

Die Akustikpaneele SoundLeaves sorgen für eine ruhige Umgebung am Arbeitsplatz. Sie eignen sich besonders für offen gestaltete Büros. Der Nutzer kann ein oder mehrere Paneele bequem an seinem Schreibtisch platzieren. Auf der einen Seite wird so Lärm absorbiert und gleichzeitig Privatsphäre, beispielsweise für Gespräche, geschaffen. Auf der anderen Seite bleibt trotzdem der Sichtkontakt zu Kollegen erhalten. Die organisch gestalteten Elemente sind in verschiedenen Ausführungen, etwa als Modell für den Schreibtisch oder die Wand, und in unterschiedlichen Farben erhältlich.

Statement by the jury
The design of SoundLeaves is aimed at improving the acoustics of office areas. In addition, the organic shape of the acoustic panels is pleasing.

Begründung der Jury
Die Gestaltung von SoundLeaves ist auf die akustische Verbesserung in Büroräumen ausgerichtet. Darüber hinaus gefällt die organische Formensprache der Akustikpaneele.

Volum Art
Storage Furniture
Stauraummöbel

Manufacturer
Steelcase, Madrid, Spain
In-house design
Web
www.steelcase.com

The Volum Art storage furniture is defined by high versatility in conjunction with a clean design and a robust structure. The Volum Art family supports a full range of needs, from individual pedestals to mid-size cupboards and large cabinets. The individual elements can be combined to create user-oriented office environments and with their modern aesthetics stylishly blend into any interior. With the possibility of having a mix of different materials, a unique and personalised look can be achieved.

Statement by the jury
The Volum Art storage furniture skilfully finds the balance between practicable usability and timeless appeal.

Große Variabilität verbunden mit einer klaren Gestaltung und robuster Beschaffenheit machen die Stauraummöbel Volum Art aus. Die Produktfamilie bietet alle erdenklichen Aufbewahrungsmöglichkeiten, von individuellen Containern bis zu halbhohen Auszieh- oder großen Aktenschränken. Die einzelnen Elemente können zu anwendungsorientierten Bürolandschaften kombiniert werden und fügen sich mit ihrer zeitgemäßen Ästhetik überall harmonisch ein. Dank vielfältiger Auswahlmöglichkeiten zwischen unterschiedlichen Materialien wird dem persönlichen Stil Ausdruck verliehen.

Begründung der Jury
Die Stauraummöbel Volum Art halten gekonnt die Balance zwischen praktikabler Anwendung und zeitloser Anmutung.

Masterbox
Multi Furniture System (Office)
Multifunktionales Möbelsystem (Büro)

Manufacturer
Inwerk GmbH, Meerbusch, Germany
In-house design
Karl Bell, Jens Hohenbild
Web
www.inwerk.de
www.inwerk-bueromoebel.de

Purist in design, the Masterbox furniture system proves to be exceptionally multifunctional. Thanks to manifold configuration options, the cubic storage space furniture allows the realisation of individual office and room planning. A filigree geometry is combined with functional features and stability: the foamed steel construction allows setups with a width of up to 160 cm without requiring dividing walls or rear walls. The boxes can be stacked horizontally as well as vertically, in line or staggered, while in combination with a cushioning element, they also offer workplace-oriented seating.

Puristisch in der Gestaltung, erweist sich das Möbelsystem Masterbox als ausgesprochen multifunktional. Dank der vielfältigen Konfigurationsoptionen kann mit den kubischen Stauraummöbeln eine individuelle Büro- und Raumplanung realisiert werden. Filigrane Geometrie verbindet sich mit guten Gebrauchseigenschaften und Stabilität: Bis zu einer Breite von 160 cm erlaubt die ausgeschäumte Stahlkonstruktion eine Ausführung ohne Trenn- und Rückwand. Die Boxen sind horizontal wie vertikal gerade und versetzt stapelbar. In Kombination mit einem Polsterelement dienen sie zugleich als arbeitsplatznahe Sitzmöbel.

Statement by the jury
The combination of purist design and high functionality qualifies the Masterbox furniture system for individual and flexible room planning.

Begründung der Jury
Die Kombination aus puristischer Gestaltung und hoher Funktionalität qualifizieren das Möbelsystem Masterbox für die individuelle und flexible Raumplanung.

FrameFour
Office Furniture System
Büromöbelsystem

Manufacturer
Steelcase Werndl AG,
Rosenheim, Germany
In-house design
Web
www.steelcase.com

The construction of the FrameFour office furniture system is fully geared to and equipped for modern work routines. The individual modules are carefully attuned to one another and with a consistent design convey a uniform appearance. Flexibly combinable, they provide a suitable setting for different work situations. Practical features such as the Storage Leg store bags and personal items in a lockable compartment and thus keep the work surface uncluttered. The integrated power outlets allow users to charge three devices simultaneously.

Die Konstruktion des Büromöbelsystems FrameFour ist ganz auf den modernen Arbeitsalltag aus- und eingerichtet. Die einzelnen Module sind sorgfältig aufeinander abgestimmt und vermitteln mit ihrer konsistenten Gestaltung ein einheitliches Bild. Flexibel zu kombinieren, geben sie unterschiedlichen Arbeitssituationen den passenden Rahmen. Praktische Elemente wie das Storage Leg bringen Taschen und persönliche Gegenstände in einem abschließbaren Fach unter und halten so die Arbeitsfläche frei. Die ebenfalls integrierten Steckdosen ermöglichen es, bis zu drei verschiedene Geräte gleichzeitig aufzuladen.

Statement by the jury
The FrameFour office furniture system is fully adjusted to the requirements of the user. The modular construction allows a high degree of creativity.

Begründung der Jury
Das Büromöbelsystem FrameFour ist ganz auf die Bedürfnisse des Nutzers abgestimmt. Der modulare Aufbau lässt ein hohes Maß an Kreativität zu.

Cable Outlet
Kabeldurchführung

Manufacturer
Confurn Export GmbH, Bad Oeynhausen,
Germany
In-house design
Web
www.confurn.eu

Timeless design and technical sophistication characterise this cable outlet with inductive charging function. Available in a large variety of high-quality surfaces, it convincingly blends into any work and living environment. An integrated brush organises and discreetly conceals the cables. Compatible end devices such as mobile phones can be charged through protective covers up to 3 mm in thickness without difficulty. If no receiving device is within range, the induction coil turns itself off automatically.

Statement by the jury
Clear and consistent in its design, the cable outlet with inductive technology blends very well into different environments.

Zeitloses Design und technische Ausgereiftheit prägen die Kabeldurchführung mit induktiver Ladefunktion. In vielfältigen, hochwertigen Oberflächen erhältlich, fügt sie sich überzeugend in jede Arbeits- und Wohnumgebung ein. Eine integrierte Bürste ordnet die Kabel und lässt sie diskret verschwinden. Kompatible Endgeräte wie Mobiltelefone können auch mit bis zu 3 mm starken Schutzhüllen problemlos aufgeladen werden. Ist kein Empfänger in Reichweite, schaltet sich die Induktionsspule automatisch ab.

Begründung der Jury
Klar und konsequent in der Formgebung, fügt sich die Kabeldurchführung mit Induktionstechnologie sehr gut in ihr Nutzungsumfeld ein.

Binditz / Cord Ring
Cord Wrap
Kabelring

Manufacturer
Rubbo International, Inc.,
California, USA
In-house design
Kevin Chen
Web
www.ut-wire.com

The design of the Binditz cable ring focuses on a simple and user-oriented solution for efficient cable management. It is characterised by its stretchable material that also ensures its slim and compact form. The oval end can be pulled over plugs of any size. It can be flexibly moved over the cables and positioned without coming off the cords. This allows to bundle and route cables effortlessly and cleanly in only a few easy steps. The cable ring fits cables of any size, from charging devices to heavy-duty cables.

Statement by the jury
The cable ring especially pleases with its easy and convenient handling. The simple design is fully targeted on purposeful use.

Eine einfache und nutzungsorientierte Lösung für ein effizientes Kabelmanagement stand bei der Gestaltung des Kabelrings Binditz im Mittelpunkt. Sein dehnbares Material macht ihn aus und ermöglicht seine schlanke und kompakte Form. Das ovale Ende lässt sich über Stecker jeglicher Größe ziehen, flexibel über die Kabel bewegen und positionieren, ohne abzurutschen. So können Kabel mit wenigen Handgriffen mühelos gebündelt und geordnet geführt werden. Dabei ist der Kabelring für alle Kabelgrößen geeignet, von Ladegeräten bis hin zu Hochleistungskabeln.

Begründung der Jury
Der Kabelring gefällt besonders seiner einfachen und praktischen Handhabung wegen. Das schlichte Design ist ganz auf den Verwendungszweck ausgerichtet.

Tandscape
Stationery Organiser
Organizer

Manufacturer
Shiang Design Studio,
New Taipei City, Taiwan
In-house design
Chewei Shiang, Yulin Chen
Web
www.shiangdesign.com
Honourable Mention

The design of this desktop stationery organiser was modelled on nature. Its forms evoke a mountain silhouette. Clear lines and "mountains" different in height form a versatile usable space for keeping office stationery as well as personal accessories such as jewellery. This "landscape" stores pens, rulers and sharpeners safely and clearly arranged. With its sculptural appeal, the organiser also has a decorative character, which catches the eye even without stationery.

Statement by the jury
The Tandscape stationery organizer appeals with its functional and unusual form, which constantly appears in a new light as the viewing angle changes.

Sein Vorbild hat der Schreibtisch-Organizer Tandscape in der Natur. Seine Formen sind einer Bergsilhouette nachempfunden. Klare Linien und unterschiedlich hohe „Berge" bilden eine flexibel nutzbare Fläche zur Aufbewahrung von Büroutensilien sowie persönlichen Accessoires wie Schmuck. In dieser „Landschaft" lagern Stifte, Lineal und Anspitzer sicher und geordnet. Der skulptural anmutende Organizer hat zudem einen dekorativen Charakter, der auch ohne Utensilien zur Geltung kommt.

Begründung der Jury
Der Schreibtisch-Organizer Tandscape besticht durch seine funktionale und ungewöhnliche Form, die abhängig vom Winkel der Betrachtung jeweils eine neue Wirkung entfaltet.

Mr. Punch
2-Hole Punch
Locher

Manufacturer
CARL Manufacturing Co., Ltd.,
Tokyo, Japan
In-house design
Web
www.carl.co.jp
Honourable Mention

The design objective of the Mr. Punch 2-hole punch was to create a timeless and minimalist appearance. The flat, rectangular shape of the lever area has a light and elegant appeal. This impression is further enhanced by the use of aluminium, a material not commonly used in punches. In this way, Mr. Punch sets a new emphasis in the workplace, blending in next to a computer or tablet in a visually coherent way. The punch is also effortless to use. Two levers reinforce the leverage power, making punching considerably easier and more efficient.

Statement by the jury
Mr. Punch merges clear lines and a well thought-through construction, marking itself as a sophisticated office utensil.

Das Gestaltungsziel bei dem Locher Mr. Punch war eine zeitlose und minimalistische Anmutung. Die flache, rechteckige Form seines Griffbereichs wirkt leicht und elegant. Verstärkt wird dieser Eindruck noch durch das gewählte und für Locher nicht übliche Material Aluminium. So setzt Mr. Punch am Arbeitsplatz neue Akzente und fügt sich optisch stimmig neben Computer und Tablet ein. Zugleich ist der Locher mühelos zu bedienen. Zwei Hebel verstärken seine Wirkkraft, was das Ausstanzen deutlich erleichtert und effizienter macht.

Begründung der Jury
Die klare Linienführung und die durchdachte Konstruktion verschmelzen bei dem Locher Mr. Punch zu einem anspruchsvollen Büroutensil.

LAMY screen
Stylus

Manufacturer
C. Josef Lamy GmbH,
Heidelberg, Germany

Design
GR Design, Barcelona, Spain

Web
www.lamy.com

reddot award 2017
best of the best

Modern writing

Even in our highly modern work environments, people often jot down notes on paper while using their smartphones with the other hand. Adapting to this phenomenon, the LAMY screen fascinates with its cleverly thought-out functionality. It houses an innovative dual-pivoting mechanism that comprises a standard ballpoint refill on one end and a silicone-tip stylus for use on capacitive surfaces on the other. A dual-mechanism on the inside serves to extend and retract the two tips on opposing ends. The device thus meaningfully merges the function of a ball pen and a stylus into one single writing tool. The LAMY screen features a compact housing with a shape that was designed to match the most common electronic devices on the market. It is made of anodised aluminium, which makes it durable and pleasing to the touch. In order to make handling the pen as convenient as possible, it features a ribbed section on the writing pen end to provide ergonomically supportive holding grip as well as a slightly protruded logo plate to prevent the pen from rolling on flat surfaces. Apart from that, the pen does without a clip for enhanced usability when used with smart phones and tablets. The LAMY screen rests safely and comfortably in the hand. This multifunction writing tool is available in four colours and fascinates time and again with both its aesthetic and strikingly logical functionality.

Modern Writing

Im modernen Arbeitsleben macht man sich noch immer oft handschriftliche Notizen, während man zugleich den Touchscreen seines Smartphones bedient. Der LAMY screen passt sich dem an und verblüfft dabei mit einer klug durchdachten Funktionalität. In seinem Inneren befindet sich eine innovative Doppel-Drehmechanik, die eine Standard-Kugelschreibermine und eine Silikonspitze für kapazitive Oberflächen bereitstellt. Die Doppelmechanik wird zum Ein- und Ausfahren beider sich gegenüberliegenden Spitzen eingesetzt. Auf diese Weise werden die Funktionen Kugelschreiber und Stylus sinnvoll in einem Schreibgerät kombiniert. Der LAMY screen ist gestaltet mit einem kompakten Gehäuse, wobei seine Form im Einklang mit den gängigen elektronischen Geräten entwickelt wurde. Er besteht aus eloxiertem Aluminium, was ihn haptisch angenehm und langlebig macht. Damit die Handhabung für den Nutzer möglichst praktikabel ist, dient eine Profilierung auf der Kugelschreiberseite als ergonomisch sinnvolle Greifunterstützung, eine Logoplakette verhindert das Wegrollen. Bewusst verzichtet wurde zudem zugunsten der komfortablen Handhabung mit Smartphones und Tablets auf einen störenden Clip. Der LAMY screen liegt gut austariert und sicher in der Hand des Nutzers. Das Multifunktionsschreibgerät ist in vier Farbvarianten erhältlich und begeistert immer wieder mit seiner Ästhetik und bestechend logischen Funktionalität.

Statement by the jury

The design of the LAMY screen reflects the spirit of our time. In a convincing manner, it lends itself as a mix between a traditional ball pen and a tool for touch screens. The clear and plain design emphasises only essential elements and fascinates users. There is nothing redundant or impractical about this stylus. It is highly functional and rests ergonomically well-balanced in the hand. It is an ideal companion for everyday office work.

Begründung der Jury

Der LAMY screen reflektiert mit seiner Gestaltung den Spirit unserer Zeit. Auf überzeugende Weise bietet er einen Mix aus traditionellem Stift und einem Tool für Touchscreens. Sein einfaches und klares Design, das die wesentlichen Elemente akzentuiert, begeistert. Nichts an diesem Stylus ist überflüssig oder unpraktisch. Er ist überaus funktional und liegt ergonomisch perfekt in der Hand. Damit ist er der ideale Begleiter für den Büroalltag.

Designer portrait
See page 38
Siehe Seite 38

Forever Pininfarina Aero
Stylus
Stift

Manufacturer
Napkin, Ravenna, Italy
Design
Pininfarina Extra srl (Paolo Pininfarina),
Cambiano (Turin), Italy
Web
www.napkinforever.com
www.pininfarina.it

The special feature of the Forever Pininfarina Aero stylus is its tip. Made of Ethergraph, a special metal alloy, it allows writing without ink. The pen itself is made of the aluminium alloy Ergal. Its appearance is defined by the empty core of its body, which is encompassed by a filigree, slightly twisted frame. This design is inspired by the symbol for eternity. The pen is complemented by a concrete base, which forms a deliberate contrast to its delicate form.

Statement by the jury
The carefully conceived Forever Pininfarina Aero stylus impresses with the successful implementation of a sophisticated design idea.

Die Besonderheit des Stifts Forever Pininfarina Aero ist seine Spitze. Gefertigt aus der Metalllegierung Ethergraf ermöglicht sie tintenloses Schreiben. Der Stift selbst ist aus der Aluminiumlegierung Ergal geformt. Sein Erscheinungsbild wird durch die leere, transparente Körpermitte geprägt, die von einem filigranen, leicht in sich gedrehten Rahmen umgeben ist. Diese Linienführung ist angelehnt an das Symbol für Unendlichkeit. Komplettiert wird der Stift durch eine Halterung aus Beton, die im bewussten Kontrast zu seiner feingliedrigen Form steht.

Begründung der Jury
Der mit Bedacht konzipierte Stift Forever Pininfarina Aero beeindruckt durch die gelungene Umsetzung einer anspruchsvollen Gestaltungsidee.

TORSION
Ballpoint Pen
Kugelschreiber

Manufacturer
Premec SA, Cadempino, Switzerland
In-house design
Web
www.premec.ch
Honourable Mention

Inspired by the profiles of Italian sport cars, the Torsion ballpoint pen presents an intriguing and dynamic design. Corresponding to its name, the body of the pen is defined by a slight twist that leads to an ergonomic and comfortable handhold. In this way, the pen rests well in the hand and ensures smooth writing. Barrel, clip and push can be individually mixed and matched out of twelve standard colours, lending each individual pen a unique appearance.

Statement by the jury
Its dynamic and consequent design turns the Torsion ballpoint pen into a stylish writing utensil.

Inspiriert vom Profil italienischer Sportwagen, zeigt der Kugelschreiber Torsion eine spannungsvolle, dynamische Linienführung. Seinem Namen entsprechend prägt den Stiftkörper eine leichte Drehung, die in einen ergonomischen und komfortablen Griff mündet. So liegt der Stift gut in der Hand und lässt sich leicht führen. Drücker, Clip und Schaft können individuell aus zwölf Standardfarben gewählt und kombiniert werden, was jedem einzelnen Exemplar ein eigenes Erscheinungsbild verleiht.

Begründung der Jury
Seine schwungvolle und konsequente Formgebung macht den Kugelschreiber Torsion zu einem stilvollen Schreibgerät.

Monoset Bespoke Stationery
Personalised Stationery Collection
Personalisiertes Briefpapier

Manufacturer
Monoset, Dublin, Ireland
In-house design
Web
www.monoset.com

The Monoset Bespoke personalised stationery sets a mark for the tradition of letter writing in an increasingly digital world. Each set includes letter writing paper, notecards as well as individually embossed envelopes made of high-quality, environmentally-friendly paper with a subtly textured writing canvas. The storage box converts to an elegant desk stand, protecting and presenting the papers and envelops in an appealing, well-organised and ready-to-hand way. The set is available in the six different styles Traditional, Industrial, Minimalist, Modern, Natural and Neon.

Statement by the jury
The stationery set makes the value of handwritten conversation visible with its elegant appearance and bespoke design.

Das personalisierte Briefpapierset Monoset Bespoke Stationery setzt ein Zeichen für die Tradition des Briefeschreibens in einer zunehmend digitalisierten Zeit. Jedes Set umfasst Briefpapier, Grußkarten sowie individuell geprägte Umschläge aus hochwertigem, umweltfreundlichem Papier mit leicht strukturierter Oberfläche. Die Aufbewahrungsbox fungiert als edel anmutende Halterung, die Papiere und Umschläge schützt, ansprechend geordnet präsentiert und griffbereit hält. Das Set gibt es in den sechs unterschiedlichen Stilen Traditional, Industrial, Minimalist, Modern, Natural und Neon.

Begründung der Jury
Das Briefpapierset macht den Wert handgeschriebener Konversation mit seiner eleganten Anmutung und der individualisierten Umsetzung sichtbar.

OWSPACE
Desk Calendar 2017
Calendar
Kalender

Manufacturer
Owspace, Beijing, China
In-house design
Xiaonan Liu, Fan Zhang
Web
www.owspace.com

The Owspace Desk Calendar 2017 is a vintage style desk calendar. The design, with a clearly defined frame as well as the layout of the individual pages, is inspired by traditional Chinese almanacs. Each page shows the date and features quotes of famous personalities. This classic approach is combined with modern augmented reality technology: impressive videos lead users via smartphone to recommended extended reading. The Owspace Calendar App gives access to the calendar at any time and from anywhere.

Statement by the jury
The desk calendar convinces with its successful combination of classical traditions and modern technologies. Its design appears tidy and clear.

Der Owspace Desk Calendar 2017 ist ein Tischkalender im Vintage-Stil. Die Gestaltung mit klar abgesetzten Rahmen sowie die Aufteilung der einzelnen Seiten sind angelehnt an traditionelle chinesische Almanache. Jedes Blatt zeigt das Datum und beinhaltet zudem Zitate berühmter Persönlichkeiten. Dieser klassische Ansatz wird mit moderner Augmented-Reality-Technologie verbunden: Eindrucksvolle Videos führen den Nutzer über das Smartphone zu empfohlener weiterführender Lektüre. Mit der Owspace Calendar App kann orts- und zeitunabhängig auf den Kalender zugegriffen werden.

Begründung der Jury
Der Tischkalender überzeugt durch eine gelungene Verbindung klassischer Traditionen und moderner Technologien. Dabei wirkt seine Gestaltung aufgeräumt und übersichtlich.

Industry and crafts
Industrie und Handwerk

FLIR Exx-Series
Thermal Imaging Camera
Wärmebildkamera

Manufacturer
FLIR Systems,
Täby, Sweden

In-house design
Anton Hoffman,
Christian Högstedt,
Adam Sjöberg,
Mikael Erlandsson

Design
Howl,
Nacka, Sweden

Web
www.flir.com
www.howlstudio.se

reddot award 2017
best of the best

Professional inspection

Thermal imaging cameras can provide valuable information for the assessment of the energy efficiency of buildings, the detection of deficiencies in electrical installations and other similar tasks. The professional thermal imaging cameras of the innovative FLIR Exx-Series enable sophisticated building inspections. Based on an easy to understand point-and-shoot approach to operation, the camera allows users in their daily work to search for and identify invisible problems in constructions and analyse them in depth. The design of the camera impresses with a large and clearly arranged display with an optimised graphical user interface that continuously supports the users' crucial decisions. The interface promotes the most-wanted and relevant information in every specific moment, resulting in highly goal-oriented work processes. Giving users the possibility to utilise and manoeuvre the camera and its functions with one hand, with thick protective gloves or via the touchscreen, the FLIR Exx-Series covers a wide range of user scenarios and adapts easily to deliver in a myriad of different situations. The camera is protected by a durable and compact body that can easily withstand impacts and shocks in tough industrial work environments. This thermal imaging camera helps to prevent fire as well as other dangerous occurrences, as well as to save energy and costs. It inspires the user with its cleverly thought-out and at any time self-explanatory design.

Professionell überwacht

Für die Beurteilung der Energieeffizienz von Gebäuden, die Feststellung von Mängeln in elektrischen Anlagen und ähnliche Aufgaben können Wärmebildkameras wertvolle Informationen liefern. Die professionellen Wärmebildkameras der innovativen FLIR Exx-Serie ermöglichen eine anspruchsvolle Bauüberwachung. Ihre Bedienung basiert auf einem leicht verständlichen Point-and-Shoot-Ansatz, der es den Anwendern erlaubt, bei ihrer täglichen Arbeit unkompliziert Probleme zu ermitteln und differenziert zu analysieren. Die Gestaltung der Kamera begeistert mit einem großen und übersichtlichen Display, dessen optimierte grafische Benutzeroberfläche den Anwender laufend unterstützt bei entscheidenden Beurteilungen. Diese stellt die wichtigsten und relevanten Informationen zu jedem Zeitpunkt bereit, weshalb mit ihr sehr zielgerichtet gearbeitet werden kann. Durch die Möglichkeit, die Kamera und ihre hochmodernen Funktionen auch mit nur einer Hand, mit dicken Schutzhandschuhen oder über den Touchscreen zu bedienen, deckt die FLIR Exx-Serie eine Vielzahl von Anwendungsszenarien ab und kann sich damit leicht unterschiedlichen Situationen anpassen. Geschützt wird die Kamera durch ein robustes und kompaktes Gehäuse, das problemlos Stößen und Erschütterungen in rauen industriellen Umgebungen standhält. Diese Wärmebildkamera trägt dazu bei, Feuer und andere Gefahren zu vermeiden sowie Energie und Kosten zu sparen. Sie begeistert den Nutzer dabei mit ihrem klug durchdachten und jederzeit selbsterklärenden Design.

Statement by the jury

The thermal imaging cameras of the FLIR Exx-Series impress with their perfect and successful integral design. They are distinguished by a distinctive appearance and impressive latest state-of-art functionality. Solid materials not only give this product its scope of use, they also underline its high degree of professionalism. Ergonomically very well thought-out, the camera, with its pistol grip, can be easily operated to perform various tasks.

Begründung der Jury

Die Wärmebildkameras der FLIR Exx-Serie überzeugen durch ihre auf perfekte Weise gelungene integrale Gestaltung. Sie zeichnen sich durch ein markantes Erscheinungsbild und eine beeindruckende Funktionalität auf dem neuesten Stand der Technik aus. Solide Materialien geben diesem Produkt seinen Rahmen und unterstreichen zugleich das hohe Maß an Professionalität. Ergonomisch sehr gut durchdacht, kann die Kamera mit ihrem Pistolengriff einfach bedient und sehr variabel eingesetzt werden.

Designer portrait
See page 40
Siehe Seite 40

DeWALT Rotary Laser
Rotationslaser

Manufacturer
Stanley Black & Decker, Southington, USA
In-house design
Vincent Cook
Design
Michael Matteo, Chicago, USA
Web
www.stanleyblackanddecker.com

The DeWalt rotary laser is able to withstand more than one fall from a height
of two metres. Its sensitive electronic
components are protected by a kind of
roll cage featuring an extremely durable
polycarbonate frame and handles of
overmoulded urethane foam to optimally
absorb impact forces. The handles meet
high ergonomic standards and, with
their clever positioning, ensure optimal
tactile feedback as well as easy access
to the battery compartments and
control elements.

Statement by the jury
The distinctive protection frame makes
this rotary laser impressively tough,
while also giving it high recognition
value.

Der Rotationslaser von DeWalt übersteht
auch mehrere Stürze aus zwei Metern
Höhe. Seine empfindlichen elektronischen
Bauteile sind durch eine Art Überrollkäfig
geschützt. Dieser besteht aus einem hoch-
stabilen Rahmen aus Polycarbonat und
Griffen, die mit Polyurethanschaum um-
spritzt sind und die Stoßkräfte bei einem
Aufprall optimal absorbieren. Die Griffe
erfüllen hohe ergonomische Ansprüche
und garantieren durch ihre geschickte
Platzierung ein optimales haptisches Feedback sowie einen einfachen Zugang zu den
Akkufächern und den Bedienelementen.

Begründung der Jury
Der prägnante Schutzrahmen macht den
Rotationslaser beeindruckend belastbar
und verleiht ihm darüber hinaus einen
hohen Wiedererkennungswert.

Apecrafts
Laser Rangefinder
Laser-Entfernungsmesser

Manufacturer
Beijing Ximi Technology Co., Ltd.,
Beijing, China
Design
LKK Design Shenzhen Co., Ltd. (Yonggao
Li, Hongyao Lu, Yichao Li, Jianhui Zhang),
Shenzhen, China
Web
www.apecrafts.com
www.lkkdesign.com

Thanks to its simple design and high user-friendliness, the compact, intelligent Apecrafts laser rangefinder is easy to use for both professionals and laypeople. With the help of an app, the measurements can be converted into a three-dimensional layout, which automatically shows the respective floor plan. In addition, the user can decorate the rooms in the app and thus get a preview of possible renovations.

Statement by the jury
The Apecrafts laser rangefinder impresses with its premium look, which results from the contrast between its softly gleaming housing and black interface.

Der handliche, intelligente Laser-Entfernungsmesser Apecrafts kann durch seine schlichte Gestaltung und hohe Bedienfreundlichkeit sowohl von professionellen Anwendern als auch von Laien problemlos verwendet werden. Mithilfe einer App werden die Messwerte in ein dreidimensionales Layout verwandelt, das automatisch den entsprechenden Grundriss abbildet. Darüber hinaus kann der Nutzer die Räume in der App dekorieren und so eventuelle Renovierungen vorab erfahrbar machen.

Begründung der Jury
Der Entfernungsmesser Apecrafts besticht durch seine edle Anmutung, die durch das matt schimmernde Gehäuse im Kontrast zu dem schwarzen Interface vermittelt wird.

RAL COLORCATCH NANO
Colorimeter
Farbmessgerät

Manufacturer
COLORIX AG, Neuchâtel, Switzerland
In-house design
David Maurer
Web
www.colorix.com

The RAL Colorcatch Nano colorimeter measures up to five colours simultaneously and identifies the corresponding shade in the world-renowned RAL colour collection. Thanks to the camera and its optics, the device magnifies an image sixfold and measures colour starting at just a few pixels. The shade is displayed with digital colour values and directly applied to an object using an app. During the colour measurement, all non-dominant shades as well as shadows or dirt are automatically eliminated.

Statement by the jury
The RAL Colorcatch Nano colorimeter combines advanced technology in an aesthetic of simplicity, which attests to high-level design skills.

Das Farbmessgerät RAL Colorcatch Nano misst bis zu fünf Farben gleichzeitig und findet den dazu passenden Farbton in den weltweit anerkannten RAL-Farbsammlungen. Dank der Kamera und ihrer Optik vergrößert das Gerät ein Bild sechsfach und misst Farbe schon ab wenigen Pixeln. Der Farbton wird mit digitalen Farbwerten angezeigt und über eine App direkt auf ein Objekt übertragen. Während der Farbmessung werden alle nicht dominierenden Farbtöne sowie Schatteneffekte oder Schmutzpartikel automatisch eliminiert.

Begründung der Jury
Anspruchsvolle Technologie wurde bei dem Farbmessgerät RAL Colorcatch Nano in eine Ästhetik der Einfachheit überführt, die von hohem gestalterischem Können zeugt.

Nix Pro Color Sensor
Colorimeter
Farbmessgerät

Manufacturer
Nix Sensor Ltd., Hamilton,
Ontario, Canada
In-house design
Matthew Sheridan
Web
www.nixsensor.com

The Nix Pro Color Sensor is a wireless colorimeter that measures the exact colour of surfaces and transmits the digital colour values to a smartphone or tablet using Bluetooth. The colour data can then be used to match to physical colours such as paints, leathers, cosmetics, plastics and dyes. The device blocks all ambient light, shines a calibrated white light at the surface and then measures only the light reflected back. With its superior accuracy, the colorimeter provides objective and reliable colour measurement to professionals worldwide.

Statement by the jury
The Nix Pro Color Sensor colorimeter features a diamond shape with a matt-black surface, which makes it an exciting eye-catcher.

Das Nix Pro Color Sensor ist ein kabelloses Farbmessgerät, das die exakte Farbe von Oberflächen misst und die digitalen Farbwerte über Bluetooth an ein Smartphone oder Tablet sendet. Die Farbdaten können dann verwendet werden, um sie physikalischen Farbtönen von Lacken, Leder, Kosmetika, Kunst- und Farbstoffen zuzuordnen. Das Gerät entfernt sämtliches Umgebungslicht, beleuchtet die Oberfläche mit Weißlicht und misst dann nur das reflektierte Licht. Mit seiner sehr hohen Genauigkeit bietet das Kolorimeter eine professionelle und zuverlässige Farbmessung für Fachleute weltweit.

Begründung der Jury
Das Farbmessgerät Nix Pro Color Sensor besitzt die Form eines Diamants mit mattschwarzer Oberfläche, was ihn zu einem aufregenden Blickfang macht.

Contour Honing Tool
Konturhonwerkzeug

Manufacturer
ELGAN-Diamantwerkzeuge
GmbH & Co. KG,
Nürtingen, Germany

Design
Design Tech,
Ammerbuch, Germany

Web
www.elgan.de
www.designtech.eu

reddot award 2017
best of the best

The elegance of precision

The process of honing is a common working step in technical production processes, used for example for accurate machining in engine construction. The Contour Honing Tool is a highly developed diamond tool for manufacturing special borehole shapes in engine cylinders and counteracts hole deformation during operation. This reduces the oil consumption as well as friction and thus reduces the emissions from state-of-the-art combustion engines. The innovative design of the Contour Honing Tool achieves significantly improved grip and feel in the operating area. This makes it much easier to handle, as tools in this work area generally get oily and dirty during use. Another innovative aspect is the positioning of the air measuring tube in the interior, which eliminates the risk of tearing or damage. Owing to the possibility of colour coding the identification plates, the tools can be quickly and clearly arranged for the appropriate processes at hand. Moreover, this measure is also supported by the use of an optional RFID chip (Radio-Frequency Identification). The highly sophisticated design of the Contour Honing Tool thus has lead to its optimised functionality, which contributes to a decisive improvement in the daily operation of motors.

Die Eleganz der Präzision

Der Vorgang des Honens ist in technischen Produktionsprozessen ein gängiger Arbeitsschritt, der etwa für die Feinbearbeitung im Motorenbau genutzt wird. Das Konturhonwerkzeug ist ein hochentwickeltes Diamantwerkzeug für die Erzeugung spezieller Bohrungsformen bei Zylindern von Motoren, um der Gefahr der Bohrverformung im Betrieb entgegenzuwirken. Dies reduziert den Ölverbrauch sowie die Reibung und verringert so die Emissionen hochmoderner Verbrennungsmotoren. Die innovative Gestaltung des Konturhonwerkzeugs führt dabei zu einer wesentlich verbesserten Griffigkeit und Haptik im Bedienbereich des Werkzeugs. Es ist damit angesichts der meist verölten und verschmutzten Werkzeuge in diesem Arbeitsumfeld viel leichter handhabbar. Eine weitere Innovation ist die Verlegung der Luftmessschläuche nach innen, wodurch keine Abrisse oder Beschädigungen mehr vorkommen. Durch die Möglichkeit, die Identifizierungsplatten farblich zu kennzeichnen, können die Werkzeuge zudem schnell und eindeutig dem jeweiligen Arbeitsgang zugeordnet werden. Optional kann dies auch durch den Einsatz eines RFID-Chips (Radio-Frequency Identification) unterstützt werden. Die überaus durchdachte Gestaltung des Konturhonwerkzeugs führt auf diese Weise zu dessen optimierter Funktionalität, was dazu beiträgt, den täglichen Betrieb von Motoren entscheidend zu verbessern.

Statement by the jury

This diamond tool for creating special boreholes for cylinders of engines inspires with the accuracy of its design as well as the high-quality appearance of the materials, making them harmonise very well with the shape. The design is perfect for both the details as well as in the implementation of the surfaces. The Contour Honing Tool is a successfully crafted product that conveys both high quality and precision.

Begründung der Jury

Bei diesem Diamantwerkzeug, mit dem spezielle Bohrungsformen bei Zylindern von Motoren erzeugt werden können, begeistert die Genauigkeit der Gestaltung sowie die hochwertige Materialanmutung, wobei Material und Form sehr gut harmonieren. Die Gestaltung ist bis in die Details und auch bei den Oberflächen perfekt ausgeführt. Das Konturhonwerkzeug ist ein sehr gelungenes Produkt, das Hochwertigkeit und Präzision gleichermaßen zum Ausdruck bringt.

Designer portrait
See page 42
Siehe Seite 42

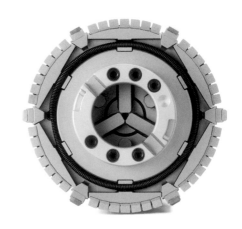

133

Leatherman Skeletool RX
Rescue Multitool
Multifunktionswerkzeug für
den Rettungseinsatz

Manufacturer
Leatherman Tool Group, Inc.,
Portland, USA
In-house design
Web
www.leatherman.de

The Leatherman Skeletool RX rescue multitool features a glass breaker and an extra-strong combination blade for hard materials such as leather or canvas. Further features are standard and pointed pliers, wire cutters, screwdrivers and bit holders, including Phillips-head screwdriver. The tools are accessible from the outside and thus enable one-handed operation. The stainless-steel body with its Cerakote coating and the aluminium alloy of the grip elements are very robust.

Statement by the jury
The individual components of the Leatherman Skeletool RX are clearly visible and sensibly arranged. Thus, the right tool is always at one's fingertips.

Das Leatherman Skeletool RX für den Rettungseinsatz verfügt über einen Glasbrecher und eine extra starke feststellbare Kombiklinge für harte Materialien wie Leder oder Canvas. Weiterhin gehören eine normale und eine Spitzzange, Drahtschneider, Schraubendreher und Bithalter inkl. Kreuzschlitzschraubendreher zur Ausstattung. Die Werkzeuge sind von außen zugänglich und ermöglichen so die Bedienung mit einer Hand. Der Edelstahlkorpus mit Cerakote-Beschichtung und die Alulegierung der Griffschalen sind sehr robust.

Begründung der Jury
Die Einzelteile des Leatherman Skeletool RX sind von allen Seiten hervorragend einsehbar und sinnvoll angeordnet. So hat man das richtige Werkzeug stets schnell zur Hand.

HAZET 5108 VDE, HAZET 5109 VDE
VDE Torque Wrenches
VDE-Drehmomentschlüssel

Manufacturer
HAZET-WERK,
Hermann Zerver GmbH & Co. KG,
Remscheid, Germany
In-house design
Kai Kowitz, Peter Welp
Web
www.hazet.com
Honourable Mention

The torque wrenches have been developed for working on live components. In contrast to conventional VDE torque wrenches, which cannot be disassembled and reassembled due to their sheathing, the 5108 VDE and 5109 VDE can be readjusted and recalibrated. The interchangeable square drive enables both right and left tightening. The achievement of the set torque value is signalled palpably with a close-gap release and audibly with a "click" sound.

Statement by the jury
The slim torque wrenches impress with their disassembly feature, which makes them particularly durable and sustainable.

Die Drehmomentschlüssel sind für Arbeiten an spannungsführenden Bauteilen konzipiert. Im Gegensatz zu herkömmlichen VDE-Drehmomentschlüsseln, die wegen ihrer Ummantelung nicht demontiert und wieder zusammengesetzt werden können, sind der 5108 VDE und 5109 VDE wieder justier- und kalibrierbar. Der Umsteck-Vierkant erlaubt das Anziehen sowohl nach rechts als auch nach links. Ist der eingestellte Drehmomentwert erreicht, wird dies haptisch mit Kurzwegauslösung und akustisch durch ein „Klick"-Geräusch signalisiert.

Begründung der Jury
Die schlank gestalteten Drehmomentschlüssel überzeugen durch ihre Demontierbarkeit. Dadurch sind sie besonders langlebig und nachhaltig.

LiftUp 26one®
Magazine Bit Holder
Magazin-Bithalter

Manufacturer
Wiha Werkzeuge GmbH,
Schonach, Germany
In-house design
Web
www.wiha.com

The LiftUp 26one magazine bit holder features 13 double bits, thus combining 26 of the most common drive profiles in a single tool. Bit selection, removal and return are easily carried out at the touch of a button. Moreover, the novel packaging design provides a clear overview of the bit range while at the same time protecting it. The ergonomic SoftFinish handle enables a very good transmission of force, making it possible to also loosen stuck screws.

Statement by the jury
The integration of the bits in the handle is a clever innovation. Individual bits are thus well stowed and always at hand.

Der Magazin-Bithalter LiftUp 26one vereint mit seinen 13 Doppelbits 26 der gängigsten Abtriebsprofile in einem Werkzeug. Die Auswahl, Entnahme und Rückführung der Bits funktioniert schnell und einfach per Knopfdruck. Zudem sorgt das neuartige Verpackungsdesign dafür, dass das Bitsortiment nicht nur übersichtlich präsentiert, sondern auch geschützt wird. Der ergonomische SoftFinish-Griff ermöglicht eine sehr gute Kraftübertragung, um auch festsitzende Schrauben zu lösen.

Begründung der Jury
Die Integration von Bits in den Griff stellt eine clevere Innovation dar. So gehen die einzelnen Bits nicht verloren und sind immer schnell verfügbar.

imonkey 24-in-1
Screwdriver Set
Schraubenzieher-Set

Manufacturer
Zhuhai imonkey technology Co., Ltd.,
Shanghai, China
In-house design
Web
www.imonkey.com.cn

The 24 bits of the imonkey 24-in-1 screwdriver set have been carefully selected to cover most of the screws in the home. The case is made of an aluminium alloy and lends the set a high-quality appearance. A special mechanism makes the product easy to open and close. The bits are attached to the case using magnets. In addition, the bit handle is also made of an aluminium alloy and thus more robust than conventional plastic handles.

Statement by the jury
The screwdriver set stages the bits as select individual items. The monochrome colour scheme highlights the premium look.

Die 24 Bits des Schraubenzieher-Sets imonkey 24-in-1 sind mit Sorgfalt ausgewählt und decken die gängigsten Schraubengrößen im Haushalt ab. Das Etui besteht aus einer Aluminiumlegierung und verleiht dem Set eine qualitativ hochwertige Anmutung. Ein spezieller Mechanismus ermöglicht das einfache Öffnen und Schließen, die Bits sind mit Magneten in dem Etui befestigt. Der Bitgriff besteht ebenfalls aus einer Aluminiumlegierung und ist somit robuster als herkömmliche Plastikgriffe.

Begründung der Jury
In dem Schraubenzieher-Set werden die Bits als erlesene Einzelstücke inszeniert. Die monochrome Farbgebung unterstreicht den edlen Look.

01
Dimensioning Instrument
Dimensionierungsinstrument

Manufacturer
Stars Microelectronics, Ayutthaya, Thailand
Design
InstruMMents Inc. (Mladen Barbaric),
Montreal, Canada
Web
www.starsmicro.com
www.instrumments.com

The dimensioning instrument called 01 measures the length, height and width of any real object. The sensor side of the instrument is moved along the contours of an object and wirelessly transmits the measurements to a smartphone. Complex surfaces of objects like furniture or clothing can also be easily captured in this way. The instrument is available in three versions: with a ballpoint pen, pencil or stylus at the tapering end.

Statement by the jury
The 01 dimensioning instrument presents a fascinating new way of capturing dimensions. At the same time, it returns to the traditional form of a writing utensil.

Das wie ein Stift geformte Dimensionierungsinstrument 01 vermisst Länge, Höhe und Breite eines jeden beliebigen realen Objekts. Die Sensorseite des Instruments wird entlang der Konturen eines Objekts bewegt und überträgt die Messungen drahtlos an ein Smartphone. Auch komplexe Oberflächen wie bei Möbeln oder Kleidungsstücken können so problemlos erfasst werden. Das Instrument steht in drei verschiedenen Ausführungen zur Verfügung: mit einem Kugelschreiber, Bleistift oder Stylus am sich verjüngenden Ende.

Begründung der Jury
Das Dimensionierungsinstrument 01 stellt eine faszinierende neue Art dar, Maß zu nehmen. Gleichzeitig besinnt es sich zurück auf die traditionelle Form eines Stifts.

transotype® Red Aluminium Cutter PRO
Cutter
Cuttermesser

Manufacturer
Holtz Office Support, Wiesbaden, Germany
In-house design
Tobias Liliencron
Web
www.holtzofficesupport.com

The transotype Red Aluminium Cutter Pro was developed for professional graphics work. It ensures even edges when cutting paper, cardboard and paperboard. The blade rests in a stable metal guide. The foldaway function and the safety locking mechanism enable safe use of the cutter. The tool is made of powder-coated aluminium and has a heavy weight, so that it sits comfortably in the hand. Thanks to its eye-catching red colour, it is hard to lose.

Statement by the jury
The precision of the cutter is skilfully reflected in its technical appearance. The signal red colour adds a relaxed element to the professional look.

Das Cuttermesser transotype Red Aluminium Cutter Pro für professionelle Grafikarbeiten gewährleistet saubere Schnittkanten beim Schneiden von Papier, Pappe und Karton. Die Klinge sitzt in einer stabilen Metallführung. Die Klappfunktion und die Sicherheitsverriegelung ermöglichen einen sicheren Umgang mit dem Messer. Das Werkzeug besteht aus pulverbeschichtetem Aluminium und hat ein hohes Eigengewicht, sodass es gut in der Hand liegt. Dank seiner auffälligen roten Farbe geht es nicht so schnell verloren.

Begründung der Jury
Die Präzision des Cuttermessers spiegelt sich gekonnt in seiner technischen Anmutung wider. Aufgelockert wird der professionelle Look durch das Signalrot.

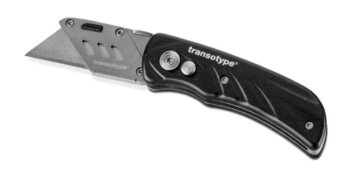

ORSY System Cases
ORSY System-Koffer

Manufacturer
Adolf Würth GmbH & Co. KG,
Künzelsau, Germany
In-house design
Wolfgang Hohl
Design
Busse Design + Engineering GmbH (Felix Timm),
Elchingen, Germany
Web
www.wuerth.com
www.busse-design.com

The Orsy System Cases are characterised by their standardised modular dimensions, making all storage items compatible with each other. The cases can be vertically stacked and coupled together, and they fit into additional storage units like shelves and workshop or vehicle racks. The handle is integrated into the front of the case, thus allowing for especially convenient carrying. The glossy and structured surfaces of the body and the lid lend the cases a modern appearance. The functional elements are encoded in the red company colour.

Die Orsy System-Koffer zeichnen sich durch ein definiertes Rastermaß aus, dadurch sind alle Lagerkomponenten miteinander kompatibel. Die Koffer können aufeinandergestapelt und verrastet werden und passen in weitere Lagereinheiten wie Regale, Betriebs- und Fahrzeugeinrichtungen. Der Griff ist an der Front angebracht, was das Tragen besonders komfortabel macht. Korpus und Deckel sorgen durch ihre glänzenden und rauen Flächen für ein modernes Erscheinungsbild. Die Funktionselemente sind durch die unternehmenstypische rote Farbe gekennzeichnet.

Statement by the jury
The Orsy System Cases with their high-quality finish impress with a modular design concept, which enables versatile and individual use.

Begründung der Jury
Die hochwertig verarbeiteten Orsy System-Koffer überzeugen durch ihr modulares Gestaltungskonzept, das eine flexible und individuelle Benutzung ermöglicht.

DeWALT Demolition Hammer
Abbruchhammer

Manufacturer
Stanley Black & Decker, Southington, USA
In-house design
Tolga Caglar, Vincent Cook
Web
www.stanleyblackanddecker.com

The handle grip of the demolition hammer by DeWalt is made of three different materials. The first layer absorbs vibration, the second layer creates a durable structure and the third layer provides grip and comfort. The hammer head is cast in one piece and has a design that optimally shifts the weight onto the striking surface, which ensures minimal bounce. The patented section between the claw at the hammer head and the lower claw is sharpened and able to rip out drywall.

Statement by the jury
The functionality of this demolition hammer is sophisticatedly engineered. The different profile surfaces lend the tool a distinctive character.

Der Griff des Abbruchhammers von DeWalt besteht aus drei unterschiedlichen Materialien. Die erste Schicht absorbiert Vibrationen, die zweite Schicht sorgt für eine langlebige Struktur und die dritte Schicht dient dem Halt und Komfort. Der aus einem Guss hergestellte Hammerkopf ist so entworfen, dass die Belastung optimal auf die Schlagfläche verlagert wird, was einen minimalen Rückstoß gewährleistet. Der patentierte Abschnitt zwischen der Klaue am Hammerkopf und der unteren Klaue wurde scharf geschliffen und ist in der Lage, Trockenwandmaterialien aufzubrechen.

Begründung der Jury
Die Funktionalität des Abbruchhammers ist bis ins Detail durchdacht. Die unterschiedlichen Profilflächen verleihen dem Werkzeug einen markanten Charakter.

TE 60-ATC/AVR
Combihammer
Kombihammer

Manufacturer
Hilti Corporation, Schaan, Liechtenstein
In-house design
Design
Matuschek Design & Management,
Aalen, Germany
Web
www.hilti.com
www.matuschekdesign.de

The TE 60-ATC/AVR combihammer with an electro-pneumatic hammer mechanism is the fourth generation of hammer drills by the Hilti brand in the 6–7 kg class. It is ideal for drilling holes up to a diameter of 40 mm and is primarily used in concrete with a high risk of hitting steel reinforcing bars. In addition to drilling, the tool is also used for chiselling work such as removing tiles or creating channels for laying cables. Moreover, the current model also features a detachable power cable.

Der Kombihammer TE 60-ATC/AVR mit elektro-pneumatischem Schlagwerk ist die vierte Generation in der 6–7-kg-Klasse von Bohrhämmern der Marke Hilti. Er ist ideal für das Bohren von Löchern bis zu einem Durchmesser von 40 mm und kommt vornehmlich in Betonuntergründen mit einem hohen Risiko von Eisentreffern zum Einsatz. Außer zum Bohren wird das Gerät auch zum Meißeln genutzt, um Kacheln und Platten zu entfernen oder Kabelkanäle vorzubereiten. Darüber hinaus verfügt das aktuelle Modell über ein abnehmbares Kabel.

Statement by the jury
With its eye-catching silhouette and the contrasting functional surfaces, the TE 60-ATC/AVR combihammer conveys the impression of a powerful tool.

Begründung der Jury
Durch seine prägnante Silhouette und die kontrastreichen Funktionsflächen vermittelt der Kombihammer TE 60-ATC/AVR den Eindruck eines kraftvollen Arbeitsgeräts. .

TE 3-M
Rotary Hammer Drill
Bohrhammer

Manufacturer
Hilti Corporation, Schaan, Liechtenstein
In-house design
Web
www.hilti.com

Weighing only 3.1 kg, the TE 3-M rotary hammer drill is a lightweight tool used for medium-duty drilling work in concrete and masonry. A corded tool in classic pistol-grip design, the rotary hammer drill also features a chiselling function, thus making it an all-rounder. Moreover, a dust-collection device was developed specifically for this model, which protects the user from the drilling dust generated, especially when working overhead, as well as a quick-release chuck, enabling a quick exchange of drill bits.

Der Bohrhammer TE 3-M ist mit seinem Gewicht von 3,1 kg ein leichtes Gerät, das bei mittelschweren Bohrarbeiten in Beton und Mauerwerk angewendet wird. Als Kabelgerät mit klassischem Pistolengriff verfügt der Bohrhammer zusätzlich über eine Meißelfunktion und ist damit universell einsetzbar. Des Weiteren wurde speziell für dieses Modell eine Staubfang-Vorrichtung entwickelt, die den Anwender insbesondere bei Überkopfarbeiten vor entstehendem Bohrstaub schützt, sowie eine Schnellspannaufnahme, die den schnellen Wechsel der Aufsätze ermöglicht.

Statement by the jury
With is compact design, the TE 3-M rotary hammer drill appears neither heavy nor bulky, but conveys safety and lightness thanks to its balanced proportions.

Begründung der Jury
Der Bohrhammer TE 3-M wirkt in seiner Kompaktheit weder schwer noch massiv, sondern strahlt durch ausgewogene Proportionen Sicherheit und Leichtigkeit aus.

SID 8-A22
Cordless Impact Screwdriver
Akku-Schlagschrauber

Manufacturer
Hilti Corporation, Schaan, Liechtenstein
In-house design
Design
Proform Design, Winnenden, Germany
Web
www.hilti.com
www.proform-design.de

The SID 8-A22 cordless impact screwdriver is based on 22-volt battery technology and has been developed for drilling and for driving screws into wood. The tangential impact mechanism with intelligent electronic control develops a maximum torque of 500 newton metres and protects the user against excessive impact resulting from the torque reaction during operation. The specifically designed handle area has been optimised for working with protective gloves. The 7/16" hex chuck with lip ensures easy bit changing.

Der Akku-Schlagschrauber SID 8-A22 basiert auf einer 22-Volt-Akku-Technologie und ist für Bohr- und Schraubarbeiten in Holz bestimmt. Das Tangential-Schlagwerk, das über eine intelligente Elektronik gesteuert wird, entwickelt dabei ein maximales Drehmoment von 500 Newtonmetern und schützt den Anwender vor zu großer Belastung durch das Reaktionsmoment während der Anwendung. Der speziell gestaltete Griffbereich ist für das Arbeiten mit Schutzhandschuhen optimiert. Die 7/16"-Sechskantaufnahme mit Lippe garantiert einen einfachen Wechsel des Werkzeugs.

Statement by the jury
Its dynamic lines lend the SID 8-A22 cordless impact screwdriver character and a distinct silhouette. The elaborate design of the handle enables very comfortable use.

Begründung der Jury
Die dynamischen Linien verleihen dem Akku-Schlagschrauber SID 8-A22 Charakter und ein prägnantes Profil. Der deutlich ausgearbeitete Griff sorgt für eine sehr gute Handhabung.

TE-YX
Drill Bits for Concrete
Betonbohrer

Manufacturer
Hilti Corporation, Schaan, Liechtenstein
In-house design
Web
www.hilti.com

The high-performance TE-YX drill bit for concrete is available in two versions, featuring a head with either six or four cutting edges. The newly designed head with six cutting edges for diameters in the 35–55 mm range provides consistent high performance and less catching and jamming when striking steel reinforcing bars. The classic four-edged drill bit features narrower helical flutes and even more durable cutting edges than its predecessors. A special design feature of the flutes is the company logo, which runs all the way around.

Den leistungsstarken Betonbohrer TE-YX gibt es in zwei Ausführungen: mit Sechs-schneidkopf oder Vierschneidkopf. Der neuartige Sechsschneidkopf für Durch-messer von 35 bis 55 mm bietet eine kon-stant hohe Bohrleistung und weniger Verhaken oder Klemmen bei Eisentreffern. Der klassische Bohrer mit Vierschneidkopf verfügt über eine schmalere Wendel und noch widerstandsfähigere Schneidkanten des Bohrkopfes als die Vorgängermodelle. Ein besonderes Gestaltungsmerkmal der Wendel stellt das umlaufende Firmenlogo dar.

Statement by the jury
The well-thought-out geometry of the TE-YX drill bits for concrete provides effective results. The high-quality finish ensures extended durability.

Begründung der Jury
Die durchdachte Geometrie der Beton-bohrer TE-YX bringt effektive Ergebnisse. Die hochwertige Verarbeitung sorgt für ausgesprochene Langlebigkeit.

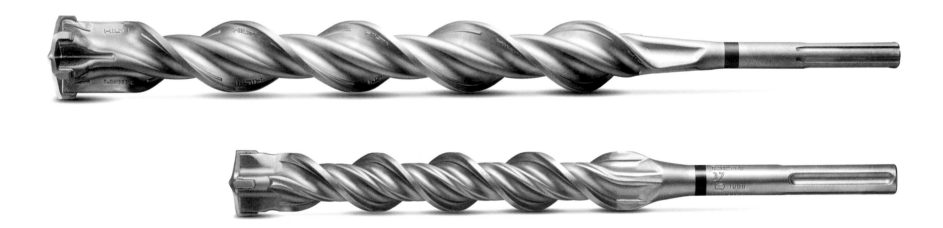

WORX Switchdriver 20V
Cordless Drill & Driver
20V MAX Akku-Switchdriver WX176.9
Cordless Drill Driver
Akku-Bohrschrauber

Manufacturer
Positec Technology, Suzhou, China
In-house design
Web
www.positecgroup.com
www.worx.com

The Worx Switchdriver 20V Cordless
Drill & Driver is characterised by its
rotating chuck, thanks to which users
may switch between two bits. One
side of the chuck can be equipped with
a drill, while the other holds a bit. This
enables interruption-free work and the
user can continue holding the workpiece
in place during the switch. An LED work
light provides good visibility in dark
working environments.

Der 20V Max Akku-Switchdriver WX176.9
zeichnet sich durch sein drehbares Bohrfutter aus, mit dem der Anwender zwischen
zwei verschiedenen Aufsätzen hin- und
herwechseln kann. So lässt sich die eine
Seite des Bohrfutters mit einem Bohrer,
die andere mit einem Bit bestücken. Dies
erlaubt ein unterbrechungsfreies Arbeiten
und der Anwender kann das Werkstück
während des Wechsels weiterhin festhalten.
Ein LED-Arbeitslicht sorgt für eine gute
Sicht in dunklen Arbeitsbereichen.

Statement by the jury
This cordless drill driver impresses with
its high ease of use. The option of
switching quickly between bits saves a
lot of time.

Begründung der Jury
Der Akku-Bohrschrauber punktet durch
seine hohe Bedienfreundlichkeit. Die
Möglichkeit des sehr schnellen Aufsatz-
wechsels spart viel Zeit.

WORX 20V MAX Lithium Smart Drill
WORX 20V MAX Akku-Bohrschrauber Smart-Drill
Cordless Drill Driver
Akku-Bohrschrauber

Manufacturer
Positec Technology, Suzhou, China
In-house design
Web
www.positecgroup.com
www.worx.com

The Worx 20V Max Lithium Smart Drill features an electronic torque control, which stops the motor when the screw is sunk to the selected depth. The drill chuck automatically self-centres the bits and provides 50 per cent more tightening torque as compared to conventional chucks. In addition, the drill driver features a pulse assist mode that rotates the chuck in small steps. This makes it possible, among other things, to drill into hard surfaces.

Der Worx 20V Max Akku-Bohrschrauber Smart-Drill verfügt über eine elektronische Drehmomentkontrolle, die den Motor stoppt, wenn die Schraube ideal versenkt ist. Die Bohrfutterarretierung zentriert die Bits automatisch und verleiht ihnen 50 Prozent mehr Halt als ein herkömmliches Bohrfutter. Darüber hinaus ist der Bohrschrauber mit einem zuschaltbaren Pulse-Modus ausgestattet, der das Bohrfutter in kleinen Schritten rotiert. Dies erlaubt u. a. das Bohren in harte Oberflächen.

Statement by the jury
The WORX 20V MAX Lithium Smart Drill features an impressive design that has managed to incorporate versatile technology in an extremely compact form.

Begründung der Jury
Bei dem WORX 20V MAX Akku-Bohrschrauber Smart-Drill ist es auf beeindruckende Weise gelungen, vielseitige Technik in eine äußerst kompakte Form zu überführen.

WORX WX655 Vibrafree
Rotary Sander
Exzenterschleifer

Manufacturer
Positec Technology, Suzhou, China
In-house design
Web
www.positecgroup.com
www.worx.com

The Worx WX655 Vibrafree rotary sander features a dual oscillating pattern, with two separate sanding sheets rotating in opposing directions. The patented Vibrafree technology reduces vibrations and thus the vibrational strain on the user. The integrated CDS dust extraction system ensures a clean work environment and an unobstructed view of the workpiece. Once the dust box is full, it can be quickly emptied at the touch of a button.

Statement by the jury
The design of the rotary sander is characterised by narrow radii and slim edges, which give rise to a dramatic and powerful look.

Der Exzenterschleifer Worx WX655 Vibrafree arbeitet mit einem dual oszillierenden Schwingmuster, wobei sich zwei getrennte Schleifblätter in gegensätzliche Richtungen drehen. Diese patentierte Vibrafree-Technologie reduziert die Vibrationen und damit die Schwingungsbelastung für den Anwender. Das integrierte CDS-Staub-Absaugsystem sorgt für eine saubere Arbeitsumgebung und freie Sicht auf das Werkstück. Ist die Staubbox voll, lässt sie sich schnell und einfach per Knopfdruck entleeren.

Begründung der Jury
Die Bauform des Exzenterschleifers ist von engen Radien und schmalen Kanten geprägt, die ein spannungsreiches, kraftvolles Erscheinungsbild erzeugen.

Mirka® AOS-B
Cordless Sander
Akku-Schleifmaschine

Manufacturer
Oy KWH Mirka Ab, Jeppo, Finland
In-house design
Caj Nordström
Design
Veryday (Hans Himbert, Pelle Reinius), Bromma, Sweden
Web
www.mirka.com
www.veryday.com

The Mirka AOS-B is a brushless, battery-powered sander used for repairing minor damage to paintwork. Thanks to cordless operation, the machine can be easily used in areas that are hard to access. The ergonomic handle enables fatigue-free work. Moreover, the spot-repair sander has very low noise and vibration levels. The lithium-ion battery charges in only 45 minutes and has an operating time of up to 16 hours.

Statement by the jury
The colour contrast of the Mirka AOS-B sander effectively defies the minimalist design, while simultaneously highlighting its comfortable proportions.

Bei der Mirka AOS-B handelt es sich um eine bürstenlose akkubetriebene Schleifmaschine, die zum Ausbessern kleinerer Lackschäden verwendet wird. Dank des kabellosen Betriebs lässt sich die Maschine auch an schwer erreichbaren Stellen leicht führen. Der ergonomische Griff erlaubt ein ermüdungsfreies Arbeiten. Zudem läuft der Spot-Repair-Schleifer sehr geräusch- und vibrationsarm. Der Lithium-Ionen-Akku ist in nur 45 Minuten aufgeladen und hat eine Betriebslaufzeit von bis zu 16 Stunden.

Begründung der Jury
Der Farbkontrast der Schleifmaschine Mirka AOS-B durchbricht wirkungsvoll ihre reduzierte Gestaltung und betont gleichzeitig ihre angenehmen Proportionen.

PURLOGIC® PREMIUMpress
PU-Foam Gun
PU-Schaumpistole

Manufacturer
Adolf Würth GmbH & Co. KG,
Künzelsau, Germany
Design
Designtotale, Milan, Italy
Web
www.wuerth.com
www.designtotale.com

The Purlogic PremiumPress PU-foam gun has been developed for one-component polyurethane foam applications. The controllable foam dispensing function and the conical valve ensure controlled spraying of the material as well as an even spray pattern. Thanks to its ergonomic shape, the gun sits well in the hand. In addition, the low weight of the device enables fatigue-free use. The functional elements have been colour-coded for ease of use.

Statement by the jury
The clear design language communicates that this foam gun is a precision tool. Furthermore, it combines high ergonomic quality with convenient use.

Die Schaumpistole Purlogic PremiumPress dient zur Verarbeitung von 1-komponentigem Polyurethanschaum. Der dosierbare Schaumaustritt und die konische Düse ermöglichen ein kontrolliertes Austreten des Materials und ein sauberes Spritzbild. Durch die ergonomische Griffform liegt die Pistole angenehm in der Hand. Darüber hinaus gewährleistet das geringe Eigengewicht des Geräts ein ermüdungsfreies Arbeiten. Die Funktionselemente sind farblich hervorgehoben, was die Bedienung erleichtert.

Begründung der Jury
Die klare Formensprache der Schaumpistole vermittelt gekonnt, dass es sich um ein Präzisionswerkzeug handelt. Zudem vereint sie gute Ergonomie mit Komfort.

Pro One
Air Blow Gun
Druckluftpistole

Manufacturer
Silvent, Borås, Sweden
In-house design
Rasmus Tibell
Design
Veryday (Anna Carell, Hans Himbert,
Fredrik Ericsson), Bromma, Sweden
Web
www.silvent.com
www.veryday.com

The Pro One air blow gun is characterised by its low use of energy and reduced noise level. The volume is reduced by half as compared to conventional models, which minimises strain on the user's ears. The components are manufactured using the latest technologies. The stainless-steel valve, for instance, is created using a precise 3D printing method. Optimally balanced weight distribution and the flexible handle enable fatigue-free use.

Statement by the jury
The Pro One air blow gun impresses with its high-quality workmanship and minimalist design, which puts a focus on seamless transitions.

Die Druckluftpistole Pro One zeichnet sich durch einen geringen Energieverbrauch und niedrigen Geräuschpegel aus. Gegenüber herkömmlichen Modellen ist die Lautstärke um die Hälfte reduziert, was das Gehör des Anwenders deutlich entlastet. Die Bauteile sind mithilfe modernster Technologien gefertigt, die Edelstahldüse beispielsweise entsteht durch ein präzises 3D-Druckverfahren. Eine optimal austarierte Gewichtsverteilung und der flexible Handgriff ermöglichen ein ermüdungsfreies Arbeiten.

Begründung der Jury
Die Druckluftpistole Pro One besticht durch ihre qualitativ hochwertige Ausführung und zurückgenommene Gestaltung, welche die nahtlosen Übergänge in den Fokus rückt.

Sievert Professional Heating Tools Range
Sievert Professionelles Heizgeräte-Sortiment

Manufacturer
Sievert AB, Solna, Sweden
Design
Yellon AB (Martin Sallander, Måns Sjöstedt),
Jönköping, Sweden
Web
www.sievert.se
www.yellon.se

The professional heating tools range by Sievert comprises the lightweight and ergonomic hot-air hand tool DW 3000, the Powerjet torch system with replaceable burner and the Handyjet multipurpose torch line, which features an innovative preheating tube. The range is aligned to the corporate design, for instance incorporating the brand's colours of orange, grey and black. Furthermore, slim proportions and a contrast-rich surface structure made of hard plastic and soft rubber fosters a uniform appearance.

Das professionelle Heizgeräte-Sortiment von Sievert umfasst das leichte und ergonomische Heißluft-Handgerät DW 3000, das Lötlampen-System Powerjet mit austauschbarem Brenner und die vielseitig einsetzbare Lötlampen-Linie Handyjet, die über ein neu entwickeltes Vorwärmrohr verfügt. Das Sortiment entspricht dem Corporate Design, u. a. werden die markentypischen Farben Orange, Grau und Schwarz aufgegriffen. Darüber hinaus sorgen schlanke Proportionen und eine kontrastreiche Oberflächenstruktur aus festem Kunststoff und weichem Gummi für ein einheitliches Erscheinungsbild.

Statement by the jury
This heating tools range captivates with its striking colour and material contrasts, which highlight the tools' slim contours. The operating elements are clearly highlighted.

Begründung der Jury
Das Heizgeräte-Sortiment besticht durch markante Farb- und Materialkontraste, welche die schlanke Kontur der Werkzeuge betont. Die Bedienelemente sind klar hervorgehoben.

Racing Creeper
Mechanics Creeper
Montagerollbrett

Manufacturer
Ersson, Taichung, Taiwan
In-house design
Miles Liu
Web
www.ersson.com.tw

The Racing Creeper features foam pads for the neck and back in order to enable comfortable use over longer periods of time. The castors made from thermoplastic polyurethane are particularly resistant against oil and chemicals. They have an extended lifespan as compared to conventional PU castors. The full ball bearings provide smooth rolling properties. Practical storage surfaces on both sides enable comfortable work with either the left or right hand.

Der Racing Creeper verfügt über Polster für Nacken und Rücken, um ein bequemes Arbeiten über längere Zeiträume zu gewährleisten. Die Laufrollen aus thermoplastischem Polyurethan sind besonders widerstandsfähig gegen Öl und Chemikalien und im Vergleich zu herkömmlichen PU-Rollen extra verschleißfest. Die Vollkugellager sorgen für ein gleichmäßiges Rollverhalten. Praktische Ablageflächen auf beiden Seiten ermöglichen das komfortable Arbeiten sowohl mit der linken als auch mit der rechten Hand.

Statement by the jury
The Racing Creeper meets the highest ergonomic standards. In terms of form, its racy curves and contrasting colours are reminiscent of motorsports.

Begründung der Jury
Der Racing Creeper erfüllt hohe Ansprüche an die Ergonomie. Seine schnittigen Kurven und die kontrastierenden Farben schaffen eine formale Brücke zum Motorsport.

RC 4/36
Job-Site Radio Charger
Baustellenradio-Ladegerät

Manufacturer
Hilti Corporation, Schaan, Liechtenstein
In-house design
Design
Matuschek Design & Management,
Aalen, Germany
Web
www.hilti.com
www.matuschekdesign.de

The RC 4/36 is a powerful job-site radio
charger, which not only plays music but
also recharges lithium-ion batteries of
various sizes. The charger can be connected to a wide variety of devices like
smartphones using Bluetooth or the
USB port. The black rubberised edges
make the charger particularly robust by
providing impact protection, and both
speakers are shielded by strong metal
grilles. The unit can play music using
either mains or battery power.

Statement by the jury
The RC 4/36 features distinct edges that
give it a powerful look. Thanks to its
compact dimensions, the radio requires
very little space.

Das RC 4/36 ist ein leistungsstarkes Bau-
stellenradio, das nicht nur Musik abspielt,
sondern auch Lithium-Ionen-Akkus unterschiedlicher Größe auflädt. Die Station
kann via Bluetooth oder USB-Anschluss mit
verschiedensten anderen Geräten wie beispielsweise einem Smartphone vernetzt
werden. Die schwarzen gummierten Kanten
machen die Ladestation äußerst robust gegen Stöße, beide Lautsprecher sind durch
stabile Metallgitter geschützt. Zum Musik-
hören bezieht das Radio Strom aus der
Steckdose oder von den Akkus.

Begründung der Jury
Das RC 4/36 gefällt durch seine Ecken und
Kanten, die ihm ein markiges Aussehen
verleihen. Dank der kompakten Maße
nimmt das Radio nur wenig Platz ein.

Janus
Distribution Board
Stromverteilerkasten

Manufacturer
Palazzoli S.p.A., Brescia, Italy
Design
Marco Gaudenzi, Pesaro, Italy
Web
www.palazzoli.it
www.marcogaudenzi.it

The mobile Janus distribution board was designed for use in challenging building site conditions. It is easy to transport and can either be placed on the ground or attached to the wall folded out. Its design with two front panels is inspired by Janus, the ancient god with two faces. The lower cable holders prevent the cables from accidentally being pulled out and thus interrupting the power supply.

Statement by the jury
With its two front panels, the well-structured Janus distribution board confidently stands out from other devices both visually and functionally.

Der mobile Stromverteilerkasten Janus wurde für den anspruchsvollen Einsatz auf Baustellen entwickelt. Er ist einfach zu transportieren und kann entweder auf den Boden gestellt oder auseinandergeklappt und an einer Wand befestigt werden. Seine Gestaltung mit zwei Fronten ist inspiriert von Janus, dem antiken Gott mit zwei Gesichtern. Die unteren Kabelhalterungen verhindern, dass die Kabel versehentlich herausgerissen werden und dadurch die Stromversorgung unterbrochen wird.

Begründung der Jury
Der übersichtlich gestaltete Stromverteilerkasten Janus hebt sich durch seine zwei Fronten optisch und funktional souverän von anderen Geräten ab.

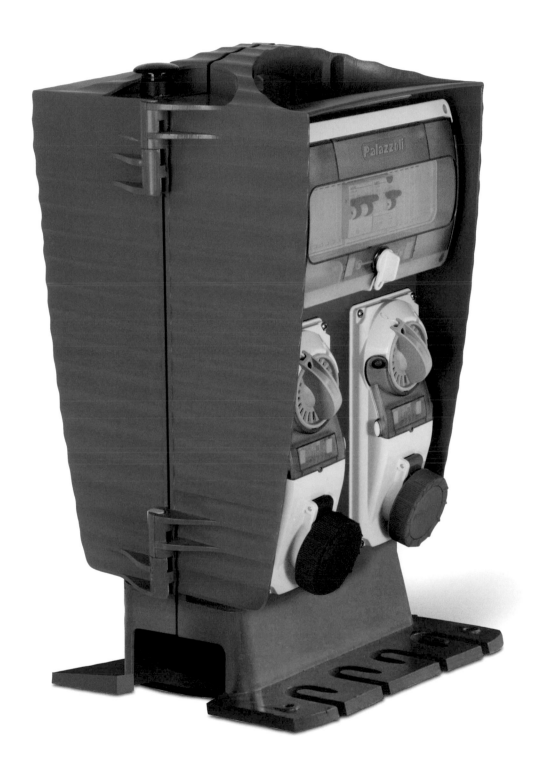

Univet 5.0
Safety Glasses with Augmented Reality
Schutzbrille mit erweiterter Realität

Manufacturer
Univet, Rezzato (Brescia), Italy
In-house design
Fabio Borsani
Web
www.univet-optic.com

The Univet 5.0 safety glasses add augmented reality to the wearer's visual field. Aided by waveguide technology, holographic projections are displayed right in front of the wearer's eyes. This provides useful information about the tasks at hand without having to divert the gaze or interrupt the work being done. The glasses' ergonomic design makes them comfortable to wear even over prescription glasses. The lens can be interchanged quickly and provides maximum protection against mechanical impact.

Die Schutzbrille Univet 5.0 fügt dem realen Sichtfeld eine erweiterte Realität hinzu. Mithilfe von Wellenleiter-Technologie werden in der Brille holografische Projektionen direkt vor dem Auge des Trägers angezeigt. Dadurch erhält er nützliche Informationen zu seiner Tätigkeit, ohne den Blick abwenden und die Arbeit unterbrechen zu müssen. Das ergonomische Design sorgt für einen angenehmen Tragekomfort, auch über einer Korrekturbrille. Die Scheibe kann mit wenigen Handgriffen gewechselt werden und gewährleistet maximalen Schutz gegen mechanische Einwirkungen.

Statement by the jury
The Univet 5.0 safety glasses combine pioneering technology with a well-engineered design, which is fascinatingly lightweight and unobtrusive.

Begründung der Jury
Die Schutzbrille Univet 5.0 vereint zukunftsweisende Technologie mit einer ausgereiften Gestaltung, die faszinierend leicht und dezent ist.

Jigtech Pro Jig
Installation Tool
Montagewerkzeug

Manufacturer
Dale Hardware, Ossett, Great Britain
Design
AME Group Ltd., Sheffield, Great Britain
Web
www.dalehardware.com
www.ame-group.co.uk

The Jigtech Pro Jig installation tool enables the quick installation of door handles and latches. It takes less than five minutes, because the drill holes do not have to be measured and marked out. The drilling jig can be used for doors with different thicknesses due to the self-centring clamp, and features an adjustable drill hole for the latch, which both mark out and guide drilling. The intuitive backset adjuster enables the user to easily switch between two different latch length settings.

Das Montagewerkzeug Jigtech Pro Jig ermöglicht einen schnellen Einbau von Türgriffen und -riegeln. Die Montage dauert weniger als fünf Minuten, da die Bohrlöcher nicht extra ausgemessen und eingezeichnet werden müssen. Die Bohrschablone kann dank der selbstzentrierenden Klemme für unterschiedlich dicke Türen verwendet werden und verfügt über ein einstellbares Bohrloch für den Riegel; Klemme und Bohrloch geben die Bohrposition und -richtung vor. Die intuitive Einstellung des Dornmaßes ermöglicht dem Benutzer einen einfachen Wechsel zwischen zwei unterschiedlichen Riegellängen.

Statement by the jury
Its high utility value and intuitive usability make the Jigtech Pro Jig installation tool a convincing product solution.

Begründung der Jury
Der hohe Gebrauchswert und die intuitive Bedienbarkeit machen das Montagewerkzeug Jigtech Pro Jig zu einer überzeugenden Produktlösung.

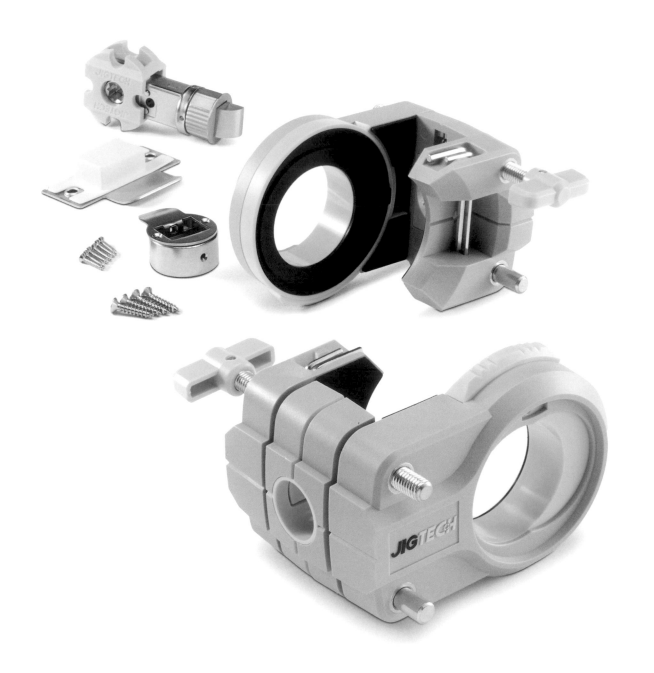

WINBAG CONNECT
Inflatable Shim
Aufpumpbares Montagekissen

Manufacturer
Red Horse, Skanderborg, Denmark
In-house design
Web
www.winbag.eu

The Winbag Connect inflatable shim is suited to various uses, such as levelling windows, positioning doors and installing cabinets. The maximum lifting capacity is 135 kg; by connecting several shims it can be increased to 450 kg. The specifically developed hand pump enables intuitive use with just one hand. Thanks to the fibre-reinforced material, the shim is tough and durable but does not leave any scratches on sensitive surfaces.

Mit dem aufpumpbaren Montagekissen Winbag Connect lassen sich beispielsweise Fenster ausrichten, Türen positionieren oder Schränke einbauen. Die maximale Hebekraft beträgt 135 kg. Werden mehrere Kissen verbunden, kann die Tragfähigkeit auf 450 kg erhöht werden. Die speziell entwickelte Handpumpe ermöglicht eine intuitive Bedienung mit nur einer Hand. Durch das faserverstärkte Material ist das Kissen hart und langlebig, ohne auf empfindlichen Oberflächen Kratzer zu hinterlassen.

Statement by the jury
The Winbag Connect inflatable shim is extremely robust, functional and – when empty – saves space. The hand pump is positioned to provide easy accessibility.

Begründung der Jury
Das aufpumpbare Montagekissen Winbag Connect ist äußerst robust, funktional und – im leeren Zustand – platzsparend. Die Handpumpe ist gut zugänglich positioniert.

HAWK PEN
Tattoo Machine
Tätowiermaschine

Manufacturer
MT.DERM GmbH, Berlin, Germany
In-house design
Web
www.cheyenne-tattoo.de

In contrast to conventional tattooing machines, the Hawk Pen is significantly quieter and vibrates less, while nevertheless featuring high puncturing power and frequency. By rotating the grip, the optimal needle protrusion can be continuously set and altered. The pen-like form gives the user the feeling of drawing. The exterior consists of anodised aluminium, thus the surface is hard and particularly scratch-resistant.

Der Hawk Pen ist gegenüber herkömmlichen Tätowiermaschinen erheblich leiser und vibrationsärmer. Dennoch verfügt er über eine hohe Einstechkraft und Stechfrequenz. Durch das Drehen des Griffs kann der optimale Nadelherausstand stufenlos eingestellt und verändert werden. Die stiftähnliche Form gibt dem Anwender das Gefühl, er würde zeichnen. Die Außenseite besteht aus eloxiertem Aluminium, somit ist die komplette Oberfläche hart und besonders kratzfest.

Statement by the jury
The Hawk Pen fascinates with its markedly simple design, which also conveys the sensuality associated with the art of tattooing.

Begründung der Jury
Der Hawk Pen fasziniert durch eine betont schlichte Gestaltung, die auch die Sinnlichkeit transportiert, die man mit der Tätowierkunst verbindet.

Precision Paintbrush
Paintbrush
Malerpinsel

Manufacturer
Orkla House Care AB, Bankeryd, Sweden
Design
Catino, Stockholm, Sweden
Web
www.orklahousecare.com
www.catino.se

The Precision Paintbrush was designed to provide the feel of an artist brush. Its innovative filaments enable high precision when painting details and still carry lots of paint. Three different grip zones meet the requirements of a wide range of work situations; the triangular grip at the front of the paintbrush provides stability for precision tasks, the circular grip in the middle allows the painter to rotate the brush while painting and the rearmost grip is designed for longer reach and stability.

Der Malerpinsel Precision Paintbrush wurde entworfen, um dem Anwender das Gefühl zu vermitteln, er arbeite mit einem Künstlerpinsel. Seine innovativen Borsten erlauben ein präzises Lackieren von Details und eine sehr gute Farbaufnahme. Die drei Griffzonen werden unterschiedlichen Arbeitssituationen gerecht: Der vordere Dreipunktgriff sorgt für Stabilität bei Präzisionsarbeiten, der mittlere kreisförmige Griff erleichtert das Drehen des Pinsels während des Lackierens und der hintere Griff ist auf eine größere Reichweite und Stabilität ausgelegt.

Statement by the jury
Thanks to its elegant form and the three grip zones, the Precision Paintbrush appeals to the visual and tactile senses in a pleasing way.

Begründung der Jury
Durch seine elegante Form und die drei Griffzonen spricht der Malerpinsel Precision Paintbrush auf reizvolle Weise den visuellen wie den Tastsinn an.

MidRanger
RFID Reader for Libraries
RFID-Lesegerät für Bibliotheken

Manufacturer
Nedap N.V.,
Groenlo, Netherlands

In-house design
Erik Veurman

Web
www.ncdap.com

reddot award 2017
best of the best

Mediator of knowledge

The great libraries of the world, such as that of the time-honoured Trinity College in Dublin or the modern National Library of China in Beijing, are distinctive places for disseminating crucial knowledge. With an ambitious design, the MidRanger aims to accelerate sharing this knowledge. The reader offers a user-friendly alternative for library staff and visitors that would otherwise spend a lot of time manually checking in and out every book. The reader is at the core of an innovative RFID (Radio-Frequency Identification) system for libraries, enabling librarians and visitors to quickly and effortlessly scan books and other media remotely. It is made of high-quality materials that make it reliable and robust to process and withstand millions of transactions. The MidRanger can be laid on top of a desk or mounted below one. Featuring a flowing stainless steel design, the scanner allows users to easily slide books over the robust reader. Its solid weight and rubber feet ensure that the product does not move when used for scanning. The combination of beautiful materials and the thin feel of the product make it a well thought-out solution that easily blends into any library environment. With an up-to-date design concept, the MidRanger RFID reader supports libraries in continuing to play their role in the information age.

Mittler des Wissens

Die großen Bibliotheken dieser Welt wie etwa die des altehrwürdigen Trinity College in Dublin oder die moderne Chinesische Nationalbibliothek in Beijing sind besondere Orte der Wissensvermittlung. Mit einem ambitionierten Design schließt das Lesegerät MidRanger daran an und beschleunigt die Verbreitung dieses Wissens. Vor dem Hintergrund, dass Bibliotheksmitarbeiter und Nutzer viel Zeit für den manuellen Ausleihvorgang aufwenden müssen, bietet es eine anwenderfreundliche Alternative. Das Lesegerät steht im Mittelpunkt eines innovativen RFID-Systems (Radio-Frequency Identification), das es Bibliotheken und Besuchern ermöglicht, Bücher und andere Medien aus der Entfernung zu scannen. Es besteht aus hochwertigen Materialien und ist deshalb, auch angesichts der Vielzahl von Ausleihvorgängen, zuverlässig und robust. Der MidRanger kann auf einem Schreibtisch platziert oder darunter montiert werden. Da der Scanner eine fließende Form aus Edelstahl hat, können die Anwender ihre Bücher einfach darüber schieben. Ein solides Gewicht und die Gestaltung mit Gummifüßen sorgen dafür, dass er nicht verrutscht. Die Kombination aus ansprechenden Materialien und einer schlanken Formensprache macht dieses Gerät zu einer durchdachten Lösung, die sich in jede Bibliotheksumgebung einfügen kann. Mit einem zeitgemäßen Gestaltungskonzept unterstützt das RFID-Lesegerät MidRanger Bibliotheken dabei, auch im Informationszeitalter ihrer Rolle gerecht zu werden.

Statement by the jury

The MidRanger RFID reader embodies the idea of the library as a key place of discovery in an impressive manner. Featuring a clear and high-quality design, it simplifies the process of borrowing and returning media. The reader is astonishingly simple to use and gives positive, immediate feedback. The process remains transparent. The device can be used in various settings and is highly robust yet aesthetically appealing.

Begründung der Jury

Auf eindrucksvolle Weise verkörpert das RFID-Lesegerät MidRanger die Idee von der Bibliothek als zentralem Ort der Begegnung. Klar und sehr hochwertig gestaltet, vereinfacht es den Vorgang der Ausleihe und Rückgabe. Die Benutzung ist denkbar unkompliziert, wobei es sehr positiv ist, dass eine sofortige Rückmeldung erfolgt. Der Vorgang bleibt damit transparent. Das Gerät kann variabel eingesetzt werden und ist dabei ebenso ästhetisch ansprechend wie solide.

Designer portrait
See page 44
Siehe Seite 44

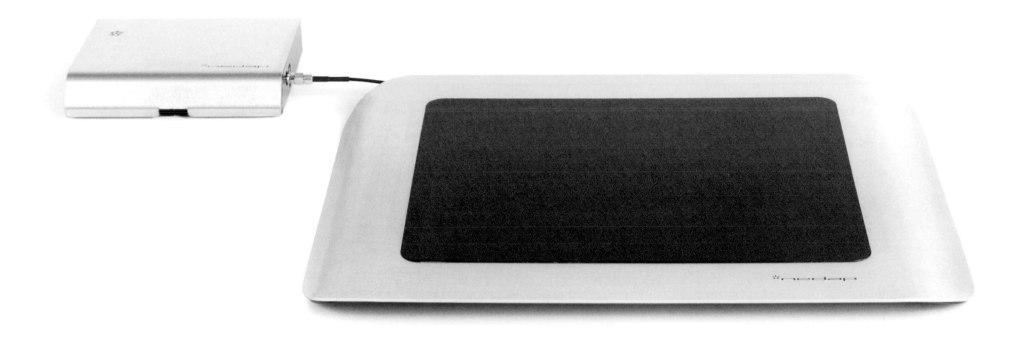

BEETLE / iSCAN EASY
Smart Pay
Self-Checkout POS System
Selbstbedienungskasse

Manufacturer
Diebold Nixdorf, Berlin, Germany
In-house design
Bernd Kruse
Web
www.dieboldnixdorf.com

The Beetle / iScan Easy Smart Pay self-checkout POS system enables consumers to scan and bag their items and quickly pay using cards or mobile wallet solutions, for example using NFC-enabled smartphones. Guided by an intuitive user interface and automated audiovisual prompts, consumers can rapidly complete their retail journey, even if they aim to buy items that are not pre-tagged with barcodes. This self-checkout POS system is distinguished by a compact footprint and complies with industry regulations covering ergonomic standards for self-service terminals.

Statement by the jury
With its simple, elegant design, this self-checkout POS system makes a tidy and friendly impression and blends in with any environment.

Mit der Selbstbedienungskasse Beetle / iScan Easy Smart Pay können Kunden ihre Einkäufe selbst scannen, einpacken und wahlweise mit Karte oder Mobile-Wallet-Lösungen bezahlen, z. B. über NFC-fähige Smartphones. Die intuitive Benutzerführung und audiovisuellen Bedienhinweise ermöglichen den schnellen Abschluss des Einkaufs, auch wenn Artikel ohne festen Barcode dazugehören. Die Selbstbedienungskasse zeichnet sich durch eine kompakte Stellfläche aus und erfüllt die ergonomischen Anforderungen an SB-Terminals gemäß den Industrievorschriften.

Begründung der Jury
Die Selbstbedienungskasse macht durch ihr schlichtes, elegantes Design einen ansprechend aufgeräumten Eindruck und passt in jede Umgebung.

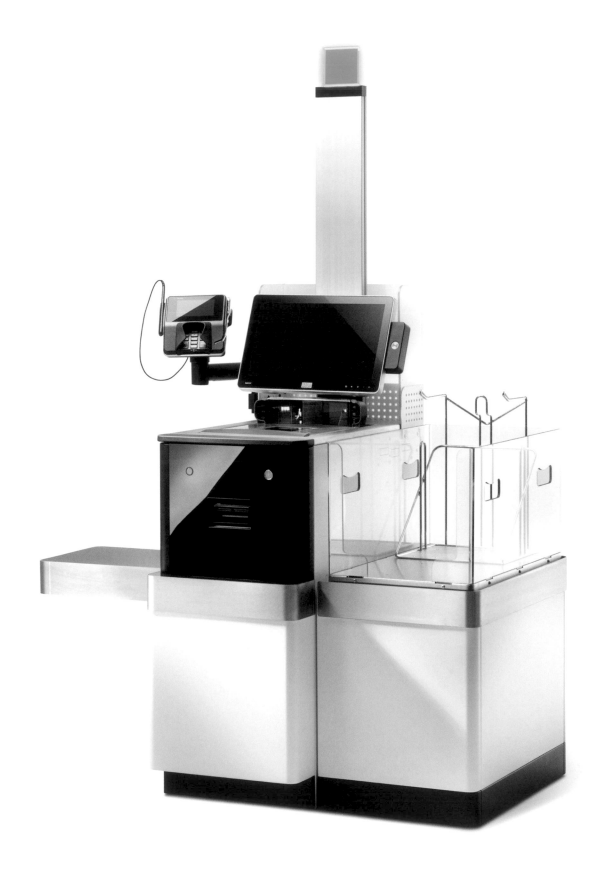

BEETLE / iSCAN EASY eXpress
Self-Checkout POS System
Selbstbedienungskasse

Manufacturer
Diebold Nixdorf, Berlin, Germany
In-house design
Gregor Pollmann, Dominik Widmaier
Web
www.dieboldnixdorf.com

The Beetle/iScan Easy eXpress self-checkout POS System is distinguished by a compact design and meets the demand of retail companies for a miniaturised footprint. It offers payment options with cards or mobile wallet solutions, e.g. using NFC-enabled smartphones. The audiovisual prompts allow consumers to rapidly and intuitively complete the payment process. Alternatively, the terminal can be used as an in-store kiosk system to quickly and easily gather additional information on products sold in a store or to take advantage of value-added services.

Die Selbstbedienungskasse Beetle/iScan Easy eXpress zeichnet sich durch ein kompaktes Design aus und erfüllt die Anforderung von Handelsunternehmen nach minimaler Stellfläche. Sie bietet Bezahloptionen per Karte oder Mobile-Wallet-Lösungen, z. B. über NFC-fähige Smartphones. Die audiovisuellen Bedienhinweise führen den Kunden schnell und intuitiv durch den Bezahlvorgang. Alternativ kann das Terminal auch als In-Store-Kiosksystem eingesetzt werden, um schnell und einfach zusätzliche Informationen zu Produkten und dem Filialsortiment zu bekommen oder um Mehrwertdienstleistungen anzubieten.

Statement by the jury
The self-checkout POS system features excellent functionality in the smallest of spaces. The seamless design lends expression to its high quality.

Begründung der Jury
Die Selbstbedienungskasse bietet hervorragende Funktionalität auf kleinstem Raum. Das nahtlose Design bringt eine hohe Qualität zum Ausdruck.

SWING
POS Tablet
Tablet-POS

Manufacturer
AURES Technologies, Lisses, France
Design
ID'S – Design Stratégique (Bertrand Médas), Lyon, France
Web
www.aures.com
www.id-s.fr

Swing is a multifunctional POS tablet that enables numerous configurations. The slightly curved housing, which features a laterally attached elastic band, optimally distributes the weight between the hand and lower arm. The case has a particularly soft feel and offers ease of use and strong protection if the tablet is dropped. With its specifically developed POGO fastening and locking system, the tablet can be automatically positioned and mounted in three different ways: in addition to the desk version, it can be placed on its docking station, on its mini pole or on the wall.

Swing ist ein multifunktionales POS-Tablet, das zahlreiche Konfigurationen ermöglicht. Das leicht gewölbte Gehäuse mit einem seitlich platzierten elastischen Band verteilt das Gewicht optimal auf Hand und Unterarm. Die Hülle fühlt sich besonders weich an und bietet eine komfortable Handhabung und einen guten Schutz, falls das Tablet herunterfällt. Mit seinem eigens entwickelten Befestigungs- und Verriegelungssystem POGO lässt sich das Tablet automatisch positionieren und auf drei verschiedene Arten anbringen: Zusätzlich zur Platzierung auf einem Tisch, kann es auf einer Dockingstation, einer Minisäule oder an der Wand befestigt werden.

Statement by the jury
Swing has many clever functional details that give the design of the POS tablet a fresh and original look.

Begründung der Jury
Swing bietet viele clevere funktionale Details, die dem Tablet-POS auf gestalterischer Ebene ein frisches und eigenwilliges Aussehen verleihen.

i5 Series
i5-Serie
POS System

Manufacturer
SENOR TECH Co., Ltd.,
New Taipei City, Taiwan
In-house design
Web
www.senortech.com

The POS system of the i5 Series is characterised by a slim and fanless design, which ensures quiet and reliable operation. The touchscreen is tiltable by 60 degrees. The bezel around the screen is replaceable and can be customised to suit individual preferences. The terminal features several optional extras. In addition, there is enough space for a receipt printer or barcode scanner between the base and the mount.

Statement by the jury
With a choice of different coloured bezels and many available accessories, the i5 Series demonstrates an exceptional degree of flexibility.

Das POS-Kassensystem der i5-Serie zeichnet sich durch eine schlanke Bauweise mit einem lüfterlosen Gehäuse aus, das einen leisen und zuverlässigen Betrieb garantiert. Der Touchscreen lässt sich um 60 Grad kippen, die Blende um den Bildschirm kann ausgetauscht und individuellen Wünschen angepasst werden. Das Terminal bietet zahlreiche Optionen, um weiteres Zubehör zu ergänzen. Zusätzlich befindet sich zwischen Sockel und Halterung genug Platz für einen Bondrucker oder Barcodescanner.

Begründung der Jury
Die i5-Serie zeigt mit ihren farblich variablen Blenden und den vielen Erweiterungsmöglichkeiten ein außergewöhnliches Maß an Flexibilität.

T1 PRO
POS System

Manufacturer
Shanghai Sunmi Technology Co., Ltd.,
Shanghai, China
In-house design
Guihong Chen, David Protet
Web
www.sunmi.com

The T1 Pro is a point of sale system that has been developed especially for fashion shops, high-end department stores and restaurants. In contrast to conventional POS systems this device conveys a much more pleasant shopping experience thanks to its organically rounded forms and orange-coloured accents. The aluminium body simultaneously serves as the outer housing and main chassis for all technical components. Thus the device is particularly resource-saving.

Statement by the jury
With its soft lines and fresh colour accents the POS system T1 Pro appeals to the user on an emotional level. Its display and body form a harmonious unit.

Das T1 Pro ist ein Point-of-Sale-System, das speziell für Modegeschäfte, High-end-Kaufhäuser und Restaurants entwickelt wurde. Im Vergleich zu herkömmlichen POS-Systemen vermittelt das Gerät durch seine organisch gerundeten Formen und die orangefarbenen Akzente ein sehr viel menschlicheres Kauferlebnis. Der Korpus aus Aluminium dient gleichzeitig als Außengehäuse und Hauptchassis für alle technischen Komponenten. Dadurch ist das Gerät besonders ressourcenschonend.

Begründung der Jury
Das POS-System T1 Pro emotionalisiert den Nutzer durch seine sanfte Linienführung und die frischen Farbakzente. Display und Korpus bilden eine harmonische Einheit.

Mini POS
POS System

Manufacturer
Compal Electronics Company,
Taoyuan, Taiwan
Design
Avalue Technology Inc.,
New Taipei, Taiwan
Web
www.compal.com
www.avalue.com.tw

The POS system Mini POS combines two displays: a full flat 10.1" touchscreen facing the sales staff and an adjustable 5" touchscreen on the customer end. Also integrated into the system is a built-in thermal printer with auto cut functionality. The bottom of the device features a gap that serves as a channel for cables and also protects the electrical connectors. The system supports connectivity via both data cable and Wi-Fi.

Statement by the jury
The Mini POS captivates with its triangular form, which not only offers functional and ergonomic advantages, but also creates an iconographic design.

Das POS-System Mini POS kombiniert zwei Displays: einen vollständig flachen 10,1"-Touchscreen auf der Verkäuferseite und einen verstellbaren 5"-Touchscreen auf der Kundenseite. Zudem verfügt das System über einen eingebauten Thermodrucker mit Auto-Cut-Funktion. An der Unterseite des Geräts befindet sich ein Zwischenraum, der als Kabelkanal und zum Schutz der elektrischen Anschlüsse dient. Das System unterstützt sowohl eine Verbindung per Datenkabel als auch per Wi-Fi.

Begründung der Jury
Das Mini POS besticht durch seine dreiwinkelige Form, die nicht nur funktionale und ergonomische Vorzüge bietet, sondern auch ein ikonografisches Design schafft.

DCR
POS Terminal

Manufacturer
Posbank, Seoul, South Korea
Design
IDnComm (Hyung Sub Kim),
Seoul, South Korea
Web
www.posbank.com
www.idncomm.com

The DCR combines a PC, a touchscreen and a printer in a single point-of-sale terminal. Thanks to its compact size, it is suitable for the restricted space in smaller shops and restaurants. The integrated printer facing the staff and the card reader allow even untrained operators to control the POS terminal as intuitively as possible. The touchscreen that is tilted towards the operator and the stable base enable ergonomic and fatigue-free working.

Das DCR vereint einen PC, einen Touchscreen und einen Drucker in einem einzigen Point-of-Sale-Terminal. Durch seine kompakte Größe ist es an die beengten Raumverhältnisse in kleineren Geschäften und Restaurants angepasst. Der dem Verkäufer zugewandte integrierte Drucker und das Kartenlesegerät sind darauf ausgelegt, dass sie auch von ungeübtem Personal intuitiv bedient werden können. Der angeschrägte Touchscreen und der stabile Standfuß ermöglichen ein ergonomisches und ermüdungsfreies Arbeiten.

Statement by the jury
The practical POS terminal fascinates with its puristic, contemporary style. The extremely slim base lends it visual lightness.

Begründung der Jury
Das handliche POS-Terminal gefällt durch seinen puristischen, zeitgemäßen Stil. Der äußerst schmale Standfuß sorgt für visuelle Leichtigkeit.

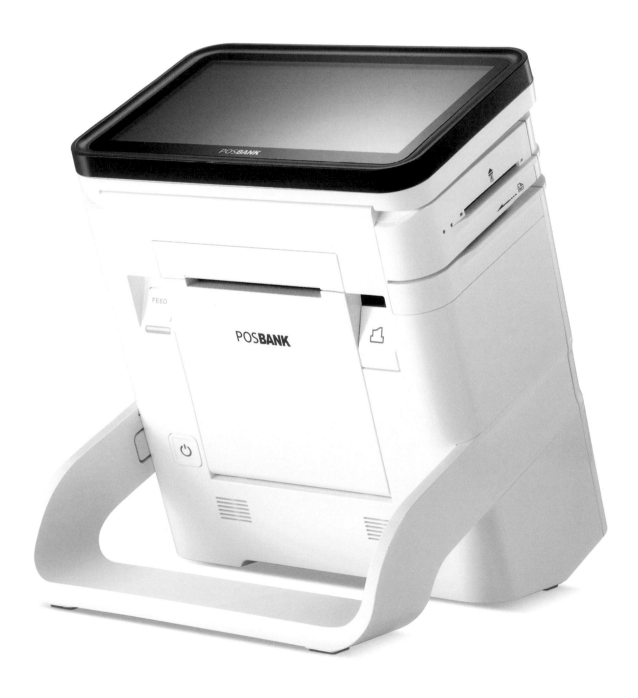

S302
POS System

Manufacturer
Shenzhen iBoxpay Co., Ltd.,
Shenzhen, China
In-house design
Qiuding Li, Bingbing Xu
Web
www.iboxpay.com

The intelligent POS system S302 was developed to manage mobile payment services for small businesses. It supports a large variety of contactless transaction modes, such as Apple Pay, NFC and QR code payments. In addition to functioning as a point-of-sale terminal, the system also enables e-commerce applications like the accumulation of loyalty points or the preparation of business reports. The 5.5" touchscreen and the Android operating system provide a smartphone-like user experience.

Statement by the jury
The elegant POS system S302 features a touchscreen that has been harmoniously integrated into the housing. The communication interfaces can be identified at a glance.

Das intelligente POS-System S302 wurde für den mobilen Zahlungsverkehr in kleineren Geschäften entwickelt. Es unterstützt eine Vielzahl von kontaktlosen Transaktionsarten wie Apple Pay, NFC- oder QR-Code-Zahlungen. Neben der Point-of-Sale-Kassenfunktion sind mit dem System auch verschiedenste E-Commerce-Anwendungen möglich, wie das Sammeln von Treuepunkten oder die Erstellung von Geschäftsberichten. Der 5,5"-Touchscreen und das Android-Betriebssystem erzeugen ein Smartphone-ähnliches Nutzererlebnis.

Begründung der Jury
Bei dem eleganten POS-System S302 ist der Touchscreen äußerst stimmig in das Gehäuse integriert. Die Kommunikationsschnittstellen können auf einen Blick erfasst werden.

PX7
POS Terminal

Manufacturer
PAX Computer Technology Co., Ltd.,
Shenzhen, China
Design
Shenzhen ND Industrial Design Co., Ltd.
(Jingzhou Wen, Tianyu Xiao),
Shenzhen, China
Web
www.pax.com.cn
www.sz-nd.com

In addition to providing the functions of a modern payment system, the POS terminal PX7 also supports multimedia applications. Company-specific advertising content or information for customers can be shown on the 7" colour touchscreen. Customers are able to sign with a finger directly on the display, even without a pen. The open software structure and the many communication interfaces enable full or partial integration into the existing in-store payment system.

Statement by the jury
The POS terminal PX7 places interaction with the customer centre stage. The flat, seamless design with radiused edges has a premium look.

Das POS-Terminal PX7 unterstützt neben den Funktionen eines modernen Bezahlsystems auch Multimedia-Anwendungen. Auf dem 7"-Farbtouchscreen können unternehmensspezifische Werbeinhalte oder Kundeninformationen abgespielt werden. Der Kunde kann seine Unterschrift direkt mit dem Finger auf dem Bildschirm tätigen, auch ohne Eingabestift. Die offene Software-Architektur und die vielfältigen Kommunikationsschnittstellen ermöglichen eine volle oder teilweise Integration in das bestehende Kassensystem.

Begründung der Jury
Das POS-Terminal PX7 rückt die Interaktion mit dem Kunden in den Fokus. Das flache, nahtlose Design mit abgerundeten Kanten wirkt sehr hochwertig.

iZettle Reader
Contactless Card Reader
Kontaktloser Kartenleser

Manufacturer
iZettle AB, Stockholm, Sweden
In-house design
Nino Höglund, Tomas Prochazka
Design
Howl (Gustav Müller Nord, Oscar Karlsson),
Nacka, Sweden
Web
www.izettle.com
www.howlstudio.se

The iZettle Reader is a mobile card reader that enables merchants to accept credit cards and contactless payments. The card reader connects to smartphones and tablet PCs via Bluetooth. The high-contrast concave buttons ensure good visibility and tactile quality. The OK button and branded tab on the side set colourful accents. The card reader can be used in conjunction with the optional iZettle Dock, which simultaneously serves as a charging station.

Statement by the jury
Thanks to its minimalist style, the iZettle not only looks particularly attractive but is also extremely easy to use.

Der iZettle Reader ist ein mobiler Kartenleser, der Händlern die Möglichkeit gibt, Kreditkarten und kontaktlose Zahlungen anzunehmen. Der Kartenleser wird via Bluetooth mit einem Smartphone oder Tablet-PC gekoppelt. Die kontrastreichen konkaven Tasten sind gut zu sehen und leicht zu ertasten. Die Bestätigungstaste und der seitliche Reiter mit dem Firmenlogo setzen farbliche Akzente. Der Kartenleser kann optional mit der Halterung iZettle Dock verwendet werden, die gleichzeitig Ladestation ist.

Begründung der Jury
Durch seinen minimalistischen Stil sieht der iZettle Reader nicht nur besonders gut aus, sondern ist auch ausgesprochen einfach zu handhaben.

QR100
POS Terminal

Manufacturer
PAX Computer Technology Co., Ltd.,
Shenzhen, China
Design
TGS Design Consultancy (Weixue Liao,
Hangdong Wang), Shenzhen, China
Web
www.pax.com.cn
www.chinatgs.com

The wireless POS terminal QR100 supports contactless payment methods via scan code and NFC chip. Customers simply position their smartphone briefly above the scanner in order to complete the transaction. The POS terminal features Internet connectivity and an Android operating system, which provides familiar user guidance. Moreover, it can be flexibly customised to the respective business requirements.

Statement by the jury
The POS terminal QR100 takes a convincing approach to combining the latest technology with a contemporary aesthetic inspired by smartphones.

Das kabellose POS-Terminal QR100 unterstützt kontaktlose Bezahlverfahren per Scancode und NFC-Chip. Der Kunde muss das Smartphone lediglich kurz über das Kartenlesegerät halten, um die Transaktion abzuwickeln. Das POS-Terminal ist internetfähig und verwendet ein Android-Betriebssystem, das dem Anwender eine vertraute Menüführung bietet. Darüber hinaus kann es flexibel an die jeweilige Geschäftssituation angepasst werden.

Begründung der Jury
Das POS-Terminal QR100 kombiniert auf überzeugende Weise aktuelle Technologie mit einer zeitgemäßen, von Smartphones inspirierten Ästhetik.

DS8100 Series
DS8100-Serie
Barcode Scanners
Barcodescanner

Manufacturer
Zebra Technologies, Holtsville, USA
In-house design
Mark Fountain
Design
Intelligent Product Solutions,
Hauppauge, USA
Thinkable Studio, Offenburg, Germany
Web
www.zebra.com
www.intelligentproduct.solutions
www.thinkablestudio.com

The cordless and corded barcode scanners of the DS8100 series can instantly read even damaged barcodes as well as electronic barcodes on poorly lit displays. Thanks to the scan range of up to 61 cm, a high-resolution image sensor and a bright aiming light, checkout terminal operators can scan products in the customer's trolley without having to leave the terminal area. The scanners display the current power status of the battery and, thanks to the ergonomic handle, rest comfortably in the user's hand.

Statement by the jury
The technical and simultaneously elegant look of the DS8100 series effectively highlights the practical value of these barcode scanners.

Die kabellosen und kabelgebundenen Barcodescanner der DS8100-Serie erfassen auch beschädigte Barcodes und elektronische Barcodes auf schlecht beleuchteten Displays sofort. Durch die Scanreichweite von bis zu 61 cm, einen hochauflösenden Bildsensor und einen hellen Zielpunkt können Kassenmitarbeiter Artikel im Einkaufswagen des Kunden scannen, ohne den Kassenbereich verlassen zu müssen. Die Scanner zeigen den aktuellen Stromstatus des Akkus an und liegen mit ihrem ergonomischen Griff angenehm in der Hand.

Begründung der Jury
Die technische und zugleich elegante Anmutung der DS8100-Serie bringt den hohen Gebrauchswert der Barcodescanner gekonnt zur Geltung.

HTDB-100FM
Handheld Barcode Scanner
Tragbarer Barcodescanner

Manufacturer
IEI Integration Corp., New Taipei City, Taiwan
In-house design
Liao Ying Hsiu, Han Tsung Yuan
Web
www.ieiworld.com

The HTDB-100FM handheld barcode scanner has been developed for the specific requirements of healthcare. Medical personnel can access important data by scanning the barcode on patients' wristbands or medicine bottles. An antimicrobial coating prevents bacterial contamination and can be easily disinfected. Thanks to its elegant and well-balanced curved form, the scanner sits well in the hand and can be set down in a stable position. The symmetrically placed head of the scanner is suited for left- and right-handed operation alike.

Der tragbare Barcodescanner HTDB-100FM wurde für die besonderen Anforderungen im Medizinbereich entwickelt. Das medizinische Personal kann damit Barcodes auf dem Patientenarmband oder auf Arzneimittelflaschen scannen und somit wichtige Daten einsehen. Eine antimikrobielle Beschichtung schützt vor Keimen und kann problemlos desinfiziert werden. Dank seiner eleganten, ausbalancierten Kurvenform liegt der Scanner gut in der Hand und lässt sich stabil ablegen. Der symmetrisch platzierte Scanknopf kann sowohl von Rechtsals auch von Linkshändern bedient werden.

Statement by the jury
The well-proportioned HTDB-100FM barcode scanner with its soft contours instils trust in patients and enables ergonomic use for operating personnel.

Begründung der Jury
Der formschöne Barcodescanner HTDB-100FM mit seinen sanften Konturen vermittelt dem Patienten Vertrauen und ermöglicht dem Anwender ein ergonomisches Arbeiten.

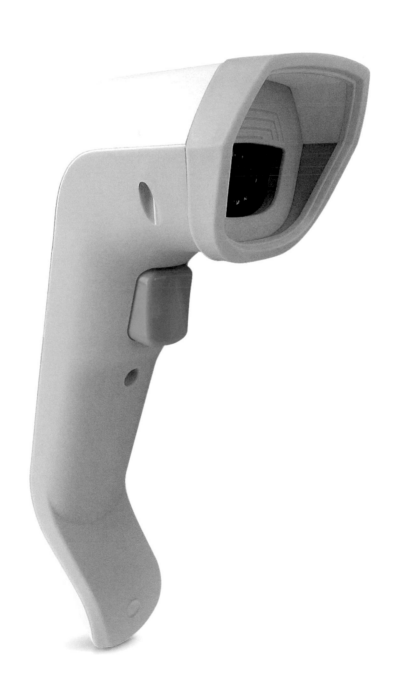

FX3-LX
Label Printer
Etikettendrucker

Manufacturer
SATO Corporation, Tokyo, Japan
In-house design
Yuji Saito
Design
AXIS (Taichi Ozawa), Tokyo, Japan
Web
www.satoworldwide.com
www.axisinc.co.jp

The FX3-LX is a label printer, which can be customised to the client's requirements. A cloud solution minimises downtime through preventive maintenance and ensures that the applications are always up-to-date. The large touchscreen enables simple and intuitive printing without a PC, allowing clients to reduce costs and minimise the required working space. Moreover, the printer features an antibacterial coating and is drip-proof, making it suitable for use in a wide range of industries.

Der FX3-LX ist ein Etikettendrucker, der nach Kundenwunsch angepasst werden kann. Eine Cloud-Lösung minimiert Ausfallzeiten durch vorbeugende Wartung und stellt sicher, dass die Anwendungen immer aktuell sind. Der große Touchscreen bietet ein einfaches und intuitives Drucken ohne PC, wodurch der Kunde Kosten spart und weniger Arbeitsfläche benötigt. Zudem ist der Drucker antibakteriell beschichtet und tropfwassergeschützt, sodass er flexibel in verschiedensten Branchen eingesetzt werden kann.

Statement by the jury
With its straight lines and minimalist design, this label printer strongly radiates professionalism and practicality.

Begründung der Jury
Der Etikettendrucker strahlt durch sein geradliniges und reduziertes Erscheinungsbild in hohem Maße Professionalität und Sachlichkeit aus.

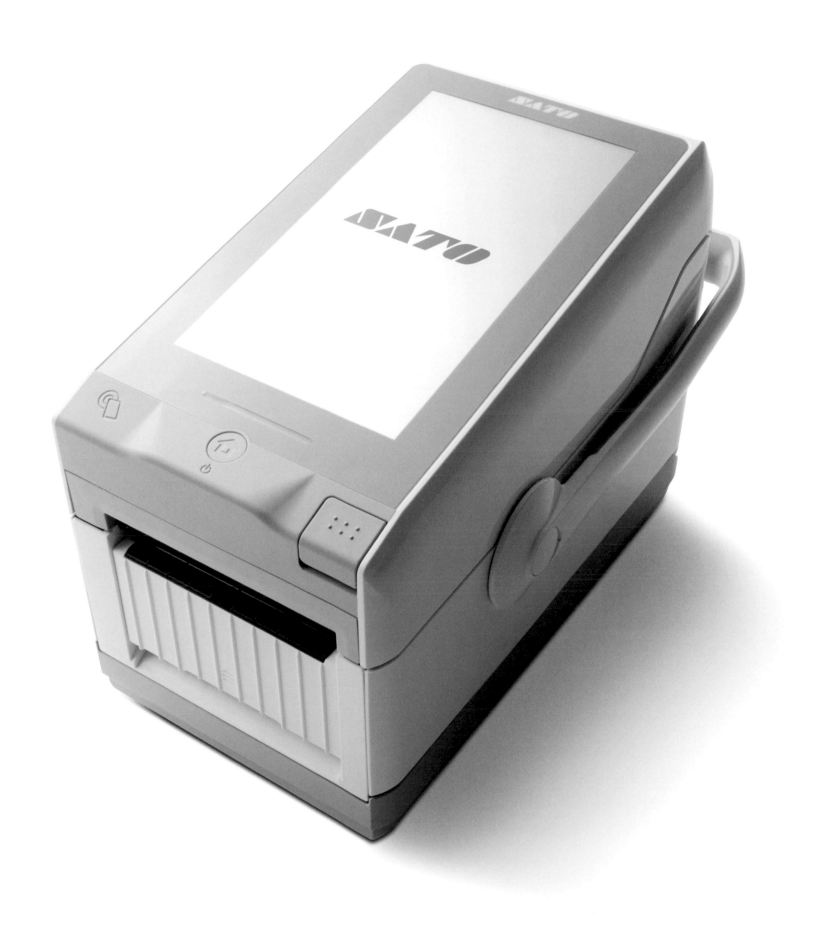

Smart Item Label
Digital Price Label
Digitales Preisschild

Manufacturer
Solu-M, Suwon, South Korea
In-house design
Solu-M Design Group
Web
www.solu-m.com

The Smart Item Label (SIL) shows product details as well as price, sale and stock inventories on an e-paper display. By utilising WAN (Wide Area Network), retailers can change information on smart labels in multiple stores from a central location in real time, without the labels needing to be manually adjusted or replaced. The SIL system allows the matching of accurate prices at an item level between online and offline retailing. With its sleek appearance, the SIL also draws attention to brand equity and enhances the visibility of the products in stores.

Statement by the jury
The Smart Item Label is surprisingly thin and flexible. The strong colours add a relaxed element to the greatly simplified design language.

Das Smart Item Label (SIL) zeigt Produktdetails sowie Preis-, Verkaufs- und Lagerbestände auf einem E-Paper-Display an. Durch die Nutzung von WAN (Wide Area Network) können Einzelhändler von einem zentralen Standort aus die Informationen auf den intelligenten Preisschildern in mehreren Filialen in Echtzeit ändern, ohne dass die Etiketten per Hand überschrieben oder ersetzt werden müssen. Das SIL-System ermöglicht die artikelgenaue Preisanpassung zwischen Online- und Offline-Handel. Zudem lenkt das SIL durch sein apartes Erscheinungsbild den Blick auf den Markenwert und steigert die Sichtbarkeit der Produkte in den Geschäften.

Begründung der Jury
Das Smart Item Label ist überraschend dünn und flexibel. Seine stark vereinfachte Formensprache wird durch die kräftigen Farben aufgelockert.

VISS NX
LED Floor Display
LED-Bodendisplay

Manufacturer
VISS Lighting, Shenzhen, China
Design
21g Product Design Co., Ltd.
(Haiping Zheng, Baiqiu Liu, Bingyun Su),
Shenzhen, China
Web
www.viss.cn
www.design21g.com

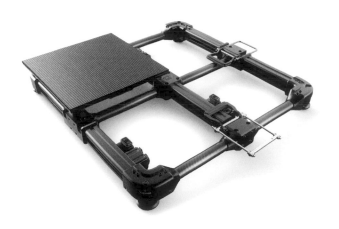

The VISS NX LED floor display was developed for uneven terrain in particular and is for instance suited to sports events or motor shows. In order to simplify installation, the 50 x 50 cm panels are not set into the ground individually but are first inserted into a 100 x 100 cm mount. This allows four panels to be installed simultaneously and results in an even surface. The LED display made of carbon and aluminium is robust, lightweight and waterproof.

Statement by the jury
The VISS NX convinces with its extremely practical mounting system, which ensures short installation times and high stability.

Das LED-Bodendisplay VISS NX wurde speziell für unebenes Gelände entwickelt und eignet sich z. B. für Sportveranstaltungen oder Motorshows. Um die Montage zu vereinfachen, werden die 50 x 50 cm großen Panels nicht einzeln in den Boden eingelassen, sondern zunächst in eine 100 x 100 cm große Halterung eingesetzt. Dadurch können immer vier Panels gleichzeitig installiert werden und es entsteht eine gleichmäßige Fläche. Das LED-Display aus Carbon und Aluminium ist robust, leicht und wasserdicht.

Begründung der Jury
Das VISS NX überzeugt durch sein überaus praktisches Halterungssystem, das für kurze Installationszeiten und hohe Stabilität sorgt.

VISS ES5/7
LED Wall Display
LED-Wanddisplay

Manufacturer
VISS Lighting, Shenzhen, China
Design
21g Product Design Co., Ltd.
(Haiping Zheng, Baiqiu Liu, Bingyun Su),
Shenzhen, China
Web
www.viss.cn
www.design21g.com

The LED wall display VISS ES5/7 is easy to transport and quick to install. It only takes one minute for a single person to install it on a surface area of 1 sqm. The frame made of carbon fibre has a low weight and provides enhanced rigidity. The electronic components are made of an aluminium alloy, which protects them from transport damage and ensures good heat dissipation. The cables are designed for good accessibility.

Statement by the jury
The VISS ES5/7 is surprisingly easy to handle and features a very simple construction. The installation is carried out in no time at all.

Das LED-Wanddisplay VISS ES5/7 ist einfach zu transportieren und schnell zu installieren. Für die Installation auf einer Fläche von 1 qm benötigt eine einzige Person nur eine Minute. Der Rahmen aus Carbonfaser sorgt für ein geringes Gewicht und eine hohe Steifigkeit. Die elektronischen Teile bestehen aus einer Aluminiumlegierung, die vor Transportschäden schützt und für eine gute Wärmeableitung sorgt. Die Kabel sind leicht zugänglich.

Begründung der Jury
Das VISS ES5/7 ist überraschend leicht zu handhaben und besonders einfach konstruiert. Die Installation gelingt im Handumdrehen.

CRUISER 2 LED
LED Industrial Luminaire
LED-Industrieleuchte

Manufacturer
LUG Light Factory Sp. z o.o.,
Zielona Góra, Poland
In-house design
Web
www.lug.com.pl

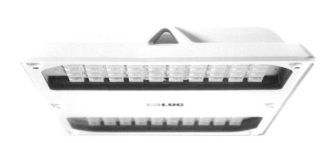

The Cruiser 2 LED industrial luminaire has been designed for production plants, warehouses and sports facilities. Its radiator provides optimised heat circulation in high temperatures and dusty environments. The luminaire is IP66-certified and thus can be easily cleaned using a water jet. Moreover, it may be installed in six different ways. Small parts that could get lost during installation have been eliminated. The luminaire is 98 per cent recyclable.

Statement by the jury
The Cruiser 2 LED looks particularly bright and friendly. Its markedly flat housing creates a sense of space and expanse.

Die Industrieleuchte Cruiser 2 LED ist für Produktionsstätten, Lagerhallen und Sportanlagen konzipiert. Der Kühler sorgt für eine optimale Wärmezirkulation bei hohen Temperaturen und in staubigen Umgebungen. Die Leuchte erfüllt die Schutzklasse IP66 und lässt sich schnell und einfach mit einem Wasserstrahl säubern. Zudem kann sie auf sechs verschiedene Arten montiert werden. Kleinteile, die bei der Installation verloren gehen könnten, wurden eliminiert. Die Leuchte ist zu 98 Prozent recycelbar.

Begründung der Jury
Die Cruiser 2 LED wirkt ausgesprochen hell und freundlich. Ihr besonders flaches Gehäuse schafft Raum und Weite.

Carbon
LED Display Series
LED-Display-Serie

Manufacturer
ROE Visual Co., Ltd., Shenzhen, China
In-house design
Chen Lu, Danhu Cai, Zhanqiang Li,
Hong Zhang
Web
www.roevisual.com

Carbon is the first LED display series by the ROE brand to incorporate carbon-fibre technology. The material is particularly lightweight, impact-proof, shock-resistant and robust. Its low weight and slim design reduce transport and rigging costs, making the display optimally suitable for touring shows in particular – in both indoor and outdoor settings. The elements are simply fastened using magnets and quick-release connectors, which enable easy installation and maintenance.

Statement by the jury
The LED display series Carbon is impressively robust and lightweight, thus featuring excellent portability.

Carbon ist die erste LED-Display-Serie der Marke ROE mit Kohlefaser-Technologie. Das Material ist besonders leicht, schlagfest, schockresistent und stabil. Aufgrund des geringen Gewichts und des schlanken Designs reduzieren sich die Kosten für Transport und Aufbau, sodass das Display insbesondere für Tourneen optimal geeignet ist – sowohl im Innen- als auch im Außenbereich. Die Elemente werden lediglich mithilfe von Magneten und Schnellverschlüssen fixiert, was eine einfache Installation und Wartung ermöglicht.

Begründung der Jury
Die LED-Display-Serie Carbon ist beeindruckend robust und leicht, sodass sie über eine hervorragende Portabilität verfügt.

Diamond Series P3.91
Indoor LED Display

Manufacturer
Shenzhen BAKO Optoelectronics Co., Ltd.,
Shenzhen, China
Design
LKK Design Shenzhen Co., Ltd. (Shuai Ma,
Jianhui Zhang, Junxian Chen, Jianjian Xu),
Shenzhen, China
Web
www.szbako.com
www.lkkdesign.com

The LED display Diamond Series P3.91 for indoor use has a characteristic diamond relief, which adds an extravagant design element to its otherwise technical look. The housing with radiused edges and a large handle enables safe use. A small integrated screen indicates the voltage, temperature, current duration of usage and overall utilisation period of the display. The cordless design enables fast and easy installation.

Statement by the jury
With its smooth transitions and diamond relief, the Diamond Series P3.91 demonstrates a sense of style and emotionality in an otherwise technical environment.

Der LED-Display Diamond Series P3.91 für den Innenbereich hat ein charakteristisches Diamant-Relief, das dem ansonsten technischen Look ein extravagantes Gestaltungselement hinzufügt. Das Gehäuse mit abgerundeten Kanten und einem breiten Haltegriff erlaubt eine sichere Handhabung. Ein integrierter LED-Bildschirm zeigt Stromspannung, Temperatur, die aktuelle Nutzungsdauer und die Gesamtnutzungszeit des Displays an. Das kabellose Design ermöglicht eine schnelle und einfache Montage.

Begründung der Jury
Die Diamond Series P3.91 beweist durch fließende Übergänge und das Diamant-Relief Stilbewusstsein und Emotionalität in einem ansonsten technischen Umfeld.

ROAD READY
LED Display

Manufacturer
Coleder Display Co., Ltd., Shenzhen, China
Design
LKK Design Shenzhen Co., Ltd. (Junxian
Chen, Hao Tian, Gang Wang, Jianhui Zhang),
Shenzhen, China
Web
www.coleder.com
www.lkkdesign.com

The Road Ready LED display features an innovative connector system that is cordless and tool-free. It is assembled and ready for operation in just 2.8 seconds. The adjustable connectors enable gapless transitions between the display units. Due to the fact that the power supply, receiving card and hub board are directly installed on the back panel, faulty parts can be replaced very quickly. The LED tiles may be removed from the magnetic front with a simple push.

Statement by the jury
The LED display Road Ready is impressively easy to install. All components are quickly accessible via the back panel.

Das LED-Display Road Ready wird über ein innovatives Verschlusssystem kabellos und werkzeugfrei verbunden. Es ist in 2,8 Sekunden montiert und einsatzbereit. Die justierbaren Verbindungsstücke ermöglichen lückenlose Übergänge zwischen den Bildschirmen. Dadurch, dass das Netzteil, die Empfangskarte und das Hub Board direkt in der Rückwand verbaut sind, lassen sich defekte Teile besonders schnell austauschen. Die LED-Kacheln können aus der magnetischen Front durch einfachen Druck herausgenommen werden.

Begründung der Jury
Das LED-Display Road Ready ist begeisternd einfach zu montieren. Alle Komponenten sind über die Rückwand sehr leicht zugänglich.

TC51/56
Industrial Handheld Computer
Mobiler Industriecomputer

Manufacturer
Zebra Technologies, Holtsville, USA
In-house design
Mu Kai Shen, Mark Fountain
Web
www.zebra.com

The TC51/56 industrial handheld computer keeps working reliably even after having been submerged in water, dropped onto concrete or when used in dusty environments. The unibody design provides effective impact-protection for its sophisticated electronics. The 5" touchscreen enables use with or without gloves, with a stylus and even in wet conditions. Unique dedicated keys can be created on either side of the display for one-touch access to the most frequently used device features.

Statement by the jury
The TC51/56 impresses with its robust design. The outer frame provides effective protection and is a distinctive eye-catcher at the same time.

Der mobile Industriecomputer TC51/56 funktioniert auch noch zuverlässig, wenn er in Wasser untergetaucht wird, auf Beton fällt oder in staubigen Umgebungen eingesetzt wird. Das Unibody-Design bietet einen wirksamen Stoßschutz für die anspruchsvolle Elektronik. Über das 5"-Touchscreen lässt sich das Gerät mit oder ohne Handschuhe, mit Eingabestift und sogar bei Nässe bedienen. Auf beiden Seiten des Displays befinden sich individuell programmierbare Tasten, die einen direkten Zugriff auf die meistgenutzten Funktionen ermöglichen.

Begründung der Jury
Der TC51/56 imponiert durch sein robustes Design. Der äußere Rahmen ist effektiver Schutz und markanter Hingucker zugleich.

DS2
Rugged Handheld Computer
Robuster Handcomputer

Manufacturer
DSIC Co., Ltd., Seoul, South Korea
Design
DESIGN NID Corp. (Seonhoon Kim, Taesung Yoon), Seoul, South Korea
Web
www.dsic.co.kr
www.nidd.co.kr

Thanks to its pocket-size format, the DS2 rugged handheld computer can be comfortably operated with one hand. The computer withstands repeated drops onto concrete without damage. Furthermore, it is dust- and water-resistant. The 5" multitouch display provides sufficient working space. Like many smartphones, the computer uses an Android operating system, thus users do not require extensive training to operate the unit. The device is also available with an integrated barcode scanner as an optional extra.

Statement by the jury
The DS2 rugged handheld computer skilfully combines the user-friendly aesthetics of a smartphone with the indestructibility of an industrial device.

Der robuste Handcomputer DS2 ermöglicht durch sein Taschenformat die komfortable Bedienung mit nur einer Hand. Der Computer übersteht auch wiederholte Stürze auf Beton ohne Schaden, zudem ist er staub- und wasserdicht. Das 5"-Multitouch-Display bietet ausreichend Platz zum Arbeiten. Wie viele Smartphones läuft der Computer mit einem Android-Betriebssystem, sodass es keiner aufwendigen Schulung bedarf, um ihn bedienen zu können. Optional ist das Gerät mit einem integrierten Barcodescanner erhältlich.

Begründung der Jury
Der robuste Handcomputer DS2 vereint souverän die bedienfreundliche Ästhetik eines Smartphones mit der Unverwüstlichkeit eines Industriegeräts.

G60
Mobile Inspection Assistant
Mobiler Inspektionsassistent

Manufacturer
AMobile Intelligent Corp.,
New Taipei City, Taiwan
In-house design
Cheng-Cheng Chen
Web
www.amobile-solutions.com

The G60 mobile inspection assistant combines thermal imaging and push-to-talk technology in an industrial mobile computer designed for inspections. The dual-lens thermal camera and the laser pointer enable accurate recording of temperature changes in electrical equipment. Further features include a pogo pin for reading and writing data and a docking station for simultaneous charging and data transfer. The device has IP67 certification.

Statement by the jury
The G60 incorporates elaborate technical features in a surprisingly small device, while the large screen offers high ease of use.

Der Inspektionsassistent G60 vereint Thermographie- und Push-to-talk-Technologie in einem mobilen Industriecomputer, der für Inspektionen konzipiert wurde. Die Dual-Linsen-Wärmebildkamera und der Laserpointer ermöglichen eine präzise Aufzeichnung von Temperaturveränderungen in Elektrogeräten. Zur weiteren Ausstattung gehören ein Federkontaktstift zum Lesen und Schreiben von Daten und eine Dockingstation, die gleichzeitig lädt und Daten überträgt. Das Gerät ist nach Schutzklasse IP67 zertifiziert.

Begründung der Jury
Der G60 überführt eine technisch aufwendige Ausstattung in ein überraschend kleines Gerät, während der großzügige Bildschirm einen hohen Bedienkomfort bietet.

MaxiSys® MS906
Automotive Diagnostic Device
Diagnosegerät für Fahrzeuge

Manufacturer
Autel Intelligent Technology Corp., Ltd.,
Shenzhen, China
In-house design
Prof. Juntian Jiang, Prof. Boming Lu
Web
www.autel.com

The MaxiSys MS906 automotive diagnostic device offers diagnostic processes for a wide range of vehicle manufacturers, thus making it possible to carry out comprehensive analyses efficiently. The device features an exceptionally fast hexa-core processor, a high-resolution 8" LED touchscreen and a wireless communication module that works over long distances. The ergonomic design with rubberised exterior protection is optimally suited to rough working conditions in the workshop.

Statement by the jury
The compact MaxiSys MS906 diagnostic device makes an extremely robust impression. The touchscreen interface impresses with its high ease of use.

Das Diagnosegerät MaxiSys MS906 bietet Diagnoseverfahren für eine sehr große Bandbreite an Fahrzeugherstellern, sodass umfangreiche Analysen effizient durchgeführt werden können. Das Gerät ist mit einem außergewöhnlich schnellen Sechskernprozessor, einem hochauflösenden 8"-LED-Touchscreen und einem auch über lange Distanzen leistungsfähigen kabellosen Kommunikationsmodul ausgestattet. Das ergonomische Design mit gummiertem Außenschutz ist optimal auf die rauen Arbeitsbedingungen in der Werkstatt abgestimmt.

Begründung der Jury
Das handliche Diagnosegerät MaxiSys MS906 macht einen äußerst robusten Eindruck. Das Touchscreen-Interface überzeugt durch seine Bedienfreundlichkeit.

MaxiSys® Pro
Automotive Diagnostic Platform
Diagnoseplattform für Kraftfahrzeuge

Manufacturer
Autel Intelligent Technology Corp., Ltd.,
Shenzhen, China
In-house design
Prof. Juntian Jiang
Web
www.autel.com

The MaxiSys Pro automotive diagnostic platform enables extremely fast scans and intuitive handling. The system consists of a tablet, functioning as central processor and monitor for the system, and an automotive diagnostic interface, which enables access to the vehicle data. The interface is coupled with the vehicle and can be connected to the tablet or another PC. The vehicle data may be transferred wirelessly using Bluetooth or with a cable.

Statement by the jury
The comprehensive technical MaxiSys Pro diagnostic platform provides a high degree of functionality. In addition, mechanics can move freely through the workshop while using the device.

Die Diagnoseplattform für Kraftfahrzeuge MaxiSys Pro ermöglicht extrem schnelle Scanzeiten und eine intuitive Bedienung. Das System besteht aus dem Tablet, das als zentraler Prozessor und Monitor für das System fungiert, und der Fahrzeugdiagnoseschnittstelle, die den Zugriff auf die Fahrzeugdaten ermöglicht. Die Schnittstelle wird an das Fahrzeug angeschlossen und kann mit dem Tablet oder einem anderen PC verbunden werden. Die Fahrzeugdaten können sowohl via Bluetooth als auch über ein Kabel übermittelt werden.

Begründung der Jury
Die technisch umfangreiche Diagnoseplattform MaxiSys Pro bietet ein hohes Maß an Funktionalität. Der Mechaniker kann sich zudem frei mit dem Gerät durch die Werkstatt bewegen.

AFL3-W19C-ULT3
All-in-One Panel PC

Manufacturer
IEI Integration Corp., New Taipei City, Taiwan
In-house design
Li Po Han, Tong Yu Shen
Web
www.ieiworld.com

The all-in-one panel PC AFL3-W19C-ULT3 has been developed for harsh industrial environments. The front panel is resistant to dust and water, thus making the device suitable for both indoor and outdoor use. The device is touchscreen-operated, which correlates with the habits of users. The symmetrical monitor frame enables flexible positioning in portrait or landscape mode. In addition, there are several modular expansions available for the PC, allowing for cost-effective upgrades. The design features only a few screws, thus enabling fast maintenance.

Der All-in-one-Panel-PC AFL3-W19C-ULT3 wurde für die raue industrielle Umgebung entwickelt. Die Front ist gegen Staub und Wasser resistent, sodass das Gerät sowohl im Innen- als auch im Außenbereich verwendet werden kann. Entsprechend den Nutzergewohnheiten wird es über einen Touchscreen gesteuert. Der symmetrische Monitorrahmen erlaubt eine flexible Platzierung im Hoch- oder Querformat, zudem bietet der PC mehrere Modulerweiterungen, sodass das System kostengünstig nachgerüstet werden kann. Die Konstruktion mit wenigen Schrauben ermöglicht eine einfache Wartung.

Statement by the jury
This industrial panel PC impresses with its simple, flat design. In addition, it also easily withstands extreme environmental conditions.

Begründung der Jury
Der Industrie-Panel-PC begeistert durch sein schlichtes, flaches Design. Er hält auch extremen Umweltbedingungen problemlos stand.

S21WP
Industrial Computer
Industriecomputer

Manufacturer
noax Technologies AG,
Ebersberg, Germany
In-house design
Web
www.noax.com

The S21WP industrial computer consists of a frameless, zero-bezel glass front and a completely sealed chassis made of finely brushed stainless steel, which optimally protects all internal components. The full HD display with integrated LED keys is easy to read even in adverse lighting conditions. The touch surface is made of extremely resistant, heat-strengthened safety glass, which can also be operated with protective gloves.

Statement by the jury
The seamless and gapless design of the S21WP industrial computer combines impressive functionality with high durability.

Der Industriecomputer S21WP besteht aus einer rahmenlosen Ganzglasfront und einem komplett geschlossenen Gehäuse aus fein geschliffenem Edelstahl, das alle Komponenten im Inneren optimal schützt. Das Full-HD-Display mit integrierten LED-Bedientasten lässt sich auch unter ungünstigen Lichtbedingungen einwandfrei ablesen. Die Touch-Oberfläche ist aus einem extrem widerstandsfähigen, thermisch gehärteten Sicherheitsglas gefertigt, das auch mit Schutzhandschuhen bedient werden kann.

Begründung der Jury
Die Konstruktion des Industriecomputers S21WP ohne Fugen und Spalten verbindet eine beeindruckende Funktionalität mit einer hohen Belastbarkeit.

The new S-Line
Die neue S-Line
Industrial Panel PC

Manufacturer
CRE Rösler Electronic GmbH,
Hohenlockstedt, Germany
In-house design
Web
www.cre-electronic.de

This industrial panel PC series is particularly flat, compact and lightweight. The new S-Line is tailored to meet customer-specific requirements and offers an impressively high degree of modularity. Thanks to the innovative housing design, individual components such as a CPU, RFID reader, barcode scanner and Wi-Fi can be quickly replaced, added or upgraded. Using its innovative adapter, the device can be easily mounted to a wide range of support arm systems by various manufacturers.

Statement by the jury
The new S-Line is highly adaptable due to its flat construction and open design. Its robust housing is very durable.

Diese Panel-PC-Serie ist besonders flach, kompakt und hat ein sehr geringes Gewicht. Die neue S-Line setzt auf kundenspezifische Anforderungen und besticht durch einen hohen Grad an Modularität. Durch den innovativen Gehäuseaufbau können einzelne Komponenten wie CPU, RFID-Lesegerät, Barcodescanner oder Wi-Fi jederzeit schnell ersetzt, ergänzt oder aktualisiert werden. Mithilfe des innovativen Anschlussadapters lässt sich das Gerät bequem an diverse Tragarmsysteme von verschiedenen Herstellern montieren.

Begründung der Jury
Die neue S-Line ist aufgrund ihrer flachen Bauweise und offenen Architektur sehr anpassungsfähig. Das robuste Gehäuse hält auch hohen Belastungen stand.

MK350N PLUS
Handheld Spectrometer
Tragbares Spektrometer

Manufacturer
United Power Research Technology Corp.,
Zhunan Township, Miaoli County, Taiwan
In-house design
Web
www.uprtek.com

The MK350N Plus handheld spectrometer provides key data on the colour and quality of an LED light source. It enables snapshot and ongoing measurements in four different recording modes. The recorded parameters can be saved to an SD memory card, displayed as a measurement log or output for further data processing. The measurements are displayed both numerically and graphically in a colour spectrum on the 3.5" LCD touchscreen.

Statement by the jury
The compact MK350N Plus spectrometer comes in all black, thus providing a strong, distraction-free contrast to the colours shown on the display.

Das Spektrometer MK350N Plus liefert die wichtigsten lichttechnischen Daten zur Farbe und Qualität eines LED-Leuchtmittels. Dabei sind sowohl Moment- als auch Dauermessungen in vier verschiedenen Erfassungsmodi möglich. Die erfassten Parameter können auf eine SD-Speicherkarte aufgezeichnet, als Messprotokoll oder für die weitere Datenverarbeitung ausgegeben werden. Die Messungen werden auf dem 3,5"-LCD-Touchscreen sowohl numerisch als auch grafisch in einem Farbspektrum dargestellt.

Begründung der Jury
Das handliche Spektrometer MK350N Plus ist ganz in Schwarz gehalten. Dadurch bietet es einen starken Kontrast zu den dargestellten Farben auf dem Display, ohne abzulenken.

G7
Personal Gas Detector
Gaswarngerät für den Personenschutz

Manufacturer
Blackline Safety, Calgary, Canada
Design
Advanta Design, Calgary, Canada
Web
www.blacklinesafety.com
www.advantadesign.com

Not only does the G7 personal gas detector warn the user about toxic or combustible gases; it also sends out distress signals. These safety alerts are transmitted to a monitoring team in real time, enabling them to initiate the appropriate emergency response. The speakerphone and the two-way text messaging system allow direct communication with the person involved. All alerts are managed within a cloud-hosted monitoring portal complete with mapping of the employee's location.

Das Gaswarngerät G7 warnt den Benutzer nicht nur vor giftigen oder brennbaren Gasen, sondern versendet auch Notrufe. Alle Sicherheitsalarme werden live an ein Überwachungsteam übermittelt, um entsprechende Notfallmaßnahmen einzuleiten. Über die Freisprechfunktion und das 2-Wege-Benachrichtigungssystem kann direkt mit der Person kommuniziert werden. Alle Alarme werden über das cloudbasierte Überwachungsportal mit integrierter Ortung des Aufenthaltsorts der Person bearbeitet.

Statement by the jury
With its expanded range of features, the G7 personal gas detector can save lives. In addition, the cartridges can be replaced very easily and quickly.

Begründung der Jury
Mit seiner erweiterten Funktionalität kann das Gaswarngerät G7 Leben retten. Darüber hinaus können die Module besonders einfach und schnell ausgetauscht werden.

MaxSHOT 3D
Optical Measuring System
Optisches Koordinatenmesssystem

Manufacturer
Creaform Inc, Lévis, Québec, Canada
In-house design
François Lessard, Nicolas Lebrun
Web
www.creaform3d.com

With the MaxShot 3D optical measuring system, even users with little experience can benefit from the highest measurement accuracy and repeatability when measuring large objects. The device and its proprietary operating software offer step-by-step guidance through the entire process. The 3D photogrammetry camera has a well-positioned centre of gravity so that shots can be easily and comfortably taken from several angles and hand positions.

Das optische Koordinatenmesssystem MaxShot 3D macht es aufgrund der hohen Messgenauigkeit und der Wiederholbarkeit selbst für wenig erfahrene Anwender möglich, große Objekte zu vermessen. Das Gerät und die eigens entwickelte Verarbeitungssoftware führen Schritt für Schritt durch den gesamten Prozess. Die 3D-Fotogrammetrie-Kamera hat einen gut positionierten Schwerpunkt, damit die Aufnahme von Bildern aus mehreren Winkeln und aus verschiedenen Handpositionen einfach und komfortabel gelingt.

Statement by the jury
The MaxShot 3D represents an accomplished interplay of geometric forms. Moreover, thanks to its optimally balanced centre of gravity, the device rests well in the hand.

Begründung der Jury
Das MaxShot 3D stellt ein gelungenes Zusammenspiel geometrischer Formen dar. Zudem liegt das Gerät dank seines optimal austarierten Schwerpunktes gut in der Hand.

Nivo-i
Digital Measuring Station
Digitale Vermessungsstation

Manufacturer
Nikon-Trimble Co., Ltd., Tokyo, Japan
In-house design
Shota Nikaido
Web
www.nikon-trimble.co.jp

The digital measuring station Nivo-i makes it possible to obtain digital images and precise positioning data simultaneously. The device can be used in many areas ranging from infrastructure management to disaster prevention, including the detection and inspection of cracks in a concrete bridge, the monitoring of landslides and the alignment of steel frames. Thanks to its compact and lightweight design, the station is easy to use and can also be carried for extended distances without major exertion.

Die digitale Vermessungsstation Nivo-i ermöglicht es, gleichzeitig digitale Bilder und präzise Positionsdaten abzurufen. Das Gerät kann vom Infrastrukturmanagement bis zum Katastrophenschutz in vielen Bereichen eingesetzt werden, ob es um die Erkennung und Untersuchung von Rissen in einer Betonbrücke, die Überwachung von Erdrutschen oder die Anleitung bei der Ausrichtung von Stahlrahmen geht. Durch ihre kompakte und leichte Gestaltung ist die Station einfach zu bedienen und lässt sich ohne große Kraftanstrengung auch über längere Strecken tragen.

Statement by the jury
Nivo-i embodies a new generation of digital measuring technology. Thanks to a profile that is dynamically arched forward and distinctive colouring, it has an original appearance.

Begründung der Jury
Nivo-i verkörpert eine neue Generation digitaler Messtechnik. Durch ihr dynamisch nach vorne gewölbtes Profil und die markante Farbgebung erhält sie ein eigenständiges Äußeres.

ORLAS CREATOR
3D Metal Printing
3D-Metall-Drucker

Manufacturer
O.R. Lasertechnologie GmbH, Dieburg,
Germany
Design
andré stocker design, Offenbach am Main,
Germany
Web
www.or-laser.com
www.andre-stocker.de

The Orlas Creator has succeeded in introducing metal 3D printing technology,
previously only used in industrial environments, to offices and studios. It can
process a wide range of metals, thus
providing many application options in
areas such as jewellery-making and aviation. The device is controlled via a tablet attached to the front of the housing,
featuring a specifically developed software. This tablet can be easily removed
from its mount in order to monitor one
or more units via cloud computing.

Statement by the jury
The seamless transitions of its design
give the Orlas Creator an appealing
aesthetic. The side panels with circumferential edges highlight the unit's
compactness.

Der Orlas Creator überführt die aus dem
industriellen Umfeld stammende Metall-
3D-Druck-Technologie in die Büro- und
Atelierumgebung. Er kann unterschiedlichste Metalle verarbeiten und bietet damit viele Einsatzmöglichkeiten, z.B. im
Schmuckhandwerk oder in der Luftfahrt.
Zur Bedienung der Anlage ist ein Tablet
mit eigens entwickelter Software an der
Gehäusevorderseite angebracht. Dieses
Tablet kann sehr leicht aus der Halterung
genommen werden, um eine oder mehrere
Anlagen über Cloud-Computing zu überwachen.

Begründung der Jury
Beim Design des Orlas Creator schaffen
nahtlose Übergänge eine ansprechende
Ästhetik. Die Seitenpaneele mit umlaufenden Kanten betonen die Kompaktheit der
Anlage.

LIX PEN
3D Printing Pen
3D-Druckerstift

Manufacturer
LIX PEN Ltd, London, Great Britain
In-house design
Anton Suvorov, Ismail Baran
Web
www.lixpen.com

The Lix Pen is a particularly small 3D printer in the shape of a pen, allowing free-standing objects to be drawn by hand. The pen is filled at the top using a plastic rod. The plastic is heated and comes out in molten form at the lower end of the pen. It can be shaped as desired until it sets after a short period of time. The pen has a housing made of anodised aluminium that is available in black and silver. The pen is powered via a USB port.

Statement by the jury
The Lix Pen surprises because it feels as familiar as a writing utensil. Since it is so small and practical, it can be used anywhere at any time.

Der Lix Pen ist ein besonders kleiner 3D-Drucker in Stiftform, mit dem frei stehende Objekte per Hand gezeichnet werden können. Der Stift wird am oberen Ende mit einem Kunststoffdraht befüllt. Der Kunststoff wird erwärmt und tritt in geschmolzener Form am unteren Stiftende wieder aus. Er kann nach Belieben geformt werden, bis er nach kurzer Zeit aushärtet. Der Stift besitzt ein Gehäuse aus eloxiertem Aluminium und ist in Schwarz und Silber erhältlich. Über einen USB-Anschluss wird er mit Strom versorgt.

Begründung der Jury
Der 3D-Drucker Lix Pen verblüfft, weil er sich so vertraut wie ein Stift anfühlt. Da er so klein und handlich ist, kann er jederzeit und überall verwendet werden.

Form 2
3D Printer
3D-Drucker

Manufacturer
Formlabs Inc., Somerville, USA
In-house design
Web
www.formlabs.com

The 3D printer Form 2 uses high-resolution stereolithography technology. This creates complex geometries from synthetic resins for a wide range of applications, including dentistry and mechanical engineering. An innovative peel mechanism and a heated resin tank ensure a reliable printing process, both for large, solid components and small, intricate details. Thanks to its compact dimensions, the printer is ideal for engineering companies and design studios.

Statement by the jury
The 3D printer Form 2 combines high technical standards with an extremely simple design: two cubes that harmoniously complement each other.

Der 3D-Drucker Form 2 basiert auf der hochauflösenden Stereolithografie-Technologie. Diese erzeugt komplexe Geometrien aus Kunstharzen für verschiedenste industrielle Anwendungsgebiete wie die Zahnmedizin oder den Maschinenbau. Ein innovativer Ablösemechanismus und ein beheizter Harztank sorgen sowohl bei großen, soliden Teilen als auch kleinen, komplexen Details für einen zuverlässigen Ablauf des Druckprozesses. Dank seiner kompakten Abmessungen ist der Drucker ideal für Ingenieurunternehmen und Designstudios geeignet.

Begründung der Jury
Der 3D-Drucker Form 2 verbindet hohen technischen Anspruch mit einer denkbar einfachen Gestaltung – zwei Kuben, die sich stimmig ergänzen.

You can also find this product on
Dieses Produkt finden Sie auch auf
Page 384
Seite 384

Océ Colorado 1640
Wide-Format Production Printer
Großformatdrucksystem

Manufacturer
Océ-Technologies, Venlo, Netherlands
In-house design
Web
www.oce.com

The digital wide-format production printer Océ Colorado 1640 prints applications such as posters and banners at a high printing speed. The UV-hardening ink gels instantly on contact with the print medium, thus preventing colours from bleeding. The heavy, sturdy frame, the special torsional stiffness and the industrial components all ensure high durability. The automatic two-roll system allows users to choose from two media types and formats without manual intervention.

Das digitale Großformatdrucksystem Océ Colorado 1640 produziert Anwendungen wie Plakate oder Banner in extrem hoher Druckgeschwindigkeit. Die UV-härtende Tinte wird bei Kontakt mit dem Druckmedium sofort fixiert und verhindert so ein Ineinanderlaufen der Farben. Der schwere, robuste Rahmen, die spezielle Verwindungsfestigkeit und die Industriekomponenten sorgen für eine hohe Lebensdauer. Durch eine Zwei-Rollen-Automatik kann zwischen zwei Medientypen und Formaten ohne manuelle Eingriffe gewechselt werden.

Statement by the jury
The striking design of the Océ Colorado 1640 visualises its advanced technology. The seamless transparent cover makes the printing process come alive in front of the user's eyes.

Begründung der Jury
Die markante Formensprache des Océ Colorado 1640 visualisiert die hochentwickelte Technologie. Die nahtlose transparente Abdeckung macht den Druckprozess erlebbar.

Soil Scanner
Bodenscanner

Manufacturer
SoilCares,
Wageningen, Netherlands

Design
Scope Design & Strategy bv
(Pim Jonkman),
Amersfoort, Netherlands

Web
www.soilcares.com
www.scopedesign.nl

reddot award 2017
best of the best

Groundbreaking interpretation
Faced with food shortages in many developing countries, researchers are looking for new ways to produce more food. The innovative Soil Scanner makes it easy for smallholder farmers to increase their agricultural yields due to rapid soil diagnostics. Easy to use and user-friendly, the scanner works with a ground sensor that can be intuitively activated by just one button. The collected data is then transmitted wirelessly to a smartphone app for analysis, whereupon the scanner gives advice on how to optimally fertilise the farmland and which type of crop can best be grown. The combination of Soil Scanner and smartphone thus turns into a functional unit that provides instant fertilising advice to the farmer. The aim of the design was to express the characteristics of a high-quality device and combine that with the expectations maintained toward an agricultural product. The metal elements are consistently integrated into the form to disperse the intense heat of the internal near-infrared light source. The innovative concept of combining a robust, reliable scanner for soil analysis with an app for the smartphone impresses in both form and function – especially for smallholder farmers in developing countries, it offers a very good way to utilise their soil profitably.

Zukunftsweisend interpretiert
Angesichts der Nahrungsmittelknappheit in vielen Ländern suchen Forscher nach neuen Wegen, mehr Nahrung zu erzeugen. Der innovative Bodenscanner ermöglicht es Kleinbauern auf einfache Weise, ihre landwirtschaftlichen Erträge aufgrund einer schnellen Bodendiagnose zu steigern. Leicht zu bedienen und nutzerfreundlich, arbeitet der Scanner mit einem Bodensensor, der sich intuitiv über nur einen einzigen Knopf aktivieren lässt. Die ermittelten Daten werden dann drahtlos an eine Smartphone-App übermittelt und analysiert, woraufhin die Landwirte eine Empfehlung erhalten, wie sie ihr Ackerland optimal düngen können oder welche Arten von Gewächsen am besten auf ihrem Boden gedeihen. Bodenscanner und Smartphone werden so zu einer funktionalen Einheit, die dem Bauern beratend zur Seite steht. Die Zielsetzung der Gestaltung war es dabei, die Eigenschaften eines hochwertigen Gerätes mit den Erwartungen an ein landwirtschaftliches Produkt zu vereinen. Die Metallelemente sind schlüssig in die Form integriert, um die intensive Hitze der inneren Nahinfrarot-Lichtquelle zu zerstreuen. Das innovative Konzept der Kombination eines robusten, zuverlässigen Bodenscanners mit einer App für das Smartphone beeindruckt in Form und Funktionalität – insbesondere für die Kleinbauern in Entwicklungsländern bietet sich eine sehr gute Möglichkeit, ihren Boden ertragreich zu nutzen.

Statement by the jury
The Soil Scanner captivates with the innovative idea of combining a scanner with an app for monitoring soil data in agriculture. Uncomplicated and functional, it features a robust design suitable for the work area, operates reliably and is easy to clean. The possibility offered by the Soil Scanner to manage cultivation more efficiently breaks new ground for the future of many people around the world.

Begründung der Jury
Der Bodenscanner besticht mit der innovativen Idee, einen Scanner mit einer App für die Bestimmung von Bodendaten in der Landwirtschaft zu verbinden. Unkompliziert einsetzbar und funktional, bietet er eine für diesen Bereich sehr robuste Gestaltung, er arbeitet zuverlässig und lässt sich leicht reinigen. Die mit dem Bodenscanner verbundene Möglichkeit, den Anbau wesentlich effizienter zu bewerkstelligen, ist für die Zukunft vieler Menschen weltweit richtungsweisend.

Designer portrait
See page 46
Siehe Seite 46

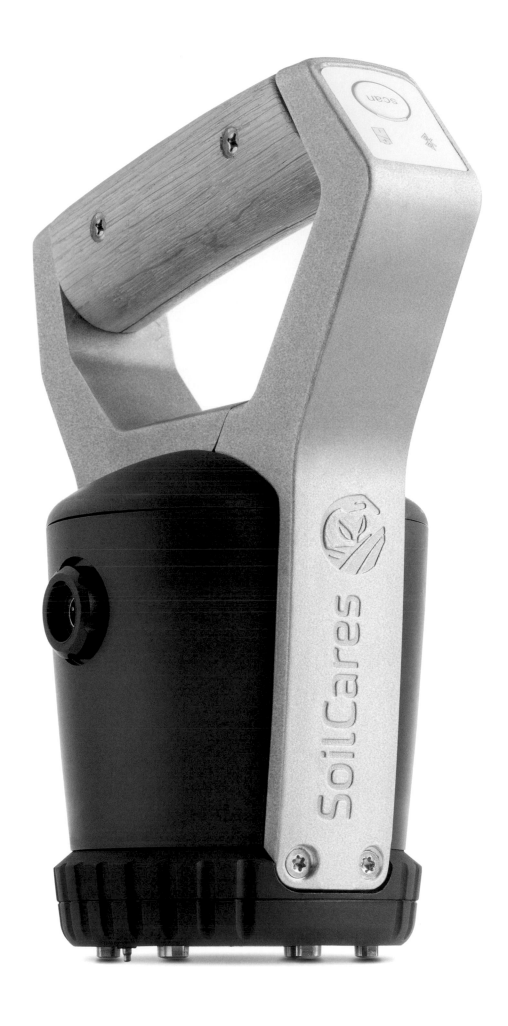

Drill Core Analyser
Bohrkernanalysator

Manufacturer
Orexplore, Stockholm, Sweden
Design
Semcon (Tue Beijer), Stockholm, Sweden
Web
www.orexplore.com
www.semcon.com

The Drill Core Analyser enables the mineral analysis of rock samples directly on site. The device has an outer layer of steel, which protects it from the harsh mining environment. During the drilling process it communicates through light, which is perceptible even in loud environments. The samples are placed in one-metre-long tubes, which are then fed into the revolving chamber of the analyser in groups of four. A single rotary push button and a user-friendly graphic interface suffice for user input, providing high ease of use in both the mine and the laboratory.

Statement by the jury
The monolithic shape of the Drill Core Analyser is contrasted by the tapering surfaces and precise lines in an especially dramatic way.

Der Bohrkernanalysator ermöglicht eine Mineralienanalyse von Gesteinsproben direkt vor Ort. Seine äußere Stahlschicht schützt das Gerät vor dem rauen Umfeld im Bergbau. Es kommuniziert während des Bohrvorgangs durch Licht, da dies auch in einer lauten Umgebung wahrgenommen werden kann. Die Proben werden in ein Meter lange Röhren platziert und dann in Vierergruppen in die rotierende Kammer des Analysegeräts eingesetzt. Für die Bedienung genügen ein einziger Knopf und eine grafische Benutzerschnittstelle, die sowohl unter Tage als auch im Labor ein komfortables Nutzererlebnis bietet.

Begründung der Jury
Die monolithische Form des Bohrkernanalysators wird auf besonders spannungsreiche Weise durch die sich verjüngenden Flächen und präzisen Linien durchbrochen.

C-MAG HS 7
Magnetic Stirrer
Magnetrührer

Manufacturer
IKA-Werke GmbH & Co. KG,
Staufen, Germany
In-house design
Web
www.ika.com

The C-MAG HS 7 is a magnetic stirrer with a temperature range between 50 and 500 degrees centigrade, able to withstand even the most extreme applications. Colour changes in the medium can be easily observed on the square ceramic mounting plate. The glass surfaces of the top section enable easy cleaning. In order to save space at the front of the device, the display is positioned between the ergonomic buttons, allowing them to be easily associated with the displayed values.

Statement by the jury
The C-MAG HS 7 magnetic stirrer convinces with a well-thought-out selection of materials and a coherent design that communicates clean work processes.

Der C-MAG HS 7 ist ein Magnetrührer mit einem Temperaturbereich von 50 bis 500 Grad Celsius, der auch extremen Anwendungen problemlos standhält. Auf der quadratischen Aufstellplatte aus Keramik lassen sich Farbumschläge im Medium besonders gut beobachten. Die Glasflächen im Gehäuseoberteil ermöglichen eine leichte Reinigung. Um an der Gerätefront Platz zu sparen, wurde das Display zwischen den ergonomischen Knöpfen positioniert, so lassen sich zudem die Knöpfe den angezeigten Werten eindeutig zuordnen.

Begründung der Jury
Der Magnetrührer C-MAG HS 7 überzeugt durch die durchdachte Materialwahl und eine übersichtliche Gestaltung, die saubere Arbeitsabläufe kommuniziert.

Omni
Digital Microscope and
Measurement System
Digitales Inspektions- und
Messmikroskop

Manufacturer
Ash Technologies Limited, Naas, Ireland
In-house design
Sean O'Neill, Martin Cahill
Design
Dolmen (Christopher Murphy, Lyndsey Bryce, Mark Murray), Dublin, Ireland
Web
www.ash-vision.com
www.dolmen.ie

The digital microscope and measurement system Omni is used for the quality inspection of small precision components. The robust digital camera with detachable lighting module can be connected between any standard screen and camera mount to magnify images up to 120 times. Thanks to its digital technology, the device is much smaller and lighter than microscopes with optical lenses, allowing it to be used directly at the production line. Its key design feature is the rotary control dial.

Statement by the jury
Omni has been inspired by the shape of optical microscopes. At the same time, its digital technology imbues the classic form with a new expression.

Das Inspektions- und Messmikroskop Omni wird für die Qualitätskontrolle kleiner Präzisionsteile verwendet. Die robuste Digitalkamera mit abnehmbarem Lichtmodul kann zwischen jedem Standardbildschirm und Kamerahalter angeschlossen werden, um Bilder auf das bis zu 120-Fache zu vergrößern. Durch die Digitaltechnologie ist das Gerät sehr viel kleiner und leichter als Mikroskope mit optischen Linsen, wodurch es direkt am Fließband eingesetzt werden kann. Gestalterisches Herzstück ist das Rotationskontrollrad.

Begründung der Jury
Omni ist inspiriert von der Gestalt optischer Mikroskope. Gleichzeitig lässt seine Digitaltechnik die klassische Form neu erscheinen.

Leica BLK360
Imaging Laser Scanner
Bildgebender Laserscanner

Manufacturer
Leica Geosystems AG,
Heerbrugg, Switzerland
Design
platinumdesign (Matthias Wieser),
Stuttgart, Germany
Web
www.leica-geosystems.com
www.platinumdesign.com

The Leica BLK360 imaging laser scanner produces high-definition 3D spherical images of its surroundings. The measuring range is 60 metres for 360-degree scans. The compact device is small, light and can be easily transported in a typical messenger bag. The scanner is operated via a single button and is specifically designed to work in conjuction with the iPad Pro. An app filters and records scan data in real time and exports it to many different applications.

Der bildgebende Laserscanner Leica BLK360 erstellt hochauflösende 3D-Panoramabilder seiner Umgebung. Die Messreichweite beträgt 60 Meter für 360-Grad-Scans. Das kompakte Gerät ist klein, leicht und passt in eine gewöhnliche Umhängetasche. Der Scanner wird über eine einzige Taste bedient und ist speziell für das iPad Pro ausgelegt. Eine App filtert und registriert die Scandaten in Echtzeit und macht sie für zahlreiche Anwendungen zugänglich.

Statement by the jury
The Leica BLK360 imaging laser scanner translates advanced technology into an extremely simple and stylish form that is consistently geared towards compactness.

Begründung der Jury
Der bildgebende Laserscanner Leica BLK360 überführt fortschrittliche Technik in eine denkbar einfache und stilvolle Form, die konsequent auf Kompaktheit ausgelegt ist.

xetto®
Innovative Transport and Loading System
Innovatives Beladekomfort-System

Manufacturer
HOERBIGER Automotive
Komfortsysteme GmbH,
Schongau, Germany

Design
Design Tech,
Ammerbuch, Germany

Web
www.hoerbiger.com
www.designtech.eu

reddot **award** 2017
best of the best

New approach

In many areas, heavy materials or components need to be loaded and unloaded with great effort to transport them to the right location. xetto was designed against the backdrop that this process traditionally requires several pieces of equipment such as a forklift and pallet truck. Implementing an innovative concept, this system reduces this to one piece of equipment. It only takes one person a few simple steps to load the transport and loading system along with the items being hauled – without exertion. The key component is a powerful system of microhydraulics and kinematics. The newly developed hydraulic unit makes high power density possible. The scissor system, electrical system and energy storage device have room in the smallest of spaces. To keep the system safely in place, it features a solid floor unit, which can be stored in the chassis for horizontal movements. In an impressive manner, lifting to a height of 80 cm takes only 20 seconds. The innovative principle also allows a variety of application variants for trade, business and industry. Following a fundamentally new approach, the design of xetto improves working conditions. The system eliminates the need for transhipping, which saves time and manpower, and it reduces the risk of accidents.

Neue Wege

In vielen Bereichen müssen schwere Materialien oder Bauteile mit großem Kraftaufwand verladen oder entladen werden, um sie an den richtigen Ort zu transportieren. xetto wurde vor dem Hintergrund gestaltet, dass für diesen Vorgang meist mehrere Geräte wie Stapler und Hubwagen gleichzeitig zum Einsatz kommen. Auf der Grundlage eines innovativen Konzepts ist damit der Einsatz nur eines Gerätes möglich. Das Transport- und Beladesystem lässt sich von einer einzelnen Person mit wenigen Handgriffen und ohne großen Kraftaufwand mit der Transportware verladen. Schlüsselkomponente ist ein leistungsstarkes System aus Mikro-Hydraulik und Kinematik. Das neu entwickelte Hydraulik-Aggregat ermöglicht eine hohe Leistungsdichte. Scherensystem, Elektrik und der Stromspeicher finden auf kleinstem Raum Platz. Für den sicheren Stand des Systems sorgt eine stabil gestaltete Bodengruppe, die zum horizontalen Bewegen im Chassis des Gerätes Platz findet. Auf beeindruckende Weise geschieht das Heben auf 80 cm Höhe in 20 Sekunden. Das innovative Prinzip ermöglicht zudem eine Vielzahl von Varianten des Einsatzes für Handwerk, Gewerbe und Industrie. Mit einem grundlegend neuen Ansatz verbessert die Gestaltung von xetto die Arbeitsbedingungen. Das System reduziert durch den Wegfall des Umladens den Zeitbedarf, den Personalaufwand sowie das Unfall- und Verletzungsrisiko.

Statement by the jury

The innovative transport and loading system xetto impresses with a design that has found a clever way to simplify the difficult task of the handling of heavy loads. The system's innovative, ergonomically well thought-out concept is an expression of user-oriented thinking. The system combines efficiency with a new kind of safety. Its design has been precisely adapted to the demands of users working with it on construction sites.

Begründung der Jury

Das innovative Beladekomfort-System xetto beeindruckt mit einer Gestaltung, die einen cleveren Weg gefunden hat, das Schwierige, nämlich den Umgang mit schweren Lasten, entscheidend zu vereinfachen. Sein innovatives, auch ergonomisch sehr gut durchdachtes Konzept ist Ausdruck eines nutzerorientierten Denkens. Das System vereint Effektivität mit einer neuen Art von Sicherheit. Seine Gestaltung wurde exakt den Ansprüchen derjenigen angepasst, die auf Baustellen mit ihm arbeiten.

Designer portrait
See page 48
Siehe Seite 48

SIMILAGO II
Roller Mill
Walzenmühle

Manufacturer
Alapala Makina, Çorum, Turkey
Design
Italdesign Giugiaro, Turin, Italy
Web
www.alapala.com
www.italdesign.it

The Similago II roller mill has been developed for the continuous and consistent milling of grain. The frame is made of high-quality carbon steel, with the bearings and grinding roll attached directly to the frame. This robust construction enables continuous use of the machine without a decrease in performance or reliability over time. In order to ensure continuous monitoring and control of the parameters, it features a touchscreen on both sides.

Statement by the jury
Thanks to its high-grade materials and precise finish, the Similago II exceeds the elevated quality standards of the food industry.

Die Walzenmühle Similago II ist für ein kontinuierliches und gleichmäßiges Mahlen von Getreide ausgelegt. Der Rahmen besteht aus hochwertigem Carbonstahl, die Lager und die Mahlwalzen sind direkt am Rahmen montiert. Diese robuste Bauweise ermöglicht den Dauereinsatz der Maschine, ohne dass sie mit der Zeit an Leistung oder Zuverlässigkeit einbüßt. Um eine kontinuierliche Überwachung und Steuerung der Parameter zu gewährleisten, befindet sich auf beiden Seiten je ein Touchscreen.

Begründung der Jury
Die Similago II wird durch ihre hochwertigen Materialien und präzise Verarbeitung den hohen Qualitätsansprüchen in der Lebensmittelindustrie mehr als gerecht.

TOS FRU
Machining Centre
Bearbeitungszentrum

Manufacturer
TOS Kuřim – OS, a.s., Brno, Czech Republic
Design
Martin Tvarůžek Design,
Brno, Czech Republic
Tomáš Klíma (External Design Engineer),
Brno, Czech Republic
Web
www.tos-kurim.cz
www.tvaruzekdesign.com
www.kkmetal.eu

The Tos Fru machining centre has been designed for the machining of complex workpieces such as steam turbines, marine engines and aircraft components. The gantry has been incorporated into the machining centre, enabling optimum use of the working space. The dark areas of the machine are made from fine-meshed expanded metal and contribute to motor cooling. The control room with lighting ramp is slightly raised and travels vertically to provide better visual control over the machining process.

Statement by the jury
The design of the Tos Fru looks open and accessible. The individual areas of this machining centre are characterised by visual clarity.

Das Bearbeitungszentrum Tos Fru ist für die Bearbeitung komplexer Werkstücke wie Dampfturbinen, Schiffsmotoren oder Flugzeugkomponenten ausgelegt. Das Portal ist in das Gantry-System integriert, dadurch wird die Arbeitsfläche optimal ausgenutzt. Die dunklen Maschinenbereiche sind aus feinmaschigem Streckmetall gefertigt und tragen zur Motorkühlung bei. Die Steuerkabine mit der Beleuchtungsrampe ist leicht erhöht und fährt vertikal, um eine bessere visuelle Kontrolle über die Prozesse zu haben.

Begründung der Jury
Die Architektur des Tos Fru wirkt offen und zugänglich. Die einzelnen Bereiche des Bearbeitungszentrums sind von optischer Klarheit geprägt.

MultiBloc® MBE
Multifunctional Gas Control
Gas-Mehrfachstellgerät

Manufacturer
Karl Dungs GmbH & Co. KG,
Urbach, Germany
Design
Design Tech, Ammerbuch, Germany
Web
www.dungs.com
www.designtech.eu

The multifunctional gas control MBE consists of a body and two step-motor drives. The functionally distinct step-motor drives provide great flexibility and intelligent controls. The individual components create a harmonious whole of die-cast body and translucent cover. The vertical fillets at the front turn into ribs at the back, which facilitate heat dissipation and give the multifunctional gas control a robust appearance.

Statement by the jury
The MBE is characterised by a sense of formal tension, resulting from a clear design structure combined with the components and body merging into one.

Das Gas-Mehrfachstellgerät MBE besteht aus einem Gehäuse und zwei Schrittmotorantrieben. Die funktional unterschiedlichen Schrittmotorantriebe ermöglichen eine große Flexibilität und intelligente Regelung. Die Einzelkomponenten bilden eine formale Einheit aus Druckgusskörper und lichtdurchlässiger Abdeckung. Frontseitig vertikal verlaufende Hohlkehlen gehen auf der Rückseite in die Verrippungen über, welche die Wärmeabfuhr unterstützen und dem Gas-Mehrfachstellgerät ein robustes Erscheinungsbild verleihen.

Begründung der Jury
Das MBE ist charakterisiert durch eine formale Spannung, die durch die klare Gliederung und gleichzeitige Verschmelzung der Bauteile mit dem Korpus hervorgerufen wird.

Oxyple
Oxygen Generator
Sauerstoffgenerator

Manufacturer
Juvair Co., Ltd., Seoul, South Korea
Design
BDCI (Seomin Lee), Seoul, South Korea
Web
www.juvair.com
www.bdci.co.kr

The Oxyple oxygen generator creates oxygen with high purity as used, for instance, in medical applications or fish farming. Due to its modular design, the system can be expanded with further modules according to the desired capacities and specific applications. In addition, it can be delivered in a disassembled condition to allow assembly on site. The client may thus freely choose the location in which to install the generator.

Statement by the jury
The Oxyple provides great flexibility with regard to configuration and use. The modules are distinctly characterised by a rounded roof.

Der Sauerstoffgenerator Oxyple erzeugt Sauerstoff in hoher Reinheit, wie er z. B. in der Medizin oder in der Fischzucht verwendet wird. Aufgrund seines modularen Aufbaus kann das System entsprechend der gewünschten Kapazitäten und spezifischen Anwendungen um weitere Module ergänzt werden. Zudem lässt es sich im auseinandergebauten Zustand ausliefern, um dann vor Ort montiert zu werden. Der Kunde kann den Standort des Generators dementsprechend frei wählen.

Begründung der Jury
Der Oxyple bietet großartige Flexibilität in der Konfiguration und Nutzung. Die Module sind auf prägnante Weise durch ein abgerundetes Dach charakterisiert.

Sensepoint XCL
Gas Detector

Manufacturer
Honeywell, Bracknell, Great Britain
In-house design
Honeywell Design Team
Design
Design Partners, Bray, Ireland
Web
www.honeywell.com
www.designpartners.com

The intelligent gas detector Sensepoint XLC detects dangerous concentrations of toxic gases such as carbon monoxide, ammonia or methane in the surrounding air. It is used in places such as boiler rooms or underground car parks. The product development focused on an optimised user experience, from simple installation on the wall to mobile control. The detector connects via Bluetooth to a smartphone, where an app enables time- and cost-saving initial start-up, maintenance and management by a single person.

Der intelligente Gasdetektor Sensepoint XCL erkennt eine gefährliche Konzentration von toxischen Gasen wie Kohlenmonoxid, Ammoniak oder Methan in der Umgebungsluft. Er wird beispielsweise in Heizkellern oder Tiefgaragen verwendet. Bei der Geräteentwicklung stand eine optimierte Benutzererfahrung im Fokus – von der einfachen Wandmontage bis hin zur mobilen Steuerung. Der Detektor wird via Bluetooth mit einem Smartphone verbunden. Eine App ermöglicht die zeit- und kostensparende Inbetriebnahme, Wartung und Verwaltung durch eine einzige Person.

Statement by the jury
Operating the Sensepoint XCL via smartphone is not only easy but also makes buttons and keys unnecessary, thus creating an appealing, minimalist design.

Begründung der Jury
Die Bedienung des Sensepoint XCL via Smartphone ist nicht nur sehr einfach, sondern macht auch Knöpfe und Tasten überflüssig, sodass ein ansprechend minimalistisches Design entsteht.

Sensepoint XRL Industrial
Gas Detector

Manufacturer
Honeywell, Bracknell, Great Britain
In-house design
Honeywell Design Team
Design
Design Partners, Bray, Ireland
Web
www.honeywell.com
www.designpartners.com

The intelligent gas detector Sensepoint XRL Industrial protects staff and goods in explosion-prone environments such as manufacturing, storage and production facilities. The device meets international safety standards and is explosion-proof. It is controlled wirelessly via a smartphone app, allowing a single user to manage the detector without requiring monitoring by another person in a control room. Moreover, the app simplifies the creation of system reports, which are necessary in order to meet legal regulations.

Der intelligente Gasdetektor Sensepoint XRL Industrial dient dazu, Personen und Güter in explosionsgefährdeten Umgebungen wie Fertigungs-, Lager- und Produktionsanlagen zu schützen. Das Gerät erfüllt die internationalen Sicherheitsstandards und ist explosionsgeschützt. Es wird kabellos über eine Smartphone-App bedient, so kann ein einziger Anwender den Detektor verwalten, ohne dass eine weitere Person in einem Kontrollraum erforderlich ist. Zudem vereinfacht die App die Erstellung von Systemberichten, die für die Einhaltung gesetzlicher Vorschriften notwendig sind.

Statement by the jury
The Sensepoint XRL Industrial is a highly modern system visually as well as technologically. The robust housing is ideally suited for a demanding industrial environment.

Begründung der Jury
Der Sensepoint XRL Industrial ist ein visuell wie technologisch hochmodernes System. Mit seinem robusten Gehäuse ist es prädestiniert für ein anspruchsvolles Industrieumfeld.

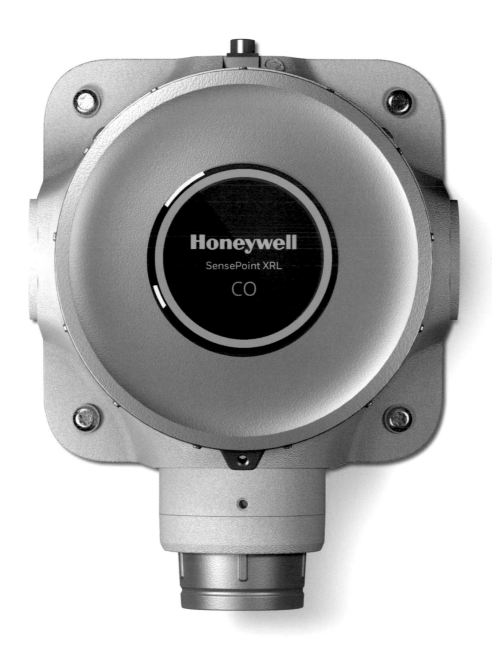

Amtrol-Alfa High Pressure CoMet Cylinder
Amtrol-Alfa Hochdruck-CoMet Zylinder

Manufacturer
Amtrol-Alfa S.A., Guimarães, Portugal
In-house design
Design
Escritório de Design (Prof. Carlos Aguiar), Arouca, Portugal
Web
www.amtrol-alfa.com
www.escritorio-de-design.blogspot.pt

The Amtrol-Alfa High Pressure CoMet Cylinder for industrial gases represents a lightweight, user-friendly design, achieving a new level of mobility and universal use. It has a fully dismountable body made of high-density polyethylene that is equipped with a carbon-fibre-reinforced steel liner, internal foam shock absorbers and heavy-duty wheels. The highly positioned wide front handle allows improved ergonomics and ease of use.

Statement by the jury
Thanks to its sophisticated structural qualities and the special materials employed, the Amtrol-Alfa High Pressure CoMet Cylinder achieves excellent mobility and ergonomics.

Der Amtrol-Alfa Hochdruck-CoMet Zylinder für Industriegase zeichnet sich durch ein leichtes, bedienerfreundliches Design aus, das einen neuen Grad an Mobilität und universelle Einsatzmöglichkeiten bietet. Er verfügt über einen vollständig demontierbaren Korpus aus hochdichtem Polyethylen, der mit einem carbonfaserverstärkten Stahleinsatz, innen liegenden Stoßdämpfern aus Schaumstoff sowie Schwerlasträdern ausgestattet ist. Der hoch positionierte, breite Griff sorgt für eine bessere Ergonomie und Bedienbarkeit.

Begründung der Jury
Dank seiner ausgereiften baulichen Eigenschaften und des besonderen Materials erreicht der Amtrol-Alfa Hochdruck-CoMet Zylinder eine hervorragende Mobilität und Ergonomie.

SUN2000
Photovoltaic Inverter
Photovoltaik-Wechselrichter

Manufacturer
Huawei Technologies Co., Ltd., Shenzhen, China
In-house design
Yu Guan
Design
No Picnic AB (Kenny Wong, Mikael Edoff), Stockholm, Sweden
Web
www.huawei.com
www.nopicnic.com

The Sun2000 photovoltaic inverter converts the direct current produced in photovoltaic cells into grid-compliant alternating current. The horizontal layout improves heat dissipation. All inductors, connectors and screws have been concealed behind the aluminium housing, thus creating a surface without visual interruptions. The inverter is IP65-certified and thus well equipped for all weather conditions. Several handles simplify both transport and assembly.

Statement by the jury
The Sun2000 inverter is characterised by its premium look, which is the result of the seamless surfaces and the elegant frame.

Der Wechselrichter Sun2000 wandelt den in Photovoltaikzellen erzeugten Gleichstrom in netzkonformen Wechselstrom um. Der horizontal ausgerichtete Korpus verbessert die Wärmeableitung. Alle Induktoren, Steckverbindungen und Schrauben liegen hinter dem Gehäuse aus Aluminium verborgen, sodass eine Fläche ohne optische Unterbrechungen geschaffen wurde. Der Wechselrichter erfüllt die Schutzklasse IP65 und ist damit für alle Wetterbedingungen gerüstet. Mehrere Griffe vereinfachen den Transport und die Montage.

Begründung der Jury
Der Wechselrichter Sun2000 zeichnet sich durch eine besonders hochwertige Optik aus, die durch die nahtlose Beschaffenheit der Flächen und den eleganten Rahmen erzielt wird.

V1000MMD
Frequency Inverter
Frequenzumrichter

Manufacturer
Yaskawa Europe GmbH, Eschborn, Germany
In-house design
John Colreavey
Design
Christian Bunse, Hagen, Germany
Web
www.yaskawa.eu.com

The V1000MMD frequency inverter can be mounted onto a motor or installed in a horizontal or vertical position independently of the drive. In order to ensure optimum usability, the operating areas are located on top of the housing. The circular signal indicates the diverse operating conditions, clearly visible even from a distance. Identical connectors on the lateral surfaces further increase installation flexibility.

Statement by the jury
The frequency inverter impresses with its distinctively curved silhouette. All elements are perfectly matched to one another in regard to function and design.

Der Frequenzumrichter V1000MMD kann auf einen Motor montiert oder – räumlich unabhängig vom Antrieb – in horizontaler oder vertikaler Lage eingebaut werden. Um eine optimale Bedienbarkeit unabhängig von der Einbaulage zu gewährleisten, sind die Bedienflächen auf der Oberseite angeordnet. Das ringförmige Signal zeigt auch aus der Entfernung gut sichtbar unterschiedliche Betriebszustände an. Die identischen Anschlussfelder auf den Seitenflächen erhöhen zusätzlich die Flexibilität beim Einbau.

Begründung der Jury
Der Frequenzumrichter besticht durch seine prägnant gebogene Silhouette. Alle Elemente sind funktional und gestalterisch hervorragend aufeinander abgestimmt.

Synconta 900
Wastewater Lifting Station
Abwasserfertigschacht

Manufacturer
Sulzer, Wexford, Ireland
In-house design
Ben Breen, Michael Burke, Otto Genz,
Barry McDonald
Design
Dolmen (Martin Bruggemann, Colin Conlon),
Dublin, Ireland
Web
www.sulzer.com
www.dolmen.ie

The Synconta 900 is made of high-
quality synthetics and has been designed
for installation below ground. Its purpose is to dispose of wastewater and
sewage that has accumulated below
the backflow level. The pumps are pre-
assembled outside the tank and then
lowered into the chamber once the tank
has been positioned in the ground.
The technician in charge of installation
and maintenance does not have to
climb inside the tank, which especially
increases safety.

Statement by the jury
The Synconta 900 wastewater lifting
station is a clever solution requiring
minimal installation effort. The material
is highly corrosion-resistant.

Der Synconta 900 aus hochwertigem
Synthetik ist für die Installation im Boden
vorgesehen. Sein Zweck besteht in der
Schmutz- und Abwasserentsorgung aus
Räumen unterhalb der Rückstauebene.
Die Pumpen werden außerhalb des Tanks
vorinstalliert und in die Kammer abge-
senkt, sobald der Tank in den Boden eingelassen wurde. Der für die Installation und
Wartung zuständige Arbeiter muss nicht in
den Tank steigen, was sich vor allem positiv
auf die Sicherheit auswirkt.

Begründung der Jury
Der Abwasserfertigschacht Synconta 900
stellt eine clevere Lösung mit geringem
Installationsaufwand dar. Das Material ist
überaus korrosionsbeständig.

ServoLine
Press Line
Pressenlinie

Manufacturer
Schuler AG, Göppingen, Germany
Design
TEAMS Design, Esslingen, Germany
Web
www.schulergroup.com
www.teamsdesign.com

The ServoLine press line is characterised by a high output of 16 to 23 strokes per minute. The fully automated exchange of die and tooling enables quick product changes. The modularly designed system can be flexibly adapted to individual production requirements. The dark outside edges are the key design element, bordering the lighter, central area like a frame and lending the press line a high-quality and compact appearance. This impression is further enhanced by the circumferential horizontal line in the blue colour so typical of the brand.

Die Pressenlinie ServoLine zeichnet sich durch eine hohe Ausbringungsleistung von 16 bis 23 Hüben pro Minute aus. Der vollautomatische Wechsel von Pressformen und Werkzeugen ermöglicht kurzfristige Produktwechsel. Die modular aufgebaute Anlage kann flexibel an den jeweiligen Produktionsbedarf angepasst werden. Das Hauptgestaltungselement bilden die dunklen Außenkanten, die den helleren zentralen Bereich wie ein Rahmen einfassen, was die Pressenlinie kompakt und hochwertig erscheinen lässt. Dieser Eindruck wird durch die umlaufende horizontale Linie im markentypischen Blau verstärkt.

Statement by the jury
The orthogonal silhouette of the ServoLine is highly effectively highlighted by the dark borders and distinct lines.

Begründung der Jury
Die orthogonale Silhouette der ServoLine wird durch die dunklen Einrahmungen und die prägnanten Linien äußerst wirkungsvoll in Szene gesetzt.

HB400
Wire Electrical Discharge Machine
Drahterodiermaschine

Manufacturer
Suzhou Sanguang Science & Technology Co.,
Ltd., Suzhou, China
Design
Dongzhi Industrial Design Co., Ltd.
(Yue Jiao, Zonghui Zhang, Dongyang Lu),
Beijing, China
Web
www.ssgedm.com
www.dzdesign.com.cn

The HB400 wire electrical discharge machine cuts all kinds of metal. Its electrode is a thin wire with which complex shapes can be realised even when processing the hardest types of steel, for instance in components for aviation, aerospace, medical technology and the automotive industry. The machine's language of form is reduced to simple lines. The design does without any decorative elements in order to visualise the precision and efficiency of the machine.

Statement by the jury
The HB400 wire electrical discharge machine features a monolithic design. The very slender substructure gives rise to an impression of floating.

Die Drahterodiermaschine HB400 schneidet alle Arten von Metall. Als Bearbeitungselektrode dient ein dünner Draht, mit dem sich komplexe Geometrien realisieren lassen, selbst wenn härteste Stähle bearbeitet werden, z. B. bei Bauteilen für die Luft- und Raumfahrt, Medizintechnik oder Automobilindustrie. Die Formensprache der Maschine ist auf einfache Linien reduziert. Auf dekorative Gestaltungselemente wurde bewusst verzichtet, um die Präzision und Effizienz der Maschine zu visualisieren.

Begründung der Jury
Die Drahterodiermaschine HB400 imponiert durch ihre monolithische Bauweise. Aufgrund der schmaleren Unterkonstruktion wirkt sie so, als würde sie schweben.

E line
Single-Spindle Honing Machine
Einspindel-Honmaschine

Manufacturer
Kadia Produktion GmbH + Co., Nürtingen,
Germany
Design
Design Tech, Ammerbuch, Germany
Web
www.kadia.de
www.designtech.eu

The E line single-spindle honing machine is suitable for prototype building and small series production. Thanks to the intelligently placed maintenance openings, it can be positioned close to a wall, thus requiring little space. Generous access to the machining area, offset in dark colours, and the reduction to basic elements of form are among the design aspects characteristic of the company. The tidy design language conveys the machine's high-precision standards.

Statement by the jury
With its convex form, the honing machine appears particularly generous and very user-friendly. At the same time, it features impressive compactness.

Die Einspindel-Honmaschine E line eignet sich für den Musterbau und die Kleinserienfertigung. Die durchdacht platzierten Wartungsöffnungen ermöglichen eine wandnahe Aufstellung der Maschine, sodass sie nur wenig Platz in Anspruch nimmt. Die großzügigen, dunkel abgesetzten Zugangsbereiche zum Bearbeitungsraum und die Reduktion auf einfache Grundformen gehören zu den unternehmenstypischen Gestaltungsmerkmalen. Die aufgeräumte Formensprache vermittelt den Präzisionsanspruch der Maschine.

Begründung der Jury
Die Honmaschine mutet durch ihre vorgewölbte Form ausgesprochen großzügig und überaus benutzerfreundlich an. Gleichzeitig beeindruckt sie durch ihre Kompaktheit.

Briquetting Machine
Brikettiermaschine

Manufacturer
Beijing Aoke Ruifeng Energy-saving
Technology Co., Ltd., Beijing, China
Design
Beijing Top Industrial Design Co., Ltd.,
Beijing, China
Web
www.akrfjn.com
www.designt.cn

The briquetting machine compresses straw from wheat, corn and other crops into fuel briquettes. Crop material that would usually be classified as waste can thus be used as a CO_2-neutral energy source for heat and electricity generation and replace non-renewable fossil fuels such as coal. The machine's low centre of gravity compensates for vibrations as well as any noise caused in the process. Moreover, the machine guarantees high production security and operator safety.

Statement by the jury
This briquetting machine makes an important contribution to sustainable energy generation and displays a substantial throughput rate.

Die Brikettiermaschine presst Stroh aus Weizen, Getreide und anderen Nutzpflanzen zu Brennstoffbriketts. Pflanzenmaterial, das sonst Abfall darstellt, kann dadurch als CO_2-neutraler Energieträger für die Wärme- und Stromerzeugung verwertet werden und endliche fossile Brennstoffe wie Kohle ersetzen. Der niedrige Schwerpunkt der Maschine kompensiert Schwingungen und Vibrationslärm. Darüber hinaus gewährleistet die Anlage einen hohen Produktions- und Personenschutz.

Begründung der Jury
Die Brikettiermaschine leistet einen wichtigen Beitrag zur nachhaltigen Energiegewinnung und zeigt eine beträchtliche Durchsatzleistung.

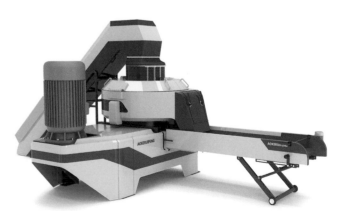

8 Series
Serie 8
Mobile Air Compressors
Fahrbare Druckluftkompressoren

Manufacturer
Atlas Copco, Antwerp, Belgium
In-house design
Web
www.atlascopco.com

The mobile air compressors of the 8 Series all weigh less than 750 kg. This allows them to be towed by a normal passenger car, without needing a special driving licence. The canopy consists of a non-corrosive polyethylene "HardHat" and withstands the harshest conditions. All of the compressors consume, on average, 12 per cent less fuel than comparable models. They are simple and quick to service: all components are easily accessible and the filters are threaded for simple connection.

Die Druckluftkompressoren der Serie 8 wiegen alle unter 750 kg. Deshalb können sie ohne besonderen Führerschein als Anhänger von einem normalen Pkw transportiert werden. Die Haube besteht aus einem „HardHat" aus korrosionsfreiem Polyethylen und widersteht selbst härtesten Bedingungen. Alle Kompressoren der Serie verbrauchen durchschnittlich 12 Prozent weniger Kraftstoff als vergleichbare Modelle. Ihre Wartung ist problemlos, da sämtliche Teile leicht zugänglich sind und die Filterung ein einfaches Aufschraubsystem nutzt.

Statement by the jury
The powerful 8 Series air compressors captivate with their lightweight design, allowing them to be used in many different contexts.

Begründung der Jury
Die leistungsstarken Druckluftkompressoren der Serie 8 begeistern durch ihre Leichtbauweise, dank derer sie in vielen Bereichen angewendet werden können.

RM 120GO!
Mobile Impact Crusher
Mobiler Prallbrecher

Manufacturer
RUBBLE MASTER HMH GmbH, Linz, Austria
In-house design
Heinz Jank
Design
Freiform (Karl Norbert Grasberger),
Salzburg, Austria
Web
www.rubblemaster.com
www.freiform.at

The mobile impact crusher RM 120GO! crushes construction and demolition waste, asphalt, concrete and natural stone. Its compact external dimensions enable easy transport even in urban areas. Weighing in at only 35 tonnes while producing an output of up to 350 tonnes per hour, the machine is the most compact impact crusher of its kind. A diesel-electric drive concept enables the direct drive of the crusher. High efficiency is achieved through optimised crusher geometry. The drive and crush functions are operated securely via remote control.

Der mobile Prallbrecher RM 120GO! bricht Bauschutt, Asphalt, Beton sowie Naturstein. Seine kompakten Außendimensionen ermöglichen einen einfachen Transport auch im städtischen Raum. Mit einer Durchsatzleistung von bis zu 350 Tonnen pro Stunde und einem Gesamtgewicht von nur 35 Tonnen ist die Maschine der kompakteste Prallbrecher seiner Baugröße. Durch ein diesel-elektrisches Antriebskonzept wird ein Direktantrieb ermöglicht. Eine optimierte Brechgeometrie sorgt für hohe Effizienz. Der Fahr- und Brechbetrieb wird mittels Funkfernbedienung sicher gesteuert.

Statement by the jury
The crusher RM 120GO! impresses with its balanced proportions and dynamic lines, which effectively highlight its mobility.

Begründung der Jury
Der Prallbrecher RM 120GO! beeindruckt durch seine ausgewogenen Proportionen und dynamische Linienführung, die seine Mobilität wirkungsvoll unterstreicht.

VRS 30
Friction Welding Machine
Reibschweißmaschine

Manufacturer
KUKA Industries GmbH, Augsburg, Germany
In-house design
Michael Büchler, Otmar Fischer
Web
www.kuka.com

The VRS 30 vertical friction welding machine is characterised by a large machining room paired with a small footprint. The large maintenance doors and the platform installed at half height make it easy to reach the hydraulic control block and main drive. Thanks to the sophisticated hydraulic-numerical process axis and the wide speed-load range, the machine is suitable for a wide spectrum of welding applications. Operation is intuitive and large-scale status lights indicate the respective operating status.

Die vertikale Rotationsreibschweißmaschine VRS 30 zeichnet sich durch einen großzügigen Arbeitsraum bei sehr geringer Standfläche aus. Die großen Wartungstüren und eine auf halber Höhe angebrachte Plattform ermöglichen ein unproblematisches Erreichen des hydraulischen Steuerblocks und Hauptantriebs. Dank der ausgeklügelten hydraulisch-numerischen Prozessachse und des großen Drehzahl-Last-Bereichs ist die Maschine für vielfältige Schweißbereiche geeignet. Die Bedienung erfolgt intuitiv, großflächige Statusleuchten zeigen den jeweiligen Betriebszustand an.

Statement by the jury
The VRS 30 friction welding machine fascinates with its unusual vertical orientation, which takes up little space while providing excellent accessibility.

Begründung der Jury
Die Reibschweißmaschine VRS 30 fasziniert durch ihre ungewöhnliche vertikale Ausrichtung. Diese nimmt wenig Raum ein und bietet ausgezeichnete Zugänglichkeit.

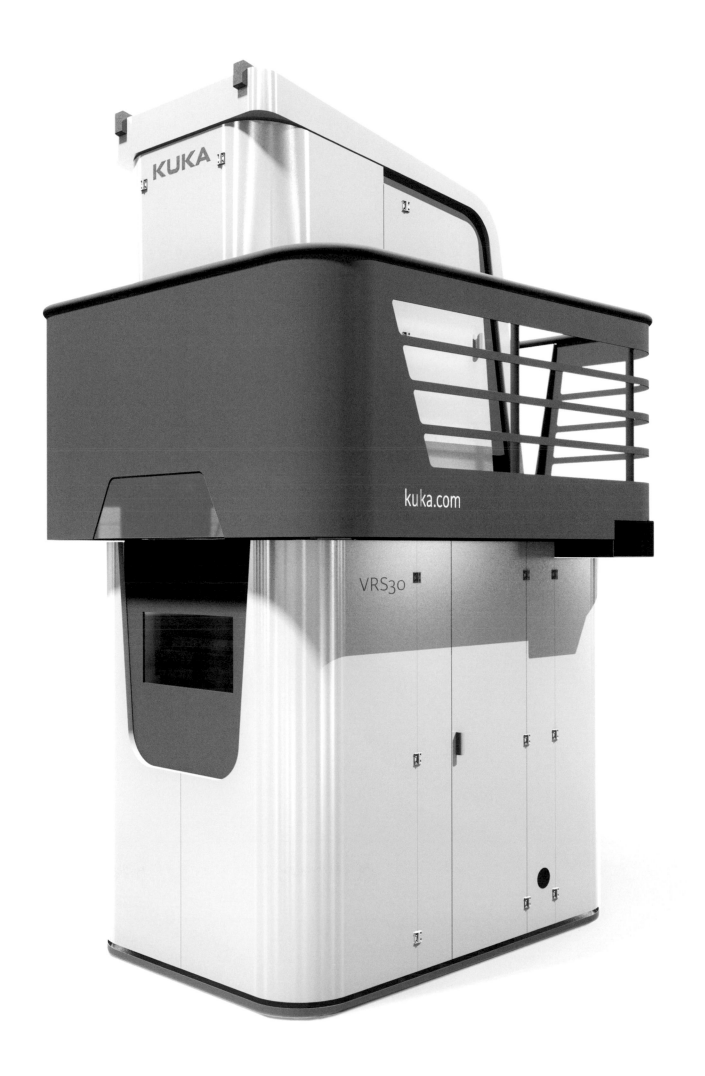

FL3015 Fiber
Laser Cutting Machine
Laserschneidmaschine

Manufacturer
HK Co., Ltd., Hwaseong, South Korea
In-house design
Hyeonjoo Lee, Eunhye Oh
Web
www.hk-global.com

The FL3015 Fiber is a high-performance laser cutting machine with a long cutting bridge. The wide-opening door enables convenient loading of the machine with raw materials. Processing can be monitored continuously through the window. The large, rounded edges of the machine create a friendly work environment. In conjunction with the design, the company logo and the signal lamp communicate a strong brand identity.

Statement by the jury
The highly productive FL3015 Fiber laser cutting machine impresses with incisive colour contrasts and distinctive lines, thus presenting an attractive appearance on the plant floor.

Die FL3015 Fiber ist eine Hochleistungs-Laserschneidmaschine mit einer langen Schneidebrücke. Dank der weit zu öffnenden Tür lässt sich die Maschine komfortabel mit dem Rohmaterial beladen. Über das Fenster kann der Bearbeitungsvorgang permanent überwacht werden. Die großen abgerundeten Kanten der Maschine schaffen eine freundliche Arbeitsumgebung. Firmenlogo und Signallampe ergeben zusammen mit der Bauform eine ausdrucksstarke Markenidentität.

Begründung der Jury
Die leistungsstarke Laserschneidmaschine FL3015 Fiber besticht durch prägnante Farbkontraste und markante Linien, die in der Maschinenhalle einen reizvollen Anblick bieten.

PS3015 Fiber
Laser Cutting Machine
Laserschneidmaschine

Manufacturer
HK Co., Ltd., Hwaseong, South Korea
In-house design
Hyeonjoo Lee, Bokeum Choi
Web
www.hk-global.com

The PS3015 Fiber high-speed laser cutting machine features a short cutting bridge that enables it to freely process hard materials like mild steel and stainless steel. The integrated database for all cutting parameters ensures precise results and non-contact cutting makes post-processing unnecessary. The folding door is easy to open with just one hand. The machine is encompassed by a dark frame structure, giving it a powerful and sturdy appearance.

Statement by the jury
Its self-contained design gives the PS3015 Fiber laser cutting machine a harmonious homogeneity, which at the same time communicates safe processes.

Die Hochgeschwindigkeits-Laserschneidmaschine PS3015 Fiber mit einer kurzen Schneidebrücke ermöglicht es, harte Materialien wie Baustahl und Edelstahl frei zu bearbeiten. Die integrierte Datenbank für alle Laserschneidparameter ermöglicht präzise Ergebnisse und das berührungslose Schneiden macht eine Nachbearbeitung unnötig. Die Flügeltür ist leicht mit einer Hand zu öffnen. Als Einfassung dient eine dunkle Rahmenkonstruktion, die der Maschine ein kraftvolles und stabiles Erscheinungsbild verleiht.

Begründung der Jury
Die Laserschneidmaschine PS3015 Fiber zeigt durch ihre in sich geschlossene Architektur eine harmonische Einheitlichkeit, die zugleich sichere Abläufe kommuniziert.

Highcon Beam
Digital Cutting and Creasing Machine
Digitale Schneide- und Rillmaschine

Manufacturer
Highcon Systems Ltd., Yavne, Israel
Design
Taga Innovations Ltd (Yaniv Adir), Tel Aviv, Israel
Web
www.highcon.net
www.tagapro.com

The Highcon Beam is a digital cutting and creasing machine for packaging converters and printers. The machine delivers improved responsiveness, design flexibility and the ability to perform a wide range of applications in-house. It replaces the expensive and slow conventional die-making and setup process with digital technology. The machine is suited to a variety of substrates and processes up to 5,000 sheets per hour.

Statement by the jury
Its successful combination of open and closed areas in conjunction with colour contrasts gives the Highcon Beam a clear structure.

Die Highcon Beam ist eine digitale Schneide- und Rillmaschine für Kartonverarbeitungsbetriebe und Druckereien. Die Maschine bietet eine verbesserte Reaktionsfähigkeit, mehr Flexibilität beim Design und die Möglichkeit, eine große Bandbreite an Anwendungen im eigenen Haus durchzuführen. Sie ersetzt den teuren und langsamen konventionellen Stanz- und Einrichtungsprozess durch digitale Technologie. Die Maschine eignet sich für eine Vielzahl von Substraten und Prozessen bis zu 5.000 Bogen pro Stunde.

Begründung der Jury
Ein gelungenes Zusammenspiel aus offenen und geschlossenen Bereichen in Verbindung mit Farbkontrasten sorgt bei der Highcon Beam für eine klare Struktur.

CDI Crystal 5080 XPS
Machine for the Production of Flexo Printing Plates
Anlage zur Herstellung von Flexodruckplatten

Manufacturer
Esko-Graphics Imaging GmbH,
Itzehoe, Germany
Design
designship (Thomas Starczewski),
Ulm, Germany
Web
www.esko.com
www.designship.de

The CDI Crystal 5080 XPS renders the image to be printed with a computer-controlled laser onto a flexo printing plate made of polymer, which functions as a printing plate. The machine combines digital imaging and UV platesetting in one device. Glass surfaces reduce the volume of the machine. The front purposely tilts towards the operator in order to enable ergonomic use.

Statement by the jury
In the CDI Crystal 5080 XPS combination machine, imagers and platesetters are cleanly separated and at the same time combined harmoniously in a visually appealing way.

Die Anlage CDI Crystal 5080 XPS überträgt das zu druckende Bild computergesteuert mit einem Laser auf eine Flexodruckplatte aus Polymer, die die Funktion einer Druckplatte erfüllt. Die Anlage kombiniert die digitale Bebilderung und UV-Belichtung in einem Gerät. Glasflächen lockern das Volumen des Korpus optisch auf, die Front ist dem Bediener bewusst zugeneigt, um ein ergonomisches Arbeiten zu ermöglichen.

Begründung der Jury
In der Kombinationsanlage CDI Crystal 5080 XPS sind Bebilderer und Belichter auf optisch ansprechende Weise sauber voneinander getrennt und zugleich harmonisch vereint.

NP800
Industrial Paper Scanner
Industrieller Papierscanner

Manufacturer
ABB, Dundalk, Ireland
In-house design
Cormac Doyle, Donal Sheridan,
Finian Moore
Design
Dolmen (Martin Bruggemann,
Colin Conlon, Steve King),
Dublin, Ireland
Web
www.abb.com
www.dolmen.ie

NP800 is a high-performance platform for scanning small to mid-size paper with a maximum width of 6.2 metres. All system electronics and moving parts are fully integrated into the end columns and thus safely and easily accessible for maintenance work. The robust nature of the A-beam construction provides reliable vertical, horizontal and torsional rigidity. This is essential for the precise alignment of the sensor source and detector heads.

Statement by the jury
Thanks to its minimalist design language and straight lines, the NP800 paper scanner impressively conveys efficiency and strength.

NP800 ist eine Hochleistungsplattform für das Scannen von kleinem bis mittelgroßem Papier mit einer maximalen Breite von 6,2 Metern. Die Systemelektronik und beweglichen Teile sind vollständig in die beiden Vor-Kopf-Säulen integriert und dadurch für Wartungsarbeiten sicher und einfach zugänglich. Die robuste Ausführung der A-Träger-Konstruktion bietet eine zuverlässige Vertikal-, Horizontal- und Torsionssteifigkeit. Dies ist entscheidend für die genaue Ausrichtung der Sensorquelle und der Detektorköpfe.

Begründung der Jury
Durch seine reduzierte, geradlinige Formensprache kommuniziert der Papierscanner NP800 auf eindrucksvolle Weise Leistung und Stärke.

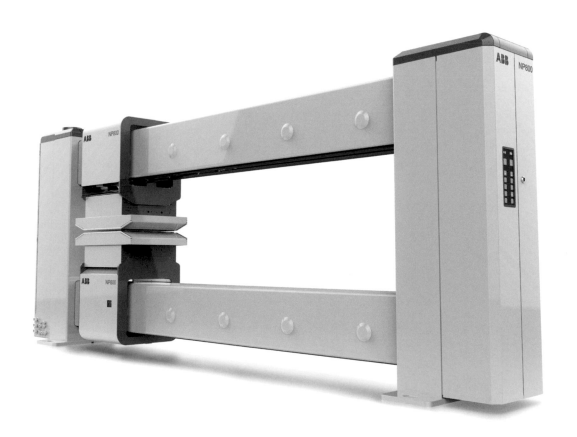

profiRounder
Deburring and Edge-Rounding Machine
Entgrat- und Kantenverrundungsanlage

Manufacturer
Karl Heesemann Maschinenfabrik GmbH & Co. KG, Bad Oeynhausen, Germany
Design
Oliver Stenzel Designfit, Ruppertsberg, Germany
Web
www.heesemann.de
www.designfit.de

The front and back of the profiRounder deburring and edge-rounding machine form a simplified H, which is both a characteristic element of the brand and a structuring formal element of the design. The controls, the mounting for the operating terminal and the workpiece infeed are integrated into the recessed areas of the H shape. The transparent front directs the focus to the interior with up to eight units. The modular character is supported by the specific unit icons on the glass doors, which at the same time conceal the feed mechanism.

Statement by the jury
Its closed form lends the profiRounder a consistent overall impression. The glass doors provide fascinating insight into the machining area.

Bei der Entgrat- und Kantenverrundungsanlage profiRounder bilden Vorder- und Rückseite ein vereinfachtes H, das sowohl ein Merkmal der Marke als auch strukturierendes Formelement darstellt. Die Bedienelemente, die Befestigung für das Bedienpanel und die Werkstückeinführung sind in die vertieften Bereiche der H-Form integriert. Die transparente Front lenkt den Fokus auf den Innenraum mit bis zu acht Aggregaten. Der modulare Charakter wird durch die spezifischen Aggregate-Icons an den Glastüren unterstützt, die gleichzeitig die Vorschubmechanik verbergen.

Begründung der Jury
Die profiRounder erzeugt durch ihre geschlossene Form ein stimmiges Gesamtbild. Die Glastüren ermöglichen faszinierende Einblicke in den Arbeitsbereich.

NetEngine9000
Industrial Router Series
Industrierouter-Serie

Manufacturer
Huawei Technologies Co., Ltd., Shenzhen, China
In-house design
Jules Parmentier, Zhongshu Hu
Web
www.huawei.com

The NetEngine9000 industrial router series features data-transfer rates of up to 160 TB/s. The air ventilation intakes at the front provide efficient airflow to cool the high-performance routers. User-friendly cable management is provided by flexible hooks, which allow users to quickly snap the fibre lines into the cable management channels. The amount of materials used has been strongly reduced as compared to previous models by replacing fixed with removable components.

Statement by the jury
The industrial router series NetEngine9000 impresses with its energy- and resource-saving design. The clear design language exudes reliability and efficiency.

Die Industrierouter-Serie NetEngine9000 arbeitet mit Datendurchsätzen von bis zu 160 TB/s. Die Lüftungsgitter auf der Frontseite sorgen für eine effiziente Luftströmung, um die Hochleistungsrouter zu kühlen. Das benutzerfreundliche Kabelmanagement besteht aus flexiblen Haken. Diese ermöglichen es, die Glasfaserleitungen schnell und sicher in die Kabelkanäle einzuklinken. Indem fixe durch abnehmbare Teile ersetzt wurden, konnte der Materialverbrauch im Vergleich zu den Vorgängermodellen stark reduziert werden.

Begründung der Jury
Die Industrierouter-Serie NetEngine9000 beeindruckt durch ihre energie- und ressourcensparende Gestaltung. Die klare Formensprache strahlt Zuverlässigkeit und Effizienz aus.

BH-1
Supervisory Device
Überwachungsgerät

Manufacturer
Azbil Corporation, Fujisawa City,
Kanagawa, Japan
In-house design
Hiroshi Koga
Web
www.azbil.com

The BH-1 supervisory device manages large quantities of information and facilitates data transfer to client PCs for effective building management. The clearly structured user interface provides a quick overview of the settings and possible error messages. The display is easy to read, even in adverse lighting conditions. The self-contained design conceals the electronics so that the user can focus on the status display without any distractions.

Statement by the jury
The BH-1 supervisory device features an extremely sophisticated design that instils trust in users and intuitively guides them in its use.

Das Überwachungsgerät BH-1 verwaltet große Informationsmengen und erleichtert die Datenübertragung auf Client-PCs für ein effektives Gebäudemanagement. Die klar gegliederte Bedienoberfläche gibt einen schnellen Überblick über die Einstellungen und mögliche Fehlermeldungen. Das Display ist auch bei schlechten Lichtverhältnissen gut lesbar. Die geschlossene Konstruktion verbirgt die Elektronik, sodass der Anwender sich ohne Ablenkungen auf die Statusanzeige konzentrieren kann.

Begründung der Jury
Das Überwachungsgerät BH-1 bietet eine hervorragend durchdachte Gestaltung, die Vertrauen zum Anwender schafft und ihn intuitiv bei der Bedienung anleitet.

WJ-1, RJ-1
Digital Controllers
Digitale Steuergeräte

Manufacturer
Azbil Corporation, Fujisawa City,
Kanagawa, Japan
In-house design
Hiroshi Koga
Web
www.azbil.com

The WJ-1 is a digital controller for building facilities such as heating, ventilation and air conditioning. It has a long lifespan and keeps energy consumption at a low level in buildings without regular maintenance. The controller can be expanded with the module RJ-1 in order to control several units simultaneously. The built-in NFC chip enables connection with a smartphone to easily manage data and reduce time spent on installation and troubleshooting on site.

Statement by the jury
The surface design of the controllers in matt grey and glossy black lends a premium elegance to their technical appearance.

Der WJ-1 ist ein digitales Steuergerät für Gebäudeanlagen wie Heiz-, Lüft- und Klimaräume. Es hat eine lange Lebensdauer und hält in Gebäuden, die nicht regelmäßig gewartet werden, den Energieverbrauch auf einem niedrigen Niveau. Das Steuergerät lässt sich um das Modul RJ-1 erweitern, um mehrere Anlagen gleichzeitig zu kontrollieren. Der eingebaute NFC-Chip ermöglicht die Verbindung mit einem Smartphone, um Daten einfach zu verwalten und die Zeiten für Installation und Fehlersuche vor Ort zu reduzieren.

Begründung der Jury
Die Oberflächengestaltung der Steuergeräte in mattem Grau und glänzendem Schwarz verleiht ihrer technisch anmutenden Form eine wertige Eleganz.

VPCF
Flow Control Valve
Durchflussregelventil

Manufacturer
Festo AG & Co. KG,
Esslingen, Germany
In-house design
Matthias Wunderling
Web
www.festo.com

The VPCF adjusts the flow rate of a
pneumatic consumer to a defined value.
It is used in painting systems for the
precise adjustment of the spray jet as
well as in fabric and foil processing and
the packaging industry. It is particularly
durable and characterised by a quick
response time and high repetition accuracy. Thanks to its compact size and
easily accessible air and power connections, the valve can be flexibly positioned and incorporated into existing
systems.

Statement by the jury
The high functionality of the flow
control valve is reflected in its clearly
defined form. It is extremely robust
and lightweight.

Das VPCF regelt den Durchfluss eines pneu-
matischen Verbrauchers auf einen definierten Wert. Es kommt in Lackieranlagen zur
präzisen Sprühstrahlregulierung sowie bei
der Stoff- und Folienverarbeitung und in
der Verpackungsindustrie zum Einsatz. Es
ist besonders langlebig und zeichnet sich
durch eine schnelle Reaktionszeit sowie
hohe Wiederholgenauigkeit aus. Durch
seine kompakte Größe und die gut zugäng-
lichen Anschlüsse für Luft und elektrische
Versorgung lässt sich das Ventil flexibel
anordnen und auch in bereits bestehende
Anlagen einbauen.

Begründung der Jury
Die hohe Funktionalität des Durchfluss-
regelventils spiegelt sich in seiner klar
definierten Form wider. Es ist äußerst
robust und leicht.

DLGF
Linear Drive
Linearantrieb

Manufacturer
Festo AG & Co. KG,
Esslingen, Germany
In-house design
Madlen Loser
Web
www.festo.com

As a flat, rodless pneumatic drive, the DLGF is suitable for a variety of uses. Typical ranges of application include special machinery construction, assembly of small parts and traditional mechanical engineering. Its main purpose is to move loads safely. As a special feature, the system has two interfaces for mounting various drive components. In addition, the drive has a compact design. Details such as the continuous lateral strip visually connect the individual components to create a compact unit.

Als flachbauender, kolbenstangenloser, pneumatischer Antrieb ist der DLGF vielfältig einsetzbar. Typische Anwendungsbereiche sind der Sondermaschinenbau, die Kleinteilemontage sowie der klassische Maschinenbau. Seine Hauptaufgabe ist das sichere Bewegen von Massen. Als Besonderheit besitzt das System zwei Schnittstellen zur Montage verschiedener Antriebskomponenten. Zudem ist der Antrieb platzsparend konstruiert. Details wie das durchlaufende seitliche Band verbinden die Einzelteile optisch zu einer kompakten Einheit.

Statement by the jury
Its self-contained design lends the DLGF a clear and unobstructed appearance. The interfaces provide flexible connection options.

Begründung der Jury
Die geschlossene Bauweise des DLGF führt zu einem klaren, unverbauten Erscheinungsbild. Die Schnittstellen bieten flexible Anbindungsmöglichkeiten.

VEVM
App-Controlled Valve
App-gesteuertes Ventil

Manufacturer
Festo AG & Co. KG,
Esslingen, Germany
In-house design
Jörg Peschel
Web
www.festo.com

The VEVM valve is an industrial platform 4.0 that combines pneumatics with electronic automation technology, sensor systems and software. With the help of apps, a wide range of applications and functions can be realised using the same hardware. The outcome of this is a valve framework with multiple degrees of freedom for actuation, as well as integrated data acquisition and processing suitable for a cyber-physical system. The combination of clearly structured shapes and organic elements provides a design tailored to the technical innovation.

Das Ventil VEVM ist eine Industrieplattform 4.0, die Pneumatik mit elektrischer Automatisierungstechnik, Sensorik und Software verbindet. Durch Apps lassen sich bei gleicher Hardware Anwendungen und Funktionen unterschiedlichster Art realisieren. So entsteht eine Ventilstruktur mit mehr Freiheitsgraden bei der Ansteuerung sowie eine integrierte Datenerfassung und Datenverarbeitung im Sinne eines cyberphysischen Systems. Die Kombination klar gegliederter Formen und organischer Elemente erzeugt eine der technischen Innovation gerecht werdende Gestaltung.

Statement by the jury
The VEVM valve is the expression of a future-oriented design concept. It combines intelligent technology with flexible functionality.

Begründung der Jury
Das Ventil VEVM ist Ausdruck eines zukunftsorientierten Gestaltungskonzepts. Es verbindet intelligente Technologie mit flexibler Funktionalität.

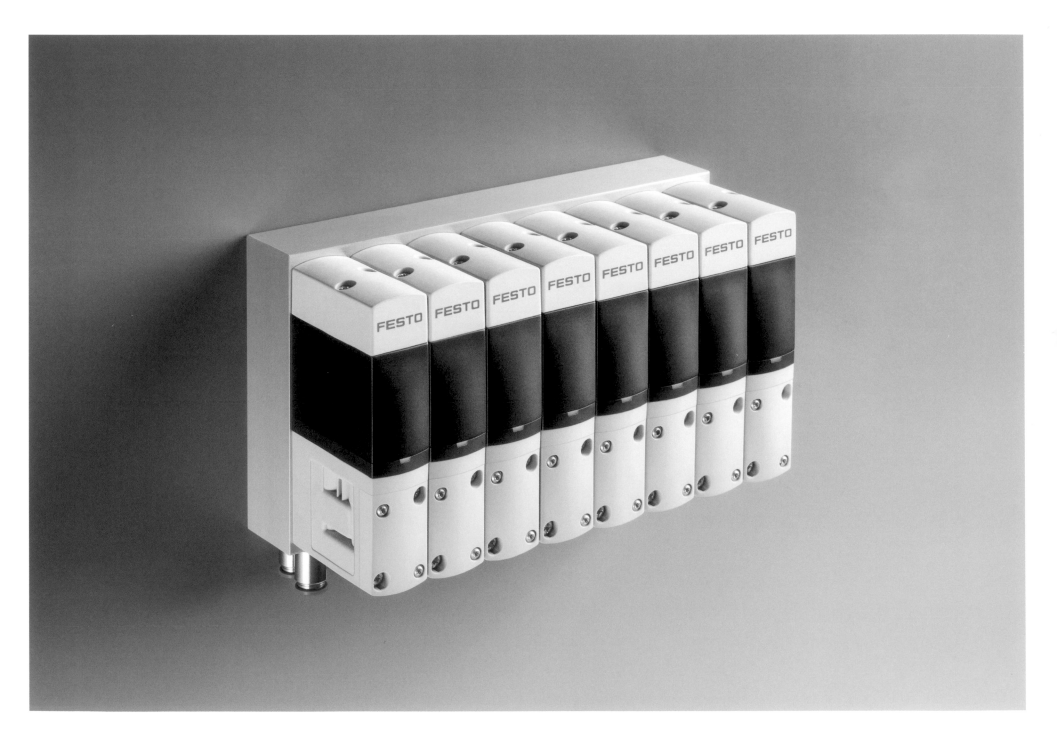

VYKA
Media-Separated Solenoid Valve
Mediengetrenntes Magnetventil

Manufacturer
Festo AG & Co. KG,
Esslingen, Germany
In-house design
Simone Mangold
Web
www.festo.com

Vyka is a media-separated solenoid valve for dosing liquid media. A current-controlled magnet enables highly precise and reliable operation. The media valve is mainly used in laboratory automation and medical technology, as well as in highly precise filling applications involving sensitive and aggressive media, for example in packaging contact lenses or in the perfume industry. The high-visibility LEDs arranged in a row form a light strip. The blue light used thus increases the recognisability of the Festo brand.

Das Vyka ist ein mediengetrenntes Magnetventil zum Dosieren von Flüssigkeiten. Ein stromgesteuerter Magnet ermöglicht hochpräzises und zuverlässiges Arbeiten. Zum Einsatz kommt das Medienventil hauptsächlich in der Laborautomatisierung und in der Medizintechnik sowie bei hochpräzisen Abfüllanwendungen mit sensiblen und aggressiven Medien, z. B. beim Verpacken von Kontaktlinsen oder in der Parfümindustrie. Die deutlich zu sehenden LEDs bilden in Reihung ein Lichtband. Das blaue Leuchten erhöht die Wiedererkennbarkeit der Marke Festo.

Statement by the jury
The self-contained design of Vyka offers optimum protection of the interior. The slim solenoid valves can be installed side by side in a highly space-saving way.

Begründung der Jury
Die geschlossene Form des Vyka bietet optimalen Schutz für das Innenleben. Die schlanken Magnetventile lassen sich äußerst platzsparend nebeneinander verbauen.

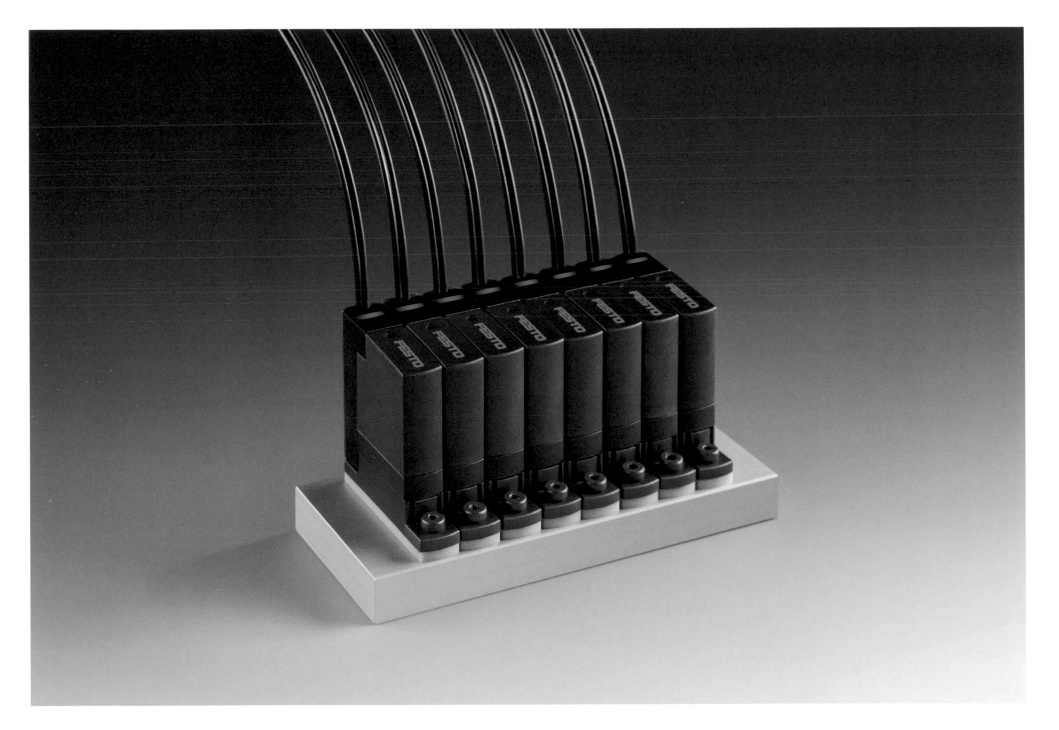

Mira 230
Wire Stripping Machine
Abisoliermaschine

Manufacturer
Komax AG, Dierikon, Switzerland
Design
Vetica Group, Lucerne, Switzerland
Web
www.komaxgroup.com
www.vetica-group.com

The Mira 230 is a benchtop machine for professional wire stripping. With numerous intelligent functions and the data storage, it supports high productivity and quality. Multi-conductor cables can be processed in one operation, saving time while using the sequence function. The large touchscreen allows intuitive use, comparable to that of a smartphone. The key functions are represented as simple icons and explained by on-screen help texts, and an ergonomic hand rest allows for comfortable working.

Die Mira 230 ist eine Tischmaschine zum professionellen Abisolieren elektrischer Leitungen. Mit zahlreichen intelligenten Funktionen und dem Datenspeicher ermöglicht die Maschine hohe Produktivität und Qualität. Die Sequenzfunktion bietet die Möglichkeit, Mehrleiterkabel zeitsparend in einem Arbeitsgang zu verarbeiten. Der große Touchscreen erlaubt eine intuitive Bedienung, vergleichbar mit der eines Smartphones. Die wichtigsten Funktionen werden als einfache Symbole dargestellt und mit Hilfetexten erklärt, eine ergonomische Handauflage sorgt für entspanntes Arbeiten.

Statement by the jury
The clear focus of the compact Mira 230 is the user interface framed in red, which impresses with its clear and ergonomic design.

Begründung der Jury
Bei der handlichen Mira 230 steht die rot eingefasste Bedienoberfläche, welche durch ihre Übersichtlichkeit und Ergonomie besticht, klar im Mittelpunkt.

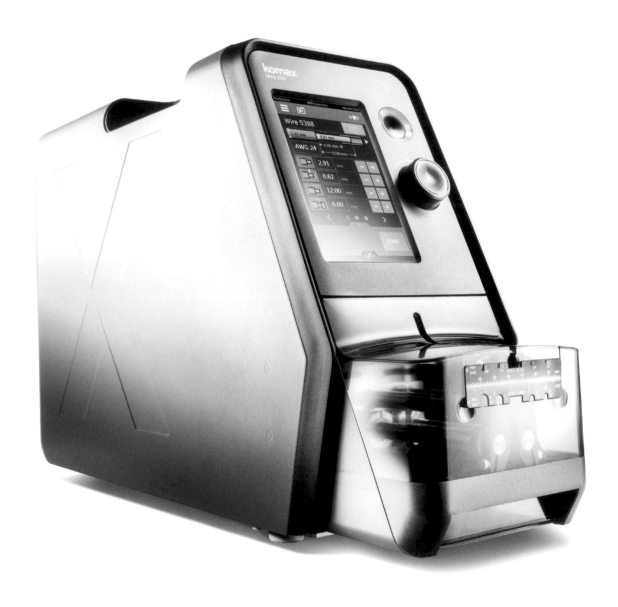

igus® CRM
Rotation Module
Drehmodul

Manufacturer
igus® GmbH, Cologne, Germany
In-house design
Web
www.igus.de

The igus CRM is a rotation module for applications requiring rotary movements up to ±180 degrees in very small spaces. It enables the guidance of a wide variety of cables and hoses without the need for inflexible rotary connections that can be prone to failure. The current angle of rotation is indicated on a scale. Furthermore, the rotation module is easy to install and can be configured online.

Statement by the jury
The rotation module convinces with its compact and smooth form. The impressed scale is not only a functional but also a visually attractive detail.

Bei dem igus CRM handelt es sich um ein Drehmodul für Anwendungen, bei denen Drehbewegungen bis ±180 Grad auf engstem Raum realisiert werden müssen. Ohne störungsanfällige und unflexible Drehdurchführungen ermöglicht es die Führung von unterschiedlichsten Leitungs- und Schlauchtypen. Der aktuelle Drehwinkel lässt sich auf einer Skala ablesen. Darüber hinaus ist das Drehmodul einfach zu installieren und kann online konfiguriert werden.

Begründung der Jury
Das Drehmodul überzeugt durch seine kompakte, bündige Form. Die eingeprägte Skala ist nicht nur ein funktionales, sondern auch gestalterisch attraktives Detail.

Hygienic Design e-chain®
Energy Chain
Energiekette

Manufacturer
igus® GmbH, Cologne, Germany
In-house design
Web
www.igus.de

This plastic e-chain is suitable for applications that require the highest hygiene standards and where cables and tubes have to be routed safely and securely. The rounded edges and absence of threaded connections ensure that there are no dead spaces in which germs can accumulate. The blue material, which is typical of plastic elements in the food industry, is also especially resistant to aggressive cleaning agents and chemicals.

Statement by the jury
From the choice of materials to its design, every detail of the energy chain is completely geared towards impeccable hygiene and cleanability.

Die Kunststoff-Energiekette ist für jeden Anwendungsbereich geeignet, wo höchste Anforderungen an die Hygiene herrschen und Leitungen und Schläuche sicher geführt werden müssen. Abgerundete Ecken und eine verschraubungsfreie Konstruktion sorgen dafür, dass keine Toträume entstehen, in denen sich Keime bilden. Der für Kunststoffelemente in der Lebensmittelindustrie typische blaue Werkstoff ist außerordentlich beständig gegen aggressive Reinigungsmittel und Chemikalien.

Begründung der Jury
Angefangen von der Materialwahl bis hin zu ihrer Geometrie – die Energiekette ist bis ins Detail auf eine einwandfreie Hygiene und Reinigbarkeit ausgelegt.

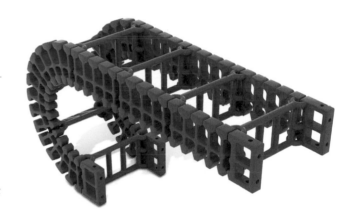

Easy & Safe
Industrial Plug and Connector
Industrie-Steckverbindungen

Manufacturer
ABB, Nyköping, Sweden
Design
Design Group Italia, Milan, Italy
Web
www.abb.com
www.designgroupitalia.com

The Easy & Safe industrial plug and connector meet high standards of reliability and safety. They are IP67-certified, which guarantees that electrical contacts are protected from dust and water. This reduces downtime and maintenance costs. The contact components of the connectors are manufactured from solid brass. The innovative design enables the contacts to self-clean and protects the contact areas from arcing.

Statement by the jury
With high-quality contacts and efficient design, the Easy & Safe industrial plug and connector are exceptionally functional and reliable.

Die Industrie-Steckverbindungen Easy & Safe erfüllen hohe Anforderungen an die Zuverlässigkeit und Sicherheit. Sie sind nach Schutzklasse IP67 zertifiziert, die gewährleistet, dass elektrische Kontakte vor Staub und Wasser geschützt sind. Dies reduziert Ausfallzeiten und Wartungskosten. Die Kontaktteile der Stecker sind aus solidem Messing gefertigt. Dank ihrer innovativen Bauform reinigen die Kontakte sich selbst und die Kontaktbereiche sind vor Funkenbildung geschützt.

Begründung der Jury
Die Steckverbindungen Easy & Safe sind durch die qualitativ hochwertigen Kontakte und die effiziente Bauform ausgesprochen funktional und zuverlässig.

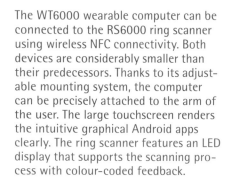

WT6000, RS6000
Industrial Wearable Computing System

Manufacturer
Zebra Technologies, Holtsville, USA
In-house design
Hoon Lim, Edward Hackett
Web
www.zebra.com

The WT6000 wearable computer can be connected to the RS6000 ring scanner using wireless NFC connectivity. Both devices are considerably smaller than their predecessors. Thanks to its adjustable mounting system, the computer can be precisely attached to the arm of the user. The large touchscreen renders the intuitive graphical Android apps clearly. The ring scanner features an LED display that supports the scanning process with colour-coded feedback.

Statement by the jury
The wearable computer WT6000 and ring scanner RS6000 fascinate with their extremely compact dimensions, which make them comfortable to wear.

Der Wearable-Computer WT6000 kann per kabelloser NFC-Konnektivität mit dem Ringscanner RS6000 gekoppelt werden. Beide Geräte sind wesentlich kleiner als ihre Vorgängermodelle. Mit einem verstellbaren Halterungssystem kann der Computer passgenau am Arm des Benutzers befestigt werden. Auf dem großen Touchscreen werden die intuitiven grafischen Android-Anwendungen gut lesbar dargestellt. Der Ringscanner verfügt über eine LED-Anzeige, die den Scanvorgang durch ein farbcodiertes Feedback unterstützt.

Begründung der Jury
Der Wearable-Computer WT6000 und der Ringscanner RS6000 begeistern durch ihre außergewöhnlich kompakten Abmessungen, wodurch sie komfortabel zu tragen sind.

Mark
Smart Working Glove
Intelligenter Arbeitshandschuh

Manufacturer
Workaround GmbH, Munich, Germany
In-house design
Hans Christian Sittig
Web
www.proglove.de

The Mark smart working glove makes manual work in manufacturing and logistics more efficient and ergonomic by enabling the reading of barcodes without an external device. The scanner is located directly on the back of the hand and is activated by the user's thumb pressing a button. The glove provides immediate visual, acoustic and haptic feedback as to whether the working step has been carried out correctly. Moreover, the hands of the wearer remain free the whole time.

Statement by the jury
The Mark smart working glove transfers the trend of wearable technology to industrial applications in an innovative way.

Der intelligente Arbeitshandschuh Mark dient dazu, die manuelle Arbeit in der Fertigung und Logistik effizienter und ergonomischer zu gestalten, indem er das Einlesen von Barcodes ohne ein externes Gerät ermöglicht. Der Scanner befindet sich direkt auf dem Handrücken und wird per Knopfdruck mit dem Daumen ausgelöst. Der Handschuh gibt ein unmittelbares optisches, akustisches und haptisches Feedback, ob der Arbeitsschritt korrekt ausgeführt wurde. Die Hände des Benutzers bleiben die ganze Zeit über frei.

Begründung der Jury
Der intelligente Arbeitshandschuh Mark überträgt den Trend der Wearables – der körpernahen Technik – auf innovative Weise in die Industrieanwendung.

AxiBlade
Axial Fan with EC Motor
Axialventilator mit EC-Motor

Manufacturer
ebm-papst Mulfingen GmbH & Co. KG,
Mulfingen, Germany
Design
Reform Design (Christoph Winkler),
Stuttgart, Germany
Web
www.ebmpapst.com
www.reform-design.de

The AxiBlade axial fan with EC motor is used in ventilation, refrigeration and air-conditioning systems. It transports the feed air in an axial direction parallel to the revolving motor shaft. The modular design concept includes fan housings in various sizes with an aerodynamically optimised inlet ring. Together, they are complemented by the profiled impeller geometry. The impellers have been designed for the various compatible motors, which increases efficiency and reduces running noise.

Der Axialventilator AxiBlade wird in Lüftungs-, Kälte- und Klimaanlagen eingesetzt. Er transportiert die Förderluft in axialer Richtung parallel zur umlaufenden Motorwelle. Das modulare Gestaltungskonzept umfasst Ventilatorengehäuse in unterschiedlicher Größe mit einem aerodynamisch optimierten Einlassring. Beides zusammen wird durch die profilierte Laufradgeometrie ergänzt. Die Laufräder sind für die verschiedenen Motoren konzipiert, mit denen sie kombiniert werden können, was die Effizienz erhöht und das Laufgeräusch reduziert.

Statement by the jury
The AxiBlade captivates with its modular structure, which sets extraordinary standards with regard to versatility and functionality.

Begründung der Jury
AxiBlade begeistert durch seinen modularen Aufbau, der in Sachen Flexibilität und Funktionalität besondere Maßstäbe setzt.

Wine AIRPCS
Air Cushion
Luftpolsterverpackung

Manufacturer
AIRBAG Packing Co., Ltd., New Taipei City, Taiwan
In-house design
Mike Liao
Web
www.airpcs.com

The Wine Airpcs inflatable air cushion protects wine bottles from breaking during transport and keeps their temperature at a constant level for a certain period of time. The air tubes are separate from each other so that the protective function remains intact even if individual tubes are damaged. Furthermore, the packaging provides enhanced protection for the particularly fragile bottleneck. When not in use, the air can be let out and the packaging stored away to save space.

Die aufblasbare Luftpolsterverpackung Wine Airpcs schützt Weinflaschen während des Transports vor Bruch und hält ihre Temperatur für eine gewisse Zeit konstant. Die Luftkammern arbeiten unabhängig voneinander, sodass die Schutzfunktion intakt bleibt, auch wenn einzelne Kammern beschädigt sind. Zudem bietet die Verpackung einen verstärkten Schutz für den besonders zerbrechlichen Flaschenhals. Bei Nichtgebrauch kann die Luft einfach herausgelassen und die Verpackung platzsparend verstaut werden.

Statement by the jury
The Wine Airpcs is an extremely clever and environmentally friendly packaging solution, which is specifically designed to accommodate the shape of wine bottles.

Begründung der Jury
Das Wine Airpcs stellt eine ausgesprochen clevere und umweltschonende Verpackungslösung dar, die genau auf die Form von Weinflaschen abgestimmt ist.

Stingray
Indoor Cleaning Tool
Innenreinigungssystem

Manufacturer
Unger Germany GmbH,
Solingen, Germany
In-house design
Jim Buckley
Design
Unger Enterprises, LLC.,
Bridgeport, Connecticut, USA
Web
www.ungerglobal.com

The Stingray indoor cleaning tool simplifies the professional cleaning of windows from the inside. The ergonomically designed Easy-Click-Pole can be extended up to a length of four metres. In combination with the cleaning pad, hard-to-reach areas also become easy to clean. The innovative pad has a triangular form, and windows and frames are cleaned simultaneously. The integrated spray system enables spraying and cleaning in one step, without any drips.

Das Reinigungssystem Stingray erleichtert die professionelle Innenreinigung von Fenstern. Die ergonomisch gestaltete Easy-Click-Stange kann auf bis zu vier Meter ausgefahren werden. In Verbindung mit dem Reinigungspad lassen sich so auch schwer zugängliche Stellen problemlos erreichen. Das innovative Pad zeichnet sich durch seine dreieckige Form aus, Fenster und Rahmen können gleichzeitig gereinigt werden. Das integrierte Sprühsystem ermöglicht es, in einem Arbeitsgang zu sprühen und zu reinigen, ohne zu tropfen.

Statement by the jury
The sophisticated design of the Stingray indoor cleaning tool effectively incorporates both ergonomic and functional aspects.

Begründung der Jury
Bei der durchdachten Gestaltung des Innenreinigungssystems Stingray wurden Aspekte der Ergonomie und der Funktionalität gleichermaßen berücksichtigt.

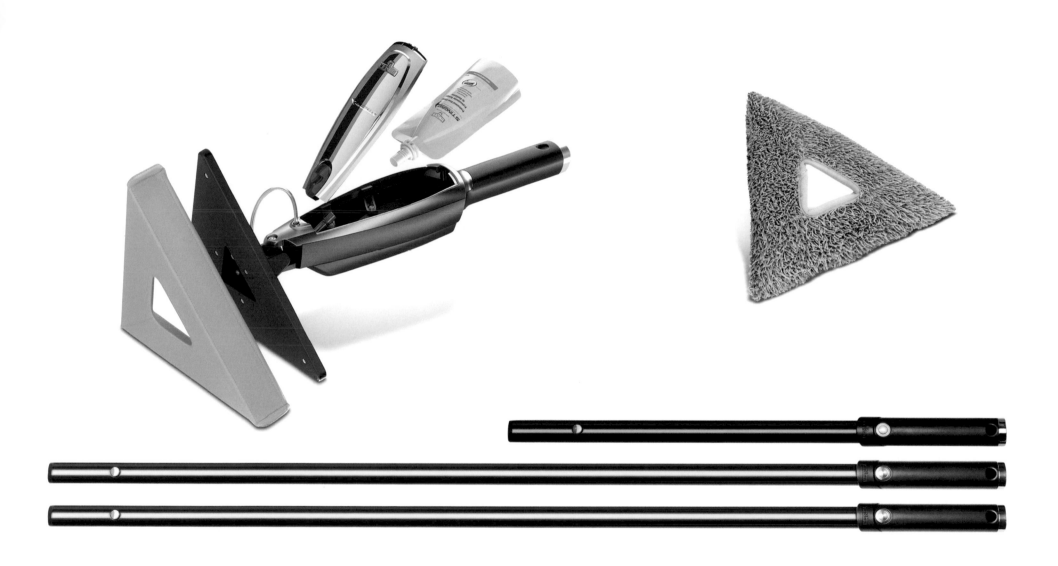

SC250
Walk-Behind Scrubber Dryer
Scheuersaugmaschine

Manufacturer
Nilfisk Production, Nagykanizsa, Hungary
Design
Nilfisk SpA, Guardamiglio, Italy
Web
www.nilfisk.com

The battery-powered SC250 walk-behind
scrubber dryer scrubs, sweeps and dries
in one working step. Cleaning can be carried out in forward and backward motion.
Attached to the handle is a structured
display along with touch sensors that ensure easy usage. The ergonomic push-bar
can be set to different positions or folded
away when the machine is not in use.
The pivoting wheels positioned under the
device ensure good manoeuvrability.

Statement by the jury
The SC250 walk-behind scrubber dryer is
extremely smooth-running and gentle on
the user's back. Its soft contours lend it a
friendly appearance.

Die batteriebetriebene Scheuersaugmaschine SC250 schrubbt, kehrt und trocknet
in einem Arbeitsgang. Die Reinigung kann
vorwärts und rückwärts durchgeführt werden. Am Griff befinden sich ein strukturier-
tes Display sowie Berührungssensoren, die
eine einfache Bedienung gewährleisten.
Der ergonomische Schubbügel lässt sich auf
verschiedene Positionen einstellen und ein-
klappen, wenn die Maschine nicht benutzt
wird. Die unter der Maschine positionierten
Schwenkräder sorgen für eine gute Manövrierfähigkeit.

Begründung der Jury
Die Scheuersaugmaschine SC250 ist außerordentlich leichtgängig und rückenscho-
nend zu bedienen. Ihre sanften Konturen
verleihen ihr ein sympathisches Äußeres.

SC100
Walk-Behind Scrubber Dryer
Scheuersaugmaschine

Manufacturer
Nilfisk Ltd., Suzhou, China
Design
Nilfisk A/S, Hadsund, Denmark
Web
www.nilfisk.com

The SC100 is an upright scrubber dryer for cleaning smaller areas. With its low scrubbing deck, the machine can also access corners that are otherwise hard to reach. All cleaning functions can be controlled using the self-explanatory symbol buttons on the handle. Operation can be stopped immediately by bringing the machine into an upright position. The robust aluminium frame is particularly durable, and the well-accessible tank can be cleaned easily and thoroughly.

Statement by the jury
Designed with a focus on the user, the SC100 walk-behind scrubber dryer is characterised by its extremely intuitive, safe and convenient operation.

Der SC100 ist ein aufrechter Scheuersauger für die Reinigung kleinerer Bereiche. Durch das niedrige Schrubbdeck erreicht die Maschine auch schwer zugängliche Stellen. Alle Reinigungsfunktionen lassen sich durch die selbsterklärenden Symboltasten am Griff steuern. Indem die Maschine in eine aufrechte Position gebracht wird, wird der Betrieb sofort gestoppt. Der robuste Rahmen aus Aluminium ist besonders langlebig, der gut zugängliche Tank lässt sich einfach und gründlich säubern.

Begründung der Jury
Gestaltet mit dem Anwender im Fokus, zeichnet sich die Scheuersaugmaschine SC100 durch ihre ausgesprochen intuitive, sichere und komfortable Bedienung aus.

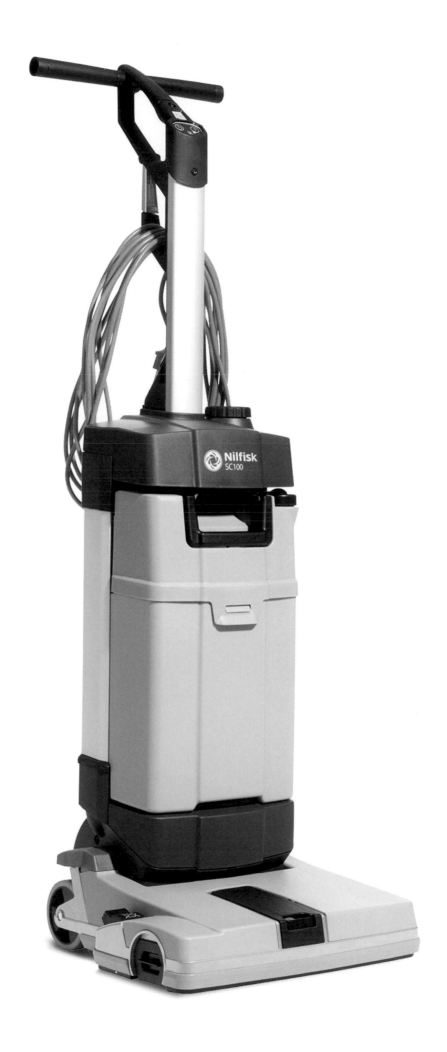

GWH Wavy
Professional Washing Machine
Professionelle Waschmaschine

Manufacturer
Grandimpianti I.L.E. – Ali S.p.A., Sospirolo, Italy
Design
Emo Design, Vittorio Veneto, Italy
Web
www.grandimpianti.com
www.emo-design.it
Honourable Mention

The GWH Wavy professional washing machine is operated via a 7" touchscreen that is ergonomically integrated into the front of the machine. The graphic icons, which are reminiscent of the visual language of smartphone apps, provides orientation while also simplifying and accelerating work in the laundry. The menu guidance adjusts to the respective user status: beginner, intermediate, specialist or technician. The machine can be controlled from anywhere via the cloud.

Die professionelle Waschmaschine GWH Wavy wird über einen 7"-Touchscreen gesteuert, der ergonomisch in die Front integriert ist. Die grafischen Icons, die sich an der Zeichensprache von Smartphone-Apps orientieren, vereinfachen und beschleunigen die Arbeit in der Waschküche. Die Menüführung ist an den jeweiligen Benutzerstatus angepasst: Anfänger, Fortgeschrittene, Fachkraft oder Techniker. Über die Cloud kann die Maschine von jedem Ort aus gesteuert werden.

Statement by the jury
With its touchscreen, the GWH Wavy professional washing machine provides contemporary ease of use. Its slanted position makes the display easier to read.

Begründung der Jury
Die professionelle Waschmaschine GWH Wavy bietet durch den Touchscreen einen zeitgemäßen Bedienkomfort. Der angeschrägte Winkel erleichtert das Ablesen des Displays.

PW 413 / 418 / 811 / 814 / 818
Commercial Washing Machines
Gewerbe-Waschmaschinen

Manufacturer
Miele & Cie. KG, Gütersloh, Germany
In-house design
Web
www.miele.de

Designed for the use in launderettes, these washing machines meet high expectations in terms of effectiveness, performance and reliability. The commercial washing machines with a load capacity of 11-18 kg offer short programme cycles and achieve good cleaning results even with temperature-sensitive textiles. The smooth running of the machines facilitates daily routines in laundries while the arrangement of the control elements follows ergonomic principles. Clearly structured fronts as well as high-quality materials convey professionalism.

Konzipiert für den Einsatz in Wäschereien, erfüllen diese Waschmaschinen hohe Erwartungen hinsichtlich Wirtschaftlichkeit, Leistung und Zuverlässigkeit. Die 11-18 kg fassenden Gewerbe-Waschmaschinen bieten kurze Programmlaufzeiten und erzielen auch bei temperaturempfindlichen Textilien gute Reinigungsergebnisse. Die Laufruhe der Maschinen erleichtert den Alltag in Wäschereien, zudem folgt die Anordnung der Bedienelemente ergonomischen Gesichtspunkten. Klar strukturierte Gerätefronten sowie hochwertige Materialien vermitteln Professionalität.

Statement by the jury
A high degree of functionality and con-vincing ease of use characterise these distinctive commercial washing machines.

Begründung der Jury
Ein hohes Maß an Funktionalität sowie ein überzeugender Bedienkomfort kennzeichnen diese markanten Gewerbe-Waschmaschinen.

Tian Qi
Smart Weather Station
Intelligente Wetterstation

Manufacturer
Beijing Insentek Technology Co., Ltd.,
Beijing, China
Design
Beijing Top Industrial Design Co., Ltd.,
Beijing, China
Web
www.insentek.com
www.designt.cn

The Tian Qi smart weather station measures seven different weather parameters: temperature, wind speed, wind direction, rainfall, UV radiation, atmospheric pressure and humidity. The data can be stored in the cloud and accessed via a web-enabled device such as a smartphone or tablet. Thanks to its mast made of carbon fibre, the station weighs only 4.1 kg and can withstand wind gusts of up to 120 kph. The design evokes associations with a spaceship and plays with the expectations as to how a scientific measuring instrument should look.

Die intelligente Wetterstation Tian Qi erfasst sieben unterschiedliche Wetterparameter: Temperatur, Windgeschwindigkeit, Windrichtung, Niederschlag, UV-Strahlung, Luftdruck und Luftfeuchtigkeit. Die Messdaten können in der Cloud gespeichert und über ein internetfähiges Endgerät wie Smartphone oder Tablet abgerufen werden. Die Station wiegt dank ihres Masts aus Carbonfaser nur 4,1 kg und hält Windböen von bis zu 120 km/h stand. Die Gestaltung weckt Assoziationen an ein Raumschiff und spielt mit den Erwartungen darüber, wie ein wissenschaftliches Messinstrument auszusehen hat.

Statement by the jury
The Tian Qi smart weather station is characterised by its extremely flat and airy silhouette, which creates a unique aesthetic.

Begründung der Jury
Die intelligente Wetterstation Tian Qi zeichnet sich durch eine äußerst flache, schlanke und luftige Silhouette aus, die eine ganz besondere Ästhetik erzeugt.

PuduBOT
Service Robot
Serviceroboter

Manufacturer
Shenzhen Pudu
Technology Co., Ltd.,
Shenzhen, China

In-house design
Peng Chen

Web
www.pudutech.com

reddot award 2017
best of the best

Serving with personality
Robots can deliver valuable work in the often hectic area of customer service. The PuduBOT has specially been designed to work in restaurants, providing help to waiters and waitresses and, in so doing, help effectively cut labour costs. This robot boasts a very well-balanced design. Gently rounded corners and its high-quality language of form make this robot ideal for use in modern catering environments. The PuduBOT inspires with an outstanding approach toward intelligent interaction. It interacts with diners by voice and shows a variety of friendly-looking facial expressions on its display, lending it charismatic personality. It can move around smoothly and self-reliantly. Being equipped with ultra-wideband positioning, SLAM (Simultaneous Localisation and Mapping), as well as high-precision laser radar technology, make it possible for PuduBOT to navigate with high precision, allowing as many as 100 robots to be used in one single setting. This robot can also adapt to a variety of service tasks thanks to a well thought-out modular design concept. In order to cover different service tasks, it offers freely customisable modules as well as easy-to-clean trays. This ensures that all items from champagne bottles to artistically arranged desserts are always presented in an appropriate, stylish manner. With its premium design implementation and memorable appearance, this robot exudes a futuristic yet charming aura – it redefines the concept of service.

Service mit Persönlichkeit
Im oft geschäftigen Umgang mit Menschen können Roboter gute Dienste leisten. Der PuduBOT wurde speziell für die Arbeit in Restaurants konzipiert. Er soll das Bedienpersonal bei seiner Arbeit unterstützen und auf diese Weise dazu beitragen, die Kosten zu senken. Dieser Roboter ist sehr ausgewogen gestaltet. Sanft abgerundete Kanten und eine hochwertige Formensprache prädestinieren ihn dafür, in modernen Gastronomieumgebungen eingesetzt zu werden. Der PuduBOT begeistert dabei mit einer besonderen Art der intelligenten Interaktion. Sein Display zeigt eine freundlich anmutende Mimik, er interagiert per Stimme mit den Gästen und hat eine sehr persönliche Ausstrahlung. Seine Bewegung im Raum ist geschmeidig und geschieht selbsttätig. Die Ausstattung mit Ultra-Wideband-Positionsbestimmung, SLAM (Simultaneous Localisation and Mapping) und einer hochpräzisen Laserradar-Technologie ermöglicht es dem PuduBOT, sehr präzise zu navigieren, weshalb etwa 100 von ihnen gleichzeitig eingesetzt werden können. Seinen differenzierten Serviceaufgaben wird dieser Roboter auch durch eine gut durchdachte modulare Gestaltung gerecht. Er bietet für die jeweilige Serviceaufgabe frei arrangierbare Module sowie reinigungsfreundliche Tabletts. Damit gewährleistet er das stilvolle Darreichen von Champagner ebenso wie das Präsentieren und Anbieten kunstvoller Desserts. Hochwertig gestaltet mit einem einprägsamen Erscheinungsbild, verbreitet dieser Roboter im Raum eine futuristische und doch angenehme Aura – der Servicegedanke wird neu definiert.

Statement by the jury
The PuduBOT is a fascinating demonstration of the possibilities of robotics in the service sector. It is highly functional and showcases an elegant appearance. It can be used in restaurants as well as for order delivery in canteens or old people's homes. Thanks to its aesthetic design, it easily integrates into a wide range of environments. Simple and cost-effective, it embodies a sensible alternative with a pleasing design that also appeals to the emotions.

Begründung der Jury
Der PuduBOT zeigt auf faszinierende Weise die Möglichkeiten der Robotik im Servicebereich auf. Er ist sehr funktional und hat eine elegante Anmutung. Eingesetzt werden kann er in Restaurants ebenso wie etwa bei der Essensausgabe in Kantinen oder Altenheimen. Dort fügt er sich dank seiner ästhetischen Gestaltung leicht in unterschiedlichste Umgebungen ein. Einfach und kostengünstig konzipiert, stellt er eine sinnvolle Alternative dar und spricht mit seiner gefälligen Formgebung auch die Emotionen an.

Designer portrait
See page 50
Siehe Seite 50

Pudding BeanQ
Robot for Early Childhood Education
Roboter für die frühkindliche Erziehung

Manufacturer
Intelligent Steward Co., Ltd.,
Beijing, China

In-house design
Yi Chen, Feizi Ye, Tingting Xue,
Bin Zheng, Haichen Zheng,
Yong Zheng, Jian Sun, Ye Tian,
Xue Mei, Fan Li

Web
www.roobo.com

reddot award 2017
best of the best

Friendly buddy

In order to understand the world around them, children interact with it in their very own way. The Pudding BeanQ is an intelligent robot designed especially for small children in China. Symbolising the children's early development, the robot is inspired by the form of a bean to attract attention. This form is intended to visualise the concept that a bean waiting to sprout comes to earth with curiosity and is looking forward to interacting with the world. The design of this robot is concisely geared toward the principles of fun, ease of use and safety. With its colourful appearance and rounded, cute design language, it aims at inviting children to play with it. With tactile sensation in mind, its body has been designed in such a way that it feels comfortable and is reminiscent of touching a pet. The robot's actions look natural, since the included angle between the plane of rotation and the level is five degrees, allowing the body to rotate 330 degrees. Moreover, the robot is supported by a rich mimetic repertoire with easy-to-understand, characteristic emotions. This makes it enjoyable and smooth for children to have fun with and experience various interactions such as video chatting, playing games, being kept company and educated. For safety reasons, the Pudding BeanQ comes with a formally matched yet separate charging base. Its design interprets a robot in an impressive new way – it merges an inspired form with a well thought-out educational concept.

Freundlicher Kumpel

Um die sie umgebende Welt zu verstehen, interagieren Kinder mit ihr auf ihre ganz eigene Weise. Der Pudding BeanQ ist ein intelligenter Roboter, der speziell für Kleinkinder in China entworfen wurde. Deren kindliche Entwicklung symbolisch widerspiegelnd, hat er die aufmerksamkeitsstarke Form einer Bohne. Seine Gestaltung will visualisieren, dass sich eine aufkeimende Bohne neugierig darauf freut, endlich mit der Welt in Kontakt zu kommen. Dieser Roboter wurde gänzlich an den Attributen Spaß, Nutzerfreundlichkeit und Sicherheit ausgerichtet. Mit seiner rundlichen und farbigen Formensprache will er die Kinder aktiv dazu auffordern, mit ihm zu spielen. Sein Korpus ist auch haptisch rundum so gestaltet, dass er sich angenehm anfühlt und an ein Haustier erinnert. Der Pudding BeanQ wirkt in seinen Aktionen natürlich, da der Winkel zwischen Rotationsebene und Basis nur fünf Grad beträgt und sein Körper sich deshalb um 330 Grad drehen kann. Er verfügt zudem über ein reichhaltiges mimisches Repertoire mit gut nachvollziehbar dargestellten Emotionen. Mittels dieser macht er es den Kindern möglich, viel Spaß mit ihm zu haben. Sie erleben mit ihm etwa einen Videochat, er spielt mit ihnen Spiele, er begleitet und unterrichtet sie. Aus Sicherheitsgründen wurde der Pudding BeanQ mit einer formal sehr gut abgestimmten, separaten Ladestation gestaltet. Sein Design interpretiert einen Roboter auf beeindruckend neue Weise – es vereint formale Inspiration mit einer gut durchdachten Didaktik.

Statement by the jury

This robot addresses the children in a friendly way. Its aesthetic design finds a whole new form for a robot. This makes it unmistakable and not simply an imitation of existing models. Moreover, the smart functions of this robot are also perfectly adapted to the world of children. The Pudding BeanQ helps them in their daily life. It not just instructs them to go to bed, but also inspires them while playing.

Begründung der Jury

Dieser Roboter spricht die Kinder auf eine freundschaftliche Art und Weise an. Seine ästhetische Gestaltung findet eine ganz neue Form für einen Roboter. Diese macht ihn unverwechselbar und ist nicht einfach nur eine Imitation vorhandener Modelle. Die intelligenten Funktionen dieses Roboters sind zudem perfekt an die Kinderwelt angepasst. Der Pudding BeanQ hilft ihnen in ihrem täglichen Leben. So instruiert er sie, wenn sie ins Bett gehen sollen, aber er inspiriert sie auch beim Spielen.

Designer portrait
See page 52
Siehe Seite 52

JELLY
Commercial Service Robot
Kommerzieller Serviceroboter

Manufacturer
Intelligent Steward Co., Ltd., Beijing, China
In-house design
Feizi Ye, Yong Zheng, Haichen Zheng
Web
www.roobo.com

The commercial service robot Jelly can both recognise and show human emotions. Its movement sequences are based on three rotating axes. The neck is particularly flexible in order to create natural, humanoid movement. The robot can carry out a wide range of tasks, such as taking video calls, translating spoken text, sending e-mails or renting a car. It is characterised by a gender-neutral appearance that is designed to look simple and elegant. Therefore, it blends into the home and the office equally well.

Statement by the jury
Jelly fascinates with its fluid movements that emotionalise the user experience. The minimalist design skilfully puts the display centre stage as a likeable "face".

Der Serviceroboter Jelly kann menschliche Emotionen erkennen und selbst darstellen. Seine Bewegungsabläufe beruhen auf drei rotierenden Achsen. Der Hals ist besonders flexibel, um eine natürliche, humanoide Bewegung zu erzeugen. Der Roboter kann vielfältige Aufgaben ausführen, wie Videoanrufe entgegennehmen, gesprochene Texte übersetzen, E-Mails versenden oder ein Auto mieten. Er zeichnet sich durch einen geschlechtsneutralen Look aus, der auf Einfachheit und Eleganz ausgelegt ist. Dadurch passt er genauso gut in das häusliche Umfeld wie an den Arbeitsplatz.

Begründung der Jury
Jelly fasziniert durch seine flüssigen Bewegungsabläufe, die das Nutzererlebnis emotionalisieren. Die reduzierte Gestaltung rückt das Display als sympathisches „Gesicht" gezielt in den Fokus.

Midea Bubble Robot
Intelligent Voice Robot
Intelligenter Sprachroboter

Manufacturer
Midea Smart Technology Co., Ltd.,
Shenzhen, China
In-house design
Tao Xiao, Mingyu Xu
Design
Hefei XIVO Design Co., Ltd.
(Wei Gu, Min Wei), Hefei, China
Web
www.midea.com
www.xivodesign.com

The intelligent voice robot Midea Bubble Robot is based on sensor technology as well as voice and graphic recognition and is constantly learning from its experiences. It reacts to voice commands and search queries, and it controls compatible smart home devices. Moreover, the built-in HD camera can transmit video calls. The robot thus facilitates an intuitive use of the new technology, especially by children and seniors. Optionally, the voice robot can be mounted onto a mobile robot, for instance so that it can help with cleaning.

Statement by the jury
With its spherical shape, the Midea Bubble Robot attracts everyone's attention. Thanks to its display face, which is craned upward, it always looks attentive and interested.

Der intelligente Sprachroboter Midea Bubble Robot basiert auf Sensortechnologie, Sprach- sowie Bilderkennung und lernt ständig dazu. Er nimmt per Zuruf Kommandos oder Suchanfragen entgegen und steuert kompatible Smart-Home-Geräte. Außerdem kann die eingebaute HD-Kamera Videoanrufe übermitteln. So ermöglicht er vor allem Kindern und Senioren einen intuitiven Umgang mit neuen Technologien. Optional kann der Sprachroboter auf einen mobilen Roboter montiert werden, damit er z. B. beim Saubermachen hilft.

Begründung der Jury
Der Midea Bubble Robot zieht mit seiner kugeligen Gestalt alle Blicke auf sich. Mit seinem nach oben gereckten Display-Gesicht sieht er stets aufmerksam und interessiert aus.

Midea o2
Smart Home Management System
Intelligentes Heimsteuerungssystem

Manufacturer
Midea Smart Technology Co., Ltd.,
Shenzhen, China
In-house design
Mingyu Xu, Tao Xiao
Design
Hefei XIVO Design Co., Ltd.
(Chao Jing, Jiuzhou Zhang), Hefei, China
Web
www.midea.com
www.xivodesign.com

Midea o2 is a smart home management system with a graphical user interface. It is operated through voice recognition and takes over the central wireless management of various smart devices in the household. Via the integrated speakers, the system can play music or videos. The two identical hemispherical bodies create strong acoustics. The head is flexible and can swivel, while at the same time looking identical from every angle.

Statement by the jury
Thanks to its humanoid look, the smart home management system Midea o2 exudes a likeability that fosters trust and lowers any reservations about the technology.

Midea o2 ist ein intelligentes Heimsteuerungssystem mit einer grafischen Benutzeroberfläche. Es wird über Spracherkennung gesteuert und übernimmt die kabellose zentrale Bedienung zahlreicher intelligenter Endgeräte im Haushalt. Über die integrierten Lautsprecher kann das System Musik oder Videos abspielen. Die zwei identischen halbkugelförmigen Körper schaffen einen guten Klangraum. Das Kopfteil ist beweglich und kann sich drehen, dabei sieht es aus jedem Winkel stets gleich aus.

Begründung der Jury
Durch seine humanoide Anmutung strahlt das intelligente Heimsteuerungssystem Midea o2 eine Verbindlichkeit aus, die Vertrauen schafft und Berührungsängste mit der Technik abbaut.

Zenbo
Home Robot
Heimroboter

Manufacturer
ASUSTeK Computer Inc., Taipei, Taiwan
In-house design
Web
www.asus.com

The Zenbo home robot moves independently through the home and follows voice commands. Its face functions as a touchscreen and can express a range of emotions. The robot is thus particularly suited for entertaining children with games or supporting seniors in their daily lives. Thanks to an integrated camera, it also takes over the security surveillance of the home. Connected to other smart home devices, such as light switches or the TV, it serves as a central control unit.

Statement by the jury
With its spherical body and cute face, Zenbo appeals to all age groups. Its voice-operated command and control system helps it to appear even more human.

Der Heimroboter Zenbo bewegt sich selbständig durch das Zuhause und hört auf Sprachkommandos. Sein Gesicht funktioniert als Touchscreen und kann verschiedene Emotionen ausdrücken. Der Roboter ist insbesondere dazu geeignet, Kinder mit Spielen zu unterhalten oder Senioren in ihrem Alltag zu unterstützen. Dank seiner integrierten Kamera übernimmt er zudem die Heimüberwachung. Verbunden mit anderen intelligenten Heimgeräten wie Lichtschaltern oder dem Fernseher dient er als zentrale Steuerungseinheit.

Begründung der Jury
Mit seinem kugeligen Körper und dem niedlichen Gesicht weckt Zenbo Sympathie bei Jung und Alt. Dass er durch Sprachbefehle gesteuert wird, lässt ihn noch menschlicher wirken.

Midea Home
Smart Voice Robot
Intelligenter Sprachroboter

Manufacturer
Midea Smart Technology Co., Ltd.,
Shenzhen, China
In-house design
Tao Xiao, Mingyu Xu, Ao Li
Web
www.midea.com

The design of the smart voice robot Midea Home is inspired by Japanese teru teru bōzu dolls. They are said to have the magic skill of being able to invoke good weather for the following day. When given a voice command, the robot plays music, shows the weather forecast and much more. It also understands gestures and is able to identify different persons based on facial recognition technology. Moreover, it can take over the control of networked devices in the home, such as air conditioning and refrigeration.

Statement by the jury
Its design, which was modelled after a doll, gives the voice robot a markedly playful character, which skilfully encourages users to interact with it.

Die Gestaltung des intelligenten Sprachroboters Midea Home ist inspiriert von japanischen „Teru teru bōzu"-Puppen. Diesen wird die magische Fähigkeit nachgesagt, schönes Wetter für den kommenden Tag herbeizuführen. Der Roboter spielt auf Zuruf Musik ab, ruft ein Taxi, zeigt den Wetterbericht an und vieles mehr. Zudem versteht er Gesten und kann per Gesichtserkennung verschiedene Personen identifizieren. Des Weiteren kann er die Heimsteuerung vernetzter Geräte wie Klimaanlage oder Kühlschrank übernehmen.

Begründung der Jury
Die einer Puppe nachempfundene Gestaltung verleiht dem Sprachroboter einen betont verspielten Charakter. Dies animiert dazu, mit ihm in Interaktion zu treten.

Krypton 7
Educational Robot
Lernroboter

Manufacturer
Shanghai PartnerX Robotics Co., Ltd.,
Abilix Educational Robots, Shanghai, China
In-house design
Web
www.partnerx.cn
www.abilix.com

The components of the Krypton 7 education robot can be attached along all six faces, which offers almost infinite possibilities for mechanical creation. The controller is not only superior in its computing speed, but also in terms of voice and face recognition. There are six motors and 26 sensors of different varieties in the robot, providing diverse functionality. It also offers four apps that enable users, regardless of age and education, to accomplish their projects.

Statement by the jury
The educational robot Krypton 7 introduces users of all ages to the world of technology in a playful way. Its modular structure greatly promotes creativity.

Die Bausteine des Lernroboters Krypton 7 lassen sich von allen sechs Seiten miteinander verbinden und bieten so nahezu unbegrenzte mechanische Gestaltungsmöglichkeiten. Die Steuereinheit zeigt nicht nur eine außergewöhnliche Leistung in ihrer Rechnergeschwindigkeit, sondern auch bei der Stimm- und Gesichtserkennung. In dem Roboter stehen sechs Motoren und 26 Sensoren mit unterschiedlichsten Funktionen zur Verfügung. Zudem helfen vier Apps Benutzern jeden Alters und jeder Lernstufe dabei, ihre Projekte zu verwirklichen.

Begründung der Jury
Der Lernroboter Krypton 7 bringt Benutzern jeden Alters die Welt der Technik spielend näher. Sein modulares Baukastenprinzip fördert in hohem Maß die Kreativität.

Sineva Service Robot
Commercial Service Robot

Manufacturer
Beijing Sineva Technology Co., Ltd.,
Beijing, China
Design
LKK Design Beijing Co., Ltd.,
Beijing, China
Web
www.sineva.com
www.lkkdesign.com

The commercial service robot by Sineva can be used in shopping malls, banks and other public places to give advice to customers, point them in the right direction, provide information or connect them with a service staff member by way of video. The robot uses speech and facial recognition to communicate. Thanks to intelligent localisation and mapping functions, it knows its exact position and is able to move around independently indoors as well as drive around any obstacles.

Statement by the jury
The energetic design language of this service robot skilfully emphasises its mobility. The vertically aligned display allows communication at eye level with the user.

Der Serviceroboter von Sineva kann in Einkaufszentren, Banken und anderen öffentlichen Bereichen eingesetzt werden, um Kunden zu beraten, ihnen den Weg zu weisen, Auskünfte zu erteilen oder sie per Videofunktion mit einem Servicemitarbeiter zu verbinden. Der Roboter nutzt Sprach- und Gesichtserkennung zur Kommunikation. Durch intelligente Lokalisierungs- und Mappingfunktionen kennt er seinen genauen Standort und ist in der Lage, sich in Innenräumen frei zu bewegen und Hindernisse zu umfahren.

Begründung der Jury
Die schwungvolle Formensprache des Serviceroboters unterstreicht gekonnt seine Mobilität. Das vertikal ausgerichtete Display erlaubt dem Benutzer eine Kommunikation auf Augenhöhe.

360 Smart Assistant A1
Smart Voice Assistant
Intelligenter Sprachassistent

Manufacturer
Shenzhen Fenglian Technology Co., Ltd.,
Shenzhen, China
In-house design
Xueyong Zhang
Web
www.ifenglian.com

The 360 Smart Assistant A1 connects to the home network via Wi-Fi and recognises voice commands. It is operated via the Lulu voice control software, which is activated by the words "Hey Lulu". When prompted, the device plays music or sends voice messages. Thus children or older people for instance, who are not familiar with the use of a smartphone, may communicate with their relatives. Furthermore, the device can function as the main controller of a networked home.

Statement by the jury
This voice assistant impresses with its purist aesthetic, which highlights how uncomplicated it is to use and allows it to blend in seamlessly with modern home decor.

Der 360 Smart Assistant A1 wird via Wi-Fi mit dem Heimnetzwerk verbunden und erkennt gesprochene Befehle. Die Bedienung über die Sprachsteuerung Lulu wird mit den Worten „Hey Lulu" aktiviert. Auf Kommando spielt das Gerät Musik ab oder versendet Sprachnachrichten. So können beispielsweise Kinder oder ältere Personen, die nicht mit der Bedienung eines Smartphones vertraut sind, mit ihren Angehörigen kommunizieren. Des Weiteren kann das Gerät die Steuerung in einem vernetzten Haushalt übernehmen.

Begründung der Jury
Der Sprachassistent besticht durch seine puristische Ästhetik, die den unkomplizierten Umgang mit dem Gerät unterstreicht und dank der er sich nahtlos in ein modernes Wohnambiente einfügt.

Unibot
Modular Home Robot
Modularer Heimroboter

Manufacturer
ECOVACS Robotics Co., Ltd., Suzhou, China
In-house design
Xiaowen Li
Web
www.ecovacs.com

The Unibot is a modular home robot featuring four functions: floor cleaning, smart housekeeping, air humidification and air purification. It is possible to implement the modules either independently or in combination with the others, allowing several tasks to be carried out simultaneously. The user can control the robot remotely with the help of a smartphone app and thus retains full control at all times.

Statement by the jury
The dot pattern, which symmetrically fades out, gives the Unibot an iconographic appearance, stylishly highlighting its technical character.

Der Heimroboter Unibot besteht aus vier Funktionsmodulen: Bodenreinigung, intelligente Heimsteuerung, Luftbefeuchtung und Luftreinigung. Die Module lassen sich unabhängig voneinander einsetzen oder miteinander kombinieren, um mehrere Aufgaben gleichzeitig zu erledigen. Der Benutzer kann den Roboter mithilfe einer Smartphone-App auch aus der Ferne steuern und hat dadurch jederzeit die volle Kontrolle.

Begründung der Jury
Der Unibot erhält durch das symmetrisch auslaufende Punktmuster ein ikonografisches Erscheinungsbild, das seinen technischen Charakter stilvoll unterstreicht.

Smart Pro Compact
Robotic Vacuum Cleaner
Saugroboter

Manufacturer
Philips, Eindhoven, Netherlands
In-house design
Philips Design
Web
www.philips.com

The Smart Pro Compact robotic vacuum cleaner is equipped with an extra-wide nozzle that spans the whole length of the device. The blue edges of the nozzle are visible from above, which manifests their dimensions. The high suction power is visualised by the circularly aligned ribs on the dust cover. The robot is only 6 cm tall and removes dust even under pieces of furniture with low clearance. Thanks to its four-wheel-drive system, it easily navigates carpet edges or transitions between rooms.

Statement by the jury
The Smart Pro Compact impresses with its flat design. The basic design element is a circle, which consistently and coherently recurs in the language of form.

Der Saugroboter Smart Pro Compact ist mit einer extra breiten Düse ausgestattet, die sich über die gesamte Länge des Geräts erstreckt. Die blauen Kanten der Düse sind von oben sichtbar, um ihre Ausmaße erfahrbar zu machen. Die hohe Saugleistung wird durch die kreisförmig angeordneten Rippen auf der Abdeckung visualisiert. Der Roboter ist nur 6 cm hoch und entfernt den Staub auch unter niedrigen Möbeln. Dank des Antriebssystems mit vier Rädern bewältigt er mühelos Teppichkanten oder Raumübergänge.

Begründung der Jury
Der Smart Pro Compact punktet durch sein flaches Design. Das gestalterische Grundelement ist ein Kreis, der in der Formensprache konsequent und stimmig immer wieder aufgegriffen wird.

Roomba® 980
Vacuuming Robot
Saugroboter

Manufacturer
iRobot, Bedford, USA
In-house design
Web
www.irobot.com

The Roomba 980 vacuuming robot supports cleaner floors throughout the entire home. It seamlessly navigates an entire level of a home, keeping track of its location and recharging as needed until the job is done. The AeroForce Cleaning System with Carpet Boost automatically increases power on carpets where it is needed the most. With the iRobot HOME App, it is easy to schedule and start cleaning jobs remotely, and to see what the robot cleaned with Clean Map reports.

Statement by the jury
The Roomba 980 vacuuming robot has an extremely compact and high-quality design. Thanks to its sophisticated features, it provides very efficient cleaning results.

Der Saugroboter Roomba 980 sorgt für saubere Böden im gesamten Haus. Er bewegt sich problemlos auf einer ganzen Etage, merkt sich seinen Standort und lädt sich so oft wieder auf, bis er seine Arbeit erledigt hat. Das AeroForce-Reinigungssystem mit Turbo-Teppich-Modus erhöht auf Teppichen bei Bedarf automatisch seine Leistung. Mit der iRobot HOME-App kann die Reinigung einfach von unterwegs geplant und gestartet werden; Clean-Map-Berichte zeigen an, wo der Roboter gesaugt hat.

Begründung der Jury
Der Saugroboter Roomba 980 ist äußerst kompakt und wertig gestaltet. Dank seiner ausgefeilten technischen Ausstattung sorgt er für sehr gründliche Reinigungsergebnisse.

Braava jet™
Mopping Robot
Bodenwischroboter

Manufacturer
iRobot, Bedford, USA
In-house design
Web
www.irobot.com

The Braava jet mopping robot cleans hard floors, including hardwood, tile and stone. With its compact, smart design and iAdapt 2.0 navigation system, it mops and sweeps hard-to-reach places, like under kitchen cabinets and around toilets. The robot automatically customises cleaning based on pad type. In wet mopping and damp sweeping modes, the Precision Jet Spray and Vibrating Cleaning Head tackle dirt and stains. In dry sweeping mode, the robot traps and locks away dust, dirt and pet hair.

Statement by the jury
The Braava jet mopping robot inspires with its extraordinarily simple one-button operation. Thanks to its practicable contours, it can access any space.

Der Saugroboter Braava jet reinigt Hartböden, einschließlich Hartholz, Fliesen und Stein. Mit seinem kompakten, intelligenten Design und dem iAdapt-2.0-Navigationssystem wischt und fegt er schwer zu erreichende Orte, z. B. unter Küchenschränken und um Toiletten herum. Der Roboter wählt anhand des Tuchtyps automatisch die richtige Reinigungsmethode. Im Nass- und Feuchtwischmodus lösen der Präzisionssprühstrahl und der vibrierende Reinigungskopf Schmutz und Flecken. Im Trockenwischmodus zieht der Roboter Staub, Schmutz und Tierhaare an und hält sie fest.

Begründung der Jury
Der Bodenwischroboter Braava jet begeistert durch seine außergewöhnlich simple Ein-Tasten-Bedienung. Mit seiner praxistauglichen Bauform kommt er überall hin.

KR 3 AGILUS
Small Robot
Kleinroboter

Manufacturer
KUKA AG, Augsburg, Germany
In-house design
Christoph Groll, Wolfgang Mayer
Design
Selic Industriedesign,
Augsburg, Germany
Web
www.kuka.com
www.selic.de

The KR 3 Agilus small robot is used in the manufacturing and assembly of tiny components and for products that must be produced in the smallest of spaces. As one of the fastest robots in the 3 kg class, it is characterised by very short cycle times and high repetition accuracy. Moreover, the robot achieves high acceleration values thanks to its low weight. Its internal energy supply, protected interfaces on the arm and minimal disruptive contours enable flexible movements, even in tight spaces.

Der Kleinroboter KR 3 Agilus findet Einsatz bei der Herstellung und Montage kleinster Bauteile oder bei Produkten, die auf engstem Raum produziert werden müssen. Als einer der schnellsten Roboter in der 3-kg-Klasse zeichnet er sich durch sehr kurze Taktzeiten und eine hohe Wiederholgenauigkeit aus. Zudem erreicht der Roboter durch sein geringes Eigengewicht hohe Beschleunigungswerte. Die innen liegende Energiezuführung, geschützte Schnittstellen am Arm sowie geringe Störkonturen ermöglichen flexible Bewegungen auch dort, wo wenig Platz ist.

Statement by the jury
Thanks to its human-like joint positions and flowing contours, the KR 3 Agilus small robot appears very alive and thus radiates a high degree of agility.

Begründung der Jury
Mit seinen menschlich anmutenden Gelenkpositionen und durch seine fließenden Konturen wirkt der Kleinroboter KR 3 Agilus sehr lebendig und strahlt ein hohes Maß an Agilität aus.

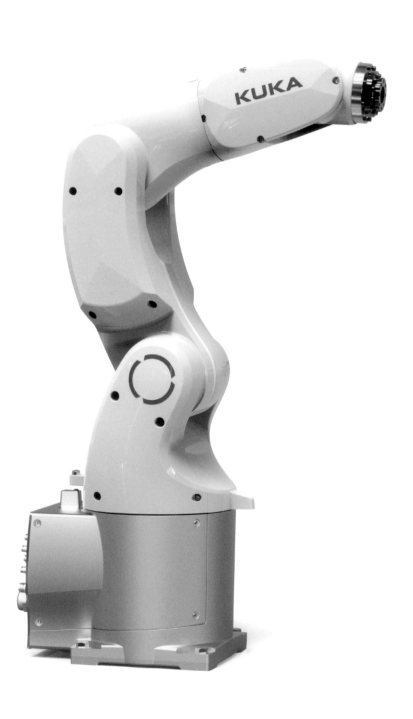

KR 20 CYBERTECH
Industrial Robot
Industrieroboter

Manufacturer
KUKA AG, Augsburg, Germany
In-house design
Günther Merk, Leander Eisenwinter
Design
Selic Industriedesign,
Augsburg, Germany
Web
www.kuka.com
www.selic.de

The KR 20 Cybertech is suitable for processing and handling large components as well as for assembly, palletising and inert gas welding. Thanks to its small volume and compactness, the robot is fast, agile and does precise work even at maximum speed. With a range of 2,100 mm, it bridges distances that could not be reached by its predecessors. The sparing use of materials reduces the energy input and underlines the sustainability. The robot can be installed on the ground, the wall or the ceiling, as well as at a particular angle.

Der Industrieroboter KR 20 Cybertech eignet sich zum Bearbeiten und Handhaben großer Bauteile sowie zum Montieren, Palettieren und Schutzgasschweißen. Durch seine volumenreduzierte Kompaktheit ist er schnell, beweglich und arbeitet auch bei maximalem Tempo exakt. Mit einer Reichweite von 2.100 mm überbrückt der Roboter Distanzen, die für die Vorgängermodelle nicht möglich waren. Der sparsame Materialeinsatz reduziert den Energieaufwand und unterstreicht die Nachhaltigkeit. Der Roboter kann am Boden, an der Wand, an der Decke oder in einem bestimmten Winkel montiert werden.

Statement by the jury
With its slim, long silhouette, the KR 20 Cybertech industrial robot pushes the boundaries of what is possible with regard to speed and range.

Begründung der Jury
Der Industrieroboter KR 20 Cybertech mit seiner schlanken, langgestreckten Silhouette reizt die Grenzen des Möglichen aus, was Geschwindigkeit und Reichweite angeht.

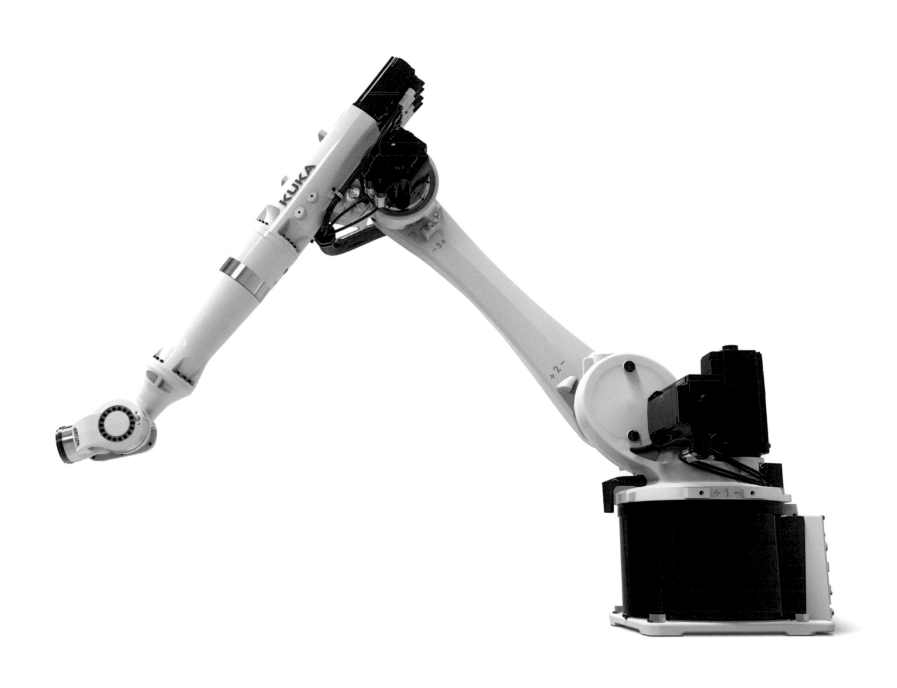

Moving HRC System
MRK-Mitfahrwagen

Manufacturer
Daimler AG, Sindelfingen, Germany
Design
defortec GmbH (Stefan Grobe, Lionel Linke),
Dettenhausen, Germany
Web
www.daimler.com
www.defortec.de

The intelligent Moving HRC System enables human robotic collaboration (HRC) in the field of automotive manufacturing. Being constantly in motion, the device recognises human beings in its surroundings and therefore prevents collision. By sorting, isolating and transferring the material to the robots head, the Moving HRC System is able to execute complex tasks independently. The integrated light channels indicate the operational status. The service areas have been optimised for quick accessibility and easy use.

Der intelligente Mitfahrwagen ermöglicht die Mensch-Roboter-Kollaboration (MRK) im Bereich der Automobilfertigung. Selbst während fortlaufender Bewegungsabläufe erkennt das Gefährt Menschen in seiner Umgebung und ist in der Lage, Kollisionen zu vermeiden. Dabei führt der Wagen komplexe Tätigkeiten wie das Sortieren, Vereinzeln und Übergeben der Montageelemente an den Roboterkopf aus. Die integrierten Lichtkanäle geben hierbei Auskunft über den jeweiligen Betriebszustand. Die Servicebereiche und Bedienelemente sind für einen schnellen Zugriff und eine einfache Bedienung konzipiert.

Statement by the jury
The unobtrusive aesthetic of the Moving HRC System, with its soft contours and light colours, introduces a friendly atmosphere into the work environment.

Begründung der Jury
Die zurückhaltende Ästhetik des Mitfahrwagens mit seinen weichen Konturen und hellen Farben bringt eine freundliche Atmosphäre in das Arbeitsumfeld.

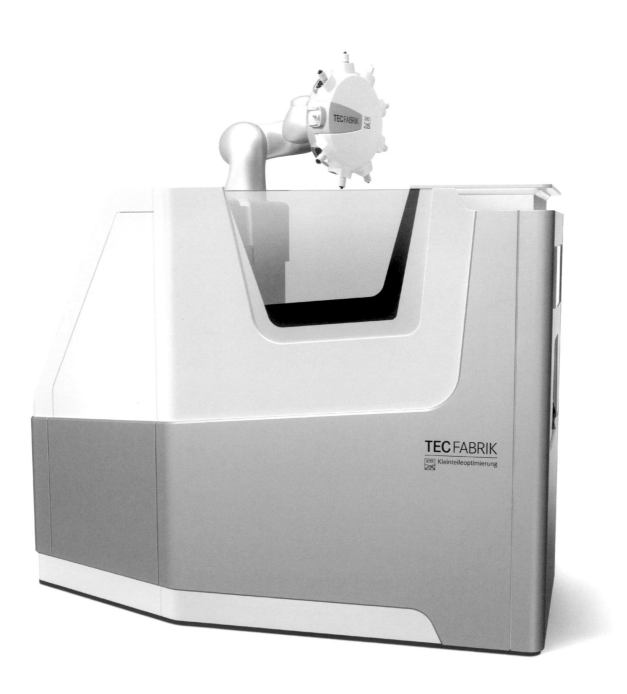

Dexmo
Exoskeleton for Virtual Reality Applications
Exoskelett für Virtual-Reality-Anwendungen

Manufacturer
Dexta Robotics Inc., Elko, USA/Shenzhen, China
Design
Hefei XIVO Design Co., Ltd. (Wenbao Chu, Chao Jing),
Hefei, China
Web
www.dextarobotics.com
www.xivodesign.com

Dexmo is a mechanical exoskeleton, which has been developed for virtual reality applications. In combination with a VR headset, it transfers the hand and finger movements of the wearer into the digital world, while simultaneously providing tactile feedback in real time. Wearers can feel the shape, quality and weight of the virtual objects they touch. The exoskeleton is encased in cuffs made of lightweight plastic. They are precisely adapted to the rounded shapes of the internal motors, creating an overall slim design.

Dexmo ist ein mechanisches Exoskelett, das für Virtual-Reality-Anwendungen entwickelt wurde. In Verbindung mit einem VR-Headset überträgt es die realen Hand- und Fingerbewegungen des Trägers in die digitale Welt und liefert gleichzeitig ein haptisches Feedback in Echtzeit. Der Träger kann Form, Beschaffenheit und Gewicht eines virtuell ergriffenen Gegenstands real spüren. Das Exoskelett ist von Manschetten aus leichtem Kunststoff umhüllt. Diese sind passgenau auf die gerundete Form der innen liegenden Motoren abgestimmt, sodass die Konstruktion insgesamt schlank bleibt.

Statement by the jury
The Dexmo exoskeleton creates an intense user experience by giving the wearer a tactile experience of the virtual world. Its design is strikingly reminiscent of a human skeleton.

Begründung der Jury
Das Exoskelett Dexmo schafft eine intensive Nutzererfahrung, indem es die virtuelle Welt haptisch erfahrbar macht. Seine Gestaltung erinnert auf prägnante Weise an ein menschliches Skelett.

Heating and air conditioning technology
Heiz- und Klimatechnik

S-BOX
Air Purifier
Luftreiniger

Manufacturer
Haier Group, Qingdao, China

In-house design
Haier Innovation Design Center
(Dai Nanhai, Zhou Shu,
Fei Zhaojun, Feng Zhiqun,
Zhao Tianyu)

Web
www.haier.com

reddot award 2017
best of the best

Fresh air

Air purifiers are an important element in interiors as they can make a valuable contribution to the health and well-being of people. The design of the S-BOX air purifier has emerged with a novel and appealing shape for this type of device. It catches the eye at first glance with its rounded edges and wooden base. This lends the unit an appearance of a 1950s piece of furniture, an impression that is further enhanced by the use of a fresh colour scheme. The wooden base is highly functional as it can be easily assembled and transformed into three different versions, allowing the purifier to meet different operating conditions. A special innovative aspect is that the fan part can be taken off and put into a vacuum cleaner as its own fan. Equipped with a click-joint design, this allows users to easily change the filter and replace it with any other filter matching the 300 mm x 300 mm size. When in use, the air purifier takes air in from the top and blows it out from the bottom. In this way, all dirt on the floor is blown into the air and can be completely purified. Another useful feature is that the unit features a battery and thus can be operated anywhere without any cables that could get tangled up. Incorporating a new interpretation, this air purifier has turned into a highly functional as well as stylish device for the home environment, an item that users can always enjoy looking at.

Fresh Air

Ein Luftreiniger ist ein wichtiger Bestandteil des Interieurs, da er einen wertvollen Beitrag für die Gesundheit und das Wohlbefinden leistet. Die Gestaltung der S-BOX findet für diese Art von Gerät eine neue und ansprechende Formensprache. Auf den ersten Blick verblüfft dieser Luftreiniger mit seinen abgerundeten Konturen sowie der Tatsache, dass er auf einem Ständer aus Holz ruht. Dies verleiht ihm die Anmutung eines Möbelstücks der 1950er Jahre, was durch eine frische Farbgebung noch unterstrichen wird. Der Holzständer ist zudem sehr funktional, da er leicht zu montieren ist und drei unterschiedliche Standversionen möglich sind, wodurch der Luftreiniger variabel einsetzbar ist. Eine besondere Innovation ist auch, dass die Ventilator-Einheit abgenommen und in einen Staubsauger eingesetzt werden kann. Eine Klick-Verbindung erlaubt den einfachen Filtertausch, wobei alle Filter im Format 300 x 300 mm verwendet werden können. In Betrieb saugt der Luftreiniger die Luft von oben ein und bläst sie unten wieder aus. Auf diese Weise wird der Schmutz auf dem Boden aufgewirbelt und effektiv aufgenommen. Sehr praktisch ist außerdem, dass das Gerät mit einer Batterie und ohne störende Kabel überall betrieben werden kann. Neu interpretiert, wird der Luftreiniger so zu einem überaus funktionalen und auch stylischen Gegenstand im häuslichen Umfeld, den man immer wieder gern ansieht.

Statement by the jury

The S-BOX air purifier literally delivers a fresh breeze to almost any interior. Showcasing a homely and friendly design appearance, it appeals to the senses. Its consistent functionality is impressive and has made it emerge as a highly user-friendly unit for a variety of uses. Uncomplicated to operate, it also offers the possibility to easily change the filters. This air purifier is an expression of a bold, future-oriented design.

Begründung der Jury

Der Luftreiniger S-BOX bringt buchstäblich eine frische Brise in seine Umgebung. Mit seiner ebenso wohnlich wie freundlich anmutenden Gestaltung spricht er die Emotionen an. Beeindruckend ist die schlüssige Funktionalität, die diesen Luftreiniger sehr nutzerfreundlich und variabel macht. Er ist unkompliziert zu handhaben und bietet eine einfache Möglichkeit des Filterwechsels. Dieser Luftreiniger ist Ausdruck eines mutigen und zukunftsweisenden Designs.

Designer portrait
See page 54
Siehe Seite 54

S-Box air purifier_2
Air Purifier
Luftreiniger

Manufacturer
Haier Group, Qingdao, China
In-house design
Haier Innovation Design Center
(Dai Nanhai, Zhou Shu, Fei Zhaojun,
Feng Zhiqun, Zhao Tianyu, Sun Luning)
Web
www.haier.com

The S-Box air purifier_2 features a
base whose shape may be modified and
adapted to different application areas.
The fan can be taken off and put into
a vacuum cleaner. Thanks to click connections, all filters with a size of up to
300 x 300 mm fit into the air purifier.
The device takes the air in from above
and blows it out at the bottom. In this
way, dust is whirled up from the ground,
then sucked into the device for cleaning.
The air purifier includes a rechargeable
battery and can thus be placed anywhere.

Statement by the jury
With its original design, this air purifier is
setting accents. The airflow direction
efficiently filters dust out of the air and
is another intelligent solution.

Der Luftreiniger S-Box air purifier_2 besitzt
einen Standfuß, dessen Form verändert
und an unterschiedliche Einsatzbereiche
angepasst werden kann. Der Ventilator lässt
sich abnehmen und in einen Staubsauger
einsetzen. Dank Klickverbindungen passen
alle Filter mit Maßen bis 300 x 300 mm in
den Luftreiniger. Das Gerät saugt die Luft
oben an und bläst sie unten heraus. So wird
der Staub zunächst am Boden aufgewirbelt,
dann vom Gerät eingesaugt und schließlich
gereinigt. Da der Luftreiniger einen Akku
besitzt, kann er überall aufgestellt werden.

Begründung der Jury
Mit seiner eigenwilligen Formgebung setzt
dieser Luftreiniger Akzente. Intelligent
gelöst ist die Führung des Luftstroms, dank
derer Staub effizient aus der Luft gefiltert
wird.

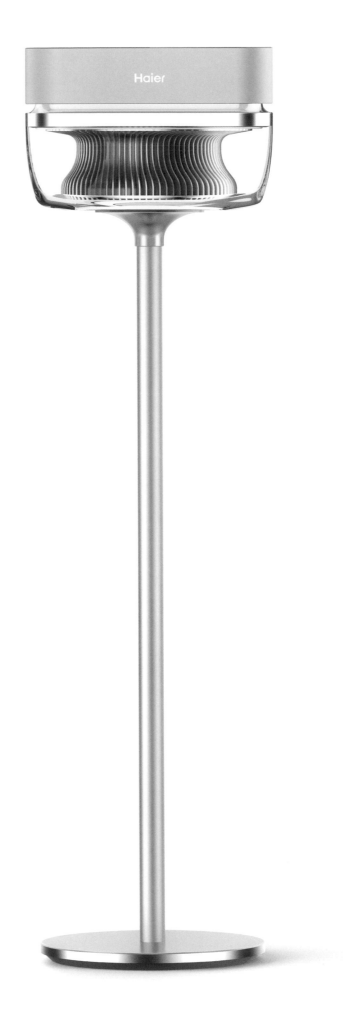

AirVibe
Air Quality Sensor
Luftsensor

Manufacturer
Philips, Eindhoven, Netherlands
In-house design
Philips Design
Web
www.philips.com

The AirVibe is a digital sensor for monitoring air quality in rooms, allowing for remote operation via an app on mobile devices. In addition to temperature and humidity, it monitors levels of fine dust, volatile organic compounds, CO_2 and formaldehyde in the air. With its elegant, compact design, it can be set up as standing device or mounted to a wall using the detachable knob on the rear. The user interface enables intuitive operation and good readability of measurement results.

Statement by the jury
Thanks to its small size and discreet design, AirVibe can be placed virtually anywhere.

AirVibe ist ein digitaler Luftsensor, der die Luftqualität in Räumen überwacht und dabei den Zugriff per App von Mobilgeräten aus erlaubt. Neben Temperatur und Feuchtigkeit misst er auch den Gehalt an Feinstaub, flüchtigen organischen Verbindungen, CO_2 und Formaldehyd in der Luft. Mit seiner eleganten, kompakten Gestalt kann er aufgestellt oder – wenn der Knopf auf der Rückseite abgenommen wird – an eine Wand gehängt werden. Die Benutzerschnittstelle gewährleistet die intuitive Bedienung und leichte Ablesbarkeit der Werte.

Begründung der Jury
Dank seiner geringen Größe und zurückhaltenden Formgebung lässt sich AirVibe überall aufstellen oder anbringen.

Air Purifier Series 2000
Luftreiniger-Serie

Manufacturer
Philips, Eindhoven, Netherlands
In-house design
Philips Design
Web
www.philips.com

This series of air purifiers was designed to provide users with a high degree of security with regard to air quality in the surrounding environment. Three preconfigured modes serve to remove either pollutant particles, allergens or bacteria and viruses from the air, making it easy to achieve the desired result. The three air inlets and outlets guarantee a high filter performance, while the intuitive display precisely indicates air quality.

Statement by the jury
This series is characterised by a strong degree of user-friendliness, which is underscored by its congenial appearance.

Geräte dieser Serie von Luftreinigern sind darauf ausgelegt, dem Anwender hinsichtlich der Luftqualität in seiner Umgebung eine hohe Sicherheit zu geben. Mit drei vorkonfigurierten Modi werden wahlweise Schmutzpartikel, Allergene oder Bakterien und Viren aus der Luft gefiltert. Dadurch ist es für den Benutzer kein Aufwand, das gewünschte Ergebnis zu erreichen. Die drei Luftein- und -auslässe gewährleisten eine hohe Filterleistung, während das intuitive Display die Luftqualität präzise anzeigt.

Begründung der Jury
Die Serie zeichnet sich durch eine hohe Anwenderfreundlichkeit aus, was durch ihre sympathische Anmutung unterstrichen wird.

LA502
Air Purifier
Luftreiniger

Manufacturer
Dongguan Lifa Air Technology Limited,
Dongguan, China
In-house design
Yao Jia Xing
Web
www.lifa-air.com
Honourable Mention

The LA502 air purifier was conceived for indoor use. It is equipped with a Smart Controller that constantly monitors levels of various substances: fine dust, CO_2, temperature, relative humidity and optionally either formaldehyde or volatile organic compounds. The monitor automatically controls the air purifier, depending on the levels measured. Using an app, air quality can be monitored and controlled remotely.

Statement by the jury
The air purifier excels with its range of functions since it monitors not only common data like CO_2 or air humidity, but also fine dust and formaldehyde.

Der Luftreiniger LA502 wurde für die Verwendung im Innenbereich entwickelt. Er ist mit einem Smart Controller bestückt, der permanent verschiedene Werte misst: Feinstaub, CO_2, Temperatur, Luftfeuchtigkeit und wahlweise Formaldehyd oder flüchtige organische Verbindungen. Das Gerät wird dann in Abhängigkeit der gemessenen Werte automatisch gesteuert. Per App lässt sich die Luftqualität auch von unterwegs kontrollieren und das Gerät entsprechend regulieren.

Begründung der Jury
Der Luftreiniger gefällt mit seinem Funktionsumfang, da er nicht nur übliche Werte wie CO_2 oder Luftfeuchtigkeit erfasst, sondern auch Feinstaub oder Formaldehyd.

LG Montblanc-D
Air Purifier
Luftreiniger

Manufacturer
LG Electronics Inc., Seoul, South Korea
In-house design
Kyeongchul Cho, Yoojeong Han,
Seungho Baek
Web
www.lg.com

The Montblanc-D air purifier unites the functions of air purification and air circulation and is thus able to effectively cover a wider space. The blower either expels the purified air in a desired direction or distributes it evenly throughout the room. The lower part of the device cleans the air at a height where children are usually situated. Moreover, the cylindrical shape prevents children from being injured in case they bump against the device.

Statement by the jury
This air purifier excels with its wellthought-out design, which takes the concerns of both children and adults into account.

Der Luftreiniger Montblanc-D vereint die Funktionen Luftreinigung und Luftumwälzung, dadurch kann er einen größeren Raum effektiv abdecken. Das Gebläse bläst die gereinigte Luft wahlweise in eine gewünschte Richtung oder verteilt sie gleichmäßig im Raum. Im unteren Bereich des Geräts wird die Luft in einer Höhe gereinigt, in der sich gewöhnlich Kinder aufhalten. Die zylindrische Form verhindert zudem, dass sich Kinder verletzen, wenn sie an das Gerät stoßen.

Begründung der Jury
Der Luftreiniger begeistert mit seiner durchdachten Gestaltung, die auf die Belange von Kindern wie Erwachsenen Rücksicht nimmt.

Mushroom
Household Oxygenerator
Haushaltsluftreiniger

Manufacturer
Yuwell, Nanjing, China
Design
Shenzhen ND Industrial Design Co., Ltd.
(Jingzhou Wen, Tianyu Xiao),
Shenzhen, China
Web
www.yuyue.com.cn
www.sz-nd.com

With its rounded, soft appearance, the Mushroom household oxygenerator is reminiscent of a mushroom, newly defining the design language of this sort of device. The wooden top gives reference to pieces of furniture, facilitating integration into the domestic environment. The oxygenerator is operated via an intuitively conceived user interface thanks to the large backlit display. With its compact dimensions, the unit can be placed anywhere.

Statement by the jury
Mushroom scores with its original shape, which is appealing while also ensuring seamless integration of the device into living room interiors.

Der Haushaltsluftreiniger Mushroom erinnert mit seiner rundlichen, weichen Erscheinung an einen Pilz und definiert damit die Formensprache derartiger Geräte neu. Die Oberseite aus Holz stellt einen Bezug zu Möbelstücken her, wodurch sich das Gerät ganz einfach in das häusliche Umfeld einfügen lässt. Der Luftreiniger wird über eine intuitiv konzipierte Benutzerschnittstelle bedient, was sich dank des großen, hinterleuchteten Displays einfach gestaltet. Aufgrund seiner kompakten Maße findet er überall Platz.

Begründung der Jury
Mushroom punktet mit seiner originellen Form, die zum einen sympathisch wirkt, zum anderen gewährleistet, dass sich das Gerät wie selbstverständlich in Wohnräume einfügt.

Super L
Air Purifier
Luftreiniger

Manufacturer
SK magic, Seoul, South Korea
In-house design
Dongsu Kim, Dongwook Yoon
Web
www.skmagic.com

The Super L is a smart air purifier that measures the degree of indoor air pollution, recording the values and then performing an automatic cleaning function. It is equipped with a learning function that calculates when air pollution mainly occurs in order to then clean the air according to a specific pattern. Thanks to its GPS functionality, the air purifier can be controlled from a smartphone and also, for example, be activated directly prior to the user's arrival at home. With its small wooden base, it is reminiscent of a piece of furniture, thus harmonising with the surrounding space.

Statement by the jury
Smart functions allow the user to keep an eye on air cleaning at any time, reducing to a minimum the necessity of manual intervention.

Super L ist ein intelligenter Luftfreiniger, der den Grad der Luftverschmutzung in Innenräumen misst, aufzeichnet und dann automatisch die Reinigung durchführt. Er ist mit einer Lernfunktion ausgestattet und berechnet, wann die Luft hauptsächlich belastet ist, um sie dann nach einem bestimmten Muster zu reinigen. Aufgrund seiner GPS-Funktion kann der Luftfreiniger über ein Smartphone gesteuert und beispielsweise aktiviert werden, bevor der Benutzer nach Hause kommt. Mit seinen kleinen Holzfüßen erinnert er an ein Möbelstück und fügt sich harmonisch in den Raum ein.

Begründung der Jury
Die intelligenten Funktionen erlauben dem Benutzer, die Luftreinigung jederzeit im Blick zu behalten. Die Notwendigkeit, selbst einzugreifen, wird auf ein Minimum reduziert.

Tower XQ600
Air Purifier
Luftreiniger

Manufacturer
WINIX Manufacturing Company,
Seongnam, South Korea
In-house design
Chan Wook Yeo, Seung Ho Kim
Web
www.winixcorp.com

The Tower XQ600 air purifier is conceived for use in rooms of up to 60 sqm. Thanks to its vertical design, it can be placed in smaller rooms, and with its rounded edges, it resembles an interior furnishing item. A display in the upper part of the device shows the air quality in numerical and graphic figures. When the display is not needed, it can be turned off. An integrated UV LED sterilises air channels and the ventilator as soon as the corresponding button is pushed.

Statement by the jury
With its unobtrusive, friendly design, this air purifier can be ideally placed in small- to medium-sized rooms without attracting attention.

Der Luftreiniger Tower XQ600 ist für den Einsatz in Räumen bis 60 qm konzipiert. Dank seiner vertikalen Bauweise kann er auch in kleineren Räumen aufgestellt werden. Zudem ähnelt er mit seinen gerundeten Kanten einem Einrichtungsgegenstand. Ein Display im oberen Bereich des Geräts zeigt die Luftqualität numerisch und grafisch an. Wird das Display nicht benötigt, lässt es sich abschalten. Eine integrierte UV-LED sterilisiert die Luftkanäle und den Ventilator, sobald der entsprechende Knopf gedrückt wird.

Begründung der Jury
Mit seiner unaufdringlichen, freundlichen Formgebung kann der Luftreiniger auch in kleinen bis mittleren Räumen ideal platziert werden, ohne aufzufallen.

Smart-Mi Degerm
Humidifier
Luftbefeuchter

Manufacturer
Beijing Zhimi Electronic Technology Co., Ltd.,
Beijing, China
In-house design
Jun Su
Web
www.zhimi.com

This ultrasonic air humidifier provides a comfortable indoor climate and removes bacteria from the air. It is easily operated, as water can be refilled from above as soon as the appropriate sensor indicates a low water level. If it is not possible for the humidifier to be immediately refilled, it automatically moves into standby mode to prevent overheating. The ambient air is analysed by the temperature and humidity sensor, with the degree of nebulisation and ventilator speed being adjusted accordingly.

Statement by the jury
The well-thought-out technical design makes it easy for the user to ensure good air quality with only little effort in operating the device.

Dieser Ultraschall-Luftbefeuchter sorgt für ein angenehmes Raumklima und reinigt die Luft von Bakterien. Die Handhabung ist einfach, denn sobald der entsprechende Sensor einen niedrigen Wasserstand meldet, lässt sich das Wasser bequem von oben nachfüllen. Sollte dies gerade nicht möglich sein, schaltet das Gerät auf Standby, um nicht heiß zu laufen. Über den Temperatur- und Feuchtigkeitssensor wird die Umgebungsluft analysiert, woraufhin Zerstäubungsgrad und Geschwindigkeit des Lüfters angepasst werden.

Begründung der Jury
Die durchdachte technische Ausstattung macht es dem Anwender leicht, für eine gute Luftqualität zu sorgen. Der Aufwand bei der Bedienung bleibt dabei erfreulich gering.

Storm (AP-1516A)
Air Purifier
Luftreiniger

Manufacturer
Coway Co., Ltd., Seoul, South Korea
In-house design
Jingyu Seo, Jongho Choi
Web
www.coway.com

This air purifier with circulator function cleanses the air particularly fast and releases the purified air in an efficient way. To optimise air circulation, the filtered air can be expelled, as required, to the front as well as upward. An air jet of up to ten metres can be blown out from the front circular opening. Storm is also suitable for operation in living rooms with adjacent kitchens, whereby the air purification can be flexibly adapted to the dwellers' needs.

Statement by the jury
Storm convinces with its high degree of functionality and, as a standing unit with a characteristic design, creates a striking effect.

Dieser Luftwäscher mit Umwälzfunktion reinigt die Raumluft besonders schnell und gibt die gereinigte Luft auf effektive Weise frei. Um die Luftzirkulation zu optimieren, kann die gefilterte Luft bei Bedarf sowohl vorne als auch oben ausgestoßen werden. Aus der vorderen Öffnung der Gerätefront kann ein bis zu zehn Meter reichender Luftstrahl entweichen. Storm eignet sich u. a. für den Einsatz in Wohnräumen mit angrenzender Küche, wobei sich die Luftwäsche flexibel auf die Bedürfnisse der Bewohner einstellen lässt.

Begründung der Jury
Storm überzeugt aufgrund seiner hohen Funktionalität und wirkt als charakteristisch gestaltetes Standgerät sehr prägnant.

AirBrain
Intelligent Hardware

Manufacturer
GD Midea Air-Conditioning Equipment Co., Ltd., Foshan, China
In-house design
Jinpeng Shao, Sanxin Li
Web
www.midea.com

The AirBrain is an intelligent indoor climate control centre for households. Devices such as air conditioners, ventilators, air washers and humidifiers are monitored through voice control. Moreover, it enables two-way communication and, thanks to the 360-degree speaker, turns into a hub for playing music. As a playful detail, it includes an LED lamp on the vertical aluminium ring, which changes colour depending on speech volume.

Statement by the jury
The iconic design of the AirBrain is reminiscent of a microphone and thus highlights one of its central functions in an original way.

AirBrain ist eine intelligente Steuerzentrale für das Raumklima im Haushalt. Per Sprachsteuerung werden Geräte wie Klimaanlagen, Ventilatoren, Luftwäscher oder Luftentfeuchter bedient. Zudem ermöglicht sie die 2-Wege-Kommunikation und wird dank des 360-Grad-Lautsprechers zur Musikanlage. Als spielerisches Detail besitzt sie eine LED-Leuchte auf dem vertikalen Aluminiumring, die ihre Farbe je nach Sprachlautstärke wechselt.

Begründung der Jury
Die ikonische Gestaltung von AirBrain erinnert an ein Mikrofon und betont damit auf originelle Weise eine ihrer zentralen Funktionen.

Super Mini
Air Purifier
Luftreiniger

Manufacturer
SK magic, Seoul, South Korea
In-house design
Dongsu Kim, Dongwook Yoon
Web
www.skmagic.com

This interactive air purifier may be combined with other air purifying devices. Information with regard to air pollution can be exchanged between the devices to ensure optimum air purification. In this way, indoor air quality in the entire house can be improved rapidly. Moreover, measured values can be read off remotely with a smartphone, also allowing the user to change settings on the devices. With its modern, reduced design and light colouring, the device symbolises purity and freshness.

Der interaktive Luftreiniger lässt sich mit anderen Luftreinigern vernetzen. So können Informationen über die Luftbelastung zwischen den Geräten ausgetauscht werden, um eine optimale Luftreinigung zu gewährleisten. Auf diese Weise lässt sich die Raumluft im gesamten Haus rasch verbessern. Zudem können via Smartphone Messwerte von unterwegs abgelesen und Einstellungen an den Geräten vorgenommen werden. Mit seiner modernen, reduzierten Gestaltung und den hellen Farben symbolisiert das Gerät Reinheit und Frische.

Statement by the jury
This air purifier with its minimalist design blends into any interior and, thanks to information exchange among the devices, offers a high degree of benefit and comfort.

Begründung der Jury
Der zurückhaltend gestaltete Luftreiniger fügt sich in jeden Raum ein und bietet dank Vernetzung ein hohes Maß an Nutzen und Komfort.

Venta Airwasher LW62T
Venta Luftwäscher LW62T
Indoor Air Humidifier and
Purifier with Water Filter
Raumluft-Befeuchter und
Reiniger mit Wasserfilter

Manufacturer
Venta Luftwäscher GmbH, Weingarten, Germany
In-house design
Fred Hitzler
Design
Vision Produktgestaltung (Michael Leggewie),
Pfaffenhofen, Germany
Web
www.venta-luftwaescher.de
www.vision-produktgestaltung.de

The Venta Airwasher LW62T is designed for rooms of up to 250 sqm. Its mode of action is based on the principle of natural cold evaporation: the air passes through rotating disc stacks in the water and thus becomes humidified and purified simultaneously. The design pays close attention to a timeless appearance with high recognition value, generated by the circumferential lattice structure. The device is operated either via the swivelling touch display, a remote control or via Wi-Fi with an app and mobile device.

Der Venta Luftwäscher LW62T ist für Räume bis 250 qm ausgelegt. Seine Wirkungsweise beruht auf dem Prinzip der natürlichen Kaltverdunstung: Die Luft wird durch im Wasser rotierende Plattenstapel geleitet und dadurch sowohl befeuchtet als auch gereinigt. Bei der Gestaltung wurde auf ein zeitloses Erscheinungsbild geachtet, das durch die umlaufende Gitterstruktur zudem einen hohen Wiedererkennungswert aufweist. Bedient wird das Gerät über das schwenkbare Touchdisplay, über eine Fernbedienung oder dank Wi-Fi mittels App über ein mobiles Endgerät.

Statement by the jury
The Venta Airwasher LW62T excels with its unmistakable design and comfortable operating options.

Begründung der Jury
Der Venta Luftwäscher LW62T besticht durch seine unverwechselbare Formgebung und die komfortablen Möglichkeiten, ihn zu bedienen.

Buderus Logatherm WLW196i AR T
Air-to-Water Heat Pump
Luft-Wasser-Wärmepumpe

Manufacturer
Bosch Thermotechnik GmbH,
Buderus Deutschland,
Wetzlar, Germany

Design
designaffairs GmbH,
Erlangen, Germany

Web
www.buderus.de
www.designaffairs.com

reddot award 2017
best of the best

Smart elegance

Heating with air-to-water heat pumps is a process based on absorbing heat from the air and transferring it into a heating system. Thus taking advantage of a regenerative source of energy, this approach is future-oriented and helps conserve limited natural resources. The air-to-water heat pump by Buderus is a smart, high-performance system for this type of energy generation. In an impressive manner, the design of the system succeeds in making its high inner technical quality clearly visible on the outside. Marked by the high-quality material Titanium glass, the system has an unobtrusive and elegant appearance. Featuring a compact housing, it takes up only little space in the home and fascinates with its purist design. The heat pump is operated via a touch-sensitive control unit that is consistently fitted onto the housing and sits behind an ergonomically arranged flap, which makes even complex settings particularly simple. Moreover, an integrated Internet gateway offers uncomplicated and intuitive operation via mobile devices such as smartphones and tablets. Following a modular approach, this air-to-water heat pump can also be easily extended with additional renewable energy sources. Available in black and white, the path-breaking design of this system sets new standards in the market for heat pumps.

Smarte Eleganz

Das Heizen mit einer Luft-Wasser-Wärmepumpe basiert auf der Nutzung der Umgebungsluft, der Wärme entzogen wird. Als regenerative Energiequelle schont dies die begrenzt vorhandenen Ressourcen und ist deshalb zukunftsweisend. Die Luft-Wasser-Wärmepumpe von Buderus ist eine smarte, für diese Art der Energiegewinnung sehr leistungsfähige Wärmepumpe. Ihrer Gestaltung gelingt es dabei auf beeindruckende Weise, die hohe technische Qualität mittels der äußeren Form zu transportieren. Geprägt durch das hochwertige Material Titanium-Glas, wirkt sie unaufdringlich und elegant. Mit ihrem kompakten Gehäuse benötigt sie im Haus nur sehr wenig Standfläche und begeistert dort mit ihrer puristischen Formensprache. Die Wärmepumpe wird über eine schlüssig in das Gehäuse eingepasste, hinter einer ergonomisch angeordneten Klappe befindlichen Bedieneinheit mit Sensortasten gesteuert, wodurch auch komplexe Einstellungen besonders einfach vorgenommen werden können. Eine integrierte Internet-Schnittstelle ermöglicht zudem eine unkomplizierte und intuitive Bedienung über mobile Geräte wie Smartphones oder Tablets. Dank eines modularen Ansatzes kann diese Luft-Wasser-Wärmepumpe problemlos um zusätzliche erneuerbare Energiequellen erweitert werden. Mit ihrer wegweisenden Gestaltung setzt die in den Farben Schwarz und Weiß verfügbare Anlage neue Standards im Segment der Wärmepumpen.

Statement by the jury

This air-to-water heat pump by Buderus fits into almost any domestic environment thanks to its clear, unobtrusive elegance. It thus opens up new architectural possibilities in planning and arranging domestic heating systems. Well-thought-through to the last detail, the design not only manages to communicate the high utility value of this heat pump, it also draws attention to its uncompromising quality and sophisticated technology. Moreover, it fascinates with an ease of operation that places the user centre stage.

Begründung der Jury

Diese Luft-Wasser-Wärmepumpe von Buderus kann sich durch ihre klare, unaufdringliche Eleganz in jedes Ambiente einfügen. Dadurch eröffnen sich architektonisch neue Möglichkeiten bei der Planung von Heizungsanlagen. Der bis ins Detail durchdachten Gestaltung gelingt es, den hohen Gebrauchswert dieser Wärmepumpe zu vermitteln und dabei auf ihre kompromisslose Qualität und ausgereifte Technologie hinzuweisen. Zudem begeistert ein Bedienkomfort, der den Nutzer in den Mittelpunkt stellt.

Designer portrait
See page 56
Siehe Seite 56

Buderus Logano plus
Floorstanding Gas/Oil Condensing Boiler
Bodenstehender Gas-/Öl-Brennwertkessel

Manufacturer
Bosch Thermotechnik GmbH, Buderus Deutschland,
Wetzlar, Germany
Design
designaffairs, Erlangen, Germany
Web
www.buderus.de
www.designaffairs.com

The Logano plus condensing boiler combines attractive and modern design with efficient heating using oil or gas. The unique Titanium-glass design represents state-of-the-art technology in the modern world of heating devices, underscoring the high technological quality of the boiler. The glass front is not only robust but also easily cleaned. The condensing boiler is operated via a user-friendly control unit or, thanks to the integrated Internet gateway, via mobile devices.

Der Brennwertkessel Logano plus verbindet eine attraktive und moderne Gestaltung mit effizientem Heizen mit Öl oder Gas. Das einzigartige Titanium-Glas-Design repräsentiert den Stand der Technik in der modernen Welt von Heizgeräten und unterstreicht die technologische Qualität des Geräts. Zudem ist die Front aus Glas nicht nur stabil, sondern auch leicht zu reinigen. Gesteuert wird der Brennwertkessel über eine benutzerfreundliche Bedienoberfläche oder, dank des integrierten Internet-Gateways, über Mobilgeräte.

Statement by the jury
With its contemporary design, the Logano plus condensing boiler represents high technical standards with regard to modern heating with traditional fuels.

Begründung der Jury
Mit seiner zeitgemäßen Gestaltung steht der Brennwertkessel Logano plus für den hohen technischen Anspruch an modernes Heizen mit traditionellen Brennstoffen.

Bosch Condens 7000i W
Wall-Hung Condensing Gas Boiler
Gas-Brennwertkessel für
die Wandmontage

Manufacturer
Bosch Thermotechnik GmbH,
Wernau, Germany
Design
designaffairs, Erlangen, Germany
Web
www.bosch-thermotechnik.de
www.designaffairs.com

The Bosch Condens 7000i W wall-hung
condensing gas boiler is very compact
and can even be placed in a kitchen cabinet. The device is compatible with existing water connections and controllers,
enabling effortless installation. With its
high modulation rate, it is particularly
suitable for modern apartments with low
heating demands, yet powerful enough
to ensure an optimum warm water
supply.

Statement by the jury
Thanks to its discreet design with harmoniously rounded edges, this wall-
hung condensing boiler blends into any
domestic environment.

Der Gas-Brennwertkessel für die Wandmontage Bosch Condens 7000i W ist überaus kompakt und findet sogar in einem
Küchenschrank Platz. Das Gerät ist kompatibel zu bestehenden Wasseranschlüssen
und Reglern und daher mühelos zu installieren. Dank seines hohen Modulations-
bereichs ist es besonders für moderne
Wohnungen mit geringem Heizbedarf geeignet, aber dennoch leistungsfähig genug,
um eine optimale Versorgung mit warmem
Wasser zu garantieren.

Begründung der Jury
Das Wandheizgerät passt dank seiner
zurückhaltenden Gestaltung mit freundlich gerundeten Kanten in jedes häusliche
Umfeld.

Bosch Gaz 7200i W
Wall-Hung Gas Boiler
Gas-Wandheizgerät

Manufacturer
Bosch Thermotechnology (Shanghai)
Co., Ltd., Shanghai, China
In-house design
Xuefei Liu
Web
www.bosch-climate.cn

This wall-hung gas boiler is characterised
by a glass front with a precious appearance, underlining its technical quality.
It is available in black or white to meet
different demands. The high-contrast
LCD display with bright white digits can
be read effortlessly, even under difficult
lighting conditions. The boiler is energy
efficient and offers the option of
switching back and forth between energy-saving and comfort modes. It can
also be remotely controlled via an app.

Statement by the jury
The Bosch Gaz 7200i W is Internet-
capable and, with its different heating
modes, provides the flexibility desired
by modern users.

Das Gas-Wandheizgerät zeichnet sich
durch eine edel wirkende Glasfront aus,
die seine technische Qualität unterstreicht.
Es ist in Schwarz und Weiß verfügbar, um
unterschiedlichen Bedürfnissen gerecht zu
werden. Das kontrastreiche LCD-Display
mit hellen weißen Ziffern lässt sich auch
bei schwierigen Lichtverhältnissen leicht
ablesen. Das Gerät arbeitet energieeffizient
und bietet die Möglichkeit, zwischen einem
Energiespar- und einem Komfortmodus zu
wechseln. Bedienen lässt es sich auch per
App von unterwegs.

Begründung der Jury
Das Bosch Gaz 7200i W ist internetfä-
hig und bietet mit seinen verschiedenen
Heizmodi die Flexibilität, die modernen
Anwendern entgegenkommt.

OSA
Wall-Hung Condensing Gas Boiler
Gas-Brennwertkessel für die Wandmontage

Manufacturer
Unical AG S.p.A., Castel d'Ario (Mantua), Italy
In-house design
Ilaria Jahier, Igor Zilioli, Sergio Fiorani, Gianluca Angiolini
Web
www.unical.eu
www.artudesignstudio.com

The OSA condensing gas boiler combines aesthetics and function in an independent way. It obtains its design appeal from the combination of different materials: the smooth front is in acrylic glass, while the sides are in carbon steel. The front is available in six different colours. The OSA condensing boiler, with all its connections concealed and merely 18 cm deep, is laid out for comfortable operation via wired interface or Wi-Fi with a dedicated app for smartphone or tablet. The device also includes indoor and outdoor temperature sensors, thus enabling energy-efficient heating.

Der Gas-Brennwertkessel OSA verbindet Ästhetik und Funktion auf eine eigenständige Weise. Seinen gestalterischen Reiz bezieht er aus der Kombination unterschiedlicher Materialien: Die glatte Vorderseite besteht aus Acrylglas, während die Einfassung aus Carbonstahl gefertigt ist. Zudem ist die Front in sechs verschiedenen Farben erhältlich. Auch die Bedienung des nur 18 cm tiefen OSA-Brennwertkessels mit seinen komplett verdeckten Anschlüssen ist komfortabel. Sie erfolgt über eine kabelgebundene Schnittstelle oder per Wi-Fi über eine eigene App für Smartphone oder Tablet. Das Gerät verfügt weiterhin über Sensoren, die die Innen- und Außentemperatur messen und das energieeffiziente Heizen ermöglichen.

Statement by the jury
With its minimalist design, the OSA condensing boiler can be integrated into virtually any room. A refined detail is the circumferential edge structuring that contrasts the front and side while highlighting the different materials.

Begründung der Jury
Mit seiner minimalistischen Gestaltung lässt sich der Brennwertkessel OSA in nahezu jeden Raum integrieren. Ein feines Detail ist die umlaufende Kante, die Front und Seite voneinander absetzt und die unterschiedlichen Materialien betont.

Tower Heater
Heizlüfter

Manufacturer
GD Midea Environment Appliances
Manufacturing Co., Ltd., Zhongshan, China
In-house design
Meng Yi Lang, Tong Ying
Web
www.midea.com

The Tower Heater is conceived for year-round use. In winter the heater expels warm air, while in summer cold air is blown into the room. In spring and autumn, the device can be used as a ventilator. Since the heater is compact and portable, it can be conveniently placed in any desired space and stowed away when not in use. The heater is available in various sizes to meet different demands.

Statement by the jury
The functional Tower Heater is a ventilator for every occasion. The rotary knob at the top enables easy operation.

Der Tower Heater ist für den ganzjährigen Einsatz konzipiert. Im Winter stößt der Heizlüfter warme Luft aus, im Sommer wird kalte Luft in den Raum geblasen. In Frühling und Herbst kann das Gerät als Ventilator verwendet werden. Da der Heizlüfter kompakt und tragbar ist, kann er leicht an jedem gewünschten Ort aufgestellt werden und lässt sich gut verstauen, wenn er nicht gebraucht wird. Er ist in verschiedenen Größen erhältlich und wird somit unterschiedlichen Anforderungen gerecht.

Begründung der Jury
Der funktional gehaltene Tower Heater ist ein Ventilator für jede Gelegenheit. Über Drehregler an der Oberseite lässt er sich einfach bedienen.

Tower PTC Heater-Series
Heater Series
Heizlüfterserie

Manufacturer
GD Midea Environment Appliances
Manufacturing Co., Ltd., Zhongshan, China
In-house design
Hou Wei, Meng Yi Lang, Tong Ying
Web
www.midea.com

This series of heaters features devices in three different sizes conceived for use in rooms of various dimensions. The tall version is suitable for large living spaces, the medium-sized version for small- to midsized bedrooms, while the small version can be placed, for example, on a desk. The air channels are arranged in such a way that the air is expelled vertically, thus solving the problem of low heating performance found in conventional heaters. As the heaters are column-shaped, they require only little floor space.

Statement by the jury
This series offers heaters with different capacities, allowing users to equip all of their rooms with uniformly designed heating units.

Diese Serie von Heizlüftern umfasst Geräte in drei Größen, die für den Einsatz in unterschiedlich großen Räumen konzipiert wurden. Die hohe Ausführung eignet sich für große Wohnräume, die mittlere für kleinere Schlafzimmer und die kleine kann z. B. auf dem Schreibtisch platziert werden. Die Luftkanäle sind so angelegt, dass die Luft vertikal ausgestoßen wird, was das Problem der geringen Heizleistung von traditionellen Heizgeräten löst. Da die Heizlüfter säulenförmig gestaltet sind, benötigen sie nur wenig Standfläche.

Begründung der Jury
Die Serie stellt Heizlüfter mit unterschiedlichen Kapazitäten bereit. So können sämtliche Räume mit einheitlich gestalteten Geräten ausgestattet werden.

auroSTOR/uniSTOR plus/exclusive
Hot Water Cylinders
Warmwasserspeicher

Manufacturer
Vaillant GmbH, Remscheid, Germany
In-house design
Design
Noto GmbH, Cologne, Germany
Web
www.vaillant.com
www.noto.design

The auroSTOR/uniSTOR plus/exclusive product family consists of indirect hot water cylinders characterised by a clear design along with user- and eco-friendliness. With capacities of up to 500 litres and variable configurations, they enable the storage of excess energy as thermal energy produced by solar systems or heat pumps. The clearly arranged user interfaces display important figures such as the water temperature, as well as information about the charge level and system connectivity for the LED variant.

Die Produktfamilie auroSTOR/uniSTOR plus/exclusive besteht aus indirekten Warmwasserspeichern, die sich durch eine klare Formgebung sowie durch Nutzer- und Umweltfreundlichkeit auszeichnen. Mit Kapazitäten bis zu 500 Litern und variabler Ausstattung ermöglichen sie die Speicherung von überschüssiger Energie als Wärmeenergie, die von Solaranlagen oder Wärmepumpen erzeugt wird. Die übersichtlich gestalteten Bedienschnittstellen zeigen wichtige Werte wie die Wassertemperatur, bei der LED-Variante außerdem Informationen zum Ladezustand und zur System-Konnektivität.

Statement by the jury
These hot water cylinders combine future-oriented, sustainable technology with a user-friendly, appealing design.

Begründung der Jury
Die Warmwasserspeicher verbinden eine zukunftsorientierte, nachhaltige Technologie mit einer nutzerfreundlichen, attraktiven Gestaltung.

16HQS Gas Water Heater
16HQS Gas-Warmwasser-bereiter

Manufacturer
Wuhu Midea Kitchen and Bath Appliances
Manufacturing Co., Ltd., Wuhu, China
In-house design
Design
Kurz Kurz Design China, Foshan, China
Web
www.midea.com
www.kkdesign.cn

The 16HQS gas water heater features a special heating method for efficient operation and reduction of harmful gas. Its minimalist design in matt colours signifies reliability and a long life cycle. Redundant design elements have been dispensed with, enabling easy cleaning and maintenance. A user-oriented interface indicates operational status, facilitating smooth handling and temperature monitoring.

Statement by the jury
This gas water heater is a successful example of a reduction to bare essentials. It offers a high degree of functionality and signalises dependability.

Im Gas-Warmwasserbereiter 16HQS kommt ein besonderes Heizverfahren zum Einsatz, das effizient ist und schädliche Abgase reduziert. Seine minimalistische Gestaltung in matten Farben vermittelt Zuverlässigkeit und eine lange Nutzungsdauer. Da auf überflüssige Designelemente verzichtet wurde, ist das Gerät leicht zu pflegen und zu reinigen. Eine Benutzerschnittstelle zeigt den Betriebszustand an, gewährleistet die einfache Bedienung und ermöglicht die Überwachung der Temperatur.

Begründung der Jury
Dieser Gas-Warmwasserbereiter ist ein gelungenes Beispiel für die Reduzierung auf das Wesentliche. Gleichzeitig bietet er eine hohe Funktionalität und signalisiert Verlässlichkeit.

BasicVent Enthalpie
Central Ventilation System
Zentrales Lüftungssystem

Manufacturer
WATERKOTTE GmbH, Herne, Germany
Design
industrialpartners GmbH,
Frankfurt/Main, Germany
Web
www.waterkotte.de
www.industrialpartners-communication.de

The BasicVent Enthalpie ventilation unit presents a modern, reduced design. The control display stands out with its colour scheme, ensuring easy retrieval of all important information. It also shows current measurement values. An integrated enthalpy heat exchanger allows the recovery of heat and air humidity from exhaust air. The transfer of smells and germs is ruled out. An app allows comfortable control via smartphone, PC or tablet.

Statement by the jury
This ventilation unit is characterised by a discreet design that focuses the user's attention on the essentials.

Das Lüftungssystem BasicVent Enthalpie zeigt eine moderne, reduzierte Formgebung. Das Bediendisplay tritt durch seine Farbgestaltung deutlich hervor und gewährleistet den einfachen Abruf aller wichtigen Informationen. Zudem zeigt es aktuelle Messwerte an. Ein integrierter Enthalpie-Wärmetauscher ermöglicht die Rückführung der Wärme und der Luftfeuchte aus der Abluft. Gerüche und Keime werden dabei nicht übertragen. Eine App erlaubt die bequeme Steuerung über Smartphone, PC oder Tablet.

Begründung der Jury
Das Lüftungsgerät zeichnet sich durch eine schlichte Gestaltung aus, die den Blick des Anwenders auf das Wesentliche lenkt.

EcoVent Enthalpie
Central Ventilation System
Zentrales Lüftungssystem

Manufacturer
WATERKOTTE GmbH, Herne, Germany
Design
industrialpartners GmbH,
Frankfurt/Main, Germany
Web
www.waterkotte.de
www.industrialpartners-communication.de

The EcoVent Enthalpie ventilation unit regulates air temperature, air humidity, CO_2 content and air circulation. The integrated enthalpy heat exchanger transfers both heat and humidity from exhaust air into a current of fresh air. The separation of airflow ensures a flawless solution with regard to hygiene. Additional functions are a summer bypass and the fireplace function, enabling the operation of a fireplace in parallel to the ventilation system. The display shows measurement values in real time, with three status LEDs providing additional orientation.

Statement by the jury
EcoVent Enthalpie impresses with its range of functions and the option of operating a fireplace at the same time.

Das Lüftungssystem EcoVent Enthalpie regelt Lufttemperatur, Luftfeuchtigkeit, CO_2-Gehalt und Luftbewegung. Der integrierte Enthalpie-Wärmetauscher überträgt sowohl Wärme als auch Feuchtigkeit aus der Abluft in den frischen Zuluftstrom. Die Trennung der Luftströme garantiert dabei eine hygienisch einwandfreie Lösung. Zusätzliche Funktionen sind ein Sommerbypass und die Feuerstätten-Funktion, die parallel zur Lüftungsanlage den Betrieb einer Feuerstätte erlaubt. Das Display zeigt Messwerte in Echtzeit an, drei Status-LEDs dienen zur zusätzlichen Orientierung.

Begründung der Jury
EcoVent Enthalpie beeindruckt mit seinem Funktionsumfang und der Möglichkeit, gleichzeitig eine Feuerstätte zu betreiben.

Q6
Electric Water Heater
Elektrischer Warmwasserbereiter

Manufacturer
Guangdong Vanward Electric Co., Ltd.,
Foshan, China
In-house design
Chu Peng Lu, Yu Cong Lu, Jin Kui Yuan
Design
Fangkuai Industrial Design Co., Ltd.
(Wei Tao Chen, Bai Yu Li), Hefei, China
Web
www.chinavanward.com
www.sq-id.com

The Vanward Q6 electric water heater has a high degree of efficiency and features a minimalist design. Thanks to the redefined user interface, it is simple to operate by elderly users as well. Its side part can be customized in different colours or adapted with individual decors. Inside, the tank is coated with a special diamond enamel in order to significantly reduce its weight.

Statement by the jury
The minimalist design of this water heater hints at its uncomplicated handling. Another clever idea is the control panel serving as a stand.

Der elektrische Warmwasserbereiter Vanward Q6 besitzt einen hohen Wirkungsgrad und zeichnet sich durch eine reduzierte Gestaltung aus. Dank der überarbeiteten Benutzerschnittstelle lässt er sich auch von älteren Personen leicht bedienen. Sein Seitenteil kann in verschiedenen Farben ausgeführt oder mit Dekoren individuell angepasst werden. Der Tank ist innen mit einer speziellen Diamantbeschichtung überzogen, wodurch sein Gewicht wesentlich reduziert werden konnte.

Begründung der Jury
Die minimalistische Gestaltung des Warmwasserbereiters verweist auf die unkomplizierte Bedienung. Eine clevere Idee ist auch das als Ständer dienende Bedienpanel.

Max Warmer
Electric Warmer
Elektrischer Wärmer

Manufacturer
Shenzhen Stylepie Lifestyle Co., Ltd.,
Shenzhen, China
In-house design
Neo Bie
Web
www.stylepie.com

The Max Warmer is an electric warmer specifically designed to warm the user's hands on the go. Two devices can be connected with the practical magnetic fastener for warming up larger surfaces as well, such as parts of the body or a bed. With its smooth surface, flat shape and rounded edges, the Max Warmer can be placed in a way most comfortable for the user. Heat emission is monitored with a temperature sensor in a range from 42 to 50 degrees centigrade.

Statement by the jury
With just a few movements, the Max Warmer can be transformed into either a smaller or larger version, offering more options for mobile and domestic use.

Der Max Warmer ist ein elektrischer Wärmer, mit dem sich unterwegs Hände wärmen lassen. Werden zwei Geräte mit dem praktischen Magnetverschluss zusammengesteckt, können aber auch größere Flächen wie Körperteile oder ein Bett gewärmt werden. Mit seiner glatten Oberfläche, der flachen Form und den gerundeten Kanten lässt sich der Max Warmer so platzieren, dass es für den Benutzer angenehm ist. Die Hitzeabstrahlung wird über einen Temperatursensor geregelt und kann auf einen Wert zwischen 42 und 50 Grad Celsius eingestellt werden.

Begründung der Jury
Der Max Warmer lässt sich mit wenigen Handgriffen in eine kleinere oder größere Variante verwandeln, was mehr Möglichkeiten bei der Verwendung unterwegs oder zu Hause bietet.

iPump
Heat Pump
Wärmepumpe

Manufacturer
IDM Energiesysteme GmbH, Matrei, Austria
Design
Phormolog OG, Kuchl, Austria
Web
www.idm-energie.at
www.phormolog.at

The iPump is a comprehensive heat pump system consisting of indoor and outdoor units for heating, cooling and hot water supply. The outdoor unit displays a language of form inspired by modern architecture and can thus be perceived as part of a facade. Its design has also been adapted to the large U-shaped evaporator to minimise noise level. With its small footprint, it allows flexible positioning in many places and comparatively easy transportation as well. The iPump is available for brine/groundwater or air.

Statement by the jury
The iPump picks up aspects of design elements that are usually found in outdoor areas. The device thus blends seamlessly into many different environments.

Die iPump ist ein Wärmepumpen-Komplettgerät, bestehend aus Innen- und Außengerät, das heizt, kühlt und warmes Wasser bereitstellt. Das Außengerät zeigt eine an moderne Architektur angelehnte Formensprache und kann daher als Teil einer Fassade wahrgenommen werden. Seine Gestaltung wurde darüber hinaus an den großflächigen u-förmigen Verdampfer angepasst, um niedrige Schallwerte zu erzielen. Dank seiner geringen Stellfläche findet es an vielen Orten Platz und lässt sich zudem vergleichsweise einfach transportieren. Die iPump ist sowohl als Luft-, Grundwasser oder Erdwärmepumpe verfügbar.

Begründung der Jury
Die iPump greift gestalterische Aspekte von Elementen auf, die üblicherweise im Außenbereich zu finden sind. Dadurch fügt sich das Gerät in zahlreiche Umgebungen problemlos ein.

Cigsor
Humidor Sensor

Manufacturer
Cigsor AG, Tägerwilen, Switzerland
In-house design
Web
www.cigsor.com

Cigsor is a humidor sensor that measures humidity and temperature and sends these data to the Cigsor app. The app user is automatically notified if values outside predetermined limits are being measured. With its cigar-shaped design, the device takes up only little space and can be placed directly beside or above the cigars. Its elegant appearance is brought about by the nearly seamless design with symmetrically placed slits along the upper surface.

Statement by the jury
The elegant Cigsor sensor meets high demands with regard to both function and design.

Cigsor ist ein Humidor-Sensor, der Feuchtigkeit und Temperatur misst und diese Daten an die Cigsor-App sendet. Der App-Benutzer wird automatisch benachrichtigt, wenn Werte außerhalb der eingestellten Grenzbereiche gemessen werden. Dank seiner zigarrenförmigen Gestalt benötigt das Gerät nur wenig Platz und kann direkt neben oder auf die Zigarren gelegt werden. Seine elegante Anmutung erzielt Cigsor durch die nahezu nahtlose Gestaltung, die lediglich durch symmetrisch angeordnete Schlitze im oberen Bereich durchbrochen wird.

Begründung der Jury
Der elegante Sensor Cigsor wird in funktionaler wie auch in gestalterischer Hinsicht gehobenen Ansprüchen gerecht.

MyAir
Portable Air Sensor
Tragbarer Luftsensor

Manufacturer
Tion LLC, Novosibirsk, Russia
Design
Logeeks LLC, Novosibirsk, Russia
Web
www.tion.ru
www.logeeks.ru

The MyAir portable air sensor serves to monitor air quality and ventilation status in any given situation. The design of the device was inspired by the shape of a CO_2 molecule. To start the air quality analysis, the unit is spun in such a way that air flows through the openings, thus reaching the sensors measuring CO_2 content and temperature. Air quality is indicated by different colours. In addition, measurement results can be recorded with an intuitively operated app and shared in social networks.

Statement by the jury
MyAir convinces with its simple, self-explanatory handling. With its compact, playful shape, it is a smart companion for air-sensitive users.

Mit dem kompakten, tragbaren Gerät MyAir lässt sich die Luftqualität und Belüftungssituation in jedem Bereich überwachen. Die Gestaltung des Geräts wurde von der Form eines CO_2-Moleküls inspiriert. Um die Luftanalyse zu starten, wird das Gerät so gedreht, dass Luft durch die Einlässe gelangt und auf die Sensoren trifft. Daraufhin werden CO_2-Gehalt und Temperatur gemessen. Die Qualität der Luft wird durch verschiedene Farben angezeigt. Die Messergebnisse können zusätzlich über eine intuitiv zu bedienende App erfasst und in sozialen Netzwerken geteilt werden.

Begründung der Jury
MyAir besticht durch seine einfache, selbsterklärende Handhabung. Zudem ist der Sensor mit seiner kompakten, verspielten Form ein pfiffiger Begleiter für luftsensible Anwender.

Honeywell T Series
Honeywell T-Serie
Thermostats
Thermostate

Manufacturer
Honeywell, Golden Valley, USA
In-house design
Brian Moy, Travis Read
Web
www.honeywell.com

The thermostats of the T Series offer a consistent user experience for installation and everyday use, even in the most different fields of application. The range of functionality is oriented to a modern lifestyle and takes into account the needs of a networked, mobile target group that wants to control home technology via an app, even while out and about. The basis for this is the universal wall plate. Once installed, other thermostat models from this series can be fixed on that plate without rewiring or complicated remounting. Thanks to the square shape with its rounded edges and conically tapering base, the thermostats do not appear overly technical, creating the appearance of merging with the wall.

Thermostate der T-Serie bieten im Einbau und täglichen Gebrauch auch bei unterschiedlichen Anwendungsbereichen eine konsistente Anwendererfahrung. Ihr Funktionsumfang orientiert sich an einem modernen Lebensstil und berücksichtigt die Bedürfnisse einer vernetzten, mobilen Zielgruppe, die Haustechnik per App auch von unterwegs steuern möchte. Basis ist die universelle Wandplatte. Ist sie einmal installiert, lassen sich alle Thermostat-Modelle der Serie ohne Verkabelung oder komplizierten Einbau auf diese Platte setzen. Dank ihrer quadratischen Form mit abgerundeten Kanten und konisch zulaufender Basis wirken die Thermostate wenig technisch und verschmelzen scheinbar mit der Wand.

Statement by the jury
With their reduced design, the thermostats fit well with already existing installations like light switches or wall sockets.

Begründung der Jury
Mit ihrer reduzierten Form passen die Thermostate gut zu bereits vorhandenen Installationen wie Lichtschalter oder Steckdosen.

IAQ
Air Quality Monitor
Gerät zur Luftqualitäts-
überwachung

Manufacturer
Honeywell Sensing and Control
(China) Co., Ltd., Nanjing, China
Design
Honeywell International
(Dezhi Yang, Cui Du, Yunlien Lin),
Shanghai, China
Web
www.sensing.honeywell.com.cn
www.honeywell.com

The IAQ is a device used for monitoring air quality in households. It measures fine dust pollution as well as temperature and humidity. The semi-transparent acrylic front cover is surrounded by an illuminated ring that visually displays the values measured: a soft blue light indicates clean air; when it turns to red, it means that the air has to be purified. An app enables the user to also monitor air quality in the house from afar.

Statement by the jury
The discreet design of the IAQ with its illuminated ring as filigree detail indicates the elegance and style of this device. It blends harmoniously into any interior.

Das IAQ ist ein Gerät zur Überwachung der Luftqualität in Haushalten. Es misst sowohl die Feinstaubbelastung als auch die Temperatur und Luftfeuchtigkeit. Die halbtransparente Frontabdeckung aus Acryl ist von einem Leuchtring umgeben, der die Werte visuell darstellt: Ein sanftes blaues Licht zeigt saubere Luft an, wechselt das Licht auf Rot, bedeutet dies, dass die Luft gereinigt werden muss. Eine App ermöglicht es dem Benutzer, die Luftqualität auch aus der Ferne zu überwachen.

Begründung der Jury
Das dezent gehaltene Design des IAQ mit dem Lichtring als filigranem Detail zeugt von Eleganz und Stil. Das Gerät fügt sich harmonisch in jedes Interieur ein.

R4
Radiator
Heizkörper

Manufacturer
Tomton s.r.o.,
Velké Albrechtice, Czech Republic
Design
Descent s.r.o. industrial design (Jiří Španihel),
Kopřivnice, Czech Republic
Web
www.tomton-radiators.com
www.spanihel.cz

The R4 radiator features wood panelling, allowing it to impart a feeling of warmth on first sight. This particular kind of panelling has been made possible because the radiator does not heat up on the front side. The natural wood covers are available in a large number of wood types and shades. Moreover, several valve colours are offered and can be freely combined with any cover. At the end of its life cycle, this radiator can be fully recycled.

Statement by the jury
With the wood panelling, each radiator turns into a unique product that appears to be a piece of furniture with a natural touch.

Der Heizkörper R4 ist mit Holz verkleidet, wodurch er schon auf den ersten Blick ein Gefühl von Wärme vermittelt. Diese besondere Art der Verkleidung ist möglich, weil der Heizkörper an der Vorderseite nicht heiß wird. Die Abdeckungen aus Echtholz sind in zahlreichen Holzarten und Farbtönen erhältlich, zudem stehen diverse Ventilfarben zur Verfügung, die mit den Abdeckungen nach Belieben kombiniert werden können. Nach Nutzungsende lässt sich der Heizkörper vollständig recyceln.

Begründung der Jury
Durch die Holzabdeckung wird jeder Heizkörper zum Unikat und darüber hinaus zu einem natürlich wirkenden Einrichtungsgegenstand.

Origami
Radiator
Heizkörper

Manufacturer
Tubes Radiatori Srl, Resana, Italy
Design
Alberto Meda, Milan, Italy
Web
www.tubesradiatori.com
www.albertomeda.com

The Origami is an electrical plug and play
radiator made of aluminium which can
be adapted to any ambiance in a home.
Available in three versions, with red or
blue cable and in more than 260 RAL colours, Origami can also be combined with
accessories. In the free-standing version,
the movable modules allow it to be used
as a partition. The wall-mounted version
is offered with a single or double module.
As a double module, the device can be
transformed, if needed, into an elegant
towel warmer. In the static version, it
turns into a warming interior furnishing.

Statement by the jury
Origami captivates with its high adaptability, turning it into more than just a
pure heating element.

Origami ist ein elektrischer Plug-and-play-
Heizkörper aus Aluminium, der jedem Ambiente im Haus angepasst werden kann.
Erhältlich in drei Versionen, mit rotem oder
blauem Kabel sowie in mehr als 260 RAL-
Farben, kann Origami auch mit Accessoires
kombiniert werden. In der freistehenden
Version bieten die beweglichen Module die
Möglichkeit, ihn als Raumteiler zu verwenden. Das Wandmodell wird mit Einzel- und
Doppelmodul angeboten. In der Ausführung
als Doppelmodul kann Origami bei Bedarf
in einen zuklappbaren eleganten Handtuch-
wärmer verwandelt werden. In der statischen Version wird er zu einem wärmenden
Einrichtungsgegenstand.

Begründung der Jury
Origami besticht durch seine Wandlungs-
fähigkeit, die ihn über seine Funktion als
reines Heizelement hinaushebt.

Face_Zero Air
Flush-to-Wall Plate Radiator
Wandeinbau-Flachheizkörper

Manufacturer
Irsap SpA, Arquà Polesine (Rovigo), Italy
Design
Antonio Citterio, Sergio Brioschi,
Milan, Italy
Web
www.irsap.com

Face_Zero Air is a radiator designed for
flush-to-wall mounting. With its discreet
design and special type of installation,
it can be integrated inconspicuously into
any room. The models are available in
two heights and two lengths, as well as
in a static and an air version, thus offering a suitable solution for a wide variety
of housing situations. A low-noise forced
ventilation system modulates heat emission according to the users' needs, and
an integrated thermoregulation modu-
lating head in the heating element
ensures intelligent, comfortable control.
Thanks to the cover, which can be
opened like a book, cleaning and maintenance are easily performed.

Statement by the jury
This radiator excels with its seamless
design, accentuating the advantages of
flush-to-wall mounting.

Face_Zero Air ist ein für den Wandeinbau
konzipierter Heizkörper. Dank seiner zurückhaltenden Formensprache und der
besonderen Montageart lässt er sich unauffällig in jeden Raum integrieren. Die
Modelle sind in zwei Höhen, zwei Längen
sowie als statische und als Air-Variante mit
Ventilatoren erhältlich und bieten damit
für zahlreiche Wohnsituationen die passende Lösung. Eine geräuscharme Zwangs-
belüftung richtet die Wärmeabgabe an den
Bedürfnissen der Benutzer aus, ein integrierter Thermoregulierungsmodulkopf im
Heizelement sorgt für die intelligente, komfortable Regelung. Wartung und Reinigung
gestalten sich dank einer Klappe, die wie
ein Buch geöffnet werden kann, einfach.

Begründung der Jury
Der Heizkörper besticht durch seine nahtlose Erscheinung, dank derer die Vorteile
des Wandeinbaus gut zur Geltung kommen.

Android
Radiator
Heizkörper

Manufacturer
Antrax IT Srl, Resana, Italy
Design
Studio Daniel Libeskind (Daniel Libeskind)
Web
www.antrax.it
www.libeskind.com

Android is not a simple radiator, but rather a genuine sculpture. Edges and lines alternate to create dynamic contrasts of light and shadow. Thanks to an efficient circuit, only a small amount of water and energy is required to operate the radiator. Android can be installed horizontally or vertically and, in the vertical version, can also be equipped with a towel rail.

Statement by the jury
Android impresses with its independent design that cleverly plays with contrasts. This is particularly effective in the bathroom where, usually, there are different light sources.

Android ist kein einfacher Heizkörper, sondern präsentiert sich vielmehr als echte Skulptur. Kanten und Linien wechseln einander ab und lassen dynamisch wirkende Kontraste von Licht und Schatten entstehen. Für den Betrieb des Heizkörpers ist dank des effizienten Kreislaufs nur wenig Wasser und Energie nötig. Android kann horizontal oder vertikal installiert und bei der vertikalen Variante mit einer Stange zum Aufhängen von Handtüchern ausgestattet werden.

Begründung der Jury
Android beeindruckt mit seiner eigenständigen Gestaltung, die geschickt mit Kontrasten spielt. Dies kommt besonders gut im Bad zur Geltung, wo in der Regel unterschiedliche Lichtquellen vorhanden sind.

Pioli
Radiator
Heizkörper

Manufacturer
Antrax IT Srl, Resana, Italy
In-house design
Andrea Crosetta
Web
www.antrax.it

The Pioli is a radiator combining classic and contemporary design in a skilful way. It is wittily reminiscent of a ladder. The high versatility and practicability of this object with its thousands of years of history has come back to life in heating décor. The radiator consists of two carbon-steel rails to which the rectangular cross sections are attached in an unconventional way. Aside from black and white, 200 additional colours are available.

Statement by the jury
Pioli newly interprets the classic design language of a radiator. Its airy design is visually appealing and functional.

Pioli ist ein Heizkörper, der klassisches und zeitgemäßes Design gekonnt verbindet. Er erinnert auf originelle Weise an eine Leiter. Die hohe Funktionalität und Vielseitigkeit dieses jahrtausendealten Objekts erlebt nun in der Gestaltung von Heizungen seine Renaissance. Der Heizkörper besteht aus zwei Holmen aus Carbonstahl, an denen die rechteckigen Querstreben auf unkonventionelle Weise befestigt sind. Neben Schwarz und Weiß stehen weitere 200 Farben zur Auswahl.

Begründung der Jury
Pioli interpretiert die klassische Formensprache eines Heizkörpers neu. Seine luftige Gestaltung ist optisch ansprechend und funktional.

Bathroom Steward
Bathroom Heater
Heizgerät für das Badezimmer

Manufacturer
Kohler, Shanghai, China
In-house design
Henry Yang, River Cheng
Web
www.kohler.com

The Bathroom Steward is a heater and air purifier in one device. With its wind tunnel, it effectively heats up a bathroom, rapidly purifying the air at the same time. Once the integrated sensor measures an air humidity of 60 per cent, the dehumidifier is automatically turned on to prevent mould formation. The device can be turned on and off using an app, thus warming up the bathroom at the precise time desired by the user. With its mirrored glass surface, the unit blends harmoniously into any bathroom interior.

Statement by the jury
The smooth glass surface gives the Bathroom Steward a precious appearance. Moreover, this makes it easy to clean, which is of particular advantage in the bathroom.

Der Bathroom Steward ist Heizgerät und Luftreiniger in einem. Mit seinem Windtunnel heizt er ein Badezimmer effektiv auf und reinigt die Luft in kurzer Zeit. Misst der integrierte Sensor eine Luftfeuchtigkeit von 60 Prozent, so schaltet sich der Entfeuchter automatisch ein, um der Schimmelbildung vorzubeugen. Über eine App lässt sich die Heizung an- oder ausschalten, damit das Badezimmer zu einem gewünschten Zeitpunkt bereits warm ist. Mit seiner spiegelnden Glasoberfläche passt das Gerät zu jeglichem Badezimmer-Mobiliar.

Begründung der Jury
Die glatte Glasoberfläche verleiht dem Bathroom Steward eine edle Anmutung. Darüber hinaus ist er dadurch leicht zu reinigen, was besonders im Badezimmer vorteilhaft ist.

Wall-Mounted Air Conditioner
Klimagerät für die Wandmontage

Manufacturer
GD Midea Air-Conditioning Equipment Co., Ltd., Foshan, China
In-house design
Hailu Wang, Sanxin Li
Web
www.midea.com

This air conditioner is based on the concept of mixed air. When it is running, negative pressure is generated around the air outlet. In this way, ambient air is taken into this area, which is then uniformly mixed with the air released from the device. The result is well-tempered airflow that fulfils the purpose of air conditioning yet still feels comfortable to the resident. This overcomes the problem of being subjected to airflow that is too cold, particularly in the summertime.

Statement by the jury
The principle of gentle air intermixing is a sensible function and of particular advantage for temperature-sensitive users.

Dieses Klimagerät basiert auf einem Konzept der Mischluft. Wenn es in Betrieb ist, wird um den Luftauslass ein Unterdruck erzeugt. Dadurch wird in diesem Bereich Raumluft angesaugt und mit der vom Gerät ausgeblasenen Luft gleichmäßig vermischt. Als Ergebnis entsteht ein wohltemperierter Luftstrom, der den Zweck des Klimatisierens erfüllt, aber für den Bewohner angenehm ist. Auf diese Weise wird das Problem umgangen, dass besonders im Sommer der Luftstrom oft unangenehm kalt wird.

Begründung der Jury
Das Prinzip einer sanften Durchmischung der Luft ist eine sinnvolle Funktion, die besonders für temperaturempfindliche Anwender von Vorteil ist.

AP100 Series
Air Conditioners
Klimageräte

Manufacturer
GD Midea Air-Conditioning Equipment Co., Ltd.,
Foshan, China
In-house design
Jiabing Ye, Lilong Zhou, Hong Cheng,
Ying Ao, Zhi Liu
Web
www.midea.com

The Midea AP100 series consists of air-conditioning units combining intelligent technology and state-of-the-art design. With the objective of promoting well-being and health, they improve not only the interior atmosphere but also air quality. To keep these levels constant, an integrated filter cleans both the indoor air and the inflowing outdoor air. The filter is located at the top of the device and can easily be taken out, cleaned and put back in.

Die Serie Midea AP100 umfasst Klimageräte, die intelligente Technologie und zeitgemäßes Design zusammenführen. Mit dem Ziel, Wohlbefinden und Gesundheit zu fördern, verbessern sie nicht nur das Raumklima, sondern auch die Luftqualität. Um diese auf einem konstanten Niveau zu halten, reinigt ein integrierter Filter sowohl die Innenluft als auch die Luft, die von außen hereinströmt. Der Filter befindet sich an der Oberseite des Geräts und kann mühelos herausgenommen, gereinigt und wieder eingesetzt werden.

Statement by the jury
These air-conditioning units are characterised by unmistakable aesthetics, thus harmonising well with modern living room interiors.

Begründung der Jury
Die Klimageräte besitzen eine unverwechselbare Ästhetik, die gut mit modern eingerichteten Wohnräumen harmoniert.

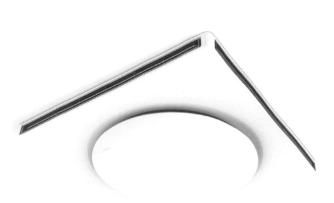

The Four-way Cassette
Air Conditioner
Klimagerät

Manufacturer
GD Midea Air-Conditioning Equipment
Co., Ltd., Foshan, China
In-house design
Xueli Huang, Sanxin Li
Web
www.midea.com

The air inlet grille of this air conditioning device for ceiling installation is concealed under the panel. This gives the device a purist appearance, as it merely seems to consist of the basic geometric forms of circle and square. At the same time, this construction prevents dust from entering the interior of the device. The air is released on all four sides, ensuring even distribution throughout the room.

Statement by the jury
The Four-way Cassette excels with its discreet design and thus subordinates itself to other ceiling installations in a harmonious way.

Bei diesem Klimagerät für die Deckenmontage verbirgt sich das Lufteintrittsgitter unter der Abdeckung. Dies verleiht dem Gerät eine puristische Anmutung, da es lediglich aus den beiden Grundformen Kreis und Quadrat zu bestehen scheint. Gleichzeitig verhindert diese Konstruktion, dass Staub in das Innere gelangt. Die Luft tritt an den vier Seiten aus, was sicherstellt, dass sie gleichmäßig im Raum verteilt wird.

Begründung der Jury
The Four-way Cassette begeistert mit seiner zurückhaltenden Formgebung, dank derer das Gerät sich problemlos anderen Deckeninstallationen unterordnet.

Healthy Air Conditioner
Klimagerät

Manufacturer
GD Midea Air-Conditioning Equipment
Co., Ltd., Foshan, China
In-house design
Xueli Huang, Sanxin Li
Web
www.midea.com

The objective pursued in the development of the Healthy Air Conditioner was a modified internal structure to redirect airflow in such a way that only a minimum of dust can enter the device. This reduces the need to clean the air conditioner frequently and less deposits build up, resulting in higher air quality. Moreover, with its slim design, the air conditioner takes up less space on the wall and blends harmoniously into living room interiors.

Statement by the jury
With its clever construction, the Healthy Air Conditioner reduces the problem of dust entering interiors, which is a common problem with many air conditioning devices.

Ziel bei der Entwicklung des Healthy Air Conditioners war eine veränderte interne Struktur, um den Luftstrom so umzuleiten, dass möglichst wenig Staub in das Innere gelangt. Dadurch muss der Anwender das Gerät nicht so häufig reinigen, zudem bilden sich weniger Ablagerungen, was der Luftqualität zugutekommt. Darüber hinaus benötigt das Klimagerät durch seine schlanke Gestalt wenig Platz an der Wand und fügt sich harmonisch in den Wohnraum ein.

Begründung der Jury
Durch seine clevere Konstruktion reduziert der Healthy Air Conditioner das bei Klimageräten grundlegende Problem von Staubeintrag ins Innere.

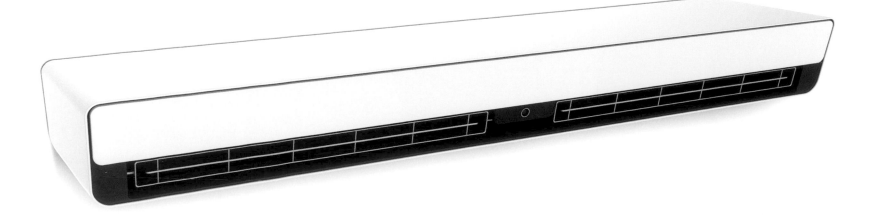

Smart Dew
Air Conditioner and Humidifier
Klimagerät und Luftbefeuchter

Manufacturer
GD Midea Air-Conditioning Equipment
Co., Ltd., Foshan, China
In-house design
Jun Wang, Sanxin Li
Web
www.midea.com

Smart Dew is an air conditioner and humidifier in one device. It automatically adjusts the air humidity to a comfortable level and thus overcomes the common problem that air conditioning devices frequently produce a dry indoor climate. The water tank is located at the front and is thus easily accessible. It is characterised by a circular shape, which contrasts with the rectangular form of the device. Smart Dew can be optionally controlled via smartphone or the integrated touchscreen.

Statement by the jury
This air conditioner combines different geometric forms in a skilful way and thus attains a high degree of design independence.

Smart Dew ist Klimagerät und Luftbefeuchter in einem. Es stellt automatisch die Luftfeuchtigkeit auf ein angenehmes Maß ein und umgeht damit das Problem, dass Klimageräte häufig trockene Luft im Raum verursachen. Der Wassertank befindet sich vorne und ist damit leicht zugänglich. Er ist durch seine Kreisform gekennzeichnet, die sich von der rechteckigen Form des Geräts abhebt. Gesteuert wird Smart Dew wahlweise kabellos per Smartphone oder über den integrierten Touchscreen.

Begründung der Jury
Das Klimagerät kombiniert geschickt unterschiedliche geometrische Formen und erzielt dadurch eine hohe gestalterische Eigenständigkeit.

Floor-standing
Air Conditioner
Klimagerät

Manufacturer
GD Midea Air-Conditioning Equipment
Co., Ltd., Foshan, China
In-house design
Qinghua Tu, Sanxin Li
Web
www.midea.com

This slim air conditioner is conceived for placement in the corner of a room. It takes up minimal floor space, allowing for many placement options. The air outlet area can be rotated in different positions to regulate the strength of airflow. Three levels of intensity – from closed to strong – are possible. Depending on the level, the front changes its appearance, enabling the user to recognise the current airflow intensity at first glance.

Statement by the jury
This air conditioner convinces with its extremely slim, elegant form. It enriches any room and can be placed virtually anywhere.

Dieses schlanke Klimagerät ist dafür gedacht, in der Ecke eines Raums aufgestellt zu werden. Es nimmt nur wenig Stellfläche in Anspruch, was viele Möglichkeiten bei der Platzierung eröffnet. Der Bereich, aus dem die Luft austritt, kann in unterschiedliche Positionen gedreht werden, um die Stärke des Luftstroms zu regeln. Drei Stufen – von geschlossen bis stark – sind hierbei möglich. Je nach Stufe ändert sich das Aussehen der Vorderseite, was auf den ersten Blick erkennen lässt, mit welcher Intensität die Luft gerade ausgestoßen wird.

Begründung der Jury
Das Klimagerät überzeugt mit seiner äußerst schlanken, eleganten Form. Damit bereichert es jeden Raum und lässt sich zudem überall aufstellen.

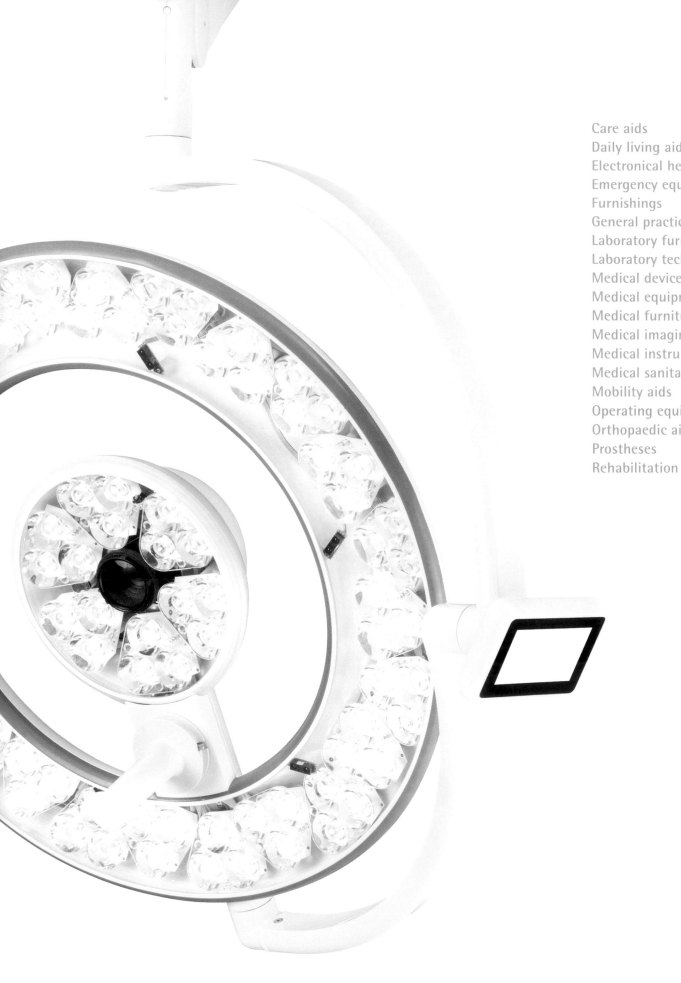

Life science and medicine
Life Science und Medizin

U scope
Stethoscope
Stethoskop

Manufacturer
Classico, Inc., Tokyo, Japan

In-house design
Arata Ohwa

Design
Yoshio Goodrich Design
(Hiroki Yoshitomi), Tokyo, Japan

Web
www.classico.co.jp
www.yoshiogoodrich.com

reddot award 2017
best of the best

Reengineered

Indispensable for medical examinations, the stethoscope has been used in an almost unchanged shape ever since its invention in 1816. For U scope, the shape and structure of such a device has been skilfully rethought and rebuilt. Guided by the idea of formal refinement, the redesign has focused on overcoming issues often experienced by health personnel during examinations, as the daily use of a stethoscope can quickly lead to troubling earaches and neck pain. The design process also included aspects of improved portability. The result is a high-quality and elegant looking tool that also fascinates in use due to its outstandingly pleasant feel. Following the principles of human engineering, its design resulted in an optimised and self-explanatory method of application. The tips of U scope emerged with an ideal shape that fits perfectly and rests well balanced in the hand, entirely eliminating the need for examiners to ever rethink the grip. In this way, the problem is solved of the stethoscope having to be aligned again with each examination step. Based on a perfectly thought-out and innovative design, U scope offers sophisticated functionality and ergonomics – its elegant aesthetic is an enrichment to daily medical work.

Neu komponiert

Das für die ärztliche Untersuchung unverzichtbare Stethoskop wird seit seiner Erfindung im Jahre 1816 in nahezu unveränderter Form eingesetzt. Für das U scope wurde die Gestaltung und Struktur eines solchen Gerätes grundsätzlich hinterfragt. Im Mittelpunkt einer feinsinnigen Neuinterpretation standen dabei die oftmals mit dieser Art der Untersuchung einhergehenden Problemstellungen. So können sich in der täglichen Arbeit mit dem Stethoskop rasch Ohrenschmerzen oder Nackenschmerzen einstellen. In den Designprozess flossen zudem Aspekte einer verbesserten Portabilität mit ein. Das Ergebnis ist ein sehr elegant und hochwertig anmutendes Instrument, das zudem im Gebrauch durch seine überaus angenehme Haptik begeistert. Den Grundsätzen des Human Engineering folgend, führte seine Gestaltung zu einer optimierten und selbsterklärenden Art der Anwendung. Das Bruststück des Stethoskops liegt gut austariert in der Hand des Untersuchenden, intuitiv kann er es verwenden, ohne darauf achten zu müssen, ob ein Umgreifen oder ein erneutes Zufassen erforderlich ist. Auf diese Weise wird das Problem gelöst, dass das Stethoskop bei jedem Untersuchungsschritt wieder ausgerichtet werden muss. Auf der Basis einer perfekt durchdachten und innovativen Gestaltung bietet das U scope eine ausgereifte Ergonomie und Funktionalität – seine elegante Ästhetik bereichert den Medizinbereich.

Statement by the jury
Featuring a sophisticated, intelligent concept, the design of U scope lends the familiar stethoscope an entirely new form and functionality. It impresses with its elegant appearance, which is based not least on a successful choice and combination of materials. All elements have been combined to form a coherent unity. In line with a sophisticated ergonomics, U scope offers an outstandingly simple and comfortable handling.

Begründung der Jury
Mit einem ausgefeilten, intelligenten Konzept verleiht die Gestaltung des U scope dem bekannten Stethoskop eine gänzlich neue Form und Funktionalität. Es beeindruckt durch seine elegante Anmutung, die nicht zuletzt auch auf einer gelungenen Kombination der eingesetzten Materialien beruht. Alle Elemente wurden zu einem stimmigen Ganzen zusammengefügt. Im Einklang mit einer ausgereiften Ergonomie bietet das U scope eine verblüffend einfache und komfortable Handhabung.

Designer portrait
See page 58
Siehe Seite 58

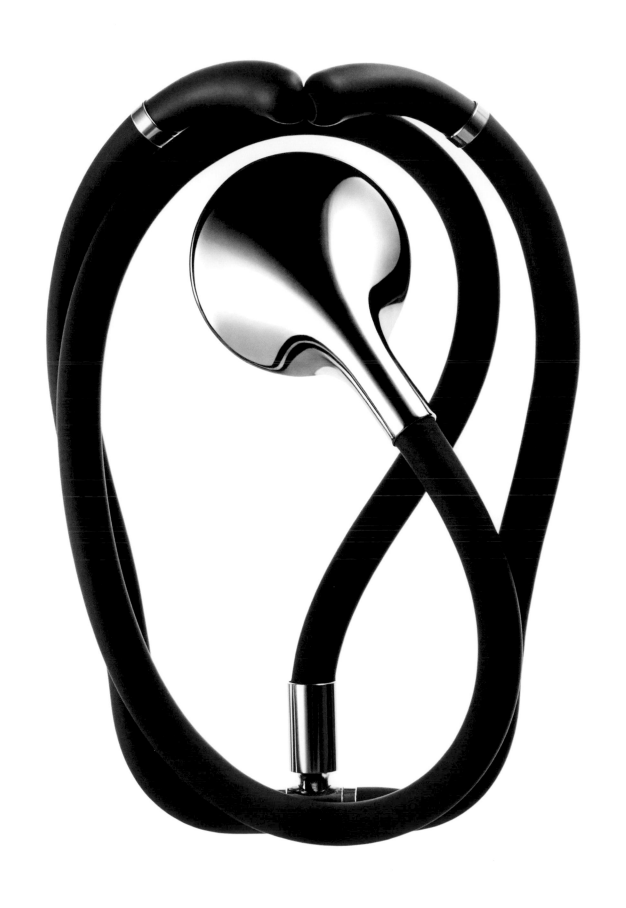

Dräger Babyleo® TN500 IncuWarmer

Manufacturer
Drägerwerk AG & Co. KGaA,
Lübeck, Germany

Design
MMID GmbH, Essen, Germany

Web
www.draeger.com
www.mmid.de

reddot award 2017
best of the best

Surrounded by care

Prematurely born babies rely on highly intensive care and life support from the outset. It can take several weeks for their vital functions to have matured enough to be self-sustaining and for the baby to be released from the clinic. The Babyleo TN500 IncuWarmer has been designed to respond to these specific requirements in an impressive manner. It provides continuous optimal thermoregulation for neonates in open care and closed care as well as in transition. With the combination of three synchronised heat sources, this device protects little patients against loss of body heat, promoting their healthy development. At the same time, the well thought-out design offers clinicians and nurses ergonomically sophisticated comfort that makes their daily workflow easier. The hood design allows opening and closing with only one finger, while the large hand ports enable caregivers to easily reach the entire patient bed area. The IncuWarmer is variably height adjustable, allowing mothers to be closer to their babies, even when sitting in a wheelchair. A user-friendly, intuitive user interface and a plethora of automated options assist clinicians, nurses and parents to fully concentrate on the small patient and provide the care needed. With its balanced and emotionalising language of form, the Babyleo TN500 IncuWarmer creates a comfortable and relaxed atmosphere for optimal care.

Rundum betreut

Frühgeborene Kinder benötigen von Anfang an eine hochgradig intensive Betreuung. Es dauert zudem oftmals eine Weile, bis ihre Vitalfunktionen die nötige Autarkie erreicht haben, um aus der Klinik entlassen werden zu können. Der Babyleo TN500 IncuWarmer wurde in seiner Gestaltung diesen spezifischen Anforderungen in beeindruckender Weise angepasst. Er ermöglicht eine konstante, optimale Thermoregulation in der offenen und in der geschlossenen Pflege von Frühgeborenen, sowie in der Übergangsphase. In ihm sind drei synchronisierte Wärmequellen integriert, die die Frühgeborenen sicher vor Wärmeverlust schützen und ihre gesunde Entwicklung fördern. Gleichzeitig bietet er den auf der Station arbeitenden Menschen einen ergonomisch ausgereiften Komfort. So erleichtert er eine durchdachte Gestaltung die täglichen Arbeitsabläufe. Die Haube lässt sich einfach öffnen und schließen, große Durchgriffsöffnungen ermöglichen es, dass alle Bereiche im Patientenraum gut zugänglich sind. Der IncuWarmer ist stufenlos höhenverstellbar, weshalb auch im Rollstuhl sitzende Mütter ihr Baby leicht erreichen können. Eine benutzerfreundliche, intuitiv erschließbare Bedienoberfläche und eine Vielzahl automatischer Optionen unterstützen Ärzte, Pflegekräfte und Eltern dabei, sich vollständig auf die kleinen Patienten zu konzentrieren. Mit seiner ausgewogenen und emotionalisierenden Formensprache schafft der Babyleo TN500 IncuWarmer die dazu notwendige ruhige und entspannte Atmosphäre.

Statement by the jury

The Babyleo TN500 IncuWarmer is an outstanding example of a highly successful interplay between design and technology. It not only supports doctors and nurses in their work but also promotes communication between a mother and her child in this first phase of its life. The clear and emotionalising design creates a pleasant atmosphere and reduces the complexity of such a device to the essential, yet fulfilling all requirements for accessibility, ergonomics and flexibility in an impressive manner.

Begründung der Jury

Der Babyleo TN500 IncuWarmer ist ein gelungenes Beispiel für ein hervorragendes Zusammenspiel von Design und Technik. Er hilft den Ärzten und Pflegekräften bei ihrer Arbeit und fördert auch die Kommunikation zwischen Mutter und Kind in dieser ersten Lebensphase. Sein klares und emotionalisierendes Design schafft eine angenehme Atmosphäre und reduziert die Komplexität eines solchen Gerätes auf das Wesentliche, die Anforderungen an Zugänglichkeit, Ergonomie und Flexibilität werden eindrucksvoll erfüllt.

Designer portrait
See page 60
Siehe Seite 60

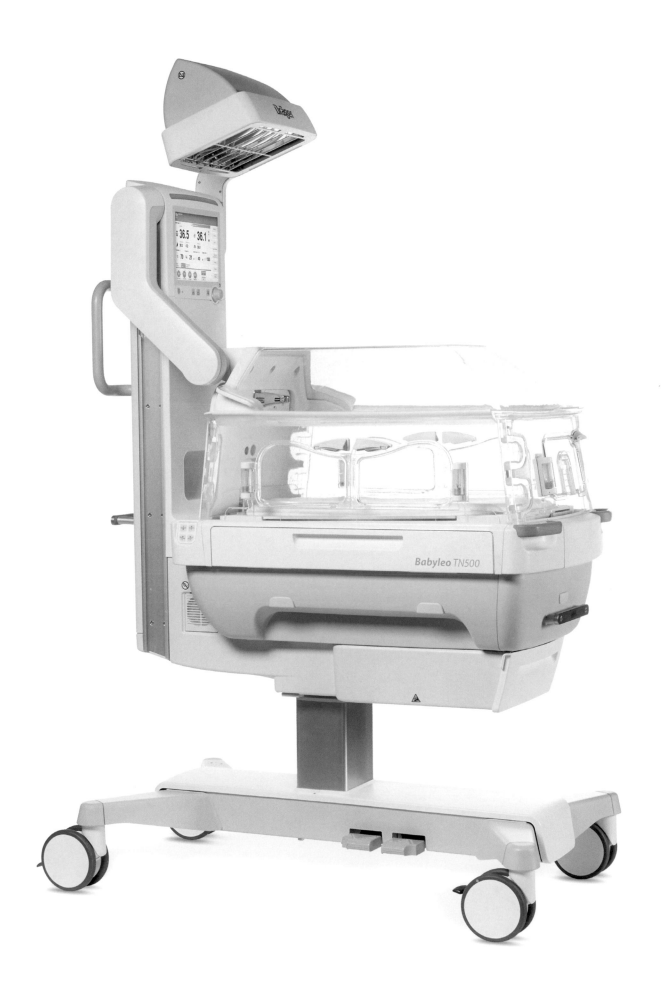

AVE 2
Birthing Bed
Entbindungsbett

Manufacturer
BORCAD Medical a.s., Fryčovice,
Czech Republic
Design
Descent s.r.o. industrial design (Jiří Španihel),
Kopřivnice, Czech Republic
Pavel Šipula product design (Pavel Šipula),
Ostrava, Czech Republic
Web
www.borcadmedical.com
www.spanihel.cz
www.sipula.eu

The Ave 2 birthing bed gives expecting mothers the option of finding the most pleasant birthing position. Thanks to the electric lifting column, the bed can be lowered to an extremely low position for easy entry and raised particularly high for medical interventions. The leg supports can be manually adjusted via a lifting and tilting mechanism without having to be removed. Doctors and midwives have optimum access to the delivering woman via the U-shaped cutout in the chair. The base can be simply pivoted underneath the main part of the bed for the birth.

Das Entbindungsbett Ave 2 bietet der werdenden Mutter die Möglichkeit, die angenehmste Geburtsposition zu finden. Über die elektrische Hubsäule kann das Bett für den Einstieg besonders niedrig oder für die ärztliche Intervention besonders hoch eingestellt werden. Die Beinstützen lassen sich manuell über einen Hebe- und Kippmechanismus verstellen, ohne extra abgenommen werden zu müssen. Arzt und Hebamme haben durch den U-förmigen Sitzausschnitt optimalen Zugang zu der Gebärenden. Das Fußteil kann für die Geburt einfach unter das Hauptteil geschwenkt werden.

Statement by the jury
The Ave 2 birthing bed with its sophisticated design and attractive colouring provides extraordinary comfort for all phases of the birthing process.

Begründung der Jury
Das bis ins Detail durchdachte und farblich ansprechende Entbindungsbett Ave 2 bietet außergewöhnlichen Komfort für jede Phase des Geburtsprozesses.

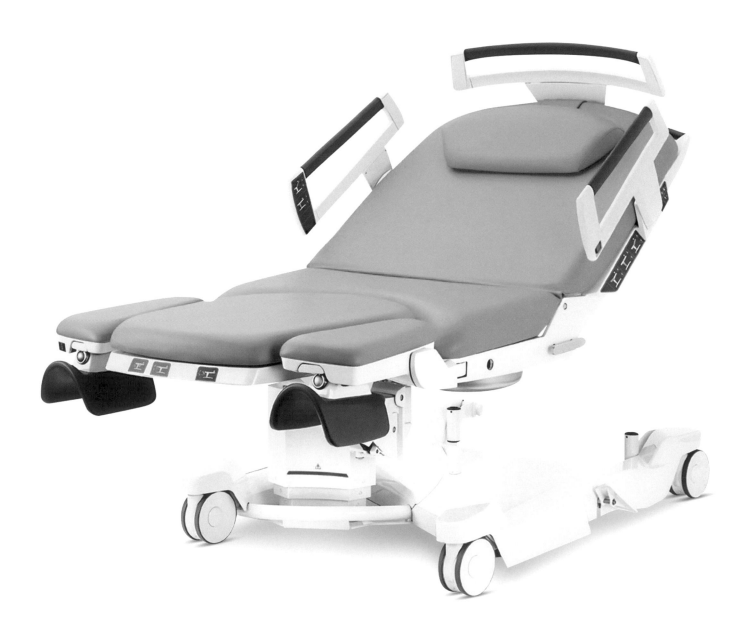

arco-matic®
Gynaecological Examination Chair
Gynäkologischer
Untersuchungsstuhl

Manufacturer
Schmitz u. Söhne GmbH & Co. KG,
Wickede/Ruhr, Germany
Design
Rainer Schindhelm Industrie-Design
(Rainer Schindhelm),
Rotthalmünster, Germany
Web
www.schmitz-soehne.com

The gynaecological examination chair arco-matic allows the treatment of patients in a reclining or sitting position. With the memory function, four chosen examination positions can be programmed and then recalled again and again. The special features of the chair are its lightweight structure, flowing forms and colourful cushion elements, which are available in many different colours. The smooth, closed spaces make the chair easy to clean and hygienic.

Statement by the jury
The soft contours, fresh colours and airy construction of the arco-matic create a friendly atmosphere and help reduce anxiety in patients.

Der gynäkologische Untersuchungsstuhl arco-matic ermöglicht eine Behandlung in sitzender oder liegender Position. Über die Memoryfunktion können vier beliebige Untersuchungspositionen gespeichert und immer wieder abgerufen werden. Besondere Gestaltungsmerkmale sind die Leichtigkeit des Aufbaus, die fließenden Formen und die bunten Polsterelemente, die in vielen verschiedenen Farben zur Verfügung stehen. Durch die glatten, geschlossenen Flächen ist der Stuhl pflegeleicht und hygienisch.

Begründung der Jury
Die weichen Konturen, frischen Farben und luftige Konstruktion des arco-matic schaffen eine freundliche Atmosphäre und helfen, Berührungsängste bei den Patientinnen abzubauen.

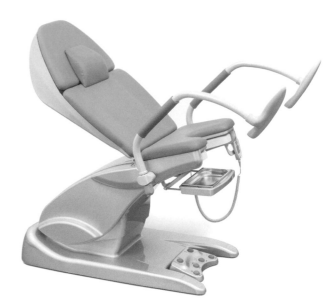

arco
Gynaecological Examination Chair
Gynäkologischer
Untersuchungsstuhl

Manufacturer
Schmitz u. Söhne GmbH & Co. KG,
Wickede/Ruhr, Germany
Design
Rainer Schindhelm Industrie-Design
(Rainer Schindhelm),
Rotthalmünster, Germany
Web
www.schmitz-soehne.com

The examination chair arco is designed for treatment in a sitting position. Its low starting height allows patients to be seated comfortably. The chair is adjusted and appropriately positioned using an electric motor operated via a foot control. The ergonomic leg and foot support system with integrated armrest ensures a relaxed examination position. Moreover, the powder-coated frame is shock- and scratch-resistant. Paint finishes and padding are available in many different colours.

Statement by the jury
The examination chair arco impresses with its open construction and colourful design, which fosters visual lightness in an otherwise functional medical environment.

Der gynäkologische Untersuchungsstuhl arco ist für eine Behandlung in sitzender Position konzipiert. Die niedrige Ausgangshöhe ermöglicht es der Patientin, bequem Platz zu nehmen. Über die Fußbedienung wird der Stuhl elektrisch verstellt und in jede gewünschte Position gebracht. Das ergonomische Bein- und Fußstützensystem mit integrierter Armauflage sorgt für eine entspannte Untersuchung. Der pulverbeschichtete Rahmen ist stoß- und kratzfest, Lackierungen und Polster sind in vielen verschiedenen Farben erhältlich.

Begründung der Jury
Der Untersuchungsstuhl arco besticht durch seine offene Konstruktion und farbenfrohe Gestaltung, die visuelle Leichtigkeit in ein ansonsten sachliches medizinisches Umfeld überführt.

Sonicaid Team 3
Fetal Monitor

Manufacturer
Huntleigh, Cardiff, Great Britain
Design
PDR, Cardiff, Great Britain
Web
www.huntleigh-diagnostics.com
www.pdronline.co.uk

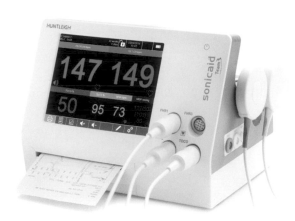

The fetal monitor Sonicaid Team 3 is intuitive to use thanks to its icon-based touchscreen. The heartbeat of mother and child are rendered separately on the display. The fetal heart frequency is displayed in large letters and is easy to read, even in the case of twins and triplets. The simple design language of the device makes it appear less dominant at the patient's bedside. The integrated battery enables continuous monitoring, even during patient transport.

Statement by the jury
The Sonicaid Team 3 has a very logical structure and is easy to use. Its minimalist design fosters a deliberately unobtrusive effect.

Der Fetalmonitor Sonicaid Team 3 bietet durch den symbolgesteuerten Touchscreen eine intuitive Bedienung. Die Herztöne von Mutter und Kind werden auf dem Display klar voneinander getrennt dargestellt. Die fetale Herzfrequenz wird gut lesbar in großen Buchstaben angezeigt, auch bei Zwillingen oder Drillingen. Durch die einfache Formensprache wirkt das Gerät weniger dominant am Bett der Patientin. Der integrierte Akku ermöglicht die kontinuierliche Überwachung, auch während die Patientin transportiert wird.

Begründung der Jury
Der Sonicaid Team 3 ist absolut logisch aufgebaut und einfach zu bedienen. Seine reduzierte Gestaltung erzielt eine bewusst unauffällige Wirkung.

Gymna 200 Series
Gymna 200 Serie
Electrotherapy Devices
Elektrotherapiegeräte

Manufacturer
GymnaUniphy n.v., Bilzen, Belgium
Design
GBO Innovation Makers, Antwerp, Belgium
Web
www.gymna.com
www.gbo.eu

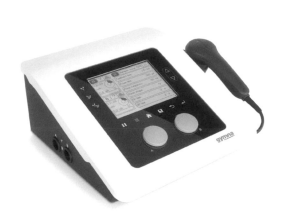

The portable electrotherapy devices of the Gymna 200 series feature modern ultrasound technology for muscle stimulation and pain treatment. The ultrasound waves reach deep into the tissue without heating the skin. The touchscreen with its logically arranged screen elements enables users to quickly access the desired settings. Furthermore, icon-based interfaces and one-touch keys make the electrotherapy devices intuitive and easy to use.

Statement by the jury
The electrotherapy devices of the Gymna 200 series fascinate with their sophisticated control concept and compact design. The units are easy to transport and can thus be taken anywhere.

Die tragbaren Elektrotherapiegeräte der Gymna 200 Serie verfügen über moderne Ultraschalltechnologie zur Muskelstimulation und Schmerzbehandlung. Die Ultraschallwellen dringen tief in das Gewebe ein, ohne dabei die Haut zu erhitzen. Der Touchscreen mit logisch angeordneten Bildschirmelementen ermöglicht es, schnell zu den gewünschten Einstellungen zu gelangen. Darüber hinaus sorgen symbolbasierte Schnittstellen und Direktwahltasten für eine intuitive und einfache Bedienung der Elektrotherapiegeräte.

Begründung der Jury
Die Elektrotherapiegeräte der Gymna 200 Serie bestechen durch ihr durchdachtes Bedienkonzept und eine kompakte Gestaltung. Die Geräte können problemlos überallhin mitgenommen werden.

FibroScan Mini 430
Device for Non-Invasive Liver Diagnosis
Gerät für die nicht-invasive Leberdiagnostik

Manufacturer
Echosens, Paris, France
Design
Nova Design (Olivier Jeanjean), Lunel, France
Web
www.echosens.com
www.nova-design.fr

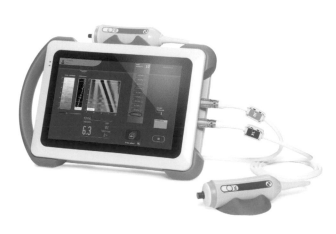

The FibroScan Mini 430 is based on a transformative and non-invasive diagnostic technology called vibration-controlled transient elastography that has improved the management of patients with chronic liver diseases, which affect over 1 billion people worldwide. Light, ultra-mobile, rugged and battery-powered, the device has been designed to conduct health screening and prevention campaigns in remote areas without access to medical facilities.

Statement by the jury
The FibroScan Mini 430 is highly portable thanks to its compact dimensions, while the large display provides strong ease of use.

Der FibroScan Mini 430 beruht auf einem transformativen und nicht-invasiven Diagnoseverfahren, das sich vibrationskontrollierte transiente Elastographie nennt. Es hat die Behandlung von Patienten mit chronischen Lebererkrankungen verbessert, von denen über eine Milliarde Menschen weltweit betroffen sind. Das leichte, hochmobile, robuste und akkubetriebene Gerät wurde speziell für den Einsatz bei Vorsorgeuntersuchungen und Präventionskampagnen in abgelegenen Gebieten ohne Zugang zu medizinischen Einrichtungen konzipiert.

Begründung der Jury
Der FibroScan Mini 430 ist dank seiner kompakten Maße hervorragend zu transportieren, während das großzügige Display einen hohen Nutzerkomfort bietet.

Vivatmo System
Asthma Monitoring Device
Asthma-Monitoring-Gerät

Manufacturer
Bosch Healthcare Solutions, Waiblingen,
Germany
In-house design
Design
Puls Produktdesign, Darmstadt, Germany
Web
www.bosch-healthcare.com
www.puls-design.de

The Vivatmo System enables asthma patients to monitor their health from home in a few simple steps. It includes the physician device Vivatmo pro, the patient device Vivatmo me and the Vivatmo app. Based on innovative sensor technology, the patient device measures the concentration of nitric oxide in the breath. The measurement data are transmitted wirelessly via Bluetooth to the patients' smartphones and automatically saved there. Patients can then forward the data to the attending physician.

Statement by the jury
The Vivatmo System makes clever use of miniaturised sensor technology and networking options in order to enhance quality of life for asthmatics.

Mit dem Vivatmo System können Asthmapatienten ihren Gesundheitszustand einfach und mit wenigen Handgriffen selbst überwachen. Es besteht aus dem Arztgerät Vivatmo pro, dem Patientengerät Vivatmo me und der Vivatmo-App. Basierend auf neuartiger Sensortechnologie misst das Patientengerät die Stickoxid-Konzentration in der Atemluft. Die Messdaten werden kabellos via Bluetooth auf dem Smartphone des Patienten gespeichert, von wo aus er diese Informationen an den behandelnden Arzt weiterleiten kann.

Begründung der Jury
Bei dem Vivatmo System werden miniaturisierte Sensortechnik und die Möglichkeiten der Vernetzung intelligent genutzt, um die Lebensqualität von Asthmatikern zu verbessern.

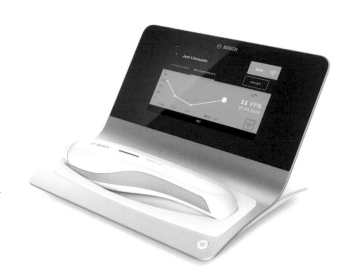

Paramon®
OR Integration System
OP-Integrationssystem

Manufacturer
TRILUX Medical GmbH & Co. KG,
Arnsberg, Germany
In-house design
Web
www.trilux-medical.com

The Paramon OR integration system takes over the entire control of cameras, lights and tables in the operating theatre. It consists of a workstation with a small footprint and an intuitive touchscreen, which is available as a standalone or in-wall unit. The integrated 4K and 3D technology enables documentation via still frames and video of the highest quality. Furthermore, the system allows data to be shared in real time with colleagues near and far in full HD or 3D on PCs, tablets and smartphones.

Statement by the jury
Paramon convinces with its clear design language, which communicates simple workflows. The graphical user interface facilitates self-explanatory interaction with the system.

Das OP-Integrationssystem Paramon übernimmt die gesamte Steuerung von Kameras, Leuchten und Tischen im Operationssaal. Es besteht aus einer Workstation, die nur wenig Standfläche einnimmt, und dem intuitiven Touchscreen, der als Standgerät oder Einbaulösung zur Verfügung steht. Die integrierte 4K- und 3D-Technologie erlaubt die Dokumentation von Standbild und Video in höchster Qualität. Darüber hinaus ermöglicht das System Daten in Echtzeit mit Kollegen nah und fern in Full-HD oder 3D auf PCs, Tablets und Smartphones zu teilen.

Begründung der Jury
Paramon überzeugt durch die klare Formensprache, die einfache Arbeitsabläufe kommuniziert. Die grafische Bedienoberfläche erlaubt eine selbsterklärende Interaktion mit dem System.

NeuViz128 CT
Computed Tomography Scanner
Computertomograph

Manufacturer
Neusoft Medical Systems Co., Ltd.,
Shenyang, China
In-house design
Jun Yu, Hai-Song Chen, He Wei, Chun-Chit Kan
Design
Designit, Munich, Germany
Web
www.neusoft.com
http://medical.neusoft.com
www.designit.com

The 128-slice computed tomography scanner called NeuViz128 CT provides precise diagnostic imaging data at low radiation doses. An illuminated ring at the gantry opening uses changes in colour to indicate which scanning phase is currently running. This keeps patients informed and reduces anxiety. Furthermore, patients are distracted from the examination by entertaining graphics. The control panels are emphasised using strong black-and-white contrasts. The control unit is dominated by an oversized rotary knob, which simplifies operation of the device.

Der 128-Zeilen-Computertomograph NeuViz128 CT liefert genaue diagnostische Bildinformationen bei niedriger Strahlendosis. Ein Lichtring in der Gantryöffnung zeigt mittels Farbveränderungen an, in welcher Scanphase das Gerät sich gerade befindet. Dies hält den Patienten informiert und verringert Ängste. Zudem wird der Patient durch unterhaltsame Grafiken von der Untersuchung abgelenkt. Die Schalttafeln sind durch starke Schwarz-Weiß-Kontraste hervorgehoben. Die Steuerungseinheit wird von einem überdimensionalen Drehknopf dominiert, der die Bedienung vereinfacht.

Statement by the jury
The NeuViz128 CT uses multimedia technology in an exemplary way in order to make the examination as pleasant as possible for the patient.

Begründung der Jury
Der NeuViz128 CT nutzt auf beispielhafte Weise multimediale Technik, um dem Patienten die Untersuchung so angenehm wie möglich zu machen.

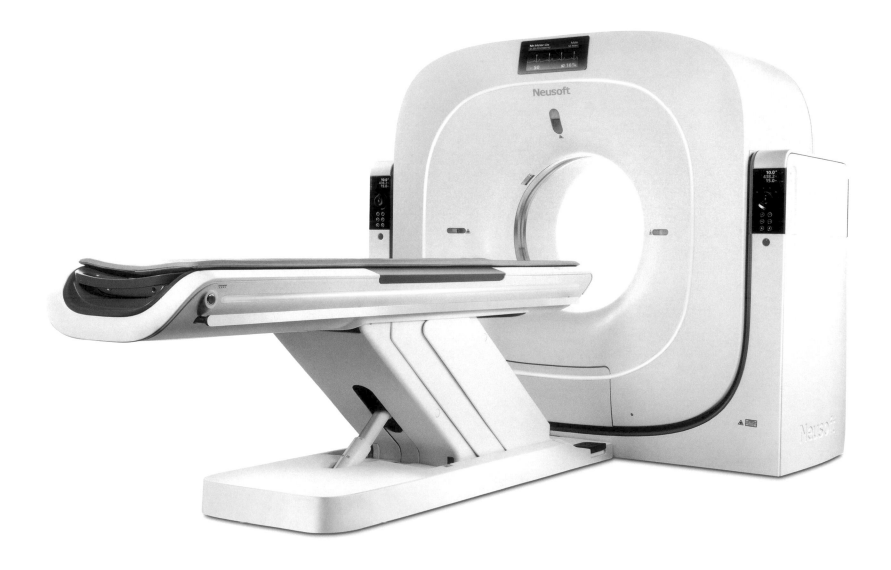

NeuSight PET/CT
PET/CT System

Manufacturer
Neusoft Medical Systems Co., Ltd.,
Shenyang, China
In-house design
Guo-Tao Zhao, Jian Ma, Chun-Chit Kan
Design
Designit, Munich, Germany
Web
www.neusoft.com
http://medical.neusoft.com
www.designit.com

The NeuSight PET/CT features state-of-the-art electronics, producing high-quality diagnostic images at rapid scanning and post-processing speeds. A variety of tactile and audiovisual feedback functions give rise to an interactive user experience. The LCD navigation integrated into the gantry precisely displays the current work status and important patient information in real time. The 72 cm gantry opening and extra-wide examination table with soft padding offer high patient comfort.

Das NeuSight PET/CT ist mit Spitzenelektronik ausgestattet, die bei schneller Aufnahme- und Nachbearbeitungsgeschwindigkeit hochwertige diagnostische Bilder ermöglicht. Verschiedene taktile und audiovisuelle Feedbackfunktionen schaffen ein interaktives Nutzererlebnis. Die in die Gantry integrierte LCD-Navigation bietet eine präzise Anzeige des aktuellen Arbeitsstatus und wichtige Patienteninformationen in Echtzeit. Die 72 cm große Gantryöffnung und der extrabreite Untersuchungstisch mit einer weichen Auflagefläche sind sehr komfortabel für den Patienten.

Statement by the jury
With its architectural and geometric design language, the NeuSight PET/CT achieves a distinctive appearance with a modern and self-confident effect.

Begründung der Jury
Das NeuSight PET/CT erzielt durch seine architektonisch-geometrische Formensprache ein eigenständiges Erscheinungsbild, das modern und selbstbewusst wirkt.

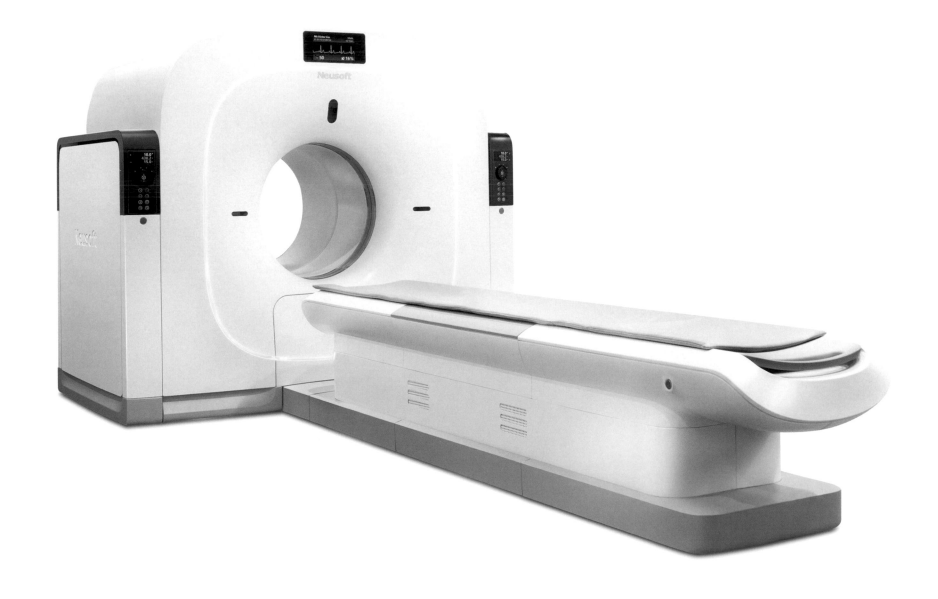

WDM Bamboo Series
Medical Imaging Devices
Medizinische Bildgebungsgeräte

Manufacturer
China Resources Wandong Medical Equipment Co., Ltd.,
Beijing, China
Design
Shenzhen ND Industrial Design Co., Ltd.
(Jingzhou Wen, Tianyu Xiao), Shenzhen, China
Web
www.wandong.com.cn
www.sz-nd.com

The design concept of the medical imaging devices in the WDM Bamboo Series is based on the traditional Chinese saying that "bamboo reports safety". This refers to a letter from the family saying that everything is fine at home. Unobtrusive bamboo edging makes the devices look friendly and inviting, thus reducing patients' fear of the examination. In addition, the use of bamboo is a unique feature in the industry, clearly referencing the oriental legacy of the brand.

Die gestalterische Idee für die medizinischen Bildgebungsgeräte der Serie WDM Bamboo beruht auf der traditionellen chinesischen Redewendung „Bambus berichtet von Sicherheit". Gemeint ist ein Brief von der Familie, der besagt, dass zu Hause alles in Ordnung ist. Durch dezente Umrandungen aus Bambus wirken die medizinischen Geräte freundlich und einladend, was die Angst der Patienten vor der Untersuchung mindert. Darüber hinaus stellt der Materialeinsatz von Bambus ein Alleinstellungsmerkmal in der Branche dar, welches auf das orientalische Erbe der Marke verweist.

Statement by the jury
The medical imaging devices of the WDM Bamboo Series have a distinctive look thanks to the bamboo accents and the soft, contour-enhancing design.

Begründung der Jury
Die medizinischen Bildgebungsgeräte der Serie WDM Bamboo erhalten durch die Akzente aus Bambus und die weiche konturverstärkende Form ein unverwechselbares Erscheinungsbild.

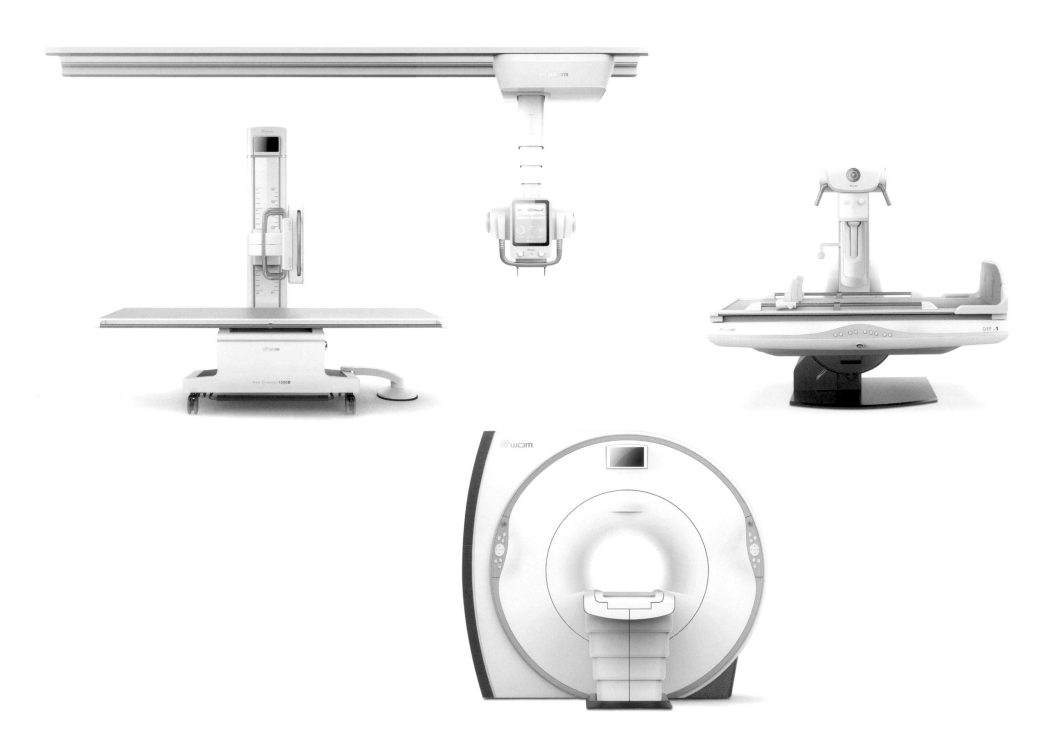

ARTIS pheno
Robot-Supported Interventional X-Ray System
Interventionelles robotergestütztes Röntgensystem

Manufacturer
Siemens Healthcare GmbH, Erlangen, Germany
In-house design
Nadja Roth
Design
at-design GbR (Tobias Reese), Fürth, Germany
Web
www.healthcare.siemens.com
www.atdesign.de

Powered by an industrial robot, the interventional X-ray system Artis pheno moves safely and flexibly around patients even in limited spaces. This enables the physician to select optimal imaging positions. The aim of the design is to reduce the robot's visual complexity and to give the system a less technical look. The surfaces feature an antimicrobial coating and are easy to clean. The illuminated tableside modules simplify use of the system for medical staff.

Angetrieben von einem industriellen Roboter, bewegt sich das interventionelle Röntgensystem Artis pheno auch bei schwierigen Platzverhältnissen sicher und flexibel um den Patienten herum. Dies ermöglicht dem Arzt optimale Aufnahme-positionen. Die Gestaltung zielt darauf ab, die visuelle Komplexität des Roboters zu reduzieren und dem System eine weniger technische Anmutung zu verleihen. Die Oberflächen sind mit einer antimikrobiellen Beschichtung versehen und leicht zu reinigen. Die beleuchteten tischseitigen Module erleichtern dem Fachpersonal die Bedienung des Systems.

Statement by the jury
The fascinating precision of movement in the robot-supported X-ray system Artis pheno is reflected in the clear design language with its smooth, flush surfaces.

Begründung der Jury
Die faszinierende Präzision der Bewegungen des robotergestützten Röntgensystems Artis pheno spiegelt sich in der klaren Formensprache mit glatten, bündigen Oberflächen wider.

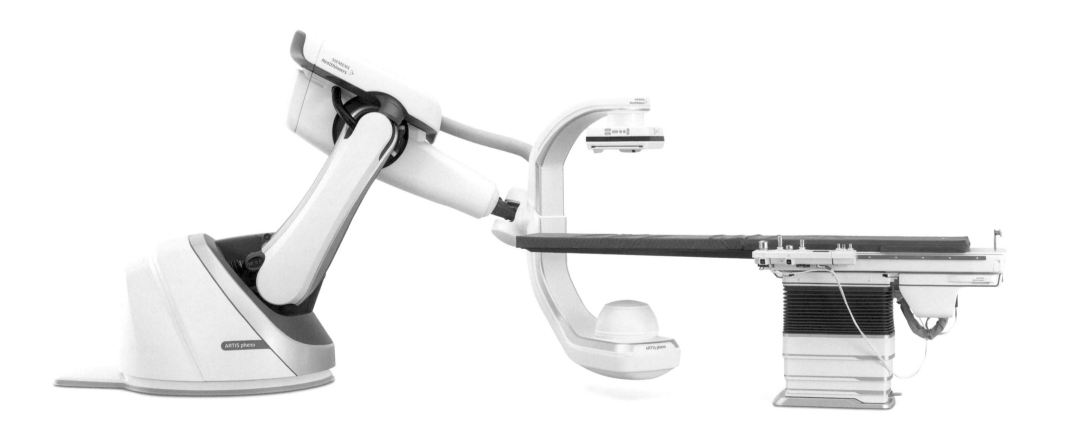

Multitom Rax
Robot-Supported 3D X-Ray Scanner
Robotergestützter 3D-Röntgenscanner

Manufacturer
Siemens Healthcare GmbH, Forchheim, Germany
In-house design
Siemens Healthineers Design Team
(Gerben ten Cate)
Design
at-design GbR, Fürth, Germany
Web
www.healthcare.siemens.com
www.atdesign.de

With the Multitom Rax robot-supported 3D X-ray scanner, a wide variety of examinations from different clinical fields can be carried out with a single system. The fully automated arms controlled by robotic technology move around the patients when they are sitting, standing or lying down. Thus, there is no need for patients to be repositioned or change rooms. The dynamic contours of the scanner put the focus on its three main functional elements: detector, X-ray head and table. The positioning of the control and display elements supports fluent use of the system.

Mit dem 3D-Röntgenscanner Multitom Rax können verschiedenste Untersuchungen aus unterschiedlichen klinischen Bereichen an nur einem System durchgeführt werden. Die durch Robotertechnik gesteuerten Arme fahren vollautomatisiert um den Patienten herum, ob dieser sitzt, steht oder liegt. Der Patient muss daher weder umgelagert werden, noch den Raum wechseln. Der dynamische Kantenverlauf des Scanners setzt den Fokus auf die drei wichtigsten Funktionsgruppen – Detektor, Röntgenkopf und Tisch. Die Positionierung der Bedien- und Displayelemente unterstützt eine einfache Handhabung des Systems.

Statement by the jury
The progressive design of the Multitom Rax skilfully conveys its innovative strength. Thanks to its openness, the extensive construction exudes a discreet presence.

Begründung der Jury
Die progressive Gestaltung des Multitom Rax transportiert gekonnt seine Innovationskraft. Die raumgreifende Konstruktion strahlt durch ihre Offenheit eine unaufdringliche Präsenz aus.

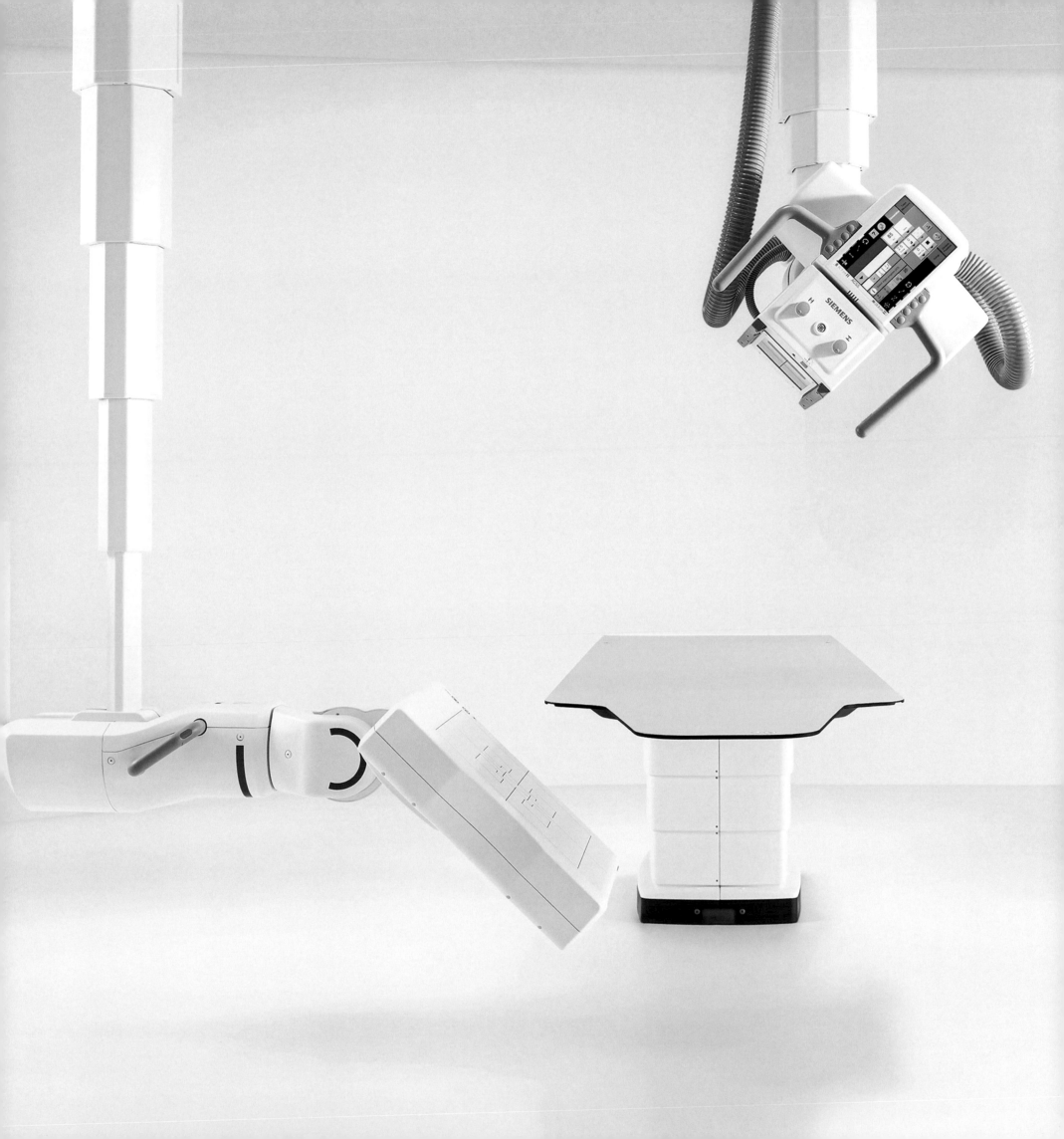

Q-Flow
Surgical Light
Operationsleuchte

Manufacturer
Merivaara Corp., Lahti, Finland
In-house design
Jyrki Nieminen, Paul Bärlund
Design
S.E.O.S. Design Oy (Pekka Kumpula),
Espoo, Finland
Web
www.merivaara.com
www.seos.fi

The form of the surgical light Q-Flow has been optimised for air circulation. It reduces the amount of twirling particles in the sterile work environment and thereby lowers the risk of infection. Moreover, the light keeps the operating theatre free of harmful gases, thus improving working conditions for medical staff. Brightness and diameter of the light are adjustable in a sterile and ergonomic way. The high colour rendering index ensures excellent visibility of tissue and blood vessels.

Statement by the jury
The open design of the Q-Flow lends it remarkable functionality. Together with the touchscreen, the light and mount create a coherent overall image.

Die Form der Operationsleuchte Q-Flow ist für die Luftzirkulation optimiert. Sie senkt die Menge herumwirbelnder Partikel im sterilen Arbeitsbereich und verringert somit die Infektionsgefahr. Zudem hält die Leuchte den OP-Bereich frei von schädlichen Gasen und verbessert so die Arbeitsbedingungen für das medizinische Personal. Helligkeit und Lichtdurchmesser sind auf sterile und ergonomische Weise verstellbar. Der hohe Farbwiedergabeindex gewährleistet eine ausgezeichnete Sichtbarkeit von Gewebe und Blutgefäßen.

Begründung der Jury
Ihre offene Bauform verleiht der Q-Flow eine außergewöhnliche Funktionalität. Leuchte und Halterung ergeben zusammen mit dem integrierten Touchscreen ein stimmiges Gesamtbild.

KINEVO 900 Robotic Visualization System

KINEVO 900 Robotisches Visualisierungssystem

Manufacturer
Carl Zeiss Meditec AG,
Oberkochen, Germany
In-house design
Frank Rudolph, Martin Schneider,
Dominik Litsch, Andreas Raab
Design
Matuschek Design & Management
(Walter Matuschek), Aalen, Germany
Web
www.zeiss.com/kinevo
www.matuschekdesign.de

The KINEVO 900 Robotic Visualization System advances user interaction and thus enhances surgical certainty through intra-operative digital imaging. With integrated 3D and 4K technology, it gives surgeons an alternative to the optical approach: the new Digital Hybrid Visualization. Surgeon-controlled robotics enables smart positioning functions like PositionMemory to minimise disruption during repositioning. QEVO, the unique Micro-Inspection Tool, expands the line of sight and helps to eliminate blind spots.

Statement by the jury
The design of the KINEVO 900, with its dynamic contours and taut lines, gives the hybrid technological approach a pioneering form.

Das robotische Visualisierungssystem KINEVO 900 erhöht durch intraoperative digitale Bildgebung die Benutzerinteraktion und damit die chirurgische Gewissheit. Die Digitale Hybride Visualisierung gewährt Entscheidungsfreiheit zwischen neuartiger 3D- und 4K-Technologie sowie optischer Visualisierung. Die vom Chirurgen gesteuerte Robotik ermöglicht intelligente Positionierungsfunktionen wie PositionMemory, wodurch Repositionierungen minimiert werden. Das QEVO Mikro-Inspektionstool erweitert die Sichtlinie und ermöglicht es, nicht einsehbare Bereiche zu erschließen.

Begründung der Jury
Bei der Gestaltung des KINEVO 900 mit seinen dynamischen Konturen und straffen Linien ist es gelungen, dem hybriden technologischen Ansatz eine wegweisende Form zu geben.

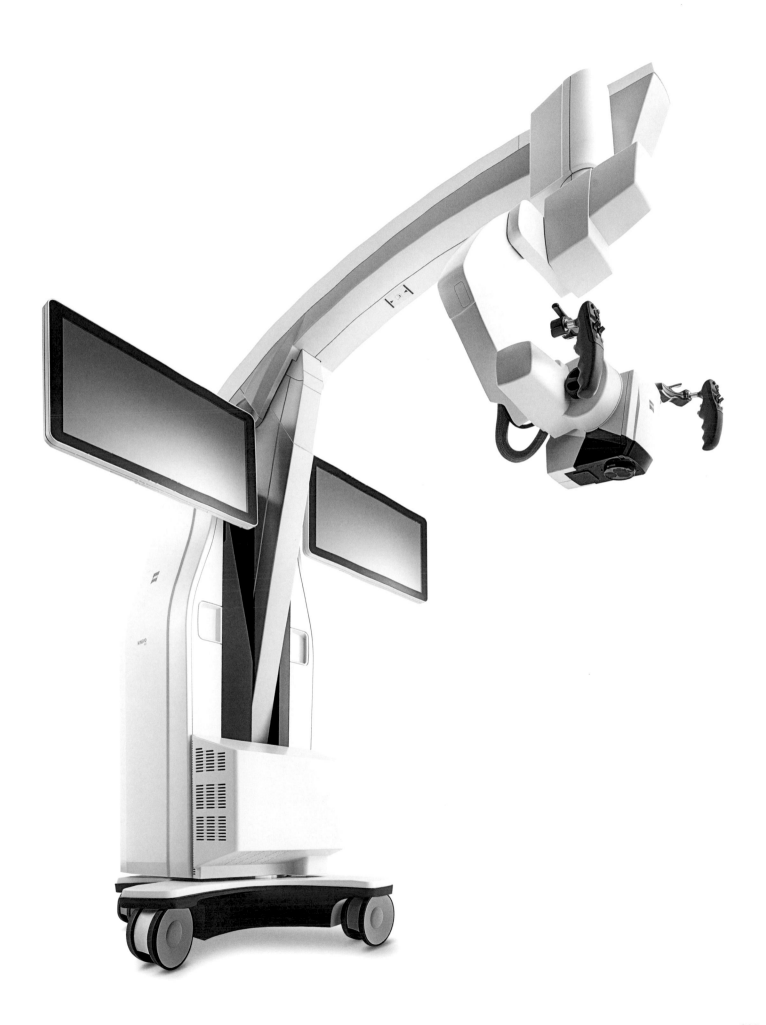

Aesculap® 3D EinsteinVision®, Aesculap® 2D SmartVue®
3D Camera Head and 2D Camera Head
3D-Kamerakopf und 2D-Kamerakopf

Manufacturer
Aesculap AG, Tuttlingen, Germany
In-house design
Rudi Zepf
Web
www.bbraun.de
www.aesculap.de

The Aesculap camera heads for 2D and 3D laparoscopy can be used interdisciplinary. The control keys are backlit in colour in order to enable intuitive use in the dimmed lighting conditions of the operating theatre. The flattened form of the 3D camera heads enables clear identification of the endoscope's direction of view. The clear form and colour design prove value and modernness. All camera heads shall ensure recognition due to consistent design elements. Moreover, the camera heads are easy to clean thanks to their smooth surfaces and flowing form.

Die Kameraköpfe von Aesculap für die 2D- und 3D-Laparoskopie können fächerübergreifend eingesetzt werden. Die Bedienknöpfe sind farbig hinterleuchtet, um eine intuitive Handhabung im abgedunkelten OP-Feld zu ermöglichen. Durch die abgeflachte Form der 3D-Kameraköpfe lässt sich die Blickrichtung des Endoskops eindeutig erkennen. Die klare Form- und Farbgestaltung vermittelt Modernität und Wertigkeit. Alle Kameraköpfe sorgen durch einheitliche Gestaltungselemente für eine hohe Wiedererkennung. Zudem sind die Kameraköpfe durch die glatten Oberflächen und fließende Formgebung einfach zu reinigen.

Statement by the jury
The compact camera heads are extremely convenient to use and also impress with their ergonomically rounded construction, featuring significant colour contrasting.

Begründung der Jury
Die kompakten Kameraköpfe sind äußerst komfortabel zu bedienen und überzeugen darüber hinaus durch ihre ergonomisch gerundete Bauform mit signifikanten Farbkontrasten.

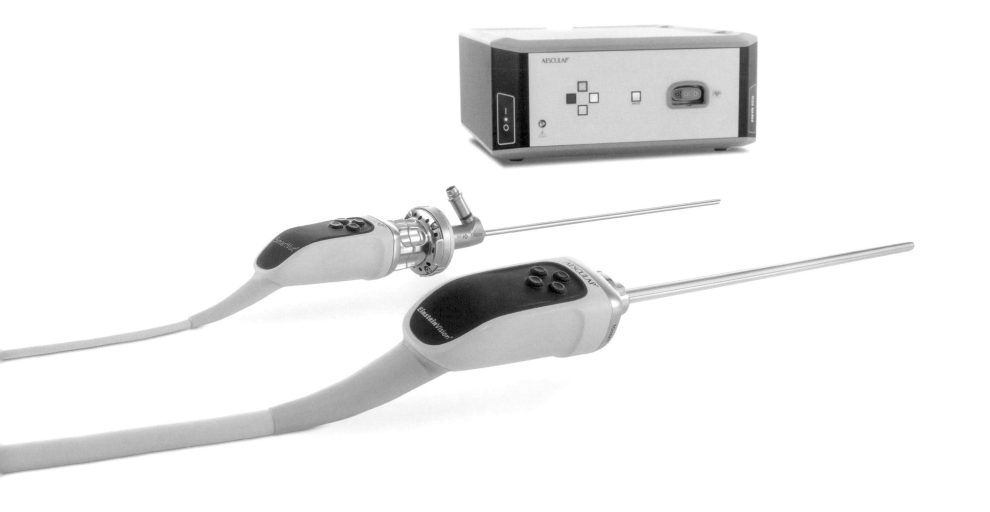

Memory Metal
Liposuction System
Liposuktionssystem

Manufacturer
Metal Industries Research & Development
Centre, Kaohsiung, Taiwan
Design
Qisda Corporation, Taipei, Taiwan
Web
www.mirdc.org.tw
www.qisda.com

The liposuction system Memory Metal
features a super-elastic cannula made
from a nickel-titanium alloy. It flexibly
adapts to the body, avoiding tissue
damage and needle deformation. After
sterilisation the needle returns to its
original shape, which significantly extends its service life. The system provides
different frequencies while maintaining
constant vibration. Coloured rings at the
needle piston and different-coloured
pipes support correct usage.

Statement by the jury
The Memory Metal inspires with its safe-
ty-related design aspects and excellent
material properties, which enable a particularly long service life.

Das Liposuktionssystem Memory Metal
verfügt über eine superelastische Hohlnadel
aus einer Nickel-Titan-Legierung. Sie passt
sich flexibel dem Körper an, die Schädigung
von Gewebe und eine Verformung der
Nadel werden vermieden. Nach der Sterilisation nimmt die Nadel ihre ursprüngliche
Form wieder an, was ihre Lebensdauer
deutlich erhöht. Das System bietet verschiedene Frequenzen bei konstanter Vibration.
Farbringe an den Nadelkolben und verschie-
denfarbige Rohre unterstützen die korrekte
Anwendung.

Begründung der Jury
Das Memory Metal punktet durch sicher-
heitstechnische Gestaltungsaspekte und
hervorragende Materialeigenschaften, die
einen besonders langlebigen Einsatz
ermöglichen.

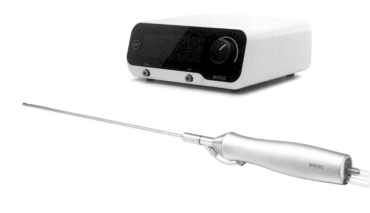

QEVO Micro-Inspection Tool
QEVO Mikro-Inspektionstool

Manufacturer
Carl Zeiss Meditec AG, Oberkochen, Germany
In-house design
Martin Fanenbruck, Roland Guckler
Design
Matuschek Design & Management
(Walter Matuschek), Aalen, Germany
Web
www.zeiss.com/kinevo
www.matuschekdesign.de

The QEVO Micro-Inspection Tool complements intraoperative microsurgical
visualisation by visualising previously
concealed areas. It helps in the recognition of structures that elude the direct
line of sight, while also making areas
visible that are hard to see, thus supporting better clinical decisions. Its angled design promotes safe use during
insertion into the body and reduces the
necessity of having to reposition the
KINEVO 900 Robotic Visualization System, which fully integrates QEVO into
its design.

Statement by the jury
Thanks to its flowing, geometrical form,
the QEVO Micro-Inspection Tool combines technological and ergonomic aspects to create a coherent unit.

Das QEVO Mikro-Inspektionstool erweitert
die intraoperative mikrochirurgische Visualisierung und ermöglicht die Darstellung
bisher verborgen gebliebener Bereiche.
Es hilft Strukturen zu erkennen, die nicht in
der direkten Sichtlinie liegen, und macht
schwer einsehbare Bereiche sichtbar, wodurch bessere medizinische Entscheidungen
getroffen werden können. Das abgewinkelte
Design unterstützt eine sichere Handhabung beim Einführen in den Situs und reduziert Repositionierungen des robotischen
Visualisierungssystems KINEVO 900.

Begründung der Jury
Durch seine fließende, geometrische Form
verbindet das QEVO Mikro-Inspektionstool
technologische und ergonomische Aspekte
zu einer stimmigen Einheit.

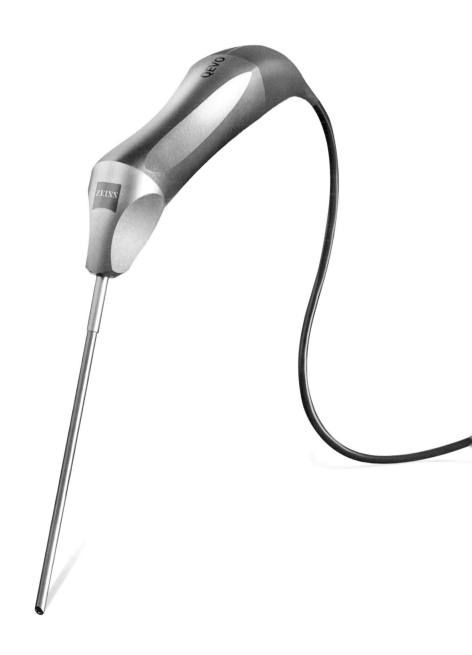

EC-760ZP-V/L
Video Endoscope
Videoendoskop

Manufacturer
FUJIFILM Corporation, Tokyo, Japan
In-house design
Kunihiko Tanaka
Web
www.fujifilm.com

The video endoscope EC-760ZP-V/L features a multi-zoom function, which enables magnification up to 135x. The newly developed instrument channel enables an enhanced transfer of force, allowing the tip to move freely. A colour code on the handle indicates the diameter of the instrument channel in order to prevent operating errors. The endoscope is powered directly via the video processor, enabling quick start-up after it is connected.

Statement by the jury
Thanks to its innovative technology, high-quality workmanship and intuitive use, the video endoscope EC-760ZP-V/L is an efficient work instrument with regard to both function and form.

Das Videoendsokop EC-760ZP-V/L ist mit einer Multi-Zoom-Funktion ausgestattet, die eine bis zu 135-fache Vergrößerung ermöglicht. Der neu entwickelte Instrumentenkanal sorgt für eine verbesserte Kraftübertragung, sodass die Spitze frei beweglich ist. Ein Farbcode am Griff zeigt den Durchmesser des Instrumentenkanals an, um mögliche Bedienfehler zu vermeiden. Das Endoskop bezieht seinen Strom direkt über den Videoprozessor. Es wird angeschlossen und kann dann sofort in Betrieb genommen werden.

Begründung der Jury
Dank innovativer Technologie, hochwertiger Verarbeitung und intuitiver Bedienbarkeit ist das Videoendsokop EC-760ZP-V/L ein funktional wie formal effizientes Arbeitsinstrument.

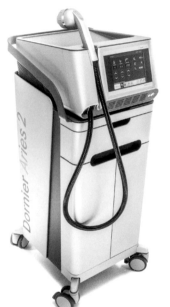

Dornier Aries 2
Shock Wave Therapy Unit
Stoßwellentherapieeinheit

Manufacturer
Dornier MedTech Systems GmbH, Weßling, Germany
In-house design
Web
www.dornier.com

The Dornier Aries 2 shock wave therapy unit creates shock waves outside the body and applies them to the area of discomfort. The lightweight applicator can be held in different ways, thus enabling comfortable and low-fatigue use. Design details such as continuous lines and the targeted integration of metal surfaces achieve a coherent design language in both the device and the trolley. The long wheelbase provides high stability and optimal manoeuvrability.

Statement by the jury
The functional look of the Dornier Aries 2 strongly exudes professionalism. Calm colours and a handleless front are skilfully combined to create a coherent design.

Die Stoßwellentherapieeinheit Dornier Aries 2 erzeugt Stoßwellen außerhalb des Körpers und appliziert diese im Bereich der Beschwerden. Der leichte Applikator erlaubt über verschiedene Griffweisen eine bequeme, ermüdungsarme Bedienung. Durch gestalterische Details wie fortlaufende Linien und den gezielten Einsatz von Oberflächen aus Metall wird eine durchgängige Formensprache zwischen Gerät und Wagen erzielt. Der weite Achsabstand der Räder sorgt für hohe Stabilität und optimale Manövrierfähigkeit.

Begründung der Jury
Die sachliche Anmutung des Dornier Aries 2 strahlt in hohem Maße Professionalität aus. Die ruhigen Farben und die grifflose Front stellen gekonnt eine gestalterische Einheit her.

CAN-Q
Image System for Cell Analysis
Bildgebungssystem für die Zellanalyse

Manufacturer
Venneos GmbH, Stuttgart, Germany
Design
defortec GmbH (Stefan Grobe, Lionel Linke), Dettenhausen, Germany
Web
www.venneos.com
www.defortec.de

CAN-Q is an image system for the analysis of biological cells. It is based on an innovative measuring approach in order to make cellular changes not optically but electronically visible. The cells grow on a silicon chip, which detects the electrical signals of the cellular changes. The signals are then processed and displayed as images reminiscent of microscopy. The main design focus has been placed on achieving ease of use and a compact form.

Statement by the jury
CAN-Q takes an impressive approach to translating complex technologies into a manageable, simple form. Operation can be intuitively grasped thanks to the clear geometric design.

CAN-Q ist ein Bildgebungssystem für die Analyse von biologischen Zellen. Es beruht auf einem innovativen Messansatz, um zelluläre Veränderungen nicht optisch, sondern elektronisch sichtbar zu machen. Die Zellen wachsen auf einem Siliziumchip, der die elektrischen Signale der zellulären Veränderungen identifiziert. Die Signale werden anschließend verarbeitet und ähnlich wie Mikroskopiebilder dargestellt. Bei dem Gestaltungskonzept standen eine einfache Handhabung und eine kompakte Bauform im Mittelpunkt.

Begründung der Jury
Auf beeindruckende Weise überführt CAN-Q komplexe Technologie in eine beherrschbare einfache Form. Die Benutzung lässt sich durch die klare geometrische Gestaltung intuitiv nachvollziehen.

3Shape X1
CBCT Scanner
DVT-Scanner

Manufacturer
3Shape A/S, Copenhagen, Denmark
Design
Eskild Hansen Design Studios,
Copenhagen, Denmark
Web
www.3shape.com
www.eskildhansen.com

The CBCT scanner 3Shape X1 produces three-dimensional X-ray images of the teeth and jaw. The device features innovative technology that generates sharp images even if the patient moves. This reduces stress for patients, because their heads do not have to be fixated during the scanning process. Furthermore, the calming ambient light and the headrest made of natural wood enhance user-friendliness. The carbon construction minimises vibrations that result from the movements of the scanner.

Statement by the jury
The CBCT scanner 3Shape X1 achieves more freedom of movement for the patient thanks to its technology and design, thus representing a new sense of lightness and openness.

Der DVT-Scanner 3Shape X1 erstellt dreidimensionale Röntgenbilder der Zähne und des Kiefers. Das Gerät verfügt über eine innovative Technologie, die scharfe Bilder generiert, auch wenn der Patient sich bewegt. Dies reduziert den Stress für den Patienten, da sein Kopf für das Scannen nicht fixiert werden muss. Darüber hinaus erhöhen das beruhigende Umgebungslicht und die Kopfstütze aus natürlichem Holz den Benutzerkomfort. Die Konstruktion aus Carbon reduziert Vibrationen durch Bewegungen des Scanners.

Begründung der Jury
Der DVT-Scanner 3Shape X1 erzielt in technischer wie gestalterischer Hinsicht mehr Bewegungsfreiheit für den Patienten und steht damit für eine neue Leichtigkeit und Offenheit.

Stretcher X
Life-Support Trolley
Notfalltransporter

Manufacturer
Novak M d.o.o., Komenda, Slovenia
In-house design
Design
Wilsonic Design, Trzin, Slovenia
Web
www.novak-m.com
www.wilsonicdesign.com

The Stretcher X life-support trolley is a stretcher for all treatment phases in the emergency department: admission, transportation and examination. The innovative diagonal shape ensures optimal access to X-ray devices from all sides of the stretcher. The large reclining surface, permeable for X-rays, allows images to be made without having to move the patient. Thanks to its short wheelbase, the trolley is easy to manoeuvre and can turn on the spot.

Statement by the jury
The Stretcher X life-support trolley convinces with its versatile functionality, high mobility and unrestricted access, which ensure smooth workflows during emergencies.

Der Notfalltransporter Stretcher X ist eine Patientenliege für alle Versorgungsphasen in der Notaufnahme – von der Aufnahme über den Transport bis hin zur Untersuchung. Die innovative Diagonalform gewährleistet von allen Seiten der Liege einen optimalen Zugang zu den Röntgengeräten. Die große, für Röntgenstrahlen durchlässige Liegefläche ermöglicht es, den Patienten zu durchleuchten, ohne ihn bewegen zu müssen. Durch den kurzen Radstand lässt sich der Transporter leicht rangieren und auf der Stelle wenden.

Begründung der Jury
Der Notfalltransporter Stretcher X überzeugt durch vielseitige Funktionalität, hohe Mobilität und uneingeschränkte Zugänglichkeit. Dadurch sorgt er für reibungslose Abläufe im Einsatz.

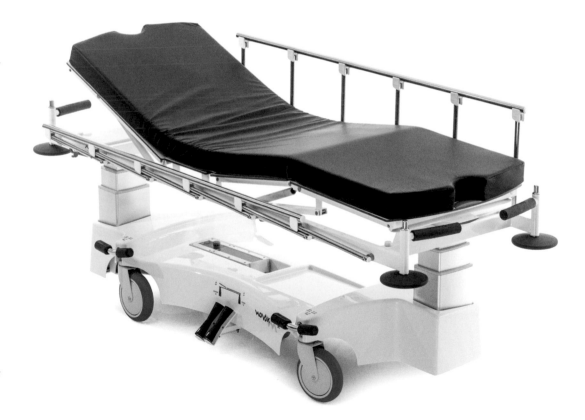

revogene™
System for Microbial Testing
System für mikrobielle Untersuchungen

Manufacturer
GenePOC Inc.,
Quebec, Canada

Design
ALTO Design Inc.,
Montreal, Canada

Web
www.genepoc-diagnostics.com
www.alto-design.com

reddot award 2017
best of the best

On the spot

In clinical everyday practice, laboratory testing results must often be determined rapidly in order to plan further therapeutic steps. Based on an innovative centripetal technology platform, the revogene system can deliver microbial analysis results within just 70 minutes. The system is suitable for testing a wide range of biological samples directly at the point of care. It is composed of one single instrument that accepts single-use cartridges, named PIE's, that have been developed to target specific infections. The instrument functions by safely performing a defined set of cycling conditions that activate the cartridge chemicals for testing the sample. The results are then displayed on the screen at the end of the analysis. Up to eight tests of different infections can be conducted simultaneously. Sophisticated in both form and function, the design of this device was designed to streamline the workflow and handling of the samples to be tested. The logically arranged uscr interface promotes safe and intuitive operation. A dissimulated LED ring permeates the otherwise opaque cover to provide visual feedback of the cycle progress during testing. Showcasing a design that is equally professional and appealing, the device offers new possibilities in sample testing and analysis – it contributes to saving lives by bringing the lab to the patient.

An Ort und Stelle

Im klinischen Alltag müssen oftmals Laborergebnisse zeitnah ermittelt werden, um weitere therapeutische Schritte planen zu können. Basierend auf einer innovativen Plattform der Zentripetaltechnologie, ermöglicht revogene mikrobielle Analysen in einem Zeitraum von nur 70 Minuten. Das System eignet sich für ein breites Spektrum biologischer Proben, die patientennah und vor Ort analysiert werden können. Es besteht aus nur einem Gerät für den Einsatz von Einwegpatronen, genannt PIE's, die speziell für das Testen bestimmter Infektionen entwickelt wurden. Das System vollzieht auf sichere Art und Weise zunächst eine vordefinierte Anzahl an Zyklusbedingungen, wodurch die Chemikalien in der Patrone aktiviert werden. Die Ergebnisse werden dann nach Abschluss der Analyse auf dem Bildschirm angezeigt. Bis zu acht Tests verschiedener Infektionen können gleichzeitig durchgeführt werden. Die in Form und Funktion ausgereifte Gestaltung des Gerätes ist dabei darauf ausgerichtet, den Arbeitsablauf und die Handhabung der Proben zu optimieren. Mittels einer logisch aufgebauten Nutzeroberfläche lässt es sich sicher und intuitiv bedienen. Ein verdeckt integrierter LED-Ring ist durch die ansonsten undurchsichtige Abdeckung hindurch sichtbar und gibt Aufschluss über den Programmstatus. Mit seinem ebenso professionellen wie ansprechenden Design bietet dieses System neue Möglichkeiten der Diagnoseerstellung – es bringt das Labor zum Patienten und kann dadurch Leben retten.

Statement by the jury

This innovative system for microbial testing allows receiving comprehensive analysis results of biological samples for many types of infections within only 70 minutes, while the patient is close by. The compact and aesthetically pleasing design corresponds to the high efficiency of the device. It features an impressive, user-friendly design that combines simple operation with the delivery of meaningful results.

Begründung der Jury

Dieses innovative System für mikrobielle Untersuchungen ermöglicht innerhalb von nur 70 Minuten eine umfassende, patientennah erfolgende Analyse von biologischen Proben im Hinblick auf Infektionskrankheiten. Die kompakte und ästhetisch ansprechende Gestaltung entspricht der hohen Effizienz des Gerätes. Beeindruckend ist seine nutzerfreundliche Konzeption, die eine einfache Bedienung mit der Bereitstellung aussagekräftiger Ergebnisse kombiniert.

Designer portrait
See page 62
Siehe Seite 62

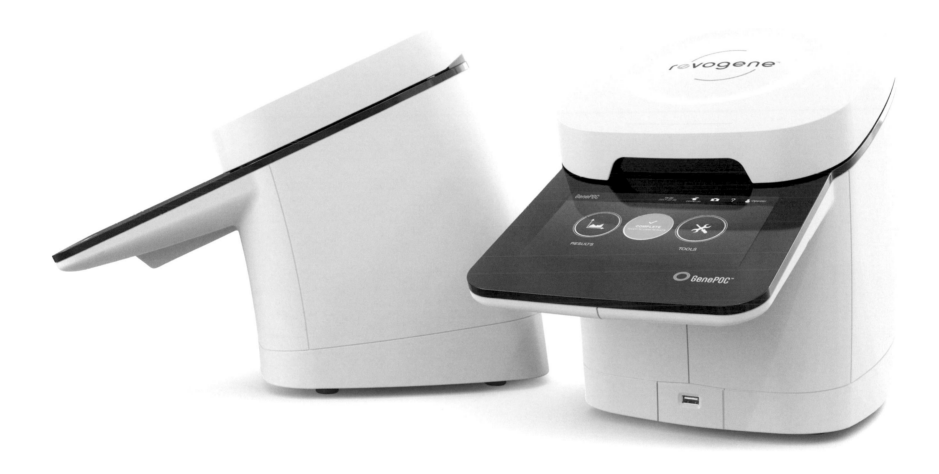

MICROJET
Microwave Autoclave
Mikrowellenautoklav

Manufacturer
ENBIO Technology Sp. z o.o.,
Suchy Dwór, Poland
Design
BRANDSPOT (Paweł Borsuk, Rafał Pelc),
Gdynia, Poland
Web
www.enbiogroup.eu
www.brandspot.pl

The Microjet microwave autoclave is designed for the sterilisation of liquid media like microbiological cultures in a laboratory. The thermal energy required for sterilisation is delivered directly to the medium. Microwaves are used as energy source, enabling immediate and uniform heating of the liquid. The sterilisation process is thus shortened to seven minutes, which is five times faster than in steam autoclaves. Each sterilisation process is automatically stored on a memory card.

Statement by the jury
The Microjet has an appealing contemporary and space-saving design, which harmoniously blends in with a modern work environment.

Der Mikrowellenautoklav Microjet dient der Aufbereitung von Flüssigmedien wie z. B. mikrobiologische Nährböden im Labor. Die für die Sterilisation notwendige Wärmeenergie wird dem Medium direkt zugeführt. Als Energiequelle dienen Mikrowellen, welche die Flüssigkeit schnell und gleichmäßig erhitzen. Dadurch verkürzt sich der Sterilisationsvorgang auf sieben Minuten, das ist fünfmal schneller als bei vergleichbaren Dampfautoklaven. Jeder Sterilisationsprozess wird automatisch gespeichert.

Begründung der Jury
Der Microjet gefällt durch seine zeitgemäße und platzsparende Gestaltung, die sich harmonisch in ein modernes Arbeitsumfeld einfügt.

STEAMJET
Steam Autoclave
Dampfautoklav

Manufacturer
ENBIO Technology Sp. z o.o.,
Suchy Dwór, Poland
Design
BRANDSPOT (Paweł Borsuk, Rafał Pelc),
Gdynia, Poland
Web
www.enbiogroup.eu
www.brandspot.pl

The Steamjet steam autoclave has been designed to process all packaged and unpackaged medical equipment that is used, for instance, in dental practices. Its compact size, quiet operation and very short sterilisation times facilitate on-demand use of the device, even directly next to the patient. All functions are controlled via the intuitive touchscreen. The legally mandated process parameters of sterilisation are automatically saved to a flash drive.

Statement by the jury
The Steamjet steam autoclave combines purist form with aesthetically exciting details, such as the unusually structured stainless-steel grille in the sterilisation chamber.

Der Dampfautoklav Steamjet ist für die Aufbereitung aller verpackten und unverpackten Medizinprodukte konzipiert, wie sie z. B. in Zahnarztpraxen verwendet werden. Durch die kompakte Größe, den geräuscharmen Betrieb und die sehr kurzen Sterilisationszeiten kann das Gerät nach Bedarf und direkt beim Patienten eingesetzt werden. Alle Funktionen werden über den intuitiven Touchscreen gesteuert. Die gesetzlich geforderten Prozessparameter der Sterilisation werden automatisch auf einem USB-Stick gespeichert.

Begründung der Jury
Der Dampfautoklav Steamjet verbindet eine puristische Form mit ästhetisch aufregenden Details wie dem außergewöhnlich strukturierten Edelstahlgitter in der Sterilisationskammer.

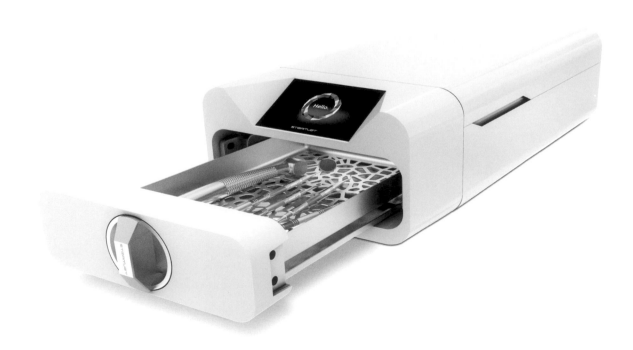

PANTHERA Series
Smart Laboratory
Microscopes
Intelligente Labormikroskope

Manufacturer
Motic China Group Co., Ltd., Xiamen, China
In-house design
Design
Cosmocolors (Xiamen) Design Ltd.,
Xiamen, China
Web
www.motic.com
www.cosmocolors.com

The smart laboratory microscopes of
the Panthera series combine optical
technologies with digital connectivity,
and they can be linked directly to an
HDMI monitor or a tablet. The appearance of the microscopes is inspired by a
large sitting cat. The LED feedback ring
at the revolving nosepiece is not only
a status indicator, but also an iconographic design characteristic of this
series. The shiny metallic surfaces, with
uniform black-anodised mechanical
components, exude elegance and clarity.

Statement by the jury
Thanks to their distinctive silhouettes,
the laboratory microscopes of the
Panthera series are an eye-catcher from
every angle. Their technological features
are groundbreaking.

Die intelligenten Labormikroskope der
Serie Panthera verbinden optische Technologien mit digitaler Konnektivität. Sie können direkt mit einem HDMI-Bildschirm
oder einem Tablet verbunden werden.
Das Aussehen der Mikroskope ist inspiriert
von der Gestalt einer sitzenden Großkatze.
Der LED-Feedback-Ring am Objektivrevol-
ver dient nicht nur als Statusanzeige,
sondern auch als ikonografisches Gestaltungsmerkmal dieser Serie. Die glänzenden
metallischen Oberflächen mit einheitlich
schwarz eloxierten mechanischen Komponenten strahlen Eleganz und Klarheit aus.

Begründung der Jury
Die Labormikroskope der Serie Panthera
sind durch ihre prägnante Silhouette
aus jedem Blickwinkel ein Hingucker. Ihre
technologische Ausstattung ist zukunftsweisend.

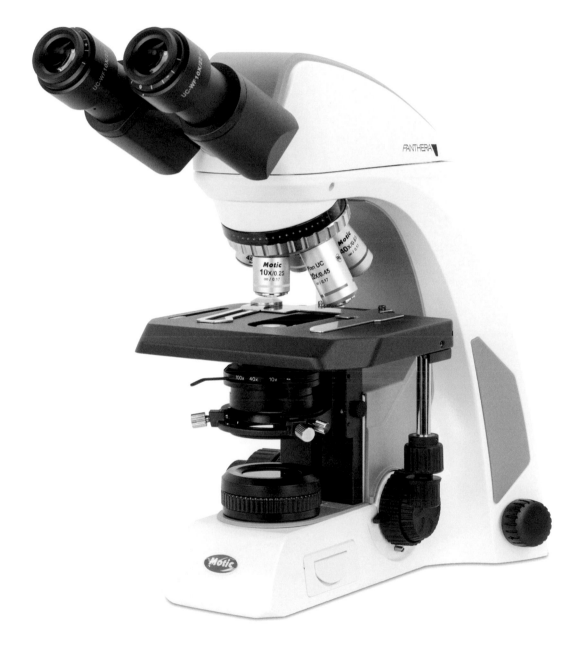

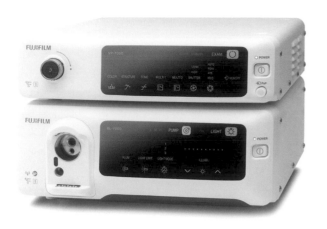

BL-7000, VP-7000
Light System and Video Processor for Endoscopic Imaging
Lichtsystem und Videoprozessor für die endoskopische Bildgebung

Manufacturer
FUJIFILM Corporation, Tokyo, Japan
In-house design
Kunihiko Tanaka
Web
www.fujifilm.com

The 4 LED multi-light system BL-7000 uses state-of-the-art, image-optimised endoscopy technology to better visualise mucosal surfaces and vascular structures in the gastrointestinal tract. The video processor VP-7000 provides images and video sequences in full HD quality. With their rounded shape, the consoles are designed for easy cleaning and to reduce patients' fear of the examination. The LED display against a black background ensures good readability.

Statement by the jury
The light system and video processor make a particularly compact and tidy impression. All interfaces are at the front, ensuring optimum accessibility.

Das 4-LED-Multi-Lichtsystem BL-7000 setzt modernste Techniken der bildoptimierten Endoskopie ein, um Schleimhautoberflächen und Gefäßstrukturen im Magen-Darm-Trakt besser zu visualisieren. Der Videoprozessor VP-7000 liefert Bilder und Videosequenzen in Full-HD-Qualität. Die Konsolen sind durch ihre gerundete Form auf eine einfache Reinigung ausgelegt und darauf, dem Patienten die Angst vor der Untersuchung zu nehmen. Die LED-Anzeige vor schwarzem Hintergrund sorgt für gute Lesbarkeit.

Begründung der Jury
Das Lichtsystem und der Videoprozessor machen einen besonders kompakten und aufgeräumten Eindruck. Alle Schnittstellen befinden sich an der Front, was für optimale Zugänglichkeit sorgt.

SP-900, CP-900, RS-900
Endoscopic Ultrasound Probe System
Endoskopisches Ultraschallsondensystem

Manufacturer
FUJIFILM Corporation, Tokyo, Japan
In-house design
Kunihiko Tanaka
Web
www.fujifilm.com

The endoscopic ultrasound probe system consists of the SP-900 ultrasound processor, the CP-900 control pad and the RS-900 scanner. The system is used in conjunction with a light source and a video processor. The display of the ultrasound processor, the operating elements of the control pad and the probe connector of the scanner are all designed in black in order to ensure easy recognition. The devices are characterised by a rounded construction with smooth surfaces, which are thus easy to clean.

Statement by the jury
With their markedly simple, user-friendly design, the individual components of the endoscopic ultrasound probe system are harmoniously coordinated.

Das endoskopische Ultraschallsondensystem besteht aus dem Ultraschallprozessor SP-900, dem Steuerpult CP-900 und dem Scanner RS-900. Das System wird in Kombination mit einer Lichtquelle und einem Videoprozessor verwendet. Das Display des Ultraschallprozessors, die Bedienelemente des Steuerpults und der Sondenstecker des Scanners sind schwarz gestaltet, wodurch sie schnell erkannt werden. Die Geräte zeichnen sich durch eine abgerundete Bauform mit glatten Oberflächen aus, wodurch sie einfach zu reinigen sind.

Begründung der Jury
Die einzelnen Komponenten des endoskopischen Ultraschallsondensystems sind in ihrer betont schlichten und benutzerfreundlichen Gestaltung ausgesprochen harmonisch aufeinander abgestimmt.

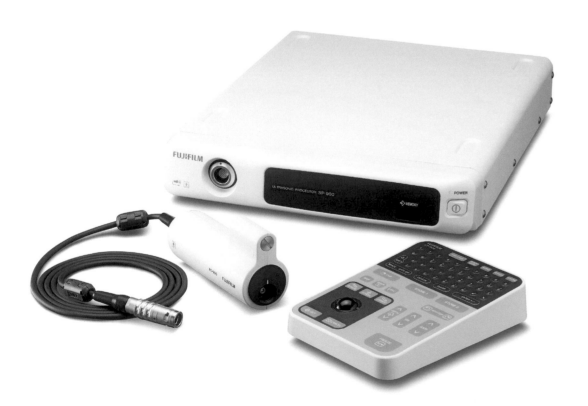

PORT X-IV
Portable Dental X-Ray Camera
Tragbare Dentalröntgenkamera

Manufacturer
GENORAY Co., Ltd.,
Seongnam, South Korea
In-house design
Design
we'd design, Seongnam,
South Korea
Web
www.genoray.com
www.wed-design.com

With the portable dental X-ray camera Port X-IV, dentists are entirely independent and able to take X-rays from any position and at any place. Thanks to the low dosage of radiation, the camera is safe for both patients and doctors. The housing with its rounded edges has deliberately been kept simple in order to improve acceptance by the patient. The examination process is shown on the graphic LCD display. The X-ray images can be transmitted via Wi-Fi.

Statement by the jury
The design language of the Port X-IV draws on the aesthetics of modern consumer electronics in a fascinating way, which makes it particularly easy to use.

Mit der tragbaren Dentalröntgenkamera Port X-IV sind Zahnärzte komplett unabhängig, sie können Röntgenbilder aus jeder Position und an jedem Ort aufnehmen. Durch die geringe Strahlung ist die Kamera sowohl für den Patienten als auch für den Arzt sicher. Das Gehäuse mit seinen abgerundeten Kanten ist bewusst einfach gehalten, um die Akzeptanz durch die Patienten zu verbessern. Der Ablauf der Untersuchung wird auf dem grafischen LCD-Display angezeigt, die Röntgenbilder können per Wi-Fi übertragen werden.

Begründung der Jury
Die Formensprache der Port X-IV ist auf faszinierende Weise an die Ästhetik moderner Unterhaltungselektronik angelehnt, was zu einer besonders angenehmen Bedienung führt.

Implantmed
Dental Drive Unit
Dental-Antriebseinheit

Manufacturer
W&H Dentalwerk Bürmoos GmbH,
Bürmoos, Austria
In-house design
Web
www.wh.com

The Implantmed modular drive unit was developed for dental implantology. The simple design with its clear lines is tailored to the hygienic working conditions found in dental clinics. The high-quality materials ensure easy and thorough cleaning of the surfaces. The targeted use of green elements highlights the intuitive use of the device. Thanks to a wireless foot control, surgeons can freely choose their treatment position.

Statement by the jury
The controls of the Implantmed drive unit focus on the essentials, thus creating an extremely calm appearance that exudes efficiency and clarity.

Die modular aufgebaute Antriebseinheit Implantmed wurde für die dentale Implantologie entwickelt. Das schlichte Design mit seinen klaren Linien ist an die hygienischen Arbeitsbedingungen einer zahnärztlichen Praxis angepasst. Die hochwertigen Materialien ermöglichen eine leichte und gründliche Reinigung der Oberflächen, der gezielte Einsatz grüner Elemente unterstreicht die intuitive Benutzung des Geräts. Dank der kabellosen Fußsteuerung kann der Chirurg seine Behandlungsposition frei wählen.

Begründung der Jury
Die Bedienelemente sind bei der Antriebseinheit Implantmed auf das Wesentliche konzentriert, sodass ein ausgesprochen ruhiges Erscheinungsbild entsteht, das Effizienz und Klarheit ausstrahlt.

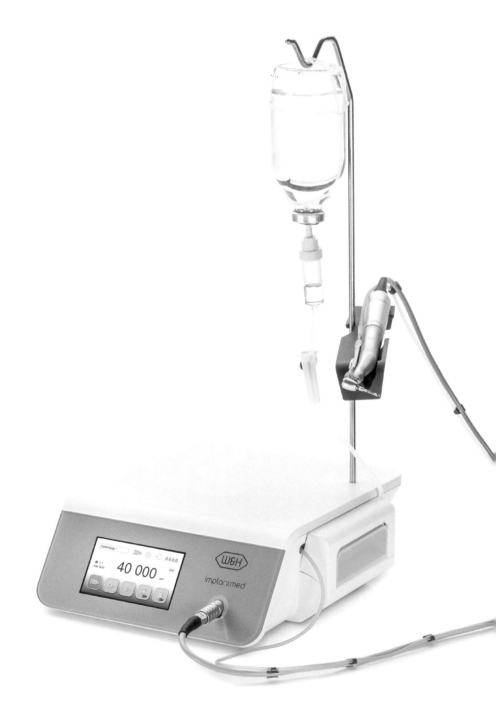

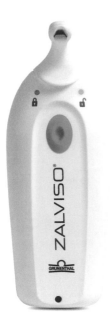

Zalviso®
Application System for Pain Treatment
Applikationsgerät zur Schmerzbehandlung

Manufacturer
AcelRx Pharmaceuticals, Inc.,
Redwood City, California, USA
In-house design
Web
www.acelrx.com

Zalviso is an innovative, pre-programmed, non-invasive, handheld system that allows adult hospital patients with acute moderate to severe post-operative pain to self-dose with sufentanil sublingual tablets to manage their pain. The dispenser was designed to allow for convenient sublingual application of sufentanil, while the controller is kept plain and simple to ensure intuitive and easy usage by patients.

Statement by the jury
The minimalist design of the Zalviso application system makes it highly intuitive to use. The ergonomically shaped mouthpiece simplifies administration of the tablets.

Zalviso ist ein innovatives, vorprogrammiertes, nicht-invasives System, mit dessen Hilfe sich erwachsene Krankenhauspatienten mit akuten, mäßig starken bis starken postoperativen Schmerzen Sufentanil-Sublingualtabletten selbst verabreichen können, um ihre Schmerzen zu behandeln. Die Dispensiereinheit wurde für die komfortable und einfache sublinguale Anwendung von Sufentanil designt. Die Steuerungseinheit ist schlicht gehalten, um eine intuitive Nutzung durch den Patienten zu gewährleisten.

Begründung der Jury
Die reduzierte Gestaltung des Applikationsgeräts Zalviso ist in hohem Maß auf eine intuitive Bedienung ausgelegt. Das ergonomisch geformte Mundstück erleichtert die Tablettengabe.

RaplixaSpray®
Haemostat
Sprühgerät zur Wundversorgung

Manufacturer
ProFibrix BV, Leiden, Netherlands
In-house design
Jos Grimbergen, Eliane Schutte
Design
Team Consulting Ltd (John Burke, Paul Greenhalgh, Oliver Harvey), Cambridge, Great Britain
Web
www.profibrix.com
www.team-consulting.com

The RaplixaSpray is used to stem bleeding during surgical procedures. To this end, a dry powder is applied – a two-component adhesive that seals the wound. The device features an intuitive fingertip control, which enables the physician to precisely distribute the powder. Each operating element is clearly marked in colour. The handpiece is a combination of pen and pistol grip for open or minimally invasive procedures.

Statement by the jury
The RaplixaSpray impresses with its balanced proportions and clearly structured individual functional areas, thus facilitating smooth use.

Das RaplixaSpray wird während operativer Eingriffe verwendet, um Blutungen zu stoppen. Dafür wird ein Trockenpulver appliziert – ein Zweikomponentenkleber, der die Wunde versiegelt. Das Gerät verfügt über eine intuitive Fingerspitzensteuerung, die es dem Arzt ermöglicht, das Pulver genau zu verteilen. Jedes Bedienelement ist farblich klar gekennzeichnet. Das Handstück ist eine Kombination aus Füller- und Pistolengriff für offene oder minimal-invasive Eingriffe.

Begründung der Jury
Das RaplixaSpray besticht durch ausgewogene Proportionen und eine klare Strukturierung der einzelnen Funktionsbereiche, was eine reibungslose Handhabung ermöglicht.

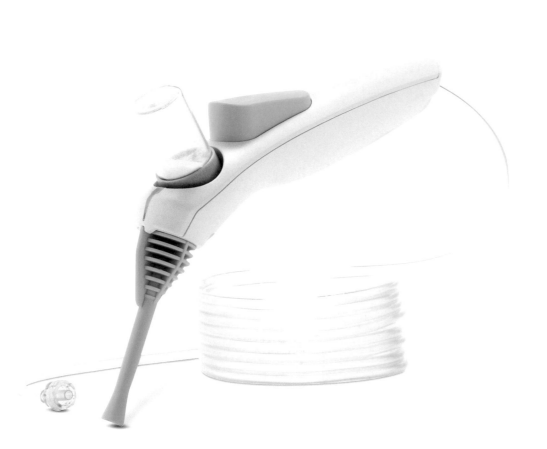

XPR Precision Balances
XPR-Präzisionswaagen

Manufacturer
Mettler-Toledo GmbH,
Greifensee, Switzerland
In-house design
Daniel Mock, Hansjörg Rotach
Design
Held + Team (Fred Held, Thilo Hogrebe),
Hamburg, Germany
Web
www.mt.com
www.heldundteam.de

The XPR precision balances feature a SmartPan weighing pan. This minimises the impact of airflow on the weighing results, thus clearly improving settling times and repeatability. Thanks to the high stability of the weighing pan, results are delivered up to twice as fast as in comparable models, even in harsh production environments. A status light on the terminal indicates to the user that the balance is ready to use.

Statement by the jury
Featuring straight line management, the XPR precision balances present clear structures that skilfully highlight their accuracy and create a distinctive look.

Die XPR-Präzisionswaagen sind mit der innovativen SmartPan-Waagschale ausgestattet. Diese minimiert eine Beeinflussung der Wägeresultate durch Luftströme auf die Wägezelle und verbessert so deutlich Einschwingzeiten und Wiederholbarkeit. Durch die hohe Stabilität der Waagschale können Resultate sogar in rauen Produktionsumgebungen bis zu doppelt so schnell geliefert werden wie bei vergleichbaren Modellen. Ein Statuslicht auf dem Terminal zeigt dem Benutzer an, dass die Waage wägebereit ist.

Begründung der Jury
Die XPR-Präzisionswaagen weisen mit ihrer geraden Linienführung klare Strukturen auf, die ihre Akkuratesse visuell gekonnt unterstreichen und für ein prägnantes Erscheinungsbild sorgen.

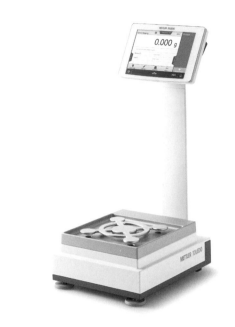

C-KUP
Specimen Container
Probenbehälter

Manufacturer
Bonraybio Corporation, Taichung, Taiwan
In-house design
Hsi-Wen Huang
Web
www.bonraybio.com

The C-KUP specimen container was developed especially for storing male seminal fluid. The ergonomic curve and wide opening facilitate easy sample collection. The innovative dripper design and flexible container material enable precisely dosed sample extraction, without having to open the lid completely. The distance between the flow channel in the bottom of the lid and the convex bottom of the cup allows the condition of the seminal fluid to be examined.

Statement by the jury
The ergonomic and functional design of the C-KUP is particularly user-friendly, which has a very positive effect on medical examination conditions.

Der Probenbehälter C-KUP wurde speziell für die Aufbewahrung von männlicher Samenflüssigkeit entwickelt. Die ergonomische Krümmung und breite Öffnung erleichtern die Abgabe der Probe. Die innovative Pipettieröffnung und das elastische Material ermöglichen eine feindosierte Entnahme der Probe, ohne den Deckel ganz öffnen zu müssen. Der Abstand zwischen dem im Deckelboden angebrachten Fließkanal und dem konvexen Gefäßboden gestattet es, den Zustand der Samenflüssigkeit zu betrachten.

Begründung der Jury
Die ergonomische und funktionale Gestaltung des C-KUP ist besonders anwenderfreundlich, was sich sehr positiv auf die medizinischen Untersuchungsbedingungen auswirkt.

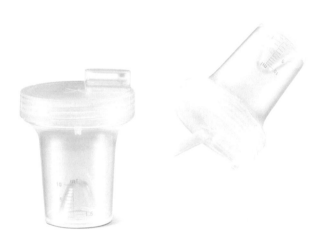

asipco
Sterilising Container System
Sterilisations-Container-System

Manufacturer
AS Medizintechnik GmbH,
Tuttlingen, Germany
Design
Barski Design GmbH,
Frankfurt/Main, Germany
Web
www.as-medizintechnik.de
www.barskidesign.com

The asipco sterilising container system is made of high-quality materials that provide stability and durability. The permanent germ barrier system does not require disposables, thus reducing follow-up costs. There are two slots integrated into the handle plate at the front of the container, which are designed to hold identification labels. Small viewing slits in the lid reveal whether the germ barrier system has been correctly inserted into the container.

Statement by the jury
Thanks to its carefully selected materials and high-quality workmanship, asipco is carefully designed to meet the elevated hygienic standards of a clinical environment.

Das Sterilisations-Container-System asipco ist aus hochwertigen Materialien gefertigt, die für Stabilität und Langlebigkeit sorgen. Das permanente Keimrückhaltesystem kommt ohne Verbrauchsmaterial aus und reduziert dadurch die Folgekosten. An der Stirnseite der Container befinden sich jeweils zwei in der Griffplatte integrierte Felder für Kennzeichnungsschilder. Durch kleine Sichtschlitze im Deckel ist jederzeit erkennbar, ob das Keimrückhaltesystem ordnungsgemäß in den Container eingesetzt ist.

Begründung der Jury
asipco ist durch seine sorgfältig ausgewählten Materialien und eine qualitätsvolle Verarbeitung konsequent auf die hohen hygienischen Anforderungen in der Klinik ausgelegt.

Quick Claw®
Quick Fixing Claw
Schnellspannvorrichtung

Manufacturer
W. Krömker GmbH, Bückeburg, Germany
In-house design
Web
www.kroemker.com

The quick fixing claw by the name of Quick Claw is particulary designed for installing devices on standard rails and round tubes. The combination of the ergonomic ball handle and the release lever enables simple and quick adjustments as well as safe fastening. The system meets the requirements of the DIN standard for road ambulances and features an optional Fix-Safe function that gives the user audible and tactile feedback during tightening, indicating that the claw has been firmly and securely fastened.

Die Schnellspannvorrichtung Quick Claw ist besonders zum Anbringen von Geräten an Normschienen und Rundrohren geeignet. Die Kombination aus dem ergonomischen Ballengriff und dem Auslösehebel ermöglicht eine einfache Schnellverstellung und ein sicheres Arretieren. Das System erfüllt die DIN-Norm für den Rettungswageneinsatz und verfügt optional über eine Fix-Safe-Funktion. Diese gibt dem Anwender beim Anziehen eine hör- und spürbare Rückkopplung, dass die Klaue sicher und fest angebracht ist.

Statement by the jury
The extremely functional design of the Quick Claw accelerates assembly in the field of emergency medical services, an environment where every second counts.

Begründung der Jury
Die überaus funktionale Gestaltung der Quick Claw beschleunigt die Montage im rettungsdienstlichen Umfeld, wo es auf jede Sekunde ankommt.

Enobio 2 StarStim
Brain-Monitoring Helmet
Haube zur Überwachung
der Gehirnaktivität

Manufacturer
Neuroelectrics, Barcelona, Spain
Design
ÀNIMA design, ÀNIMA Barcelona,
Barcelona, Spain
Web
www.neuroelectrics.com
www.anima.design

The cordless Enobio 2 StarStim brain-monitoring helmet was designed for use in clinical settings and research, for instance in the treatment of pain or re-habilitation after a stroke. The system enables three different applications; it measures the electrical currents in the brain, stimulates the brain with direct current and tracks physical activity. The recordings can be stored on an SD card or transmitted to a computer via Bluetooth.

Statement by the jury
The sophisticated design of the Enobio 2 StarStim combines cutting-edge tech-nology with extremely high wearing comfort. Moreover, the helmet enables a seamless integration of the electrodes.

Die kabellose Kopfhaube Enobio 2 StarStim wurde für den Einsatz in Klinik und Forschung entwickelt. Sie wird z. B. zur Behandlung von Schmerzen oder zur Rehabilitation nach einem Schlaganfall eingesetzt. Das System ermöglicht drei unterschiedliche Anwendungen: Es misst die elektrischen Ströme des Gehirns, sti-muliert das Gehirn mit Gleichstrom und zeichnet körperliche Aktivitäten auf. Die Aufnahmen können auf SD-Karte gespei-chert oder via Bluetooth an einen Com-puter übertragen werden.

Begründung der Jury
Die ausgereifte Gestaltung von Enobio 2 StarStim vereint hochmoderne Technologie mit einem äußerst angenehmen Trage-komfort. Zudem ermöglicht die Haube eine nahtlose Integration der Elektroden.

Biatain Silicone
Wound Dressing
Wundverband

Manufacturer
Coloplast A/S, Humlebæk, Denmark
In-house design
Web
www.coloplast.com

The Biatain Silicone wound dressing optimally adjusts to the shape of the body. The 3D foam structure curves towards the wound bed and provides superior absorption for optimal moist wound healing. The silicone adhesive extends across the entire surface of the dressing, so that it fits securely and can be removed with minimal pain. In contrast to conventional dressings which attempt to imitate skin colour, this product is kept in a discreet grey tone. The matt surface structure ensures less friction against clothing.

Statement by the jury
Thanks to its form and materiality, the Biatain Silicone wound dressing provides excellent and close skin adhesion, which restricts the patient as little as possible.

Der Wundverband Biatain Silicone passt sich der Körperform optimal an. Die 3D-Schaumstruktur wölbt sich zum Wund-grund hin und verfügt über eine ausge-zeichnete Saugkraft für eine optimale feuchte Wundheilung. Die Silikonhaftung erstreckt sich über die gesamte Fläche des Verbandes, sodass dieser sicher hält und schmerzarm entfernt werden kann. Im Gegensatz zu herkömmlichen Verbänden, die versuchen die Hautfarbe zu imitieren, ist das Produkt in einem dezenten Grauton gehalten. Die matte Oberflächentextur sorgt für geringe Reibung an der Kleidung.

Begründung der Jury
Der Wundverband Biatain Silicone bietet dank seiner Form und Materialität eine hervorragende körpernahe Haftung, die den Patienten so wenig wie möglich einschränkt.

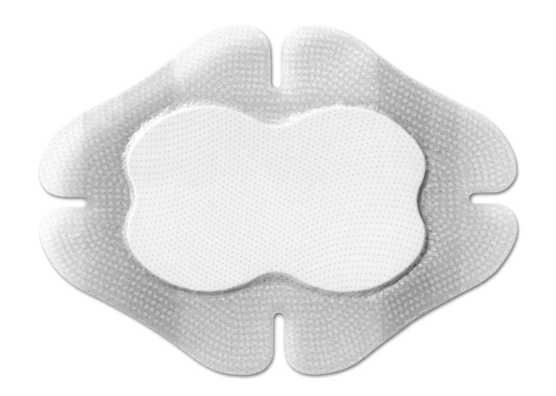

ITS-L
Endoscopic System
Endoskopie-System

Manufacturer
InTheSmart Co., Ltd., Seoul, South Korea
In-house design
Web
www.itsnuh.com

The ITS-L endoscopy system has been designed with surgeons' needs in mind and is meant to serve as their eyes during laparoscopic operations. The LED-lit touchscreen displays essential information and allows for intuitive control of the light settings. The anodised finish of the aluminium case is durable and allows for easy disinfection. The side panel gives convenient access to internal components for maintenance. Created from an autoclavable, ultralight plastic compound, the camera head is designed to complement various wrist positions, thus reducing fatigue during prolonged operations.

Das Endoskopie-System ITS-L wurde nach den Bedürfnissen des Chirurgen gestaltet und dient als dessen Augen während eines laparaskopischen Eingriffs. Der LED-Touchscreen zeigt alle wichtigen Informationen an und erlaubt eine intuitive Kontrolle der Lichteinstellungen. Das Gehäuse aus eloxiertem Aluminium ist widerstandsfähig und leicht zu desinfizieren. Die Seitenteile bieten einfachen Zugang zu den innen liegenden Wartungskomponenten. Der Kamerakopf ist aus einem autoklavierbaren, ultraleichten Kunststoff gefertigt und unterstützt verschiedene Handgelenkspositionen, was ein ermüdungsfreies Arbeiten gewährleistet.

Statement by the jury
The high-quality finish of the ITS-L endoscopic system shows very clear control structures, which ensure high functionality and ergonomic quality.

Begründung der Jury
Das hochwertig verarbeitete Endoskopie-System ITS-L zeigt sehr klare Bedienstrukturen, die in hohem Maße für Funktionalität und Ergonomie sorgen.

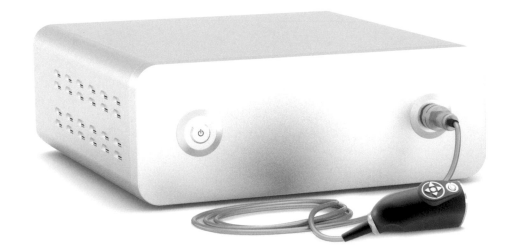

RAYDENT Studio
Dental 3D Printer
Dental-3D-Drucker

Manufacturer
Ray Co., Ltd., Hwaseong, South Korea
Design
Woofer Design Co., Ltd., Seoul, South Korea
Web
www.raymedical.com
www.wooferdesign.com

With the Raydent Studio dental 3D printer, dental practices and laboratories can produce customised dental prostheses, surgical stents and orthodontic appliances themselves. The featured LCD and UV technologies enable precise printing results and significant energy savings. Thanks to its simple and compact design, the printer can be integrated into any work environment. The oval, curved silhouette deliberately stands out from the aesthetics of conventional medical devices. Moreover, the sealed front cover protects the user from harmful UV light.

Mit dem Dental-3D-Drucker Raydent Studio können Zahnarztpraxen und Dentallabore kundenspezifische Zahnprothesen, chirurgische Stents und kieferorthopädische Hilfsmittel selbst anfertigen. Die verwendeten LCD- und UV-Technologien ermöglichen präzise Druckergebnisse und sparen Energie. Durch die einfache und kompakte Bauweise kann der Drucker in jede beliebige Arbeitsumgebung integriert werden. Die ovale, kurvenförmige Silhouette hebt sich bewusst von der Ästhetik herkömmlicher Medizingeräte ab. Die versiegelte Frontabdeckung schützt den Benutzer vor schädlichem UV-Licht.

Statement by the jury
This dental 3D printer fascinates with its sculptural look, which is the result of its self-contained and softly curved design in puristic white.

Begründung der Jury
Der Dental-3D-Drucker fasziniert durch seine skulpturale Anmutung, die durch die geschlossene und sanft geschwungene Bauform in puristischem Weiß erzielt wird.

Arc InstaTemp MD
Non-Touch Thermometer
Kontaktloses Thermometer

Manufacturer
ARC Devices USA, Inc,
Boca Raton, Florida, USA
In-house design
Design
Design Partners (David Fleming,
Eugene Canavan, Terence Kealy,
Peter Murphy), Bray, Ireland
Web
www.arcdevices.com
www.designpartners.com

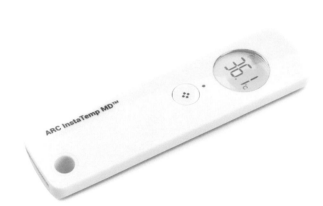

The Arc InstaTemp MD digital non-touch thermometer measures body core temperature without skin contact. The taking of temperature without touching the person simplifies medical care, especially in developing countries, since it is not necessary to disinfect the device after each use. The simple one-button control minimises the training effort required. The device features an infrared sensor and is held close to the forehead to carry out the measurement. Depending on the temperature, the LED light will illuminate in green, orange or red.

Statement by the jury
Thanks to its advanced non-touch measuring technology, the Arc InstaTemp MD features a flat and smooth design that is surprisingly different from other thermometers.

Das digitale Thermometer Arc InstaTemp MD misst die Körperkerntemperatur ohne Hautkontakt. Vor allem in Entwicklungsländern erleichtert das berührungslose Temperaturmessen die medizinische Versorgung, da das Gerät nicht nach jedem Gebrauch desinfiziert werden muss. Die simple Ein-Tasten-Bedienung minimiert den Schulungsaufwand. Das Gerät ist mit einem Infrarotsensor ausgestattet und wird für die Messung nah an die Stirn gehalten. Je nach Temperaturwert leuchtet die LED grün, orange oder rot.

Begründung der Jury
Das Arc InstaTemp MD besitzt durch seine fortschrittliche berührungslose Messtechnik eine flache, ebene Form, die sich auf überraschende Weise von anderen Thermometern unterscheidet.

tyson bio TP100
Continuous Patch-Type
Clinical Thermometer
Patch-Thermometer
für die kontinuierliche
Temperaturkontrolle

Manufacturer
Tyson Bioresearch Inc., Zhunan Township,
Miaoli County, Taiwan
In-house design
Web
www.tysonbio.com

The thermometer tyson bio TP100 enables the continuous monitoring of body temperature besides working as a typical clinical thermometer. The measurement data are transmitted directly to a smartphone via Bluetooth. The duo-link design facilitates good wearing comfort as well as accurate measurement and reliable data transfer. The thermally insulating gel patch stays safely attached to the skin. The device measures not only temperature but also activity level, thus providing useful additional information, for instance on sleep quality.

Statement by the jury
The tyson bio TP100 appeals with its unusual design, which makes this device look more like a trendy lifestyle product and less like a medical one.

Das Thermometer tyson bio TP100 ermöglicht neben dem herkömmlichen Fiebermessen eine kontinuierliche Überwachung der Körpertemperatur. Die Messdaten werden via Bluetooth direkt an das Smartphone gesendet. Das Duo-Link-Design mit zwei Hautkontaktstellen sorgt sowohl für ein gutes Tragegefühl als auch eine präzise Messung und korrekte Übertragung der Daten. Das thermisch isolierende Gelpatch hält sicher auf der Haut. Das Gerät misst nicht nur die Temperatur, sondern auch das Aktivitätslevel und liefert dadurch nützliche Zusatzinformationen, z. B. zur Schlafqualität.

Begründung der Jury
Das tyson bio TP100 gefällt durch seine ungewöhnliche Form, die es mehr wie ein hippes Lifestyleprodukt und weniger medizinisch aussehen lässt.

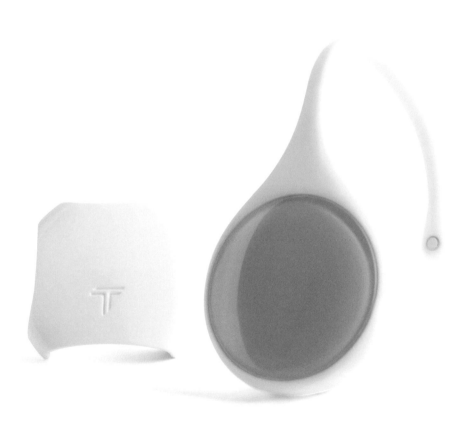

Q-tube Wi-Fi Teeth Scope Pro, Q-tube Wi-Fi Otoscope Pro
Teeth Scope and ENT Otoscope
Zahn-Otoskop und
HNO-Otoskop

Manufacturer
Quanta Computer Inc., Taoyuan, Taiwan
In-house design
Po-Hsian Tseng, Chu-Fu Wang,
Chang-Ta Miao, Guo-Chyuan Chen
Web
www.quantatw.com

With Q-tube Wi-Fi Teeth Scope Pro and
Q-tube Wi-Fi Otoscope Pro, dentists or
ENT physicians can show a video stream
of the examination live on a monitor
and thus more strongly involve patients
in their treatment. A blue illuminated
ring indicates that the device is in operation. The camera head is smooth and
rounded to instil confidence in the patient. The elliptically shaped housing
consists of rubberised and sandblasted
surfaces, which have a pleasant feel.
The power button is colour-contrasted
with the control buttons.

Statement by the jury
The digital technology of the otoscopes
is used effectively to improve doctor-
patient communication. With their organic lines, the devices appear as if cast
in one piece.

Mit Q-tube Wi-Fi Teeth Scope Pro und
Q-tube Wi-Fi Otoscope Pro können Zahnärzte bzw. HNO-Ärzte die Untersuchung
per Videostream live auf einen Bildschirm
übertragen und den Patienten so stärker
in die Behandlung einbinden. Ein blauer
Leuchtring zeigt an, dass das Gerät in Betrieb ist. Der Kamerakopf ist glatt und
gerundet, um Vertrauen zum Patienten zu
schaffen. Das elliptisch geformte Gehäuse
besteht aus gummierten und sandgestrahl-
ten Oberflächen, die sich angenehm an-
fühlen. Die Power-Taste setzt sich farblich
von den Bedientasten ab.

Begründung der Jury
Die digitale Technik wird bei den Otoskopen
auf sinnvolle Weise für eine bessere Arzt-
Patienten-Kommunikation genutzt. Mit
ihrer organischen Linienführung wirken die
Geräte wie aus einem Guss.

Moxi Now
Hearing Aid
Hörgerät

Manufacturer
Unitron, Kitchener,
Ontario, Canada

In-house design
Unitron Product & Design Team

Design
AWOL Company,
Calabasas, USA

Web
www.unitron.com
www.awolcompany.com

reddot award 2017
best of the best

Aesthetic and comfort

The need to wear hearing aid can change one's life. To start feeling at ease with such a device usually requires a certain period of adjustment. Moxi Now is an innovative wireless RIC (Receiver-in-Canal) hearing aid that merges highly advanced functionality and technology with outstanding aesthetics. A design that focused on the needs of wearers led to impressive new features for a hearing aid. Moxi Now is very small and features a minimalist, organic shape that lends it the look of a beautiful accessory. Thanks to this ergonomic shape, the device provides all-day wearing comfort without users even noticing the device. In addition, it has a fully automatic amplification system offering improved, natural sound quality with a special focus on conversation. This is complemented by the ability to individually adjust the performance of the device using modern smart device media. Moxi Now captures objective data about the user's listening lifestyle and allows wearers to share their reactions to the device's performance via a cloud-based app. Based on these data, clinicians have the opportunity to better adapt the device to the individual needs of the wearer. With its clear language of form and sophisticated technology, the Moxi Now hearing aid sets new standards in hearing aid acoustics – users experience this as high wearing comfort and enduring performance.

Ästhetik und Komfort

Die Notwendigkeit ein Hörgerät tragen zu müssen, kann das Leben verändern. Um sich mit diesem Hilfsmittel wohlzufühlen, ist eine gewisse Eingewöhnungszeit erforderlich. Moxi Now ist ein innovatives wireless RIC-Hörgerät (Receiver-in-Canal), das eine hochentwickelte Funktionalität und Technologie mit einer bestechenden Ästhetik vereint. Eine die Bedürfnisse der Träger in den Mittelpunkt rückende Gestaltung führt zu beeindruckend neuen Eigenschaften für ein Hörgerät. Moxi Now ist sehr klein, wobei seine minimalistische, ausgewogene Form ihm die Anmutung eines schönen Accessoires verleiht. Aufgrund seiner ergonomischen Gestaltung kann man es bequem den ganzen Tag lang tragen, ohne es überhaupt zu bemerken. Es verfügt zudem über ein vollautomatisches Hörsystem, das vor allem in Gesprächssituationen eine verbesserte, natürliche Klangqualität bietet. Dies geht einher mit der Möglichkeit einer individuellen Anpassung der Hörleistung mithilfe zeitgemäßer Medien. Moxi Now sammelt objektive Daten über den Höralltag und erlaubt es dem Träger, über eine cloudbasierte App jederzeit eigene Bewertungen der Hörleistung abzugeben. Aufgrund dieser Informationen haben Akustiker die Möglichkeit, besser auf die individuell variierenden Bedürfnisse ihrer Kunden einzugehen. Mit seiner klaren Formensprache und ausgefeilten Technologie setzt das Hörgerät Moxi Now neue Maßstäbe in der Hörgeräteakustik – die Träger spüren täglich seinen hohen Komfort und die große Leistungsfähigkeit.

Statement by the jury

The Moxi Now hearing aid impresses with its clear, functional design and the high degree of miniaturisation allowing it to be worn almost invisibly. In a remarkable manner, it embodies a reduction to the essentials through the use of advanced technology. Its fully automatic amplification system delivers outstanding acoustic quality while its sophisticated ergonomic design lends it an outstanding wearing comfort.

Begründung der Jury

Das Hörgerät Moxi Now beeindruckt durch seine klare, funktionale Gestaltung und den hohen Miniaturisierungsgrad, sodass es nahezu unsichtbar getragen werden kann. Auf bemerkenswerte Weise verkörpert es so eine Reduktion auf das Wesentliche durch die Verwendung avancierter Technologie. Mit seinem vollautomatischen Hörsystem bietet es eine hervorragende akustische Qualität, und dank der ausgereiften ergonomischen Formgebung ist der Tragekomfort ausgezeichnet.

Designer portrait
See page 64
Siehe Seite 64

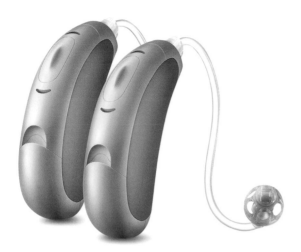

Stride M
Hearing Aid
Hörgerät

Manufacturer
Unitron, Kitchener, Ontario, Canada
In-house design
Unitron Product & Design team
Design
AWOL Company, Calabasas, California, USA
Web
www.unitron.com
www.awolcompany.com

The Stride M behind-the-ear hearing aid is the smallest in its product family. It enables natural hearing in all situations of daily life. The design concept is geared towards discretion in order to increase acceptance by the wearer. With the help of software, the device collects objective data about the daily listening conditions and allows wearers to give their own ratings about the hearing aid's performance using a cloud-based app. On the basis of this information, the audiologist can individually adjust the device.

Statement by the jury
The Stride M is fascinatingly small and unobtrusive to wear. It utilises an innovative technological approach in order to document and enhance the auditory experience of the user.

Das Hinter-dem-Ohr-Hörgerät Stride M ist das kleinste seiner Produktfamilie. Es gewährleistet ein natürliches Hören in allen Situationen des Alltags. Das Gestaltungskonzept ist auf Diskretion ausgelegt, um die Akzeptanz beim Träger zu erhöhen. Mithilfe einer Software sammelt das Gerät objektive Daten über den Höralltag und ermöglicht dem Träger, über eine cloudbasierte App die Hörleistungen selbst zu bewerten. Auf Basis dieser Informationen kann der Akustiker das Gerät individuell anpassen.

Begründung der Jury
Das Stride M ist faszinierend klein und unauffällig zu tragen. Es nutzt einen innovativen technologischen Ansatz, um das Hörerlebnis des Benutzers zu dokumentieren und zu verbessern.

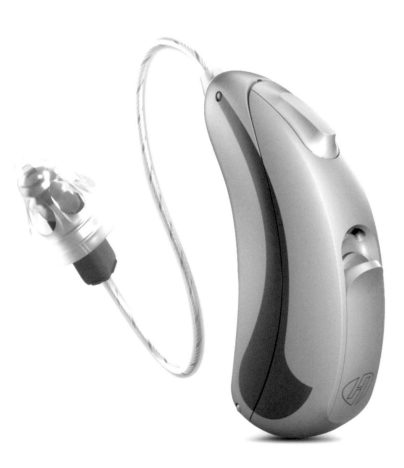

sound SHD S312
Digital Hearing System
Digitales Hörsystem

Manufacturer
Hansaton Akustik GmbH,
Hamburg, Germany
Design
Pilotfish, Munich, Germany
Web
www.hansaton.de
www.pilotfish.eu

The digital hearing system called sound SHD S312 features high-performance sensors that detect the acoustic environment of the wearer and automatically adjust to the respective hearing conditions. The gentle contours of the housing provide a comfortable wearing experience. Thanks to its distinctive form, the push-button is easy to feel and operate. The specially designed battery compartment sets visual accents and makes it easy to change batteries and switch the hearing system on and off.

Statement by the jury
The sound SHD S312 impresses with its tactile qualities, which make it very user-friendly. The sweeping horizontal line lends the hearing system a distinctive character.

Das digitale Hörsystem sound SHD S312 ist mit Hochleistungssensoren ausgestattet, die das akustische Umfeld des Benutzers erkennen und sich der jeweiligen Hörsituation automatisch anpassen. Die weichen Konturen des Gehäuses sorgen für ein angenehmes Tragegefühl. Der Taster ist durch seine markante Form gut spürbar und leicht zu bedienen. Die ausgearbeitete Batterielade setzt optische Akzente und dient einem einfachen Batteriewechsel sowie dem leichten Ein- und Ausschalten des Hörsystems.

Begründung der Jury
Das sound SHD S312 punktet durch besondere taktile Eigenschaften, die es sehr nutzerfreundlich machen. Die schwungvolle Horizontallinie verleiht dem Hörsystem einen eigenständigen Charakter.

Oticon Opn™
Hearing Aid
Hörgerät

Manufacturer
Oticon, Smørum, Denmark
In-house design
Web
www.oticon.global

The Oticon Opn hearing aid features innovative BrainHearing technology, designed to support the brain's natural way of perceiving and processing sounds, even in complex acoustic situations. The placement of the slim push-button on the device allows for easy and discreet adjustment of volume and change of programme. The extra-large battery compartment is especially well accessible. All essential components are nano-coated on the inside and outside, thus protecting the hearing aid from water and dirt.

Statement by the jury
The Oticon Opn hearing aid successfully incorporates its complex technology in a surprisingly small and reduced structural form, thus fostering high aesthetic quality.

Das Hörgerät Oticon Opn verfügt über eine innovative BrainHearing-Technologie. Diese unterstützt die natürliche Art und Weise, wie das Gehirn Klänge auch in komplexen Hörsituationen wahrnimmt und verarbeitet. Der schlanke Taster ist so an dem Gerät positioniert, dass Lautstärke und Programme einfach und diskret eingestellt werden können. Das extra große Batteriefach ist besonders gut zugänglich. Alle wesentlichen Komponenten sind innen und außen nanobeschichtet, sodass das Hörgerät vor Wasser und Schmutz geschützt ist.

Begründung der Jury
Die komplexe Technologie wird bei dem Hörgerät Oticon Opn in eine überraschend kleine und reduzierte Bauform überführt, die eine hohe ästhetische Qualität schafft.

SL 70
Snore Stopper
Schnarchstopper

Manufacturer
Beurer GmbH, Ulm, Germany
Design
VVFLY Electronics Co., Ltd. (Johnson Luo), Shenzhen, China
Web
www.beurer.com

The SL 70 provides gentle snoring therapy. If it detects a snoring sound, then it emits tone and vibration pulses, which, for instance, trigger a change in lying position. The pulse intensity can be individually adjusted using an app. The on/off switch and the info LEDs for battery and Bluetooth are highlighted by a light-grey border. A micro USB connection for charging is incorporated into the underside of the device. The earplugs are supplied in three different sizes.

Statement by the jury
The soft shape of the SL 70 perfectly adjusts to the user's ear anatomy. The utilisation of cutting-edge digital technology constitutes real added value for the user.

Der SL 70 dient der sanften Schnarchtherapie. Erkennt er ein Schnarchgeräusch, so sendet er Ton- und Vibrationsimpulse, die z. B. eine Änderung der Liegeposition auslösen. Die Impulsintensität kann über eine App individuell eingestellt werden. Die Ein-/Aus-Taste und die Info-LEDs zu Akku und Bluetooth werden durch eine hellgraue Umrandung hervorgehoben. An der Unterseite befindet sich ein Micro-USB-Anschluss zum Wiederaufladen des Geräts. Es werden Ohrstöpsel in drei verschiedenen Größen mitgeliefert.

Begründung der Jury
Die sanfte Form des SL 70 ist perfekt an die Anatomie des Ohrs angepasst. Die Verwendung modernster digitaler Technologie stellt einen echten Mehrwert für den Gebrauch dar.

F&P Brevida
Nasal Pillows Mask
Nasalkissenmaske

Manufacturer
Fisher & Paykel Healthcare Limited,
Auckland, New Zealand
In-house design
Bruce Walls, Jason Huang, Arvin Gardiola,
Jeremy Young, Jonathan Sng
Web
www.fphcare.co.nz

The F&P Brevida nasal pillows mask prevents breathing obstruction during sleep by creating positive pressure. An innovative air pillow seals the area in and around the nose gently and effectively. The mask is fastened with a headband that can be individually adjusted, ensuring a secure fit. The air diffuser, which reduces noise and air draft, is washable and durable. The most important interfaces are highlighted in blue.

Die Nasalkissenmaske F&P Brevida verhindert Atemaussetzer während des Schlafs, indem sie einen Überdruck erzeugt. Ein innovatives Luftkissen dichtet den Bereich in der Nase und um die Nase sanft und wirksam ab. Die Maske wird mit einem Kopfband fixiert, das sich individuell anpassen lässt und dafür sorgt, dass sie sicher sitzt. Der Luftverteiler, der Geräusche und Luftzug reduziert, ist waschbar und langlebig. Die wichtigsten Benutzerschnittstellen sind durch blaue Markierungen hervorgehoben.

Statement by the jury
With its especially high wearing comfort and very effective air pillow seal, the F&P Brevida nasal pillows mask makes an essential contribution to healthy sleep.

Begründung der Jury
Durch ihren besonders hohen Tragekomfort und die sehr effektive Luftkissenabdichtung leistet die Nasalkissenmaske F&P Brevida einen entscheidenden Beitrag zu einem gesunden Schlaf.

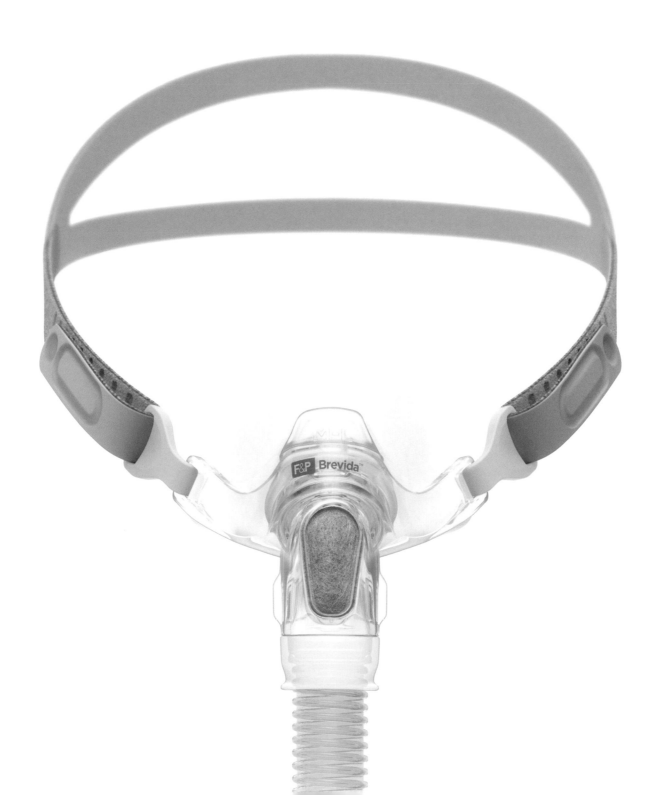

Raycop RX
Allergen Vacuum
Allergen-Sauger

Manufacturer
Raycop Japan Inc., Tokyo, Japan
In-house design
Web
www.raycop.com
www.raycop.co.jp
www.raycop.co.kr
www.raycop.com.cn

The cordless vacuum Raycop RX frees the sleeping environment from allergens, mites and viruses. In deodorising mode, it eliminates bacteria that cause bad odours. The unique contours provide optimal weight distribution and cover large surface areas to achieve especially effective cleaning. The vacuum recognises the texture of textiles and automatically adjusts the suction level and its brush rotation. It also uses heated air to create an uninhabitable environment for mites.

Statement by the jury
The Raycop RX fascinates with a remarkable shape that is practical and stylish at once. The many useful functions provide allergy sufferers with particularly comprehensive protection.

Der kabellose Sauger Raycop RX befreit die Schlafumgebung von Allergenen, Milben und Viren. Im Desodorierungsmodus entfernt er zudem Bakterien, die schlechte Gerüche verursachen. Die einzigartigen Konturen sorgen für eine optimale Verteilung des Gleichgewichts und decken große Oberflächen ab, wodurch der Sauger besonders effektiv reinigt. Er erkennt die Beschaffenheit von Textilien und passt seine Saugleistung sowie Bürstenrotation automatisch an. Durch Heißluft schafft er eine unbewohnbare Umgebung für Milben.

Begründung der Jury
Der Raycop RX besticht durch seine außergewöhnliche Form, die praktisch und stylish zugleich ist. Seine Vielzahl an sinnvollen Funktionen bietet Allergikern einen besonders umfassenden Schutz.

Air Dragon
Air Monitoring Device
Gerät zur Überwachung der Luftqualität

Manufacturer
Beijing Coilabs Co., Ltd., Beijing, China
Design
LKK Design Beijing Co., Ltd., Beijing, China
Web
www.coilabs.com
www.air-dragon.cn
www.lkkdesign.com

The Air Dragon is a portable device that measures and analyses air quality. It is equipped with the air quality sensor CCS811, which detects harmful substances like spent breathing air, nicotine, solvents or paint in the room's air. This enables the user to react quickly if safety limits are exceeded. The device is designed like a fashion accessory that can also be used discreetly in public space.

Statement by the jury
The Air Dragon impresses with its practical, organically shaped housing, which features a stylish shell. Its function is deliberately concealed by its exceptional aesthetic.

Air Dragon ist ein tragbares Gerät, das die Luftqualität misst und analysiert. Es ist mit dem Luftqualitätssensor CCS811 ausgestattet, der Schadstoffe wie z. B. verbrauchte Atemluft, Nikotin, Lösungsmittel oder Lacke in der Raumluft erkennt. Dies ermöglicht dem Benutzer schnell zu reagieren, falls Grenzwerte überschritten werden. Das Gerät ist wie ein modisches Accessoire gestaltet, das der Benutzer auch an öffentlichen Orten unauffällig verwenden kann.

Begründung der Jury
Air Dragon imponiert durch sein handliches, organisch geformtes Gehäuse mit einer schnittigen Umhüllung. Ganz bewusst wird seine Funktion durch die edle Ästhetik kaschiert.

i-Mu Smart Blood Pressure Instrument
i-Mu intelligentes Blutdruck-messgerät

Manufacturer
i-Mu Technology Co., Ltd., Shenzhen, China
In-house design
Web
www.i-mu.com.cn

The i-Mu Smart Blood Pressure Instrument measures blood pressure while simultaneously monitoring heart rate. It features a photoelectric pulse sensor, which shines light onto the blood vessels in the finger. The measured values are calculated within 15 seconds by a special algorithm and shown on a digital display. The data can be transferred to a smartphone or tablet via Bluetooth and then saved and analysed in an app.

Statement by the jury
The i-Mu Smart Blood Pressure Instrument impresses with its purist aesthetic. The bezelless display almost completely merges with the entirely flat front.

Das intelligente Blutdruckmessgerät von i-Mu misst den Blutdruck und überwacht gleichzeitig die Herzfrequenz. Es ist mit einem fotoelektrischen Impulssensor ausgestattet, der die Blutgefäße im Finger belichtet. Die Messergebnisse werden innerhalb von 15 Sekunden durch einen speziellen Algorithmus berechnet und auf dem digitalen Display angezeigt. Via Bluetooth können die Daten auf ein Smartphone oder Tablet übertragen und in einer App gespeichert und analysiert werden.

Begründung der Jury
Das intelligente Blutdruckmessgerät von i-Mu besticht durch seine puristische Ästhetik. Das rahmenlose Display verschmilzt nahezu mit der völlig flachen Front.

SpeediCath Flex
Catheter for Men
Katheter für Männer

Manufacturer
Coloplast A/S, Humlebæk, Denmark
In-house design
Web
www.coloplast.com

SpeediCath Flex is a soft catheter with a protective sleeve and a flexible ball tip, which has been developed especially for men. Thanks to the elastic handle, the ball tip can be easily positioned at the entrance of the urethra without touching it. The protective sleeve makes it possible to insert the catheter without direct contact. After the treatment, the catheter can be resealed and, due to its neutral packaging, disposed of in a discreet and hygienic way.

Statement by the jury
SpeediCath Flex reflects a sophisticated combination of functionality and aesthetics. The sensitive handling of the users' needs becomes apparent in the choice of materials as well as in the colour scheme.

SpeediCath Flex ist ein weicher Katheter mit einer Schutzhülle und flexibler Kugelspitze, der speziell für Männer entwickelt wurde. Durch den elastischen Griff kann die Kugelspitze einfach am Harnröhreneingang positioniert werden, ohne sie zu berühren. Die Schutzhülle ermöglicht es, den Katheter ohne direkten Kontakt einzuführen. Nach der Anwendung wird der Katheter wieder verschlossen und in seiner neutralen Verpackung diskret und hygienisch entsorgt.

Begründung der Jury
SpeediCath Flex vereint auf hohem Niveau Funktion und Ästhetik. Der sensible Umgang mit den Bedürfnissen des Nutzers zeigt sich sowohl in der Wahl des Materials als auch in der Farbgebung.

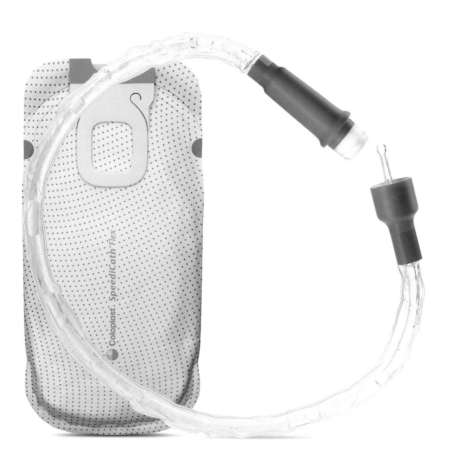

SmartLife Care Flex Handheld Transmitter
Handsender für SmartLife Care Flex

Manufacturer
Swisscom (Schweiz) AG, Bern, Switzerland
In-house design
Web
www.swisscom.ch
www.smartlife-care.ch

This handheld transmitter is an additional accessory for the emergency GPS tracker SmartLife Care Flex. At the touch of a button, the handheld transmitter triggers an emergency call. It is water-resistant, has a range of up to 200 metres and a battery life of up to five years. The device can be worn on the wrist or around the neck: a white necklace, a black stretch wristband and a cord are included. The playful designs make the handheld transmitter look like a watch, allowing users to enjoy wearing the device and feel less stigmatised.

Bei diesem Handsender handelt es sich um ein Zubehörteil für das GPS-Notrufgerät SmartLife Care Flex. Auf Knopfdruck löst der Handsender einen Notruf aus. Er ist wasserfest und hat eine Reichweite von bis zu 200 Metern, die Akkulaufzeit beträgt fünf Jahre. Das Gerät kann am Handgelenk oder um den Hals getragen werden: Ein weißes Armband, ein schwarzes Stretcharmband und eine Kordel gehören zum Lieferumfang. Die verspielten Designs lassen den Handsender wie eine Uhr aussehen, so hat der Benutzer Freude am Tragen und fühlt sich nicht stigmatisiert.

Statement by the jury
The SmartLife Care Flex handheld transmitter surprises with its many fashionable designs, which make it appear like a piece of jewellery, thus encouraging greater acceptance in the wearer.

Begründung der Jury
Der Handsender für SmartLife Care Flex überrascht durch seine vielfältigen modischen Designs, die ihn gezielt wie ein Schmuckstück erscheinen lassen, was beim Träger die Akzeptanz erhöht.

System Electric Greifer DMC VariPlus
System-Elektrogreifer DMC VariPlus
Hand Prosthesis
Handprothese

Manufacturer
Otto Bock Health Care
Products GmbH, Vienna, Austria

In-house design
Annette Sting

Web
www.ottobock.com

reddot award 2017
best of the best

Sensitive support

Grabbing and holding objects effortlessly with the hand is a highly complex but natural set of movements that people who receive a prosthesis have to relearn and practice patiently. The innovative design of the System Electric Greifer DMC VariPlus provides reliable support for wearers of hand prostheses. Its gripping function is based on a sophisticated concept, helping users work with precision and enabling a powerful grip. It allows users to independently switch between their myoelectric hand prosthesis and the System Electric Greifer. In this way, the functionality of the Greifer can be adjusted to the relevant requirements in just a few seconds. The device showcases a strikingly clear aesthetic that lends it a modern, almost fashionable appearance. The premium finish and colour design also safely protects against dirt, which allows wearers to also use the prosthesis for handling tools and objects in a workshop, for instance. An additional LED torch function enables ideal illumination of the work area. This is an important added value for users who, due to also having lost the sense of touch in the hand, have to rely all the more on visual feedback. Boasting design that is perfectly adapted to the needs of people wearing a hand prosthesis, the System Electric Greifer DMC VariPlus incorporates a highly effective tool that also captivates with an attractive design as well as high user comfort.

Sensibel unterstützt

Das oftmals als Selbstverständlichkeit empfundene mühelose Greifen nach Dingen mit der Hand ist ein komplexer Vorgang, den Menschen mit einer Prothese erst üben müssen. Der System-Elektrogreifer DMC VariPlus bietet Trägern von Handprothesen mit einer innovativen Gestaltung eine zuverlässige Unterstützung. Seine Greiffunktion basiert auf einem ausgeklügelten Konzept und ermöglicht ein präzises Arbeiten und kraftvolles Zugreifen. Der Anwender kann selbständig zwischen seiner myoelektrischen Handprothese und dem System-Elektrogreifer wechseln. Auf diese Weise lässt sich die Funktionalität des Greifers innerhalb weniger Sekunden an die jeweilige Anforderung anpassen. Dies geht einher mit einer eindringlich klaren Ästhetik, die ihm ein neues, modisches Erscheinungsbild verleiht. Eine hochwertige Farb- und Oberflächengestaltung schützt zudem sicher vor Verschmutzungen, weshalb der Anwender mit ihm etwa auch in einer Werkstatt hantieren kann. Die Ausstattung mit einer zusätzlichen LED-Lampe ermöglicht dabei eine ideale Ausleuchtung des Arbeitsbereiches. Dies ist ein wichtiger Mehrwert für Anwender, da diese aufgrund der fehlenden Sensibilität auf das visuelle Feedback umso mehr angewiesen sind. Mit seiner perfekt auf die Bedürfnisse von Menschen mit Handprothese abgestimmten Gestaltung verkörpert der System-Elektrogreifer DMC VariPlus ein sehr effektives Werkzeug, das auch durch sein attraktives Design und hohen Komfort besticht.

Statement by the jury

The System Electric Greifer DMC VariPlus combines a compact and easy-to-clean design with the user-friendliness of optimal adaptation. This hand prosthesis allows the gripping force and function to be precisely directed and adapted smoothly. It features an exemplary design in terms of material technology and functionality. It supports users in carrying out detailed gripping tasks and handling objects again independently.

Begründung der Jury

Der System-Elektrogreifer DMC VariPlus vereint eine kompakte und reinigungsfreundliche Bauweise mit einer optimal angepassten Nutzerfreundlichkeit. Mit dieser Handprothese können die Kräfte und Greiffunktionen fließend und sehr präzise dirigiert und entsprechend eingestellt werden. Dabei ist sie materialtechnisch und in ihrer Funktionalität vorbildlich gestaltet. Sie gibt den Menschen die Möglichkeit, viele Handhabungen und Tätigkeiten wieder selbständig ausführen zu können.

Designer portrait
See page 66
Siehe Seite 66

Confetti
Prosthetic Leg Cover
Prothetische Beinverkleidung

Manufacturer
ETHNOS Produtos Ortopédicos,
Rio de Janeiro, Brazil

Design
Furf Design Studio,
Curitiba, Brazil

Web
www.ethnos.com.br
www.furf.com.br

reddot award 2017
best of the best

The democratisation of self-esteem
Many wearers of all too familiar prosthetic leg covers perceive them to be stigmatising. Against this backdrop, the design of Confetti inspires with a novel, highly colourful approach. As a committed reinterpretation, it completely replaces the generic concept of elaborately tailor-made covers in skin colour. This polyurethane leg prosthesis cover is a high-quality and cost-effective product, boasting a material that is not only durable but above all also pleasant to the touch. Confetti is the result of comprehensive anatomical studies. This resulted in an ergonomic shape that offers wearers a high degree of comfort and functionality. Incorporating a well thought-out scaling system, the prosthesis cover can be perfectly adjusted to the wearer's leg measurements. It therefore features a set of predefined internal guiding lines on the inside. These allow the cover to be cut in a self-explanatory manner to adjust it to both the height of the wearer and the dimensions of the most familiar prostheses. The stylish appearance is further underlined by the cover being available in a choice of different colours. Users can thus customise the cover to their taste and liking. Based on a socially engaged design concept, the Confetti prosthetic leg cover promotes patient rehabilitation in a life-affirming manner and conveys a new sense of self-esteem – with its emotionalising design it positively influences the ability to enjoy life for people who have had to undergo an amputation.

Die Demokratisierung des Selbstwertgefühls
Viele Träger empfinden die gängigen Beinverkleidungen für ihre Prothesen als stigmatisierend. Die Gestaltung von Confetti begeistert hier mit einem neuen, sehr farbenfrohen Ansatz. Als engagierte Neuinterpretation löst sie sich gänzlich vom gängigen Konzept aufwendiger hautfarbener Spezialanfertigungen. Diese Beinprothesenabdeckung aus Polyurethan ist ein hochwertiges und kosteneffizientes Produkt, wobei das verwendete Material haptisch angenehm und langlebig ist. Confetti ist das Ergebnis langwieriger anatomischer Studien. Daraus resultiert eine ergonomische Form, die dem Träger ein hohes Maß an Komfort und Funktionalität bietet. Auf der Grundlage einer durchdachten Maßskala kann die Prothesenabdeckung zudem perfekt den Maßen des jeweiligen Trägers angeglichen werden: Auf ihrer Innenseite ist sie mit vordefinierten Schnittkanten ausgestattet. Mittels dieser lässt sie sich selbsterklärend der Größe des Trägers anpassen, wobei sie auch den Maßen der gängigen Prothesen entspricht. Ihre stilvolle Anmutung wird dadurch noch unterstrichen, dass sie in einer Auswahl verschiedener Farben erhältlich ist. Der Nutzer kann sie seinem eigenen Geschmack anpassen. Basierend auf einem engagierten Gestaltungskonzept fördert die prothetische Beinverkleidung Confetti so auf lebensbejahende Weise die Rehabilitation und vermittelt ein neues Selbstvertrauen – mit ihrem emotionalisierenden Design verändert sie das Lebensgefühl von Menschen, die sich einer Amputation unterziehen mussten.

Statement by the jury
This leg prosthesis covering has emerged from a combination of innovative design with the application of a 3D printing process, leading to a remarkably individual product. Thanks to the emotionalising design idiom and fresh colour choice, Confetti has a positive effect on the self-esteem of people who have to live with an amputation. The formal as well as functional simplicity is impressive and has been implemented in an outstandingly smart way, contributing to the well-being of users.

Begründung der Jury
Bei dieser Beinprothesenverkleidung führt ein innovatives Design in Kombination mit der Anwendung eines 3D-Druckverfahrens zu einem bemerkenswert individuellen Produkt. Dank der emotionalisierenden Formensprache und einer Auswahl frischer Farben hat Confetti einen positiven Effekt auf das Selbstwertgefühl von Menschen, die mit einer Amputation leben müssen. Beeindruckend ist die formale wie funktionale Einfachheit, die, auf äußerst clevere Art und Weise umgesetzt, zum Wohl des Nutzers beiträgt.

Designer portrait
See page 68
Siehe Seite 68

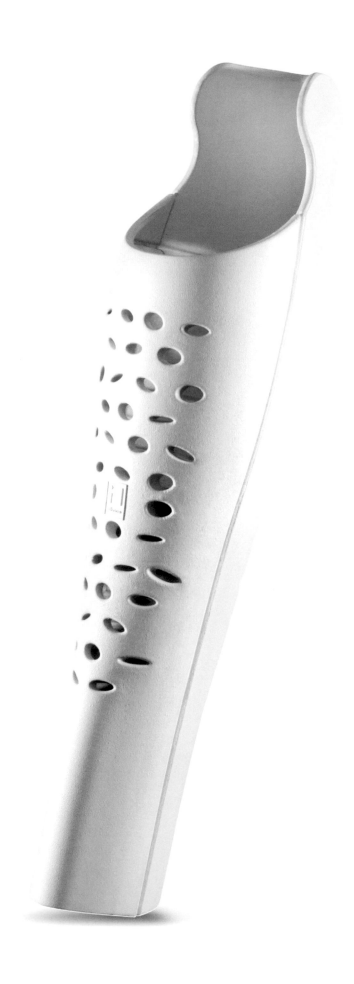

Challenger
Prosthetic Sport Foot
Sportprothesenfuß

Manufacturer
Otto Bock HealthCare LP,
Salt Lake City, USA
In-house design
Carsten Mönicke, Darshan Rane
Web
www.ottobock.com

The Challenger prosthetic sport foot was developed for the varying demands of recreational sports. Its curved main spring made of carbon fibre absorbs impact loads and provides high energy return. At the same time, the base spring, combined with individually adjustable heel wedge damping, ensures stability and control during fast movements as well as when standing and walking. The prosthetic sport foot is suitable for use in low-top sports shoes without a foot shell.

Statement by the jury
With its sophisticated design and special material properties made of carbon fibre, the Challenger creates an unrivalled level of functionality.

Der Sportprothesenfuß Challenger wurde für unterschiedliche Belastungen im Freizeitsport entwickelt. Seine geschwungene Hauptfeder aus Carbon dämpft Stoßbelastungen ab und sorgt für eine hohe Energierückgabe. Gleichzeitig gewährleistet die Basisfeder in Kombination mit einer individuell einstellbaren Fersenkeildämpfung Stabilität und Kontrolle bei schnellen Bewegungen sowie beim Stehen und Gehen. Der Sportprothesenfuß ist zur Verwendung ohne Hülle in niedrig geschnittenen Sportschuhen geeignet.

Begründung der Jury
Der Challenger schafft durch sein ausgeklügeltes Design in Kombination mit den besonderen Materialeigenschaften von Carbon eine Funktionsvielfalt, die ihresgleichen sucht.

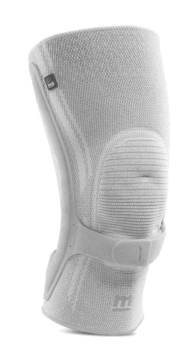

Genumedi® PSS
Knee Support
Kniebandage

Manufacturer
medi GmbH & Co. KG, Bayreuth, Germany
In-house design
Web
www.medi.de

The Genumedi PSS is a knee support designed to relieve strain on the patellar tendon entheses. Its offset strap system ensures a well-balanced pressure distribution. The two-part pad system with 3D profile provides an additional massaging effect. The coating with silicone dots ensures a firm hold. In addition, each product package contains an exercise wedge, with which patients can perform physiotherapy exercises at home that are suitable for patellar tip syndrome.

Statement by the jury
The Genumedi PSS impresses with a sporty look that whets the user's appetite for movement. The offset strap positioning ensures an exceptional fit of the knee support.

Die Genumedi PSS ist eine Kniebandage zur Entlastung der Patellasehnenansätze. Das versetzt verlaufende Gurtsystem sorgt für eine ausgewogene Druckverteilung. Das zweigeteilte Pelottensystem mit 3D-Profil bietet einen zusätzlichen Massageeffekt. Die Beschichtung mit Silikonpunkten gewährleistet einen sicheren Halt der Bandage. Jeder Verpackung liegt zudem ein Übungskeil bei, mit dem die Patienten zu Hause Physioübungen durchführen können, die für die Indikation Patellaspitzensyndrom geeignet sind.

Begründung der Jury
Die Genumedi PSS begeistert durch ihr sportliches Aussehen, das Lust auf Bewegung macht. Die versetzte Gurtanordnung sorgt für einen außergewöhnlich guten Sitz der Kniebandage.

mediven 550®
Fashion-Elements
Compression Stocking
Kompressionsstrumpf

Manufacturer
medi GmbH & Co. KG, Bayreuth, Germany
In-house design
Web
www.medi.de

The flat-knit compression stocking called mediven 550 Fashion-Elements is available in nine variants: in three different patterns (animal, crosses, ornaments) and three colour combinations (grey, brown, berry). The two-coloured patterns result from innovative technology that combines different production methods. First the patterns are knitted into the stockings using a special yarn. This then allows the two colours to emerge once the stockings are subsequently dyed.

Statement by the jury
The innovative manufacturing technology of this compression stocking has been used to create an attractive product that gives its wearer self-confidence.

Der flachgestrickte Kompressionsstrumpf mediven 550 Fashion-Elemente steht in neun Varianten zur Auswahl: in drei unterschiedlichen Mustern (Animal, Crosses, Ornaments) und in drei verschiedenen Farbkombinationen (Grau, Braun, Beere). Die zweifarbigen Muster entstehen durch eine innovative Technologie, die verschiedene Verfahren miteinander kombiniert. Zunächst werden die Muster eingestrickt, dabei wird ein spezielles Garn verwendet. Dadurch werden die Strümpfe beim anschließenden Färben zweifarbig.

Begründung der Jury
Die innovative Fertigungstechnologie wird bei diesem Kompressionsstrumpf genutzt, um ein attraktives Produkt zu schaffen, das seiner Trägerin Selbstbewusstsein verleiht.

Hipsafety
Hip Protector Shorts
Hüftschutzhose

Manufacturer
Doctor Lundh AB, Sundsvall, Sweden
Design
Idag Design Studio, Sundsvall, Sweden
Web
www.hipsafety.com
www.idagdesignstudio.com

The Hipsafety hip protector shorts, designed for senior citizens, reduce the risk of injury in the case of a tumble. The protective padding at the hips absorbs the impact of a fall. It is so thin that it can also be worn comfortably while sleeping and easily removed for washing. Due to the generous opening with three Velcro fasteners, the shorts are easy to put on and take off. The silicone strips on the inside prevent incontinence aids from slipping out of position.

Statement by the jury
Thanks to their modern design and pleasant, light fabric, the Hipsafety hip protector shorts are particularly discreet and comfortable to wear.

Die Hüftschutzhose Hipsafety wurde für ältere Menschen konzipiert und reduziert das Risiko von Verletzungen im Falle eines Sturzes. Die Schutzpolster an den Hüften absorbieren den Aufprall beim Fallen. Sie sind so dünn, dass sie auch zum Schlafen bequem zu tragen sind, und lassen sich zum Waschen einfach herausnehmen. Die großzügige Öffnung mit drei Klettverschlüssen erleichtert das An- und Ausziehen der Hose. Die innen liegenden Silikonstreifen verhindern, dass verwendete Inkontinenzhilfen verrutschen.

Begründung der Jury
Dank ihres modernen Schnitts und des angenehm leichten Stoffs ist die Hüftschutzhose Hipsafety besonders diskret und komfortabel zu tragen.

BEMER VET
Therapy Device for Horses
Therapiegerät für Pferde

Manufacturer
BEMER International AG,
Triesen, Liechtenstein
Design
Flink GmbH (Maurin Bisaz, Remo Frei),
Chur, Switzerland
Web
www.bemergroup.com
www.flink.ch

The Bemer Vet therapy device promotes the regeneration of horses in case of injury or illness as well as after training or competitions. It consists of an adjustable horse blanket and cuff for the targeted treatment of a horse's leg or neck. Signal transmission takes place via the highly flexible, stitched-in magnetic coils. The signal controller is simple, robust, waterproof and intuitive to use. Thanks to the powerful battery, therapy can be carried out during transport as well.

Statement by the jury
The Bemer Vet impresses with its high-quality workmanship and individually adjustable fit. The rechargeable battery enables flexible use in any given location.

Das Therapiegerät Bemer Vet fördert die Regeneration von Pferden bei Verletzung oder Krankheit, nach Trainings oder Wettkämpfen. Es besteht aus einer verstellbaren Pferdedecke und einer Manschette für die gezielte Behandlung eines Beins oder der Halsregion des Pferdes. Über eingestickte, hochflexible Magnetspulen werden die Signale übertragen. Die Signalsteuerung ist leicht, robust, wasserdicht und intuitiv zu bedienen. Dank des leistungsstarken Akkus können die Pferde auch unterwegs behandelt werden.

Begründung der Jury
Das Bemer Vet punktet durch eine qualitativ hochwertige Verarbeitung mit individuell einstellbarer Passform. Der Akku ermöglicht den flexiblen Einsatz unter allen Ortsbedingungen.

Bimeo PRO
Stroke Rehabilitation Device
Rehabilitationsgerät nach
Schlaganfall

Manufacturer
Kinestica d.o.o., Ljubljana, Slovenia
Design
Gigodesign d.o.o., Ljubljana, Slovenia
Web
www.kinestica.com
www.gigodesign.com

The Bimeo Pro stroke rehabilitation device encourages stroke patients to use their more affected arm through supportive movements of the less affected arm. The activities with the rehabilitation device are synchronised with the activities of the cursor on a computer monitor. The exercises are closely oriented to situations from daily life. The sensors in the device capture objective data, providing insight into the patient's progress.

Statement by the jury
The Bimeo Pro stroke rehabilitation device playfully encourages patients to actively participate in their rehabilitation. The indentations in the surface make gripping significantly easier.

Das Rehabilitationsgerät Bimeo Pro ermutigt Schlaganfallpatienten dazu, ihren stärker beeinträchtigten Arm durch unterstützende Bewegungen des weniger beeinträchtigten Arms zu benutzen. Die Aktivitäten mit dem Rehabilitationsgerät werden mit den Aktivitäten des Cursors auf einem Computerbildschirm synchronisiert. Die Übungsaufgaben orientieren sich an Situationen des alltäglichen Lebens. Die Sensoren in dem Gerät erfassen objektive Daten, die Einblicke in die Fortschritte des Patienten geben.

Begründung der Jury
Auf spielerische Weise motiviert das Rehabilitationsgerät Bimeo Pro den Patienten zum Mitmachen. Die Vertiefungen auf der Oberfläche erleichtern maßgeblich das Greifen.

APEX
Wheelchair
Rollstuhl

Manufacturer
Motion Composites,
Saint-Roch-de-l'Achigan, Canada
In-house design
Motion Composites Design Team
Web
www.motioncomposites.com

The wheelchair Apex, with its carbon-fibre construction, is one of the lightest rigid-frame models in the world. It weighs only 4.2 kg thanks to its cutting-edge technology. Moreover, it is characterised by high strength and durability. The design is fully based on a modular structure. Its laser-etched markings allow users to easily adjust key components and specify their exact positioning. The rear bar, which supports rigidity, optimises ride performance.

Statement by the jury
The wheelchair Apex is extremely lightweight and robust. Thanks to the modular structure, it perfectly adjusts to the specific requirements of each individual.

Der Rollstuhl Apex aus Carbon ist eines der leichtesten Starrrahmen-Modelle weltweit. Er wiegt dank seiner hochmodernen Fertigungstechnologie nur 4,2 kg. Darüber hinaus zeichnet er sich durch seine hohe Stabilität und Langlebigkeit aus. Die Konstruktion ist komplett modular aufgebaut. Mithilfe der lasergeätzten Markierungen lassen sich die Schlüsselkomponenten einfach ein-stellen und ihre genaue Positionierung festlegen. Die hintere Versteifungsstange optimiert die Fahrleistung.

Begründung der Jury
Der Rollstuhl Apex ist extrem leicht und robust. Dank seines modularen Aufbaus lässt er sich hervorragend an die individuellen Anforderungen des Benutzers anpassen.

HALT
Table for an Independent Life
Tisch für ein selbständiges Leben

Manufacturer
MORMOR, etage8 GmbH, Leipzig, Germany
In-house design
Web
www.mormor.de

With its surrounding wooden handrail, the HALT table provides safe support, even in the middle of a room. Therefore, it offers a reliable aid for people with reduced mobility. The clear and straightforward design is intuitively understood by all generations. The rounded corners and edges, pleasant-to-touch shapes and antibacterial surfaces support the users in their daily lives without stigmatising them.

Der Tisch HALT bietet durch seinen umlaufenden Handlauf aus Holz auch mitten im Raum sicheren Halt. Dadurch wird eine feststehende Stütze für Menschen geboten, deren Mobilität eingeschränkt ist. Das klare und eindeutige Design wird von allen Generationen intuitiv verstanden. Die abgerundeten Ecken und Kanten, haptisch angenehme Formen und antibakterielle Oberflächen unterstützen die Nutzer zusätzlich in ihrem Alltag, ohne sie zu stigmatisieren.

Statement by the jury
The sophisticated design of the table displays a deep understanding of people with restricted mobility and their desire to lead a self-determined life.

Begründung der Jury
Die durchdachte Gestaltung des Tischs zeugt von einem tiefen Verständnis für Menschen mit eingeschränkter Mobilität und ihrem Bedürfnis, ein selbstbestimmtes Leben zu führen.

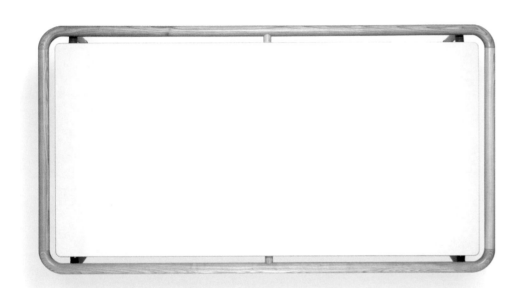

ImpressionIST 4
3D Video Centring System
3D-Videozentriersystem

Manufacturer
Rodenstock GmbH, Munich, Germany
Design
Brandis Industrial Design, Nuremberg,
Germany
Web
www.rodenstock.com
www.brandis-design.com

The 3D video centring system
ImpressionIST 4 captures all relevant
data for the optimal fitting of spectacle
lenses. To this end, the user looks in
the mirror and is recorded by two cameras. Individual parameters, including
the pupil diameter, are measured precisely using a single shot. The innovative
light concept ensures homogeneous
illumination over the entire measurement range. The red illuminated on/off
switch communicates the corporate
design of the brand.

Statement by the jury
The elegant free-standing video centring
system ImpressionIST 4 convinces with its
clear design language that intuitively
instructs users how to position themselves.

Das 3D-Videozentriersystem
ImpressionIST 4 erfasst alle relevanten
Daten für die optimale Anpassung von
Brillengläsern. Dazu blickt der Benutzer in
den Spiegel und wird von zwei Kameras
erfasst. Anhand einer einzigen Aufnahme
werden individuelle Parameter, inklusive
des Pupillendurchmessers, präzise vermessen. Das innovative Lichtkonzept sorgt
für eine homogene Ausleuchtung des gesamten Messbereichs. Der rot beleuchtete
Ein-/Aus-LED-Schalter kommuniziert das
Corporate Design der Marke.

Begründung der Jury
Das elegant frei stehende 3D-Video-
zentriersystem ImpressionIST 4 überzeugt,
weil es dem Benutzer durch seine klare
Formensprache intuitiv vorgibt, wie er sich
zu positionieren hat.

Luna EMG
Rehabilitation Robot
Rehabilitationsroboter

Manufacturer
EgzoTech Sp. z o.o., Gliwice, Poland
In-house design
Design
Husarska Design Studio
(Jadwiga Husarska-Sobina),
Krakow, Poland
Web
www.egzotech.com
www.husarska.pl

Through electrodes attached to the patient, the Luna EMG reads the electrical activity from inside the muscle tissue. It thus helps to develop innovative therapeutic methods for treating neurological disorders. The ergonomic and sleek design ensures intuitive usability and mobility. Gamified exercises with an interactive tablet and a visually appealing organic design create a trustworthy environment for even the youngest patients.

Statement by the jury
The playful training approach of the Luna EMG is skilfully reflected by its modern appearance. The slim design allows excellent accessibility.

Das Luna EMG kann durch am Patienten angebrachte Elektroden die elektrische Aktivität aus dem Innern des Muskelgewebes auslesen. Dadurch hilft es dabei, innovative therapeutische Methoden zur Behandlung von neurologischen Störungen zu entwickeln. Das ergonomische und schlanke Design garantiert intuitive Bedienbarkeit und Mobilität. Durch die Gamifizierung der Übungen mit einem interaktiven Tablet und einem optisch ansprechenden, organischen Design wird ein vertrauenerweckendes Umfeld für die jüngsten Patienten geschaffen.

Begründung der Jury
Der spielerische Trainingsansatz des Luna EMG spiegelt sich gekonnt in seinem modernen Erscheinungsbild wider. Die schlanke Konstruktion bietet hervorragende Zugänglichkeit.

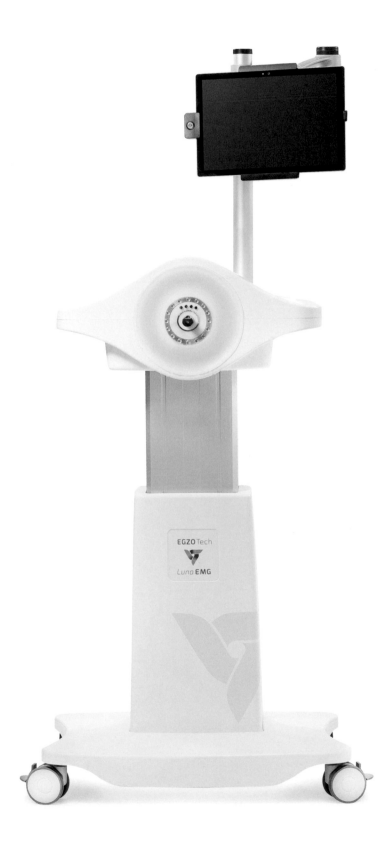

Computers and information technology
Computer und Informationstechnik

Dell Canvas 27
Interactive Computer Work Surface
Interaktive Computer-Arbeitsfläche

Manufacturer
Dell Inc., Round Rock,
Texas, USA

In-house design
Experience Design Group

Web
www.dell.com

reddot award 2017
best of the best

Form for creativity

Today, both creative work and creative interactive exchange between people heavily rely on computers. This offers the advantage that the results can easily be integrated into existing work processes. By questioning the principles underlying these media, the design of the Dell Canvas 27 has emerged as a strikingly new version of a digital workspace. The work surface features the innovation of a horizontal layout that complements the users' vertical view surfaces and thus offers innovative ease of use. The 27" touchscreen provides creative users with a lot of space for drawing. In the initial position, the Dell Canvas rests almost flat on the desktop, while its fold-out stand gives it a ten-degree incline. The innovation of this interactive computer work surface is also due to the fact that the display and input media merge into one formal as well as functional unit. This allows seamless navigation across two planes by touch, pen, mouse or dial and knob totem. The Dell Canvas also inspires with a sleek-looking design idiom. Thanks to its flat design, it allows users from a wide range of fields to interact with their systems in a multidimensional environment. Promoting fascinating new possibilities for interactive work with a computer desktop, the Dell Canvas 27 has emerged to embody an outstanding mediator of creativity.

Form für die Kreativität

Kreatives Arbeiten und der damit verbundene interaktive Austausch geschehen heute oftmals am Computer. Dies birgt den Vorteil, dass sich die Ergebnisse leichter in bestehende Arbeitsprozesse einbringen lassen. Indem seine Gestaltung das Prinzip der dafür genutzten Medien hinterfragt, stellt das Dell Canvas 27 eine bestechend neue Version einer digitalen Arbeitsfläche dar. Es ist auf innovative Weise horizontal ausgerichtet und bietet dem Nutzer eine intuitiv erschließbare Oberfläche, die durch eine vertikale Betrachtungsfläche ergänzt wird. Das 27" große Touch-Display stellt dem Kreativen viel Fläche zum Zeichnen bereit. In der Ausgangsposition liegt das Dell Canvas nahezu flach auf dem Tisch, sein ausklappbarer Standfuß gibt ihm eine Neigung von zehn Grad. Die Innovation dieser interaktiven Computer-Arbeitsfläche liegt auch darin begründet, dass Anzeige- und Eingabemedium zu einer formalen wie funktionalen Einheit verschmelzen. Dies erlaubt ein nahtloses Navigieren über zwei Ebenen per Finger, Maus, Eingabestift oder Totem (Drehregler). Das Dell Canvas begeistert mit einer schnittig anmutenden Formensprache. Dank seiner flachen Bauform können Nutzer aus den unterschiedlichsten Bereichen mit ihrem System in einer mehrdimensionalen Umgebung interagieren. Mittels faszinierend neuer Möglichkeiten für die interaktive Arbeit mit einer Computer-Arbeitsfläche wird das Dell Canvas 27 so zu einem hervorstechenden Mittler der Kreativität.

Statement by the jury

The Dell Canvas 27 impresses with its integrated concept, which opens up new possibilities for communication and visualisation. Following a consistent, user-oriented design, it has emerged as an innovative tool for designers and engineers. It allows them to intuitively make use of the different operating modes, including the conveniently designed rotary knobs. Reduced to the essential, the Dell Canvas has been carefully crafted to support creative, interactive work.

Begründung der Jury

Das Dell Canvas 27 beeindruckt durch sein integratives Konzept, durch das es der Visualisierung und Kommunikation neue Möglichkeiten eröffnet. Eine stringente, nutzerorientierte Gestaltung führt hier zu einem innovativen Tool für Designer und Ingenieure. Intuitiv können diese die unterschiedlichen Bedienungsarten einschließlich der komfortabel gestalteten Drehregler für sich nutzen. Das Dell Canvas ist für das kreative, interaktive Arbeiten wunderbar durchdacht und auf das Essentielle reduziert.

Designer portrait
See page 70
Siehe Seite 70

Dell XPS 27
All-in-One PC

Manufacturer
Dell Inc., Round Rock, Texas, USA
In-house design
Experience Design Group
Web
www.dell.com

The Dell XPS 27 provides a design that is elegant and space-saving at the same time. The UltraSharp 4K Ultra HD display, vivid and accurate Adobe RGB colour and a strong audio system cater to the most discerning visual demands. The adjustable stand of the touch display allows easy positioning for the needs of office work or gaming. Easily accessible, laterally situated ports facilitate quick connection of a telephone for data synchronisation or uploading of pictures from a camera, without the need to reach behind the screen of the device.

Statement by the jury
With its technically sophisticated display, the Dell XPS 27 all-in-one PC satisfies high demands for an immersive picture experience.

Der Dell XPS 27 zeigt eine elegante und zugleich platzsparende Gestaltung. Das UltraSharp-4K-Ultra-HD-Display, eine lebendige und exakte Adobe-RGB-Farbraumabdeckung sowie das sehr gute Audiosystem werden hohen optischen Ansprüchen gerecht. Der verstellbare Standfuß des Touch-Displays ermöglicht eine einfache Einstellung für die Bedürfnisse im Office- wie auch im Spielebereich. Gut zugängliche seitliche Anschlüsse erlauben die schnelle Verbindung mit einem Telefon zum Datenabgleich oder das Hochladen von Bildern aus einer Kamera, ohne dass ein Zugriff auf die Rückseite des Geräts notwendig ist.

Begründung der Jury
Mit seinem technisch ausgereiften Display wird der All-in-One-PC Dell XPS 27 hohen Ansprüchen an ein immersives Bilderlebnis gerecht.

Dell 24 Touch Monitor P2418HT

Manufacturer
Dell Inc., Round Rock, Texas, USA
In-house design
Experience Design Group
Web
www.dell.com

Innovative touch technology called Advanced In-Cell Touch (AIT) is integrated into the Dell 24 Touch Monitor P2418HT, by means of which the conventional glass cover can be eliminated. This reduces reflection, lessens power consumption and facilitates a thin, light construction. Since the monitor is mainly desk-bound for various usage situations, it has been equipped with an articulating stand with convenient tilt and swivel features.

Statement by the jury
A glare-free screen with touchscreen functionality and ergonomically attractive adjustability attest to the userfriendliness of the Dell 24 Touch Monitor P2418HT.

Bei dem Dell 24 Touch Monitor P2418HT wurde die innovative Touch-Technologie Advanced In-Cell Touch (AIT) integriert, mit der auf die herkömmliche Glas-Abdeckscheibe verzichtet werden kann. Das vermindert Reflexion, senkt den Stromverbrauch und ermöglicht eine schmale, leichte Bauweise. Da der Monitor hauptsächlich auf dem Schreibtisch für unterschiedliche Nutzungsmuster Einsatz findet, wurde er mit einem gelenkartigen Standfuß mit komfortabler Neige- und Schwenkfähigkeit ausgestattet.

Begründung der Jury
Ein blendfreier Bildschirm mit Touchscreen-Funktion und ergonomisch ansprechender Justierbarkeit zeugen von der Benutzerfreundlichkeit des Dell 24 Touch Monitor P2418HT.

Philips Entertainment Monitor 356M6QSB

Manufacturer
TPV Technology Group,
New Taipei City, Taiwan
Design
TPV Technology Design Team,
Amsterdam, Netherlands
Web
www.philips.com

The Philips Entertainment Monitor 356M6QSB is aimed at a target group with high demands with regard to both performance and optical appearance. The decorative aluminium stand is produced from a single rod, which is bent at three places and thereby ensures stability for standing on the table at three points. Taking into account that many components of the device can be recycled, pure metal has been used for the manufacture of the monitor and stand as far as possible.

Statement by the jury
The Philips Entertainment Monitor 356M6QSB is appealing due to its contemporary aesthetics and the materials that have been chosen with a view towards ecological compatibility.

Der Philips Entertainment Monitor 356M6QSB richtet sich an ein Zielpublikum, das hohe Ansprüche sowohl an die Leistungsfähigkeit wie auch an das optische Erscheinungsbild stellt. Der zierliche Aluminiumständer ist aus einer einzelnen Stange gebildet, die an drei Stellen gebogen wurde und somit an drei Punkten auf dem Tisch für stabilen Stand sorgt. Unter der Berücksichtigung, dass viele Teile des Gerätes dem Recycling zugeführt werden können, wurde möglichst weitgehend Echtmetall bei der Herstellung von Monitor und Ständer verwendet.

Begründung der Jury
Der Philips Entertainment Monitor 356M6QSB gefällt durch seine zeitgemäße Ästhetik und die Materialauswahl mit Bedacht auf ökologische Verträglichkeit.

Philips Consumer Monitor

Manufacturer
TPV Technology Group,
New Taipei City, Taiwan
Design
TPV Technology Design Team,
Amsterdam, Netherlands
Web
www.philips.com

The Philips Consumer Monitor meets several demands: it fulfils contemporary requirements in technology, its design communicates high performance and it blends in with modern homes at the same time. The stand in particular fits the latter requirement well, thanks to its visual lightness. Details on the monitor, for instance the height adjustment and the back cover, complete the pleasant overall impression. Where possible, only metal has been used for the monitor and the stand in order to increase the ecological compatibility of the device.

Statement by the jury
Monitors are part of everyday life for many people and should provide up-to-date performance along with a pleasant appearance. The Philips Consumer Monitor delivers both of these attributes.

Der Philips Consumer Monitor wird mehreren Ansprüchen gerecht: Er erfüllt zeitgemäße Erfordernisse an die Technologie, seine Gestaltung kommuniziert hohe Leistung und zugleich fügt er sich in ein modernes Zuhause ein. Insbesondere der Ständer verwirklicht dank seiner optischen Leichtigkeit den letztgenannten Anspruch. Details am Monitor wie die Höhenjustierung und die Rückseite runden den Gesamteindruck ab. Nach Möglichkeit wurden für den Monitor wie für den Ständer echte Metalle verwendet, um die ökologische Verträglichkeit des Geräts zu erhöhen.

Begründung der Jury
Monitore gehören zum Alltag vieler Menschen und sollen zeitgemäße Leistung wie auch einen erfreulichen Anblick bieten. Beides erbringt der Philips Consumer Monitor.

EX3200R
Curved Monitor
Gekrümmter Monitor

Manufacturer
BenQ Corporation, Taipei, Taiwan
In-house design
Web
www.benq.com

Featuring a 1800R curvature and a 31.5" monitor, the EX3200R is designed for the most striking visual experience possible. A connector cover conceals the cables and thus ensures a tidy look. The device supports a refresh rate of 144 Hz and smooth moving images thanks to FreeSync technology. The high contrast ratio of 3000:1 guarantees an excellent colour gradient. Multitasking is made possible by a split screen and picture-in-picture functions. Low blue light technology filters out harmful blue light and thus protects the eyes from irritation.

Statement by the jury
The curved monitor EX3200R ensures an impressive cinema experience, which allows film aficionados to become immersed in the action.

Mit einer 1800R-Krümmung und einem 31,5"-Monitor ist der EX3200R für ein möglichst eindringliches Seherlebnis konzipiert. Eine Anschlussabdeckung versteckt die Kabel und sorgt so für einen ordentlichen Eindruck. Das Gerät unterstützt durch eine Bildwiederholrate von 144 Hz und FreeSync-Technologie flüssig laufende Bilder. Die hohe Kontrastrate von 3000:1 sorgt für einen sehr guten Farbverlauf. Multitasking wird ermöglicht durch Bildschirmaufteilungs- und Bild-in-Bild-Funktionen. Die Low-Blue-Light-Technologie filtert schädliches blaues Licht heraus und beugt so Augenirritationen vor.

Begründung der Jury
Der gekrümmte Monitor EX3200R sorgt für ein eindrucksvolles Kinoerlebnis, das Filmliebhaber mitten ins Geschehen eintauchen lässt.

OMEN X
Curved Monitor
Gekrümmter Monitor

Manufacturer
HP Inc., Palo Alto, USA
In-house design
HP Inc. PS Industrial Design Team
Design
Native Design, London, Great Britain
Web
www.hp.com

This 35" monitor with a format of 21:9 has a curvature radius of 1800R. With a GTG reaction time of 4 ms and an ultra-wide QHD resolution of 3440 x 1440, it masters even demanding games trouble-free and in superb picture quality. The stand bracket is adjustable, thus increasing ergonomic comfort. The ambient lighting gives rise to an appealing effect, which compensates for the contrast between a very bright display and a dark room.

Statement by the jury
The curved monitor Omen X impresses with excellent picture quality and imposing dimensions, which ensure a truly immersive gaming experience.

Dieser 35"-Monitor im Format 21:9 zeigt einen Krümmungsradius von 1800R. Mit einer GTG-Reaktionszeit von 4 ms und einer Ultra-Wide-QHD-Auflösung von 3440 x 1440 bewältigt er selbst anspruchsvolle Spiele störungsfrei und in hervorragender Bildqualität. Die Halterung des Ständers ist justierbar, was den ergonomischen Komfort erhöht. Für einen ansprechenden Effekt sorgt das Umgebungslicht, das den Kontrast zwischen einem sehr hellen Display und einem dunklen Raum herabsetzt.

Begründung der Jury
Der gekrümmte Monitor Omen X beeindruckt mit einer hervorragenden Bildqualität und imposanten Dimensionen, die für ein wahrhaft immersives Spieleerlebnis sorgen.

ThinkVision X27q
Monitor

Manufacturer
Lenovo, Morrisville, North Carolina, USA
In-house design
Web
www.lenovo.com

The design concept of the ThinkVision X27q is based on clear lines and a sense of timelessness. From a technical perspective, it offers a 27" display in 2560 x 1440 high-resolution QHD picture quality. Colour depth of 1.07 billion with a response time of 4 ms facilitates a high-quality and accurate viewing experience in 2K wide-angle format. A slimline chrome stand gives the screen an almost floating effect. The narrow panel makes the monitor appear nearly frameless, whereas a wider panel at the bottom edge imparts calm and stable aesthetics.

Das Gestaltungskonzept des ThinkVision X27q baut auf klare Linien und Zeitlosigkeit. In technischer Hinsicht bietet er ein 27"-Display in 2560 x 1440 hochauflösender QHD-Bildqualität. Eine Farbtiefe von 1,07 Milliarden bei einer Bildaufbauzeit von 4 ms gewährleistet ein hochwertiges und akkurates Bilderleben in 2K-Weitwinkel-Güte. Ein schlanker Ständer aus Chrom verleiht dem Bildschirm einen nahezu schwebenden Effekt. Die schmale Blende lässt den Monitor fast rahmenlos erscheinen, eine breitere Blende an der Unterkante vermittelt hingegen eine ruhige und stabile Ästhetik.

Statement by the jury
In its premium, almost frameless design, the ThinkVision X27q blends into any environment – from a small home office to a large conference room.

Begründung der Jury
In seiner edlen, nahezu rahmenlosen Gestaltung passt der ThinkVision X27q in jede Umgebung – vom kleinen Homeoffice bis hin zum großen Besprechungsraum.

ThinkVision P27q
Monitor

Manufacturer
Lenovo, Morrisville, North Carolina, USA
In-house design
Web
www.lenovo.com

The ThinkVision P27q Monitor appears to be almost borderless, and the surrounding bezel of the QHD display is extremely narrow and hardly noticeable. Prominent in this discreet frame are both the ThinkVision logo and the easily operated keys for activating the on-screen display along the lower strip. The stand is easy to mount and makes it possible to adjust the height of the screen, to pivot, swivel and tilt it. The stand is also removable so that the monitor, which complies with VESA standards, can be mounted on the wall. The red clip at the back of the stand is an eye-catcher and is used for cable management.

Nahezu randlos erscheint der Bildschirm des ThinkVision P27q, extrem schmal und kaum wahrnehmbar ist die um das QHD-Display herum verlaufende Blende. Hervorgehoben in dieser dezenten Einfassung sind das ThinkVision-Logo sowie die einfach steuerbaren Tasten zur Aktivierung des On-Screen-Displays an der unteren Leiste. Der Ständer ist leicht anzubringen und ermöglicht es, den Bildschirm in der Höhe zu justieren, zu drehen, zu schwenken und zu kippen. Er kann auch abgenommen und der Monitor, der den VESA-Standards entspricht, an der Wand montiert werden. Die rote Klammer an der Rückseite des Fußes stellt einen Blickfang dar, der zum Kabelmanagement verwendet wird.

Statement by the jury
The concept of the ThinkVision P27q is delightful, since the fine bezel lends the on-screen content of the monitor a sense of floating.

Begründung der Jury
Das Konzept des ThinkVision P27q begeistert, denn durch die feine Umrahmung scheinen die Bilder auf diesem Monitor förmlich zu schweben.

Asus MZ Monitor Series

Manufacturer
ASUSTeK Computer Inc., Taipei, Taiwan
In-house design
Web
www.asus.com

The design focus of the Asus MZ Monitor Series is placed on sound quality and formal simplicity. The monitor is only 7 mm thick; the frameless edge-to-edge screen offers QHD resolution. Clear lines and the rounded speaker base emphasise the very light and sleek design. The elegant speaker pattern in the flat metal foot provides a further design feature. Integrated there is a woofer with high-performance Harman Kardon audio technology.

Statement by the jury
The frameless edge-to-edge screen of the Asus MZ Monitor Series displays a convincing style, and the sound quality of the Harman Kardon speakers is delightful.

Der gestalterische Fokus der Serie Asus MZ Monitor liegt auf Klangqualität und formaler Einfachheit. Der Monitor ist nur 7 mm dick, der rahmenlose Edge-to-Edge-Bildschirm verfügt über QHD-Auflösung. Klare Linien und der runde Lautsprecherfuß betonen die sehr leichte und schlanke Gestaltung. In den flachen Metallfuß liefert das elegante Lautsprechermuster ein weiteres Gestaltungselement. Darin integriert ist ein Woofer mit leistungsstarker Harman-Kardon-Audiotechnologie.

Begründung der Jury
Der rahmenlose Edge-to-Edge-Bildschirm der Serie Asus MZ Monitor zeigt überzeugend Stil. Auch die Klangqualität der Harman-Kardon-Lautsprecher begeistert.

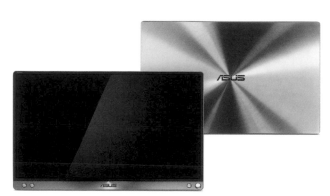

Asus ZenScreen
Portable Monitor
Tragbarer Monitor

Manufacturer
ASUSTeK Computer Inc., Taipei, Taiwan
In-house design
Web
www.asus.com

The Asus ZenScreen is particularly thin and, together with a 14.6" monitor, weighs only 800 grams. It features a C-type USB port. The noble design of the aluminium housing features a characteristic circle-line pattern on the back, and the screen switches automatically between landscape and portrait formats. The protective cover made of PU leather folds out into a stand in both horizontal and vertical positions. The device can also be used lying horizontally for typing. Due to a laterally located recess, designed to hold a pen or pencil, the monitor can be supported in a standing position even without the protective cover.

Statement by the jury
Thanks to its exceptionally slim form and low weight, the portable Asus ZenScreen monitor impresses in terms of aesthetics as well as functionality.

Der Asus ZenScreen ist besonders dünn und wiegt mit einem 15,6"-Bildschirm nur 800 Gramm. Er verfügt über einen USB-Anschluss Typ C. Das edel gestaltete Aluminiumgehäuse zeigt an der Rückseite ein charakteristisches Kreislinienmuster, der Bildschirm wechselt automatisch zwischen Hoch- und Querformat. Der Schutzdeckel aus PU-Leder dient umgeklappt als Aufsteller in horizontaler wie vertikaler Position. Das Gerät kann auch horizontal liegend zum Tippen genutzt werden. Durch eine seitlich platzierte Aussparung, in die ein Stift eingesteckt werden kann, lässt sich der Bildschirm auch ohne Schutzdeckel stehend positionieren.

Begründung der Jury
Der tragbare Monitor Asus ZenScreen weiß dank ausnehmend schlanker Formgebung und geringem Gewicht in ästhetischer wie funktionaler Hinsicht zu beeindrucken.

Arthur Holm DB2
Retractable Monitor
Versenkbarer Monitor

Manufacturer
Arthur Holm, Albiral Display Solutions SL, Barcelona, Spain
In-house design
Web
www.arthurholm.com

After use, the Arthur Holm DB2 retractable monitor glides back into a recess made in the furniture with a calm and smooth gesture. The monitor is retracted and raised by means of an intuitively operable button, which is flush with and adjacent to the retraction aperture. Since the monitor is only 20 mm thick, it is easily integrated, for instance in meeting or conference rooms. When not in use, the screen remains almost invisible in the recess without cover.

Statement by the jury
With stylish aesthetics, the Arthur Holm DB2 rises out of the furniture and retracts back in again – a truly elegant solution.

Nach der Verwendung gleitet der versenkbare Monitor Arthur Holm DB2 in einer ruhigen und gleichförmigen Bewegung zurück in eine in das Mobiliar eingearbeitete Versenkung. Mittels einer intuitiv bedienbaren Taste, die bündig neben dem Einzugsschlitz installiert ist, wird der Bildschirm ein- bzw. ausgefahren. Mit nur 20 mm Stärke ist der Bildschirm einfach zu integrieren, etwa in einen Besprechungstisch in Sitzungs- oder Konferenzräumen. Ist er nicht in Benutzung, bleibt der Bildschirm ohne Abdeckung in der Versenkung nahezu unsichtbar.

Begründung der Jury
Mit stilvoller Ästhetik taucht der Arthur Holm DB2 aus dem Mobiliar auf und versinkt ebenso dorthin wieder – eine wahrhaft elegante Lösung.

32UD99
Monitor

Manufacturer
LG Electronics Inc., Seoul, South Korea
In-house design
Jaeneung Jung, Sooyoung Park
Web
www.lg.com

The front of this monitor with a resolution in UHD format was designed without a bezel, and all other unnecessary decorative elements have also been omitted. This minimalist design concept fosters a high-quality impression, placing a focus on the screen-immersion experience. Under this aspect, provisions have also been made for height adjustment and tilt angle of the monitor to be very easily attainable at the stand base. By pressing a button, the foot can be quickly detached.

Statement by the Jury
The high-performance 32UD99 monitor convincingly supports the creation or reproduction of HDR content and allows films to be enjoyed in the same impressive quality.

Bei diesem Monitor mit einer Auflösung im UHD-Format wurde die Front ohne Blende konstruiert, so wie auch auf alle anderen überflüssigen dekorativen Elemente verzichtet wurde. Dieses minimalistische Gestaltungskonzept sorgt für eine hochwertige Anmutung und stellt das unmittelbare Filmerlebnis ganz in den Fokus. Unter diesem Aspekt wurde auch dafür gesorgt, dass die Justierung von Höhe und Neigungswinkel des Bildschirms durch den Standfuß sehr einfach gelingen kann. Durch das Betätigen eines Knopfes kann dieser auch leicht ganz abgenommen werden.

Begründung der Jury
Der leistungsstarke Monitor 32UD99 unterstützt überzeugend bei der Erstellung oder Wiedergabe von HDR-Inhalten, und in ebenso beeindruckender Qualität lassen sich Filme damit genießen.

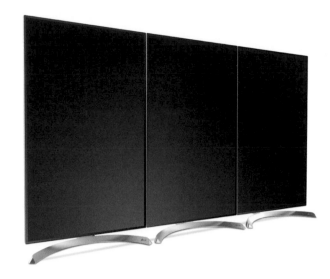

HP ENVY Curved All-in-One
Computer

Manufacturer
HP Inc., Palo Alto, USA
In-house design
HP Inc. PS Industrial Design Team
Design
Native Design, London, Great Britain
Web
www.hp.com

The HP Envy Curved All-in-One enables an intensive sound and picture experience and, with its reduced design, conveys a premium and high-quality impression. The curved monitor with its 34" micro-edge display in Ultra WQHD quality seems to literally be floating between the plain aluminium stand and the upper soundbar by Bang & Olufsen. The monolithically designed base conceals PC components of the newest generation and houses discretely integrated control elements.

Statement by the jury
The HP Envy Curved All-in-One delights due to a completely harmonious overall appearance with sophisticated aesthetics.

Der HP Envy Curved All-in-One sorgt für ein intensives Ton- und Bilderlebnis und vermittelt in seiner reduzierten Gestaltung eine edle und hochwertige Anmutung. Der gekrümmte Monitor mit 34"-Micro-Edge-Display in Ultra-WQHD-Qualität scheint zwischen dem schlichten Aluminiumstandfuß und der oberen Soundbar von Bang & Olufsen förmlich zu schweben. Die monolithisch gestaltete Basis verbirgt PC-Komponenten der neuesten Generation und enthält diskret eingearbeitete Steuerungselemente.

Begründung der Jury
Der HP Envy Curved All-in-One begeistert durch ein vollendet harmonisches Gesamterscheinungsbild in ausgereifter Ästhetik.

38UC99-W
Curved Monitor
Gekrümmter Monitor

Manufacturer
LG Electronics Inc., Seoul, South Korea
In-house design
Jaeneung Jung, Sooyoung Park
Web
www.lg.com

This monitor offers a particularly large 38" LED display and an exceptionally wide 2300 R curvature. The curved monitor thus solves the problem of image distortion in the case of large-format files, offers a very good viewing angle and almost immediate screen immersion. Renouncement of unnecessary decorative elements in the design gives the product a high-quality, minimalist impression. The form of the stand base is shaped as a narrow crescent, where the monitor is conveniently adjustable in height and tilt angle.

Statement by the jury
The 38UC99-W monitor delights with its innovative display technology. Thanks to an astonishing curvature of 2300 R, it provides a screen-immersion experience.

Dieser Monitor bietet ein besonders großes 38"-LED-Display und eine ausnehmend weite Kurvatur von 2300 R. Der gekrümmte Monitor löst somit das Problem der Bildverzerrung bei großformatigen Dateien und bietet einen sehr guten Blickwinkel sowie ein nahezu unmittelbares Filmleben. Der Verzicht auf überflüssige dekorative Elemente in der Gestaltung verleiht dem Produkt eine hochwertige minimalistische Anmutung. Die Form des Standfußes deutet einen schmalen Halbmond an, mit ihm lässt sich der Monitor bequem in der Höhe und im Neigungswinkel justieren.

Begründung der Jury
Der Bildschirm 38UC99-W begeistert mit seiner innovativen Displaytechnologie. Dank einer erstaunlichen Kurvatur von 2300 R lässt sich mitten ins Bilderleben eintauchen.

MacBook Pro 13"
Notebook

Manufacturer
Apple, Cupertino, USA
In-house design
Web
www.apple.com

The housing of the new MacBook Pro 13" is manufactured largely using recyclable aluminium in a unibody construction. This creates a particularly rigid and dense notebook that clearly appears light and slim. Its side dimensions are 30.41 x 21.24 cm with a height of only 1.49 cm, providing premium aesthetics. The model is available in the discreet, modern colours of silver and space grey. The display contains neither mercury nor arsenic, and in terms of reducing the environmental impact, the notebook is also free of brominated flame retardants, PVC and beryllium.

Das Gehäuse des neuen MacBook Pro 13" ist vollständig aus weitgehend recycelbarem Aluminium im Unibody-Bauprinzip gefertigt. Auf diese Art entsteht ein besonders festes und dicht gefertigtes Notebook, das ausgesprochen leicht und dünn ausfällt. Seine Seitenlängen von 30,41 x 21,24 cm bei einer Höhe von nur 1,49 cm verleihen ihm eine edle Ästhetik. Das Modell ist in den dezenten modernen Farbtönen Silber und Space Grau erhältlich. Das Display enthält weder Quecksilber noch Arsen, in Hinblick auf die Reduktion von Umweltbelastungen ist das Notebook außerdem frei von bromhaltigen Flammschutzmitteln, PVC und Beryllium.

Statement by the jury
The fine and elegant design of the MacBook Pro 13" gives rise to convincing aesthetics. The environmentally friendly features are also impressive.

Begründung der Jury
Die feine und elegante Gestaltung des MacBook Pro 13" beweist überzeugende Ästhetik. Auch das Augenmerk auf Umweltverträglichkeit beeindruckt.

MacBook Pro 15"
Notebook

Manufacturer
Apple, Cupertino, USA
In-house design
Web
www.apple.com

The new edition of the MacBook Pro 15" presents a particularly bright and colourful retina display with LED backlighting and IPS technology, featuring a native resolution of 2506 x 1600 pixels at 227 ppi in the P3 colour gamut. The Touch Bar – a multitouch strip of glass in retina quality – is integrated into the keyboard, allowing direct access to tools. With a single touch, a selection can be made between short commands and text prompting. In full-picture mode, it is possible to swipe through a video timeline, and photos can be processed by touch. This interface replaces the traditional row of function keys.

Die neue Version des MacBook Pro 15" zeigt ein besonders strahlendes und farbenreiches Retina-Display mit LED-Hintergrundbeleuchtung und IPS-Technologie, einer nativen Auflösung von 2506 x 1600 Pixeln bei 227 ppi im P3-Farbraum. In die Tastatur integriert ist die Touch Bar – eine Multi-Touch-Leiste aus Glas in Retina-Qualität, die direkten Zugriff auf Tools ermöglicht. Mit einer Berührung kann etwa zwischen Kurzbefehlen und Textvorschlägen gewählt werden. Im Vollbildmodus kann man durch eine Video-Timeline streichen, Fotos lassen sich mit einem Tipp bearbeiten. Diese Schnittstelle ersetzt die traditionelle Leiste mit Funktionstasten.

Statement by the jury
The MacBook Pro 15" displays special innovation by introducing the intuitively understandable Touch Bar in retina quality.

Begründung der Jury
Das MacBook Pro 15" zeigt besondere Innovation durch Einführung der intuitiv erfassbaren Touch Bar in Retina-Qualität.

Spin 7
Convertible Notebook

Manufacturer
Acer Incorporated, New Taipei City, Taiwan
In-house design
Web
www.acer.com

The polished, silver-coloured hinges of the Spin 7 facilitate use as a laptop, positioner, tent or tablet. This matt-black convertible notebook is very slim at only 10.98 mm and weighs just under 1.2 kg. The battery has a running capacity of up to eight hours. Performance is provided by a 7th generation Intel Core i7 processor with up to 8 GB of memory as well as a fast 256 GB SSD. Thanks to a fingerprint scanner the user can log in securely and password-free.

Statement by the jury
The Spin 7 proves to be a useful companion for people who are often out and about, and who wish to present and manage their work flexibly.

Die polierten, silberfarbenen Scharniere des Spin 7 machen den Einsatz in Form eines Laptops, Aufstellers, Zeltes oder Tablets möglich. Das mattschwarze Convertible Notebook ist mit 10,98 mm sehr schmal und wiegt nur knapp 1,2 kg. Die Batterielaufzeit beträgt bis zu acht Stunden. Für Leistung sorgen ein 7th-Generation-Intel-Core-i7-Prozessor, bis zu 8 GB Speicherkapazität sowie ein schnelles 256 GB-SSD. Mittels Fingerabdruckscanner meldet sich der Nutzer sicher und passwortfrei an.

Begründung der Jury
Das Spin 7 erweist sich als nützlicher Begleiter für Menschen, die viel unterwegs sind und ihre Arbeiten flexibel präsentieren und verwalten möchten.

Acer Chromebook Spin 11
Convertible Chromebook

Manufacturer
Acer Incorporated, New Taipei City, Taiwan
In-house design
Web
www.acer.com

The Acer Chromebook Spin 11 was specially designed for the classroom and is equipped with a stylus using Wacom EMR technology. As a convertible unit, it can be used in four different positions and therefore be well adjusted to each learning situation. Additional resources are downloadable as Android apps from the Google Play Store. Due to its rugged construction, the device can be handed around among many users.

Statement by the jury
The Acer Chromebook Spin 11 is predestined for use in schools thanks to its stable construction, the possibility of using it with a stylus and its flexibility as a convertible unit.

Das Acer Chromebook Spin 11 wurde speziell für die Verwendung im Unterricht konzipiert und ist mit einem Stift in Wacom-EMR-Technologie ausgestattet. Als Convertible lässt sich das Gerät in vier unterschiedlichen Stellungen verwenden und somit gut der jeweiligen Lernsituation anpassen. Zusätzliche Ressourcen können als Android-Apps von Google Play Store heruntergeladen werden. Durch die widerstandsfähige Bauart des Geräts ist es möglich, es durch viele Hände gehen zu lassen.

Begründung der Jury
Die stabile Bauweise, die Möglichkeit, auch mit einem Stift zu arbeiten, sowie der flexible Einsatz als Convertible prädestinieren das Acer Chromebook Spin 11 für die Verwendung im Schulbereich.

Acer Chromebook 11 N7

Manufacturer
Acer Incorporated, New Taipei City, Taiwan
In-house design
Web
www.acer.com

Designed as an educational tool, the Acer Chromebook 11 N7 presents numerous features that reflect high stability. The device has been tested by dropping it from a height of 122 cm, it has a splashproof keyboard and it conforms to the standard MIL-STD 810G. A fanless design increases operational reliability and ensures a quiet working environment. Furthermore, the Chromebook can be easily carried around, such as for presentations. The 11.6" display is available with or without an IPS touchscreen.

Statement by the jury
The Acer Chromebook 11 N7 proves to be very sturdy and quiet. It thus fulfils important criteria for efficient use in classrooms.

Als Unterrichtsmittel konzipiert, weist das Acer Chromebook 11 N7 zahlreiche Merkmale für eine hohe Beständigkeit auf. So ist das Gerät auf Fall aus 122 cm getestet, verfügt über eine spritzwassergeschützte Tastatur und entspricht der Norm MIL-STD 810G. Ein lüfterloses Design erhöht die Betriebssicherheit und gewährleistet eine ruhige Arbeitsatmosphäre. Darüber hinaus lässt sich das Chromebook z. B. für Präsentationen einfach umhertragen. Das 11,6"-Display gibt es mit oder ohne IPS-Touchscreen.

Begründung der Jury
Das Acer Chromebook 11 N7 erweist sich als sehr robust und leise. Damit erfüllt es wichtige Kriterien für den effizienten Einsatz im Unterricht.

Acer Switch 3
Two-in-One Notebook
2-in-1-Notebook

Manufacturer
Acer Incorporated, New Taipei City, Taiwan
In-house design
Web
www.acer.com

In work contexts, the Acer Switch 3 is used as a laptop, while for entertainment it is detached to become a tablet. Entries can be made on the 12" display if required by using the accompanying Acer active pen, for which there is a holder at the side. On the screen, a U-shaped kickstand is integrated, which can be opened at an angle of up to 165 degrees, allowing a suitable viewing angle for work or gaming. The sleek, metallic top cover with distinctive edges lends the device a dynamic and vivid impression.

Statement by the jury
The Acer Switch 3 convinces with its versatility. This is demonstrated by the various functions and many intelligent, helpful details.

Für das Arbeiten wird das Acer Switch 3 als Laptop verwendet, für die Unterhaltung wird es auseinandergenommen und zum Tablet. Die Eingabe auf dem 12"-FHD-Display erfolgt auf Wunsch mittels mitgeliefertem Acer Active Pen, für den es eine seitliche Halterung gibt. Der im Bildschirm integrierte u-förmige Kickständer kann auf bis zu 165 Grad geöffnet werden, womit sich der geeignete Blickwinkel für die Arbeit oder zum Spielen finden lässt. Die glatte metallische Abdeckung mit deutlich hervorgehobenen Kanten verleiht dem Gerät eine dynamische und lebhafte Anmutung.

Begründung der Jury
Der Acer Switch 3 überzeugt durch seine Vielseitigkeit. Sie zeigt sich in den verschiedenen Funktionen und in zahlreichen intelligenten, hilfreichen Details.

Acer TravelMate Spin B1
Convertible Notebook

Manufacturer
Acer Incorporated, New Taipei City, Taiwan
In-house design
Web
www.acer.com

Behind the design of the Acer TravelMate Spin B1 is a fundamental didactic idea. The hinge is designed in an innovative way, so that the screen can be rotated by 360 degrees. The device can therefore be used as a laptop, stand, tent or tablet for educational purposes. A special water-drainage system and an impact-resistant frame protect the notebook in case of rough usage, whereby entries are possible by using a pen.

Statement by the jury
The Acer TravelMate Spin B1 proves to be a functionally sophisticated learning tool, which upgrades every modern classroom.

Hinter der Gestaltung des Acer TravelMate Spin B1 steht ein didaktischer Grundgedanke. Das Scharnier ist auf eine innovative Weise gestaltet, sodass sich der Bildschirm in einem 360-Grad-Radius bewegen lässt. Das Gerät kann somit in Form eines Laptops, Aufstellers, Zeltes oder Tablets im Unterricht verwendet werden. Ein spezielles Wasserableitungssystem und ein stoßfester Rahmen schützen das Notebook bei starker Beanspruchung, in das auch die Eingabe mittels Pen möglich ist.

Begründung der Jury
Das Acer TravelMate Spin B1 erweist sich als funktional ausgereifte Unterrichtsausstattung, die jedes moderne Klassenzimmer aufzuwerten weiß.

Kangaroo Notebook

Manufacturer
Kangaroo by Infocus, New Taipei City, Taiwan
In-house design
Chia Jung Liu, Yi Ru Lai
Web
www.kangaroo.cc

With the Kangaroo Notebook and the associated Kangaroo Mini, users receive two independent PCs that share one 11.6" HD screen. This allows, for example, the device to be used as a family PC and a fully fledged work device or at school in different classes. To use the Kangaroo Mini, it is simply plugged into the left side of the dock. It provides 2 GB RAM, 32 GB eMMC of memory and an Intel Z8350 Cherrytrail processor.

Statement by the jury
The Kangaroo Notebook provides a clever solution for several people sharing one notebook for quite different applications.

Mit dem Kangaroo Notebook und dem dazugehörigen Kangaroo Mini erhalten Nutzer zwei unabhängige PCs, die sich einen 11,6"-HD-Bildschirm teilen. Damit lässt sich das Gerät zum Beispiel als Familien-PC und vollwertiges Arbeitsgerät oder an einer Schule in unterschiedlichen Klassen einsetzen. Um das Kangaroo Mini zu verwenden, wird es einfach an der linken Seite des Docks angesteckt. Es bietet 2 GB RAM, 32 GB eMMC-Speicherplatz und einen Intel-Z8350-Cherrytrail-Prozessor.

Begründung der Jury
Das Kangaroo Notebook bietet eine clevere Lösung, wenn sich mehrere Personen ein Notebook für ganz unterschiedliche Anwendungen teilen.

ThinkPad X1 Yoga
Convertible Notebook

Manufacturer
Lenovo, Morrisville, North Carolina, USA
In-house design
Web
www.lenovo.com

The new ThinkPad X1 Yoga is a slim convertible for a modern work environment that requires greater mobility. Thanks to its material properties, it is extremely durable and lightweight at the same time. The device has an innovative, high-quality OLED display, with the 2K touchscreen displaying sharp picture contrast with high colour fidelity. Thanks to the innovative Lift 'n' Lock technology, the notebook can be converted to a tablet which includes a stylus: the keyboard is raised behind the monitor and automatically locked. At the same time, the keyboard frame lifts, so that this side forms a plain back for the tablet that conveniently rests on any surface.

Das neue ThinkPad X1 Yoga ist ein schlankes Convertible für ein modernes Arbeitsumfeld, das nach hoher Mobilität verlangt. Dank seiner Materialeigenschaften ist es äußerst stabil bei gleichzeitig geringem Gewicht. Als Innovation weist das Gerät ein hochwertiges OLED-Display auf, dadurch zeigt der 2K-Touchscreen scharfe Bildkontraste bei hoher Farbtreue. Dank innovativer Lift-'n'-Lock-Technologie lässt es sich einfach vom Notebook zum Tablet, zu dem auch ein Eingabestift gehört, umgestalten: Die Tastatur wird hinter den Bildschirm geklappt und automatisch in ihrer Funktion gesperrt. Zugleich hebt sich der Tastaturrahmen an, sodass diese Ebene eine plane Rückseite des Tablets bildet, die auf jeder Unterlage bequem aufliegt.

Statement by the jury
The ThinkPad X1 Yoga impresses with its innovative Lift 'n' Lock technology, making the conversion from notebook to tablet surprisingly easy to achieve.

Begründung der Jury
Das ThinkPad X1 Yoga beeindruckt mit seiner innovativen Lift-'n'-Lock-Technologie, mit der der Wechsel vom Notebook zum Tablet denkbar einfach gelingt.

ThinkPad T470
Notebook

Manufacturer
Lenovo, Morrisville, North Carolina, USA
In-house design
Web
www.lenovo.com

The ThinkPad T470 is equipped with a high-performance Intel Core i7 processor and thus provides sufficient resources for effortlessly switching between various applications that assist in productivity, creativity or entertainment. The device was tested against military standards and effortlessly withstands the intense stress of a demanding, mobile workday. Thanks to fingerprint recognition, security is ensured without needing a password. Two batteries and Power Bridge technology facilitate a long running time of up to 18 hours. An HD webcam and high-quality microphones with background noise reduction guarantee trouble-free communication.

Das ThinkPad T470 ist mit einem leistungsstarken Intel-Core-i7-Prozessor ausgestattet und verfügt somit über ausreichend Ressourcen, um mühelos zwischen verschiedenen Anwendungen zu switchen, die der Produktivität, der Kreativität oder der Unterhaltung dienen. Das nach Militärstandards getestete Gerät hält hohen Belastungen in einem anspruchsvollen mobilen Arbeitsalltag mühelos stand. Dank Fingerabdruckerkennung ist die Sicherheit ohne Passwort gewährleistet. Zwei Batterien und Power-Bridge-Technologie ermöglichen eine lange Laufzeit von bis zu 18 Stunden. Für störungsfreie Kommunikation sorgen eine HD-Webkamera und hochwertige Mikrofone mit Rauschunterdrückung.

Statement by the jury
The ThinkPad T470 convinces with its high performance and its many well-conceived functions, which impart a sense of impressive versatility.

Begründung der Jury
Das ThinkPad T470 überzeugt mit seiner hohen Leistung und seinen zahlreichen durchdachten Funktionen, die ihm eine beeindruckende Vielseitigkeit verleihen.

ThinkPad X1 Carbon
Notebook

Manufacturer
Lenovo, Morrisville, North Carolina, USA
In-house design
Web
www.lenovo.com

The design of the new ThinkPad X1 Carbon is defined by a slim wedge shape, an extremely narrow bezel and a small footprint. The carbon-fibre-reinforced body with a protective frame of magnesium alloy can withstand extreme conditions. It was tested against twelve military-grade requirements and is splashproof as well as resistant to impact and vibration. Thanks to its materials, the notebook is nevertheless especially lightweight. The classic ThinkPad look with red accents and a black silhouette is retained, in this version, however, with a more refined, modernised expression.

Die Gestaltung des neuen ThinkPad X1 Carbon definiert sich über eine schlanke Keilform, eine äußerst schmale Bildschirmeinfassung sowie eine geringe Stellfläche. Das kohlefaserverstärkte Gehäuse mit einem Schutzrahmen aus Magnesiumlegierung hält extremen Bedingungen stand. Es wurde auf zwölf militärische Spezifikationen getestet und ist spritzwasserfest, hält Stößen und Erschütterungen stand. Dank seines Materials ist das Notebook überdies besonders leicht. Der klassische ThinkPad-Look mit roten Akzenten und schwarzer Silhouette bleibt bestehen, erhält in dieser Version jedoch einen verfeinerten, modernisierten Ausdruck.

Statement by the jury
The new ThinkPad X1 Carbon, thanks to it outstanding material properties, supports any enterprise in an efficient way.

Begründung der Jury
Das neue ThinkPad X1 Carbon unterstützt dank hervorragender Materialeigenschaften jedes Unternehmen auf effiziente Weise.

Asus Pro B9440
Ultrabook

Manufacturer
ASUSTeK Computer Inc., Taipei, Taiwan
In-house design
Web
www.asus.com

With twelve hours of battery life and a weight of less than 1 kg, the Asus Pro B9440 ranks in the ultrabook line for the business sector. A special hinge lifts the keyboard when opening, creating an ergonomic typing angle. An anti-glare screen allows users to work from the laptop more comfortably. With a bezel of 4.3 mm and a 14" screen, the footprint is relatively compact. A fingerprint scanner ensures efficiency and security. Stable magnesium alloys make this ultrabook a reliable and sturdy working tool.

Statement by the jury
The reduced weight, despite high-quality materials, and the slightly angled keyboard make the Asus Pro B9440 an efficient ultrabook in the business sector.

Mit zwölf Stunden Akkulaufzeit und einem Gewicht von unter 1 kg reiht sich das Asus Pro B9440 in die Ultrabook-Linie für den Geschäftsbereich ein. Ein spezielles Scharnier hebt die Tastatur beim Öffnen an, wodurch ein ergonomisch angenehmer Eingabewinkel entsteht. Ein blendfreier Bildschirm unterstützt das bequeme Arbeiten zusätzlich. Mit einem Rahmen von 4,3 mm und einem 14"-Bildschirm fällt die Standfläche relativ gering aus. Ein Fingerabdruckscanner-System sorgt für Effizienz und Sicherheit. Stabile Magnesiumlegierungen machen das Ultrabook zu einem zuverlässigen und belastbaren Arbeitsgerät.

Begründung der Jury
Geringes Gewicht trotz hochwertiger Materialien sowie die leicht angewinkelte Tastatur machen das Asus Pro B9440 zu einem effizienten Ultrabook im Geschäftsbereich.

HP EliteBook x360
Convertible Notebook

Manufacturer
HP Inc., Palo Alto, USA
In-house design
HP Inc. PS Industrial Design Team
Design
Native Design, London, Great Britain
Web
www.hp.com
www.native.com

A CNC-manufactured aluminium chassis, polished hinge surfaces with engraved logo and a moulded slot antenna along the top edge of the screen make the HP EliteBook x360 a business convertible with a premium appearance. The keyboard is bowl-shaped, embedded in the case and, together with the smooth glass clickpad, engenders an elegant impression. Thanks to its discreet, silver-coloured surface, the device blends well with any environment.

Statement by the jury
With its elegant design, the HP EliteBook x360 provides skilful aesthetics combined with a high level of functionality.

Ein CNC-gefertigtes Aluminiumgehäuse, polierte Scharnierflächen mit eingraviertem Logo sowie ein in die obere Kante des Bildschirms eingebetteter Antennenstreifen machen das HP EliteBook x360 zu einem Businessconvertible mit edler Ausstrahlung. Die Tastatur ist schalenförmig in das Gehäuse eingelassen und erzeugt zusammen mit dem geschmeidigen Glas-Clickpad eine elegante Anmutung. Dank seiner dezenten silberfarbenen Oberfläche fügt sich das Gerät gut in jede Umgebung ein.

Begründung der Jury
In seiner anmutigen Gestaltung beweist das HP EliteBook x360 gekonnte Ästhetik, die überzeugend mit hoher Funktionalität verbunden ist.

HP Envy 13
Notebook

Manufacturer
HP Inc., Palo Alto, USA
In-house design
HP Inc. PS Industrial Design Team
Design
Native Design, London, Great Britain
Web
www.hp.com
www.native.com

A slim silhouette, a scratch-resistant edge-to-edge screen, an all-metal chassis and a special technology that distinguishes the notebook when it is opened: these are the primary design characteristics of the HP Envy 13. Precisely engineered hinges position the keyboard at an ergonomically pleasant working angle, which also ensures improved air circulation. An IPS display and a sound system by Bang & Olufsen facilitate an impressive film experience. The battery runs up to 14 hours.

Statement by the jury
With its impressive quality of picture and sound, along with premium aesthetics, the HP Envy 13 is an eye-catcher in any environment.

Eine schlanke Silhouette, ein kratzresistenter rahmenloser Bildschirm, ein Vollmetallgehäuse und eine spezielle Technologie, die das Notebook beim Öffnen anhebt: Das sind die primären Gestaltungselemente des HP Envy 13. Präzise gearbeitete Scharniere positionieren die Tastatur in einem ergonomisch angenehmen Arbeitswinkel, was auch für eine bessere Luftzirkulation sorgt. Ein IPS-Display und ein Soundsystem von Bang & Olufsen sorgen für ein eindrucksvolles Filmerlebnis. Die Akkulaufzeit beträgt bis zu 14 Stunden.

Begründung der Jury
Mit einer beeindruckenden Bild- und Klangqualität und einer hochwertigen Ästhetik zieht das HP Envy 13 in jeder Umgebung anerkennende Blicke auf sich.

LG Gram
Ultrabook

Manufacturer
LG Electronics Inc., Seoul, South Korea
In-house design
Heechang Lee, Taejin Lee
Web
www.lg.com

This 13.3" ultrabook weighs only 980 grams, much lighter than traditional notebooks with a generous screen, thus allowing it to be comfortably carried around. An aesthetically discreet yet functionally efficient backlit keyboard makes work in the dark easy. When fully charged, the device achieves a working time of up to 21 hours without requiring a power adaptor.

Statement by the jury
The LG Gram ultrabook displays highly efficient functionality, especially considering the low weight of less than 1 kg and the long-running battery time.

Dieses 13,3"-Ultrabook wiegt gerade einmal 980 Gramm. Viel leichter als traditionelle Notebooks mit großem Bildschirm kann dieses Gerät also bequem mitgenommen werden. Eine ästhetisch dezente, jedoch funktional effiziente hinterleuchtete Tastatur erleichtert das Arbeiten bei Dunkelheit. In voll aufgeladenem Zustand schafft das Gerät eine Arbeitszeit von bis zu 21 Stunden, ohne es an einen Netzadapter anschließen zu müssen.

Begründung der Jury
Besonders durch das geringe Gewicht von nicht einmal 1 kg und die lange Akkulaufzeit beweist das Ultrabook LG Gram hocheffiziente Funktionalität.

Dell Latitude 2-in-1
Two-in-One Notebook

Manufacturer
Dell Inc., Round Rock, Texas, USA
In-house design
Experience Design Group
Web
www.dell.com

The slim and light Dell Latitude 2-in-1 presents a high-resolution display and an innovative, wirelessly charging keyboard. In combination with the Dell Wireless Charging Mat and the similarly wireless WiGig Docking Station, users can easily carry the device with them, without the need to disconnect cables or docking stations. It is simply laid on the mat of the nearest desk, where charging and connectivity with the WiGig dock start automatically. The Dell Active Pen, a stylus with three functions, is attached to the notebook with magnets.

Statement by the jury
The Dell Latitude 2-in-1 impresses with well-conceived peripheral products, which efficiently support mobile users in everyday life.

Das dünne und leichte Dell Latitude 2-in-1 verfügt über ein hochauflösendes Display und ein innovatives kabellos aufladbares Keyboard. In Kombination mit der kabellosen Dell Lademattte und der ebenfalls kabellosen WiGig Docking Station können Benutzer das Gerät einfach mitnehmen, ohne es von Kabeln oder Docks abkoppeln zu müssen. Auf dem nächsten Schreibtisch wird es wieder auf die Lademattte gelegt, Ladevorgang und Verbindung mit dem WiGig-Dock starten automatisch. Der Dell Active Pen, ein Stylus mit drei Funktionstasten, haftet magnetisch an dem Notebook.

Begründung der Jury
Das Dell Latitude 2-in-1 beeindruckt mit seiner durchdachten Produktperipherie, die mobile Benutzer in ihrem Alltag effizient unterstützt.

Samsung Odyssey
Gaming Notebook

Manufacturer
Samsung Electronics, London, Great Britain
In-house design
Samsung Design Europe (Jusuek Lee, Hyuntaik Lim)
Web
www.samsung.com
www.design.samsung.com

The Samsung Odyssey is a gaming notebook with a design that appears outwardly subtle and elegant; internally, however, the device is packed full of sophisticated functions. It is suitable for various gamer types, whether they play very intensively and often or only occasionally. The corporately developed HexaFlow cooling system keeps the notebook at the right temperature. It is located at the bottom of the device and is easily removed to ensure quick access when upgrading hard drives or working memory.

Statement by the jury
With the Samsung Odyssey, the combination of a functionally true gaming notebook and an elegant visual presentation is successfully achieved.

Mit dem Samsung Odyssey wurde ein Gaming-Notebook konzipiert, das äußerlich subtil und elegant wirkt, im Inneren jedoch vollgepackt ist mit ausgefeilten Funktionen. Das Gerät ist für unterschiedliche Spielertypen geeignet, ob diese nun sehr intensiv und häufig spielen oder nur gelegentlich. Das eigens entwickelte Kühlsystem HexaFlow hält das Notebook auf Temperatur. Es liegt an der Unterseite des Geräts und lässt sich herausnehmen, um den einfachen Zugriff zum Aufstocken von Festplatten- oder Arbeitsspeicher zu gewährleisten.

Begründung der Jury
Dem Samsung Odyssey gelingt die Kombination aus einem funktional veritablen Gaming-Notebook und einem eleganten optischen Auftritt.

Predator 21 X
Gaming Notebook

Manufacturer
Acer Incorporated, New Taipei City, Taiwan
In-house design
Web
www.acer.com

The Predator 21 X Gaming Notebook presents a 21" curved display as innovative feature. Particularly in combination with the integrated Tobii eye-tracking technology, an intensively immersive gaming experience is possible. The device also incorporates a powerful Intel Core CPU of the 7th generation, among other features. Up to four 512 GB SSDs in RAID 0 configuration and a 1 TB hard drive with 7,200 rpm ensure ample memory capacity. The housing is made of deep-black, high-quality solid aluminium.

Statement by the jury
Convincingly powerful functionality, impressive imaging technology and high-quality engineering catapult the Predator 21 X into the premium segment.

Das Gaming Notebook Predator 21 X umfasst als innovative Ausstattung ein 21"-Curved-Display. Besonders in Kombination mit der integrierten Tobii-Eye-Tracking-Technologie wird so ein intensiv immersiv wirkendes Spielerlebnis möglich. Weiterhin verfügt das Gerät unter anderem über einen leistungsstarken Intel-Core-Prozessor der siebten Generation. Bis zu vier 512 GB große SSDs in RAID-0-Konfiguration und eine 1 TB große Festplatte mit 7.200 Umdrehungen/Min. sorgen für großzügigen Speicherplatz. Das Gehäuse besteht aus tiefschwarzem hochwertigem Vollaluminium.

Begründung der Jury
Überzeugend leistungsstarke Funktionen, beeindruckende bildgebende Technologie sowie eine hochwertige Verarbeitung katapultieren den Predator 21 X ins Premiumsegment.

ASUS ROG GX501
Gaming Notebook

Manufacturer
ASUSTeK Computer Inc., Taipei, Taiwan
In-house design
Web
www.asus.com

With its minimised thickness of 16.5 mm and reduced weight, the Asus ROG GX501 can be easily taken anywhere. When opened, a hinge system enlarges the special cooling module. The device has a solid metal chassis with a composition including magnalium to enhance both its appearance and functionality. The surface with the variously running hairline pattern is clearly split by a transverse line. The copper-coloured edges are applied to the aerolite-hued surface in a two-phase anodising process.

Statement by the jury
The Asus ROG GX501, with its high-performance cooling system, makes the gaming experience possible anytime and anywhere. Furthermore, the concise look is enthralling.

Mit seiner geringen Dicke von 16,5 mm und leichtem Gewicht kann das Asus ROG GX501 gut überallhin mitgenommen werden. Im geöffneten Zustand vergrößert ein Scharniersystem das spezielle Kühlmodul. Das Gerät verfügt über ein Vollmetallgehäuse mit einem Anteil Magnalium, um Aussehen wie auch Funktionalität zu verstärken. Die Oberfläche im unterschiedlich verlaufenden Haarlinien-Muster ist klar durch eine schräge Linie getrennt. In einem zweiphasigen Anodisierungsverfahren wurden die kupferfarbenen Kanten an der aerolitfarbenen Oberfläche aufgebracht.

Begründung der Jury
Das Asus ROG GX501 mit seinem leistungsstarken Kühlsystem macht Spielerlebnisse zu jeder Zeit an jedem Ort möglich und auch der prägnante Look begeistert.

ASUS ROG STRIX
GL502/702 Series
Gaming Notebooks

Manufacturer
ASUSTeK Computer Inc., Taipei, Taiwan
In-house design
Web
www.asus.com

The design of this series is extremely slim and light, providing proof that gaming notebooks must not be heavy and bulky. The V-shaped cooling system integrated into the A-part ensures very good temperature stability, allowing the device to be used intensively for extended periods without problems. The colourfully highlighted WASD keys additionally provide orientation for gamers. The grooved surface lends the series an exciting sense of aesthetics.

Statement by the jury
The slim design in combination with the structured surface lends the gaming notebooks of this series an appearance that is both impressing and elegant.

Diese Serie zeigt eine schlanke und äußerst leichte Gestaltung, mit der sie den Beweis antritt, dass Gaming-Notebooks nicht schwer und klobig sein müssen. Ein im A-Teil integriertes v-förmiges Kühlungssystem sorgt für sehr gute Temperaturstabilität, sodass ein Gerät auch bei langer und intensiver Nutzung problemlos verwendet werden kann. Zusätzlich unterstützen die farblich hervorgehobenen WASD-Tasten die Spieler bei der Orientierung. Die gerillte Oberfläche verleiht der Serie eine aufregende Ästhetik.

Begründung der Jury
Das schlanke Design in Verbindung mit der strukturierten Oberfläche verschafft den Gaming Notebooks dieser Serie ein beeindruckendes wie auch elegantes Auftreten.

Wacom Cintiq Pro 13
Creative Pen Display
Kreatives Stift-Display

Manufacturer
Wacom Co. Ltd., Tokyo, Japan
Design
dingfest | design (Volker Hübner), Erkrath, Germany
Web
www.wacom.com
www.dingfest.de

The 13,3"-LCD display of the Wacom Cintiq Pro 13 offers full HD resolution. With a very wide colour range of 87 per cent of the Adobe RGB selection, an almost true-colour representation is possible. The associated Wacom Pro Pen 2 has pronounced pressure sensitivity and works precisely without lag. Integrated supports at the back of the display position it at a pleasant angle. Simple gesture control facilitates the pivoting, zooming or rotating of the drawing.

Statement by the jury
The high standard of functionality evident in the interplay between the Wacom Cintiq Pro 13 and the Wacom Pro Pen 2 clearly results in a working tool for professional artists and designers.

Das 13,3"-LCD-Display des Wacom Cintiq Pro 13 bietet eine Full-HD-Auflösung. Mit einer sehr weiten Farbskala von 87 Prozent der Adobe-RGB-Palette wird eine nahezu farbgetreue Darstellung möglich. Der dazugehörige Wacom Pro Pen 2 hat eine ausgeprägte Druckempfindlichkeit und arbeitet präzise ohne Übertragungsverzögerung. Integrierte Stützen an der Rückseite des Displays positionieren dieses in einem angenehmen Winkel. Eine einfache Gestensteuerung ermöglicht Schwenken, Zoomen oder Rotieren des Gezeichneten.

Begründung der Jury
Die hochwertige Funktionsweise im Zusammenspiel von Wacom Cintiq Pro 13 und Wacom Pro Pen 2 ergibt eindeutig ein Arbeitsgerät für professionelle Künstler und Gestalter.

Wacom Intuos Pro Paper Edition
Creative Pen Tablet
Kreatives Stifttablett

Manufacturer
Wacom Co. Ltd., Tokyo, Japan
In-house design
Mitchell Giles, Novi Rahman
Web
www.wacom.com

The Wacom Intuos Pro Paper Edition, which is only 8 mm thick, processes data like a modern graphics tablet, with the difference, however, that it is possible to write on normal paper. This is attached to a fastening strip above the tablet, available in two sizes for A5 and A4. While or after the drawing is being consigned to paper with the special finetip pen or ballpoint pen, it is synchronised via USB or Bluetooth with the special Inkspace app on the computer and can be further processed via conventional creative formats.

Statement by the jury
Wacom Intuos Pro Paper Edition impressively succeeds in bridging the gap between traditionally creative work on paper and the convenience of digital image processing.

Das nur 8 mm dicke Wacom Intuos Pro Paper Edition verarbeitet Dateien wie ein modernes Grafiktablett, jedoch mit dem Unterschied, dass auf normalem Papier gezeichnet werden kann. Dieses wird mittels Klemmleiste über dem Tablett befestigt, welche es in zwei Größen für A5 und A4 gibt. Während oder nachdem die Zeichnung mit dem speziellen Finetip Pen oder einem Ballpoint Pen auf Papier gebracht wurde, wird sie über USB oder Bluetooth mit der speziellen Inkspace-App auf dem Computer synchronisiert und kann mit den üblichen Creative-Formaten weiterbearbeitet werden.

Begründung der Jury
Dem Wacom Intuos Pro Paper Edition gelingt in beeindruckender Weise der Brückenschlag zwischen der traditionellen kreativen Arbeit auf Papier und dem Komfort digitaler Bildbearbeitung.

DTK-1651
Pen Display
Stift-Display

Manufacturer
Wacom Co. Ltd., Tokyo, Japan
In-house design
Naoya Nishizawa
Web
www.wacom.com

The DTK-1651 is a pen display which makes it possible for users to authorise and edit digital documents easily. The sleek design and the 3-in-1 cable assure an orderly appearance. On the 15.6" full HD LCD display, A4 documents or letters can be rendered in portrait or landscape alignment without size reduction or scrolling, either lying flat on the desk or standing vertically with the 15-degree stand. The magnetic pen holder and the pen compartment ensure convenient operation. Thanks to modern encryption, transactions are secure.

Statement by the jury
The sleek DTK-1651 pen display impresses with its generously dimensioned screen, which allows for convenient processing of large-format documents.

Das DTK-1651 ist ein Stift-Display und ermöglicht Anwendern, digitale Dokumente einfach zu autorisieren und zu bearbeiten. Das schlanke Design und das 3-in-1-Kabel sorgen für ein geordnetes Erscheinungsbild. Auf dem 15,6"-Full-HD LCD Display lassen sich A4- oder Letter-Dokumente ohne Verkleinerung oder Scrollen im Hoch- oder Querformat anzeigen, flach auf dem Tisch liegend oder mit dem integrierten 15-Grad-Standfuß in aufrechtstehendem Zustand. Der magnetische Stifthalter und das Stiftfach sorgen für eine komfortable Bedienung. Dank moderner Verschlüsselung gelingt eine sichere Transaktion.

Begründung der Jury
Das schlanke DTK-1651 Stift-Display beeindruckt mit seinem großzügigen Bildschirm, durch den auch größere Dokumente bequem bearbeitet werden können.

Bamboo Duo
Stylus for Touchscreens and Paper
Stylus für Touchscreens und Papier

Manufacturer
Wacom Co. Ltd., Tokyo, Japan
Design
Human Spark (Scott Lehman),
Roswell, USA
Web
www.wacom.com
www.humanspark.com

The Bamboo Duo is a two-in-one stylus. A carbon-fibre tip facilitates smooth navigation, writing and drawing on touchscreens. The black ballpoint pen at the other end is suitable for writing on paper. Both elements are interchangeable. The ergonomic triangular design and the soft-touch surface assure that the stylus is well balanced and rests comfortably in the hand. The housing is made of aluminium, has a soft finish and is available in four fashionable colours. The Bamboo Duo is compatible with touch devices based on iOS, Android or Windows.

Statement by the jury
The Bamboo Duo impresses with its innovative two-in-one solution, thanks to which ideas can be reproduced both analogue and digitally.

Der Bamboo Duo ist ein 2-in-1-Stylus. Eine Carbonfaser-Spitze an einem Ende ermöglicht geschmeidiges Navigieren, Schreiben und Zeichnen auf Touchscreens. Mit der schwarzen Kugelschreibermine am anderen Ende kann man auf Papier schreiben. Beide Elemente sind austauschbar. Das ergonomische dreieckige Design und die Soft-Touch-Oberfläche sorgen dafür, dass der Stylus gut ausbalanciert und komfortabel in der Hand liegt. Das Gehäuse aus Aluminium mit sanftem Finish ist in vier modischen Farben erhältlich. Der Bamboo Duo ist kompatibel mit Touch-Geräten auf iOS-, Android- oder Windows-Basis.

Begründung der Jury
Der Bamboo Duo besticht durch seine innovative 2-in1-Lösung, dank der sich kreative Ideen digital wie auch analog festhalten lassen.

STU-540
Signature Pad
Unterschriftenpad

Manufacturer
Wacom Co. Ltd., Tokyo, Japan
In-house design
Mitchell Giles
Web
www.wacom.com

The STU-540 signature pad offers institutes like banks, retail outlets or hospitals strong security when it comes to electronically generated handwritten signatures. The device provides a wide range of connectivity options, including virtual desktop environments. The light pad with its small footprint has a high-resolution 5" colour LCD screen. The tempered, non-reflective glass surface imparts a good feeling when writing. The light pen requires no battery and records 1,024 pen pressure levels.

Statement by the jury
A signature pad should offer security and pleasant use – the STU-540 fulfils both criteria with flying colours.

Das STU-540 Unterschriftenpad bietet Institutionen wie Banken, dem Einzelhandel oder Krankenhäusern hohe Sicherheit bei der elektronischen Erfassung handschriftlicher Signaturen. Das Gerät bietet eine breite Palette von Anschlussmöglichkeiten einschließlich virtueller Desktopumgebungen. Das leichte Pad mit geringer Stellfläche hat einen hochauflösenden 5"-Farb-LCD-Bildschirm. Die gehärtete, entspiegelte Glasoberfläche verleiht ein gutes Schreibgefühl. Der leichte, batterielose Stift erfasst 1.024 Druckstufen.

Begründung der Jury
Ein Unterschriftenpad soll Sicherheit und eine angenehme Handhabung bieten – beide Kriterien erfüllt das STU-540 mit Bravour.

Logitech K780
Multi-Device Wireless Keyboard
Kabellose Multi-Device-Tastatur

Manufacturer
Logitech, Newark,
California, USA

In-house design
Logitech,
Lausanne, Switzerland

Design
Feiz Design (Khodi Feiz),
Amsterdam, Netherlands

Web
www.logitech.com
www.feizdesign.com

reddot award 2017
best of the best

Mediator of communication

The keyboard has evolved steadily in parallel with the computer in both its form and functionality. For the human being, it is a mediator of communication. The Logitech K780 multi-device wireless keyboard captivates with an innovative design concept that allows users to type on computers, tablets and smartphones. The circular keys are large and scooped for typing comfort and precision. A functionally well-designed numeric key block facilitates easy input of numbers. The keyboard can connect with up to three devices and features an Easy-Switch button for quickly switching between the connected devices, embracing the rising trend of multitasking across devices. An integrated rubber slot with a soft finish securely cradles a variety of differently sized mobile devices at a perfect reading angle, from smartphones to the 12.9" iPad Pro. With its balanced language of form, the K780 keyboard blends very well into both private environments as well as modern office environments. As a successful reinterpretation of a wireless keyboard, it responds to the zeitgeist and provides the user with a new way of interacting with their smart devices.

Mittler der Kommunikation

Die Tastatur hat sich in ihrer Form und Funktionalität parallel zum Computer stetig weiterentwickelt, für den Menschen ist sie der Mittler der Kommunikation. Die kabellose Multi-Device-Tastatur K780 von Logitech begeistert mit einem innovativen Gestaltungskonzept und ist gleichermaßen für Computer, Smartphones und Tablets geeignet. Die Tasten sind groß und leicht konkav für ein komfortables und präzises Tippen. Ein funktional durchdachter Ziffernblock erleichtert die Eingabe von Zahlen. Die Tastatur kann mit bis zu drei Geräten verbunden werden, wobei eine Easy-Switch-Taste einen raschen Wechsel zwischen den verbundenen Geräten erlaubt und so dem aktuellen Trend hin zum Multitasking folgt. Ein integrierter Gummischlitz mit weicher Oberfläche bietet den unterschiedlich dimensionierten Geräten, vom Smartphone bis hin zu einem 12,9" großen iPad Pro, sicheren Halt in einem perfekten Lesewinkel. Mit ihrer ausgewogenen Formensprache fügt sich die Tastatur K780 überaus gut in das private Umfeld ebenso wie in eine moderne Büroumgebung ein. Als gelungene Neuinterpretation einer kabellosen Tastatur folgt sie dem Zeitgeist und bietet dem Nutzer eine neue Art von Interaktion mit seinen Endgeräten.

Statement by the jury

The Logitech K780 keyboard embodies an entirely new version of a cordless keyboard. It is also highly convenient for use with smartphones and tablets – allowing connecting of up to three devices at the same time. The design of its numeric key block and the graphical implementation of the key lettering are impressively well solved. In addition, the keys are pleasantly large and very quiet when typing. All the elements of this keyboard merge to form an artistically attractive unity.

Begründung der Jury

Die Tastatur Logitech K780 verkörpert eine gänzlich neue Version einer kabellosen Tastatur. Überaus komfortabel lässt sie sich auch für Smartphones und Tablets verwenden – sie kann mit bis zu drei Geräten gleichzeitig verbunden werden. Bestechend gut gelöst sind die Gestaltung ihres Zahlenblocks und die grafische Umsetzung der Tastenbeschriftung, zudem sind die Tasten angenehm groß und sehr leise im Anschlag. Sämtliche Elemente dieser Tastatur fügen sich zu einer künstlerisch anmutenden Einheit zusammen.

Designer portrait
See page 72
Siehe Seite 72

349

MasterKeys Lite L Combo
Gaming Keyboard and Mouse
Gaming-Tastatur und Maus

Manufacturer
Cooler Master Technology Inc., New Taipei City, Taiwan
In-house design
Web
www.coolermaster.com

By means of illuminated RGB colour zones, the keyboard of the MasterKeys Lite L Combo can be set to any individual colour the user wishes. The special Mem-chanical keys are characterised by durability and ensure clearly felt tactile feedback when typing, whereby the keyboard feels almost like a mechanical device. Furthermore, the keyboard is splashproof. The mouse has two RGB light zones to choose from. It also includes two thumb buttons and a Teflon-coated underside, allowing for use on very different surfaces.

Mit den beleuchteten RGB-Farbzonen lässt sich die Tastatur des MasterKeys Lite L Combo gemäß den individuellen Farbton-Wünschen des Nutzers anpassen. Die speziellen Mem-chanical-Tasten zeichnen sich durch Dauerhaftigkeit aus und sorgen für ein deutlich spürbares taktiles Feedback beim Tippen, wodurch sich die Tastatur fast wie ein mechanisches Gerät anfühlt. Zudem ist die Tastatur spritzwassergeschützt. Bei der Maus stehen zwei RGB-Lichtzonen zur Auswahl. Außerdem verfügt sie u. a. über zwei Daumentasten sowie eine teflonbeschichtete Unterseite, mit der sie auf sehr unterschiedlichen Unterlagen benutzt werden kann.

Statement by the jury
The ingenious formal construction of the Mem-chanical keys of the MasterKeys Lite L Combo facilitates an impressive feel while gaming.

Begründung der Jury
Der ausgeklügelte formale Aufbau der Mem-chanical-Tasten beim MasterKeys Lite L Combo sorgt für eine eindrucksvolle Haptik während des Spielens.

HP Premium Keyboard and Mouse
Tastatur und Maus

Manufacturer
HP Inc., Palo Alto, USA
In-house design
HP Inc. PS Industrial Design Team
Design
Native Design, London, Great Britain
Web
www.hp.com
www.native.com

The HP Premium Keyboard is made of forged aluminium with an anodised finish. It is thus very stable and facilitates precise typing. To make entries convenient, great attention has been paid to key size, spacing and pleasant feedback characteristics. The long-lasting battery has a very flat design. It enables a gentle, elevated angle for the keyboard, relieving the wrist. The accompanying mouse has a seamlessly designed back and is easy to navigate.

Statement by the jury
This ensemble of keyboard and mouse convinces with its ergonomically sophisticated construction of high-quality materials.

Das HP Premium Keyboard besteht aus gehämmertem Aluminium mit eloxiertem Finish. Dadurch ist es sehr stabil und ermöglicht präzises Tippen. Für eine komfortable Eingabe wurde großes Augenmerk auf Tastengröße, Abstände und ein angenehmes Eingabefeedback gelegt. Die dauerhafte Batterie ist sehr flach gestaltet. Sie ermöglicht einen sanften Anstiegswinkel in der Tastatur, die das Handgelenk entlastet. Die dazugehörige Maus hat einen nahtlos gestalteten Rücken und lässt sich bequem führen.

Begründung der Jury
Dieses Ensemble aus Tastatur und Maus überzeugt durch seine ergonomisch ausgereifte Konstruktionsweise aus hochwertigen Materialien.

Logitech G 810 Orion Spectrum
Gaming Keyboard
Gaming-Tastatur

Manufacturer
Logitech, Newark, California, USA
In-house design
Design
Design Partners, Bray, Ireland
Web
www.logitech.com
www.designpartners.com

The actuation speed of the special Romer-G mechanical switches of this gaming keyboard is greater than that of standard mechanical keyboards. These and other elements are precisely engineered – from the matte surface texture, the fingerprint masking and the sturdy, braided cable to the RGB lighting, which can be personalised. By means of the Logitech Gaming software, the individual keyboard lights may be selected from a spectrum of 16.8 million colours and can synchronise lighting effects with other Logitech G devices.

Statement by the jury
The highly efficient engineering of the Logitech G 810 Orion Spectrum facilitates almost immediate responses during challenging gaming sessions.

Die Auslösegeschwindigkeit der speziellen mechanischen Romer-G Switches dieser Gaming-Tastatur ist höher als jene bei mechanischen Standardtastaturen. Diese und weitere Elemente sind präzise gefertigt – von der matten Oberflächentextur über die Fingerabdruck-Maskierung bis hin zum robust ummantelten Kabel oder der personalisierbaren RGB-Beleuchtung. Mithilfe der Logitech Gaming Software lassen sich die einzelnen Tastaturlichter aus einem Spektrum von bis zu 16,8 Millionen Farben auswählen und Lichteffekte mit anderen Logitech-G-Geräten synchronisieren.

Begründung der Jury
Die hocheffiziente Ausarbeitung des Logitech G 810 Orion Spectrum ermöglicht nahezu augenblickliche Reaktion bei herausfordernden Gaming-Sessions.

Smart Commander
Decoding Network Keyboard
Steuerung für Videoüberwachungssysteme

Manufacturer
Zhejiang Dahua Technology Co., Ltd., Hangzhou, China
In-house design
Yahui Liu, Li Chen
Web
www.dahuatech.com

The Smart Commander has a particularly sleek design. Numerous man-machine simulation tests have resulted in a design with a high degree of user-friendliness. Touchscreen and keyboard can be detached from each other, and the angle of the device supports an ergonomically natural arm position. The unit furthermore offers a liquid crystal display and 4K HDMI output, while also supporting Wi-Fi and Bluetooth connectivity.

Statement by the jury
The sleek design of the Smart Commander is aesthetically impressive, which is also reflected by its well-conceived ergonomic design.

Der Smart Commander ist besonders schlank gestaltet. Eine Vielzahl an Mensch-Maschine-Simulationstests ermöglichte eine Gestaltung unter dem Aspekt hoher Nutzerfreundlichkeit. Touchscreen und Tastatur lassen sich voneinander trennen und die Neigung des Geräts unterstützt eine ergonomisch natürliche Armhaltung. Das Gerät bietet darüber hinaus eine Flüssigkristallanzeige sowie einen 4K-HDMI-Ausgang und unterstützt Wi-Fi- und Bluetooth-Verbindungen.

Begründung der Jury
Durch sein schlankes Design weiß der Smart Commander ästhetisch zu beeindrucken, zugleich beweist sich darin seine ergonomisch durchdachte Gestaltung.

HyperX Pulsefire FPS
Gaming Mouse
Gaming-Maus

Manufacturer
Kingston Technology, HyperX, Fountain Valley, USA
In-house design
Web
www.kingston.com
www.hyperxgaming.com

Comfort was the focus when designing the HyperX Pulsefire FPS gaming mouse. For this reason, it is especially light and ergonomically well adapted, avoiding weariness even when gaming for long periods. The mouse fits comfortably in the hand, and the lateral soft-touch texture has a pleasant feel and ensures the desired grip, whether the mouse is held with a more relaxed or a tighter grip. Large and sturdy skates on the bottom are conceived for heavy use.

Statement by the jury
Thanks to ergonomically ingenious details, with the HyperX Pulsefire FPS users are equipped for all situations during intensive gaming.

Komfort stand im Fokus bei der Gestaltung der Gaming-Maus HyperX Pulsefire FPS. Aus diesem Grund ist sie besonders leicht und ergonomisch gut angepasst, sodass der Nutzer auch bei ausdauerndem Spielen nicht ermüdet. Die Maus passt bequem in eine Hand, die Soft-Touch-Textur an den Seiten ist haptisch angenehm und sorgt für den gewünschten Grip, ob die Maus nun eher entspannt oder mit festem Griff gehalten wird. Große und robuste Kufen an der Unterseite sind für hohe Beanspruchung konzipiert.

Begründung der Jury
Dank der ergonomisch ausgeklügelten Details sind Gamer mit der HyperX Pulsefire FPS für alle Situationen eines intensiven Spiels gerüstet.

M720 Triathlon Mouse
Wireless Mouse
Kabellose Maus

Manufacturer
Logitech, Newark, California, USA
Design
Design Partners, Bray, Ireland
Web
www.logitech.com
www.designpartners.com

The M720 Triathlon Mouse was conceived to facilitate working without complications across multiple screens and operating systems (Windows, Mac OS, Chrome OS, Android and Linux). The mouse pairs with up to three devices simultaneously and allows easy switching between them at the touch of a button. Due to its form and rubberised surface, it rests gently in the hand. The robust design is able to cope with ten million clicks. Using Logitech Options software, user-defined commands and mouse gestures can be assigned to each button.

Statement by the jury
The M720 Triathlon Mouse proves to be a functionally impressive and efficient tool in challenging work situations.

Die M720 Triathlon Mouse wurde entworfen, um unkompliziert auf mehreren Bildschirmen und Betriebssystemen (Windows, Mac OS, Chrome OS, Android und Linux) arbeiten zu können. Die Maus lässt sich mit bis zu drei Geräten gleichzeitig koppeln und ermöglicht mit nur einem Tastendruck einen einfachen Wechsel zwischen diesen. Durch ihre Form und eine gummierte Oberfläche liegt sie weich in der Hand. Das strapazierfähige Design ist für bis zu zehn Millionen Klicks ausgelegt. Mittels Logitech Options kann jede Taste mit benutzerdefinierten Befehlen und Mausgesten belegt werden.

Begründung der Jury
Die M720 Triathlon Mouse beweist sich als funktional beeindruckendes und effizientes Instrument in herausfordernden Arbeitssituationen.

Party Collection
Wireless Mouse Collection
Kabellose Maus-Kollektion

Manufacturer
Logitech, Newark, California, USA
In-house design
Web
www.logitech.com

Inspired by the Memphis design of the 1980s, with its bright, contrasting colours and graphics, the Party Collection offers a colourful mix of watermelon, flamingos, popsicles and patterns. In terms of form, this mouse collection is well suited to ergonomic hand motions at the desk. The scroll wheels allow smooth and easy navigation. With the nano USB receiver, wireless roaming of up to ten metres is possible.

Statement by the jury
The wild patterns and motifs of the Party Collection enliven the atmosphere and are able to skilfully pep up any computer workstation.

Inspiriert vom Memphis-Design der 1980er-Jahre mit seinen hellen, kontrastierenden Farben und Grafiken, bietet die Party Collection einen bunten Mix an Wassermelonen, Flamingos, Eis am Stiel und Mustern. In ihrer Formgebung sind die Mäuse gut der ergonomischen Handbewegung am Schreibtisch angepasst. Die Scrollräder ermöglichen ein weiches und einfaches Navigieren. Mittels Nano-USB-Empfänger ist eine kabellose Übertragung aus bis zu zehn Metern möglich.

Begründung der Jury
Die wilden Muster und Motive der Party Collection verbreiten gute Laune und wissen jeden Computerarbeitsplatz gekonnt aufzupeppen.

Think Wireless Mouse
Kabellose Maus

Manufacturer
Lenovo, Morrisville, North Carolina, USA
In-house design
Web
www.lenovo.com

When developing the Think Wireless Mouse, the main focus was placed on user-friendliness. The mouse can be held comfortably in the left or right hand and provides wireless 2.4 GHz technology. Two AA batteries are sufficient to last for up to six months of constant use. The batteries are located under the top cover, which is easily opened and closed thanks to a magnetic mechanism. This saves the user from having to fumble awkwardly with the bottom of the mouse. A wireless dongle can be inserted into the battery chamber in case of need when out and about.

Bei der Entwicklung der Think Wireless Mouse stand die Nutzerfreundlichkeit im Mittelpunkt. Die Maus kann mit der linken sowie mit der rechten Hand bequem gehalten werden und bietet eine kabellose 2,4-GHz-Technologie. Zwei AA-Batterien reichen für eine permanente Laufzeit von bis zu sechs Monaten. Die Batterien befinden sich unter einem Deckel an der Oberseite, der mithilfe eines Magnetmechanismus einfach geöffnet und geschlossen wird. Dadurch bleibt dem Nutzer umständliches Hantieren mit dem Bodenteil der Maus erspart. In dem Batteriefach lässt sich auch ein Mini-USB-Empfänger einstecken, etwa um diesen unterwegs sicher zu verwahren.

Statement by the jury
The user-friendly Think Wireless Mouse with its sophisticated details enormously helps to meet the challenges of a modern workday.

Begründung der Jury
Die nutzerfreundliche Think Wireless Mouse mit ihren raffinierten Details unterstützt enorm dabei, die Herausforderungen eines modernen Arbeitsalltags zu bewältigen.

Logitech G Prodigy Series
PC Gaming Mouse, Keyboard and Headset
Gaming-Maus, -Tastatur und Headset für PC

Manufacturer
Logitech, Newark, California, USA
In-house design
Design
Design Partners, Bray, Ireland
Web
www.logitech.com
www.designpartners.com

The Logitech G Prodigy Series consists of two mice, a keyboard and a headset. Both mice offer long-lasting comfort, are up to eight times faster than a standard mouse and include a particularly advanced gaming mouse sensor. The spill-resistant keyboard has five personalisable RGB lighting zones, with a spectrum of up to 16.8 million colours. The headset, with its slim earcups made of washable performance material, offer hours of comfortable wear and provide high-quality stereo sound.

Die Logitech G Prodigy Series umfasst zwei Mäuse, eine Tastatur und ein Headset. Beide Mäuse bieten einen langanhaltenden Komfort, sind bis zu achtmal schneller als eine Standardmaus und verwenden einen besonders fortschrittlichen Gaming-Maus-Sensor. Die spritzwassergeschützte Tastatur hat fünf personalisierbare RGB-Beleuchtungsbereiche mit einem Spektrum von bis zu 16,8 Millionen Farben. Das Headset mit seinen schlanken Ohrmuscheln aus waschbarem Funktionsmaterial bietet stundenlangen Tragekomfort und liefert hochqualitativen Stereoklang.

Statement by the jury
The Logitech G Prodigy Series facilitates accelerated and extended play for gaming enthusiasts. The personalisation options of the keyboard's RGB zones suit the innovative, overall picture.

Begründung der Jury
Die Logitech G Prodigy Series ermöglicht Game-Enthusiasten schnelles und langes Spielen. Die individualisierbaren RGB-Bereiche an der Tastatur passen gut ins innovative Gesamtbild.

Kensington Ultimate Presenter

Manufacturer
Kensington, San Mateo, USA
In-house design
Kensington Industrial Design Team
(Nojan Sadri, Eli Huang)
Web
www.kensington.com

An elegant, organic form that pays particular attention to good ergonomic handling characterises the Kensington Ultimate Presenter. The user interface is designed at an angle and can be positioned parallel to the stretched arm. The device can thus be held ergonomically; unnatural hand-positioning is avoided. The handle fits comfortably in the palm of the hand, preventing any pressure points.

Statement by the jury
Thanks to its pleasant ergonomic properties, the speaker who is using the Kensington Ultimate Presenter can concentrate on the presentation with reassurance.

Eine elegante organische Formgebung, die auf eine gute ergonomische Handhabung besonderen Bedacht nimmt, kennzeichnet den Kensington Ultimate Presenter. Die Benutzeroberfläche ist in einem Winkel konstruiert und kann daher parallel zum ausgestreckten Arm positioniert werden. Dadurch kann das Gerät auf ergonomisch angenehme Weise gehalten werden, eine unnatürliche Handhaltung wird vermieden. Der Griff liegt gut in der Hand und es entstehen keinerlei Druckpunkte.

Begründung der Jury
Dank seiner angenehmen ergonomischen Eigenschaften können sich Redner mit dem Kensington Ultimate Presenter beruhigt auf ihren Vortrag konzentrieren.

Spotlight
Presenter

Manufacturer
Logitech, Newark, California, USA
In-house design
Web
www.logitech.com

The Spotlight presenter exceeds the function of a laser pointer and makes it possible to highlight and magnify screen content. The highlights are visible both for the live audience and for video conferences. From up to a distance of 30 metres it is possible to navigate through slides, play videos and interact with screen content. If required, Spotlight reminds the speaker of the end of the presentation by vibrating.

Statement by the jury
Spotlight offers sophisticated functions to captivate the audience all the way up to the end of the presentation.

Der Presenter Spotlight geht über die Funktion eines Laserpointers hinaus und ermöglicht es, Bildschirminhalte hervorzuheben und zu vergrößern. Die Hervorhebungen sind sowohl für ein Live-Publikum als auch per Videokonferenz sichtbar. Aus bis zu 30 Metern Entfernung lässt sich durch Folien navigieren, können Videos abgespielt und kann mit Bildschirminhalten interagiert werden. Spotlight erinnert den Vortragenden auf Wunsch durch Vibrieren an das Ende der Redezeit.

Begründung der Jury
Spotlight bietet ausgeklügelte Funktionen, um das Publikum bis zum Ende eines jeden Vortrags zu fesseln.

MasterCase Pro 6
PC Chassis
Computergehäuse

Manufacturer
Cooler Master Technology Inc., New Taipei City, Taiwan
In-house design
Web
www.coolermaster.com

With the modular FreeForm system of the MasterCase Pro 6, the PC can be adjusted, adapted and upgraded. Behind the flat, smooth wall panels and a large side window, which can be easily removed and replaced using a magnet, it is possible to install additional elements for improved PC performance in the home, at gaming locations or in the office. Thin air slits at all four corners assure good ventilation, which can be additionally increased by letting the wall panels above and at the front spring open by gently lifting them. A removable rear component can conceal untidy hanging cables.

Mit dem modularen FreeForm System des MasterCase Pro 6 kann der PC adjustiert, angepasst und hochgerüstet werden. Hinter den flachen glatten Wänden und einem großen Seitenfester, die mittels Magneten einfach entfernt und eingesetzt werden, ist es möglich, Zusatzelemente für eine verbesserte PC-Leistung im Home-, Gaming- oder Office-Bereich unterzubringen. Dünne Entlüftungsöffnungen an vier Ecken sorgen für gute Ventilation, die zusätzlich verstärkt werden kann, wenn man die Wände oben und an der Vorderseite durch leichtes Anheben weiter herausspringen lässt. Ein herausnehmbarer Rückenteil verbirgt andernfalls unordentlich herumhängende Kabel.

Statement by the jury
The MasterCase Pro6 assures clean and elegant aesthetics for technically upgraded computers. The device also gains merit due to its easy manageability.

Begründung der Jury
Das MasterCase Pro6 sorgt für eine cleane und elegante Ästhetik bei technisch hochgerüsteten Computern. Das Gerät punktet auch durch seine einfache Handhabbarkeit.

ThinkCentre M910 Tower
Computer

Manufacturer
Lenovo, Morrisville, North Carolina, USA
In-house design
Web
www.lenovo.com

To facilitate positioning of the
ThinkCentre M910 Tower anywhere
in the office or to conveniently
relocate it, a sturdy handle has been
integrated into its frame. The easily
accessible ports at the front are located
behind an automatically retracting
door. The computer can be equipped
with up to five hard drive spaces with
up to 64 GB RAM and with four FL PCI
slot expansions. The device presents
a reduced form and has a volume of
18 litres. Moreover, 80 per cent of the
material used is recycled plastic. The
overall design of the computer is very
clear and modern, allowing it to blend
well into any office environment.

Statement by the jury
The ThinkCentre M910 Tower is appealing due to its modern design in which
practical details are skilfully integrated.

Um den ThinkCentre M910 Tower überall in
einem Büro positionieren oder bequem
umstellen zu können, ist in seinem Rahmen
ein stabiler Griff integriert. Die leicht zu-
gänglichen Anschlüsse an der Vorderseite
befinden sich hinter einer automatisch
versenkbaren Klappe. Der Computer kann
mit bis zu fünf Festplattenspeichern mit
bis zu 64 GB RAM und mit vier FL-PCI-
Erweiterungen ausgestattet werden. Das
Gerät zeigt eine reduzierte Formgebung
und besitzt ein Volumen von 18 Litern.
Der verwendete Kunststoff besteht zudem
zu 80 Prozent aus recyceltem Material.
Insgesamt ist der Computer sehr klar und
modern gestaltet, wodurch er sich gut in
jedes Büroumfeld einfügt.

Begründung der Jury
Der ThinkCentre M910 Tower gefällt durch
seine moderne Gestaltung, in die geschickt
praktische Details integriert sind.

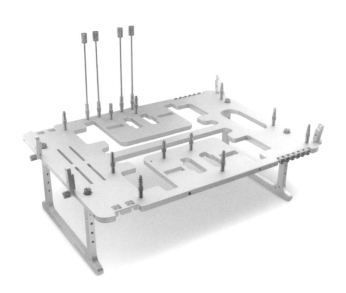

BC1 Open Benchtable
Computer Test Bed
Computer-Prüfstand

Manufacturer
Streacom, Rotterdam, Netherlands
In-house design
Shimon Simon
Web
www.streacom.com

The BC1 Open Benchtable is a portable test bed for PC components, constructed in such a way that it offers a platform for all components. However, it can still be folded up to a flat plate, facilitating easy transportation. Individual components are kept securely and without shaking in their holders during transport; no extra tools are needed to set up the Benchtable. The plate, which is milled from a single block of aluminium, the sandblasted finish and the specially made screws of stainless steel provide a noble and high-quality impression.

Statement by the jury
The light and transportable BC1 Open Benchtable is a convincingly innovative idea and possesses high functionality. The aesthetics are also convincing.

Der BC1 Open Benchtable ist ein tragbarer Prüfstand für PC-Komponenten, der so konstruiert ist, dass er eine Plattform für sämtliche Bauteile bietet, und doch zu einer flachen Platte zusammengefügt gut transportiert werden kann. Während des Transports sitzen die einzelnen Teile sicher und ohne zu rütteln in den Halterungen, zum Aufbau des Benchtables sind keine zusätzlichen Werkzeuge notwendig. Für eine edle und hochwertige Anmutung sorgen die aus einem einzelnen Aluminiumblock gefräste Platte, die sandgestrahlte Oberfläche sowie speziell angefertigte Schrauben aus rostfreiem Stahl.

Begründung der Jury
Der leichte und transportfähige BC1 Open Benchtable ist eine überzeugend innovative Idee und besitzt hohe Funktionalität. Beeindruckend ist auch seine Ästhetik.

View 27
Midi-Tower Chassis
Midi-Tower-Gehäuse

Manufacturer
Thermaltake Technology Co., Ltd., Taipei, Taiwan
In-house design
Web
www.thermaltakecorp.com

A transparent, gull-wing window panel provides inside into the View 27 interior and its mounting system for the GPU, which seems to be floating in this midi-tower chassis. Air or water cooling can be optionally fitted. A tinted front panel gives the chassis a clean look, allowing light from the LED fan to shine through. Ventilators in the side panels ensure good heat dissipation. An integrated, full-length power supply cover provides the chassis with a streamlined impression and offers additional mounting options.

Statement by the jury
The View 27 is an impressive midi-tower chassis for passionate gamers, who will enjoy showing off the technology inside.

Eine transparente flügeltürige Fensterscheibe gewährt Einblick in das Innere des View 27 und sein Montagesystem für den Grafikprozessor, der in diesem Midi-Tower-Gehäuse zu schweben scheint. Optional kann eine Luft- oder Wasserkühlung eingebaut werden. Durch das getönte Frontpanel wirkt das Gehäuse clean, LED-Ventilatoren-Licht kann hindurchscheinen. Ventilatoren in den Seitenteilen sorgen für effiziente Wärmeableitung. Eine eingebaute, durchgehende Abdeckung für die Stromversorgung lässt das Gehäuse stromlinienförmig wirken und hält zusätzliche Montageoptionen bereit.

Begründung der Jury
Das View 27 ist ein beeindruckendes Midi-Tower-Gehäuse für leidenschaftliche Gamer. Diese werden ihre Technik darin gerne gebührend zur Schau stellen.

HP Pavilion Wave
Computer

Manufacturer
HP Inc., Palo Alto, USA
In-house design
HP Inc. PS Industrial Design Team
Design
Native Design, London, Great Britain
Web
www.hp.com

The HP Pavilion Wave is a fully equipped Windows computer for use in the home. Within its triangular form there is room for all components, making the computer 85 per cent smaller than traditional tower PCs. However, it incorporates, high-performance functions, offers 4K video output and supports multiple displays. Its surfaces include premium-quality textile material. Components from Bang & Olufsen guarantee a 360-degree sound experience. Integrated far-field microphones provide hands-free voice activation.

Statement by the jury
Thanks to its impressively skilful design, the HP Pavilion Wave blends into the home like a valuable piece of furniture and is hardly recognisable as a computer.

Der HP Pavilion Wave ist ein vollausgestatteter Windows-Computer für den Gebrauch in den eigenen vier Wänden. In seiner triangulären Form finden alle Komponenten Platz und der Computer fällt so um 85 Prozent kleiner aus als traditionelle Tower-PCs. Dennoch beherbergt er Hochleistungsfunktionen, einen 4K-Videoausgang und unterstützt mehrere Bildschirme. Seine Oberflächen sind u. a. mit Stoffen hochwertig gestaltet. Für ein 360-Grad-Klangerlebnis sorgen Komponenten von Bang & Olufsen. Integrierte Fernfeld-Mikrofone ermöglichen die Sprachsteuerung des Geräts, ohne dass die Hände benutzt werden müssen.

Begründung der Jury
Dank seiner beeindruckend gekonnten Ausführung fügt sich der HP Pavilion Wave wie ein edler Einrichtungsgegenstand ins Interieur ein und ist kaum mehr als Computer wahrnehmbar.

Lenovo Smart Storage
Storage System
Speichersystem

Manufacturer
Lenovo, Morrisville, North Carolina, USA
In-house design
Web
www.lenovo.com

With Lenovo Smart Storage, authorised users can attain easy access to their data at any time. The device offers an intelligent photo management system, data security and high transfer speed. Thanks to the enormous memory capacity of up to 6 TB, a comprehensive film library can be stored. Access is simply achieved via Wi-Fi or a USB 3.0 connection. Technical components remain concealed in order to preserve minimalist aesthetics, allowing the device integrate well with any household. Large components to the inside of the casing are aligned diagonally. The cooling fan is situated at the bottom of the device.

Mit dem Lenovo Smart Storage erhalten zugriffsberechtigte Nutzer jederzeit einfachen Zugang zu ihren Daten. Das Gerät bietet ein intelligentes Foto-Management-System, Datensicherheit und hohe Übertragungsgeschwindigkeit. Dank der enormen Speicherkapazität von bis zu 6 TB lässt sich z. B. eine umfangreiche Filmbibliothek darauf ablegen. Der Zugriff gelingt einfach per Wi-Fi oder über einen USB-3.0-Zugang. Technische Komponenten bleiben zugunsten einer minimalistischen Ästhetik verborgen, sodass das Gerät gut in jedes Zuhause passt. Große Komponenten im Inneren des Gehäuses sind diagonal positioniert. Die Kühlung befindet sich am Boden des Geräts.

Statement by the jury
Lenovo Smart Storage delights with its unusually high memory capacity. All data are reliably saved and can be accessed from anywhere.

Begründung der Jury
Das Lenovo Smart Storage begeistert mit seiner außerordentlich hohen Speicherkapazität. Auf dem System sind sämtliche Daten zuverlässig gesichert und können von überallher aufgerufen werden.

TVS-873
NAS Device
NAS-Anlage

Manufacturer
QNAP Systems, Inc.,
New Taipei City, Taiwan
In-house design
Dino Wang
Web
www.qnap.com

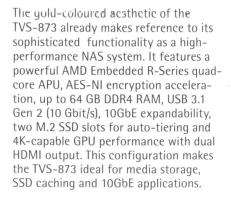

The gold-coloured aesthetic of the TVS-873 already makes reference to its sophisticated functionality as a high-performance NAS system. It features a powerful AMD Embedded R-Series quad-core APU, AES-NI encryption accelera-tion, up to 64 GB DDR4 RAM, USB 3.1 Gen 2 (10 Gbit/s), 10GbE expandability, two M.2 SSD slots for auto-tiering and 4K-capable GPU performance with dual HDMI output. This configuration makes the TVS-873 ideal for media storage, SSD caching and 10GbE applications.

Statement by the jury
The TVS-873 proves to be an impressively reliable, high-performance and energy-efficient NAS solution, which fulfils the diverse application requirements and also has a pleasing appearance.

Bereits in seiner goldfarbenen Ästhetik ver-weist das TVS-873 auf seine hochwertigen Funktionen einer Hochleistung-NAS-Anlage. Es ist ausgestattet mit einem leistungs-starken AMD-Embedded-R-Series-Vierkern-prozessor, einer AES-NI-Verschlüsselungs-engine, bis zu 64 GB DDR4 RAM, USB 3.1 Gen 2 (10 Gbits/s), 10GbE-Erweiterbarkeit, zwei M.2-SSD-Steckplätzen für Auto Tiering und einem 4K-fähigen Grafikprozessor mit dualem HDMI-Ausgang. Diese Konfiguration prädestiniert das TVS-873 zum Einsatz in der Datensicherung, beim SSD Caching und für 10GbE-Anwendungen.

Begründung der Jury
Beeindruckend zuverlässig beweist sich das TVS-873 als hochleistungsfähige und energieeffiziente NAS-Lösung, die vielfältige Einsatzanforderungen erfüllt und noch dazu gut aussieht.

Engine 27
CPU Cooler
Prozessorkühler

Manufacturer
Thermaltake Technology Co., Ltd.,
Taipei, Taiwan
In-house design
Web
www.thermaltakecorp.com

The Engine 27 CPU cooler supports the Intel Socket LGA 1150/1151/1155/1156. Its low height of 27 mm and the 60 mm compact diameter of the fan make it particularly well adaptable for small-format and slim devices. Metal blades and fins, as well as a copper base, sup-port efficient heat dissipation from the CPU. Radial slots are situated in the fan base, allowing the heat to quickly reach the rotating components. The device runs very quietly, without sacrificing performance.

Statement by the jury
Its compact dimensions make the Engine 27 CPU cooler a suitable aid for the efficient heat protection of small devices in particular.

Der Prozessorkühler Engine 27 unterstützt die Intel-Sockel LGA 1150/1151/1155/1156. Seine geringe Höhe von 27 mm sowie der kompakte Ventilatordurchmesser von 60 mm machen ihn für kleinformatige und schmale Geräte besonders gut verwendbar. Metallene Blätter und Lamellen sowie ein Kupferboden unterstützen eine starke und effiziente Wärmeableitung vom Prozessor. In den Ventilatorboden sind radiale Spalten eingearbeitet, die die Hitze schnell an die rotierenden Teile weiterleiten. Das Gerät läuft sehr leise, ohne dabei an Leistung einzubüßen.

Begründung der Jury
Seine kompakten Maße machen den Prozessorkühler Engine 27 zum geeig-neten Hilfsmittel, um effizient speziell kleine Geräte vor Hitze zu schützen.

MasterLiquid Maker 92
CPU Cooler
Prozessorkühler

Manufacturer
Cooler Master Technology Inc.,
New Taipei City, Taiwan
In-house design
Web
www.coolermaster.com

The MasterLiquid Maker 92 is a versatile CPU cooler for computer users who wish to configure the hardware of their device individually. By means of a swivel joint, the device can be adjusted to a vertical and horizontal position. Even the swivel process itself offers two variants, namely water and air cooling. The unit is easy to install compared to pure water-cooling systems. By means of the unique Silence Efficiency feature, the ventilation switches itself off as soon as the temperature reaches less than 50 per cent of the user's setting.

Statement by the jury
MasterLiquid Maker 92 represents impressive innovation in the field of CPU cooling that is convincingly implemented in terms of function.

Der MasterLiquid Maker 92 ist ein in mehrerer Hinsicht vielseitig einsetzbarer Prozessorkühler für Computernutzer, die die Hardware ihres Gerätes gerne individuell gestalten. Mittels Drehgelenk ist das Gerät zwischen vertikaler und horizontaler Lage adjustierbar. Doch auch das Kühlverfahren selbst bietet zwei Verfahren an, nämlich eine Wasser- wie auch eine Luftkühlung. Die Einheit ist im Vergleich zu reinen Wasserkühlungen einfach zu installieren. Mittels der speziellen Silence-Efficiency-Funktion schaltet sich die Lüftung ab, sobald die Temperatur bei einem Wert unter 50 Prozent der Nutzereinstellung liegt.

Begründung der Jury
Der MasterLiquid Maker 92 stellt eine beeindruckende Innovation auf dem Gebiet der Prozessorkühlung dar, die funktional überzeugend umgesetzt ist.

NVIDIA GEFORCE GTX 1080
Graphics Card
Grafikkarte

Manufacturer
NVIDIA Corporation, Santa Clara, USA
In-house design
Darren Burckhard, Hyun Kim
Web
www.nvidia.com

The Nvidia GeForce GTX 1080 graphics card is designed especially for enthusiast computer gamers. The use of tessellated surfaces cleverly imitates the polygonal shape of computer graphics. The cast aluminum body is machine finished and heat-treated to provide rigidity and durability as well as very good heat dissipation. The metal baseplate, back cover, and low-profile components assure unobstructed venting channels for reduced air resistance and better cooling, all while conforming to the strict size constraints of the PC industry. The illuminated logo provides a striking appearance inside a windowed chassis and also serves as status indicator.

Die Nvidia GeForce GTX 1080 Grafikkarte ist speziell für die Bedürfnisse enthusiastischer Computerspieler konzipiert. Die mosaikartige Oberfläche imitiert geschickt die polygonale Grundform von Computergrafiken. Der druckgegossene Aluminiumkörper ist maschinengefertigt und hitzebehandelt. Er bietet Stabilität und Dauerhaftigkeit sowie eine sehr gute Hitzeableitung. Die metallische Grundplatte, die Rückenabdeckung sowie Low-profile-Komponenten gewährleisten störungsfreie Kanäle für geringen Luftwiderstand und gute Kühlleistung unter Wahrung strikter Größenauflagen seitens der PC-Industrie. Das beleuchtete Logo sorgt in einem Gehäuse mit Fenster für ein augenfälliges Erscheinungsbild und dient als Status-Indikator.

Statement by the jury
With the Nvidia GeForce GTX 1080 graphics card, computer games become impressive and trouble-free visual experiences.

Begründung der Jury
Mit der Grafikkarte Nvidia GeForce GTX 1080 werden Computerspiele zu beeindruckenden und störungsfreien visuellen Erlebnissen.

NVIDIA GEFORCE GTX 1060
Graphics Card
Grafikkarte

Manufacturer
NVIDIA Corporation, Santa Clara, USA
In-house design
Darren Burckhard, Hyun Kim
Web
www.nvidia.com

The Nvidia GeForce GTX 1060 graphics card design, integrating polygonal design elements, caters to the high demands of computer gamers. Premium materials, such as the die-cast aluminum body, impart a solid and quality feel, while the well engineered cooler, metal baseplate, and low-profile components provide high efficiency airflow. The clearly visible logo, which also serves as a status indicator when illuminated, generates an eye-catching appearance when installed into a windowed computer chassis.

Die Grafikkarte Nvidia GeForce GTX 1060 kommt in ihrer Gestaltung aus polygonalen Elementen den hohen Ansprüchen von Computerspielern entgegen. Hochwertige Materialien wie der druckgegossene Aluminiumkörper verleihen eine feste und anspruchsvolle Haptik. Der ausgereifte Kühler, die metallische Bodenplatte und Low-profile-Komponenten gewährleisten hocheffizienten Luftdurchsatz. Das deutlich sichtbare Logo, das auch als Status-Indikator fungiert, erzeugt ein augenfälliges Erscheinungsbild, indem es aus dem transparenten Inneren eines Computerchassis herausleuchtet.

Statement by the jury
With its visually appealing, polygonal design, the Nvidia GeForce GTX 1060 graphics card adapts convincingly to the product periphery of modern gaming computers.

Begründung der Jury
In ihrer optisch ansprechenden polygonalen Gestaltung passt sich die Grafikkarte Nvidia GeForce GTX 1060 überzeugend der Produktperipherie moderner Spielecomputer an.

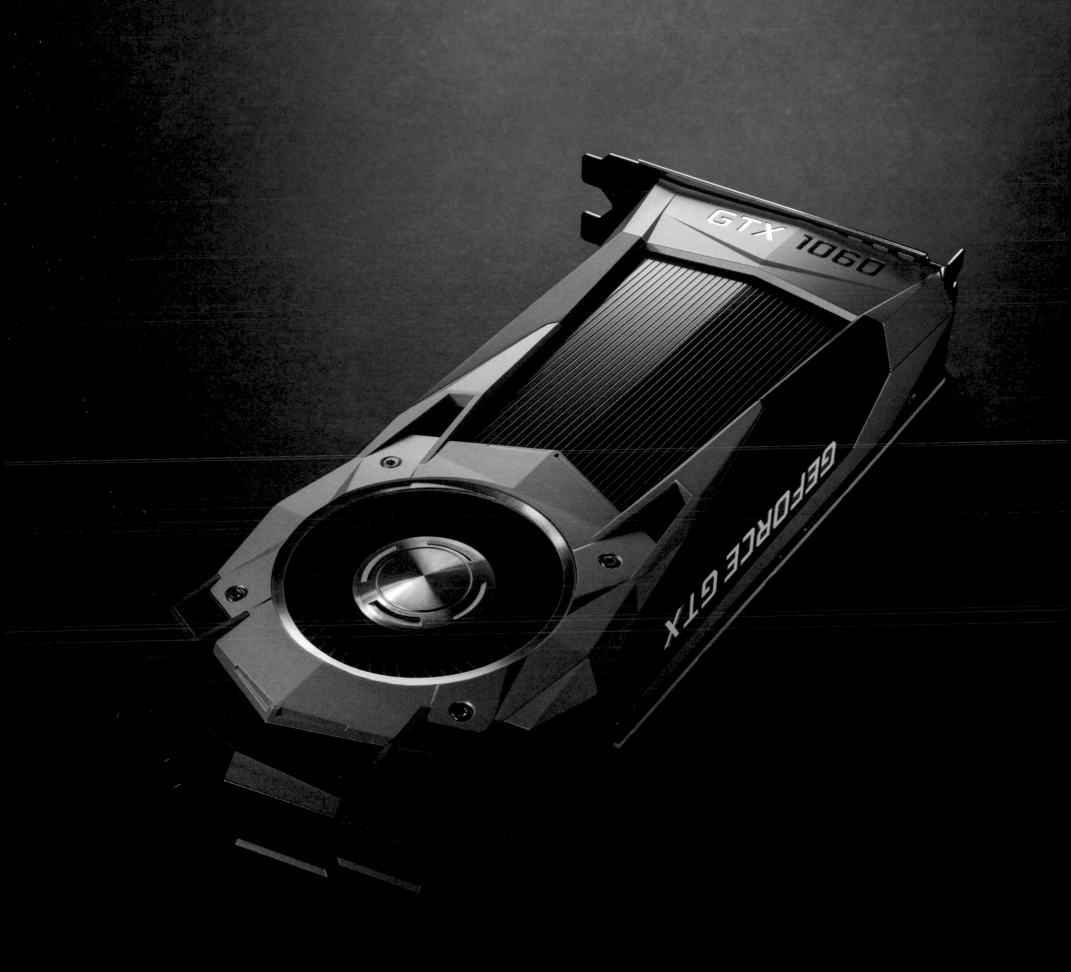

Ericsson Hyperscale Datacenter System 8000
Hyperscale Datacenter Solution
Hyperscale-Datacenter-Lösung

Manufacturer
Ericsson AB, Stockholm, Sweden
In-house design
Ericsson Industrial Design Department
Web
www.ericsson.com

The innovative Ericsson Hyperscale Datacenter System 8000 uses disaggregated hardware architecture to ensure demanding resource utilisation. The discreet design of the system makes no use of unnecessary elements. The result merges into a clear and sober design to the advantage of performance and user-friendliness. Practical hot-swap elements allow for the uncomplicated modification of individual hardware components. In order to facilitate user-friendly servicing, the design of the back was given equally great attention.

Statement by the jury
The Ericsson Hyperscale Datacenter System 8000 excels through the technically sophisticated use of disaggregated hardware architecture and impresses with aesthetic elegance.

Das innovative Ericsson Hyperscale Datacenter System 8000 nutzt disaggregierte Hardwarearchitektur, um eine anspruchsvolle Ressourcenauslastung gewährleisten zu können. Die unaufdringliche Gestaltung der Anlage verzichtet auf überflüssige Elemente. Das Resultat mündet in einem schlichten und nüchternen Design, das zugunsten der Leistungsfähigkeit und Nutzerfreundlichkeit in den Hintergrund tritt. Praktische Hot-Swap-Elemente erlauben das komplikationsfreie Umrüsten einzelner Hardwareteile. Um nutzerfreundliche Serviceeingriffe zu ermöglichen, kam der Gestaltung der Rückseite eine ebenso hohe Aufmerksamkeit zuteil.

Begründung der Jury
Das Ericsson Hyperscale Datacenter System 8000 brilliert durch die technisch ausgefeilte Nutzung disaggregierter Hardwarearchitektur und besticht dabei mit ästhetischer Eleganz.

Dell EMC PowerEdge Hard Drive Carrier
Removable Hard Drive Carrier
Austauschbarer Festplattenträger

Manufacturer
Dell EMC, Round Rock, Texas, USA
In-house design
Experience Design Group
Web
www.dell.com

With a focus on good airflow, the Dell EMC PowerEdge Hard Drive Carrier ensures operation of the server and takes into account future thermal requirements. Wherever possible, paint has been omitted in order to reduce environmental pollution, for instance with stainless-steel plates at the handle. The metal housing with formed rails supports the hard drive and provides protection through maximal air circulation. The orange-coloured circle on the unlocking button indicates that it is a hot swap component.

Statement by the jury
The EMC PowerEdge Hard Drive Carrier displays a harmonious construction in terms of both form and function, and it also impresses with its environmentally friendly approach.

Mit Augenmerk auf guten Luftdurchsatz gewährleistet der Dell EMC PowerEdge Hard Drive Carrier den Betrieb des Servers und trägt künftigen thermischen Anforderungen Rechnung. Wo es möglich war, wurde auf eine Lackierung verzichtet, um die Umweltbelastung zu reduzieren, etwa bei den Edelstahlblechen am Griff. Das Metallgehäuse mit formgerechten Schienen nimmt die Festplatte auf und bietet ihr Schutz bei maximaler Luftzirkulation. Der orangefarbene Kreis auf der Entriegelungstaste weist darauf hin, dass es sich um eine Hot-Swap-Komponente handelt.

Begründung der Jury
Der EMC PowerEdge Hard Drive Carrier zeigt einen formal wie funktional stimmigen Aufbau und beeindruckt durch seinen umweltfreundlichen Ansatz.

Dell EMC PowerEdge R740
Server

Manufacturer
Dell EMC, Round Rock, Texas, USA
In-house design
Experience Design Group
Web
www.dell.com

The holders of the Dell EMC PowerEdge R740 are integrated into the main chassis, resulting in a sturdy solution with additional space for components. The server's operating surface is constructed in a consistent and user-friendly way. The system can be wirelessly synchronised with a smartphone or tablet and controlled by apps installed on these devices. Metal edging along the top and bottom sides of the chassis underscores the structured outline and reduces the extent of painting necessary.

Statement by the jury
The Dell EMC PowerEdge R740 proves to be an innovative server that complies with modern demands for stable and reliable connectivity with the cloud.

Die Halterungen des Dell EMC PowerEdge R740 sind in das Hauptchassis integriert, was eine robuste Lösung mit zusätzlichem Platz für Komponenten ergibt. Die Server-Bedienfläche ist stimmig und nutzerfreundlich aufgebaut. Das System kann kabellos mit einem Smartphone oder Tablet synchronisiert und über Apps auf diesen Geräten gesteuert werden. Metalleinfassungen auf der Ober- und Unterseite des Chassis unterstreichen die strukturierte Gliederung und reduzieren den Lackieraufwand.

Begründung der Jury
Der Dell EMC PowerEdge R740 erweist sich als innovativer Server, indem er modernen Anforderungen an die stabile und zuverlässige Einbindung von Clouds entspricht.

H3C R4700 G3
Server

Manufacturer
Hangzhou H3C Technologies Co., Ltd., Hangzhou, China
In-house design
Kai Li, Manqian Xu
Web
www.h3c.com

Reliability of operation and maintenance friendliness were at the heart of the conception of the H3C R4700 G3 server, with the aim of achieving high performance, extended durability, reliable storage capacity and I/O properties. Intuitively understood, easy configurable functions support simple management of the server. For operational safety, high-quality metal surfaces, which also feature a linear design, confer on the device a modern aesthetic. Coloured touchscreen elements guide the user through the procedure for correct operation and upgrading, while also helping to avoid faulty operation.

Ausfallsicherheit und Wartungsfreundlichkeit standen im Fokus bei der Konzeption des Servers H3C R4700 G3, um eine hohe Leistungsfähigkeit, lange Ausdauer, zuverlässige Speicherkapazität und E/A-Eigenschaften zu erzielen. Intuitiv erfassbare, einfach konfigurierbare Funktionen unterstützen seine einfache Verwaltung. Für Betriebssicherheit sorgen hochwertige Metalloberflächen, deren gerade Linienführung dem Gerät zugleich eine moderne Ästhetik verleiht. Farbige Touchscreen-Elemente führen den Nutzer durch den Vorgang für einen korrekten Betrieb sowie für das Upgrade und helfen dabei, das Auftreten von Fehlfunktionen zu vermeiden.

Statement by the jury
The H3C R4700 G3 server ensures faultless operation and uncomplicated maintenance, thanks to the well-conceived functionality of its intuitively understandable elements.

Begründung der Jury
Der Server H3C R4700 G3 sorgt für einen reibungsfreien Betrieb und eine unkomplizierte Wartung dank durchdachter Funktionalität seiner intuitiv erfassbaren Elemente.

TRX Connected Transportation Platform
Rail Communication System
Kommunikationssystem für den Schienenverkehr

Manufacturer
Klas Telecom, Dublin, Ireland
In-house design
Frank Murray, Mark Ryan
Design
Dolmen (Christopher Murphy, James Ryan, Gerry Gillen),
Dublin, Ireland
Web
www.klastelecom.com
www.dolmen.ie

The TRX Connected Transportation Platform provides the entire communication and infotainment system of a unit in passenger and goods transportation. The construction takes into account the challenges encountered in busy trains, for instance heat, vibration and moisture. The system consists of a range of highly adaptable, modular enclosures that are equipped with an intuitive connection system for ease of installation and maintenance. To attain a small and compact form, each aluminium module also serves as a heat sink, thus reducing maintenance requirements.

Die TRX Connected Transportation Platform nimmt das gesamte Kommunikations- und Infotainment-System einer Einheit im Personen- und Güterverkehr auf. Der Aufbau berücksichtigt die Herausforderungen in viel genutzten Zügen, etwa Wärme, Vibration oder Feuchtigkeit. Das System besteht aus einer Reihe anpassungsfähiger, modularer Gehäuse, die mit einem intuitiven Verbindungssystem für leichteren Einbau und Wartung ausgestattet sind. Um eine kleine und kompakte Form zu erhalten, dient jedes Aluminiummodul zugleich als Kühlkörper, was auch den Wartungsaufwand reduziert.

Statement by the jury
The TRX Connected Transportation Platform takes an innovative approach to supporting on-board communication in rail travel while complying with functional and formal demands.

Begründung der Jury
Die TRX Connected Transportation Platform unterstützt auf innovative Weise die Bordkommunikation im Schienenverkehr und wird dabei funktionalen wie formalen Ansprüchen gerecht.

ROG Maximus IX Extreme
Motherboard

Manufacturer
ASUSTeK Computer Inc., Taipei, Taiwan
In-house design
Web
www.asus.com

The ROG Maximus IX Extreme was developed for people who often require the use of their PC at high performance for very long periods, in particular for playing computer games. In such cases, an additional water-cooling system is installed, whereby compatibility with the motherboard is usually difficult to attain. This device is a motherboard with integrated water cooler, which efficiently supports the main processor in heat dissipation. Water flow, temperature and the leakage identification sensor assist in making the performance of the motherboard easier to control. The asymmetrical design blends in well with the image world of the target group.

Statement by the jury
The ROG Maximus IX Extreme provides an impressive performance by cooling the computer system reliably, even in the case of very active gamers and hobbyists.

Das ROG Maximus IX Extreme wurde für Personen entwickelt, die ihren PC oftmals über sehr lange Zeit auf hoher Leistung beanspruchen, insbesondere für Computerspiele. In solchen Fällen werden zusätzliche Wasserkühlsysteme eingebaut, wobei die Kompatibilität mit dem Motherboard oft schwer herzustellen ist. Dieses Gerät ist ein Motherboard mit integrier-tem Wasserkühler, der den Hauptprozessor effizient bei der Wärmeableitung unterstützt. Wasserfluss-, Temperatur- und Leckerkennungssensor helfen, die Leistung des Motherboards leichter zu steuern. Das asymmetrische Design fügt sich gut in die Bilderwelt der Zielgruppe ein.

Begründung der Jury
Das ROG Maximus IX Extreme zeigt eine beeindruckende Leistung, indem es das Computersystem auch von sehr aktiven Gamern und Bastlern zuverlässig kühlt.

ROG Maximus IX APEX
Motherboard

Manufacturer
ASUSTeK Computer Inc., Taipei, Taiwan
In-house design
Web
www.asus.com

The ROG Maximus IX APEX motherboard is designed for people who wish to build their computer themselves or want to overclock it. The defining factors in the design were appearance, performance and economy. The device supports 3D printing and features an X-shaped circuit board, a DIMM.2 M.2 slot and a water-cooling sensor zone. Furthermore, the motherboard offers AURA RGB LED lighting effects as well as a clear signal-transport design.

Statement by the jury
PC enthusiasts and overclockers will find the ROG Maximus IX APEX motherboard to be an impressively efficient and visually exciting core component for their computer system.

Das Motherboard ROG Maximus IX APEX ist für Personen konzipiert, die ihren Rechner selber zusammenbauen oder übertakten möchten. Aussehen, Leistung und Wirtschaftlichkeit waren für die Gestaltung bestimmende Faktoren. Das Gerät unterstützt 3D-Druck, verfügt über eine X-förmige Leiterplatte, einen DIMM.2 M.2-Steckplatz sowie einen Wasserkühlungssensorbereich. Weiter bietet das Motherboard AURA-RGB-LED-Leuchteffekte sowie ein klares Signalübertragungsdesign.

Begründung der Jury
PC-Bastler und Übertakter finden im Motherboard ROG Maximus IX APEX ein beeindruckend effizientes wie auch optisch aufregendes Herzstück für ihr Computersystem.

Nighthawk S8000
Gaming and Media Streaming Switch
Gaming- und Medien-Streaming-Switch

Manufacturer
NETGEAR, Inc., San Jose, USA
In-house design
Ed Kalubiran
Web
www.netgear.com

The innovative Nighthawk S8000 provides consumer-friendly and advanced switching technology packaged in a sleek, modern design. The eight port gigabit Ethernet switch offers the user reliable high speed connectivity and enables trouble-free multi-user gaming, 4K video streaming, video chats in HD or streaming of HD content onto local storage, without the individual devices unevenly straining the bandwidth of the Wi-Fi network. Thanks to an intuitive user interface, the setup, configuration and optimisation are all carried out without difficulty.

Der innovative Nighthawk S8000 bietet verbraucherfreundliche und fortschrittliche Switching-Technologie, verpackt in ein schlankes, modernes Design. Der Gigabit-Ethernet-Switch mit acht Ports bietet dem Nutzer zuverlässige Gerätekonnektivität bei sehr hohen Geschwindigkeiten. So sind störungsfreies Multi-User-Gaming, 4K-Video-Streaming, Videochats in HD oder das Streamen von HD-Content auf den eigenen lokalen Speicherplatz möglich, ohne dass die einzelnen Endgeräte die Bandbreite des Wi-Fi-Netzwerkes ungleichmäßig belasten. Dank intuitiver Benutzerschnittstelle gelingen Setups, Konfigurationen und Optimierungen ohne Probleme.

Statement by the jury
Nighthawk S8000 convinces with high-performance switching technology and, thanks to the sleek, modern design, it is an eye-catcher in every home.

Begründung der Jury
Nighthawk S8000 überzeugt mit hochleistungsfähiger Switching-Technologie und ist dank seiner schnittigen modernen Gestaltung ein Blickfang in jedem Zuhause.

360 Mobile HardDrive H1
External Hard Drive
Externe Festplatte

Manufacturer
Shenzhen Fenglian Technology Co., Ltd.,
Shenzhen, China
In-house design
Xueyong Zhang
Web
www.ifenglian.com

A proportionally well-designed aluminium housing encases the external 360 Mobile HardDrive H1. Together with a resilient inner silicon covering, the device is well protected against impact and overheating. It is easily transported and, thanks to the smooth, well-proportioned metal surface with rounded corners, makes an elegant impression at the same time, so that it blends well in any work environment. The product is equipped with a fast USB 3.0 interface and offers cross-platform compatibility.

Statement by the jury
Whether in the home office or at university, the 360 Mobile HardDrive H1, with its charming and elegant design, always ensures a confident presence.

Ein ebenmäßig gestaltetes Aluminiumgehäuse umgibt die externe Festplatte 360 Mobile HardDrive H1. Zusammen mit einer federnden inneren Silikonumhüllung ist das Gerät dadurch gut bei Erschütterung und gegen Überhitzung geschützt. Leicht zu transportieren ist es dank der glatten, ebenmäßigen Metalloberfläche mit abgerundeten Ecken und erhält so gleichzeitig eine elegante Anmutung, mit der es sich gut in jede Arbeitsumgebung einfügt. Das Produkt verfügt über eine schnelle USB 3.0-Schnittstelle und bietet plattformübergreifende Kompatibilität.

Begründung der Jury
Ob im Homeoffice, im Studio oder an der Universität – in ihrer anmutigen und eleganten Gestaltung sorgt die 360 Mobile HardDrive H1 stets für einen souveränen Auftritt.

Intel Compute Card
Microcomputer

Manufacturer
Intel Corporation, Hillsboro, USA
In-house design
Intel IDXO (Aleks Magi, Dave Collins, Steve Berry)
Web
www.intel.com

The Intel Compute Card is a full computer in a compact design, measuring 95 x 55 x 5 mm. The product, rivaling the size of a credit card, is intended for use in Intel-supported devices needed in daily life and industrial environments. The device presents a pure and dynamic design, with a clear break of materials to give affordance of orientation and use. The surface is made of finely structured, sandblasted aluminum and ensures a pleasant tactile experience.

Statement by the jury
With a format almost as small as a credit card, the Intel Compute Card introduces an innovative approach and displays an extremely tasteful design.

Die Intel Compute Card ist ein vollwertiger Rechner in kompaktem Design, sie misst 95 × 55 × 5 mm, womit sie sich den Dimensionen einer Scheckkarte nähert. Vorgesehen ist sie für den Einsatz an Intel-unterstützten Geräten des täglichen Lebens und im betrieblichen Umfeld. Das Gerät zeigt ein schlichtes und dynamisches Design. Ein klarer, deutlich sichtbarer Bruch von Materialien unterstützt Orientierung und Nutzung. Die Oberfläche aus fein strukturiertem sandgestrahltem Aluminium sorgt für ein angenehmes taktiles Erlebnis.

Begründung der Jury
Mit nahezu Scheckkartenformat gibt die Intel Compute Card innovative neue Wege vor und zeigt eine äußerst geschmackvolle Gestaltung.

Elgato Thunderbolt 3 Dock
Docking Station

Manufacturer
Elgato, Munich, Germany
In-house design
Web
www.elgato.com

With the Elgato Thunderbolt 3 Dock, several devices can be integrated simultaneously with a MacBook Pro or a Windows notebook. Thanks to two Thunderbolt 3 ports, the computer can be connected and charged with a single cable, while the second port is available for other devices. It can be connected with up to two screens of 4K resolution; furthermore, the dock offers three SuperSpeed USB 3.0 ports, a one gigabit Ethernet port and separate microphone input and audio output.

Statement by the jury
The elegant Elgato Thunderbolt 3 Dock takes an exemplary approach to overcoming the frequently chaotic cable and plug entanglement of a computer workstation.

Mit dem Elgato Thunderbolt 3 Dock können mehrere Geräte gleichzeitig mit einem MacBook Pro oder Windows-Notebook verbunden werden. Dank zweier Thunderbolt-3-Anschlüsse lässt sich der Computer mit einem einzigen Kabel anschließen und aufladen, während der zweite Anschluss für andere Geräte zur Verfügung steht. Es können bis zu zwei Bildschirme in 4K-Auflösung verbunden werden, darüber hinaus bietet das Dock drei SuperSpeed-USB-3.0-Anschlüsse, einen Gigabit-Ethernet-Anschluss sowie einen separaten Mikrofoneingang und Audioausgang.

Begründung der Jury
Das elegante Elgato Thunderbolt 3 Dock bereitet dem oftmals chaotischen Kabel- und Steckersalat eines Computerarbeitsplatzes souverän ein Ende.

TeraStation TS Series
NAS Device
NAS-Anlage

Manufacturer
Buffalo Inc., Nagoya, Japan
In-house design
Hibiki Ikegami
Web
www.buffalotech.com

The TeraStation TS Series is a network-connected storage system with a high transfer rate of 10 GbE and four independent hard discs. Small and mid-sized companies can use them to protect their data reliably. The system is easy to install and manage. It has a lockable cover and therefore does not need to be shut up in a server room for security but can be situated elsewhere, for instance on a desk or an office shelf.

Die TeraStation TS Series ist eine NAS-Anlage mit einer hohen Übertragungsrate von 10 GbE und vier unabhängigen Festplatten. Kleine und mittlere Unternehmen können damit ihre Daten via Network zuverlässig schützen. Das System lässt sich einfach installieren und verwalten. Es hat ein verschließbares Verdeck und muss somit nicht aus Sicherheitsgründen in einem Serverraum versperrt werden, sondern kann außerhalb eines solchen, etwa auf einem Tisch oder in einem Regal in den Büroräumen stehen.

Statement by the jury
A pleasing advantage of the TeraStation TS Series is that data can be kept reliably secure without a server room, in addition to the design focus on home offices and small companies.

Begründung der Jury
Bei der TeraStation TS Series gefällt, wie das gestalterische Augenmerk auf Home-offices und kleine Unternehmen gelegt wurde, die ihre Daten damit auch ohne Serverraum zuverlässig sichern können.

HP Elite Slice
Computer

Manufacturer
HP Inc., Palo Alto, USA
In-house design
HP Inc. PS Industrial Design Team
Design
Native Design, London, Great Britain
Web
www.hp.com
www.native.com

The HP Elite Slice includes all the components of a fully fledged computer in a remarkably small chassis. With this space-saving concept, it addresses the conditions of many modern work environments, for example those of a home office or an open space environment. The computer is easily configured; it supports teamwork and prevents untidy cable entanglement. Furthermore, it is constructed in compliance with VESA standards and can thus be mounted directly on a monitor to save space.

Statement by the jury
The HP Elite Slice packs high performance and functionality into a very small space. This makes it first choice in all places where there is no room for bulky computer chassis.

Der HP Elite Slice bietet alle Komponenten eines vollwertigen Computers in einem denkbar kleinen Gehäuse. Mit dieser platzsparenden Ausführung wird er den Gegebenheiten vieler moderner Arbeitsumgebungen gerecht, etwa der eines Homeoffice oder eines Open-Space-Umfelds. Der Computer lässt sich einfach konfigurieren, er unterstützt beim Teamwork und vermeidet unschönes Kabelwirrwarr. Zudem ist er gemäß VESA-Standards konstruiert und kann somit nochmals platzsparender direkt an einem Monitor montiert werden.

Begründung der Jury
Der HP Elite Slice packt Leistungsstärke und Funktionalität auf ganz kleinen Raum. Das macht ihn zum Mittel der Wahl überall dort, wo klobige Computerchassis keinen Platz finden.

HP OMEN X Desktop
Gaming Computer

Manufacturer
HP Inc., Palo Alto, USA
In-house design
HP Inc. PS Industrial Design Team
Design
Native Design, London, Great Britain
Web
www.hp.com

Two discreet supports give the HP Omen X Desktop the appearance of a computer that is tilted at 45 degrees and keeps its balance on a single edge. This innovative form adds functional advantages to the gaming computer. It is thus very easy to configure the computer or to access it without tools. The unique form also supports cooling. Nine lighting zones change colour according to the hardware used, the audio preferences or the individual settings.

Statement by the jury
Even during high performance, the HP Omen X Desktop remains well cooled – also due to its unusual and innovative design.

Zwei dezente Stützen verleihen dem HP Omen X Desktop das Aussehen eines Computers, der um 45 Grad gekippt wurde und auf einer Kante die Balance hält. Diese innovative Formgebung verbindet der Gaming-Computer mit funktionalen Vorteilen. So ist es sehr einfach, Konfigurationen vorzunehmen oder werkzeugfrei auf den Computer zuzugreifen, zudem unterstützt diese besondere Form die Kühlung. Neun Beleuchtungszonen wechseln die Farbtöne je nach Hardwarenutzung, Audiovorgaben oder nach individuellen Einstellungen.

Begründung der Jury
Selbst unter Hochleistung bleibt der HP Omen X Desktop gut gekühlt – auch dank seines außergewöhnlichen und innovativen Designs.

Asus VivoMini VC66 Series
Computer

Manufacturer
ASUSTeK Computer Inc., Taipei, Taiwan
In-house design
Web
www.asus.com

The design of the Asus VivoMini VC66 Series is inspired by modern architecture, in which simple, geometric forms are transferred into ergonomically designed curves. The power button is located in a recess with blue ambient light, aesthetically providing a sense of calm and a pleasant tactile experience. Thanks to high-quality I/O ports and specifications defined by the user, the device can be used efficiently both as a home entertainment centre and in a high-grade office environment.

Statement by the jury
The Asus VivoMini VC66 Series can aesthetically enhance any environment; particularly impressive is the skilful use of light and line management.

Die Gestaltung der Serie Asus VivoMini VC66 ist von moderner Architektur inspiriert, bei der einfache geometrische Formen in ergonomisch gestaltete Kurven übergehen. Den Bereich der Einschalttaste etwa bildet eine Mulde mit blauem Umgebungslicht, was in ästhetischer Hinsicht Ruhe vermittelt und für ein angenehmes taktiles Erlebnis sorgt. Dank hochwertiger E/A-Anschlüsse sowie benutzerdefinierbarer Spezifikationen lässt sich das Gerät effizient sowohl als Home-Entertainment-Center wie auch im gehobenen Officebereich nutzen.

Begründung der Jury
Die Serie Asus VivoMini VC66 vermag jede Umgebung ästhetisch aufzuwerten, besonders beeindruckt der gekonnte Einsatz von Licht und Linienführung.

Toughpower DPS G RGB
PC Power Supply Unit
PC-Netzteil

Manufacturer
Thermaltake Technology Co., Ltd.,
Taipei, Taiwan
In-house design
Web
www.thermaltakecorp.com

A 256-colour RGB fan is pre-installed in the Toughpower DPS G RGB with 80 PLUS titanium certification. The PSU is monitored via a special software interface and three intelligent platforms. The SPM platform offers three warning functions in case of fan failure, overheating or abnormal voltage level. This helps users to reduce the risk of their PC and internal components overheating. The energy efficiency of the PC is thus improved and the CO_2 emissions reduced.

Statement by the jury
The Tougxhpower DPS G RGB is equipped with a fan system, providing the degree of innovation shown in the device. The management of energy efficiency is also remarkable.

In dem Toughpower DPS G RGB mit 80-PLUS-Titanium-Zertifizierung ist ein 256-Farben-RGB-Lüfter bereits installiert. Über eine spezielle Software-Schnittstelle und drei intelligente Plattformen lässt sich das Netzteil überwachen. Die SPM-Plattform bietet drei Warnfunktionen für einen Lüfterausfall, bei Übertemperatur oder im Fall eines anormalen Spannungspegels. Das hilft Benutzern, die Möglichkeit der Überhitzung Ihres PCs und der internen Komponenten zu reduzieren. Dadurch wird auch die Energieeffizienz des PCs verbessert und der CO_2-Ausstoß reduziert.

Begründung der Jury
Den Toughpower DPS G RGB mit einem Lüftungssystem auszustatten, zeugt vom Innovationsgrad des Gerätes. Bemerkenswert ist auch die Ausrichtung auf Energieeffizienz.

MasterWatt Maker 1200 MIJ
PC Power Supply Unit
PC-Netzteil

Manufacturer
Cooler Master Technology Inc., New Taipei City, Taiwan
In-house design
Web
www.coolermaster.com

The MasterWatt Maker 1200 MIJ high-performance PC power supply unit possesses an 80-plus titanium certification, guaranteeing a typical efficiency of 94 per cent. This is achieved by technically sophisticated cabling and a technology that supports the minimisation of heat loss. The integrated semi-passive fan is quiet, has low power consumption and, in conjunction with a honeycomb mesh grille, ensures optimal ventilation. Furthermore, it is activated only when 600 watts of power are reached. Premium engineered outer components give the product extended durability.

Das hochleistungsfähige PC-Netzteil MasterWatt Maker 1200 MIJ verfügt über eine 80-Plus-Titanium-Zertifizierung, was einen typischen Wirkungsgrad von 94 Prozent garantiert. Möglich ist dies durch eine technisch sehr ausgereifte Verkabelung und eine Technologie, die die Verringerung von Wärmeverlusten unterstützt. Der eingebaute semi-passive Lüfter ist geräuscharm, verbraucht nur sehr wenig Strom und sorgt in Verbindung mit dem Wabengitter für eine optimale Belüftung. Zudem wird er erst ab einer Last von 600 Watt aktiviert. Hochwertig verarbeitete Außenteile verleihen dem Produkt eine lange Lebensdauer.

Statement by the jury
The MasterWatt Maker 1200 MIJ impresses with a design that is of high quality in terms of both form and materials, and also with its concomitant focus on durability.

Begründung der Jury
Der MasterWatt Maker 1200 MIJ beeindruckt durch seine formal wie materiell hochwertige Ausführung und durch den damit verbundenen Fokus auf Langlebigkeit.

FoldIT® USB
USB Flash Drive
USB-Stick

Manufacturer
CustomUSB, Wheeling, Illinois , USA
Design
ClevX, LLC, Kirkland, Washington, USA
Web
www.folditusb.com
www.customusb.com
www.clevx.com

The FoldIT USB is extremely thin and therefore can be easily carried inside a wallet, a credit card compartment, attached as a paper clip or used as a key fob. When folded along the centre crease, the 1.2 mm flash drive can be inserted into a standard 2.4 mm USB port. Moreover, the device is made with eco-friendly material and can be recycled or shredded.

Statement by the jury
In times of increasing mobility, the FoldIT USB is pleasing with its innovative, thin design, thanks to which it can be simply integrated in the work documents underway.

Der FoldIT USB ist extrem dünn und kann daher einfach in einer Brieftasche, in einem Scheckkartenfach, als Heftklammer oder Schlüsselanhänger mitgenommen werden. Am mittleren Falz entlang gefaltet, passt der 1,2 mm dünne Stick in einen gewöhnlichen 2,4-mm-USB-Port. Zudem ist das Gerät mit umweltfreundlichen Materialien hergestellt und kann recycelt oder geschreddert werden.

Begründung der Jury
In Zeiten zunehmender Mobilität gefällt der FoldIT USB mit seiner innovativen dünnen Gestaltung, dank der er zur Mitnahme einfach in die Arbeitsunterlagen integriert wird.

Tile Slim
Bluetooth Tracker
Bluetooth-Suchgerät

Manufacturer
Tile, Inc., San Mateo, USA
Design
fuseproject, San Francisco, USA
Web
www.thetileapp.com
www.fuseproject.com

When for example a wallet gets lost, Tile Slim helps to find it. The device is only 2 mm thick and fits in any pocket. The battery power lasts for up to twelve months. Via a smartphone app, the item in which the device has been placed can be easily localised. When the grey button is pressed twice, the smartphone is in turn activated and receives a call. Tile Slim operates via a network and therefore, theoretically, worldwide, since it sends its signal to any other device with a Tile app installed.

Statement by the jury
Tile Slim impresses with a clever alternative idea for finding valuables, whereby it is an asset that the effective range extends as the community expands.

Wenn etwa eine Brieftasche verloren gegangen ist, hilft Tile Slim dabei, sie zu suchen. Das Gerät ist nur 2 mm dick und passt in jede Tasche, die Batterie hält bis zu zwölf Monate. Mittels Smartphone-App lässt sich der Gegenstand, in dem das Gerät platziert wurde, einfach lokalisieren. Mittels zweifachem Druck auf den grauen Knopf wird wiederum das Smartphone aktiviert und erhält einen Anruf. Tile Slim funktioniert über ein Netzwerk und damit theoretisch weltweit, denn es sendet sein Signal zu jedem anderen Gerät mit einer Tile-App.

Begründung der Jury
Tile Slim beeindruckt als eine clevere innovative Idee zum Wiederfinden von Wertgegenständen, wobei auch gefällt, dass sich der Wirkradius mit anwachsender Community vergrößert.

SD700
External SSD
Externe SSD

Manufacturer
ADATA Technology Co., Ltd., New Taipei City, Taiwan
In-house design
Web
www.adata.com

The external SSD SD700 fits into one hand and weighs only 75 grams. It operates quietly and without heat emission. Incorporating 3D NAND flash technology, it offers a capacity of 256 GB, 512 GB or 1 TB. A multilayered enclosure guarantees the protection class IP68 and reliably prevents penetration of dust and water. It also passes US Army MIL-STD-810G 516.6 shock and drop resistance standard, ensuring a high degree of shock proofing. Connectivity via a USB 3.1 allows for trouble-free 4K streaming. The average read and write data transfer speed is 440 MB per second. The data storage disc offers plug-and-play compatibility for Windows, Mac OS and Android.

Die externe SSD SD700 passt in eine Handfläche und wiegt nur 75 Gramm. Sie arbeitet leise und ohne Wärmeabgabe. Mit 3D-NAND-Flash-Technik bietet sie eine Kapazität von 256 GB, 512 GB oder 1 TB. Eine mehrschichtige Umhüllung gewährleistet die Schutzart IP68 und verhindert zuverlässig das Eindringen von Staub und Wasser. Zudem erfüllt sie in Bezug auf Erschütterungen und Fallen US-Army-MIL-STD-810G 516.6 und zeigt damit einen hohen Grad an Stoßfestigkeit. Das Gerät verbindet mittels USB 3.1, das erlaubt ein störungsfreies 4K-Streaming. Die durchschnittliche Read/Write-Datenübertragungsrate liegt bei 440 MB pro Sekunde. Der Datenträger bietet Plug-and-Play-Kompatibilität für Windows, Mac OS und Android.

Statement by the jury
Thanks to its compact dimensions and reduced weight, the SD700 can be carried everywhere and also convinces from a functional standpoint.

Begründung der Jury
Die SD700 lässt sich dank ihrer kompakten Maße und ihres geringen Gewichts einfach überallhin mitführen und überzeugt auch in funktionaler Hinsicht.

Logitech Base
Charging Stand
Ladehalterung

Manufacturer
Logitech, Newark, California, USA
In-house design
Web
www.logitech.com

The Logitech Base allows the iPad Pro to be charged and simultaneously held at an angle from which it is easily read. The special Smart Connector positions the tablet at the right place by means of a magnet, thus avoiding the annoying search for the charging port. With its aluminium surface and sleek form, the device blends well in any environment, be it within one's own four walls or in the office. With this charging stand, the iPad Pro can also be used as a second screen.

Statement by the jury
The Logitech Base always keeps the iPad Pro at a convenient viewing angle, whether reading recipe apps or working in the office. The connection is made conceivably easy via the Smart Connector.

Mit der Logitech Base wird das iPad Pro aufgeladen und zugleich in einem gut ablesbaren Blickwinkel gehalten. Der spezielle Smart Connector positioniert das Tablet mittels Magneten am richtigen Platz, damit wird umständliches Suchen nach dem Ladeanschluss vermieden. Mit seiner Oberfläche aus Aluminium und einer schlichten Formgebung fügt sich das Gerät gut in jede Umgebung ein, sei es in den eigenen vier Wänden oder im Büro. Mit dieser Ladehalterung kann das iPad Pro auch als Zweitbildschirm verwendet werden.

Begründung der Jury
Die Logitech Base hält das iPad Pro stets in einem angenehmen Blickwinkel, ob beim Ablesen der Rezepte-App oder Arbeiten im Büro. Der Anschluss mittels Smart Connector gelingt denkbar einfach.

Kensington Laptop Locking Station 2.0
Laptopschloss

Manufacturer
Kensington, San Mateo, USA
In-house design
Kensington Industrial Design Team
(Alex Klinkman, Wilson Tse)
Web
www.kensington.com

Thanks to its extending arms, the Kensington Laptop Locking Station 2.0 protects both 13.3" and 15.6" devices from theft. The laptop is easily locked and unlocked with the Kensington Security Slot located on the side of the device. The base is seamlessly manufactured from extruded aluminium, with its dark-grey design, sandblasted and anodised, imparting a high-quality impression. They are complemented by side arms with a matt-black finish. Silicon pads protect the contact areas of the laptop. The device is fairly flat, with a height of only 28 mm.

Statement by the jury
The Kensington Laptop Locking Station 2.0 offers functionally convincing security and is pleasing due to its sleek, flat design.

Dank ausziehbarer Arme lassen sich mit der Kensington Laptop Locking Station 2.0 sowohl 13.3"- als auch 15.6"-Geräte vor Diebstahl sichern. Über den seitlich angebrachten Kensington Security Slot wird das Laptop einfach ge- und entsperrt. Der Sockel ist als nahtlose Form aus stranggepresstem Aluminium gefertigt, dessen dunkles Grau in sandgestrahlter und eloxierter Ausführung hochwertig anmutet. Dazu ergänzen sich die Seitenarme aus mattschwarzer Oberfläche. Silikonpolsterungen schützen das Laptop an den Auflageflächen. Mit nur 28 mm Höhe ist das Gerät ziemlich flach.

Begründung der Jury
Die Kensington Laptop Locking Station 2.0 bietet funktional überzeugende Sicherheit und gefällt durch ihre geschmeidige flache Ausführung.

Lenovo Smart Assistant
Smart Home Controls
Smart-Home-Steuerung

Manufacturer
Lenovo, Morrisville, North Carolina, USA
In-house design
Web
www.lenovo.com

The Lenovo Smart Assistant is a practical, everyday aid for the smart home. A great variety of tasks can be performed by voice activation, for example ordering a delivery service or taxi and controlling household appliances. Eight microphones ensure accurate voice recognition and good sound quality in large rooms. In order to underscore the smart character of the device, only the volume is regulated by control elements. Various warm, modern shades of colour and a discreet, cylindrical form convey an attractive feel, thus making communication easier.

Statement by the jury
The Lenovo Smart Assistant conveys trust and can be intuitively operated, so that commands are gladly given without hesitation.

Der Lenovo Smart Assistant ist ein praktischer Alltagshelfer für das Smart Home. Die verschiedensten Aufgaben lassen sich durch Stimmbefehle erledigen, etwa einen Lieferservice oder ein Taxi zu bestellen oder auch intelligente Haushaltsgeräte zu steuern. Acht Mikrofone sorgen für präzise Stimmerkennung und gute Tonqualität in großen Räumen. Um den Smart-Charakter des Geräts zu unterstreichen, wird lediglich die Lautstärke mit Steuerungselementen geregelt. Unterschiedliche warme, modische Farbtöne und eine dezente zylindrische Form verleihen dem Gerät eine sympathische Ausstrahlung, wodurch die Kommunikation erleichtert wird.

Begründung der Jury
Der Lenovo Smart Assistant vermittelt Vertrautheit und lässt sich intuitiv bedienen, sodass man ohne zu zögern gerne Sprachbefehle an ihn übermittelt.

vSolution Cam
Desktop Visualiser

Manufacturer
WolfVision GmbH, Klaus, Austria
In-house design
Johannes Fraundorfer, Thomas Zangerle
Design
Schindler-Design (Christoph Schindler),
Wolfurt, Austria
Christian Natter, Au, Austria
Web
www.wolfvision.com
www.schindler-design.de
Honourable Mention

Books, photos, three-dimensional objects, notes and other materials can be presented quickly and easily to a large group via the vSolution Cam without the need for extended preparation. The items used are positioned under the HD camera and thus presented to the group via a connected monitor or projector. An HD camera and a LED lighting system are both integrated into the arm of the portable device; control is intuitive and requires no additional manual adjustment.

Statement by the jury
The vSolution Cam delights with its intuitively operated functions, achieving the presentation of ideas to a group in an easy and trouble-free way.

Bücher, Fotos, dreidimensionale Objekte, Notizen und andere Materialien lassen sich mit der vSolution Cam schnell und einfach einer größeren Gruppe präsentieren, ohne dass dafür längere Vorbereitungszeit nötig ist. Die betreffenden Elemente werden unter der HD-Kamera positioniert und so mittels einem verbundenen Monitor oder Projektor der Gruppe vorgestellt. HD-Kamera und LED-Lichtsystem sind beide im Arm des tragbaren Geräts integriert, die Steuerung gelingt intuitiv und bedarf keiner zusätzlichen manuellen Justierung.

Begründung der Jury
Die vSolution Cam begeistert durch ihre intuitiv einsetzbaren Funktionen, mit denen ganz einfach und unbeschwert die Präsentation von Ideen in einem Team gelingt.

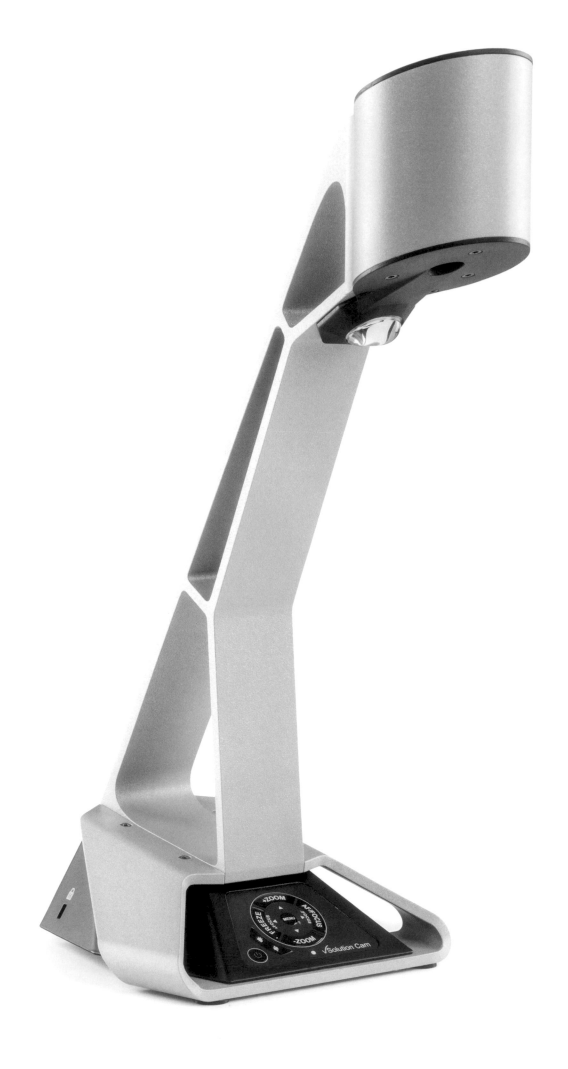

FL-T01
Interactive Tabletop Projector
Interaktiver Tisch-Projektor

Manufacturer
Sony Corporation, Tokyo, Japan
In-house design
Yusuke Tsujita
Web
www.sony.net

With this projector, pictures can be projected onto a tabletop or some other support surface and processed there interactively by means of software with gesture recognition. The device recognises items placed on the table and measures their dimensions and positions. The projector evinces a minimalist structure like a lab tool, with very good shape for heat release, a height-adjusting lock mechanism, and a stand built to help manage cords.

Mit diesem Projektor können Bilder auf eine Tischplatte oder eine andere Unterlage projiziert und dort mittels einer Software für Gestenerkennung interaktiv bearbeitet werden. Gegenstände, die auf dem Tisch platziert werden, erfasst das Gerät und es erkennt Maße und Ausrichtung derselben. Der Projektor ist wie ein Laborgerät minimalistisch gestaltet. Dadurch leitet die Form die Wärme sehr gut ab, ein Arretierungsmechanismus unterstützt die Höhenjustierung, der Ständer das Kabelmanagement.

Statement by the jury
The FL-T01 is able to transform the table into an interactive screen – an impressively innovative and functionally sophisticated idea.

Begründung der Jury
Der FL-T01 vermag den Tisch in einen interaktiven Bildschirm zu verwandeln – eine beeindruckend innovative wie auch funktional ausgereifte Idee.

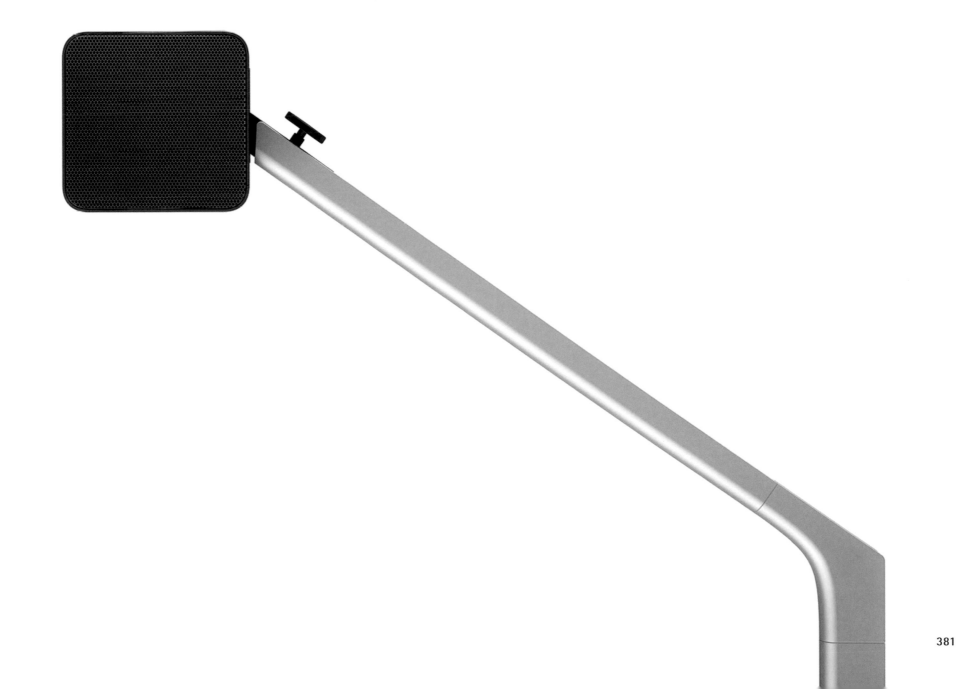

Witbox Go!
3D Printer
3D-Drucker

Manufacturer
Mundo Reader, S.L., Las Rozas de Madrid, Spain
In-house design
Eduard Villar, Julen Pejenaute, Ricardo Barriendos
Web
www.bq.com

Witbox Go! is a 3D printer which can be made available to the general public thanks to its simple operability. As an innovation, it integrates a Qualcomm processor on an Android platform. Connection to the cloud in turn assures reliable wireless communication. The device can be operated intuitively from any mobile device. With a clear, sleek design and a cubic form with rounded corners, Witbox Go! imparts easiness and fun. Due to the clear, white colouration, it also blends very well into household environments.

Witbox Go! ist ein 3D-Drucker, mit dem diese Technologie durch einfache Bedienbarkeit einem breiteren Zielpublikum zugänglich gemacht werden kann. Er integriert als Innovation einen Qualcomm-Prozessor auf Androidbasis, für zuverlässige drahtlose Kommunikation sorgt die Anbindung an eine Cloud. Das Gerät kann von jedem mobilen Gerät aus intuitiv gesteuert werden. Mit einer klaren, schlichten Gestaltung und einer kubischen Formgebung mit abgerundeten Ecken vermittelt Witbox Go! Leichtigkeit und Unbeschwertheit. Auch durch die klare weiße Farbgebung fügt er sich gut in den häuslichen Bereich ein.

Statement by the jury
With Witbox Go!, 3D printing technology confidently integrates into the living environment, thanks to intuitive operation and aesthetics suitable to everyday life.

Begründung der Jury
Mit Witbox Go! hält die Technologie des 3D-Drucks dank intuitiver Bedienbarkeit und einer alltagstauglichen Ästhetik souverän Einzug in die Wohnumgebung.

Form 2
3D Printer
3D-Drucker

Manufacturer
Formlabs Inc., Somerville, USA
In-house design
Web
www.formlabs.com

Form 2 brings the innovative technology of the 3D printer to a wide range of industries such as dentistry, handicraft, education, design or engineering. By means of high-resolution stereolithography technology, laser-sharp prints with a very good surface finish are created. Operation remains, however, simple and intuitive; the device works reliably and very accurately. Using a touchscreen, print models can be easily uploaded via Wi-Fi.

Form 2 bringt die innovative Technologie des 3D-Drucks in eine große Bandbreite von Branchen wie etwa die Zahntechnik, das Kunsthandwerk, die Bildung, das Design oder den Maschinenbau. Mithilfe hochauflösender Stereolithografie-Technologie werden laserscharfe Drucke mit sehr guter Oberflächenbeschaffenheit erzeugt. Die Bedienung bleibt dabei einfach und intuitiv, das Gerät arbeitet zuverlässig und sehr präzise. Mittels Touchscreen-Oberfläche können Druckvorlagen einfach über Wi-Fi hochgeladen werden.

Statement by the jury
Thanks to sophisticated technology, the Form 2 works with surprising accuracy. Operation and transmission of printing data succeed in a very uncomplicated way.

Begründung der Jury
Dank ausgefeilter Technologie arbeitet der Form 2 erstaunlich präzise. Die Bedienung und die Übermittlung der Druckdaten gelingen ganz unkompliziert.

You can also find this product on
Dieses Produkt finden Sie auch auf
Page 181
Seite 181

HP PageWide Pro
700 Series
Multifunction Printers
Multifunktionsdrucker

Manufacturer
HP Inc., Vancouver, USA
In-house design
HP Design (Danny Han, Pete Hwang)
Web
www.hp.com

The A3 multifunction printers of the
HP PageWide Pro 700 series focus on
integration in mobile communication
systems and in the cloud. When developing the operating elements, modern
IT consumer expectations were taken
into account. Similarly, the device ful-
fills demands placed on the operational
safety of premium office equipment.
Soft curves and self-contained planar
elements confer a modern impression.

Statement by the jury
With the simple involvement of mobile
devices and cloud systems, the HP
PageWide Pro 700 series integrates surprisingly well with peripheral products.

Die A3-Multifunktionsdrucker aus der Serie
HP PageWide Pro 700 legen verstärktes
Augenmerk auf die Einbindung in mobile
Kommunikationssysteme und in eine
Cloud. In der Ausarbeitung der Bedienele-
mente wurden moderne IT-gewohnte
Konsumentenerwartungen berücksichtigt,
ebenso erfüllt das Gerät die Ansprüche an
die Betriebssicherheit einer hochwertigen
Büroausstattung. Sanfte Kurven und flä-
chig abschließende Elemente verleihen ihm
eine moderne Anmutung.

Begründung der Jury
Mit der einfachen Implikation von mobilen
Endgeräte und Cloudsystemen lässt sich
die Serie HP PageWide Pro 700 erstaunlich
gut in die Produktperipherie einbinden.

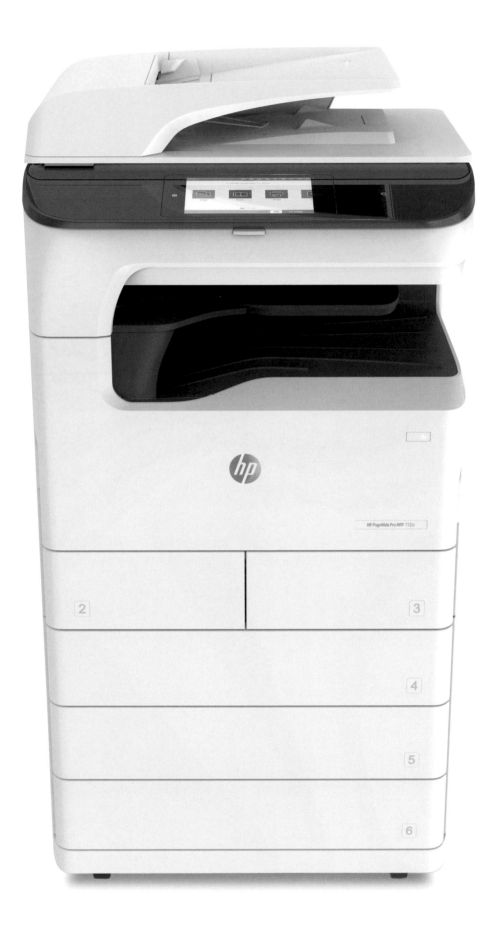

Blackmagic Broadcast Suite
Broadcast Equipment

Manufacturer
Blackmagic Design Pty Ltd,
Melbourne, Australia

In-house design
Blackmagic Design Pty Ltd

Web
www.blackmagicdesign.com

reddot award 2017
best of the best

Perfectly integrated

Productions in the field of media are often highly complex. The Blackmagic Broadcast Suite is a modular range of over 20 products designed specifically for video productions like news gathering, sporting events and concerts. In an innovative manner, it combines professional video format conversion, live switching, recording and playback. As a highly cost-effective solution, it allows the creation of tailor-made systems for specific individual workflows, while also providing the necessary flexibility for those systems to adapt to changing needs. Moreover, it features innovative thermal management, since such systems are often mounted in hot, confined spaces such as outside broadcast vehicles. The "crossflow" cooling system enables all units in the suite to work together to effectively move cold air, providing optimal heat dissipation even when the units are mounted side-by-side. Compact and versatile, the individual components of the series can be used as stand-alone desktop products or rack mounted side-by-side for larger broadcast systems. The Broadcast Suite impresses with a minimal yet coherent visual appearance as well as an intuitive control layout. It thus provides error-free operation even in high-pressure, volatile live production scenarios. Emerging from following an outstandingly logical and consistent approach, this highly advanced modular system opens up new horizons to the media sector.

Perfekt integriert

Produktionen im Medienbereich sind oft sehr komplex. Die Blackmagic Broadcast Suite ist ein modulares Sortiment aus über 20 Produkten, das speziell für Videoproduktionen wie Nachrichtensendungen, Sportveranstaltungen oder Konzerten entwickelt wurde. Auf innovative Weise bündelt es professionelle Videoformatkonvertierung, Liveschaltung, Aufnahme und Wiedergabe. Als sehr kosteneffiziente Lösung ermöglicht es maßgeschneiderte Systeme für individuell variierende Workflows und weist dabei auch die notwendige Flexibilität auf, um sich an verändernde Bedürfnisse anzupassen. Da derartiges Equipment oft in engen, wärmeintensiven Räumen wie beispielsweise Übertragungswagen eingesetzt wird, wurde ein innovatives Wärmemanagement entwickelt. Mit dem „Crossflow"-Kühlsystem arbeiten alle Geräte so zusammen, dass sie die kühle Luft effektiv bewegen und eine perfekte Wärmeableitung auch dann bieten, wenn sie Seite an Seite montiert sind. Kompakt und vielseitig, können die einzelnen Komponenten als eigenständige Geräte ihre Funktion erfüllen, oder für größere Sendesysteme nebeneinander im Rack montiert zum Einsatz kommen. Die Broadcast Suite beeindruckt dabei mit einem minimalistischen, in sich stimmigen Erscheinungsbild sowie einer intuitiv bedienbaren Steuerung. Dadurch erlaubt sie einen fehlerfreien Betrieb auch in hektischen Liveproduktionen. Ein in seiner Stringenz und Logik beeindruckender gestalterischer Ansatz führt hier zu einem hochentwickelten modularen System, das dem Medienbereich neue Horizonte erschließt.

Statement by the jury
The Blackmagic Broadcast Suite fascinates with the perfect organisation of all elements. Packed into a portable and effective system, its design is compact and geared toward enabling highly adaptable settings. The purist and consistent language of form is highly convincing, as it is complemented by an intuitive ease of operation that is outstanding for devices in this field. This innovative, highly user-friendly system is ideally suited to professional live production scenarios.

Begründung der Jury
Bei der Blackmagic Broadcast Suite begeistert die perfekte Organisation aller Elemente. Eine kompakte und auf Vielseitigkeit ausgerichtete Gestaltung vereint diese zu einem effektiven und transportablen System. Besonders überzeugt auch die puristische und konsistente Formensprache, die einhergeht mit einer für diesen Bereich ausgesprochen intuitiven Art der Bedienung. Dieses innovative, äußerst nutzerfreundliche System ist bestens geeignet für den professionellen Einsatz.

Designer portrait
See page 74
Siehe Seite 74

DaVinci Resolve Micro Panel
Motion Picture Colour Grading System
Colour Grading System für Film

Manufacturer
Blackmagic Design Pty Ltd, Melbourne, Australia
In-house design
Web
www.blackmagicdesign.com

With the DaVinci Resolve Micro Panel, motion picture footage can be processed for light and colour. The well-conceived trackballs support the interplay of hand, eye and graphical user interface. Users thus achieve control over the nuances of mood and colour in a film scene. Manually operated setting buttons provide access to important functions, thus inviting experimentation. The device is light, compact and effortlessly transportable and can therefore be carried to any set without problems. Creative control of light and colour is thus possible in challenging and remote film locations.

Mit dem DaVinci Resolve Micro Panel kann Filmmaterial in Bezug auf Licht und Farbe bearbeitet werden. Drei durchdacht konstruierte Trackballs unterstützen das Zusammenspiel von Hand, Auge und grafischer Benutzerschnittstelle. So erhalten Anwender die Kontrolle über die Justierung von Stimmung und Farbnuancen einer Filmszene. Manuelle Einstellknöpfe bieten Zugang zu wichtigen Funktionen, was zum Experimentieren einlädt. Das Gerät ist leicht, kompakt und mühelos zu transportieren und kann daher problemlos zu jedem Set mitgenommen werden. Die kreative Kontrolle von Licht und Farbe wird so auch an herausfordernden und abgelegenen Drehorten möglich.

Statement by the jury
The DaVinci Resolve Micro Panel offers a functionally sophisticated colour grading system for independent contractors and also for large film productions.

Begründung der Jury
Das DaVinci Resolve Micro Panel bietet ein funktional ausgereiftes Colour Grading System für Freiberufler wie auch für große Filmproduktionen.

DaVinci Resolve Mini Panel
Motion Picture Colour Grading System
Colour Grading System für Film

Manufacturer
Blackmagic Design Pty Ltd, Melbourne, Australia
In-house design
Web
www.blackmagicdesign.com

The DaVinci Resolve Mini Panel is equipped with three professional trackballs and a row of buttons in order to switch between individual tools, make colour corrections and navigate through the system. In addition, the device has two colour LCD screens displaying menus as well as control and parameter settings for each of the active tools. Manual setting buttons offer access to special DaVinci functions. The device, with its dynamic construction, sets itself clearly apart from a workspace that is usually quite rational, while also imparting a professional and trustworthy impression.

Das DaVinci Resolve Mini Panel ist mit drei professionellen Trackballs sowie mit einer Reihe von Knöpfen ausgestattet, um zwischen einzelnen Werkzeugen zu wechseln, Farbkorrekturen durchzuführen und durch das System zu navigieren. Zusätzlich besitzt das Gerät zwei farbige LCD-Bildschirme, auf denen Menüs sowie Kontroll- und Parametereinstellungen für das jeweils aktive Werkzeug angezeigt werden. Manuelle Einstellknöpfe bieten Zugang zu speziellen DaVinci-Funktionen. In seinem dynamischen Aufbau hebt sich das Gerät deutlich ab von einem üblicherweise recht rationalen Arbeitsplatz und vermittelt eine professionelle und vertrauenswürdige Anmutung.

Statement by the jury
The essence of image editing requires instinctive recognition and correction of nuances. The DaVinci Resolve Mini Panel is superbly suitable for this.

Begründung der Jury
Zum Wesen der Bildkorrektur gehört das intuitive Erfassen und Korrigieren von Nuancen. Das DaVinci Resolve Mini Panel ist dafür hervorragend geeignet.

The jury 2017
International orientation and objectivity
Internationalität und Objektivität

The jurors of the Red Dot Award: Product Design
All members of the Red Dot Award: Product Design jury are appointed on the basis of independence and impartiality. They are independent designers, academics in design faculties, representatives of international design institutions, and design journalists.

The jury is international in its composition, which changes every year. These conditions assure a maximum of objectivity. The members of this year's jury are presented in alphabetical order on the following pages.

Die Juroren des Red Dot Award: Product Design
In die Jury des Red Dot Award: Product Design wird als Mitglied nur berufen, wer völlig unabhängig und unparteiisch ist. Dies sind selbstständig arbeitende Designer, Hochschullehrer der Designfakultäten, Repräsentanten internationaler Designinstitutionen und Designfachjournalisten.

Die Jury ist international besetzt und wechselt in jedem Jahr ihre Zusammensetzung. Unter diesen Voraussetzungen ist ein Höchstmaß an Objektivität gewährleistet. Auf den folgenden Seiten werden die Jurymitglieder des diesjährigen Wettbewerbs in alphabetischer Reihenfolge vorgestellt.

01

David Andersen
Denmark
Dänemark

David Andersen, born in 1978, graduated from Glasgow School of Art and the Fashion Design Academy in 2003. Until 2014, he developed designs for ready-to-wear clothes, shoes, perfume, underwear and home wear and emerged as a fashion designer working as chief designer at Dreams by Isabell Kristensen as well as designing couture for the royal Danish family, celebrities, artists etc. under his own name. In 2007, he debuted his collection "David Andersen". He has received many awards and grants for his designs, e.g. a grant from the National Art Foundation. David Andersen is also known for his development of sustainable clothing with his collection, Zero Waste, and has received several awards for his work on ecology and sustainable productions. Today, he works as Vice President for Design at Rosendahl Design Group, a multi-brand house with seven brands including: Rosendahl, Holmegaard, Kay Bojesen Denmark, Bjørn Wiinblad Denmark, Lyngby Porcelain, Arne Jacobsen Clocks and Juna. Furthermore, David Andersen is a guest lecturer at different schools and colleges.

David Andersen, 1978 geboren, studierte an der Glasgow School of Art und der Fashion Design Academy, wo er 2003 sein Examen machte. Bis 2014 fertigte er Designs für Konfektionsware, Schuhe, Parfüm, Unterwäsche und Homewear. Daraus entwickelte sich eine Karriere als Modedesigner und er begann, bei Dreams von Isabell Kristensen als Chefdesigner zu arbeiten sowie unter seinem eigenen Namen Couture für die dänische Königsfamilie, Prominente, Künstler etc. zu entwerfen. Im Jahr 2007 stellte er erstmals seine eigene „David Andersen"-Kollektion vor. Für seine Entwürfe hat David Andersen bereits viele Auszeichnungen und Fördergelder erhalten, darunter ein Stipendium der National Art Foundation (Nationale Kunststiftung). David Andersen hat sich auch mit „Zero Waste", einer Kollektion nachhaltiger Kleidung, einen Namen gemacht, und er hat mehrere Auszeichnungen für seine Arbeit im Bereich Umwelt und nachhaltiger Produktion erhalten. Heute arbeitet er als Vizepräsident für Design bei der Rosendahl Design Group, einem Mehrmarkenkonzern mit sieben Marken: Rosendahl, Holmegaard, Kay Bojesen Denmark, Bjørn Wiinblad Denmark, Lyngby Porzellan, Arne Jacobsen Uhren und Juna. Darüber hinaus ist David Andersen Gastdozent an verschiedenen Schulen und Hochschulen.

01 Rosendahl Penta
thermos jug
With an insulating glass core and
a push-button lid for easy pouring
Rosendahl Penta Thermoskanne
Mit Isolierglaskern und Druckknopf-
deckel, um das Ausschenken zu
erleichtern

02 **Rosendahl wine ball**
A multi-functional design that in-
geniously combines a corkscrew,
foil cutter, wine stopper and bottle
opener
Rosendahl Weinkugel
Ein multifunktionales Design, das
auf geniale Weise einen Korken-
zieher, Folienschneider, Weinstöpsel
und Flaschenöffner vereint

02

"People prefer products with
an impressive history. As a
designer, you need to develop
products which combine design,
functionality and quality."
„Menschen bevorzugen Produkte
mit einer beeindruckenden Geschichte. Als Designer muss man
Produkte entwickeln, die Design,
Funktionalität und Qualität in
Einklang bringen."

In your opinion, what makes for good design?
Good design is not only interesting because of its
colour, shape or function, but because there is a story
behind it. A designer must be able to take in impres-
sions and signals from his or her daily life and then
convert that into great ideas.

**How has the role played by design in our everyday
lives changed?**
In the past, the design industry was dominated by
mass production. Nowadays, we all like to show ourselves through e.g. design objects. Therefore, craftsmanship and originality have become two important
factors in good design.

**What attracts you to the role of Red Dot jury
member?**
It is very inspiring to see designs from all over the
world and to follow the development. It is a pleasure
to be a juror together with such competent designers.

**What does winning the Red Dot say about a
product?**
An interesting product that has a good story and hits
the zeitgeist.

Was macht Ihrer Ansicht nach gutes Design aus?
Gutes Design ist nicht nur wegen seiner Farbe, Form
oder Funktion interessant, sondern weil eine Geschich-
te dahintersteckt. Ein Designer muss Eindrücke und
Signale aus dem Alltag verwenden und in großartige
Ideen verwandeln können.

**Inwieweit hat sich die Rolle, die Design in unserem
täglichen Leben spielt, verändert?**
Früher wurde die Designbranche von Massenproduk-
tion beherrscht. Heutzutage geben wir uns alle gerne
z. B. durch Designobjekte zu erkennen. Deshalb sind
Handwerkskunst und Originalität zu zwei wichtigen
Faktoren für gutes Design geworden.

Was reizt Sie an der Arbeit als Red Dot-Juror?
Es ist sehr inspirierend, Entwürfe aus der ganzen Welt
zu sehen und ihre Entwicklung zu verfolgen. Zudem
ist es ein Vergnügen, Jurymitglied in einer Gruppe so
fachkundiger Designer zu sein.

**Was sagt eine Auszeichnung mit dem Red Dot über
das Produkt aus?**
Dass es ein interessantes Produkt ist, auf einer guten
Geschichte basiert und den Zeitgeist trifft.

01

Prof. Masayo Ave
Japan/Germany
Japan/Deutschland

Professor Masayo Ave, an architect and designer, founded her own design studio "Ave design corporation" in 1992 and since 2001 has been a leader in advanced sensory design research. From 2004 to 2007, she had a guest professorship at the Berlin University of the Arts, where she founded the Experimental Design Institute of Haptic Interface Design. Afterwards she was professor and head of the product design department at the Estonian Academy of Arts. From 2012 to 2013, she was a guest professor at the textile and surface design department at Weißensee Academy of Art Berlin. She has also held a teaching position at the Kanazawa College of Arts in Japan, since 2009. Since 2006, her design studio "MasayoAve creation" and the Haptic Interface Design Institute have been based in Berlin. Masayo Ave is actively involved in educational design programmes for children and young people in cooperation with design institutes such as the DesignSingapore Council and the Red Dot Design Museum Essen, Germany. In October 2016, she was appointed professor and head of product design department of BAU International Berlin – University of Applied Sciences.

Professorin Masayo Ave, Architektin und Designerin, eröffnete 1992 ihr Designstudio „Ave design corporation" und nimmt seit 2001 eine Führungsposition in sensorischer Designforschung ein. Von 2004 bis 2007 hatte sie eine Gastprofessur an der Universität der Künste Berlin, wo sie das experimentelle Designinstitut „Haptic Interface Design" gründete. Anschließend war sie Professorin und Leiterin des Produktdesign-Instituts der Estonian Academy of Arts und von 2012 bis 2013 Gastprofessorin in Textildesign und Oberflächengestaltung an der Weißensee Kunsthochschule Berlin. Außerdem unterrichtet sie seit 2009 am Kanazawa College of Arts in Japan. Seit 2006 sind ihr Designstudio „MasayoAve creation" und das Haptic Interface Design Institute in Berlin ansässig. Masayo Ave beschäftigt sich mit der Designlehre von Kindern und Jugendlichen in Kooperation mit Designinstituten wie dem DesignSingapore Council und dem Red Dot Design Museum Essen. Im Oktober 2016 wurde sie zur Professorin und Leiterin der Fakultät Produktdesign an die BAU International Berlin – University of Applied Sciences berufen.

01 BLOCK
Modular sofa made from an
open-cell foam based on polyester, launched in her own
collection "MasayoAve creation",
1999/2000
Modulares Sofa, hergestellt aus
einem offenporigen Schaum,
basierend auf Polyester, erschienen in ihrer eigenen Kollektion
„MasayoAve creation", 1999/2000

02 COOL
Cushions made from an open-
cell foam based on polyester,
launched in her own collection
"MasayoAve creation",
1999/2000
Kissen, hergestellt aus einem
offenporigen Schaum, basierend
auf Polyester, erschienen in ihrer
eigenen Kollektion „MasayoAve
creation", 1999/2000

02

"Good design reduces the invisible stress of daily life."

„Gutes Design reduziert den unsichtbaren Stress des täglichen Lebens."

In your opinion, what makes for good design?
Right materials to touch, right forms to handle, the right function which follows a vision.

What attracts you to the role of Red Dot jury member?
Discovering new proposals for updating our daily life.

What does winning the Red Dot say about a product?
It allows the product to share the intercultural value of design with a wide audience across the world.

Which topics are most likely to influence design in the coming years?
Bionics, new printing and knitting technology.

Which area of design do you feel has the greatest potential for development for the future?
Sensory enhancements, such as acoustic management and haptic interfaces.

Was macht Ihrer Ansicht nach gutes Design aus?
Die richtigen Materialien zum Anfassen, die richtigen Formen für die Handhabung, die richtige Funktion, die einer Vision folgt.

Was reizt Sie an der Arbeit als Red Dot-Juror?
Neue Ideen zu entdecken, die unser tägliches Leben auf den aktuellsten Stand bringen.

Was sagt eine Auszeichnung mit dem Red Dot über das Produkt aus?
Es ermöglicht dem Produkt, den interkulturellen Wert von Design mit einem breiten Publikum in der ganzen Welt zu teilen.

Welche Themen werden das Design in den kommenden Jahren besonders beeinflussen?
Die Bionik, neue Druck- und Stricktechniken.

In welchem Designbereich sehen Sie das größte Entwicklungspotenzial für die Zukunft?
Bei Verbesserungen, die die Sinne ansprechen, wie z. B. das Akustik-Management oder haptische Schnittstellen.

01

Chris Bangle
USA / Italy
USA / Italien

Chris Bangle studied at the University of Wisconsin, graduated from the Art Center College of Design in Pasadena, California and began his career at Opel in 1981. In 1985 he moved on to Fiat, before becoming the first American Chief of Design at BMW in 1992, where he was in charge of the designs for BMW, Mini Cooper and Rolls-Royce. In 2007 he was awarded, together with the Design Team BMW Group, the honorary title "Red Dot: Design Team of the Year" for his outstanding overall design achievements. Since leaving the automotive industry in 2009 Chris Bangle has continued his own design projects and innovations in his design studio Chris Bangle Associates s.r.l. (CBA) near Clavesana in Piemonte, Italy. As Managing Director of CBA he currently heads a team of designers and engineers, who use the studio as a design residence and creative think tank together with the staff of its clients. His 25 years of experience and competence make Chris Bangle a sought-after speaker. He frequently travels around the world to give lectures, teach design and consult clients.

Chris Bangle studierte an der University of Wisconsin, machte seinen Abschluss am Art Center College of Design in Pasadena, Kalifornien, und begann seine Karriere 1981 bei Opel. 1985 wechselte er zu Fiat, bevor er 1992 der erste „American Chief of Design" bei BMW wurde und für die Entwürfe von BMW, Mini Cooper und Rolls-Royce verantwortlich zeichnete. 2007 wurde ihm für seine herausragende gestalterische Gesamtleistung zusammen mit dem Design Team BMW Group der Ehrentitel „Red Dot: Design Team of the Year" verliehen. Seit seinem Ausstieg aus der Automobilbranche 2009 führt Chris Bangle eigene Gestaltungsvorhaben und Innovationen in seinem Studio Chris Bangle Associates s.r.l. (CBA) bei Clavesana im Piemont, Italien, fort und leitet derzeit als Managing Director von CBA ein Team von Designern und Ingenieuren, die das Studio gemeinsam mit den Mitarbeitern der Auftraggeber als Designresidenz und kreative Ideenfabrik nutzen. Seine 25-jährige Erfahrung und Kompetenz machen Chris Bangle zu einem gefragten Referenten. Er reist regelmäßig um die Welt, um Vorträge zu halten, Design zu lehren und seine Kunden zu beraten.

01 Bunny
01 Bunny
"Bunny" is a robotic cocktail waitress in development with an Italian research centre. The project applies car design techniques and philosophy to a service robot to give it character and identity without creating a humanoid architecture and a formal solution.

„Bunny" ist eine Roboter-Cocktail-Kellnerin, die zurzeit mit einem italienischen Forschungszentrum entwickelt wird. Das Projekt basiert auf Automobildesign-Techniken und wendet die gleiche Philosophie für einen Service-Roboter an, um ihm eine Persönlichkeit und eine Identität zu geben, ohne eine menschenähnliche Architektur und eine formale Lösung zu schaffen.

02 Illusions
Collection of stones for Swarovski
Kollektion von Steinen für Swarovski

02

"I enjoy the company of these important designers in the Red Dot jury as we discuss design – it is very invigorating!"
„Mir macht die Gesellschaft dieser führenden Designer in der Red Dot-Jury große Freude. Wir unterhalten uns über Design. Das ist sehr anregend."

In your opinion, what makes for good design?
Good design is the embodiment of Truth, Beauty, and Love. By "embodiment" I mean that, when considering all the factors that went into the making of this artefact of design, it is evident that these three elements were prioritised. I am interested in the story behind the design.

How has the role played by design in our everyday lives changed?
Design has become a "thing unto itself" which of course it was never meant to be when our predecessors set out to improve their world. Through the rise of branding, the design itself has become a co-branding phenomenon and this is something we are still trying to come to grips with.

Which area of design do you feel has the greatest potential for development for the future?
I have always held that the expanded application of "car design" practices into all the other "design areas" would be a good thing for all concerned.

Was macht Ihrer Ansicht nach gutes Design aus?
Gutes Design ist die Verkörperung von Wahrheit, Schönheit und Liebe. Mit „Verkörperung" meine ich, dass diese drei Eigenschaften eindeutig bei der Gestaltung des Produkts vorrangig waren, wenn man alle Faktoren, die die Herstellung des Gegenstandes beeinflusst haben, berücksichtigt. Mich interessiert die Geschichte hinter dem Design.

Inwieweit hat sich die Rolle, die Design in unserem täglichen Leben spielt, verändert?
Design ist zu einem „Ding an sich" geworden, was natürlich niemals so beabsichtigt war, als unsere Vorgänger anfingen, ihre Welt zu verbessern. Durch zunehmendes Branding ist Design selbst zu einem Co-Branding-Phänomen geworden. Das ist etwas, was wir noch in den Griff zu bekommen versuchen.

In welchem Designbereich sehen Sie das größte Entwicklungspotenzial für die Zukunft?
Ich bin schon immer der Meinung gewesen, dass die erweiterte Anwendung von Automobildesign-Praktiken in allen anderen Designbereichen eine gute Sache für alle Beteiligten wäre.

01

Dr Luisa Bocchietto
Italy
Italien

Dr Luisa Bocchietto, architect and designer, graduated from the Milan Polytechnic. She has worked as a freelancer undertaking projects for local development, building renovations and urban planning. As a visiting professor she teaches at universities and design schools, she takes part in design conferences and international juries, publishes articles and organises exhibitions on architecture and design. Over the years, her numerous projects aimed at supporting the spread of design quality. From 2008 until 2014, she was National President of the ADI, the Italian Association for Industrial Design. Currently, she is a board member of the World Design Organization (formerly Icsid) and is President Elect for the period from 2017 to 2019.

Dr. Luisa Bocchietto, Architektin und Designerin, graduierte am Polytechnikum Mailand. Sie arbeitet freiberuflich und führt Projekte für die lokale Entwicklung, Gebäudeumbauten und Stadtplanung durch. Als Gastprofessorin lehrt sie an Universitäten und Designschulen, sie nimmt an Designkonferenzen und internationalen Jurys teil, veröffentlicht Artikel und betreut Ausstellungen über Architektur und Design. Ihre zahlreichen Projekte über die Jahre hinweg verfolgten das Ziel, die Verbreitung von Designqualität zu unterstützen. Von 2008 bis 2014 war sie Nationale Präsidentin der ADI, des italienischen Verbandes für Industriedesign. Aktuell ist sie Gremiumsmitglied der World Design Organization (ehemals Icsid) und President Elect für den Zeitraum 2017–2019.

01|02

Renovation of the Palazzo Gromo
Losa in the Piazzo historical
centre of Biella, Italy, restructur-
ing the ancient cellars into an
exhibition centre
Renovierung des Palazzo Gromo
Losa im historischen Zentrum
Piazzo in Biella, Italien, wobei die
antiken Keller in ein Ausstellungs-
zentrum umgestaltet wurden

02

"Sustainability, caring for the environment and design for all are the topics that are most likely to influence design in the coming years."

„Nachhaltigkeit, Umweltschutz und Design für alle werden die Themen sein, die das Design in den kommenden Jahren besonders beeinflussen werden."

In your opinion, what makes for good design?
Innovation, less impact on the planet, an appropriate form.

How has the role played by design in our everyday lives changed?
By contributing to the creation of a better world for everyone.

What importance does design quality have for the economic success of companies?
Great importance, because design can combine a technical and aesthetical vision and can be understood and loved by all.

Which area of design do you feel has the greatest potential for development for the future?
Service design, social design and a new form of transportation design.

Which country do you consider to be a pioneer in product design, and why?
I love Italian design, and I think that it is really always changing and redefining the goals – without limits.

Was macht Ihrer Ansicht nach gutes Design aus?
Innovation, eine geringere Auswirkung auf den Planeten, eine angemessene Form.

Inwieweit hat sich die Rolle, die Design in unserem täglichen Leben spielt, verändert?
Es trägt dazu bei, eine bessere Welt für alle zu schaffen.

Welche Bedeutung hat Designqualität für den wirtschaftlichen Erfolg von Unternehmen?
Eine große Bedeutung, denn Design kann eine technische und ästhetische Vision miteinander verbinden und von allen verstanden und geliebt werden.

In welchem Designbereich sehen Sie das größte Entwicklungspotenzial für die Zukunft?
Service-Design, Social Design und eine neue Form von Transportation Design.

Welche Nation ist für Sie Vorreiter im Produktdesign und warum?
Ich liebe italienisches Design und glaube, dass es sich kontinuierlich verändert und seine Ziele immer wieder neu definiert – ohne Grenzen.

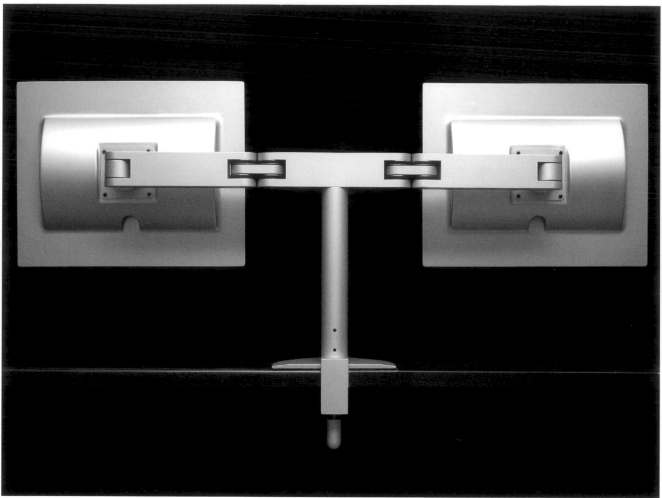

01

Gordon Bruce
USA

Gordon Bruce is the owner of Gordon Bruce Design LLC and has been a design consultant for 40 years working with many multinational corporations in Europe, Asia and the USA. He has worked on a very wide range of products, interiors and vehicles – from aeroplanes to computers to medical equipment to furniture. From 1991 to 1994, Gordon Bruce was a consulting vice president for the Art Center College of Design's Kyoto programme and, from 1995 to 1999, chairman of Product Design for the Innovative Design Lab of Samsung (IDS) in Seoul, Korea. In 2003, he played a crucial role in helping to establish Porsche Design's North American office. For many years, he served as head design consultant for Lenovo's Innovative Design Center (IDC) in Beijing. He recently worked with Bühler in Switzerland and is presently working with Huawei Technologies Co., Ltd. in China. Gordon Bruce is a visiting professor at several universities in the USA and in China and also acts as an author and design publicist. He recently received Art Center College of Design's "Lifetime Achievement Award".

Gordon Bruce ist Inhaber der Gordon Bruce Design LLC und seit mittlerweile 40 Jahren als Designberater für zahlreiche multinationale Unternehmen in Europa, Asien und den USA tätig. Er arbeitete bereits an einer Reihe von Produkten, Inneneinrichtungen und Fahrzeugen – von Flugzeugen über Computer bis hin zu medizinischem Equipment und Möbeln. Von 1991 bis 1994 war Gordon Bruce beratender Vizepräsident des Kioto-Programms am Art Center College of Design sowie von 1995 bis 1999 Vorsitzender für Produktdesign beim Innovative Design Lab of Samsung (IDS) in Seoul, Korea. Im Jahr 2003 war er wesentlich daran beteiligt, das Büro von Porsche Design in Nordamerika zu errichten. Über viele Jahre war er leitender Designberater für Lenovos Innovative Design Center (IDC) in Beijing. Bis vor Kurzem arbeitete er für Bühler, Schweiz, und ist derzeit für Huawei Technologies Co., Ltd. in China tätig. Gordon Bruce ist Gastprofessor an zahlreichen Universitäten in den USA und in China und als Buchautor sowie Publizist tätig. Kürzlich erhielt er vom Art Center College of Design den Lifetime Achievement Award.

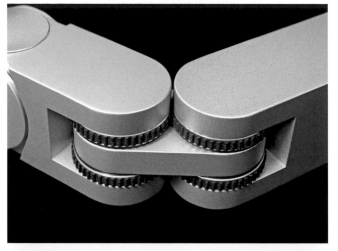

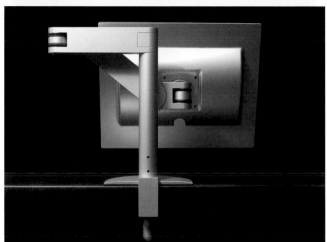

02

"Design is good when it is seamless and unintrusive in the same way that very well-designed typography becomes invisible when reading a book."

„Design ist gut, wenn es nahtlos und unaufdringlich ist, genau wie eine gut gestaltete Typografie unsichtbar wird, wenn man ein Buch liest."

In your opinion, what makes for good design?
Design is good when an idea – tangible or intangible – improves any human rituals, like reading, bicycle riding, fishing, cooking, working, education, etc., by creating a sense of fulfilment and joy while also improving the user's potential.

How has the role played by design in our everyday lives changed?
Good design continues to become more ubiquitous due to the miniaturisation and simplification of objects that embody the rapid advance of technology and the enhanced portability of power and intelligence. As such, many ideas that in the past have been separate are now coalesced.

What importance does design quality have for the economic success of companies?
Good design does many things; one of which enhances the user's experience thus creating a sense of dependability that will ultimately evolve a sense of trust. Trust is the most important quality. Trust, in turn, creates a foundation for building loyalty that enhances the economic performance of any business.

Was macht Ihrer Ansicht nach gutes Design aus?
Design ist gut, wenn eine Idee – ob konkret oder nicht – menschliche Rituale dadurch verbessert, dass ein Gefühl der Erfüllung und Freude ausgelöst und das Potenzial des Nutzers verbessert wird. Das kann Aktivitäten wie Lesen, Radfahren, Angeln, Kochen, Arbeiten, Lernen usw. einschließen.

Inwieweit hat sich die Rolle, die Design in unserem täglichen Leben spielt, verändert?
Gutes Design wird aufgrund der Miniaturisierung und Vereinfachung von Objekten, die den rasanten Fortschritt in der Technik sowie die erweiterte Mobilität von Energie und Intelligenz verkörpern, immer allgegenwärtiger. Viele Ideen, die früher unabhängig voneinander waren, sind dadurch verschmolzen.

Welche Bedeutung hat Designqualität für den wirtschaftlichen Erfolg von Unternehmen?
Gutes Design erreicht vieles. Dazu gehört ein verbessertes Nutzererlebnis, indem ein Gefühl der Zuverlässigkeit, das dann Vertrauen schafft, erweckt wird. Vertrauen ist die wichtigste Eigenschaft und bildet wiederum die Basis für die Treue, die die wirtschaftliche Leistung eines Unternehmens verbessert.

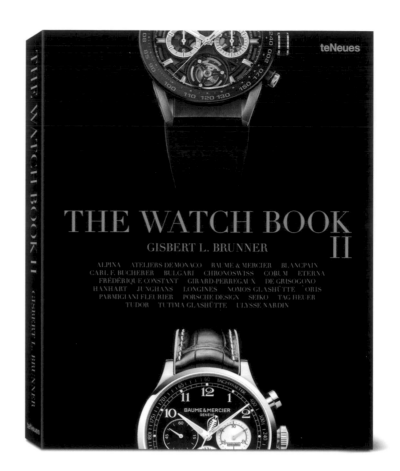

01

Gisbert L. Brunner
Germany
Deutschland

Gisbert L. Brunner, born in 1947, has been working on watches, pendulum clocks and other precision timepieces since 1964. During the quartz clock crisis of the 1970s, his love for the apparently dying-out mechanical timepieces grew. His passion as a hobby collector eventually led to the first newspaper articles in the early 1980s and later to the by now more than 20 books on the topic. Amongst others, Brunner works for magazines such as Chronos, Chronos Japan, Ganz Europa, the Handelszeitung, Prestige, Red Bulletin, Terra Mater, Uhren Juwelen Schmuck, Vectura Magazin and ZEIT Magazin. After the successful Watch Book in 2015, the teNeues publishing house published Watch Book II in 2016. In it, Gisbert L. Brunner portrays a total of 24 watch brands from Alpina to Ulysse Nardin in words and images. In June 2017, Watch Book III appeared, which was dedicated exclusively to the Rolex brand.

Gisbert L. Brunner, Jahrgang 1947, beschäftigt sich seit 1964 mit Armbanduhren, Pendeluhren und anderen Präzisionszeitmessern. Während der Quarzuhren-Krise in den 1970er Jahren wuchs seine Liebe zu den anscheinend aussterbenden mechanischen Zeitmessern. Ein leidenschaftliches Sammelhobby führte ab den frühen 1980er Jahren zu ersten Zeitschriftenartikeln und inzwischen mehr als 20 Büchern über dieses Metier. Brunner ist u. a. für Magazine wie Chronos, Chronos Japan, Ganz Europa, Handelszeitung, Prestige, Red Bulletin, Terra Mater, Uhren Juwelen Schmuck, Vectura Magazin und ZEIT Magazin tätig. Nach dem erfolgreichen Watch Book des Jahres 2015 veröffentlichte der teNeues-Verlag 2016 das Watch Book II, in dem Gisbert L. Brunner insgesamt 24 Uhrenmarken von Alpina bis Ulysse Nardin in Wort und Bild porträtiert. Im Juni 2017 erschien das ausschließlich der Marke Rolex gewidmete Watch Book III.

02

"Stringent corporate design and skilful product design increase brand and product awareness and that definitely leads to success."

„Stringentes Corporate Design und gekonntes Produktdesign steigern die Wahrnehmung von Marke und Produkt, was sich definitiv im Erfolg niederschlägt."

In your opinion, what makes for good design?
Good design is characterised by form following function. Good design is accompanied by a classic, but also future-oriented appearance, attracts the observer's attention and ensures intuitive handling of the product is a given.

How has the role played by design in our everyday lives changed?
Since time immemorial, every product has been inextricably linked with design, for design means nothing other than creation. Today, design has taken on a greater importance purely because many people have developed a greater awareness of what Max Bill once termed the "product form".

Which country do you consider to be a pioneer in product design, and why?
Japan has played a leading role in this area for quite a while. That's because people in the Land of the Rising Sun have traditionally focused intently on reducing function to the absolute essentials.

Was macht Ihrer Ansicht nach gutes Design aus?
Gutes Design ist dadurch gekennzeichnet, dass die Form der Funktion folgt. Gutes Design geht mit klassischem, aber auch zukunftsorientiertem Auftritt einher, weckt die Aufmerksamkeit des Betrachters und gewährleistet die intuitive Bedienung eines Produkts.

Inwieweit hat sich die Rolle, die Design in unserem täglichen Leben spielt, verändert?
Seit Menschengedenken verknüpft sich jedes Produkt mit Design, denn Design meint nichts anderes als Gestaltung. Heutzutage spielt Design jedoch allein schon deshalb eine größere Rolle, weil viele Menschen für das, was Max Bill einmal als Produktform bezeichnet hat, deutlich mehr Bewusstsein entwickelt haben.

Welche Nation ist für Sie Vorreiter im Produktdesign und warum?
Japan spielt hier schon seit Längerem eine herausragende Rolle, weil man sich im Land der aufgehenden Sonne traditionsgemäß sehr intensiv mit der Reduktion auf das für die Funktion unabdingbar Notwendige beschäftigt.

01

Rüdiger Bucher
Germany
Deutschland

Rüdiger Bucher, born in 1967, graduated in political science from Philipps-Universität Marburg and completed the postgraduate study course "Interdisciplinary studies on France" in Freiburg, Germany. Since 1995, he was in charge of "Scriptum. Die Zeitschrift für Schreibkultur" (Scriptum. The magazine for writing culture) at the publishing house Verlagsgruppe Ebner Ulm for five years where in 1999 he became editorial manager of Chronos, the leading German-language special interest magazine for wrist watches. As chief editor since 2005, Chronos has positioned itself internationally with subsidiary magazines and licensed editions in China, Korea, Japan and Poland. At the same time, Rüdiger Bucher established a successful corporate publishing department for Chronos. Since 2014, he has been editorial director and in addition to Chronos he has also been in charge of the sister magazines "Uhren-Magazin" (Watch Magazine), "Klassik Uhren" (Classic Watches) and the New York-based "WatchTime". Rüdiger Bucher lectures as an expert for mechanical wrist watches and is a sought-after interview partner for various media.

Rüdiger Bucher, geboren 1967, absolvierte ein Studium in Politikwissenschaft an der Philipps-Universität Marburg und das Aufbaustudium „Interdisziplinäre Frankreich-Studien" in Freiburg. Ab 1995 betreute er beim Ebner Verlag Ulm fünf Jahre lang „Scriptum. Die Zeitschrift für Schreibkultur", bevor er im selben Verlag 1999 Redaktionsleiter von „Chronos", dem führenden deutschsprachigen Special-Interest-Magazin für Armbanduhren, wurde. Ab 2005 Chefredakteur, hat sich Chronos seitdem mit Tochtermagazinen und Lizenzausgaben in China, Korea, Japan und Polen international aufgestellt. Gleichzeitig baute Rüdiger Bucher für Chronos einen erfolgreichen Corporate-Publishing-Bereich auf. Seit 2014 verantwortet er als Redaktionsdirektor neben Chronos auch die Schwestermagazine „Uhren-Magazin", „Klassik Uhren" sowie die in New York beheimatete „WatchTime". Als Experte für mechanische Armbanduhren hält Rüdiger Bucher Vorträge und ist ein gefragter Interviewpartner für verschiedene Medien.

01 Chronos
Special Uhrendesign
Published once a year in
September since 2013
Erscheint seit 2013 einmal jährlich
im September

02
Chronos is available around the
globe with different magazine
issues and special supplements
Mit verschiedenen Ausgaben und
Sonderheften ist Chronos rund um
den Globus vertreten

02

"In a society in which many already have everything they need, good design creates desires among consumers."

„In einer Gesellschaft, in der viele schon alles haben, was sie brauchen, weckt gutes Design zusätzliche Begehrlichkeiten beim Konsumenten."

What importance does design quality have for the economic success of companies?
A well-designed product is regarded as more desirable by customers and at the same time strengthens the manufacturer's credibility. As a result, the manufacturer can either increase sales or justify a better price.

What attracts you to the role of Red Dot jury member?
As a journalist, I find it fascinating to be able to exchange views with so many good designers from all over the world. I learn an awful lot in the process.

What does winning the Red Dot say about a product?
Winning a Red Dot is a bit like giving a product a knighthood. The Red Dot attests that a product is good and has been designed to a high quality, that it is quite innovative and makes you feel good.

Which topics are most likely to influence design in the coming years?
In the world of watches, the link between traditional and progressive elements will become ever more prevalent.

Welche Bedeutung hat Designqualität für den wirtschaftlichen Erfolg von Unternehmen?
Ein gut gestaltetes Produkt wird vom Konsumenten stärker begehrt und stärkt zugleich die Glaubwürdigkeit des Herstellers. Dadurch kann dieser entweder mehr Produkte verkaufen oder einen höheren Preis rechtfertigen.

Was reizt Sie an der Arbeit als Red Dot-Juror?
Für mich als Journalisten ist es faszinierend, mich mit so vielen guten Designern aus aller Welt austauschen zu können. Dabei lerne ich unheimlich viel.

Was sagt eine Auszeichnung mit dem Red Dot über das Produkt aus?
Die Verleihung des Red Dot ist ein Adelsschlag für jedes Produkt und bezeugt, dass es gut und hochwertig gestaltet ist, dass es einen gewissen Innovationsgrad besitzt und positive Emotionen weckt.

Welche Themen werden das Design in den kommenden Jahren besonders beeinflussen?
Im Segment der Uhren wird man häufiger die Verbindung von traditionellen mit zukunftsgerichteten Elementen erleben.

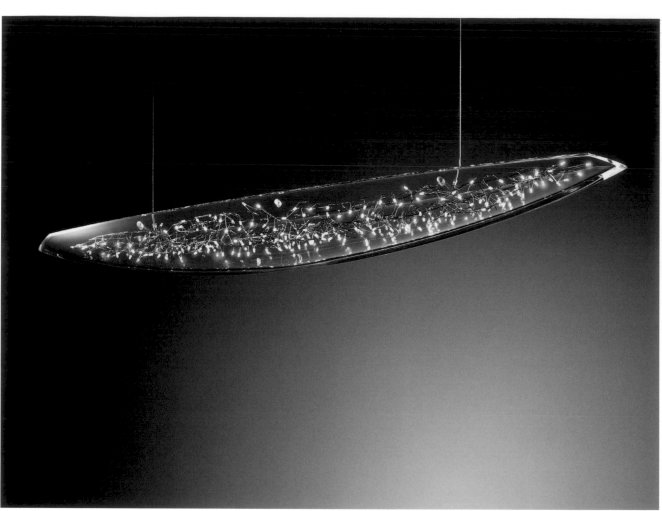

01

Prof. Jun Cai
China

Jun Cai is professor at the Academy of Arts & Design, and director of the Design Management Research Lab at Tsinghua University in Beijing. He is also external reviewer for the Aalto University and Design School of Hong Kong Polytechnic University. Professor Cai has focused on research for design strategy and design management since the 1990s. Through exploration of design-driven business innovation and user-centred design thinking by theoretical and practical research, he was a consultant for more than 60 projects for among others Motorola, Nokia, LG, Boeing, Lenovo, Coway, Fiyta and Aftershockz. Furthermore, he has published papers and publications on design research, design strategy and design management.

Jun Cai ist Professor an der Academy of Arts & Design sowie Direktor des Design Management Research Lab an der Tsinghua University in Beijing. Er ist zudem externer Referent der Aalto University und der Designschule der Polytechnic University in Hongkong. Bereits seit den 1990er Jahren konzentriert sich Professor Cai auf die Forschung in den Bereichen Designstrategie und Designmanagement. Aufgrund seiner Erforschung von designorientierter Geschäftsinnovation und benutzerzentriertem Designdenken durch theoretische und praktische Forschung war er in mehr als 60 Projekten beratend tätig, unter anderem für Motorola, Nokia, LG, Boeing, Lenovo, Coway, Fiyta und Aftershockz. Außerdem hat er bereits Abhandlungen und Veröffentlichungen über Designforschung, Designstrategie und Designmanagement verfasst.

01 Dust of Galaxy
Lighting design
Leuchtendesign

02 Journey within the air
Research and analysis framework
for a value proposition for
Chinese users on behalf of LG
Forschungs- und Analyserahmen-
konzept für das Leistungsver-
sprechen chinesischer Nutzer im
Auftrag von LG

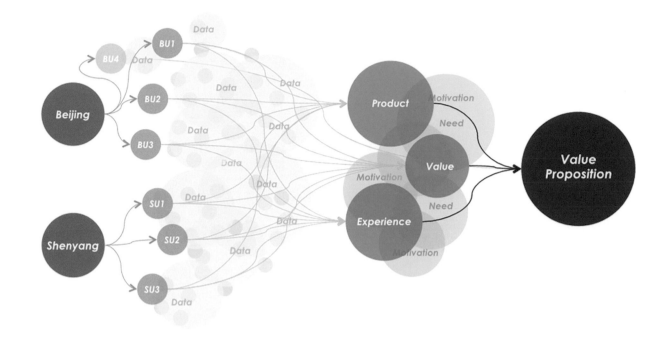

02

"Design solves problems in every aspect of our daily life. It connects technology and aesthetics, making everyday lives enjoyable."

„Design löst in jedem Bereich unseres täglichen Lebens Probleme. Es schlägt die Brücke zwischen Technik und Ästhetik und macht unseren Alltag angenehmer."

What importance does design quality have for the economic success of companies?
Good quality of design both in products and services can not only bring marketing success and make branding for companies reliable, but also strengthen their competitive position with regard to business development.

Which topics are most likely to influence design in the coming years?
IoT with AI technology will be a megatrend to future products from operation to interaction. Emotional feedback between human and machine will acquire more meaning and a cultural context. Lifestyle changes influenced by health, sports and sustainability will make product design more active in the future. Finally, 3D prints will offer more possibilities for product style and introduce new forms of aesthetics.

Welche Bedeutung hat Designqualität für den wirtschaftlichen Erfolg von Unternehmen?
Gute Designqualität für Produkte und Dienstleistungen kann nicht nur Erfolg im Marketing mit sich bringen und zuverlässiges Branding für ein Unternehmen schaffen, sondern auch seine Wettbewerbsposition mit Blick auf die Geschäftsentwicklung stärken.

Welche Themen werden das Design in den kommenden Jahren besonders beeinflussen?
Das Internet der Dinge mit der Technologie künstlicher Intelligenz wird sich zu einem Megatrend für die Produkte der Zukunft entwickeln, der vom Betrieb bis hin zur Interaktion alles steuert. Emotionales Feedback zwischen Mensch und Maschine wird an Bedeutung gewinnen und in einen kulturellen Kontext gesetzt werden. Lifestyle-Veränderungen aufgrund einer gesünderen, sportlicheren und nachhaltigeren Lebensweise werden dazu führen, dass das Produktdesign in Zukunft aktiver ist. Schließlich wird der 3D-Druck weitere Möglichkeiten für Stil und neue Formen der Ästhetik auftun.

01

Vivian Wai-kwan Cheng
Hong Kong
Hongkong

On leaving Hong Kong Design Institute after 19 years of educational service, Vivian Cheng founded "Vivian Design" in 2014 to provide consultancy services and promote her own art in jewellery and glass. She graduated with a BA in industrial design from the Hong Kong Polytechnic University and was awarded a special prize in the Young Designers of the Year Award hosted by the Federation of Hong Kong Industries in 1987, and the Governor's Award for Industry: Consumer Product Design in 1989, after joining Lambda Industrial Limited as the head of the Product Design team. In 1995 she finished her master's degree and joined the Vocational Training Council teaching product design, and later became responsible for, among others, establishing an international network with design-related organisations and schools.
Vivian Cheng was the International Liaison Manager at the Hong Kong Design Institute (HKDI) and member of the Chartered Society of Designers Hong Kong, member of the Board of Directors of the Hong Kong Design Centre (HKDC), and is board member of the World Design Organization (formerly Icsid) from 2013 to 2017. Furthermore, she has been a panel member for the government and various NGOs.

Nach 19 Jahren im Lehrbetrieb verließ Vivian Cheng 2014 das Hong Kong Design Institute und gründete „Vivian Design", um Beratungsdienste anzubieten und ihre eigene Schmuck- und Glaskunst weiterzuentwickeln. 1987 machte sie ihren BA in Industriedesign an der Hong Kong Polytechnic University. Im selben Jahr erhielt sie einen Sonderpreis im Wettbewerb „Young Designers of the Year", veranstaltet von der Federation of Hong Kong Industries, sowie 1989 den Governor's Award for Industry: Consumer Product Design, nachdem sie bei Lambda Industrial Limited als Leiterin des Produktdesign-Teams angefangen hatte. 1995 beendete sie ihren Master-Studiengang und wechselte zum Vocational Training Council, wo sie Produktdesign unterrichtete und später u. a. für den Aufbau eines internationalen Netzwerks mit Organisationen und Schulen im Designbereich verantwortlich war. Vivian Cheng war International Liaison Manager am Hong Kong Design Institute (HKDI), Mitglied der Chartered Society of Designers Hong Kong und Vorstandsmitglied des Hong Kong Design Centre (HKDC) und ist Gremiumsmitglied der World Design Organization (ehemals Icsid) von 2013 bis 2017. Außerdem war sie Mitglied verschiedener Bewertungsgremien der Regierung und vieler Nichtregierungsorganisationen.

02

"Winning a Red Dot means the design, the making and the overall quality are of a high standard, and therefore represent top quality for consumers."

„Eine Auszeichnung mit dem Red Dot bedeutet, dass Design, Herstellung und Qualität insgesamt von einem hohen Niveau sind und daher dem Verbraucher höchste Qualität bieten."

How has the role played by design in our everyday lives changed?
Design is penetrating all dimensions of our life, and has become an important part of it. The invention of the smartphone, for example, has made entertainment accessible 24 hours a day and connects us even when we are thousands of miles away. With a smartphone, we can manage our investments, as well as our assets, use various apps to process everything from shopping to drawing, and arrange scheduling and relationships.

What attracts you to the role of Red Dot jury member?
It's always a challenge to be able to reach a good judgment at design competitions. The process is not just a competition for the entries, but also a competition for the jury members with regard to time, knowledge, and an understanding of the rapidly changing world.

Which country do you consider to be a pioneer in product design, and why?
Europe is still leading the way in the development of philosophical, technological and design practices.

Inwieweit hat sich die Rolle, die Design in unserem täglichen Leben spielt, verändert?
Design durchdringt alle Aspekte unseres Lebens und ist ein wichtiger Teil dessen geworden. Die Erfindung des Smartphones zum Beispiel macht Unterhaltung 24 Stunden am Tag zugänglich und erlaubt uns, in Verbindung zu bleiben, auch wenn wir Tausende Kilometer voneinander entfernt sind. Mit einem Smartphone können wir unsere Investitionen sowie unser Vermögen verwalten, verschiedene Apps nutzen, um vom Einkauf bis zum Zeichnen alles zu handhaben, und Terminplanung ebenso wie Beziehungen organisieren.

Was reizt Sie an der Arbeit als Red Dot-Jurorin?
Es ist immer eine Herausforderung, bei Designwettbewerben ein gutes Urteil abzugeben. Der Prozess ist für die Einsendungen, aber auch für die Juroren ein Wettbewerb in Bezug auf Zeit, Wissen und Verständnis der sich so rapide verändernden Welt.

Welche Nation ist für Sie Vorreiter im Produktdesign und warum?
Europa ist in der Entwicklung von philosophischen, technologischen und Designpraktiken immer noch führend.

01

Datuk Prof.
Jimmy Choo OBE
Malaysia/
Great Britain
Malaysia/
Großbritannien

Datuk Professor Jimmy Choo is descended from a family of Malaysian shoemakers and learned the craft from his father. He studied at Cordwainers College, which is today part of the London College of Fashion. After graduating in 1983, he founded his own couture label and opened a shoe shop in London's East End whose regular customers included the late Diana, Princess of Wales. In 1996, Choo launched his ready-to-wear line with Tom Yeardye and sold his share in the business 2001 to Equinox Luxury Holdings Ltd. He now spends his time designing shoes for private clients under his new label using his Chinese name Zhou Yang Jie. He is also passionate about promoting design education through his work as an ambassador for footwear education at the London College of Fashion. He is a spokesperson for the British Council in their promotion of British Education to foreign students and is working with the non-profit programme, Teach For Malaysia. In 2003, Jimmy Choo was honoured for his contribution to fashion by Queen Elizabeth II who appointed him "Officer of the Order of the British Empire".

Datuk Professor Jimmy Choo, der einer malaysischen Schuhmacher-Familie entstammt und das Handwerk von seinem Vater lernte, studierte am Cordwainers College, heute Teil des London College of Fashion. Nach seinem Abschluss 1983 gründete er sein eigenes Couture-Label und eröffnete ein Schuhgeschäft im Londoner East End, zu dessen Stammkundschaft auch Lady Diana, die verstorbene Prinzessin von Wales, gehörte. 1996 führte Choo gemeinsam mit Tom Yeardye seine Konfektionslinie ein und verkaufte seine Anteile an dem Unternehmen 2001 an die Equinox Luxury Holdings Ltd. Heute gestaltet er unter seinem neuen Label und seinem chinesischen Namen Zhou Yang Jie Schuhe für Privatkunden. In seiner Rolle als Botschafter für Footwear Education am London College of Fashion setzt er sich leidenschaftlich für die Förderung der Designausbildung ein. Er ist ferner Sprecher des British Council für die Förderung der Ausbildung ausländischer Studenten in Großbritannien und arbeitet darüber hinaus für das gemeinnützige Programm „Teach for Malaysia". Für seine Verdienste in der Mode verlieh ihm Königin Elisabeth II. 2003 den Titel „Officer of the Order of the British Empire".

01

Chinese flower embroidered silk sling back pump. The specific gold colour is a traditional representation of the position and wealth in Malaysia, while the Chinese flower pattern represents freedom, relaxation and flying.

Ein mit chinesischen Blumen bestickter Slingback-Pumps aus Seide. Der besondere Goldton wird in Malaysia traditionell verwendet, um Position und Reichtum darzustellen, während das chinesische Blumenmuster für Freiheit, Entspannung und Fliegen steht.

02 Maroon Kelingkan embroidered pumps

Kelingkan is a style of embroidery using gold and silver metal thread dating to the 14th century and symbolising patience, diligence, perseverance and creativity.

Mit kastanienbraunen Kelingkan bestickte Pumps

Kelingkan ist eine Stilrichtung der Stickerei, die auf das 14. Jahrhundert zurückgeht und Gold- und Silber-Metallgarn verwendet, um Geduld, Fleiß, Beharrlichkeit und Kreativität zu symbolisieren.

02

"The Red Dot Award attracts the most talented and celebrated in the world of design – both as judges and entrants."

„Der Red Dot Award zieht die Begabtesten und Prominentesten der Designwelt an – sowohl als Juroren wie auch als Bewerber."

In your opinion, what makes for good design?
To catch my eye, a product must be beautiful, useful, of the highest quality, and offer something unique in the product, design or material.

What importance does design quality have for the economic success of companies?
Great importance. If a product satisfies a need, looks beautiful, is made with high-quality materials and works perfectly, then it will be a success.

Which area of design do you feel has the greatest potential for development for the future?
In fashion, sustainable and ethical fashion is growing and can't be ignored. More brands are addressing consumers' concerns about the supply chain, the product's impact on the environment and the brand's social responsibility.

Which country do you consider to be a pioneer in product design, and why?
England, particularly London, has a rich history of producing leading design talent.

Was macht Ihrer Ansicht nach gutes Design aus?
Um meine Aufmerksamkeit zu gewinnen, muss ein Produkt schön, nützlich und von höchster Qualität sein und in Design oder Material etwas Einzigartiges bieten.

Welche Bedeutung hat Designqualität für den wirtschaftlichen Erfolg von Unternehmen?
Eine große. Wenn ein Produkt ein Bedürfnis befriedigt, schön aussieht, aus hochwertigen Materialien besteht und perfekt funktioniert, wird es ein Erfolg.

In welchem Designbereich sehen Sie das größte Entwicklungspotenzial für die Zukunft?
In der Modewelt gewinnt die nachhaltige und ethische Mode an Bedeutung und kann nicht mehr ignoriert werden. Eine wachsende Anzahl von Marken geht auf die Bedenken der Konsumenten ein, was die Lieferkette, die Auswirkungen eines Produkts auf die Umwelt und die soziale Verantwortung der Marke betrifft.

Welche Nation ist für Sie Vorreiter im Produktdesign und warum?
England, besonders London, kann auf eine lange Geschichte in der Ausbildung führender Designtalente zurückblicken.

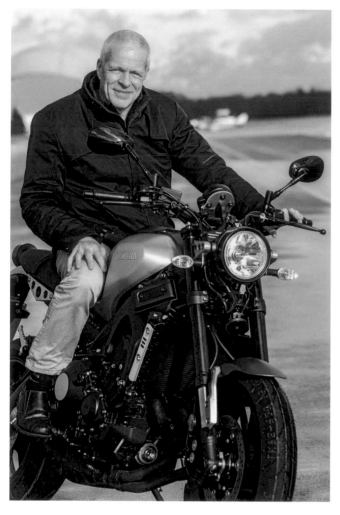

01

Vincent Créance
France
Frankreich

After graduating from the Ecole Supérieure de Design Industriel, Vincent Créance began his career in 1985 at the Plan Créatif Agency where he became design director in 1990 and developed, among other things, numerous products for high-tech and consumer markets, for France Télécom and RATP (Paris metro). In 1996, he joined Alcatel as Design Director for all phone activities on an international level. In 1999, he became Vice President Brand in charge of product design and user experience as well as all communications for the Mobile Phones BU. During the launch of the Franco-Chinese TCL and Alcatel Mobile Phones joint venture in 2004, Vincent Créance advanced to the position of Design and Corporate Communications Director. In 2006, he became President and CEO of MBD Design, one of the major design agencies in France, providing design solutions in transport design and product design. Créance is a member of the APCI (Agency for the Promotion of Industrial Creation), on the board of directors of ENSCI (National College of Industrial Creation), and a member of the Strategic Advisory Board for Strate College.

Vincent Créance begann seine Laufbahn nach seinem Abschluss an der Ecole Supérieure de Design Industriel 1985 bei Plan Créatif Agency. Hier stieg er 1990 zum Design Director auf und entwickelte u. a. zahlreiche Produkte für den Hightech- und Verbrauchermarkt, für die France Télécom oder die RATP (Pariser Metro). 1996 ging er als Design Director für sämtliche Telefonaktivitäten auf internationaler Ebene zu Alcatel und wurde 1999 Vice President Brand, zuständig für Produktdesign und User Experience sowie die gesamte Kommunikation für den Geschäftsbereich „Mobile Phones". Während des Zusammenschlusses des französisch-chinesischen TCL und Alcatel Mobile Phones 2004 avancierte Vincent Créance zum Design and Corporate Communications Director. 2006 wurde er Präsident und CEO von MBD Design, einer der wichtigsten Designagenturen in Frankreich, und entwickelte Designlösungen für Transport- und Produktdesign. Créance ist Mitglied von APCI (Agency for the Promotion of Industrial Creation), Vorstand des ENSCI (National College of Industrial Design) und Mitglied im wissenschaftlichen Beirat des Strate College.

01 Mythik
Radiator for Thermor, a company
of Groupe Atlantic
Heizkörper für Thermor, ein Unternehmen der Groupe Atlantic

02 Optifuel
Low fuel consumption trailer for
Renault Trucks
Anhänger mit geringem Kraft-
stoffverbrauch für Renault Trucks

02

"Seeing so many contemporary objects in this fantastic exhibition as a Red Dot juror is very refreshing and has the effect of a fountain of youth."

„Als Red Dot-Juror dieser phantastischen Ausstellung so viele zeitgenössische Objekte sehen zu können, ist sehr erfrischend und hat die Wirkung eines Jungbrunnens."

In your opinion, what makes for good design?
It's a pleasure to buy, then to use, and even causes some sadness when you have to replace it: emotions are always stronger than rationality when you choose something.

What does winning the Red Dot say about a product?
More than a high level of design achievement: winning a Red Dot also gives value to design within a company, rewards the commitment of all the contributors and makes them proud of their work. Moreover, it is an efficient way to compare yourself with competitors.

Which topics are most likely to influence design in the coming years?
I think that the emerging sharing economy will change the way in which we look at products over the coming years. A product will no longer be designed only for me, but also for a community. This trend will logically reinforce sustainability expectations, and desacralise the objects as a part of my identity.

Was macht Ihrer Ansicht nach gutes Design aus?
Es ist ein Vergnügen, es zu kaufen, dann zu benutzen, und macht traurig, wenn es ersetzt werden muss: Emotionen sind immer stärker als die Vernunft, wenn man etwas auswählt.

Was sagt eine Auszeichnung mit dem Red Dot über das Produkt aus?
Mehr als ein hohes Maß an Designleistung: Die Auszeichnung mit einem Red Dot verleiht dem Designprodukt auch innerhalb des Unternehmens einen Mehrwert. Sie soll das Engagement aller Mitwirkenden belohnen und sie stolz auf ihre Arbeit machen. Darüber hinaus ist es eine wirksame Methode, sich mit Konkurrenten zu messen.

Welche Themen werden das Design in den kommenden Jahren besonders beeinflussen?
Ich denke, dass die aufstrebende „Sharing Economy" unsere Perspektive auf Produkte in den kommenden Jahren verändern wird. Ein Produkt wird nicht mehr nur für mich, sondern auch für eine Gemeinschaft gestaltet. Dieser Trend wird Erwartungen an die Nachhaltigkeit logischerweise verstärken und den Objekten ihren sakralen Charakter als Teil meiner Identität nehmen.

01

Martin Darbyshire
Great Britain
Großbritannien

Martin Darbyshire founded tangerine in 1989 and under his stewardship it has developed into a global strategic design consultancy that creates award-winning solutions for internationally recognised brands such as LG, Samsung, Hyundai, Toyota, Nikon, Huawei, Virgin Australia and Cepsa. Before founding tangerine, he worked for Moggridge Associates and then in San Francisco at ID TWO (now IDEO). A design leader on the international stage, Martin Darbyshire combines his work for tangerine with a worldwide programme of keynote speeches and activities promoting the importance of design. He has served as UKT&I Ambassador for the UK Creative Industries and two terms as a board member of the World Design Organization (formerly Icsid). He was also formerly a visiting professor at Central Saint Martins. Martin Darbyshire is a trustee of the UK Design Council and a juror at the Red Dot Award and China Good Design. Recently, the UK Creative Industries Council recognised his global export success awarding him the CIC International Award 2016.

Martin Darbyshire gründete tangerine 1989. Unter seiner Leitung entwickelte sich das Büro zu einem globalen strategischen Designberatungsunternehmen, das preisgekrönte Lösungen für weltweit anerkannte Marken wie LG, Samsung, Hyundai, Toyota, Nikon, Huawei, Virgin Australia und Cepsa entwickelt. Zuvor arbeitete er für Moggridge Associates und dann in San Francisco bei ID TWO (heute IDEO). Als ein weltweit führender Designer verbindet Martin Darbyshire seine Arbeit für tangerine mit einem globalen Programm von Keynote-Referaten und -Aktivitäten, um den bedeutenden Beitrag von Design hervorzuheben. Martin Darbyshire war für das Ministerium für Handel und Investition des Vereinigten Königreichs Botschafter des Bereichs Kreativindustrie und für zwei Amtszeiten Gremiumsmitglied der World Design Organization (ehemals Icsid). Er war zudem Gastdozent an der Central Saint Martins. Martin Darbyshire ist Kurator der UK Design Council sowie Juror des Red Dot Awards und China Good Design. Vor Kurzem wurde er für seinen weltweiten Exporterfolg von der UK Creative Industries Council mit dem CIC International Award 2016 ausgezeichnet.

01
Brand repositioning of skincare
company Innisfree through the
design of a new flagship store
and retail strategy
Marken-Neupositionierung des
Hautpflege-Unternehmens Innisfree mithilfe des Designs eines
neuen Flagship-Stores und einer
neuen Verkaufsstrategie

02
A tiny revolution in Economy
Class seat comfort for Cathay
Pacific: a proprietary designed
six-way headrest that improves
lateral support during sleep
Eine winzige Revolution im Sitz-
komfort der Economy-Klasse von
Cathay Pacific: ein rechtlich
geschütztes Design für eine
Sechs-Wege-Kopfstütze, die im
Schlaf besseren seitlichen Halt
bietet

02

"With design one has to understand
the context of what is being
created, understand the challenges
and define how to create the best
result."
„Bei Design muss man den Kontext
verstehen, in dem etwas geschaffen
werden soll, und die Anforderungen
bestimmen, wie man das beste Ergebnis erzielen kann."

**What does winning the Red Dot say about a
product?**
At any stage in your career, winning a Red Dot is very
special, as a designer. It is a good feeling to know
that your peers have judged you worthy of an award,
especially a Red Dot award which carries such prestige
within the design and commercial community.

**How has the role played by design in our everyday
lives changed?**
Looking back at the early days, the focus was on form,
but now the discipline is about creating value and
desirability. The discipline itself has expanded and the
lead players in industrial design are talking about
"experiences".

**Which area of design do you feel has the greatest
potential for development for the future?**
Sustainability is absolutely fundamental, and an important part of design is getting rid of things that are
no longer needed. Every designer has a heightened
consciousness of what is going to bring a big change
in the future.

**Was sagt eine Auszeichnung mit dem Red Dot über
das Produkt aus?**
Zu jedem Zeitpunkt einer Karriere ist die Auszeichnung
mit dem Red Dot für einen Designer etwas ganz Besonderes. Es gibt einem ein gutes Gefühl zu wissen,
dass die Kollegen einen für eine Auszeichnung als wür-
dig erachten, vor allem für einen Red Dot, der in der
Design- und Geschäftswelt solches Prestige genießt.

**Inwieweit hat sich die Rolle, die Design in unserem
täglichen Leben spielt, verändert?**
Schaut man auf die Anfänge zurück, war das Augenmerk eher auf die Form gerichtet. Heutzutage geht es
um das Schaffen von Wert und darum, etwas begeh-
renswert zu machen. Die Disziplin selbst ist gewachsen
und die Branchenführer im industriellen Design reden
von „Erfahrungen".

**In welchem Designbereich sehen Sie das größte
Entwicklungspotenzial für die Zukunft?**
Nachhaltigkeit ist absolut fundamental. Ein wichtiger
Bestandteil von Design ist es, die Dinge loszuwerden,
die nicht mehr gebraucht werden. Jeder Designer hat
ein gesteigertes Bewusstsein für das, was in Zukunft
große Veränderungen mit sich bringen wird.

01

Stefan Eckstein
Germany
Deutschland

Stefan Eckstein is the founder and CEO of ECKSTEIN DESIGN in Munich. The studio focuses on industrial, interaction and corporate industrial design. Stefan Eckstein studied industrial design at the Muthesius Academy of Fine Arts and Design in Kiel and ergonomics at the Anthropological Institute of the University of Kiel, Germany. Together with his design team, he has received many design awards in national and international competitions. Today, Stefan Eckstein is recognised as a renowned designer for industrial design. In line with his principle, "reduction to the essential leads to a better result", he has developed a user-driven approach to innovation, called "Agile Design Development". It combines innovative concept- and development methods in a structured thought process. Stefan Eckstein has been a member of numerous international juries, has been a member of the Association of German Industrial Designers (VDID) for 25 years and was elected president in 2012. Under his management, the VDID CODEX was developed. Today, it serves as a model for the ethical values of the profession of industrial designers.

Stefan Eckstein ist Gründer und Geschäftsführer von ECKSTEIN DESIGN, einem Studio für Industriedesign, Interaction Design und Corporate Industrial Design in München. Er studierte Industrial Design an der Muthesius-Hochschule und Ergonomie am Anthropologischen Institut der Christian-Albrechts-Universität zu Kiel. Zusammen mit seinem Designteam erhielt er zahlreiche Auszeichnungen. Heute gehört Stefan Eckstein zu den renommierten Designern im Bereich des Industrial Designs. Gemäß seiner Philosophie „Reduzierung auf das Wesentliche führt zu einem besseren Ergebnis" entwickelte er eine nutzerorientierte Innovationsmethode, die Agile Designentwicklung. In einem besonders strukturierten Denkprozess werden dabei innovative Konzept- und Entwicklungsphasen miteinander verbunden. Stefan Eckstein ist international als Juror tätig, seit über 25 Jahren Mitglied beim Verband Deutscher Industrie Designer (VDID) und seit 2012 Präsident des Verbandes. Der VDID CODEX wurde unter seiner Leitung entwickelt und steht heute als Leitbild für die ethischen Werte des Berufsstandes.

01 ECCO 75

01 ECCO 75
The ECCO 75 by SmartRay is a high-definition, 3D sensor suitable for identifying smaller defects and for taking highly precise measurements
Der ECCO 75 von SmartRay ist ein hochauflösender 3D-Sensor für eine detailgetreue Inspektion und höchst genaue Messanwendungen

02|03 VDW.CONNECT Drive
A modern dental endoscopy machine for electronic depth measurement with accompanying mechanical file
Modernes Dental-Endoskopiegerät für die elektronische Tiefenmessung mit dazugehöriger mechanischer Feile

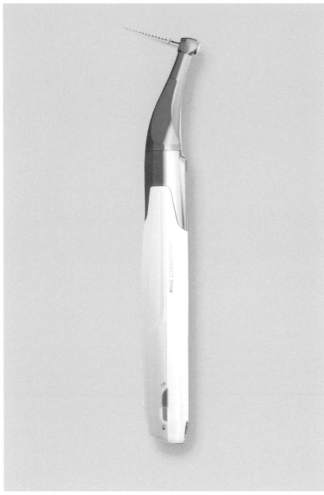

02

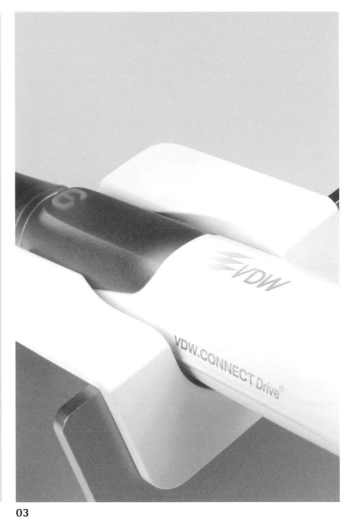

03

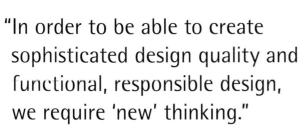

"In order to be able to create sophisticated design quality and functional, responsible design, we require 'new' thinking."
„Um anspruchsvolle Gestaltungsqualität und funktionales, verantwortungsvolles Design zu konzipieren, braucht es ‚neues' Denken."

In your opinion, what makes for good design?
For me, design is a means of understanding the world around us. It needs to be user-friendly, innovative, aesthetically pleasing and must appeal to the user's emotions.

How will the role played by design in our everyday lives change?
Design will play a leading role for products and (digital) systems and will take on an explanatory function in the years to come.

What importance does design quality have for the economic success of companies?
It is through design that technology becomes workable and understandable for users. Products do what they are meant to do and deliver the quality that their design promises. Therefore, design is an important economic driver.

What does winning the Red Dot say about a product?
That it successfully manages to combine ergonomics, usability, an idea, quality, function and aesthetics.

Was macht Ihrer Ansicht nach gutes Design aus?
Für mich ist Design eine Art und Weise, die Welt um uns herum zu begreifen. Es muss nutzerfreundlich, innovativ und ästhetisch sein und den Nutzer emotional ansprechen.

Inwieweit wird sich die Rolle, die Design in unserem täglichen Leben spielt, verändern?
Design wird in den nächsten Jahren eine Hauptrolle für Produkte und (digitale) Systeme übernehmen und eine erklärende Funktion haben.

Welche Bedeutung hat Designqualität für den wirtschaftlichen Erfolg von Unternehmen?
Erst durch Design wird Technologie funktional und für den Menschen verständlich. Die Produkte erfüllen ihre Aufgaben und lösen das Qualitätsversprechen ein, das ihr Design abgibt. Deshalb ist Design ein wichtiger Motor für die Wirtschaft.

Was sagt eine Auszeichnung mit dem Red Dot über das Produkt aus?
Dass es Ergonomie, Usability, Idee, Qualität, Funktion und Ästhetik gelungen miteinander verknüpft.

01

Robin Edman
Sweden
Schweden

Robin Edman has been the chief executive of SVID, the Swedish Industrial Design Foundation, since 2001. After studying industrial design at Rhode Island School of Design he joined AB Electrolux Global Design in 1981 and parallel to this started his own design consultancy. In 1989, Robin Edman joined Electrolux North America as vice president of Industrial Design for Frigidaire and in 1997, moved back to Stockholm as vice president of Electrolux Global Design. Throughout his entire career he has worked towards integrating a better understanding of users, their needs and the importance of design in society at large. His engagement in design related activities is reflected in the numerous international jury appointments, speaking engagements, advisory council and board positions he has held. Robin Edman served on the board of the World Design Organization (formerly Icsid) from 2003 to 2007, the last term as treasurer. Since June 2015, he is the president of BEDA (Bureau of European Design Associations).

Robin Edman ist seit 2001 Firmenchef der SVID, der Swedish Industrial Design Foundation. Nach seinem Industriedesign-Studium an der Rhode Island School of Design kam er 1981 zu AB Electrolux Global Design. Zeitgleich startete er seine eigene Unternehmensberatung für Design. 1989 wechselte Edman zu Electrolux North America als Vizepräsident für Industrial Design für Frigidaire und kehrte 1997 als Vizepräsident von Electrolux Global Design nach Stockholm zurück. Während seiner gesamten Karriere hat er daran gearbeitet, ein besseres Verständnis für Nutzer zu entwickeln, für deren Bedürfnisse und die Wichtigkeit von Design in der Gesellschaft insgesamt. Sein Engagement in designbezogenen Aktivitäten spiegelt sich in zahlreichen Jurierungsberufungen sowie in Rednerverpflichtungen und Positionen in Gremien sowie Beratungsausschüssen. Von 2003 bis 2007 war Robin Edman Mitglied im Vorstand der World Design Organization (ehemals Icsid), in der letzten Amtsperiode als Schatzmeister. Seit Juni 2015 ist er Präsident von BEDA (Bureau of European Design Associations).

01 EcoDesign Circle
Three-year EU project to increase awareness of eco-design of the Baltic Sea region's small and medium-sized companies, designers and design organisations; in collaboration with design organisations and universities from Germany, Estonia, Lithuania, Poland, Finland and Sweden, represented by SVID collaborating with Green Leap at KTH

Drei Jahre während EU-Projekt, um Aufmerksamkeit auf das Öko-design der kleinen und mittel-ständischen Unternehmen, der Designer und Designorganisationen an der Ostsee zu lenken; in Zusammenarbeit mit Designorganisationen und Universitäten aus Deutschland, Estland, Litauen, Polen, Finnland und Schweden, vertreten durch SVID in Zusammenarbeit mit Green Leap an der KTH

"Good design is seeing the opportunities and catering to the user needs in an intelligent and sustainable way."

„Gutes Design ist das Erkennen von Chancen und das Beantworten von Verbraucherbedürfnissen in einer intelligenten und nachhaltigen Form."

How has the role played by design in our everyday lives changed?
Design has become an absolute necessity to provide the solutions we expect and desire. The broader scope of design to embrace businesses as well as the public sector has made us request that design plays a role in the creation of products, services, strategies and processes.

What importance does design quality have for the economic success of companies?
Design efforts have a great impact on business success, profitability and repeat purchasing.

What does winning the Red Dot say about a product?
A Red Dot displays a seal of quality for the product and the efforts it takes to produce a winning design.

Which area of design do you feel has the greatest potential for development for the future?
The influence of design in the strategic development of businesses and the public sector.

Inwieweit hat sich die Rolle, die Design in unserem täglichen Leben spielt, verändert?
Design ist für die Lösungen, die wir erwarten und uns wünschen, zwingend notwendig geworden. Der breite Geltungsbereich, der sowohl die Wirtschaft als auch den öffentlichen Sektor umfasst, hat dazu geführt, dass wir verlangen, dass Design in der Herstellung von Produkten, Dienstleistungen, Strategien und Prozessen eine Rolle spielt.

Welche Bedeutung hat Designqualität für den wirtschaftlichen Erfolg von Unternehmen?
Designleistungen haben einen großen Einfluss auf den Geschäftserfolg, die Rentabilität und das markentreue Kaufverhalten.

Was sagt eine Auszeichnung mit dem Red Dot über das Produkt aus?
Der Red Dot ist ein Qualitätssiegel für das Produkt und die Arbeit, die in einem erfolgreichen Entwurf steckt.

In welchem Designbereich sehen Sie das größte Entwicklungspotenzial für die Zukunft?
Im Einfluss von Design auf die strategische Entwicklung von Unternehmen und öffentlichem Sektor.

01

Joachim H. Faust
Germany
Deutschland

Joachim H. Faust studied at the RWTH Aachen University as well as at the Texas A&M University in the USA with the aid of a DAAD grant. There, he obtained his diploma and masters in architecture. He has worked, among others, as design architect for Skidmore, Owings & Merrill in Houston, Texas and New York as well as for KPF Kohn, Pedersen, Fox/Eggers Group. In 1987, Joachim H. Faust took over the running of the HPP office in Frankfurt and, since 1997, has been a managing partner at the HPP Group headquarters in Düsseldorf. HPP has 400 employees and offers urban planning, architecture, interior design, general planning and project management from a total of eight offices in Germany. Internationally, HPP has independent offices in Shanghai and Istanbul. Joachim H. Faust is responsible for the company's strategic expansion in China. In 2013, he was asked to take part in the German government's reform commission for "the construction of large projects". In addition, he is an author and gives specialist lectures on architecture and interior design.

Joachim H. Faust studierte an der RWTH Aachen sowie mit einem DAAD-Stipendium an der Texas A&M University in den USA, wo er die Abschlüsse Dipl.-Ing. Architektur und Master of Architecture erlangte. Er war u. a. als Design Architect für Skidmore, Owings & Merrill in Houston, Texas, und New York tätig sowie für KPF Kohn, Pedersen, Fox/Eggers Group. 1987 übernahm Joachim H. Faust die Leitung des HPP-Büros in Frankfurt am Main, seit 1997 führt er die HPP-Gruppe am Hauptsitz Düsseldorf als geschäftsführender Gesellschafter. Mit 400 Mitarbeitern bietet HPP Stadtbereichsplanung, Architektur, Innenarchitektur, Generalplanung und Projektsteuerung in insgesamt acht Büros in Deutschland an. International ist HPP in Shanghai und Istanbul mit eigenen Gesellschaften vertreten. Joachim H. Faust begleitet die Expansion in China strategisch. 2013 wurde er in die Reformkommission „Bau von Großprojekten" der Deutschen Bundesregierung berufen. Er ist zudem als Autor tätig und hält Vorträge zu Fachthemen der Architektur und Innenarchitektur.

**01 BASF Business Center
D105, Ludwigshafen**
The employee cafeteria in the
recently completed BASF
Business Center D105 offers
cutting-edge island-based
catering and is open to all
BASF employees in the main
site in Ludwigshafen, Germany.
Das Mitarbeiter-Restaurant im
kürzlich fertiggestellten BASF
Business Center D105 bietet
modernste Inselkonzept-Gastro-
nomie und ist offen für alle
BASF-Mitarbeiter am Hauptwerk
Ludwigshafen.

**02 Shenzhen North Railway
Station Towers**
The construction of the North
Railway Station Towers in the
Chinese port city of Shenzhen
is a multi-functional complex
consisting of two towers
measuring 258 and 100 metres
respectively.
Der Bau der North Railway Station Towers in der chinesischen
Hafenmetropole Shenzhen
ist ein Multifunktionskomplex,
bestehend aus zwei Türmen
von 258 und 100 Metern Höhe.

02

"Good design is indispensable today. It shapes people's lifestyle."
„Gutes Design ist heute unverzicht-
bar und prägt den Lifestyle der
Menschen."

What importance does design quality have for the economic success of companies?
Good design quality is a must for economic success.
Outstanding design gives people confidence in a
product and leads to even greater success.

What attracts you to the role of Red Dot jury member?
The discussions with the other jury members, the
breadth of their cultural, technical but also sensory
experiences.

Which topics are most likely to influence design in the coming years?
In a time of limited resources and high environmental
pollution, the "life cycle" or "cradle to cradle" of a
product will in future become critical.

Which country do you consider to be a pioneer in product design, and why?
Italy for furniture, Japan and Germany for industrial
products, and the USA and China for communication
products. The reason for this is the prevalent culture
of creativity and craftsmanship that, through design
ideas, turns an object into a world-beater.

Welche Bedeutung hat Designqualität für den wirtschaftlichen Erfolg von Unternehmen?
Designqualität ist Pflicht für wirtschaftlichen Erfolg.
Herausragendes Design schafft Produktvertrauen und
damit noch größeren Erfolg.

Was reizt Sie an der Arbeit als Red Dot-Juror?
Die Diskussion mit den Jurykollegen und deren unterschiedliche kulturelle und technische, aber auch sinn-
liche Erfahrungshorizonte.

Welche Themen werden das Design in den kommenden Jahren besonders beeinflussen?
In Zeiten knapper Ressourcen und hoher Umwelt-
belastungen werden die Themen „Lebenszyklus" oder
auch „Cradle to Cradle" eines Produkts in Zukunft
vordringlich werden.

Welche Nation ist für Sie Vorreiter im Produktdesign und warum?
Italien bei Möbeln, Japan und Deutschland bei Industrie-
produkten, USA und China bei Kommunikationspro-
dukten. Grund dafür ist die jeweils bestehende kreative
und handwerkliche Kultur, die die Objekte durch geniale
Designideen zu den weltweit besten macht.

01

Prof. Lutz Fügener
Germany
Deutschland

Professor Lutz Fügener began his studies at the Technical University Dresden, where he completed a foundation course in mechanical engineering. He then transferred to the Burg Giebichenstein University of Art and Design in Halle/Saale, Germany, where he obtained a degree in industrial design in 1995. In the same year, he became junior partner of Fisch & Vogel Design in Berlin. Since then, the firm (today called "studioFT") has increasingly specialised in transportation design. Two years after joining the firm, Lutz Fügener became senior partner and co-owner. In 2000, he was appointed as Professor of Transportation Design/3D Design by Pforzheim University and there chairs the prestigious BA degree course in transportation design. Lutz Fügener is also active as an author and journalist for a number of different daily newspapers, weekly magazines and periodicals, as well as blogs in which he writes on mobility-related design topics.

Professor Lutz Fügener absolvierte ein Grundstudium in Maschinenbau an der Technischen Universität Dresden und nahm daraufhin ein Studium für Industrial Design an der Hochschule für Kunst und Design, Burg Giebichenstein, in Halle an der Saale auf. Sein Diplom machte er im Jahr 1995. Im selben Jahr wurde er Juniorpartner des Büros Fisch & Vogel Design in Berlin. Seit dieser Zeit spezialisierte sich das Büro (heute „studioFT") mehr und mehr auf den Bereich „Transportation Design". Zwei Jahre nach seinem Einstieg wurde Lutz Fügener Seniorpartner und gleichberechtigter Mitinhaber des Büros. Im Jahr 2000 wurde er von der Hochschule Pforzheim auf eine Professur für Transportation Design/3D-Gestaltung berufen und ist Leiter des renommierten BA-Studiengangs für Fahrzeugdesign. Lutz Fügener ist als Autor und Journalist für verschiedene Tageszeitungen, Wochenmagazine, Periodika und Blogs tätig und schreibt über Themen des Designs im Zusammenhang mit Mobilität.

02

"In my opinion, good design is
defined by a symbiotic synergy
of function and aesthetics."
„Gutes Design definiert sich aus
meiner Sicht durch ein symbio-
tisches Zusammenwirken von
Funktion und Ästhetik."

How has the role played by design in our everyday lives changed?
The superabundance in the world coexists with regions, processes and areas of work that are developing at an incredible rate. Contemporary product design must take into consideration the wide-ranging consequences of this situation.

What importance does design quality have for the economic success of companies?
Companies that are aware of the possibilities offered by design can make products that are not only aesthetically appealing, but also intuitively understandable and thereby gain a competitive advantage in the eyes of customers.

Which country do you consider to be a pioneer in product design, and why?
German designers create Asian cars just as Asian designers quite naturally work here alongside their colleagues from western countries and the Middle East.

Inwieweit hat sich die Rolle, die Design in unserem täglichen Leben spielt, verändert?
Eine Welt des Überflusses steht sich rasant in verschiedene Richtungen entwickelnden Regionen, Prozessen und Arbeitsgebieten gegenüber. Zeitgemäße Produktgestaltung muss die weitreichenden Konsequenzen dieser Situation berücksichtigen.

Welche Bedeutung hat Designqualität für den wirtschaftlichen Erfolg von Unternehmen?
Mit den Möglichkeiten des Designs vertraute Unternehmen können Produkte über einen ästhetischen Anspruch hinaus intuitiv wahrnehmbar machen und so im Wettbewerb um die Gunst des Kunden punkten.

Welche Nation ist für Sie Vorreiter im Produktdesign und warum?
Deutsche Designer gestalten asiatische Automobile ebenso wie Designer aus Asien hier selbstverständlich mit ihren Kollegen aus westlichen Ländern oder dem Nahen Osten arbeiten.

01

Hideshi Hamaguchi
USA/Japan

Hideshi Hamaguchi graduated with a Bachelor of Science in chemical engineering from Kyoto University. Starting his career with Panasonic in Japan, Hamaguchi later became director of the New Business Planning Group at Panasonic Electric Works, Ltd. and then executive vice president of Panasonic Electric Works Laboratory of America, Inc. In 1993, he developed Japan's first corporate Intranet and also led the concept development for the first USB flash drive. Hideshi Hamaguchi has over 15 years of experience in defining strategies and decision-making, as well as in concept development for various industries and businesses. As Executive Fellow at Ziba Design and CEO at monogoto, he is today considered a leading mind in creative concept and strategy development on both sides of the Pacific and is involved in almost every project this renowned business consultancy takes on. For clients such as FedEx, Polycom and M-System he has led the development of several award-winning products.

Hideshi Hamaguchi graduierte als Bachelor of Science in Chemical Engineering an der Kyoto University. Seine Karriere begann er bei Panasonic in Japan, wo er später zum Direktor der New Business Planning Group von Panasonic Electric Works, Ltd. und zum Executive Vice President von Panasonic Electric Works Laboratory of America, Inc. aufstieg. 1993 entwickelte er Japans erstes Firmen-Intranet und übernahm zudem die Leitung der Konzeptentwicklung des ersten USB-Laufwerks. Hideshi Hamaguchi verfügt über mehr als 15 Jahre Erfahrung in der Konzeptentwicklung sowie Strategie- und Entscheidungsfindung in unterschiedlichen Industrien und Unternehmen. Als Executive Fellow bei Ziba Design und CEO bei monogoto wird er heute als führender Kopf in der kreativen Konzept- und Strategieentwicklung auf beiden Seiten des Pazifiks angesehen und ist in nahezu jedes Projekt der renommierten Unternehmensberatung involviert. Für Kunden wie FedEx, Polycom und M-System leitete er etliche ausgezeichnete Projekte.

01 Cintiq 24HD
for Wacom, 2012
für Wacom, 2012

02 Toy blocks for everyone
A collection of 202 building
blocks crafted from beechwood,
available in beautifully arranged
units. Infused with the stories
of twelve elements, each unique
piece embodies a small fragment
of nature. For Felissimo, Japan,
in collaboration with Marie Uno.
Bauklötze für alle
Eine Kollektion von 202 Bauklötzen,
die aus Buchenholz gefertigt und
in attraktiv arrangierten Sets erhältlich sind. Durchtränkt mit den
Geschichten von zwölf Elementen,
verkörpert jedes einzigartige Stück
ein kleines Fragment der Natur.
Für Felissimo, Japan, in Zusammenarbeit mit Marie Uno.

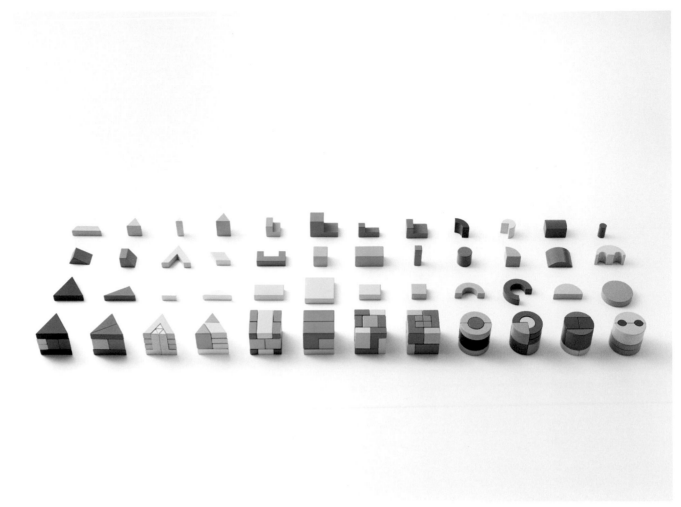

02

"Good design should be simple,
attractive and meaningful, but,
above all, it should have a beautiful
purpose."
„Gutes Design sollte schlicht, ansprechend und sinnvoll sein, aber vor
allem einen schönen Zweck haben."

How has the role played by design in our everyday lives changed?
No design, no life. Design brings stimulation to our daily life and mind.

What does winning the Red Dot say about a product?
Winning the Red Dot says the product is at its pinnacle. People can regard it as the top of a mountain and the designer can also feel as if he were at the summit.

Which area of design do you feel has the greatest potential for development for the future?
Every area has a huge potential for design development. Design development will never stop as long as humans interact with something.

Which country do you consider to be a pioneer in product design, and why?
China. Designers in China have been in a fast-learning and experimental mode for years, and this will give us a greater opportunity to develop new product design languages.

Inwieweit hat sich die Rolle, die Design in unserem täglichen Leben spielt, verändert?
Kein Design, kein Leben. Design bringt Stimulation in unser tägliches Leben und unseren Geist.

Was sagt eine Auszeichnung mit dem Red Dot über das Produkt aus?
Die Auszeichnung mit dem Red Dot bedeutet, dass ein Produkt seinen Höhepunkt erreicht hat. So können Menschen erkennen, dass es an der Spitze angekommen ist, und auch der Designer fühlt sich, als ob er den Gipfel erklommen hätte.

In welchem Designbereich sehen Sie das größte Entwicklungspotenzial für die Zukunft?
Jeder Bereich hat ein enormes Potenzial für Design-entwicklung. Die Entwicklung von Design wird nicht stillstehen, solange Menschen mit etwas interagieren.

Welche Nation ist für Sie Vorreiter im Produktdesign und warum?
China. Designer in China sind seit Jahren lern- und experimentierfreudig. So haben wir eine bessere Chance, neue Produktdesignsprachen zu entwickeln.

01

Prof. Renke He
China

Professor Renke He, born in 1958, studied civil engineering and architecture at Hunan University in China. From 1987 to 1988, he was a visiting scholar at the Industrial Design Department of the Royal Danish Academy of Fine Arts in Copenhagen and, from 1998 to 1999, at North Carolina State University's School of Design. Renke He is dean and professor of the School of Design at Hunan University and is also director of the Chinese Industrial Design Education Committee. Currently, he holds the position of vice chair of the China Industrial Design Association.

Professor Renke He wurde 1958 geboren und studierte an der Hunan University in China Bauingenieurwesen und Architektur. Von 1987 bis 1988 war er als Gastprofessor für Industrial Design an der Royal Danish Academy of Fine Arts in Kopenhagen tätig, und von 1998 bis 1999 hatte er eine Gastprofessur an der School of Design der North Carolina State University inne. Renke He ist Dekan und Professor an der Hunan University, School of Design, sowie Direktor des Chinese Industrial Design Education Committee. Er ist derzeit zudem stellvertretender Vorsitzender der China Industrial Design Association.

01 **Black sand tea set**
Design for the New Channel
Social Innovation Design project
by Cao Yuan
Design für das „New Channel
Social Innovation Design"-Projekt
von Cao Yuan

02 **Black sand tableware**
Design for the New Channel
Social Innovation Design project
by Yue Zou
Design für das „New Channel
Social Innovation Design"-Projekt
von Yue Zou

02

"Winning a Red Dot is the highest form of approval for world class design."

„Die Auszeichnung mit einem Red Dot ist die höchste Form der Anerkennung für Design von Weltklasse."

In your opinion, what makes for good design?
A user experience that surpasses the expectation of consumers.

How has the role played by design in our everyday lives changed?
The development of mobile Internet design has penetrated all aspects of our daily lives. One app design can be used all over the world simultaneously; no single physical product design was able to do that before.

What importance does design quality have for the economic success of companies?
Good design is good business; this is still a golden rule today. Design quality decides the quality of the user experiences for the products and services of any company; it is the key issue for companies' economic success.

What attracts you to the role of Red Dot jury member?
To be the first to know the best designs in the world.

Was macht Ihrer Ansicht nach gutes Design aus?
Ein Nutzererlebnis, das die Erwartungen der Verbraucher übertrifft.

Inwieweit hat sich die Rolle, die Design in unserem täglichen Leben spielt, verändert?
Die Entwicklung der Gestaltung des mobilen Internets hat alle Aspekte unseres täglichen Lebens durchdrungen. Ein App-Design kann auf der ganzen Welt gleichzeitig genutzt werden. Kein einziges physisches Produktdesign konnte das bislang schaffen.

Welche Bedeutung hat Designqualität für den wirtschaftlichen Erfolg von Unternehmen?
Gutes Design bringt wirtschaftlichen Erfolg. Das ist auch heute noch eine goldene Regel. Designqualität ist ausschlaggebend für die Art und Weise, in der der Benutzer die Produkte und Dienstleistungen eines Unternehmens qualitativ erlebt. Es ist das zentrale Thema für den wirtschaftlichen Erfolg von Unternehmen.

Was reizt Sie an der Arbeit als Red Dot-Juror?
Der Erste in der Welt zu sein, der die besten Entwürfe der Welt zu sehen bekommt.

ESCUELA DE INGENIERÍA
FACULTAD DE INGENIERÍA

01

Prof.
Carlos Hinrichsen
Chile

Professor Carlos Hinrichsen graduated as an industrial designer in Chile in 1982 and earned his master's degree in engineering in Japan in 1991. Currently, he is the Senior Managing Coordinator of Engineering Design in the School of Engineering in the P. Universidad Católica de Chile. Chile is in transition from an efficiency-based towards an innovation-based economy where the School of Engineering contributes with actions and initiatives to achieve this important aim for the country, mixing research, innovation, business, design and engineering spheres. From 2007 to 2009, Carlos Hinrichsen was president of the World Design Organization (formerly Icsid) and currently serves as senator within the organisation. In 2010, he was honoured with the distinction "Commander of the Order of the Lion of Finland". From 2014 to 2016, he was dean of the Faculty of Business, Engineering and Digital Arts at the Gabriela Mistral University in Santiago. For more than three decades he has led interdisciplinary teams to enable corporations, educational and other institutions to gain leadership and competitive positioning.

Professor Carlos Hinrichsen machte 1982 seinen Abschluss in Industriedesign in Chile und erhielt 1991 seinen Master der Ingenieurwissenschaft in Japan. Aktuell ist er leitender geschäftsführender Koordinator für Engineering Design an der P. Universidad Católica de Chile. Chile ist im Übergang von einer effizienzbasierten zu einer innovationsbasierten Wirtschaft, in der die Ingenieurschule mit Maßnahmen und Initiativen dazu beiträgt, dieses wichtige Landesziel durch eine Mischung aus Forschung, Innovation, Handel, Design und Ingenieurwesen zu erreichen. Von 2007 bis 2009 war Carlos Hinrichsen Präsident der World Design Organization (ehemals Icsid) und dient heute als Senator innerhalb der Organisation. 2010 wurde er mit der Auszeichnung „Commander of the Order of the Lion of Finland" geehrt. Von 2014 bis 2016 war er Dekan der Fakultät für Handel, Ingenieurwesen und Digitale Künste an der Gabriela-Mistral-Universität in Santiago. Seit mehr als drei Jahrzehnten leitet er interdisziplinäre Teams, um Unternehmen, Bildungsinstituten und anderen Organisationen zu helfen, eine marktführende und starke Wettbewerbsposition zu erlangen.

The School of Engineering UC with its Faculty of Engineering of the Pontificia Universidad Católica de Chile where Hinrichsen acts as Senior Managing Coordinator of Engineering Design is committed to interdisciplinary education as a key area of growth and development. The future interdisciplinary building is an evidence of this goal.

Die Ingenieurschule UC mit der Fakultät für Ingenieurwissenschaften der Pontificia Universidad Católica de Chile, wo Hinrichsen als Senior Managing Coordinator of Engineering Design tätig ist, engagiert sich für eine fachübergreifende Ausbildung, da sie diese als den wichtigsten Wachstums- und Entwicklungsbereich betrachtet. Das künftige interdisziplinäre Gebäude ist Zeugnis dieser Zielsetzung.

"The Red Dot Award is an important platform for obtaining global exposure and visibility, and is a win-win opportunity for companies and designers."

„Der Red Dot Award ist eine wichtige Plattform, um international bekannt und bemerkt zu werden. Unternehmen und Designern bietet er eine Win-win-Chance."

In your opinion, what makes for good design?
When I was child, I realised that it contributes to people's happincss, and over the years I confirmed that impression.

What importance does design quality have for the economic success of companies?
Design and innovation quality is a key factor in the fight against the general prevailing commoditisation of many product and/or service types. In this regard, those products that deserve recognition can be regarded as good evidence of a relationship between quality and a potentially successful market response.

Which area of design do you feel has the greatest potential for development for the future?
Mostly the "interdisciplinary areas" where we are able to find innovation led by design, or design led by innovation coming from the R&D sphere, and innovations associated with social and market changes, whose purpose it is to successfully respond to people's new needs and requirements.

Was macht Ihrer Ansicht nach gutes Design aus?
Schon als Kind wurde mir bewusst, dass es dazu beiträgt, Menschen glücklich zu machen. Im Laufe der Jahre hat sich dieser Eindruck bestätigt.

Welche Bedeutung hat Designqualität für den wirtschaftlichen Erfolg von Unternehmen?
Design- und Innovationsqualität ist ein zentraler Faktor für den Widerstand gegen die allgemein zunehmende Kommerzialisierung vieler Produkt- und/oder Servicetypen. In dieser Hinsicht sind die Produkte, die Anerkennung verdienen, diejenigen, die gute Beweise für einen Zusammenhang zwischen Qualität und einer potenziell erfolgreichen Marktreaktion liefern.

In welchem Designbereich sehen Sie das größte Entwicklungspotenzial für die Zukunft?
Hauptsächlich in den „interdisziplinären Bereichen", in denen wir von Design inspirierte Innovation oder von Innovation inspiriertes Design im F&E-Bereich sehen. Hinzu kommen Innovationen, die verbunden sind mit sozialen und Marktveränderungen, deren Ziel es ist, erfolgreich auf die Bedürfnisse und Anforderungen von Menschen einzugehen.

01

Simon Husslein
Germany/Switzerland
Deutschland/Schweiz

Simon Husslein was born in Werneck, Germany in 1976 and studied industrial design from 1995 to 2000 at Darmstadt University of Applied Sciences. From 2000 to 2005, he worked closely with his mentor and friend Hannes Wettstein at Wettstein's studio in Zurich. From 2005 to 2007, he completed a master's degree in Design Products at the London Royal College of Art. Subsequently, he led a number of projects in London and Shanghai and lectured at Shanghai's Tongji University. Between 2008 and 2014, he put his mark on a large number of projects at the Studio Hannes Wettstein in Zurich where he was creative director and member of the executive committee. In 2015, he founded the Atelier Simon Husslein. Simon Husslein develops products, furniture, installations and spatial design. He teaches and undertakes brand consultancy.

Simon Husslein, geboren 1976 in Werneck, studierte von 1995 bis 2000 Industrial Design an der Fachhochschule Darmstadt. Von 2000 bis 2005 arbeitete er eng mit seinem Mentor und Freund Hannes Wettstein in dessen Zürcher Studio zusammen. Von 2005 bis 2007 absolvierte er ein Masterstudium in Design Products am Royal College of Art in London. Danach betreute er eigene Projekte in London und Shanghai und unterrichtete an der Tongji-Universität in Shanghai. Zwischen 2008 und 2014 prägte er als Creative Director und Mitglied der Geschäftsleitung eine Vielzahl der Projekte des Studios Hannes Wettstein in Zürich. 2015 gründete er das Atelier Simon Husslein. Simon Husslein entwickelt Produkte, Möbel, Installationen und Raumgestaltungen. Er berät Marken und unterrichtet.

01 Braun BN0095
Wristwatch for Zeon Ltd
Armbanduhr für Zeon Ltd

02 Minimatik
Wristwatch for NOMOS
Glashütte/SA Roland Schwertner KG
Armbanduhr für NOMOS Glashütte/
SA Roland Schwertner KG

02

"No sophisticated brand can, in the long term, afford to ignore design quality."
„Keine anspruchsvolle Marke kann es sich langfristig leisten, Designqualität zu ignorieren."

How has the role played by design in our everyday lives changed?
The concentration and networking of things haven't always made everyday life easier. Design has the responsibility to provide some orientation and to create interfaces that are people-friendly.

What importance does design quality have for the economic success of companies?
Good design increases the probability that a product will be able to sustain its market position for an above-average length of time.

What attracts you to the role of Red Dot jury member?
Over the years, I have personally benefited from the attention that design prizes bring. By being a jury member and being able to contribute to the quality of the Red Dot, I am able to give something back.

Which country do you consider to be a pioneer in product design, and why?
The clarity of a classification by nation is becoming increasingly blurred.

Inwieweit hat sich die Rolle, die Design in unserem täglichen Leben spielt, verändert?
Verdichtung und Vernetzung von Dingen haben unseren Alltag nicht nur erleichtert. Design kommt die Verantwortung zu, Orientierung zu geben und Schnittstellen menschlich zu gestalten.

Welche Bedeutung hat Designqualität für den wirtschaftlichen Erfolg von Unternehmen?
Gutes Design erhöht die Chance signifikant, dass sich ein Produkt überdurchschnittlich lange in seinem Marktumfeld behaupten kann.

Was reizt Sie an der Arbeit als Red Dot-Juror?
Ich konnte in der Vergangenheit selbst wiederholt von der Aufmerksamkeit, die Designpreise auslösen, profitieren. Sich als Teil der Jury für die Qualität des Red Dot zu engagieren, gibt mir die Möglichkeit, etwas zurückzugeben.

Welche Nation ist für Sie Vorreiter im Produktdesign und warum?
Heutzutage verwischt die Klarheit einer nationalen Zuordnung.

01

Tapani Hyvönen
Finland
Finnland

Tapani Hyvönen graduated as an industrial designer from the present Aalto University School of Arts, Design and Architecture. In 1976, he founded the design agency "Destem Ltd." and was co-founder of ED-Design Ltd. in 1990. He has served as CEO and president of both agencies until 2013. He has been a visiting professor at Guangdong University of Technology in Guangzhou and Donghua University in Shanghai, China. His many award-winning designs, for which e.g. he was honoured with the Industrial Designer of the Year Award of the Finnish Association of Industrial Designers TKO in 1991 or the Pro Finnish Design Award by the Design Forum Finland, are part of the collections of the Design Museum Helsinki and the Cooper-Hewitt Museum, New York. Tapani Hyvönen was an advisory board member of the Design Leadership Programme at the University of Art and Design Helsinki 1989–2000, and a board member of the World Design Organization (formerly Icsid) 1999–2003 and 2009–2013. He was president of the Finnish Association of Designers Ornamo 2009–2012 and has been a board member of the Finnish Design Museum since 2011.

Tapani Hyvönen graduierte an der heutigen Aalto University School of Arts, Design and Architecture zum Industriedesigner. 1976 gründete er die Designagentur „Destem Ltd." und war 1990 Mitbegründer der ED-Design Ltd., die er beide bis 2013 als CEO und Präsident leitete. Er lehrt als Gastprofessor u. a. an der Guangdong University of Technology in Guangzhou und der Donghua University in Shanghai, China. Seine vielfach ausgezeichneten Arbeiten, für die er u. a. mit der Auszeichnung zum Industriedesigner des Jahres der Finnish Association of Industrial Designers TKO 1991 oder dem Pro Finnish Design Award des Design Forum Finland geehrt wurde, sind in den Sammlungen des Design Museum Helsinki und des Cooper-Hewitt Museum, New York, vertreten. Tapani Hyvönen war 1989–2000 in der Beratungskommission des Design Leadership Programme der University of Art and Design Helsinki und 1999–2003 sowie 2009–2013 Vorstandsmitglied der World Design Organization (ehemals Icsid). Er war Präsident der Finnish Association of Designers Ornamo 2009–2012 und ist seit 2011 Vorstandsmitglied des Finnish Design Museum.

01
Tableware design for Chinese
WOWDSGN 2016
01
Tableware design for Chinese
WOWDSGN 2016
Tischgeschirr-Gestaltung für das
chinesische WOWDSGN 2016

02 DOSIME
A hybrid smart home and wearable device that detects and
measures ionising radiation exposure, tracks cumulative exposure
and reports in real-time. For
Mirion Technologies, 2016.
Ein hybrides tragbares Gerät für die
intelligente Haustechnik. Es erkennt
und misst die ionisierende Strahlen-
einwirkung, zeichnet die kumulative
Belastung auf und gibt dazu in
Echtzeit Bescheid. Für Mirion
Technologies, 2016.

02

"As the purpose of design is to make things understandable and easy to use, information ergonomics will have an important role to play in future design."

„Da der Sinn von Design ist, Dinge verständlich und benutzerfreundlich zu machen, wird Informationsergo-nomie im Design der Zukunft eine wichtige Rolle spielen."

In your opinion, what makes for good design?
The most common criteria for good design are aesthetics, user friendliness, usability, sustainability, ergonomics, general efficiency etc. In good design, all
aspects are in equilibrium, but a failure of one criteria
can ruin the whole design.

What importance does design quality have for the economic success of companies?
An investment in design pays back more than many
other investments. When company management
complains about the price of the design, I usually say:
good design never costs too much, but bad design can
cost everything.

Which topics are most likely to influence design in the coming years?
Service will continue to be an important part of
product design. Digitalisation and the Internet of
Everything will be connected to most of the products.

Was macht Ihrer Ansicht nach gutes Design aus?
Die gebräuchlichsten Kriterien für gutes Design sind
Ästhetik, Nutzerfreundlichkeit, Brauchbarkeit, Nach-
haltigkeit, Ergonomie, die Leistung insgesamt usw. Bei
gutem Design sind alle diese Kriterien im Einklang.
Wenn aber eines versagt, zerstört es das ganze Design.

Welche Bedeutung hat Designqualität für den wirtschaftlichen Erfolg von Unternehmen?
Eine Investition in Design zahlt sich mehr aus als jegli-
che andere Investition. Wenn die Unternehmensleitung
über die Designkosten klagt, sage ich meist: Gutes
Design kostet nie zu viel, doch schlechtes Design kann
alles kosten.

Welche Themen werden das Design in den kommenden Jahren besonders beeinflussen?
Service wird weiterhin ein wichtiger Bestandteil von
Produktdesign sein. Die Digitalisierung und das „Internet of Everything" werden mit den meisten Produkten
verbunden sein.

01

Guto Indio da Costa
Brazil
Brasilien

Guto Indio da Costa, born in 1969 in Rio de Janeiro, studied product design and graduated from the Art Center College of Design in Switzerland in 1993. He is design director of Indio da Costa A.U.D.T, a consultancy based in Rio de Janeiro, which develops architectural, urban planning, design and transportation projects. It works with a multidisciplinary strategic-creative group of designers, architects and urban planners, supported by a variety of other specialists. Guto Indio da Costa is a member of the Design Council of the State of Rio de Janeiro, former Vice President of the Brazilian Design Association (Abedesign) and founder of CBDI (Brazilian Industrial Design Council). He has been active as a lecturer and contributing writer to different design magazines and has been a jury member of many design competitions in Brazil and abroad.

Guto Indio da Costa, geboren 1969 in Rio de Janeiro, studierte Produktdesign und machte 1993 seinen Abschluss am Art Center College of Design in der Schweiz. Er ist Gestaltungsdirektor von Indio da Costa A.U.D.T, einem in Rio de Janeiro ansässigen Beratungsunternehmen, das Projekte in Architektur, Stadtplanung, Design- und Transportwesen entwickelt und mit einem multidisziplinären, strategisch-kreativen Team aus Designern, Architekten und Stadtplanern sowie mit der Unterstützung weiterer Spezialisten operiert. Guto Indio da Costa ist Mitglied des Design Councils des Bundesstaates Rio de Janeiro, ehemaliger Vizepräsident der brasilianischen Designvereinigung (Abedesign) und Gründer des CBDI (Industrial Design Council Brasiliens). Er ist als Lehrbeauftragter aktiv, schreibt für verschiedene Designmagazine und ist als Jurymitglied zahlreicher Designwettbewerbe in und außerhalb Brasiliens tätig.

02

"Good design must bring some kind of innovation that has the potential to enhance peoples' lives and thus to improve our society."
„Gutes Design muss eine Innovation mit sich bringen, die das Potenzial hat, das Leben von Menschen und die Gesellschaft an sich zu verbessern."

How has the role played by design in our everyday lives changed?
It has deeply changed. Products have become far more complex, and usability has become a major issue.

What importance does design quality have for the economic success of companies?
Design quality has become absolutely necessary and an important requirement. Therefore, the challenge of enhancing design quality has become one of the most important factors for the economic success of companies.

What attracts you to the role of Red Dot jury member?
Firstly, it is a great experience to see the worldwide vanguard of product design every year. This is an incredible picture of the worldwide outlook on design. Secondly, the interaction with the very international jury, the exchange of points of views and the qualified discussions are extremely interesting and usually lead to new understanding and new perceptions in such a fast changing world.

Inwieweit hat sich die Rolle, die Design in unserem täglichen Leben spielt, verändert?
Sie hat sich grundlegend geändert. Produkte sind viel komplexer und Nutzerfreundlichkeit ist zu einem wichtigen Thema geworden.

Welche Bedeutung hat Designqualität für den wirtschaftlichen Erfolg von Unternehmen?
Designqualität ist absolut notwendig und zu einer wichtigen Voraussetzung geworden. Daher ist die Aufgabe, die Designqualität zu verbessern, zu einem der wichtigsten Faktoren für den wirtschaftlichen Erfolg von Unternehmen geworden.

Was reizt Sie an der Arbeit als Red Dot-Juror?
Erstens ist es ein tolles Erlebnis, jedes Jahr die weltweite Avantgarde des Produktdesigns zu sehen. Dies gibt uns einen unglaublichen Einblick in die Auffassung von Design in aller Welt. Zweitens sind die Interaktion mit der sehr internationalen Jury, der Austausch von Standpunkten und die qualifizierten Diskussionen äußerst interessant und führen üblicherweise zu einem neuen Verständnis und neuen Wahrnehmungen in dieser sich rasch verändernden Welt.

01

Prof.
Cheng-Neng Kuan
Taiwan

In 1980, Professor Cheng-Neng Kuan earned a master's degree in Industrial Design (MID) from the Pratt Institute in New York. He is currently a full professor and the vice president of Shih-Chien University, Taipei, Taiwan. With the aim of developing a more advanced design curriculum in Taiwan, he founded the Department of Industrial Design, in 1992. He served as department chair until 1999. Moreover, Professor Kuan founded the School of Design in 1997 and had served as the dean from 1997 to 2004 and as the founding director of the Graduate Institute of Industrial Design from 1998 to 2007. Professor Kuan had also held the position of the 16th chairman of the board of China Industrial Designers Association (CIDA), Taiwan. His fields of expertise include design strategy and management as well as design theory and creation. Having published various books on design and over 180 research papers and articles, he is an active member of design juries in his home country and internationally. He is a consultant to major enterprises on product development and design strategy.

1980 erwarb Professor Cheng-Neng Kuan einen Master-Abschluss in Industriedesign (MID) am Pratt Institute in New York. Derzeit ist er ordentlicher Professor und Vizepräsident der Shih-Chien University in Taipeh, Taiwan. 1992 gründete er mit dem Ziel, einen erweiterten Designlehrplan zu entwickeln, das Department of Industrial Design in Taiwan. Bis 1999 war Professor Kuan Vorsitzender des Instituts. Darüber hinaus gründete er 1997 die School of Design, deren Dekan er von 1997 bis 2004 war. Von 1998 bis 2007 war er Gründungsdirektor des Graduate Institute of Industrial Design. Zudem war er der 16. Vorstandsvorsitzende der China Industrial Designers Association (CIDA) in Taiwan. Seine Fachgebiete umfassen Designstrategie, -management, -theorie und -kreation. Neben der Veröffentlichung verschiedener Bücher über Design und von mehr als 180 Forschungsarbeiten und Artikeln ist er aktives Mitglied von Designjurys in seiner Heimat sowie auf internationaler Ebene. Zudem ist er als Berater für Großunternehmen im Bereich Produktentwicklung und Designstrategie tätig.

01 KNEESUP
A knee rehabilitation system integrating smart wearable devices and a mobile application – an example of a project that was selected as the winner of Taiwan's Young Pin Design Award 2016 for being the best of the year

Knie-Rehabilitationssystem, das tragbare intelligente Geräte und eine mobile App integriert – Beispiel eines Projekts, das als Jahresbestleistung zum Gewinner des Young Pin Design Award 2016 in Taiwan gekürt wurde

02 WisFit
A piece of intelligent magnetic fitness equipment including a commercial service system and an example of a project that was selected as a winner of Taiwan's Young Pin Design Award 2016

Intelligentes magnetisches Fitnessgerät mit einem Handels-Service-System und Beispiel für ein Gewinner-Projekt des Young Pin Design Award 2016 in Taiwan

02

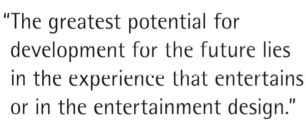

"The greatest potential for development for the future lies in the experience that entertains or in the entertainment design."

„Das größte Entwicklungspotenzial für die Zukunft liegt in Erfahrungen, die unterhalten, oder im Unterhaltungsdesign."

How has the role played by design in our everyday lives changed?
Instead of attracting attention, design is becoming a detector of cultural meanings.

What importance does design quality have for the economic success of companies?
Only through good design can a company succeed in being outstanding, as well as popularly accepted by the target market.

What does winning the Red Dot say about a product?
Authority. It makes one believe that quality design is truly good.

Which country do you consider to be a pioneer in product design, and why?
The United States, because they have three critical resources that hardly any other country can uphold simultaneously: a deeply embedded entrepreneurship, a dense multi-ethnic culture, and a big vibrant market.

Inwieweit hat sich die Rolle, die Design in unserem täglichen Leben spielt, verändert?
Anstatt Aufmerksamkeit zu erregen, wird Design zu einem Indikator für kulturelle Bedeutungen.

Welche Bedeutung hat Designqualität für den wirtschaftlichen Erfolg von Unternehmen?
Nur durch gutes Design kann es einem Unternehmen gelingen, herausragend zu sein und gleichzeitig in seinem Absatzmarkt auf allgemeine Akzeptanz zu stoßen.

Was sagt eine Auszeichnung mit dem Red Dot über das Produkt aus?
Autorität. Sie überzeugt einen davon, dass qualitativ hochwertiges Design wirklich gut ist.

Welche Nation ist für Sie Vorreiter im Produktdesign und warum?
Die Vereinigten Staaten, weil sie drei entscheidende Ressourcen haben, die kaum ein anderes Land gleichzeitig aufrechterhalten kann: einen tief verankerten Unternehmergeist, eine starke multiethnische Kultur und einen großen, dynamischen Markt.

01

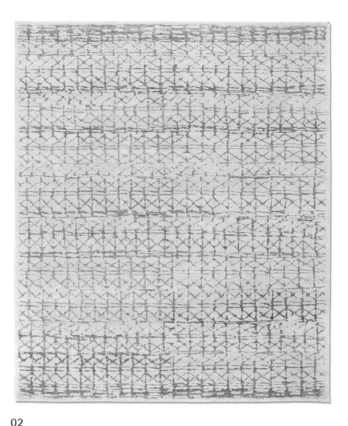

02

Kristiina Lassus
Finland/Italy
Finnland/Italien

Kristiina Lassus, born in Helsinki in 1966, graduated from the University of Industrial Arts of Helsinki with a Master of Arts in Design Leadership in 1992. This was followed by postgraduate studies in product development at the Helsinki Polytechnic in 1993, and her second MA in Interior Architecture and Furniture Design from the University of Industrial Arts in Helsinki in 1995. After working in renowned architectural practices in Finland and Australia, she developed her first products for Alessi, Poltronova and Zanotta. Her specialisation in design management and product development led to managerial positions in international design companies. She worked as Design Coordinator for Artek Oy Ab in Finland from 1994 to 1997 and as Design Manager for Alessi SpA in Italy from 1998 to 2004. In 2003, she founded Kristiina Lassus Studio which provides consultancy services in creative direction, project management, product design, brand development and design promotion. In 2007, she registered her own trademark, "Kristiina Lassus", as a symbol of independent and personal production.

Kristiina Lassus, 1966 in Helsinki geboren, graduierte 1992 an der University of Industrial Arts in Helsinki mit einem Master of Arts in Design Leadership. Ab 1993 studierte sie Product Development an der Helsinki Polytechnic und legte 1995 ihren zweiten Master of Arts in Interior Architecture und Furniture Design an der University of Industrial Arts in Helsinki ab. Sie arbeitete in renommierten Architekturbüros in Finnland und Australien, bevor sie ihre ersten Produkte für Alessi, Poltronova und Zanotta entwarf. Dank ihrer Spezialisierung auf Design Management und Product Development hatte sie geschäftsführende Positionen in internationalen Designfirmen inne. Von 1994 bis 1997 arbeitete sie als Design Coordinator für Artek Oy Ab in Finnland und von 1998 bis 2004 als Design Manager für Alessi SpA in Italien. 2003 gründete sie das Kristiina Lassus Studio, dessen Beratungstätigkeit die Bereiche Creative Direction, Projektmanagement, Produktdesign, Markenentwicklung und Designförderung umfasst. 2007 ließ sie ihre eigene Schutzmarke „Kristiina Lassus" eintragen, als Symbol einer unabhängigen und persönlichen Produktion.

01 Komo SLT
for Rugs Kristiina Lassus, Italy
für Rugs Kristiina Lassus, Italien

02 Naaba LGRH
for Rugs Kristiina Lassus, Italy
für Rugs Kristiina Lassus, Italien

03 Tau
Tray for Alessi, Italy
Tablett für Alessi, Italien

04 Adagio
Thermos for Alessi, Italy
Isolierkanne für Alessi, Italien

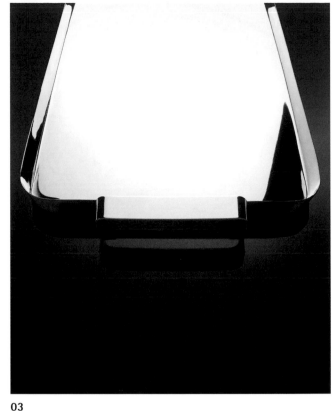

03

04

"Red Dot is a forum that helps exemplary products to stand out. It is a pleasure to be part of this jury and to give these products their well-deserved recognition."

„Red Dot ist ein Forum, das vorbildhaften Produkten hilft hervorzustechen. Es ist eine große Freude, Teil dieser Jury zu sein und diesen Produkten ihre wohlverdiente Anerkennung zu geben."

How has the role played by design in our everyday lives changed?
From concrete product design, the role of design is now moving towards abstract, intelligent and immaterial dimensions e.g. related to energy, climate, mood and atmosphere or services.

What importance does design quality have for the economic success of companies?
A fundamental importance. Design focuses on building on company strengths and opportunities and on eliminating weaknesses. It improves the overall product performance, production efficiency and the product life cycle. Research and development of new technical solutions push companies to evolve. Market leaders are innovators that have a clear mission and vision. Design quality gives companies a clear competitive advantage.

Inwieweit hat sich die Rolle, die Design in unserem täglichen Leben spielt, verändert?
Die Rolle von Design entwickelt sich vom konkreten Produktdesign weg hin zu mehr abstrakten, intelligenten und ungegenständlichen Dimensionen z. B. in Bezug auf Energie, Klima, Stimmung und Ambiente oder Dienstleistungen.

Welche Bedeutung hat Designqualität für den wirtschaftlichen Erfolg von Unternehmen?
Eine grundlegende Bedeutung. Design zielt darauf ab, auf den Stärken und Chancen eines Unternehmens aufzubauen und seine Schwächen zu beseitigen. Es verbessert die allgemeine Leistung, die Wirksamkeit und den Lebenszyklus eines Produkts. Forschung und Entwicklung neuer technologischer Lösungen treiben Unternehmen dazu an, sich weiterzuentwickeln. Marktführend sind die Unternehmen, die Wegbereiter sind und eine klare Mission und Vision haben. Designqualität gibt Unternehmen einen deutlichen Wettbewerbsvorteil.

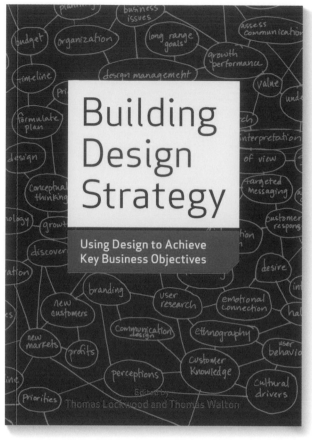

01

02

Dr Thomas Lockwood
USA

Dr Thomas Lockwood is the author of several books on design management, design strategy and design thinking. He has a PhD in design management and is recognised as a thought leader at integrating design and innovation practice into business, and building great design and UX organisations. He produced 22 conferences about design leadership, lectured and led workshops in over 20 countries, and is a design adviser to countries and companies. His design accomplishments range from creating high-tech skiwear for the US Olympic Nordic Ski Team, to corporate design programmes for Fortune 500 organisations. He is the founding partner of Lockwood Resource, an international consulting and recruiting firm specialising in design leadership. Previously he has been the president of DMI, the Design Management Institute, a corporate design director, and a partner and creative director at several design firms.

Dr. Thomas Lockwood ist der Autor mehrerer Bücher zu den Themen Designmanagement, Designstrategie und Designdenken. Er ist promovierter Designmanager und wird allgemein als Vordenker im Bereich der Integration von Design und Innovation in die Wirtschaft anerkannt. Er machte sich auch mit dem Bau von großen Design- und UX-Organisationen einen Namen. Außerdem organisierte er insgesamt 22 Konferenzen über Führung im Design, hielt in mehr als 20 Ländern Vorträge und leitete Workshops und ist als Designberater für Länder und Unternehmen aktiv. Seine Designerfolge reichen von der Gestaltung der Hightech-Skibekleidung für die olympische Nordic-Ski-Mannschaft der USA bis hin zu Corporate-Design-Programmen für Unternehmen, die zu den Fortune 500 gehören. Er ist der Gründungspartner von Lockwood Resource, einer internationalen Beratungs- und Personalbeschaffungsfirma, die sich auf Designmanagement spezialisiert hat. Davor war er Präsident des DMI (Design Management Institute), als Corporate Design Director tätig und als Partner und Creative Director bei verschiedenen Designfirmen angestellt.

"The rapidly growing international parity of design will influence the field of product design in the coming years."

„Die rasant zunehmende internationale Gleichwertigkeit von Design wird den Produktdesignbereich in den kommenden Jahren beeinflussen."

In your opinion, what makes for good design?
Good design is that which solves the right problems, with people and planet in mind.

How has the role played by design in our everyday lives changed?
Design is at the foundation of everything, and now more than ever people want to be surrounded by good design. Good design makes for good experiences; it can make us happy.

What importance does design quality have for the economic success of companies?
Design quality is fundamental to good business. Quality can be evaluated, and therefore improved, and so can design.

What attracts you to the role of Red Dot jury member?
The entire ecology – the products, process and people. Being a Red Dot judge informs my perspective of the best of global design, and stimulates my passion for design. I love the examination, the debate, the diversity of opinions, and the challenge of the entire evaluation process.

Was macht Ihrer Ansicht nach gutes Design aus?
Gutes Design löst die richtigen Probleme und verliert die Menschen und unseren Planeten nicht aus dem Blick.

Inwieweit hat sich die Rolle, die Design in unserem täglichen Leben spielt, verändert?
Design ist die Basis, auf der alles aufbaut. Mehr denn je wollen Menschen sich mit gutem Design umgeben. Gutes Design führt zu guten Erfahrungen. Es kann uns glücklich machen.

Welche Bedeutung hat Designqualität für den wirtschaftlichen Erfolg von Unternehmen?
Designqualität ist für wirtschaftlichen Erfolg von grundlegender Bedeutung. Qualität kann bewertet und daher verbessert werden. Das Gleiche gilt für Design.

Was reizt Sie an der Arbeit als Red Dot-Juror?
Die gesamte Ökologie - die Produkte, die Prozesse und die Menschen. Red Dot-Juror zu sein, beeinflusst meinen Standpunkt in Bezug auf das Beste, was globales Design zu bieten hat, und schürt meine Leidenschaft für Design. Ich liebe die Untersuchung, den Austausch, die Vielfalt der Meinungen und die Herausforderung des gesamten Bewertungsprozesses.

01

Lam Leslie Lu
Hong Kong
Hongkong

Lam Leslie Lu received a Master of Architecture from Yale University in Connecticut, USA in 1977, and was the recipient of the Monbusho Scholarship of the Japanese Ministry of Culture in 1983, where he conducted research in design and urban theory in Tokyo. He is currently the principal of the Hong Kong Design Institute and academic director of the Hong Kong Institute of Vocational Education. Prior to this, he was head of the Department of Architecture at the University of Hong Kong. Lam Leslie Lu has worked with, among others, Cesar Pelli and Associates, Hardy Holzman Pfeiffer Associates, Kohn Pedersen Fox Associates and Shinohara Kazuo on the design of the Centennial Hall of the Tokyo Institute of Technology. Moreover, he was visiting professor at Yale University and the Delft University of Technology as well as assistant lecturer for the Eero Saarinen Chair at Yale University. He also lectured and served as design critic at major international universities such as Columbia, Cambridge, Delft, Princeton, Yale, Shenzhen, Tongji, Tsinghua and the Chinese University Hong Kong.

Lam Leslie Lu erwarb 1977 einen Master of Architecture an der Yale University in Connecticut, USA, und war 1983 Monbusho-Stipendiat des japanischen Kulturministeriums, an dem er die Forschung in Design und Stadttheorie in Tokio leitete. Derzeit ist er Direktor des Hong Kong Design Institute und akademischer Direktor des Hong Kong Institute of Vocational Education. Zuvor war er Leiter des Architektur-Instituts an der Universität Hongkong. Lam Leslie Lu hat u. a. mit Cesar Pelli and Associates, Hardy Holzman Pfeiffer Associates, Kohn Pedersen Fox Associates und Shinohara Kazuo am Design der Centennial Hall des Tokyo Institute of Technology zusammengearbeitet, war Gastprofessor an der Yale University und der Technischen Universität Delft sowie Assistenz-Dozent für den Eero-Saarinen-Lehrstuhl in Yale. Er hielt zudem Vorträge und war Designkritiker an großen internationalen Universitäten wie Columbia, Cambridge, Delft, Princeton, Yale, Shenzhen, Tongji, Tsinghua und der chinesischen Universität Hongkong.

"Designs can make or break a business. User experience and functionality are keys today."

„Design ist entscheidend für Erfolg oder Misserfolg eines Unternehmens. Die Benutzererfahrung und Funktionalität sind heutzutage ausschlaggebend."

In your opinion, what makes for good design?
Form and function is still where it all starts. There is also a need for clarity – in reason, purpose, form, intuitive aspects and for me in a certain cleverness.

How has the role played by design in our everyday lives changed?
We are spoiled by mobile devices and all those apps! We now expect designs to be multi-functional and multi-use. Formal beauty is not a priority in this cycle of design evolution and less important than convenience.

What attracts you to the role of Red Dot jury member?
The humbling experience and sensory assaults when confronted with so many ideas. The experience makes you work hard to improve – it is therapy and a critique of oneself.

Was macht Ihrer Ansicht nach gutes Design aus?
Form und Funktion ist immer noch, womit alles beginnt. Es gibt auch einen Bedarf an Klarheit – bezüglich des Anlasses, des Zwecks, der Form, der intuitiven Aspekte und für mich auch einer gewissen Intelligenz.

Inwieweit hat sich die Rolle, die Design in unserem täglichen Leben spielt, verändert?
Wir werden von mobilen Endgeräten und all diesen Apps verwöhnt! Und erwarten jetzt, dass Gestaltungen multifunktional und vielseitig einsetzbar sind. Formale Schönheit hat in dieser Phase der Designentwicklung keine Priorität mehr und ist weitaus weniger wichtig als Komfort.

Was reizt Sie an der Arbeit als Red Dot-Juror?
Es ist eine Erfahrung, die einen Bescheidenheit lehrt. Man wird außerdem mit so vielen Ideen konfrontiert, dass einen die vielen sinnlichen Eindrücke überfluten. Diese Erfahrung führt dazu, dass man hart daran arbeitet, sich zu verbessern. Die Arbeit als Red Dot-Juror ist zugleich Therapie und Selbstkritik.

01

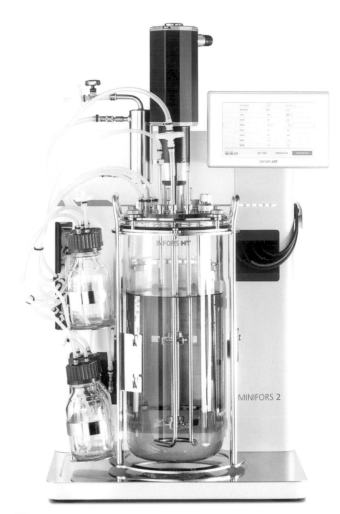

02

Wolfgang K. Meyer-Hayoz
Switzerland
Schweiz

Wolfgang K. Meyer-Hayoz studied mechanical engineering, visual communication and industrial design and graduated from the Stuttgart State Academy of Art and Design. The professors Klaus Lehmann, Kurt Weidemann and Max Bense had a formative influence on his design philosophy. In 1985, he founded the Meyer-Hayoz Design Engineering Group with offices in Winterthur, Switzerland and Constance, Germany. The design studio offers consultancy services for national as well as international companies in five areas of design competence: design strategy, industrial design, user-interface design, temporary architecture and communication design, and has received numerous international awards. From 1987 to 1993, Wolfgang K. Meyer-Hayoz was president of the Swiss Design Association (SDA). He is a member of the Association of German Industrial Designers (VDID), Swiss Marketing and the Swiss Management Society (SMG). Wolfgang K. Meyer-Hayoz also serves as juror on international design panels and supervises change management and turnaround projects in the field of design strategy.

Wolfgang K. Meyer-Hayoz absolvierte Studien in Maschinenbau, Visueller Kommunikation sowie Industrial Design mit Abschluss an der Staatlichen Akademie der Bildenden Künste in Stuttgart. Seine Gestaltungsphilosophie prägten die Professoren Klaus Lehmann, Kurt Weidemann und Max Bense. 1985 gründete er die Meyer-Hayoz Design Engineering Group mit Büros in Winterthur/Schweiz und Konstanz/Deutschland. Das Designstudio bietet Beratungsdienste für nationale wie internationale Unternehmen in den fünf Designkompetenzen Designstrategie, Industrial Design, User Interface Design, Temporäre Architektur und Kommunikationsdesign und wurde bereits vielfach ausgezeichnet. Von 1987 bis 1993 war Wolfgang K. Meyer-Hayoz Präsident der Swiss Design Association (SDA); er ist Mitglied im Verband Deutscher Industrie Designer (VDID), von Swiss Marketing und der Schweizerischen Management Gesellschaft (SMG). Wolfgang K. Meyer-Hayoz engagiert sich auch als Juror internationaler Designgremien und moderiert Change-Management- und Turnaround-Projekte im designstrategischen Bereich.

01–03 Minifors 2

01–03 Minifors 2
Compact and easy-to-use bioreactor for Infors AG, Switzerland – the unique product design and the layout of the device are optimally conceived for laboratory work processes
Kompakter und einfach zu bedienender Bioreaktor für Infors AG, Schweiz – das einzigartige Produktdesign und das Gerätelayout sind für die Arbeitsprozesse in Laboratorien optimal ausgelegt

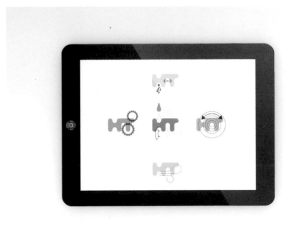

03

"Winning a Red Dot means: design quality of the highest order."

„Eine Auszeichnung mit dem Red Dot bedeutet: Designqualität auf höchstem Level."

How has the role played by design in our everyday lives changed?
Today, the desire for good design affects almost every aspect of life. What is different to the past is how design quality is defined by the DNA and positioning of a company.

What importance does design quality have for the economic success of companies?
My many years of experience in industry and in working with small, mid-sized and large companies allow me to say that there is a proven link between professional design work and the resulting success of a company.

Which area of design do you feel has the greatest potential for development for the future?
The integration of design in companies (consulting), biotechnology and the upstream and downstream processes involved, as well as the demographic challenges of the aging population in our part of the world.

Inwieweit hat sich die Rolle, die Design in unserem täglichen Leben spielt, verändert?
Der Wunsch nach guter Gestaltung hat heute praktisch alle Lebensbereiche erfasst. Was sich gegenüber früher jedoch manifestiert, ist die Definition der Designqualität über die DNA und Positionierung des Unternehmens.

Welche Bedeutung hat Designqualität für den wirtschaftlichen Erfolg von Unternehmen?
Aufgrund meiner langjährigen Erfahrung in der Industrie und der Zusammenarbeit mit kleinen, mittleren und großen Unternehmen kann ich sagen, dass die Kausalität von professioneller Designarbeit und hieraus resultierendem Unternehmenserfolg nachweisbar besteht.

In welchem Designbereich sehen Sie das größte Entwicklungspotenzial für die Zukunft?
In der Integration von Design in Unternehmen (Consulting), in der Biotechnologie und den hier vor- und nachgelagerten Prozessen sowie in den demografischen Herausforderungen der alternden Gesellschaft in unseren Breitengraden.

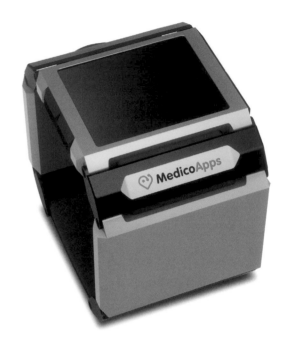

01

Prof. Jure Miklavc
Slovenia
Slowenien

Professor Jure Miklavc graduated in industrial design from the Academy of Fine Arts in Ljubljana, Slovenia and has nearly 20 years of experience in the field of design. Miklavc started his career working as a freelance designer, before founding his own design consultancy, Studio Miklavc. Studio Miklavc works in the fields of product design, visual communications and brand development and is a consultancy for a variety of clients from the industries of light design, electronic goods, user interfaces, transport design and medical equipment. Sports equipment designed by the studio has gained worldwide recognition. From 2013 onwards, the team has been working for the prestigious Italian motorbike manufacturer Bimota. Designs by Studio Miklavc have received many international awards and have been displayed in numerous exhibitions. Jure Miklavc has been involved in design education since 2005 and is currently a lecturer and head of industrial design at the Academy of Fine Arts and Design in Ljubljana.

Professor Jure Miklavc machte seinen Abschluss in Industrial Design an der Academy of Fine Arts and Design in Ljubljana, Slowenien, und verfügt über nahezu 20 Jahre Erfahrung im Designbereich. Er arbeitete zunächst als freiberuflicher Designer, bevor er sein eigenes Design-Beratungsunternehmen „Studio Miklavc" gründete. Studio Miklavc ist in den Bereichen Produktdesign, Visuelle Kommunikation und Markenentwicklung sowie in der Beratung zahlreicher Kunden der Branchen Lichtdesign, Elektronische Güter, Benutzeroberflächen, Transport-Design und Medizinisches Equipment tätig. Die von dem Studio gestalteten Sportausrüstungen erfahren weltweit Anerkennung. Seit 2013 arbeitet das Team für den angesehenen italienischen Motorradhersteller Bimota. Studio Miklavc erhielt bereits zahlreiche Auszeichnungen sowie Präsentationen in Ausstellungen. Seit 2005 ist Jure Miklavc in der Designlehre tätig und aktuell Dozent und Head of Industrial Design an der Academy of Fine Arts and Design in Ljubljana.

01 Flysentinel
Ultimate monitoring system for pilots – integral project of building a brand, corporate identity, products and packaging for the Medicoapps company
Ultimatives Überwachungssystem für Piloten – ganzheitliches Projekt zum Aufbau der Marke, der Corporate Identity, der Produkte und Verpackungen des Unternehmens Medicoapps

02 Relaxroll
Integral project of building a brand, corporate identity, products and packaging for a sports company with innovative products for the massage of athletes
Ganzheitliches Projekt zum Aufbau der Marke, der Corporate Identity, der Produkte und Verpackungen eines Sportunternehmens mit innovativen Produkten für die Massage von Athleten

02

"Winning a Red Dot is primarily confirmation of an excellent quality from invaluable impartial evaluators."

„Die Auszeichnung mit dem Red Dot ist primär eine Bestätigung hochwertiger Qualität durch unbezahlbare objektive Gutachter."

In your opinion, what makes for good design?
Sometimes, the best design is of the kind that we don't even notice. It's quietly and perfectly doing its job in anonymity like a well-mannered butler. Good design also doesn't burden people and the environment.

How has the role played by design in our everyday lives changed?
I think we live in a more artificial environment than ever before in the history of humankind. Everything around us in the urban environments is designed. That is why the importance of good-quality design is even more relevant.

Which topics are most likely to influence design in the coming years?
The development of artificial intelligence, the Internet of Things and general automation will change the way we live in the future. But the most powerful change could be that design will be bolder in taking the initiative to be the crucial social and technological innovator in the society of the future.

Was macht Ihrer Ansicht nach gutes Design aus?
Manchmal ist das beste Design das, das wir nicht einmal bemerken. Es erfüllt seine Aufgabe tadellos und in stiller Anonymität, ganz wie ein wohlgesitteter Butler. Gutes Design belastet auch Mensch und Umwelt nicht.

Inwieweit hat sich die Rolle, die Design in unserem täglichen Leben spielt, verändert?
Meiner Meinung nach leben wir in einer künstlicheren Umgebung als je zuvor in der Geschichte der Menschheit. Alles, was uns in einem städtischen Umfeld umgibt, ist von Designern gestaltet. Deshalb ist qualitativ hochwertiges Design immer wichtiger.

Welche Themen werden das Design in den kommenden Jahren besonders beeinflussen?
Die Entwicklung von künstlicher Intelligenz, das Internet der Dinge und die allgemeine Automatisierung werden unsere Lebensweise in der Zukunft verändern. Aber die größte Veränderung mag dadurch verursacht werden, dass Design in Zukunft stärker die Initiative ergreift, zum entscheidenden sozialen und technologischen Innovator der künftigen Gesellschaft zu werden.

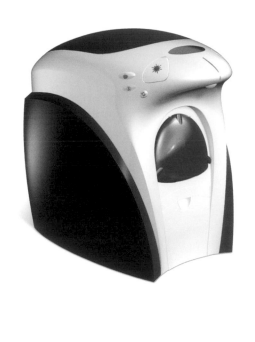

01

Prof. Ron A. Nabarro
Israel

Professor Ron A. Nabarro is an industrial designer, strategist, entrepreneur, researcher and educator. He has been a professional designer since 1970 and has designed more than 750 products to date in a wide range of industries. He has played a leading role in the emergence of age-friendly design and age-friendly design education. From 1992 to 2009, he was a professor of industrial design at the Technion Israel Institute of Technology, where he founded and was the head of the graduate programme in advanced design studies and design management. Currently, Nabarro teaches design management and design thinking at DeTao Masters Academy in Shanghai, China. From 1999 to 2003, he was an executive board member of the World Design Organization (formerly Icsid) and now acts as a regional advisor. He is a frequent keynote speaker at conferences, has presented TEDx events, has lectured and led design workshops in over 20 countries and consulted to a wide variety of organisations. Furthermore, he is co-founder and CEO of Senior-touch Ltd. and design4all. The principle areas of his research and interest are design thinking, age-friendly design and design management.

Professor Ron A. Nabarro ist Industriedesigner, Stratege, Unternehmer, Forscher und Lehrender. Seit 1970 ist er praktizierender Designer, gestaltete bisher mehr als 750 Produkte für ein breites Branchenspektrum und spielt eine führende Rolle im Bereich des altersfreundlichen Designs und dessen Lehre. Von 1992 bis 2009 war er Professor für Industriedesign am Technologie-Institut Technion Israel, an dem er das Graduiertenprogramm für fortgeschrittene Designstudien und Designmanagement einführte und leitete. Aktuell unterrichtet Nabarro Designmanagement und Design Thinking an der DeTao Masters Academy in Shanghai, China. Von 1999 bis 2003 war er Vorstandsmitglied der World Design Organization (ehemals Icsid), für die er aktuell als regionaler Berater tätig ist. Er ist ein gefragter Redner auf Konferenzen, hat bei TEDx-Veranstaltungen präsentiert, hielt Vorträge und Workshops in mehr als 20 Ländern und beriet eine Vielzahl von Organisationen. Zudem ist er Mitbegründer und Geschäftsführer von Senior-touch Ltd. und design4all. Die Hauptbereiche seiner Forschung und seines Interesses sind Design Thinking, altersfreundliches Design und Designmanagement.

01 AQ Water Bar
Water purifier, cooler and heater
for domestic and office use
Wasserreiniger, Kühl- und Heizgerät für den Einsatz im Büro und
daheim

02 Jumboard
Toddler keyboard for online
developmental computer games
Kinderkeyboard für entwicklungs-
fördernde Online-Computerspiele

02

"Design has become one of the
most important and crucial aspects
of commercial success."
„Design ist zu einem der wichtigsten
und wesentlichsten Aspekte des
wirtschaftlichen Erfolgs geworden."

In your opinion, what makes for good design?
Good design is a design that brings something important and valuable to our world. It's not just what
looks good but what performs, converts, surprises, and
is ethically and environmentally responsible. But first
and foremost it must comply with a real need.

**What attracts you to the role of Red Dot jury
member?**
As the winning products at the Red Dot Award set an
example to the design world, the most exciting part
of being a Red Dot juror is the fact that, as a juror,
you can bring your values, your ethics, your experience and your knowledge to the adjudication process
and, in doing so, influence the future of design.

**Which country do you consider to be a pioneer in
product design, and why?**
As most of the production of consumer products has
shifted to China, I believe that the natural next step
would be for Chinese designers to be the pioneers and
innovators of product design in the future.

Was macht Ihrer Ansicht nach gutes Design aus?
Gutes Design ist Design, das etwas Wichtiges und
Wertvolles zu unserer Welt beiträgt. Es geht nicht nur
darum, dass etwas gut aussieht, sondern dass es etwas
leistet, verwandelt, dass es überrascht und ethisch und
ökologisch verantwortungsvoll ist. In erster Linie muss
es aber ein wirkliches Bedürfnis erfüllen.

Was reizt Sie an der Arbeit als Red Dot-Juror?
Da die Produkte, die im Red Dot Award ausgezeichnet
werden, in der Designwelt eine Vorbildfunktion haben,
ist der aufregendste Part der Jurorenarbeit die Tatsache, dass man als Juror seine eigenen Werte, seinen
Ethos, seine Erfahrungen und sein Wissen in den
Beurteilungsprozess einbringen und so die Zukunft
von Design beeinflussen kann.

**Welche Nation ist für Sie Vorreiter im
Produktdesign und warum?**
Da sich die Produktion der meisten Konsumgüter nach
China verlagert hat, bin ich der Meinung, dass chine-
sische Designer als natürlicher nächster Schritt die
Pioniere und Wegbereiter für das Produktdesign der
Zukunft sein werden.

01

Prof. Dr. Ken Nah
Korea

Professor Dr Ken Nah graduated with a Bachelor of Science in industrial engineering from Hanyang University, South Korea, in 1983. He deepened his interest in human factors/ergonomics by earning a master's degree from Korea Advanced Institute for Science and Technology (KAIST) in 1985 and he gained a PhD from Tufts University in 1996. In addition, Ken Nah is also a USA Certified Professional Ergonomist (CPE). He is currently the dean of the International Design School for Advanced Studies (IDAS) and a professor of design management as well as director of the Human Experience and Emotion Research (HE.ER) Lab at IDAS, Hongik University, Seoul. Since 2002 he has been the director of the International Design Trend Center (IDTC). Ken Nah was the director general of "World Design Capital Seoul 2010". Alongside his work as a professor, he is also the president of the Korea Institute of Design Management (KIDM), vice president of the Korea Association of Industrial Designers (KAID) as well as the chairman of the Design and Brand Committee of the Korea Consulting Association (KCA).

Professor Dr. Ken Nah graduierte 1983 an der Hanyang University in Südkorea als Bachelor of Science in Industrial Engineering. Sein Interesse an Human Factors/Ergonomie vertiefte er 1985 mit einem Master-Abschluss am Korea Advanced Institute for Science and Technology (KAIST) und promovierte 1996 an der Tufts University. Darüber hinaus ist Ken Nah ein in den USA zertifizierter Ergonom (CPE). Derzeit ist er Dekan der International Design School for Advanced Studies (IDAS) und Professor für Design Management sowie Direktor des „Human Experience and Emotion Research (HE.ER)"-Labors an der IDAS, Hongik University, Seoul. Seit 2002 ist er zudem Leiter des International Design Trend Center (IDTC). Ken Nah war Generaldirektor der „World Design Capital Seoul 2010". Neben seiner Lehr-tätigkeit ist er Präsident des Korea Institute of Design Management (KIDM), Vizepräsident der Korea Association of Industrial Designers (KAID) sowie Vorsitzender des „Design and Brand"-Komitees der Korea Consulting Association (KCA).

01 Design Ergonomics
Co-authored with
Prof. Dr Sungjoo Cho, 2017,
Culture Code
Verfasst zusammen mit
Prof. Dr. Sungjoo Cho, 2017,
Culture Code

02 Design Innovation Note
Co-authored with
Prof. Dr Hyunsun Kim and
Hyojin Kim, 2017, Culture Code
Verfasst zusammen mit
Prof. Dr. Hyunsun Kim und
Hyojin Kim, 2017, Culture Code

02

"Design is the most effective tool for innovation. Therefore, maintaining good design quality is a must for the economic success of a company."

„Design ist das effektivste Mittel für Innovation. Deshalb muss ein Unternehmen gute Designqualität gewährleisten können, um wirtschaftlichen Erfolg zu haben."

In your opinion, what makes for good design?
To me, good design is always the optimal balance between "it looks good" and "it works well."

What does winning the Red Dot say about a product?
It is a hallmark of good design given by international design experts. It is like an internationally recognised passport for the world of design excellence.

Which topics are most likely to influence design in the coming years?
Definitely drones and robots. In the forthcoming era of Industry 4.0, these areas will explode much faster than expected.

Which country do you consider to be a pioneer in product design, and why?
For me, the Scandinavian countries are pioneers in product design, since their living standard and the awareness of design quality that ordinary people have is the highest in the world.

Was macht Ihrer Ansicht nach gutes Design aus?
Für mich ist gutes Design immer das optimale Gleichgewicht zwischen „Es sieht gut aus" und „Es funktioniert gut".

Was sagt eine Auszeichnung mit dem Red Dot über das Produkt aus?
Es ist ein Gütezeichen für gutes Design, das von internationalen Designexperten verliehen wird. Der Red Dot ist wie ein international anerkannter Pass in der Welt des Qualitätsdesigns.

Welche Themen werden das Design in den kommenden Jahren besonders beeinflussen?
Auf jeden Fall Drohnen und Roboter. In der bevorstehenden Ära der Industrie 4.0 werden diese Bereiche viel schneller wachsen als erwartet.

Welche Nation ist für Sie Vorreiter im Produktdesign und warum?
Für mich sind die skandinavischen Länder Pioniere in der Produktgestaltung, da ihr Lebensstandard und Bewusstsein für Designqualität bei der allgemeinen Bevölkerung die höchsten weltweit sind.

01

Alexander Neumeister
Germany/Brazil
Deutschland/Brasilien

Alexander Neumeister is a high-tech industrial designer, who lives both in Germany and Brazil. A graduate of the Ulm School of Design and a one-year scholarship student at the Tokyo University of Arts, he specialised in the fields of medicine, professional electronics and transportation. Among some of his best-known works are the "Transrapid" maglev trains, the German ICE trains, the Japanese Shinkansen "Nozomi 500", as well as numerous regional trains and subways for Japan, China and Brazil, and the C1 and C2 trains for the Munich underground. Aside from working on projects for large German companies, he was design consultant for Hitachi/Japan for 21 years. From 1983 to 1987 he was board member and later vice-president of the World Design Organization (formerly Icsid). In 1992, Alexander Neumeister and his team received the honorary title "Red Dot: Design Team of the Year". In November 2011, he was awarded the design prize of the city of Munich and in January 2015, he won the EU's "European Railway Award" in recognition of his contribution to railway design.

Alexander Neumeister arbeitet als Hightech-Industriedesigner und ist in Deutschland wie in Brasilien zu Hause. Als Absolvent der Hochschule für Gestaltung in Ulm und Stipendiat der Tokyo University of Arts für ein Jahr spezialisierte er sich auf die Bereiche Medizin, Professionelle Elektronik und Verkehr. Die Magnetschwebebahn „Transrapid", die deutschen ICE-Züge, der japanische Shinkansen „Nozomi 500", aber auch zahlreiche Regionalzüge und U-Bahnen in Japan, China und Brasilien sowie die U-Bahnen C1 und C2 für München zählen zu seinen bekanntesten Entwürfen. Neben Projekten für deutsche Großunternehmen war er 21 Jahre lang Designberater für Hitachi/Japan. Von 1983 bis 1987 war er Vorstandsmitglied und später Vizepräsident der World Design Organization (ehemals Icsid). 1992 wurden er und sein Team mit dem Ehrentitel „Red Dot: Design Team of the Year" ausgezeichnet. Im November 2011 erhielt er den Designpreis der Landeshauptstadt München und im Januar 2015 den „European Railway Award" der EU für seine Leistungen auf dem Gebiet des Railway-Designs.

01
C2 Generation – the new
underground trains for Munich
C2-Generation – die neue Metro
für München

02
Device for radial shockwave
therapy used in orthopaedics
Gerät zur radialen Stoßwellen-
Therapie für den orthopädischen
Bereich

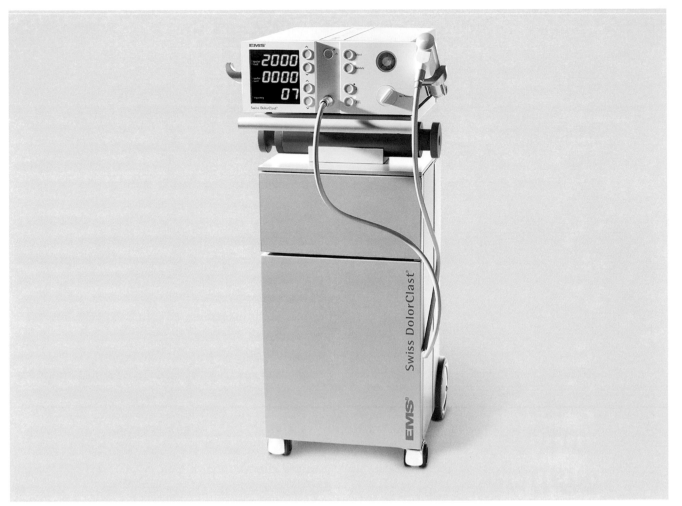

02

"In our affluent society, you will
find countless alternatives for
every product. Design awards help
consumers to decide."
„In unserer Überflussgesellschaft gibt
es für jedes Produkt unzählige Varianten. Hier helfen Designpreise dem
Käufer bei der Entscheidung."

In your opinion, what makes for good design?
The successful combination of material and function.
But also the avoidance of unnecessary decoration and
the ability for a product to fit into different environments.

**What attracts you to the role of Red Dot jury
member?**
The teamwork and the opportunity for exchange with
the other jury members from all corners of the world.

**What does winning the Red Dot say about a
product?**
The international composition of the jury shows that
the award not only addresses regional preferences, but
satisfies international standards as well.

**Which area of design do you feel has the greatest
potential for development for the future?**
New technologies have always been my first choice as
the basis for new products. This is why, in my opinion,
the combination of 3D printing technologies with
new energy-storage systems, linked to highly complex
software has the greatest development potential.

Was macht Ihrer Ansicht nach gutes Design aus?
Die gelungene Kombination von Materialaufwand
und Funktion. Aber auch der Verzicht auf unnötige
Dekoration und die Fähigkeit, sich in Umgebungen
einzuordnen.

Was reizt Sie an der Arbeit als Red Dot-Juror?
Die Arbeit im Team und die Möglichkeit, sich mit
anderen Juroren aus unterschiedlichsten Ländern
auszutauschen.

**Was sagt eine Auszeichnung mit dem Red Dot über
das Produkt aus?**
Die international zusammengesetzte Jury belegt, dass
die Auszeichnung nicht nur regionalen Präferenzen
genügt, sondern internationales Niveau erfüllt.

**In welchem Designbereich sehen Sie das größte
Entwicklungspotenzial für die Zukunft?**
Für mich standen immer neue Technologien als Basis
für neue Produkte im Vordergrund. Daher hat die
Kombination von 3D-Drucker-Technologien mit neuen
Energiespeichern und deren Verknüpfungen durch
hochkomplexe Software das optimale Entwicklungs-
potenzial für mich.

01

Simon Ong
Singapore
Singapur

Simon Ong, born in Singapore in 1953, graduated with a master's degree in design from the University of New South Wales and an MBA from the University of South Australia. He is the deputy chairman and co-founder of Kingsmen Creatives Ltd., a leading communication design and production group with 19 offices across the Asia-Pacific region and the Middle East. Kingsmen has won several awards, such as the President's Design Award, Singapore Good Design Mark, SRA Best Retail Concept Award, SFIA Hall of Fame, Promising Brand Award, A.R.E. Retail Design Award and RDI International Store Design Award USA. Simon Ong is actively involved in the creative industry as chairman of the design group of Manpower, the Skills & Training Council of Singapore Workforce Development Agency. Moreover, he is a member of the advisory board of the Singapore Furniture Industries Council, Design Business Chamber Singapore and Interior Design Confederation of Singapore. An ardent advocate of education, Simon Ong currently serves as a board director of Nanyang Academy of Fine Arts and a member of the advisory board to the School of Design & Environment at the National University of Singapore.

Simon Ong, geboren 1953 in Singapur, erhielt einen Master in Design der University of New South Wales und einen Master of Business Administration der University of South Australia. Er ist stellvertretender Vorsitzender und Mitbegründer von Kingsmen Creatives Ltd., eines führenden Unternehmens für Kommunikationsdesign und Produktion mit 19 Geschäftsstellen im asiatisch-pazifischen Raum sowie im Mittleren Osten. Kingsmen wurde vielfach ausgezeichnet, u. a. mit dem President's Design Award, Singapore Good Design Mark, SRA Best Retail Concept Award, SFIA Hall of Fame, Promising Brand Award, A.R.E. Retail Design Award und RDI International Store Design Award USA. Simon Ong ist als Vorsitzender der Designgruppe von Manpower, der „Skills & Training Council of Singapore Workforce Development Agency", aktiv in die Kreativindustrie involviert, ist unter anderem Mitglied des Beirats des Singapore Furniture Industries Council, der Design Business Chamber Singapore und der Interior Design Confederation of Singapore. Als leidenschaftlicher Befürworter von Bildung ist Simon Ong zurzeit als Vorstandsvorsitzender der Nanyang Academy of Fine Arts und als Mitglied des Beirats der School of Design & Environment an der National University of Singapore tätig.

02

"Sustainability is the key to designing for the future – especially in the areas of urban design and product design."

„Nachhaltigkeit ist der Schlüssel zur Gestaltung der Zukunft, insbesondere in den Bereichen Urban Design und Produktdesign."

In your opinion, what makes for good design?
Less is more and good design must have a purpose beyond its aesthetic value. Good design should enrich the everyday lives of end users.

How has the role played by design in our everyday lives changed?
Design permeates every aspect of our everyday lives, from urban design to product design for example. Design's role hasn't changed, but its prominence has.

Which topics are most likely to influence design in the coming years?
As the average human lifespan increases, product design will be geared towards developing solutions for aging populations. Artificial intelligence will also continue to gain momentum because the study of human behaviour is central to product design. Last but not least, sustainability will remain a priority.

Was macht Ihrer Ansicht nach gutes Design aus?
Weniger ist mehr. Gutes Design muss außerdem einen Zweck jenseits seines ästhetischen Werts erfüllen. Gutes Design sollte den Alltag des Nutzers bereichern.

Inwieweit hat sich die Rolle, die Design in unserem täglichen Leben spielt, verändert?
Design durchdringt jeden Aspekt unseres täglichen Lebens, z. B. von der Städteplanung bis zum Produktdesign. Die Rolle von Design hat sich nicht verändert, nur seine Bedeutung.

Welche Themen werden das Design in den kommenden Jahren besonders beeinflussen?
Mit dem Anstieg der durchschnittlichen menschlichen Lebensdauer wird das Produktdesign zunehmend auf die Entwicklung von Lösungen für eine alternde Bevölkerung ausgerichtet werden. Die Künstliche Intelligenz wird sich weiterhin verbreiten, weil die Untersuchung des menschlichen Verhaltens für die Produktgestaltung von zentraler Bedeutung ist. Nicht zuletzt bleibt auch die Nachhaltigkeit eine Priorität.

01

Prof. Martin Pärn
Estonia
Estland

Professor Martin Pärn, born in Tallinn in 1971, studied industrial design at the University of Industrial Arts Helsinki (UIAH). After working in the Finnish furniture industry he moved back to Estonia and undertook the role of the ambassadorial leader of design promotion and development in his native country. He was actively involved in the establishment of the Estonian Design Centre that he directed as chair of the board. Martin Pärn founded the multidisciplinary design office "iseasi", which creates designs ranging from office furniture to larger instruments and from interior designs for the public sector to design services. Having received many awards, Pärn began in 1995 with the development of design training in Estonia and is currently head of the Design and Engineering's master's programme, he established in 2010. The joint initiative of the Tallinn University of Technology and the Estonian Academy of Arts aims, among other things, to create synergies between engineers and designers.

Professor Martin Pärn, geboren 1971 in Tallinn, studierte Industriedesign an der University of Industrial Arts Helsinki (UIAH). Nachdem er in der finnischen Möbelindustrie gearbeitet hatte, ging er zurück nach Estland und übernahm die Funktion des leitenden Botschafters für die Designförderung und -entwicklung seiner Heimat. Er war aktiv am Aufbau des Estonian Design Centres beteiligt, das er als Vorstandsvorsitzender leitete. Martin Pärn gründete das multidisziplinäre Designbüro „iseasi", das Büromöbel, größere Instrumente oder Interior Designs für den öffentlichen Sektor gestaltet und Designservices anbietet. Vielfach ausgezeichnet, startete Pärn 1995 mit der Entwicklung der Designlehre in Estland und ist heute Leiter des Masterprogramms „Design und Engineering", das er 2010 aufgebaut hat. Es ist eine gemeinsame Initiative der Tallinn University of Technology und der Estonian Academy of Arts und verfolgt u. a. das Ziel, durch den Zusammenschluss Synergien von Ingenieuren und Designern zu erreichen.

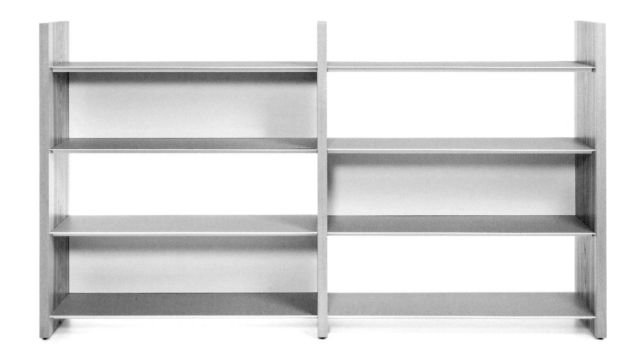

02

"I believe design at its best produces new meanings and creates promising situations that turn possible futures into pleasant everyday reality."

„Design kann im besten Falle neue Bedeutungen und verheißungsvolle Situationen schaffen, die mögliche Zukunftsszenarien zur angenehmen Realität werden lassen."

What importance does design quality have for the economic success of companies?
Design bundles the output and activities of companies together, makes these systems understandable as a whole, as well as usable and lovable. This love translates into economic success.

What attracts you to the role of Red Dot jury member?
Having been a member of the Red Dot jury for a few years in a row, gives me a fantastic archaeological overview of the changes in our everyday life. There are areas where new technologies are emerging, like robots and drones, or others where old technology is being replaced, like lighting. And, of course, sharing the judging work and experience with other judges is also a great part of being a Red Dot jury member.

Which topics are most likely to influence design in the coming years?
I believe the key role of design has always been to humanise technology. With the move towards artificial intelligence and the Internet of Things, the importance of good design will just grow.

Welche Bedeutung hat Designqualität für den wirtschaftlichen Erfolg von Unternehmen?
Design bündelt die Produktion und die Aktivitäten von Unternehmen, macht diese Systeme in ihrer Gesamtheit verständlich, verwendbar und liebenswert. Diese Liebe verwandelt sich in wirtschaftlichen Erfolg.

Was reizt Sie an der Arbeit als Red Dot-Juror?
Da ich seit einigen Jahren in Folge Mitglied der Red Dot-Jury bin, habe ich so einen phantastischen, archäologischen Überblick über die Veränderungen in unserem Alltag bekommen. Es gibt Bereiche, in denen neue Technologien entstehen, z. B. Roboter und Drohnen, oder in denen alte Technologie ersetzt wird, etwa bei der Beleuchtung. Doch auch das gemeinsame Beurteilen von Projekten und die Erfahrung mit anderen Juroren machen einen großen Teil des Reizes aus.

Welche Themen werden das Design in den kommenden Jahren besonders beeinflussen?
Ich glaube, die Schlüsselrolle des Designs war schon immer die Vermenschlichung der Technologie. Und mit dem Übergang zur künstlichen Intelligenz und dem Internet der Dinge wird gutes Design nur an Bedeutung gewinnen.

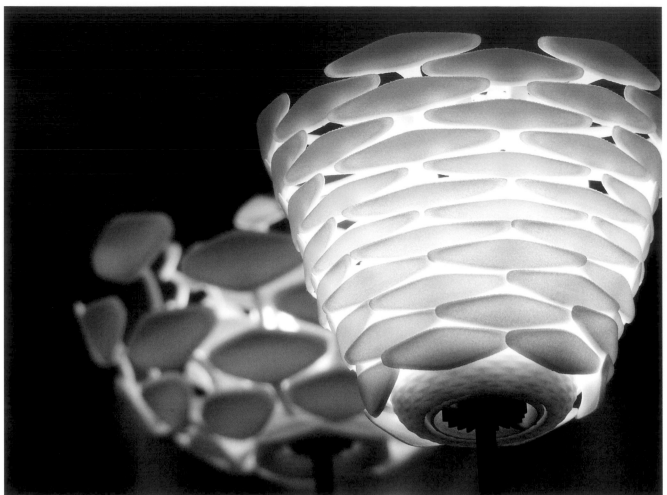

01

Dr Sascha Peters
Germany
Deutschland

Dr Sascha Peters is founder and owner of the agency for material and technology HAUTE INNOVATION in Berlin. He studied mechanical engineering at the RWTH Aachen University, Germany, and product design at the ABK Maastricht, Netherlands. He wrote his doctoral thesis at the University of Duisburg-Essen, Germany, on the complex of problems in communication between engineering and design. From 1997 to 2003, he led research projects and product developments at the Fraunhofer Institute for Production Technology IPT in Aachen and subsequently became deputy head of the Design Zentrum Bremen until 2008. Sascha Peters is author of various specialist books on sustainable raw materials, smart materials, innovative production techniques and energetic technologies. He is a leading material expert and trend scout for new technologies. Since 2014, he has been an advisory board member of the funding initiative "Zwanzig20 – Partnerschaft für Innovation" (2020 – Partnership for innovation) commissioned by the German Federal Ministry of Education and Research.

Dr. Sascha Peters ist Gründer und Inhaber der Material- und Technologieagentur HAUTE INNOVATION in Berlin. Er studierte Maschinenbau an der RWTH Aachen und Produktdesign an der ABK Maastricht. Seine Doktorarbeit schrieb er an der Universität Duisburg-Essen über die Kommunikationsproblematik zwischen Engineering und Design. Von 1997 bis 2003 leitete er Forschungsprojekte und Produktentwicklungen am Fraunhofer-Institut für Produktionstechnologie IPT in Aachen und war anschließend bis 2008 stellvertretender Leiter des Design Zentrums Bremen. Sascha Peters ist Autor zahlreicher Fachbücher zu nachhaltigen Werkstoffen, smarten Materialien, innovativen Fertigungsverfahren und energetischen Technologien und zählt zu den führenden Materialexperten und Trendscouts für neue Technologien. Seit 2014 ist er Mitglied im Beirat der Förderinitiative „Zwanzig20 – Partnerschaft für Innovation" im Auftrag des Bundesministeriums für Bildung und Forschung.

02

> "I hope that we will eventually only use materials that can be recycled indefinitely or that are completely bio-degradable."
>
> „Ich würde mir wünschen, dass wir nur noch Materialien verwenden, die unendlich oft recycelt werden können oder sich in der Natur vollständig biologisch abbauen."

What developments do you regard as particularly positive in the area of materials?
Those material developments that attempt to imitate or copy organic and natural processes. That can only be to our benefit.

What factors should designers and manufacturers consider when selecting materials?
Aside from sustainability, it would be wonderful if we could manage to make materials work in a completely closed system, thereby avoiding the creation of waste products.

What developments do you hope for in the future of materials?
The ability to integrate functions in materials by selecting the right raw materials and combining them cleverly. The use of "smart materials" would allow us to minimise the effort needed to create certain functions. Imagine if a material could take over the role of an electric motor and produce simple movements in a product.

Welche Entwicklungen im Bereich der Materialien nehmen Sie als besonders positiv wahr?
Solche Materialentwicklungen, mit denen versucht wird, organische Vorgänge und Prozesse aus der Natur nachzuahmen bzw. zu kopieren. Davon können wir nur profitieren.

Welche Faktoren sollten Designer und Hersteller bei der Wahl ihrer Materialien beachten?
Neben der Nachhaltigkeit wäre es ganz wunderbar, wenn wir es schaffen würden, Materialien vollständig in geschlossenen Kreisläufen zirkulieren zu lassen, sodass Abfälle gar nicht erst entstehen können.

Welche Entwicklungen in der Material-Branche würden Sie sich für die Zukunft wünschen?
Dass wir es durch die verwendeten Werkstoffe und deren Kombination schaffen, Funktionen in Material zu integrieren. Denn bei der Verwendung von Smart Materials würde sich der Aufwand zur Funktionsrealisierung auf ein Minimum reduzieren. Man stelle sich nur vor, ein Material könnte die Aufgabe eines Elektromotors übernehmen und leichte Bewegungsverläufe in einem Produkt realisieren.

01

Dirk Schumann
Germany
Deutschland

Dirk Schumann, born in 1960 in Soest, studied product design at Münster University of Applied Sciences. After graduating in 1987, he joined oco-design as an industrial designer, moved to siegerdesign in 1989, and was a lecturer in product design at Münster University of Applied Sciences until 1991. In 1992, he founded his own design studio Schumanndesign in Münster, developing design concepts for companies in Germany, Italy, India, Thailand and China. For several years now, he has focused on conceptual architecture, created visionary living spaces and held lectures at international conferences. Dirk Schumann has taken part in exhibitions both in Germany and abroad with works that have garnered several awards, including the Gold Prize (Minister of Economy, Trade and Industry Prize) in the International Design Competition, Osaka; the Comfort & Design Award, Milan; the iF product design award, Hanover; the Red Dot Design Award, Essen; the Focus in Gold, Stuttgart; as well as the Good Design Award, Chicago and Tokyo. In 2015 he founded Schumann&Wang in Xiamen City, the Chinese subsidiary of Schumanndesign.

Dirk Schumann, 1960 in Soest geboren, studierte Produktdesign an der Fachhochschule Münster. Nach seinem Abschluss 1987 arbeitete er als Industriedesigner für oco-design, wechselte 1989 zu siegerdesign und war bis 1991 an der Fachhochschule Münster als Lehrbeauftragter für Produktdesign tätig. 1992 eröffnete er in Münster sein eigenes Designstudio Schumanndesign, das Designkonzepte für Unternehmen in Deutschland, Italien, Indien, Thailand und China entwickelt. Seit einigen Jahren beschäftigt er sich mit konzeptioneller Architektur, entwirft visionäre Lebensräume und hält Vorträge auf internationalen Kongressen. Dirk Schumann nimmt an Ausstellungen im In- und Ausland teil und wurde für seine Arbeiten mehrfach ausgezeichnet, u. a. mit dem Gold Prize (Minister of Economy, Trade and Industry Prize) des International Design Competition, Osaka, dem Comfort & Design Award, Mailand, dem iF product design award, Hannover, dem Red Dot Design Award, Essen, dem Focus in Gold, Stuttgart, sowie dem Good Design Award, Chicago und Tokio. 2015 gründete er mit Schumann&Wang in Xiamen City die chinesische Dependance von Schumanndesign.

01 DHE-4
Instantaneous water heater for
STIEBEL ELTRON, Germany
Durchlauferhitzer für STIEBEL
ELTRON, Deutschland

02 Victrix TT
Gas-fired boiler for
IMMERGAS, Italy
Gaswärmeerzeuger für
IMMERGAS, Italien

02

"The Red Dot conveys that a product demonstrates outstanding quality of form and function, as well as a sensible use of resources."

„Der Red Dot sagt über ein Produkt aus, dass es eine exzellente Qualität in Form und Funktion sowie einen überlegten sinnvollen Umgang mit Ressourcen aufweist."

In your opinion, what makes for good design?
Spontaneous belief in a product. An aura of quality and substance. The desire to spend time on the product.

What importance does design quality have for the economic success of companies?
Design quality is a cultural statement about the responsibility companies have – towards the users of their products. Those who assume this responsibility will be successful.

Which area of design do you feel has the greatest potential for development for the future?
Communication and networking, as these areas connect people of all age groups, cultural and social background. We therefore need to find a way of making products understandable.

Which country to you consider to be a pioneer in product design, and why?
The Asia-Pacific region, because of its openness to new concepts, ideas and because of the courage companies have to implement them in a systematic way.

Was macht Ihrer Ansicht nach gutes Design aus?
Spontanes Vertrauen in das Produkt. Ausstrahlung von Qualität und Tiefgründigkeit. Der Wunsch, sich mit dem Produkt zu befassen.

Welche Bedeutung hat Designqualität für den wirtschaftlichen Erfolg von Unternehmen?
Designqualität ist ein kulturelles Statement der Verantwortlichkeit von Unternehmen – gegenüber den Nutzern ihrer Produkte. Unternehmen, die diese Verantwortung tragen, werden damit erfolgreich sein.

In welchem Designbereich sehen Sie das größte Entwicklungspotenzial für die Zukunft?
Kommunikation und Vernetzung, da in diesen Bereichen Menschen aller Altersstufen, kultureller und sozialer Herkunft verbunden sind und hier eine übergreifende Plattform der Verständlichkeit der Produkte gefunden werden muss.

Welche Nation ist für Sie Vorreiter im Produktdesign und warum?
Der Großraum Asien, durch die offene Haltung gegenüber neuen Konzepten, Ideen und dem Mut der Unternehmen, diese gezielt umzusetzen.

01

Prof. Song Kee Hong
Singapore
Singapur

Professor Song Kee Hong is a deputy head at the Industrial Design Division, National University of Singapore. He is also the design director at cross-disciplinary consultancy Design Exchange and has more than two decades of design experience, including work at global innovation consultancy Ziba in the US and at HP. He has worked with notable brands across diverse industries including Apple, Dell, Epson, HP, Intel, Lenovo, P&G, Philips, Sanyo, Sennheiser, and WelchAllyn. His portfolio lists over twenty international design awards. Until recent Song Kee Hong was executive committee member of the Design Business Chamber Singapore and served on the advisory committees of the National University of Singapore's School of Design and Environment, and of the Singapore government's Ministry of Education's Design and Technology programme. He was furthermore a member of the advisory board for Singapore Polytechnic's School of Mechanical and Manufacturing Engineering and the Singapore Design Council.

Professor Song Kee Hong ist ein stellvertretender Leiter der Industrial Design Division an der National University of Singapore. Er ist ebenfalls Designdirektor der interdisziplinären Unternehmensberatung Design Exchange und verfügt über mehr als zwei Jahrzehnte Design-erfahrung, u. a. durch Tätigkeiten bei der globalen Innovations-Unternehmensberatung Ziba in den USA und bei HP. Er arbeitete bereits mit namhaften Marken unterschiedlicher Branchen zusammen, u. a. Apple, Dell, Epson, HP, Intel, Lenovo, P&G, Philips, Sanyo, Sennheiser und WelchAllyn. Sein Portfolio verzeichnet mehr als 20 internationale Designauszeichnungen. Bis vor Kurzem war Song Kee Hong Vorstandsmitglied der Design Business Chamber Singapore und in den Fachbeiräten der Fakultät „Design und Umwelt" an der Nationaluniversität Singapur sowie des Design- und Technologieprogramms des Bildungsministeriums aktiv. Zudem saß er im Beirat der Fachhochschule für Maschinenbau und Fertigungstechnik in Singapur sowie des landeseigenen Singapore Design Councils.

01 MX W1
Wireless earphone for Sennheiser
Drahtloser Kopfhörer für Sennheiser

02 ConnectedHealth remote
Health monitoring app
App zur Fernüberwachung
des Gesundheitszustands

02

"The role of design in our everyday lives has changed insofar as it is increasingly growing beyond aesthetics and styling."

„Die Rolle von Design hat sich insofern verändert, als es zunehmend über Ästhetik und Styling hinauswächst."

How has the role played by design in our everyday lives changed?
Design is increasingly growing beyond aesthetics and styling. I think the increasing frequency of market disruptions has created more opportunities for the design industry. These days, many designers are working on ways to improve user experience and simplify the interface between people and technology, businesses and even government policies.

What importance does design quality have for the economic success of companies?
Today, almost any company can have access to the same technology and manufacturing capability. This has lowered entry barriers and saturated markets with commodity products; thus making design quality a critical differentiator against the competition.

What attracts you to the role of Red Dot jury member?
I get to see the latest and the best products from around the world and have the rare opportunity to discuss issues on the design industry with some of the world's best design talents.

Inwieweit hat sich die Rolle, die Design in unserem täglichen Leben spielt, verändert?
Design wächst zunehmend über Ästhetik und Styling hinaus. Die immer häufigeren Marktstörungen haben zu mehr Chancen für die Designbranche geführt. Heutzutage arbeiten viele Designer daran, Nutzererfahrungen zu verbessern und die Schnittstellen zwischen Mensch und Technik, Unternehmen und sogar der Regierungspolitik einfacher zu gestalten.

Welche Bedeutung hat Designqualität für den wirtschaftlichen Erfolg von Unternehmen?
Heute kann fast jedes Unternehmen Zugang zu den gleichen Technologien und Fertigungskapazitäten haben. Das hat zu niedrigeren Eintrittsbarrieren und der Überflutung von Märkten mit Rohstoffprodukten geführt. Die Designqualität ist daher zu einem wesentlichen Unterscheidungsmerkmal gegenüber der Konkurrenz geworden.

Was reizt Sie an der Arbeit als Red Dot-Juror?
Ich habe die Chance, die neuesten und besten Produkte aus aller Welt zu sehen, und die äußerst seltene Gelegenheit, mit den weltbesten Designtalenten Themen der Designbranche zu besprechen.

01

Aleks Tatic
Germany/Italy
Deutschland/Italien

Aleks Tatic, born 1969 in Cologne, Germany, is product designer and founder of Tatic Designstudio in Milan, Italy. After his studies at the Art Center College of Design in the USA and Switzerland, he specialised in the areas of sports and lifestyle products in various international agencies in London and Milan. Afterwards, he guided the multiple award-winning Italian design studio Attivo Creative Resource to international success, leading the agency for 12 years. Together with his multicultural team of designers and product specialists, he today designs and develops – amongst others – sailing yachts, sporting goods, power tools, FMCGs and consumer electronics for European and Asian premium brands. Aleks Tatic lectures on practice-oriented industrial design and innovation management at various European universities and seminars.

Aleks Tatic, geboren 1969 in Köln, ist Produktdesigner und Gründer der Agentur Tatic Designstudio in Mailand. Nach seinem Studium am Art Center College of Design in den USA und der Schweiz hat er sich zunächst in verschiedenen internationalen Büros in London und Mailand auf das Gebiet der Sport- und Lifestyleprodukte spezialisiert. Danach führte er zwölf Jahre lang das mehrfach ausgezeichnete italienische Designbüro Attivo Creative Resource zu internationalem Erfolg. Heute gestaltet und entwickelt er mit seinem multikulturellen Team von Designern und Produktspezialisten u. a. Segeljachten, Sportgeräte, Elektrowerkzeuge, FMCGs und Unterhaltungselektronik für europäische und asiatische Premiummarken. Aleks Tatic unterrichtet an verschiedenen europäischen Hochschulen und Seminaren praxisorientiertes Industriedesign und Innovationsmanagement.

01 Bosch AQT33-11
High Pressure Washer, 2015
Hochdruckreiniger, 2015

02 Gardena
Nozzle and Sprayer Range, 2002
Spritzen- und Brausensortiment, 2002

02

"Despite all the design trends, the 'Ten Principles for Good Design' by Dieter Rams have not aged at all in the last forty years."

„Trotz aller Designtrends sind die ‚Zehn Thesen für gutes Design' von Dieter Rams in den letzten vierzig Jahren kein bisschen gealtert."

How has the role played by design in our everyday lives changed?
At university, we were taught that product design would have the task to improve people's lives and work. The economic success of a company would emerge as a by-product. In the meantime, a role reversal has taken place: today, designers primarily design for the economic success of products and companies. And sometimes, a product comes out that, on the side, also improves our lives. I do not view this negatively: as companies have recognised the competitive element of design, more of design is being produced, and on all levels. Today, we are surrounded by more design, thus better products than in the past.

What does winning the Red Dot say about a product?
That the companies and the designers involved have focused on the use, handling and aesthetics of a product in an outstanding way.

Inwieweit hat sich die Rolle, die Design in unserem täglichen Leben spielt, verändert?
Im Studium wurde uns beigebracht, dass Produktdesign die Aufgabe hätte, das Leben und Arbeiten der Menschen zu verbessern, und quasi als Nebenprodukt würde der wirtschaftliche Erfolg eines Unternehmens entstehen. Inzwischen hat ein Rollentausch stattgefunden: Designer gestalten heute in erster Linie für den wirtschaftlichen Erfolg von Produkten und Unternehmen. Und manchmal kommt dabei, nebenher, ein Produkt heraus, das unser Leben verbessert. Ich sehe das nicht negativ: Dadurch, dass Unternehmen den Wettbewerbsfaktor Design erkannt haben, wird viel mehr und überall Design betrieben. Wir werden heute von mehr Design, also von besseren Produkten umgeben als früher.

Was sagt eine Auszeichnung mit dem Red Dot über das Produkt aus?
Dass sich Unternehmen und Designer ausgezeichnet mit dem Nutzen, der Handhabung und der Ästhetik eines Produktes beschäftigt haben.

465

01

02

Nils Toft
Denmark
Dänemark

Nils Toft, born in Copenhagen in 1957, graduated as an architect and designer from the Royal Danish Academy of Fine Arts in Copenhagen in 1986. He also holds a master's degree in Industrial Design and Business Development. Starting his career as an industrial designer, Nils Toft joined the former Christian Bjørn Design in 1987, an internationally active design studio in Copenhagen with branches in Beijing and Ho Chi Minh City. Within a few years, he became a partner of CBD and, as managing director, ran the business. Today, Nils Toft is the founder and managing director of Designidea. With offices in Copenhagen and Beijing, Designidea works in the following key fields: communication, consumer electronics, medicine, and graphic arts, as well as projects in business development, design strategy, graphic and exhibition design.

Nils Toft, 1957 in Kopenhagen geboren, machte seinen Abschluss als Architekt und Designer 1986 an der Royal Danish Academy of Fine Arts in Kopenhagen. Er verfügt zudem über einen Master im Bereich Industrial Design und Business Development. Zu Beginn seiner Karriere als Industriedesigner trat Nils Toft 1987 bei dem damaligen Christian Bjørn Design ein, einem international operierenden Designstudio in Kopenhagen, das mit Niederlassungen in Beijing und Ho-Chi-Minh-Stadt vertreten ist. Innerhalb weniger Jahre wurde er Partner bei CBD und leitete das Unternehmen als Managing Director. Heute ist Nils Toft Gründer und Managing Director von Designidea. Mit Büros in Kopenhagen und Beijing operiert Designidea in verschiedenen Hauptbereichen: Kommunikation, Unterhaltungselektronik, Medizin und Grafikdesign sowie Projekte in den Bereichen Geschäftsentwicklung, Designstrategie, Grafik und Ausstellungsdesign.

01–04
Four generations of
Wittenborg coffee machines
Vier Generationen der
Wittenborg Kaffeemaschinen

03

04

"As a designer, I love design.
Working as a Red Dot juror means
being in design heaven."
„Als Designer liebe ich Design.
Deshalb befinde ich mich durch die
Arbeit als Red Dot-Juror im siebten
Designhimmel."

In your opinion, what makes for good design?
Design is good when it tells a story that speaks to our emotions and opens our eyes to new possibilities and experiences.

How has the role played by design in our everyday lives changed?
Today, design is no longer an exclusive experience, but it affects all aspects of our lives. Design today can be a personal statement, a new experience, and it may define how you want to live your life.

Which topics are most likely to influence design in the coming years?
A 360 degree range of influential topics would include authenticity, transparency, artificial intelligence, industry 4.0, environment and diversity.

Which area of design do you feel has the greatest potential for development for the future?
In the near future, more and more products will be autonomous and will work with artificial intelligence. We will live alongside them and how we design them can make a big difference.

Was macht Ihrer Ansicht nach gutes Design aus?
Design ist gut, wenn es eine Geschichte erzählt, die uns emotional anspricht und unsere Augen für neue Möglichkeiten und Erfahrungen öffnet.

Inwieweit hat sich die Rolle, die Design in unserem täglichen Leben spielt, verändert?
Heute ist Design nicht mehr ein exklusives Erlebnis, sondern wirkt sich auf alle Aspekte unseres Lebens aus. Design kann heute ein persönliches Statement, eine neue Erfahrung sein und es kann bestimmen, wie man sein Leben leben will.

Welche Themen werden das Design in den kommenden Jahren besonders beeinflussen?
Ein 360-Grad-Überblick über einflussreiche Themen würde Authentizität, Transparenz, künstliche Intelligenz, Industrie 4.0, Umwelt und Vielfalt einschließen.

In welchem Designbereich sehen Sie das größte Entwicklungspotenzial für die Zukunft?
In nächster Zukunft werden immer mehr Produkte autonom und mit künstlicher Intelligenz ausgestattet sein. Wir werden direkt neben ihnen leben und es wird einen großen Unterschied machen, wie wir sie gestalten.

01

Cheng Chung Yao
Taiwan

Cheng Chung Yao studied at the Pratt Institute New York and graduated with a master's degree in architecture. In 1991, he founded the Department of Interior Space Design at Shih Chien University and has worked as a lecturer at the Graduate School of Architecture at Tam Kang University as well as at the Graduate School of Architecture at Chiao Tung University. In 1999, he founded "t1 design" where he heads a team of architects and interior designers as well as exhibition and graphic designers. The company's best-known products include the City Plaza of Taiwan Pavilion of the 2010 Shanghai Expo, the Taiwan Design Museum and the Taiwan Design Center. Furthermore, Cheng Chung Yao curated and designed the International Interior Design Exhibition for the Expo, was president of the Chinese Society of Interior Designers, chief executive of the Asia Pacific Space Designers Association, board member of the International Federation of Interior Architects/Designers and founder of the Taiwan Interior Design Award.

Cheng Chung Yao studierte Architektur am Pratt Institute New York und schloss sein Studium mit dem Master ab. 1991 gründete er die Fakultät für Interior Space Design an der Shih Chien University und war als Dozent an der Graduate School of Architecture der Tam Kang University sowie an der Graduate School of Architecture der Chiao Tung University tätig. 1999 gründete er „t1 design" und leitet dort ein Team aus Architekten, Innenarchitekten sowie Ausstellungs- und Grafikdesignern. Zu den bekanntesten Projekten des Büros zählen der City Plaza of Taiwan Pavilion der Expo 2010 in Shanghai, das Taiwan Design Museum und das Taiwan Design Center. Zudem kuratierte und gestaltete Cheng Chung Yao die International Interior Design Exhibition für die Expo, war u. a. Präsident der Chinese Society of Interior Designers, Hauptgeschäftsführer der Asia Pacific Space Designers Association und Vorstandsmitglied der International Federation of Interior Architects/Designers und gründete den Taiwan Interior Design Award.

01|02 ArtBox museum
The ArtBox museum in Taipei is a building for art exhibitions and the collection of a private foundation. It is located on the banks of the Tamsui river, between two high-rise apartment buildings. It has a steel structure with a full, matt glass facade and is illuminated at night time.

Das Museum ArtBox in Taipeh ist ein Gebäude für Kunstausstellungen und für die Sammlung einer privaten Stiftung. Es liegt am Ufer des Flusses Tamsui, zwischen zwei Hochhäusern. Es hat eine Stahlstruktur mit einer vollen, mattierten Glasfassade und wird nachts beleuchtet.

02

"The different disciplines of product design are converging and will, in future, cross traditional professional boundaries."

„Die verschiedenen Disziplinen des Produktdesigns verschmelzen miteinander und werden in Zukunft traditionelle berufliche Grenzen überschreiten."

In your opinion, what makes for good design?
Good design is not just a good answer to meeting certain needs of our times; good design is also an expression of the vision of creating a better way to live our lives.

What importance does design quality have for the economic success of companies?
The design quality of a product leads to business success and improves the image of companies. With their successful products, they become icons of their industry.

What attracts you to the role of Red Dot jury member?
The Red Dot selection process presents a comprehensive expression of the global review of the design industry's creativity. It documents contemporary design history, aesthetics and philosophy in a great way.

What does winning the Red Dot say about a product?
The Red Dot award signals advanced design quality. It gives a product a worldwide image of distinction.

Was macht Ihrer Ansicht nach gutes Design aus?
Gutes Design ist nicht nur eine gute Antwort auf bestimmte Bedürfnisse unserer Zeit. Gutes Design ist auch ein Ausdruck der Vision, einen besseren Weg zu finden, unser Leben zu leben.

Welche Bedeutung hat Designqualität für den wirtschaftlichen Erfolg von Unternehmen?
Die Designqualität eines Produkts führt zu geschäftlichem Erfolg und verbessert das Image eines Unternehmens. Mit seinen erfolgreichen Produkten wird es dadurch zu einem Kultobjekt in seiner Branche.

Was reizt Sie an der Arbeit als Red Dot-Juror?
Der Red Dot-Auswahlprozess ist der allgemeine Ausdruck des globalen Urteils über die Kreativität der Designbranche. Es ist ein großartiges Dokument der zeitgenössischen Designgeschichte, Ästhetik und Philosophie.

Was sagt eine Auszeichnung mit dem Red Dot über das Produkt aus?
Der Red Dot signalisiert fortschrittliche Designqualität. Er verleiht einem Produkt weltweit ein erstklassiges Image.

Alphabetical index manufacturers and distributors
Alphabetisches Hersteller- und Vertriebs-Register

Alphabetical index manufacturers and distributors
Alphabetisches Hersteller- und Vertriebs-Register

Alphabetical index manufacturers and distributors
Alphabetisches Hersteller- und Vertriebs-Register

Alphabetical index designers
Alphabetisches Designer-Register

Alphabetical index designers
Alphabetisches Designer-Register

Alphabetical index designers
Alphabetisches Designer-Register

Alphabetical index designers
Alphabetisches Designer-Register

Alphabetical index designers
Alphabetisches Designer-Register

reddot edition

Editor | Herausgeber
Peter Zec

Project management | Projektleitung
Sophie Angerer

Project assistance | Projektassistenz
Maren Boots
Marie Eigner
Theresa Falkenberg
Judith Lindner
Samuel Madilonga
Vivien Mroß
Louisa Mücher
Jonas Römmer
Julia Sagner

Editorial work | Redaktion
Bettina Derksen, Simmern, Germany
Eva Hembach, Vienna, Austria
Burkhard Jacob, Essen, Germany
Karin Kirch, Essen, Germany
Karoline Laarmann, Dortmund, Germany
Bettina Laustroer, Wuppertal, Germany
Kirsten Müller, Mülheim an der Ruhr, Germany
Astrid Ruta, Essen, Germany
Martina Stein, Otterberg, Germany
Corinna Ten-Cate, Wetter, Germany

Proofreading | Lektorat
Klaus Dimmler (supervision), Essen, Germany
Mareike Ahlborn, Essen, Germany
Jörg Arnke, Essen, Germany
Wolfgang Astelbauer, Vienna, Austria
Sabine Beeres, Leverkusen, Germany
Dawn Michelle d'Atri, Kirchhundem, Germany
Annette Gillich-Beltz, Essen, Germany
Eva Hembach, Vienna, Austria
Karin Kirch, Essen, Germany
Norbert Knyhala, Castrop-Rauxel, Germany
Laura Lothian, Vienna, Austria
Regina Schier, Essen, Germany
Anja Schrade, Stuttgart, Germany

Translation | Übersetzung
Heike Bors-Eberlein, Viersen, Germany
Patrick Conroy, Lanarca, Cyprus
Stanislaw Eberlein, Viersen, Germany
William Kings, Wuppertal, Germany
Tara Russell, Dublin, Ireland
Jan Stachel-Williamson, Christchurch, New Zealand
Philippa Watts, Exeter, Great Britain
Andreas Zantop, Berlin, Germany
Christiane Zschunke, Frankfurt am Main, Germany

Layout | Gestaltung
Lockstoff Design GmbH, Grevenbroich, Germany
Judith Baumann
Susanne Coenen
Katja Kleefeld
Stephanie Marniok
Iris Mecklenburg
Lena Overkamp
Saskia Rühmkorf
Nicole Slink

Photographs | Fotos
Stefano Campo Antico (BLOCK, juror Masayo Ave)
Dragan Arrigler (Relaxroll, juror Jure Miklavc)
EcoDesign Circle (EcoDesign Circle, juror Robin Edman)
Eyelike.org – Pieter Bas Doornebal
(product photo SoilCares, Netherlands; Book Working)
Kaido Haagen (Nove / Kord, juror Martin Pärn)
Alex Muchnik (portrait juror Sascha Peters)
Chih Jung Tsai (ArtBox museum, juror Cheng Chung Yao)
Wagner Ziegelmeyer (Serelepe chair, juror Indio da Costa)
Thomas Zipf (product photo biobrush GmbH, Germany;
Book Enjoying)

Page | Seite
440 Enjoying
364 Doing
442 Working
530 Living

Name
Tokyo_Institute_of_Technology_Centennial_Hall_2009
Copyright | Urheber
Wiiii
Source | Quelle
http://commons.wikimedia.org/wiki/File:Tokyo_Institute_
of_Technology_Centennial_Hall_2009.jpg

Jury photographs | Jurorenfotos
Simon Bierwald, Dortmund, Germany
Alex Muchnik, Essen, Germany

In-company photos | Werkfotos der Firmen

Production | Produktion
gelb+, Düsseldorf, Germany
Bernd Reinkens

Lithography | Lithografie
tarcom GmbH, Gelsenkirchen, Germany
Gregor Baals
Jonas Mühlenweg
Bernd Reinkens (supervision)
Gundula Seraphin

Printing | Druck
Dr. Cantz'sche Druckerei Medien GmbH,
Ostfildern, Germany

Bookbindery | Buchbinderei
CPI Moravia Books s.r.o., Pohořelice, Czechia

Red Dot Design Yearbook 2017/2018
Living: 978-3-89939-194-7
Doing: 978-3-89939-195-4
Working: 978-3-89939-196-1
Enjoying: 978-3-89939-197-8
Set (Living, Doing, Working & Enjoying): 978-3-89939-193-0

© 2017 Red Dot GmbH & Co. KG, Essen, Germany

Publisher + worldwide distribution |
Verlag + Vertrieb weltweit
Red Dot Edition
Design Publisher | Fachverlag für Design
Contact | Kontakt
Sabine Wöll
Gelsenkirchener Str. 181
45309 Essen, Germany
Phone +49 201 81418 22
Fax +49 201 81418 10
E-mail edition@red-dot.de
www.red-dot-edition.com
www.red-dot-shop.com
Book publisher ID no. | Verkehrsnummer
13674 (Börsenverein Frankfurt)

**Bibliographic information published
by the Deutsche Nationalbibliothek**
The Deutsche Nationalbibliothek
lists this publication in the Deutsche
Nationalbibliografie; detailed bibliographic
data are available on the Internet at
http://dnb.ddb.de
Bibliografische Information
der Deutschen Nationalbibliothek
Die Deutsche Nationalbibliothek verzeichnet
diese Publikation in der Deutschen
Nationalbibliografie; detaillierte
bibliografische Daten sind im Internet über
http://dnb.ddb.de abrufbar